The Coptic Encyclopedia

Editors and Consultants

Editor in Chief

Aziz S. Atiya
University of Utah

Editors

William Y. Adams
University of Kentucky

Basilios IV
Archbishop of Jerusalem

Pierre du Bourguet, S.J.
Louvre Museum, Paris

René-Georges Coquin
Collège de France, Paris

W. H. C. Frend
Glasgow University

Mirrit Boutros Ghali
Society of Coptic Archaeology, Cairo

Bishop Gregorios
Higher Institute of Coptic Studies, Cairo

Peter Grossmann
German Institute of Archaeology, Cairo

Antoine Guillaumont
Collège de France, Paris

Rodolphe Kasser
University of Geneva

Martin Krause
Westfälische Wilhelms-Universität, Münster

Subhi Y. Labib
Kiel University

Tito Orlandi
University of Rome

Marian Robertson
Utah State University

Khalil Samir
Pontifical Oriental Institute, Rome

Consultants

Labib Habachi
Egyptian Department of Antiquities, Cairo

J. M. Robinson
Institute of Antiquity and Christianity, Claremont, California

Magdi Wahba
Cairo University

Editorial Managing Committee

S. Kent Brown
Brigham Young University, Provo

Fuad Megally
Polytechnic of Central London

The Coptic Encyclopedia

Aziz S. Atiya
EDITOR IN CHIEF

Volume 7

Macmillan Publishing Company
NEW YORK
Collier Macmillan Canada
TORONTO
Maxwell Macmillan International
NEW YORK · OXFORD · SINGAPORE · SYDNEY

Macmillan Publishing Company
866 Third Avenue, New York, NY 10022

Collier Macmillan Canada, Inc.
1200 Eglinton Avenue East, Suite 200, Don Mills, Ontario M3C 3N1

Library of Congress Catalog Card No.: 90-23448

Printed in the United States of America

printing number
1 2 3 4 5 6 7 8 9 10

Library of Congress Cataloging-in-Publication Data

The Coptic encyclopedia / Aziz S. Atiya, editor-in-chief.
p. cm.
Includes bibliographical references and index.
ISBN 0-02-897025-X (set)
1. Coptic Church—Dictionaries. 2. Copts—Dictionaries.
I. Atiya, Aziz S., 1898– .
BX130.5.C66 1991 90-23448
281′.7′03—dc20 CIP

The preparation of this volume was made possible in part by a grant from the National Endowment for the Humanities, an independent federal agency.

Photographs on pages 567, 736, 754, 755, 790, 791, 876–878, 1284, 1311, and 2168 are reproduced courtesy of the Metropolitan Museum of Art. Photography by the Egyptian Expedition.

Q

QAL'AT AL-BĀBAYN (castle of the two gates), a medieval fortress on the east bank of the Nile (some 12 miles [19 km] south of Idfū), at which a few sturdy fortification walls with towers and numerous domestic buildings remain. The unusual, hook-shaped ground plan is determined by the lie of the land. The fortress falls into two parts divided by a middle wall, of which the eastern part is regarded as younger. Both parts have a gate opening on the intermediate slope.

The buildings within consist in the western section predominantly of single-story, two-roomed houses, which are set into the mountainside one above the other. In the eastern section, building development is less dense and runs parallel to the course of the wall.

The lower area accommodates several buildings with large rooms, among them a church, although only parts of the sanctuary remain. It consists of an apse with two rectangular side rooms, the spatial dimensions of which are similar to those of the Nubian churches of the tenth century from the Faras region. Furthermore, remains of the gallery floor above the two side rooms have been preserved.

One can only speculate about the date of the fortress. From the layout, it can hardly be dated to the late Roman period. The existence of a Christian church in it disproves an origin in the Islamic period. There has been no lack of support for the attempt to set it in the period of the Nubian Christian occupation of Upper Egypt (Monneret de Villard, 1938, p. 124). In that case it would go back to the first half of the tenth century.

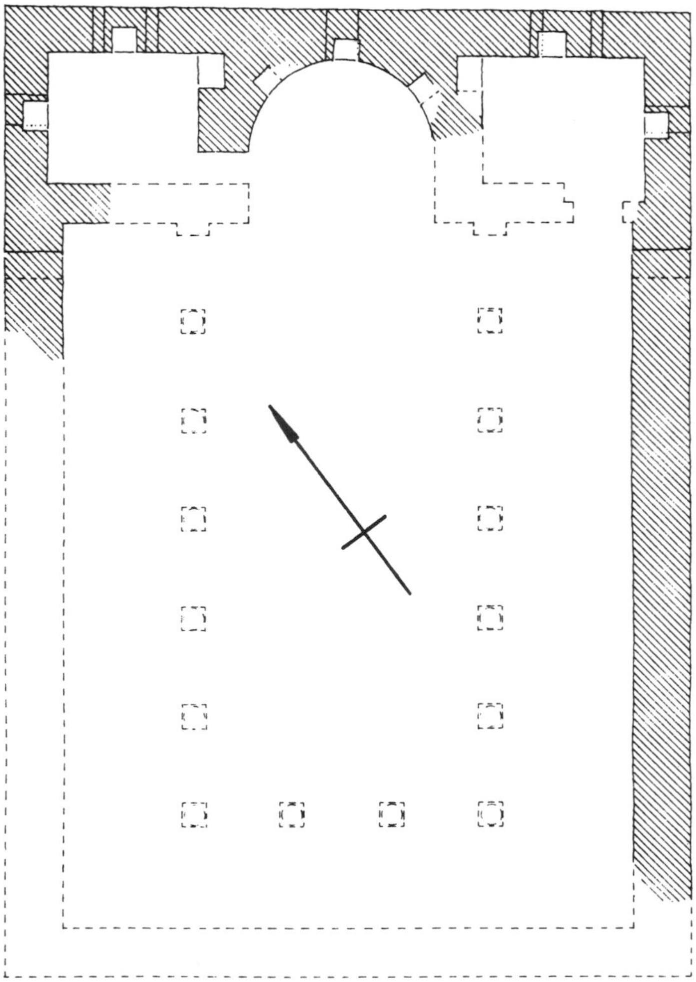

Plan of the church located in the lower area of the medieval fortress Qal'at al-Bābayn. *Courtesy Peter Grossmann.*

BIBLIOGRAPHY

Grossmann, P., and H. Jaritz. "Ein Besuch in der Festung von Qalʿat al-Babēn in Oberägypten." *Mitteilungen des deutschen archäologischen Instituts—Abteilung Kairo* 30 (1974):199–214.

Monneret de Villard, U. *Storia della Nubia Cristiana.* Rome, 1938.

PETER GROSSMANN

QALLĪN, city located in the Egyptian Delta approximately 7 miles (11 km) southwest of Kafr al-Shaykh in the Gharbiyyah Province. The city is mentioned in the SYNAXARION for 7 Ba'ūnah as the birthplace of Saint Abishkhīrun, a late third- or early fourth-century martyr.

BIBLIOGRAPHY

Amélineau, E. *La Géographie de l'Egypte à l'époque copte,* p. 390. Paris, 1893.

Ibn Mammātī. *Kitāb Qawānīn al-Dawāwīn,* ed. A. S. Atiya, p. 169. Cairo, 1943.

RANDALL STEWART

QALYŪB, a city in the Egyptian Delta, the capital of the Qalyūbiyyah Province, located approximately 8 miles (13 km) north of Cairo. A Vatican Coptic-Arabic manuscript from the seventeenth century that apparently preserves a list of thirteenth-century Egyptian bishoprics mentions Qalyūb, suggesting that the city was a bishopric by the late Middle Ages (Munier, 1943, p. 64).

BIBLIOGRAPHY

Amélineau, E. *La Géographie de l'Egypte à l'époque copte,* pp. 390–91. Paris, 1893.

Munier, H. *Recueil des listes épiscopales de l'église copte.* Cairo, 1943.

RANDALL STEWART

QAMŪLAH. *See* Pilgrimages.

QARĀRAH, early Christian settlement on the east bank of the Nile, east of the modern railway station of Maghārah (about 112 miles or 180 km south of Cairo). Apart from the remains of a few miserable houses (Ranke, 1926, p. 7, pl. 7), only the cemeteries have survived, and these afford information about an occupation extending from the fifth to the eighth century A.D. The graves themselves were oblong earth pits, without any additional casing. The dead were as usual wrapped in shrouds, but had over the head a peculiar triangular headpiece made of wood or palm branch ribs, which served to protect the head and was incorporated into the wrappings. The grave offerings were poor, for the most part fabrics as well as wood and bone carvings. In the ground of the cemetery there are also the remains of a fairly large building, which has been described by the excavators as a monastery (Bilabel, 1924, p. 4).

BIBLIOGRAPHY

Bilabel, F. *Griechische Papyri.* Heidelberg, 1924.

Ranke, H. *Koptische Friedhöfe bei Karara.* Berlin and Leipzig, 1926.

PETER GROSSMANN

QAṢR. *See* Castrum.

QAṢR IBRĪM, a fortified hilltop settlement in Lower Nubia, about 25 miles (40 km) to the north of the famous temples of Abu Simbel. A temple seems to have been built there in the Egyptian New Kingdom, and the place was intermittently occupied from that time until its final abandonment in 1811. The name appears in Meroitic texts as Pedeme; in classical texts variously as Primis, Premnis, and Prima; and in some Coptic texts as Phrim. Most Arabic sources give the name as Ibrīm or Qalʿat Ibrīm. The forename Qaṣr is seldom encountered before the nineteenth century, although it has been regularly coupled to the name of the town in the recent past.

Qaṣr Ibrīm in the beginning seems to have been primarily a religious center. In addition to the New Kingdom temple (which may never have been finished), the "Ethiopian" pharaoh Taharqa built a brick temple in the seventh century B.C. A more overt military and administrative role began when the Ptolemies occupied the place and built a massive girdle wall around it, probably around 100 B.C. They and their Roman successors apparently occupied the place for about two centuries, although a Meroitic invading force took temporary possession in 23 B.C., as recounted by Strabo and Pliny. Around A.D. 100, Qaṣr Ibrīm was returned to the control of the Meroites, who restored the Taharqa temple and built another, larger one alongside it.

Qaṣr Ibrīm retained its strategic as well as its religious importance in the post-Meroitic period. It was seized for a time by the Blemmye nomads (see BEJA TRIBES) who settled in the Nile Valley following the Meroitic collapse, and afterward by the Nobadae, who drove out the Blemmyes. Texts found at Qaṣr Ibrīm suggest that this was the earliest residence of the kings of NOBATIA; later they seem to have transferred their residence to FARAS.

Early in the sixth century the Taharqa temple was made over into a church. This may well have been the earliest church building in Nubia, for archaeological evidence suggests that its conversion preceded the "official" Christianization of Nobatia in 543, as related by John of Ephesus. Other parts of the Taharqa temple complex were apparently converted for a time into a monastery, but this was subsequently dismantled.

A bishopric was established at Qaṣr Ibrīm in the seventh century, and shortly afterward an impressive stone cathedral was begun. A smaller church was built alongside the cathedral at a later date. Meanwhile, most of the secular buildings at Qaṣr Ibrīm seem to have been leveled, and the mountaintop became primarily a religious center in the early Middle Ages. Visitors' graffiti show that it was an important pilgrimage site, as it had been in Meroitic times.

Nubia was invaded by an Ayyubid force under Shams al-Dawlah Turan Shah in 1172–1173, and the invaders temporarily seized Qaṣr Ibrīm and damaged the cathedral. This event marked a turning point in the history both of the fortress and of Nubia. The town fortifications, which had been neglected, were now restored and heightened. Secular and commercial buildings began to appear again on the mountaintop alongside the churches. The eparch of Nobatia, who had formerly resided chiefly at Faras, transferred his main headquarters to Qaṣr Ibrīm in the twelfth century. Meanwhile, the religious importance of the place continued. A bishop of Faras and Qaṣr Ibrīm was consecrated at al-Fusṭāṭ (modern-day Cairo) in 1372, and bishops of Qaṣr Ibrīm are mentioned in a number of documents of still later date.

After the medieval Nubian kingdom of MAKOURIA collapsed, its power in Lower Nubia was assumed by the splinter kingdom of DOTAWO. The capital or principal royal seat of this principality seems to have been at JABAL 'ADDĀ, but Qaṣr Ibrīm was also an important center within the kingdom. Many of the surviving documents that relate to the kingdom of Dotawo have been recovered from the excavations at Qaṣr Ibrīm. The latest of these bears the date 1464.

Qaṣr Ibrīm may have been largely abandoned by the time the Ottomans took possession of Nubia early in the sixteenth century. They reoccupied and refortified the hilltop and made it one of their two principal control points within Nubia, the other being at SAI ISLAND. Part of the old cathedral was turned into a mosque, and the remainder of the structure was allowed to deteriorate. The original Ottoman garrison, according to local tradition, was of Bosnian origin, and as a result the latter-day inhabitants of Qaṣr Ibrīm were usually termed "Bosnians" both by themselves and by their neighbors. They remained in occupation until driven out by Mamluk refugees in 1810. These in their turn were expelled by artillery fire in the following year, and the 3,000-year history of the fortress came to an end.

Excavations in the Qaṣr Ibrīm fortress were begun in 1963 and have continued intermittently. The original fortress was perched so high above the Nile Valley floor that, unlike any other site in Lower Nubia, it has not been fully inundated by the waters of Lake Nasser. It is now a small island, about 5 acres (2 hectares) in extent, projecting above the lake surface.

Some of the finds from Qaṣr Ibrīm, particularly the textual finds, are of outstanding historical importance. They include letters relating to the BAQṬ treaty, to the commercial relations of the eparchs of Nobatia, and to the late medieval kingdom of Dotawo. Also important are the intact consecration scrolls of Bishop Timotheus, one in Coptic and one in Arabic, dated 1372.

[*See also:* Nubian Church Organization.]

BIBLIOGRAPHY

Adams, W. Y. *Nubia, Corridor to Africa,* pp. 349–53, 400–404, 412–14, 464–68, 474–78, 579–80. Princeton, N.J., 1977.

______. "The 'Library' of Qaṣr Ibrim." *The Kentucky Review* 1 (1979):5–27.

______. "Qasr Ibrim, an Archaeological Conspectus." In *Nubian Studies,* ed. J. M. Plumley. Warminster, England, 1982.

Plumley, J. M. "Pre-Christian Nubia (23 B.C.–535 A.D.). Evidence from Qasr Ibrim." *Travaux du Centre d'archéologie méditerranéenne de l'Académie polonaise des sciences* 11 (1972):8–24.

______. "An Eighth-Century Arabic Letter to the King of Nubia." *Journal of Egyptian Archaeology* 61 (1975):241–45.

———. *The Scrolls of Bishop Timotheos.* Exploration Society, Texts from Excavations, First Memoir. London, 1975.

Vantini, G. *Christianity in the Sudan,* pp. 159–61. Bologna, 1981.

Publication of the archaeological results from Qaṣr Ibrīm has begun. Preliminary excavation reports will be found in *Journal of Egyptian Archaeology* 50 (1964):52 (1966); 53 (1967); 56 (1970); 60 (1974); 61 (1975); 63 (1977); 65 (1979); 69 (1983); and 71 (1985).

WILLIAM Y. ADAMS

QAṢR NISĪMAH (ʿAyn Nisīmah). About 5.5 miles (9 km) south of Khargah, Nisīmah is a tiny square site 164 × 164 feet (50 × 50 m), perched on a till of low elevation in the middle of a small cultivated plain. In addition to a small fort (qaṣr) built on a base of stones and ordinary clay mortar 50 × 32 feet (15 × 10 m; maximum extant height 24 feet or 7.5 m) and a magnificent well-preserved columbarium, one may see the leveled down remains of a small church oriented from west to east (choir rounded to the east). The entrance door is in the north side wall. In the nave, along the north side, are two median columns of octagonal sections that perhaps had matching columns along the south side. This church of small dimensions 32 × 23 feet (9.5 × 7 m) is entirely comparable to that of SHAMS AL-DĪN.

GUY WAGNER

QAṢR AL-SAYYAD. *See* Jabal al-Ṭarīf; Pilgrimages.

QAṢR AL-SHAMʿ (the Fortress of Candles), name given by the Arabs to the Roman fortress of Babylon following the ARAB CONQUEST OF EGYPT. According to al-MAQRĪZĪ, candles burned every month at the top of the tower of the fortress when the sun entered a new constellation of the zodiac. This conveyed the event to the population. In time Qaṣr al-Shamʿ came to designate a whole quarter of Old Cairo inhabited mainly by Copts.

Four Coptic churches are still to be found in that part of Cairo: Church of al-Muʿallaqah, Church of Abū Sarjah (Saint Sergius), Church of Sitt Barbārah (Saint Barbara), and Church of Mār Jirjis (Saint George). A fifth church, known as Qaṣriyyat al-Rīḥān (Church of Our Lady), burned down in 1979.

BIBLIOGRAPHY

Coquin, C. *Les Edifices chrétiens du Vieux-Caire.* Cairo, 1974.

AZIZ S. ATIYA

QATAMARUS. *See* Lectionary.

QAYS, AL-, city located in Middle Egypt on the west side of the Nile about 4 miles (6 km) southwest of Banī Mazār in Minyā Province. In Greek it was called Kynopolis ano (Upper Kynopolis).

The SYNAXARION commemorates the martyrdom of Bisādah (Psoi) from al-Qays on 24 Ṭūbah. Records indicate that the city was a bishopric in the Middle Ages. A bishop Maqārah of al-Qays attended a synod held in Cairo in 1078, and a bishop Buṭrus from the city was present at the preparation of the holy CHRISM in 1299 (Munier, 1943, pp. 27, 36).

BIBLIOGRAPHY

Amélineau, E. *La Géographie de l'Egypte à l'époque copte.* Paris, 1893.

Munier, H. *Recueil des listes épiscopales de l'église copte.* Cairo, 1943.

RANDALL STEWART

QERELLOS I. *See* Ethiopian Prelates.

QERELLOS II. *See* Ethiopian Prelates.

QERELLOS III. *See* Ethiopian Prelates.

QIFṬ (Coptos), city on the east bank of the Nile, about 25 miles (40 km) northwest of Luxor. It was already of some significance early on as the exit point of the desert routes to the Red Sea and to the quarries in the desert area. In the third century A.D. during the Palmyrene rebellion, the city fell into the hands of the Blemmyes and because of renewed resistance was besieged and destroyed by the emperor DIOCLETIAN in 292. However, the city soon recovered, although at first cities like Qūṣ and Qinā tried to take its place. Under JUSTINIAN, for a short time, it was called Justinianopolis (Kees, 1922, col. 1368), which may suggest the existence of a Chalcedonian community in the city. The city was known

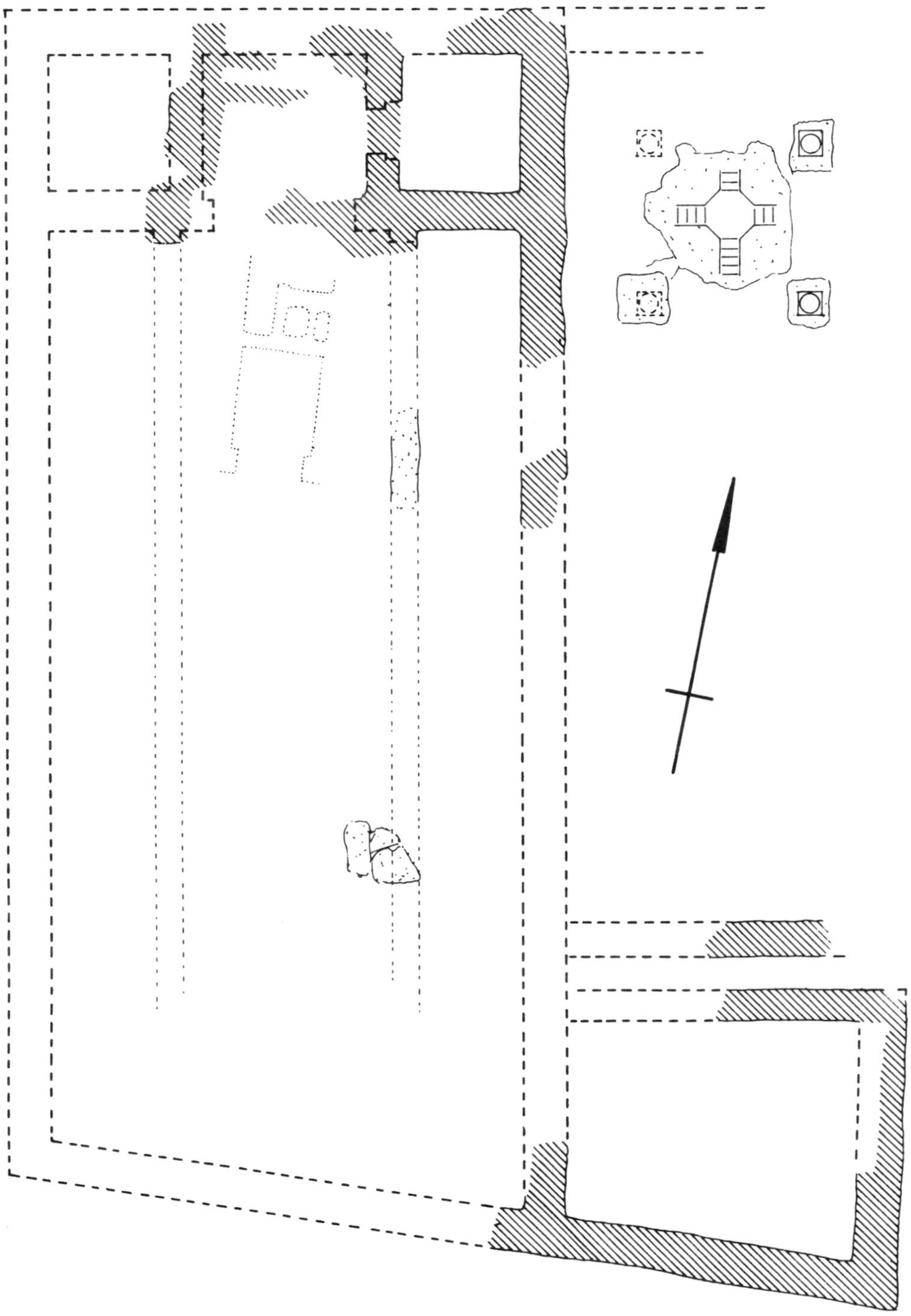

Plan of the large church of which traces are found in the old city of Qifṭ. *Courtesy Peter Grossmann.*

to be the seat of a bishop since the fifth century (Amélineau, 1893, p. 214). A bishop PHOIBAMMON from Coptos took part in the Council of EPHESUS in 431 (Munier, 1943, p. 14).

Of Christian buildings within the area of the old city, only slight traces of a church have been found, but all the same it was a structure of large proportions. Contrary to normal tradition the basilica was oriented northwestward instead of northeastward, the width of the nave being roughly 31 feet (9.5 m). The sanctuary consisted of three rectangular rooms. Apparently because of the absence of an apse, the building was not recognized as a church by Reinach (1910, p. 39). The central main room that here took the place of the apse was connected with the eastern side room by a large opening in the wall. In front of the entrance to this main room, a crypt constructed of fired bricks was found under the floor. The baptistery was accommodated in an annex on the east side of the basilica. It contained an extraordinarily large octagonal pool with steps leading down into it on four sides—a rare feature in Egypt. In addition it was surrounded by a massive ciborium supported on four large octagonal granite columns. The axle width of the columns amounted to 23 feet (7 m). The church was constructed largely of spoil material from demolished pagan temples. Consequently it goes back at the earliest to the fifth century. To judge by the capitals used in the ciborium, the baptistery was actually constructed in the sixth century.

Remains of a small, somewhat older building were found under the western section of the basilica. This also appears to have a northward orientation but only its apse has survived.

BIBLIOGRAPHY

Amélineau, E. *La Géographie de l'Egypte à l'époque copte,* pp. 213–15. Paris, 1893.

Fisher, H. G. "Koptos." In *Lexicon der Ägyptologie,* Vol. 3, cols. 737–40. Wiesbaden, 1979.

Kees, H. "Koptos." In *Realencyclopädie der classischen Altertumswissenschaft,* Vol. 11, cols. 1367–69. Stuttgart, 1922.

Munier, H. *Recueil des listes épiscopales de l'église copte.* Cairo, 1943.

Reinach, A. J. "Deuxième rapport sur les fouilles de Koptos." *Bulletin de la Societé française des fouilles archéologiques* (1910):32–40.

Weil, R. "Koptos." *Annales du Service des antiquités de l'Egypte* 11 (1911): 131–34.

PETER GROSSMANN

QINĀ, capital of Qinā Province in Upper Egypt. It is located on the east bank of the Nile about 30 miles (48 km) northeast of HIW. The city was known in Greek first as Kainopolis and then began to be called Maximanopolis in the third century.

Qinā was mentioned in a list of third-century bishoprics by George of Cyprus and occurs in medieval Coptic-Arabic scales, which suggests that the city has a long Christian tradition.

BIBLIOGRAPHY

Amélineau, E. *La Géographie de l'Egypte à l'époque copte.* Paris, 1893.

Muḥammad Ramzī. *Al-Qāmūs al-Jughrāfī lil-Bilād al-Miṣrīyyah,* Vol. 2, pt. 4. Cairo, 1953–1963.

RANDALL STEWART

QUBBAH. *See* Architectural Elements of Churches: Dome.

QUIBELL, JAMES EDWARD (1867–1935), English Egyptologist. He graduated from Christ Church, Oxford, and was appointed to the staff of the Egyptian Antiquities Service, becoming inspector in chief of antiquities in the Delta (1898). Later, as chief inspector at Saqqara, he excavated the magnificent Monastery of Saint Jeremias. He was assisted by his wife, Annie A. Quibell, who made illustrations for his publications. From 1913 to 1923 he served as keeper of the Cairo Museum and was appointed secretary-general of the Antiquities Department in 1923, retiring two years later. He has left many publications in the field of Coptic studies, listed in *A Coptic Bibliography* (Kammerer, 1950, 1969).

BIBLIOGRAPHY

Dawson, W. R., and E. P. Uphill. *Who Was Who in Egyptology,* pp. 240–41. London, 1972.

Kammerer, W., comp. *A Coptic Bibliography.* Ann Arbor, Mich., 1950; repr. New York, 1969.

AZIZ S. ATIYA

QULZUM. *See* Clysma.

QUMMUṢ. *See* Hegumenos.

QURNAT MAR'Ī. [*This entry consists of two parts: The History of Qurnat Mar'ī, and the building of the Monastery of Mark the Evangelist.*]

History

Qurnat Mar'ī is the name of ruins of a small hermitage built over an ancient tomb of a late period. It is on the north slope of the hill called Mar'ī, from the name of a Muslim saint buried on the

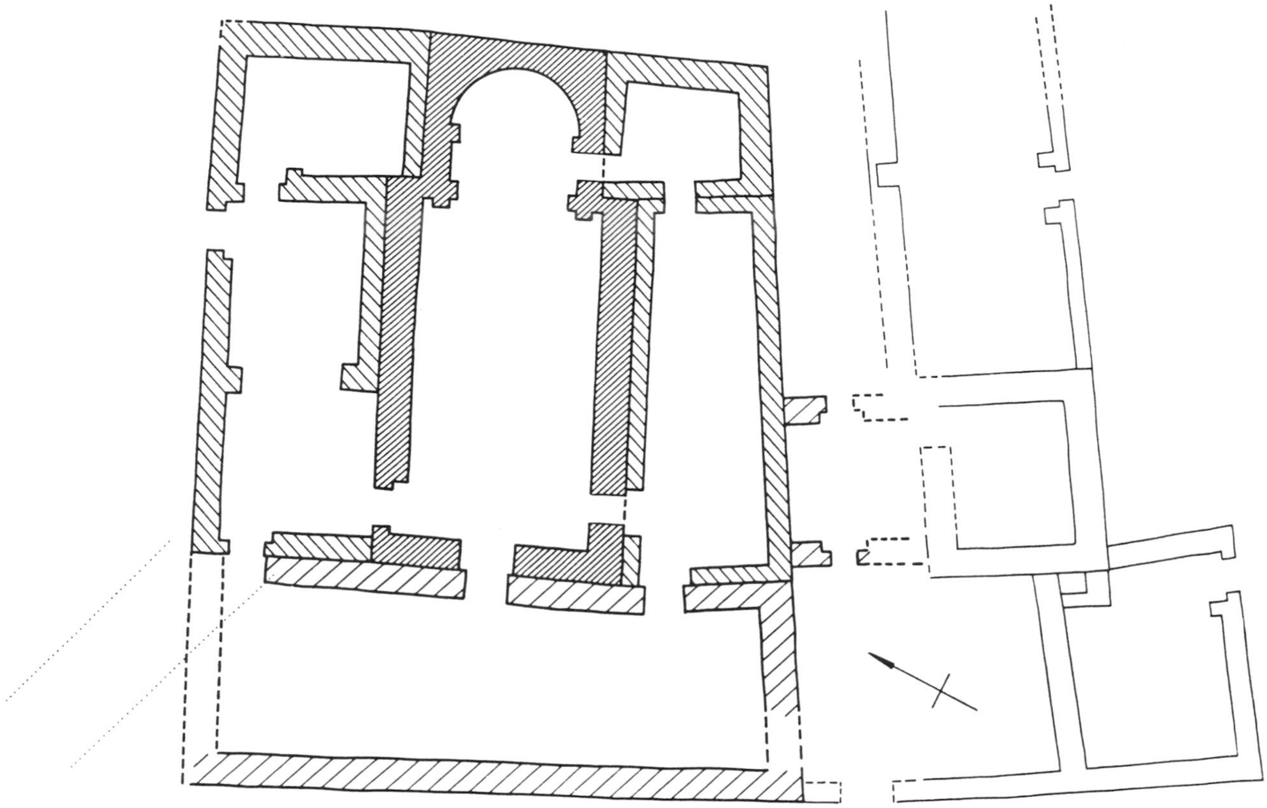

Plan of the church and adjoining monastic rooms at Qurnat Mar'ī. *Courtesy Peter Grossmann.*

summit, on the left bank of the Nile opposite Luxor. There is no ancient attestation. Winlock notes it in making his inventory of the monastic sites of the region (Winlock and Crum, Vol. 1, p. 15). U. Monneret de Villard believed he had found a church there with a plan approximating the churches of Georgia (pp. 495–500). The French Institute, which has the concession in this sector, excavated this site from 1971 to 1975, and reaped an abundant harvest of ostraca (2,000) and fragments of pottery, with and without decoration (more than 400 decorated pots that have been reassembled), but the results of this excavation have not yet been published. Only the general plan and a study of the mummies exhumed have been published (Castel, Vol. 2, pp. 121–43).

The site was called the *topos* of Saint Mark the Evangelist. The term *topos* ("place" in Greek) indicates that this was not a true monastery (besides, there is no surrounding wall) but the center where each week, on Saturday and Sunday, hermits living in the caves or tombs of the neighborhood gathered together. This *topos* was already known from the documents of the region (see Winlock and Crum, Vol. 1, p. 108), but its precise position was not known. Its superior, Mark, was a priest who wrote various documents (Winlock and Crum, Vol. 1, p. 223).

The plan published by Castel reveals a church and some adjoining rooms that are insufficient to constitute a true cenobium. Qurnat Mar'ī appears to have come to an end when the Muslim troops arrived, for the written documents do not show any Arab name. Perhaps it disappeared at the time of the Persian invasion (619–629), for a mummy of a monk shows that he died a violent death.

BIBLIOGRAPHY

Castel, G. "Etude d'une momie copte." In *Hommages à S. Sauneron,* Vol. 2, pp. 121–43. Cairo, 1979.

Monneret de Villard, U. "Una chiesa di tipo georgiano nella necropoli tebana." In *Coptic Studies in Honor of W. E. Crum,* pp. 495–500. Boston, 1950.

Sauneron, S. *Travaux de l'Institut français d'Archéologie orientale, 1969–1974.* Cairo, 1974. See pp. 40, 82–84, 120–21, 176–77 (with several photos of the site).

Winlock, H. E., and W. E. Crum. *The Monastery of Epiphanius at Thebes,* 2 vols. New York, 1926.

MAURICE MARTIN, S.J.
RENÉ-GEORGES COQUIN

Monastery of Mark the Evangelist

Set in the middle of the Theban necropolis, Qurnat Marʿī dominates the ruins of the great pharaonic temples: the Ramesseum to the east and the temple of DAYR AL-MADĪNAH to the northwest. A narrow strip of desert separates it from the cultivated areas. The monastery is built on the northeast part of the hill, near the summit. It is oriented northeast/southwest, and with its terraces covers an area of about 15 yards (14m) on each side. Its archaeological material dates it to the sixth and seventh centuries.

In its present form the monastery is composed of two buildings of mud brick. The main building, to the north and situated near the summit, occupies a natural terrace. Enclosed by high walls, it consists of communal rooms: in the center, the church with an apse; to the south, the refectory with two storage jars for water; to the west, a workroom with three loom pits; to the north, utility rooms and storage chambers. In the northwest corner of the building, an ancient pharaonic tomb drives into the rock. A small oratory is near the entrance to the tomb, and granaries occupy its lower part. The other building, south of the main building, includes three cells and a kitchen backing against the rock. These open directly on the access path to the monastery. These two buildings are separated by a passage. A spacious artificial platform to the east of the church was the monks' cemetery.

Immediately south of the cells, on a lower level, two pharaonic tombs contained some materials dating from the period of the monastery. They were inhabited by monks of the small community.

The pharaonic tomb and its court are the oldest part of the monastery. They were occupied by an anchorite, who left some graffiti in them. Then a chapel and communal buildings were built at the entrance to the tomb, in memory of this hermit. These structures underwent numerous alterations and extensions before acquiring their present appearance. The phases of construction may be summarized thus:

1. tomb and its court
2. first and second churches
3. rooms on the north, with kitchen on the outside of the monastery, to the northeast;
4. rooms on the south and west, with new kitchen to the southeast;
5. cells to the south of the main building, then eastern platform converted into a cemetery;
6. some secondary alterations when the monastery became a place of pilgrimage.

The small size of the communal buildings, the few cells (fewer than six with the two neighboring pharaonic tombs), the arrangements for work (six looms in all), and the graves in the cemetery (five or six) indicate that even in its best days the community was one of five or six monks only.

The numerous texts gathered up (about 1,400 Coptic ostraca and one in Greek) allow some insight into aspects of the daily life of this small community: weaving and trade in wine, for instance. The figure of Apa Markos, HEGUMENOS of the monastery, emerges from these letters.

The pottery (thousands of potsherds as well as 100 complete amphorae and remains of nearly 2,000 broken amphorae) includes a number of unpainted objects of various shapes: dishes, plates, cups, "pseudo-sigillate" bowls, kitchen ware, ovens, amphorae, water jars, basins, vats and mud bins. There is also another group consisting of a series of items with geometrical designs: vegetable or animal decoration. These are applied in either one or more colors, black or white on a red base, or in black or red on a lighter base (unpublished notes by Mme C. Neyret).

All these elements show that the monastery of Mark the Evangelist had several stages of development:

1. a stage intermediate between the period of absolute independence for the hermits and the period of strict organization with clearly defined community rules, characterized by a series of cells or lauras scattered around the cell of a hermit of renown who had attracted monks and become their head;
2. a stage of organized community life within an enclosed space;
3. a stage at which the monastery was no longer occupied by monks and had become a place of pilgrimage.

BIBLIOGRAPHY

Bonomi, J. "Topographical Notes on Western Thebes Collected in 1830." *Annales du Service des antiquités de l'Égypte* 7 (1906):82, no. 42.

Castel, G. "Etude d'une momie copte." In *Hommages à S. Sauneron,* Vol. 2, pp. 121–43. Cairo, 1979.

Monneret de Villard, U. "Una chiesa di tipo georgiana nella necropli Tebana." In *Coptic Studies in*

Honour of W. E. Crum, pp. 495–500. Boston, 1950.

Sauneron, S. "Travaux de l'IFAO en 1970–71." *Bulletin de l'Institut français d'Archéologie orientale* 71 (1971):236–76.

______. "Travaux de l'IFAO en 1972–1973." *Bulletin de l'Institut français d'Archéologie orientale* 72 (1973):218–263.

______. "Les Travaux de l'IFAO en 1973–1974." *Bulletin de l'Institut français d'Archéologie orientale* 73 (1974):184–233.

Winlock, H. E., and W. E. Crum. *The Monastery of Epiphanius at Thebes,* Vol. 1, p. 15. New York, 1926.

GEORGES CASTEL

QŪṢ, town known in the era of the pharaohs as Ksa or Ksi. From the Greek period onward (third century B.C.) it was known as Apollinopolis Parva. It evolved by taking advantage of the activities of QIFṬ, which the Greek kings had made the starting point for roads linking the Nile Valley and the ports on the Red Sea. But above all it was at that time a port on the Nile where the agricultural products of its environment were loaded. From the end of the third century A.D., its official name was changed to Diocletianopolis. No date can be fixed as regards the beginning of Christianity there. The SYNAXARION for 7 Tūt commemorates a family of six, martyred at Alexandria but coming from the neighborhood of the town, where they confessed their faith and because of them a crowd of people believed. It was the seat of a bishop at least from the fifth century. In about the sixth century, the city was called by its current name, Qūṣ. The ARAB CONQUEST OF EGYPT does not seem to have involved the settlement of a numerous Muslim community. Soon to be more important than Qifṭ, which remained the administrative capital, Qūṣ, which had basically a Christian population, no longer had any official role.

When the Fatimids had established their power in Egypt, one of their first concerns was to attract again, by way of the Nile, the major trade of the Indian Ocean toward the Mediterranean; they hoped to divert this commerce from the routes it was then using through Abbasid territory. The Red Sea ports were again employed. ʿAydhāb, situated at the outlet of the region of the gold mines in the Wādī al-ʿAllāqī, south of Aswan, became a busy anchorage. All the towns of Upper Egypt, and Qūṣ in particular, found new prosperity.

With the serious crises of the caliphate after 1067, the town was called upon to play a special role. The southern part of the Upper Ṣaʿīd—and above all the Aswan region, toward which the caliph's black troops retreated when they were expelled from Cairo—was for nearly a decade ill-controlled by the authorities. The turbulence of the Arab tribes, which had abandoned their obedience to the caliph, also increased the insecurity. The Qūṣ region seems to have been less troubled. It was thus natural that the ʿAydhāb caravan route, which until then had joined the Nile at Aswan, was diverted to Qūṣ. The superior officer entrusted with the maintenance of order in the Upper Ṣaʿīd established himself at Qūṣ during the last quarter of the eleventh century. The town then became the administrative center of the entire Upper Ṣaʿīd. A mint was established there in 1122, and in the second century of Fatimid rule, the military forces at the disposal of the governors of Upper Ṣaʿīd made Qūṣ into the most important station after the vizierate, a position that conferred de facto mastery of the Fatimid state. It is probable that the Shiʿite caliphate had more readily chosen Qūṣ as the new capital of Upper Ṣaʿīd because the Muslims (among whom Sunnism was still the majority faith) were small in number and the greater part of the population was Christian. If the development of trading activities, which periodically enlivened the town during the commercial season, contributed to the enrichment of the Christian community, the benefits for its services to the Fatimid authorities gave the Christian community its strength. It was probably during this period that the dozen churches of Qūṣ and its environs were built or rebuilt. These are listed in the description of the churches of Egypt that was compiled under the Ayyubids at the beginning of the thirteenth century. There Qūṣ is not separated from what is then called "the west of Qūṣ," that is, the part on the west (opposite) bank of the Nile between Naqādah and Qamūlah, and it seems that the preparation of the last recension of the SYNAXARION of Upper Egypt was made in one of the monasteries to the west of Qūṣ in the twelfth century or at the beginning of the thirteenth.

The Christian community of Qūṣ must have seen its riches and power grow. We may suppose that Christian families from other centers in the valley came to swell their ranks. From the end of the eleventh century, the bishop of Qūṣ made efforts to have it accepted that in the church he had precedence over the other bishops in the region. When subsequently around 1160, Shawār, the Muslim governor of the town, proposed to seize the vizierate by force, he thought it wise to conciliate the local

Christian community by making a vow to Saint George in his church of al-ʿAbbāsah at the gates of the town. Yāqūt, who produced his dictionary between 1215 and 1224, stated after spelling the name of the town, "it is a Coptic town."

However, one could foresee that this situation would not last. A consequence of the choice of Qūṣ as a regional center was the establishment in the town of a qāḍi (magistrate) of the Upper Ṣaʿid. And the advancement of Qūṣ had also attracted many Muslim families, some very wealthy, who had left localities like Aswan or Isnā to come and live there. The arrival of these Muslims also contributed to urban development. As was often the case at that period, the town must have had a somewhat casual and disorganized appearance due to built-up agglomerations—doubtless in part along the access roads—scattered around the old Christian center, which officially continued to be known as "the town." Significantly, the qāḍī lived "outside the town." The basic activities relating to the handling of goods arriving by road and leaving by the Nile also took place "outside the town." The residence of the governors must have been on the outskirts of "the town," not far from the Jāmiʿ al-ʿAmrī; it faced on a *maydān* (hippodrome or parade ground for the cavalry garrison), a feature characteristic of an age in which a foreign military unit of horse troops (increasingly of Turkish origin, and increasingly more dominant) put its stamp on the urban landscape. The presence of these representatives of the Muslim state also favored Islamization. The governors of the Ayyubid period increasingly surrounded themselves with educated Muslims, especially poets. Their official productions, being well received, could only strengthen the hitherto perhaps imperfect Arabic of the population and reinforce the power of attraction of the Muslim environment. Conversions to Islam took place.

Moreover, Qūṣ was not just an important spot on the main Indian Ocean trade route but also a staging-post on the way now favored by Muslim pilgrims to the Ḥijāz who wished to avoid the Crusaders' territories established in Palestine at the end of the eleventh century. Until the reconquest of Jerusalem by Ṣālaḥ al-Dīn a century later, there was no other route, and consequently pilgrims made use of it for a long time thereafter. Some of them, especially the Maghribīns (those from North Africa), having gone through the town, returned to settle there. Thus gradually a coherent Muslim environment came into being. In 1210 Qūṣ had its first *madrasah* (Islamic college). One can well imagine that during the second half of the century, under the first Mamluks, the Christian community ceased to be dominant, if not numerically then at least socially. In a town of indefinite limits, straggling between gardens, the old Christian center around the Church of Saint Stephen was for the Muslims of Qūṣ just the "Ḥārat al-Naṣārā." (The term *ḥārah* seems to have meant a distinct center of population but not a closed quarter, i.e., one of several similar sections of the agglomeration.)

The two communities in the town, one expanding and the other on the defensive, came into confrontation toward the end of the thirteenth and beginning of the fourteenth century. The situation especially lent itself to confrontation at Qūṣ, though it cannot be separated from the more general Egyptian context. At Qūṣ, as elsewhere, the dominant military class, that is, the sultan and the amirs, employed Christian secretaries who worked in the service of the *diwan* and saw to the collection of the fiscal revenues. Some elements of the taxes (e.g., those collected by the sultan himself in the whole of the northwestern part of the province of Qūṣ) were levied on a peasantry that was still in large measure Christian. In others, many conversions to Islam had occurred, and the Christian secretaries found themselves in a delicate situation when they had to show strictness against Muslims. The town Muslims in particular accused them of showing bias in the exercise of their office, especially since some of the Christian secretaries reached high financial positions in the capital, from which they could intervene. The Muslim community, however, was also represented at Cairo, where from 1295 to 1302 a Muslim from Qūṣ took on the responsibilities of the Grand *Qāḍī*. Consequently, local incidents were magnified in both directions as a result of external pressures. Often the Christian secretaries, backed by the Mamluk authorities (and therefore implicated with them), won the day. Toward the end of the thirteenth and the beginning of the fourteenth century, during the period between the two great sultanates of Qalāwūn and al-Nāṣir Muḥammad, and perhaps because power was so bitterly disputed among the amirs, the Muslim civil population became more insistent on exacting from the sultans and amirs a minimal favor from the Christian secretaries, namely, their forced conversion, and, by extension, stricter respect for the laws of Islam in an Islamic state. This was a show of opposition to the Mamluk authorities, who were ill tolerated, and a genuine religious demand.

In 1300 most of the churches in Egypt had been closed for a year. It seems that the Christian community of Qūṣ resolved to resist, gradually reopening the churches when it was possible to do so, sometimes with unwise demonstrations. They affirmed their exclusive presence in those parts of the city that they occupied, particularly in the Christian sector. To do this it was necessary on occasion to remove the Muslim places of worship that had been built among Christian dwellings. In 1307 an operation of this kind engendered a violent reaction from the Muslim population; thirteen Christian places of worship were attacked and destroyed in a single morning. The repressive action taken by the Mamluk authorities was severe, and similar events did not recur till the great crisis of 1321, which went beyond the town of Qūṣ in its scope. Then six churches were again devastated, which indicates that in the interval at least a partial reconstruction had taken place. No later incidents are known. In fact, the general administrative development of the Muslim state under al-Malik al-Nāṣir Muḥammad does not seem to have lessened the role of the Christian, or superficially converted, secretaries in the state. Quite the contrary. This is doubtless the period when Athanasius of Qūṣ referred to the ignorance of his coreligionists of their own language, and drew up in Arabic his grammar of the Coptic language. This is an indication of a decline in the knowledge of Coptic; it is also a sign that the Christians nevertheless had a place in the administrative structures of the Arab-Muslim state. At Qūṣ the destructive acts of 1307 and 1321 doubtless damaged the integrity of the Christian community, but they did not succeed in turning it into Muslim territory, which appears to have been one of the purposes for destroying churches. As to violence, which in general terms was hard on the Christians, we cannot say how the relationship between the two communities would have developed in the second part of the century had Qūṣ remained a center of attraction for the Muslims of Upper Egypt.

In fact, the position of Qūṣ gradually changed during the second half of the fourteenth century, as the town was no longer the most suitable spot in the upper valley to station troops for the maintenance of order (and in particular to control the bedouin tribesmen).

The center of control, whatever kind it might be, now had to be located in the north at Asyūṭ or, later, at Jirjā, because of the establishment of routes from the West to Sudanese Africa and of the disequilibrium this had caused in the bedouin world. This disturbance of the equilibrium, moreover, in part occasioned the disorders of 1365–1366 in the eastern desert and the closure of the ʿAydhāb route. Gradually after that date, and after a serious drought suffered by the town and its region in 1374–1375, the spice trade ceased to pass through Qūṣ. The plague of 1405–1406, which, according to al-MAQRĪZĪ, claimed 17,000 victims at Qūṣ, doubtless cleared out a good part of its population, and there was no longer anything to encourage people to come and settle. The governor of Qūṣ was of only secondary importance under the Circassian Mamluks. As the structures of the Muslim state no longer operated to the advantage of the town, the Muslim community was affected by departures or by the absence of new settlements to fill the gaps made by the epidemics. Symbolic of this eclipse was the transfer of the *qāḍī* to Qinā after the Ottoman occupation. The importance of the Christian community, therefore, began to increase in the town. This increase owed less to the exercise of fiscal service that governmental prohibitions sometimes called in question against the Christians than to the traditional activities of Qūṣ, particularly textile craftsmanship and the export of its products to the upper valley of the Nile and probably to Ethiopia. We may suppose that relations between the Christian community of Qūṣ and the Christians of Ethiopia, who were at the time feared by the Mamluk state, were not purely commercial. In 1430 a governor of Qūṣ left to take service with the negus. When the dilapidated urban environs of the medieval period gradually fell into ruins, and especially in the seventeenth century, it was initially the peripheral Muslim part of the town that was affected. The Christian center around the Church of Saint Stephen, even if penetrated little by little by the Muslims, survived. At the time of the French expedition at the end of the eighteenth century, in a town of less than 5,000 inhabitants, the proportion of Christians appeared to be significant.

The proportion declined during the nineteenth century, when Qūṣ again saw its population growing because of the rural exodus from the Islamized parts of the countryside. Some Coptic Christians became Protestants. Modern education made it possible for many to leave Qūṣ. But the situation of the Christian community of Qūṣ, which is no longer capital of the Upper Ṣaʿīd, no longer differs in any way from that of the other Christians of Upper Egypt.

BIBLIOGRAPHY

Crum, W. E. *Coptic Ostraca from the Collection of the Egypt Exploration Fund, the Cairo Museum and Others*, pp. 45 and 73. London, 1902.

______. *The Monastery of Epiphanius at Thebes*, Vol. 2, pp. 187, 224, 271. New York, 1926.

Garcin, J.-C. *Un Centre musulman de la Haute-Egypte médiévale: Qus.* Cairo, 1976.
Gril, D. "Une Emeute anti-chrétienne à Qūs au début du VIII/XIV siècles." *Annales islamologiques* 16 (1980):241–74.
Maspero, J., and G. Wiet. *Matériaux pour servir à la géographie de l'Egypte,* pp. 155ff. Cairo, 1919.
Munier, H. *Recueil des listes épiscopales de l'église Copte,* pp. 14 and 62. Cairo, 1943.
Revillout, E. "Textes coptes extraits de la correspondance de Saint Pisenthius." *Revue égyptologique,* 9 (1900):142–52 and 154.

JEAN-CLAUDE GARCIN

QUSṬANṬĪN IBN ABĪ AL-MAʻĀLĪ IBN ABĪ AL-FATḤ ABŪ AL-FATḤ, fourteenth-century Melchite of Cairo who belonged to a family of important state officials. Qusṭanṭīn must have been born around 1270, as his son was already a bishop in 1358. He knew Greek extremely well and had a fine Arabic style. He composed at least two works, both liturgical. Near the end of his life he withdrew to the Monastery of Saint Catherine on Mount Sinai. This summary of information about him derives from an autograph manuscript dated 1335 (Sinai Arabic 264, containing 206 sheets, not yet published or studied).

The first of his works, *Kitāb al-Hādī fī Maʻrifat al-Samādī,* appears not to have survived, though it is mentioned by the author in the second colophon of his *Typikon* (fol. 204b), which shows that it was composed prior to 1355. Speaking of John of Damascus he says, "For, during the vizierate of his father, at the time of the King Heraclius, Damascus was taken from the Greeks in the year 6148 of the world. Now this saint succeeded his father as vizier, as I explained in the book I composed and entitled, *Al-Hādī fī Maʻrifat al-Samādī* in the chapter of the *cheironomia.*"

The last word of the title poses a problem, since the meaning of the word *al-samādī* is not clear. For that reason, A. S. Atiya and J. N. Youssef (p. 492) read it *al-samāwī,* the heavenly. They have been followed by J. Nasrallah (1981, p. 150). But there is no doubt that it must be read *al-samādī,* for two reasons: first, because of the very clear handwriting of the autograph; and second because of the rhyme with *al-Hādī,* which is an essential element in old Arabic titles.

Qusṭanṭīn agreed to translate the *Typikon of Saint Sabas* into Arabic at the request of one who "loved virtue." The *Typikon* is the manual giving dispositions for all the liturgical ceremonies, especially the recitation of the divine office; the *Typikon of Saint Sabas* was used in the Arabic East, and was composed by Saint John of Damascus.

Qusṭanṭīn completed his translation on Tuesday, 5 December 6844 of the world/5 December A.D. 1355 (fol. 203a).

The Greek manuscript that served as a basis for Qusṭanṭīn's translation was copied by Hesychius, monk of Saint Sabas. He completed his copy on Monday, 20 April 1187. On two occasions (fols. 197a and 204b), Qusṭanṭīn states that this manuscript may have been copied from the original copy of John of Damascus.

This Greek manuscript bore an act of bequest in favor of the monastery of Saint Sabas. Nevertheless, in 1355, it was in Cairo, in the Greek quarter (ḤĀRIT AL-RŪM), in the Church of the Forty Martyrs (fol. 204b). It was there that Qusṭanṭīn translated it.

Shortly afterward, Qusṭanṭīn donated his translation to his own son, Marquṣ, the Melchite bishop of Damietta, for his use during his lifetime, on condition that it should subsequently be bequeathed to the Monastery of Saint Catherine on Mount Sinai. The act of donation is dated Wednesday, 28 February 1358. It is remarkable that Marquṣ wrote the date in Coptic cursive figures. The manuscript found its way to Sinai shortly afterward, as is indicated in a note written by the bishop of Sinai, who was also called Marquṣ and who was probably the same one mentioned in the Sinai Arabic 90. It should be noted that the bishop of Damietta speaks of his father as "the lord [my] father," which suggests a man who was highly respected socially.

After this date, Qusṭanṭīn entered the Monastery of Saint Catherine, as his wife had died and his children were already independent. He wore the monastic habit and took the name Anṭūniyūs, as is indicated in a later note added in the margin of the colophon (fol. 203b).

The manuscript contains 206 sheets, but folios 205–206, which were blank, were filled by two different hands that can be dated as the end of the fourteenth century, probably on Mount Sinai. The other folios contain the following:

Fols. 1b–2b: translator's preface in fine rhymed prose
Fols. 2b–6b: translation of the *Agrypniai,* or night vigils preceding solemn feasts
Fols. 6b–21a: translation of the Ordo of Matins
Fols. 21a–135a: translation of the ordinary of the whole year, from September to August

Fols. 135b–97a: translation of the periods of Lent, Easter, and Pentecost
Fols. 197b–99a: translator's note explaining that this is the office of monks, and indicating how this office should be adapted for lay people
Fols. 199a–203a: Six translator's notes on certain feasts, namely the Exaltation of the Cross, the Vigil of Christmas, the Vigil of the Epiphany, the Lent of the Apostles, Holy Week, and the Washing of Feet
Fols. 203a–203b: first colophon
Fols. 203b–204a: two notes concerning the eleven days on which the Liturgy of Saint Basil is celebrated, and Dissidents' Week
Fol. 204b: second colophon.

The sections composed by Qusṭanṭīn are written in an elevated style, in fine rhymed prose. Occasionally the author has employed terms so rare that readers have added explanations in the margin.

Apart from the autograph manuscript, another manuscript exists (Mār Elias Shuwayya, 30). This was copied by the deacon Sābā ibn Tādurus al-Ḥawrānī at the Monastery of Saint John the Baptist at Dūmā (Lebanon) between 4 June 1594 and 16 March 1595.

However, Qusṭanṭīn's name has been omitted, and this caused Nasrallah to think that the translation was the work of the deacon Sābā. He has recently corrected this error (Naṣrallah, 1981, p. 149, n. 195).

What is more, in the preface the copyist added an interpolation to the effect that Patriarch Gregory the Sinaite had translated the *Agrypniai* into Arabic. Since he speaks of the "deceased patriarch," Nasrallah deduced that Gregory the Sinaite, who became Melchite patriarch of Alexandria, died before 1355, the date of composition of the preface (Nasrallah, 1981, p. 149). The truth of the matter is that the two lines on Patriarch Gregory are an addition on the part of Sābā ibn Tādurus; moreover, they interrupt the sentence and spoil the rhyme. Thus Gregory died before 1594 and not before 1355.

According to Nasrallah (1963, p. 167), the end is missing in this manuscript. It lacks the translation of the periods of Easter and Pentecost and the explanations and notes composed by Qusṭanṭīn.

BIBLIOGRAPHY

Arranz, M., S.J. *Le Typicon du Monastère du Saint-Sauveur à Messine, texte grec et traduction française.* Orientalia Christiana Analecta 185, p. 446. Rome, 1969.

Atiya, A. S., and J. N. Youssef. *Catalogue Raisonné of the Mount Sinai Arabic Manuscripts* (in Arabic), pp. 490–92. Alexandria, 1970.

Nasrallah, J. *Catalogue des manuscrits du Liban,* Vol. 3, pp. 165–67. Beirut, 1963.

______. *Histoire du mouvement littéraire dans l'église melchite du Ve au XXe siècle,* Vol. 3, pt. 2, pp. 148–50. Louvain and Paris, 1981.

KHALIL SAMIR, S.J.

R

RABITAT AL-QUDS, an association that provides educational programs and administrative assistance to those who wish to visit the Holy Land as pilgrims. Established in 1944 under the presidency of the metropolitan of Jerusalem, Anbā THEOPHILUS, the association is now headquartered at Cairo. In 1972 the top of the association building was consecrated as a church by Pope Shenouda III in the presence of Anbā Basilios, the metropolitan of Jerusalem and the Near East.

ARCHBISHOP BASILIOS

RĀGHIB SAWIRUS. *See* Theological College.

RAINER, ARCHDUKE (1827–1913), Austrian collector. He was a prince of the House of Hapsburg, being the fourth son of Archduke Rainer, viceroy of Lombardy-Venice and a son of Emperor Leopold II. He assembled a large collection of papyri—hieratic, demotic, Coptic, Greek, and Arabic—originating from a large find at Arsinoë in 1877–1878. The collection was acquired by the Imperial Library of Vienna, and in 1892 an account of it was published as *Papyrus Erzherzog Rainer: Führer durch die Ausstellung*. The archduke was a patron of the Arts and Crafts Museum (1862–1898) and curator of the Academy of Sciences (1861–1913).

BIBLIOGRAPHY

Dawson, W. R., and E. P. Uphill. *Who Was Who in Egyptology*, p. 241. London, 1972.

Kammerer, W., comp. *A Coptic Bibliography*. Ann Arbor, Mich., 1950; repr. New York, 1969.

M. L. BIERBRIER

RAINER PAPYRI. *See* Papyrus Collections.

RAITHOU (al-Rāyah), ancient town, which has disappeared, 5 miles (8 km) south of al-Ṭūr, a small town on the west coast of the southern Sinai Peninsula. The information collected there by Porphyry Ouspensky in 1850 places al-Rāyah, or at least its ruins, on the edge of the sea, two hours' march south of al-Ṭūr (see also Maspero and Wiet, 1919, pp. 98–99).

In the neighborhood of this town several sites were inhabited by anchorites or cenobites. It cannot be stated with any precision at what date the first ascetics established themselves there. The APOPHTHEGMATA PATRUM mentions Raithou several times, but this collection brings together pieces of very diverse origin and period, which therefore are difficult to date. Similarly, there are no certain documents for fixing the date of the martyrdom of the forty monks at Raithou, perhaps fourth or fifth century, massacred by Blemmyes or Agarenes (Devreesse, 1940, pp. 216–21). Although it is very probable that Sinai was inhabited by monks from the fourth century on, the sources do not confirm their presence at Raithou before the beginning of the fifth century.

Amun of Raithou paid a visit to Sisoes at Clysma (*Apophthegmata patrum*, Sisoes 26); Sisoes did not install himself there before 429 (Chitty, 1966, p. 79, n. 83). Three anchorites from Raithou came before 428 to join Euthymius in his laura near Jerusalem (Festugière, 1962, p. 79). A solitary from Raithou named Zosimus became the disciple of Peter the Iberian (c. 409–489) toward the middle of the fifth century. Generally dated to the sixth century, the report of Ammonius, who was a monk of Canopus near Alexandria, and also a pilgrim to Jerusalem and then to Sinai, where he gathered up the history of the martyrs of Raithou and of Sinai, describes a semi-anchoritism at Raithou very similar to that of Egypt. Ammonius notes that at Raithou only one of the hermits "who lived separately in caves" was a Roman, which, Tillemont (1732) remarks, leads one to think that the others were autochthonous. We know that at the Council of CONSTANTINOPLE in 536 a monk-priest named Theonas represented not only the mountain of Sinai but also the "laura" (some manuscripts say the desert) of Raithou (Schwartz, Vol. 3, pp. 37, 51, 130; see the index); Eutychius (Saʿīd ibn Baṭrīq) states that a delegation of monks from Sinai asked Emperor JUSTINIAN (527–565) to build monasteries to protect them against the raids of the Blemmyes and the Arabs. The text states that a monastery was built at Rāyah (Vol. 2, pp. 202–03). It is known that the monastery of the Virgin in Sinai was completed in 556 (Stein, Vol. 2, p. 300).

The Nestorian traveler known as COSMAS INDICOPLEUSTES, whose report was written between 547 and 549, speaks of the monastery of Raithou, where Menas, one of his traveling companions, became a monk. He identifies Raithou with the biblical Elim, where twelve springs flowed.

John Climacus (c. 570–649) wrote his famous *Ladder of Divine Ascent* at the request of John, HEGUMENOS of Raithou, with whom he exchanged letters. This was perhaps the same man who is called John the Cilician in the *Pratum spirituale* of John Moschus (c. 550–619). The last source mentions three anchorites at Raithou. It was also a monk of Raithou, named Daniel, who wrote the life of John Climacus.

Apart from two rather vague references to the monk Epiphanius (perhaps in the ninth century) and to Daniel of Ephesus (in the fifteenth century), we find no further reference to monks at Raithou until the travelers of the sixteenth century.

The first sixteenth-century mention of a monastery in this part of the Sinai Peninsula is by Jean Thenaud in 1512 (p. 81). He notes that there is no potable water at al-Ṭūr; one must seek it "half a French league from there, near the sumptuous ruined monastery which Justinian once had built, the abbot of which was Saint John, to whom John Climacus addressed his book on the spiritual life (The Ladder of Paradise)." He, too, associates Raithou with the twelve springs of Elim.

In 1588, the Russian merchant Basil Posniakoff wrote of the "monastery of Saint John of Raithou, ruined from top to bottom by the accursed Turks," at "three versts [a little more than 2 miles/3 km] from al-Ṭūr" (Volkoff, p. 28).

Claude SICARD visited the site in 1720, but says very little about it; the monastery is that of John of Raithou, friend of John Climacus, and there are still gardens and caves in good condition. On his map of 1722 he places the monastery a little to the north of the well of sweet water and of Elim.

The archimandrite Ouspensky noted in 1850 that the monastery dedicated to Saint John the Baptist and founded by Justinian had been destroyed by al-Ḥākim at the beginning of the eleventh century and had become the cemetery for the Christians of al-Ṭūr. It is remarkable that all the Russian travelers designate the town of al-Ṭūr by the name of Raithou. Ouspensky notes that the ancient Raithou was at the place today called Rāyah, and that ruins are still visible: a fortress and a well of sweet water. He adds that near the Jabal Ḥammām Sidna Mūsā, three and a half hours' march northwest of al-Ṭūr, there are hermitages and a church fitted up in caves. He thus clearly distinguishes the cenobium of Justinian to the northeast and the hermitages near the sea to the northwest. The latter, of a type common in Egypt, are well described by Wellsted (1838, Vol. 2, pp. 15–19), at a place called al-Wādī.

BIBLIOGRAPHY

Chitty, D. J. *The Desert a City*. London, 1966.

Devreesse, R. "Le christianisme dans la péninsule sinaïtique, des origines à l'arrivée des musulmans." *Revue biblique* 49 (1940):205–233. (The author is wrong in placing Raithou near the Wādī Gharandal, more than 62.5 miles/100 km north of al-Ṭūr.)

Festugière, A. J. *Cyrille de Scythopolis: Vie de saint Euthyme*. Moines d'orient III/1. Paris, 1962.

Maspero, J., and G. Wiet. *Matériaux pour servir à la géographie de l'Egypte*. Mémoires de l'Institut français d'Archéologie orientale 36. Cairo, 1919.

Sicard, C. *Oeuvres*, ed. M. Martin, 3 vols. Bibliothèque d'études 83–85. Cairo, 1982.

Stein, E. *Histoire du Bas Empire*, 2 vols. Paris and Brussels, 1949–1959.

Thenaud, J. *Le Voyage d'outremer*, ed. C. Schefer. Paris, 1884.

Tillemont, L. S. le Nain de. *Mémoires pour servir à l'histoire ecclésiastique*, 16 vols. Venice, 1732.

Volkoff, O. V. *Voyageurs russes en Egypte*. Cairo, 1972.

Wellsted, J. R. *Travels in Arabia*, 2 vols. London, 1838.

RENÉ-GEORGES COQUIN
MAURICE MARTIN, S.J.

RAMSES WISSA WASSEF (1911–1974), architect born in Cairo, the eldest son of WISSA WASSEF (Pasha), the sometime speaker of the Chamber of Deputies.

In 1938 he joined the staff of the Higher School of Fine Arts at Cairo University. He was chairman of the department of architecture and art history from 1965 to 1969, when he resigned to devote himself to research.

His style was reconciled to past tradition, to the climate, and to natural materials. He excelled in designing brick vaults and domes, a form inherited from early dynasties, and in creating oriental stained glass windows from plaster and colored glass chips, for which he won the National Arts Award in 1961.

He designed a Coptic school in QAṢR AL-SHAM' in Old Cairo and the junior school of the French Lycée at Bāb-al-Lūq. He collaborated with Ḥassan Fatḥy on the village of al-Qurnah near Luxor. The best-known works of Ramses Wissa Wassef are the two Coptic cathedrals of Zamalek and Heliopolis, his own house at 'Ajūzah in Cairo, the complex of tapestry workshops at Ḥarrāniyyah, the chapel of the Dominican convent at 'Abbāsiyyah, and the Moukhtar Museum at Gezira.

The Ḥarrāniyyah workshops were the culmination of Wassef's philosophy that children have innate artistic creativity. Choosing the medium of tapestry weaving he experimented, with parental consent, with selected children from the elementary school at Qaṣr al-Sham'. He felt weaving to represent a balanced fusion between art and manual labor. The looms were vertical and simple to handle; wool came from local sources and was dipped in natural dyes. Inspiration came from within each child.

The experiments proved successful. From the first show organized by UNESCO in Paris in January 1950, exhibits were shown in Switzerland, Sweden, Denmark, Norway, the Netherlands, France, Germany, England, Italy, and the United States.

In September 1983 he was posthumously awarded the Agha Khan "Grand Prix" for the architectural ensemble conceived, created, and executed by him at Ḥarrāniyyah village in the province of Giza.

Children weaving at Ḥarraniyyah. *Courtesy Lola Atiya.*

BIBLIOGRAPHY

Forman, B., and Ramses Wissa Wassef. *Fleurs du Desert. Tapisseries d'enfants égyptiens.* Prague, 1961.

Forman, W., and J. Hoffman. "The Harrania Tapestries. New Art from an Ancient People." *Lithopenion* 34 (Summer 1974).

Juvin, R. "Notre Vérité." *Le Mur Vivant* 37 (1975).

Morineau, R. "Artisanat égyptien: La tapisserie sauvage." *L'Estampille* 59 (1974):28–31.

Ramses Wissa Wassef. *Tapisseries de la Jeune Egypte,* with photographs by W. Forman. Prague, 1972.

"Tapisseries modernes d'Egypte." *Connaissance des Arts* (March 1965):98–101.

"Une tentative d'art artisanal." *L'Art sacré* (September-October 1956):18–29.

"Tisserands, sculpteurs et poètes: les enfants du Nil." *100 Idées* 7 (April 1974).

Winslow, H. "The Child Weavers of Egypt." *Craft Horizons* (January 1958):30–33.

CÉRÈS WISSA WASSEF

RAMSHAUSEN, FRANCISCUS WILHELM VON (seventeenth century), German Coptologist. Born in the small town of Quakenbruck in Westphalia, he studied theology in the Lutheran tradition and read widely the travel works on Egypt, particularly the writings of the Jesuit Athanasius KIRCHER, whose experiences among the Copts must have influenced him greatly in his studies. He wrote and published a comprehensive doctoral thesis on the Copts and submitted it to the University of Jena in the year 1666. Written in Latin, his own work has the composite title of ⲧⲉⲕⲕⲗⲏⲥⲓⲁ ⲛⲕⲉϥϯ (tekklēsia Nkefti) *sive Exercitatio Theologica, Ecclesia Copticae, Hoc Est Christianorum Aegyptiacae Ortum, Progressum Praecipuaque Doctrinae. . . .* The book has been described by W. Kammerer in *A Coptic Bibliography* (1950, 1969) as "probably the oldest European work on the Copts," a verdict confirmed by A. Mallon in his renowned *Grammaire copte.*

Von Ramshausen's approach to the subject is systematic, original, and thorough. Starting with the definition of the word "Copt," he discussed the Coptic language in its hieroglyphic background. Then he discussed the Coptic Bibles and other Coptic manuscripts available at his time. Next, he dealt with the history of the Coptic church and Coptic persecutions and heresies in Egypt, extending his panoramic view of Coptic Egypt beyond the sixth century. Coptic dogmas, sacraments, and rituals are also treated at a time when the West was oblivious of that nation in the framework of Eastern Christianity. In this way, von Ramshausen laid a solid basis for the study of the Coptic language and Coptic church history for subsequent generations of scholars in the West. He drew attention to the antiquity of the Coptic church fathers and to the establishment of the Coptic church by Saint MARK, its first patriarch. He was outspoken in his sympathy for the ancient church. He appears to have had access to historical material no longer available, which enhances the value of his writing.

The genuine contribution of von Ramshausen's work is his objectivity in dealing with the Coptic church, which makes it overshadow subsequent works by even so great a scholar as Renaudot, whose *Liturgiarum Orientalium Collectio* (1716) was apparently more critical and unsympathetic than his predecessor's. This alone entitles von Ramshausen to a place in the story of Coptology.

BIBLIOGRAPHY

Helderman, J. "Franciscus Wilhelmus von Ramshausen Rediscovered." *Jaarbericht van het vooraziatisch-egyptisch genootschap Ex Orient Lux* 22 (1971–1972):318–34.

Trommler, C. H. *Abbildung der jakobitischen oder coptischen Kirche.* Jena, 1749.

———. *Bibliothecae Copto-Jacobiticae Specimen.* Leipzig, 1767.

Voyageurs occidentaux en Egypte (1400–1700). Series published by the Institut français d'Archéologie orientale, nos. 3, 6, 10, and 12. Cairo, 1971.

J. HELDERMAN

RAMZI TADRUS. *See* Literature, Copto-Arabic.

RANKE, HERMANN (1878–1953), German Egyptologist. He studied under A. Erman in Berlin. He moved to the United States after the Nazis came to power in Germany and was associated with the Philadelphia Museum. His publications can be found in W. Kammerer's *A Coptic Bibliography* (1950, 1969). He returned to Europe after the war and died in Freiburg.

BIBLIOGRAPHY

Dawson, W. R., and E. P. Uphill. *Who Was Who in Egyptology,* p. 242. London, 1972.

Kammerer, W., comp. *A Coptic Bibliography.* Ann Arbor, Mich., 1950; repr. New York, 1969.

AZIZ S. ATIYA

RAPHAEL, an archangel. The Hebrew word *repha'el* can mean "God has healed." Latin authors such as Gregory the Great (*Evangelia Homiliarum* 34.9) interpreted the name as "medicine of God." In a Coptic text (Kropp, 1930, Vol. 2, p. 165) it has the meaning of "cure."

The archangel Raphael appears for the first time in Tobit (3rd century B.C.), written by a Jew of the Diaspora, probably in Egypt. Here Raphael introduces himself as one of the seven angels who present the prayers of the just to God and who stand in the presence of God (Tb. 12:15). Hence the many guises under which he helps men. Under the symbolic name of Azarias ("the Lord helps"), he accompanies the young Tobias, son of Tobit, on his journey to Raguel of Medes in Ecbatana, where Tobias meets Sarah (Tb. 5:13;7:7). On the way to Raguel, Raphael frees Tobias from a monstrous fish that attacks him as he is bathing in the river Tigris (6:1–3); he later saves Sarah and Tobias from the snares of the devil Asmodeus, who has killed Sarah's previous seven husbands (6:14;8:3). Finally, as the etymology of his name indicates, he cures the blindness of Tobit, the father of Tobias (11:7–14).

In 1 *Enoch,* Raphael is one of the four archangels, together with MICHAEL, Suriel (or Uriel), and GABRIEL (1 *En.* 9.1; 10.4–8), or as one of the seven (1 *En.* 20.3). Since Raphael is the angel of men's souls, he accompanies Enoch on his heavenly journey and explains the distribution of souls in the various sections of *sheol* after death (1 *En.* 22.3–6). He also appears with Enoch in the paradise of righteousness and tells him of the tree of wisdom (1 *En.* 32.6). In Enoch's vision, the archangel Raphael is charged by God to bind Asael hand and foot and to heal earth, which the angels have corrupted (1 *En.* 10.4–8; 54.6). This charge appropriately reflects the double meaning of the root *rapha,* "to tie" and "to heal." Raphael is also said to have power over illness and wounds (1 *En.* 40.9). In the *Apocalypse of Ezra,* after Michael the archangel has departed, Raphael ministers to Ezra under the title of commander-in-chief of the angels (*Apoc. Esd.* 1.4). He is also said to be present at the end of men's lives (*Apoc. Esd.* 6.1f.). In the Apocalypse of Moses, with other angels he takes part in the burial of Abel next to Adam (*Apoc. Mos.* 40). In postbiblical Jewish literature further details are added, such as Raphael's visit to Abraham (Gn. 18; *bT Joma* 37a), his curing of pious men, and his overpowering of savage beasts. He is also said to preside over one of the four cohorts of angels surrounding the throne of God.

In Christian literature he appears as one of the four, or seven, archangels created first of all by God (*Evangelium Bartholomaei* 4.29), and, in accordance with the etymology of his name, he is held to be the angel of healing, patron of medicine (Origen *Homilies on Numbers* 14.2; *De principiis* 1.8.1), and heavenly doctor. This is why some, according to ORIGEN, represent him as a serpent (*Contra Celsum* 6.30). As with Tobias, Raphael guides men on their journeys and for their sake overpowers the demon Asmodeus. He helps them to earn their living and is present at the hour of death. With Michael, Gabriel, and other angels, he has the power to punish Satan (*Ev. Barthol.* 4.29).

In Coptic literature we know of only two encomia, undoubtedly pseudepigraphic, dedicated to the archangel Raphael. One is attributed to Saint JOHN CHRYSOSTOM and is conserved in the British Museum, ed. Budge, 1915, pp. 526–33, 1189–91 [texts]; 1034ff., 1199 [trans.]. Here, as in Tobit, Raphael binds the wicked demon Asmodeus with fetters, and his name is given the meaning of "God who guideth men." The episodes of Tobit are recalled, along with the fact that Raphael filled the poor man's house with joy and the rich man's with health (fol. 3b). Besides taking the prayer of Sarah to the seventh heaven, he is a faithful servant who accepts no payment; he is obedient to God and to the man for whom he prepares meals as a chief cook (fols. 4a–b). He is also the patron of the wedding. The appearance of Raphael to Saint JOHN CHRYSOSTOM while he was celebrating mass is narrated in this encomium (fol. 6a). Raphael is shown as the guardian angel of Chrysostom, whom he has not abandoned "for a single hour, half an hour, or the blink of an eye" (fol. 6b). Raphael sends Chrysostom to the emperor Arcadius, who builds a shrine in his honor.

The other encomium, in Sahidic, *In Raphaelem archangelum,* is attributed to the patriarch THEOPHILUS OF ALEXANDRIA; fragments are conserved in the libraries of Paris, Naples, and Vienna [identified and edited with a Latin translation by Orlandi, (1972)]. The fragments belong to two codices from the White Monastery (DAYR ANBĀ SHINŪDAH). The encomium is a homily given in the presence of Theodosius II and contains a conversation of Theophilus with the Emperor Theodosius I concerning the building of a shrine in honor of the archangel Raphael in Alexandria, and also the initiation of his cult in the city by a Roman widow called Dronice. Later the narrative tells of the building of the shrine on the island of Patres and of two miracles: the rescue of some people who were shipwrecked and the recovery of a ship, and the liberation from barbarians who wished to sack the island. The data that the homily gives concerning the construction of the shrine agree with those found in the HISTORY OF THE PATRIARCHS OF ALEXANDRIA (in Arabic, PO 1, pp. 426–30).

Five homilies in honor of Saint Raphael have been preserved in Arabic, one of which is attributed to CYRIL I of Alexandria on the feast of the consecration of the church built by Theophilus (3 Nasī/26 August) (On these homilies, see Müller, 1959, n. 131.)

Other writings in Coptic tell us that Raphael was the fourth angel to be created, after Saklitaboth, Michael, and Gabriel (*Installatio Michaelis,* ed. Müller, 1962, n. 3), and that his installation took place after that of Michael and Gabriel (Müller, 1962, n. 9); no date to commemorate this is given, however, suggesting that there was no feast to celebrate his installation. Raphael has an important role in exorcism texts (Stegemann, 1934, pp. 69–70; Kropp, 1930–1931, pp. 3 and 82). He dispenses the holy oil for healing (Coptic Evangelium Bartholomaei 85f., ed. Kropp, 1930–1931, Vol. 1, p. 80, and Vol. 2, p. 250) and he is the protector against fever and the angel of strength and good health (Kropp, 1930–1931, Vol. 1, p. 20, and Vol. 2, p. 203). He is also invoked in a blessing for success in fishing (Kropp, 1930–1931, Vol. 1, p. 33, and Vol. 2, p. 99). All the traits attributed to Raphael in these texts are derived from his activities as narrated in Tobit.

When he is mentioned with other archangels, he comes after Michael and Gabriel. In the Coptic liturgy Raphael is the third archangel. His feast is celebrated on 3 Nasī, although in the encomium attributed to Chrysostom, it was the fourth of the epagomenic (intercalary) days (4 Nasī). Sixteen doxologies or hymns in his honor are known (Müller, 1959, pp. 48–53); these emphasize that he is a servant and instrument of God. He does nothing on his own account—it is God who acts through his intercession. The chief characteristic of Raphael is joy, since he brought joy to the ancient parents of Tobias. On occasions he appears closely united to John the Baptist and the Emperor Theodosius. His cult does not appear to have been particularly widespread, since only one church is mentioned as being dedicated to him. As with other angels, the Coptic tradition relates appearances of Raphael to several saints, such as the martyrs Philotheus and Paese. He is also credited with having miraculously freed the Emperor Theodosius from being swallowed by a shark.

BIBLIOGRAPHY

Budge, E. A. T. W. *Miscellaneous Coptic Texts,* pp. 526–33, 1189–91. London, 1915.

Kropp, A. *Ausgewählte koptische Zaubertexte,* preface by Jean Capart, foreword by W. E. Crum. Brussels, 1930–1931.

Mara, M. G. "Raffaele arcangelo," In *Bibliotheca Sanctorum,* Vol. 10, pp. 1357–68. Istituto Giovanni XXIII della Pontificia Università Lateranese, Cittá Nouva Editrice. Rome, 1968.

Michl, J. "Engel VIII (Raphael)." *Reallexion für Antike und Christentum,* Vol. 5, pp. 252–54. Stuttgart, 1962.

Müller, C. D. G. *Die Engellehre der koptischen Kirche,* pp. 48–53; 239–43. Wiesbaden, 1959.

———. *Die Bücher der Einsetzung der Erzengel Michael und Gabriel.* CSCO 225–26, Scriptores Coptici, Vols. 31–32. Louvain, 1962.

Orlandi, T. "Un encomio copto di Raffaele Arcangelo." *Rivista degli Studi Orientali* 47 (1972):211–33.

Stegemann, V. *Die koptischen Zaubertexte der Sammlung Papyrus Erzherzog Rainer.* Heidelberg, 1934.

GONZALO ARANDA PÉREZ

RASHĪD (Rosetta), city in the Egyptian Delta situated west of Lake Burullus, some 26 miles (42 km) northwest of Damanhūr near the Nile mouth known as Maṣabb Rashīd. In Greek the city was known as Bolbitinē. Westerners know the place as Rosetta, a name famous for the stone found not far from the city that provided the key to the decipherment of Egyptian hieroglyphs.

In Christian-Arabic sources from the Arabic period, Rashīd is first mentioned in connection with the heresy of the BARSANUPHIANS and Gaianites (see GAIANUS). The HISTORY OF THE PATRIARCHS relates that during the patriarchate of ALEXANDER II (705–730), Bishop John of Ṣā contended successfully with at least one of these groups in Rashīd. It is not clear from the text, however, which of the two groups was active in the city.

Elsewhere in the *History* we read that in 749–750, during one of the BASHMURIC REVOLTS, the Coptic Bashmurites killed the Muslims in Rashīd and set the city on fire.

Rashīd appears in the medieval Coptic lists of Egyptian bishoprics, but it is not known when the city first became a bishopric. The first bishops of Rashīd of whom we have record were in office in the eleventh century. Bishop Yusṭus of Rashīd attended a synod in Cairo in 1086 (Munier, 1943, p. 28). Bishop Theodorus of Rashīd is mentioned for this same period, but the record does not indicate whether he was the predecessor or the successor of Yusṭus.

Historical sources for the Crusades mention Rashīd often, but they provide no information about the fate of the city's Christian inhabitants. However, the fact that a manuscript was dedicated to the Coptic Orthodox Church of Mark in Rashīd sometime around 1799 bespeaks a continuity of Coptic Christians in the city until at least the beginning of the nineteenth century.

BIBLIOGRAPHY

Amélineau, E. *La Géographie de l'Egypte à l'époque copte,* pp. 404–405. Paris, 1893.

Maspero, J. *Matériaux pour servir à la géographie de l'Egypte.* Mémoires de l'Institut français d'Archéologie orientale 36. Cairo, 1919.

Munier, H. *Recueil des listes épiscopales de l'église copte*. Cairo, 1943.

Timm, S. *Das christlich-koptische Ägypten in arabischer Zeit*, pt. 5. Wiesbaden, 1982.

RANDALL STEWART

RASHĪD AL-DĪN ABŪ SAʿĪD (Abū Saʿīd Muwaffaq al-Dīn Yaʿqūb), a thirteenth-century Christian physician from Jerusalem. His first studies were in the Arabic language, after which he applied himself to medicine under the tutelage of Rashīd al-Dīn ʿAlī ibn Khalīfah, who was in the service of the sultan al-Malik al-Muʿaẓẓam (1218–1227), and next under Muhadhdhab al-Dīn ʿAbd al-Raḥmān ibn ʿAlī. In 1235, Rashīd al-Dīn Abū Saʿīd entered the service of al-Malik al-Kāmil (1218–1238), and afterward worked as physician for al-Malik al-Ṣāliḥ Najm al-Dīn Ayyūb (1240–1249) for about nine years. While in Damascus, he became involved in a quarrel with Rashīd al-Dīn ABŪ ḤULAYQAH about the correct treatment for Najm al-Dīn, who was suffering from an ulcer. He died of palsy in Damascus, in 1248.

A book of commentaries on the great work of Abū Zakariyya al-Rāzī (865–923) is attributed to him.

PENELOPE JOHNSTONE

RECLUSION. Like ANACHORESIS, reclusion is a form of separation from the world, a fundamental element of the monastic ideal. Much practiced among the monks of Syria, it was also practiced in Egypt from the earliest days of monasticism. Saint ANTONY himself lived for a long time as a recluse before his great anachoresis in the Arabian Desert. First he spent about ten years shut up in a tomb not far from his village, provisioned by a friend who brought him bread from time to time. Thereafter he lived for about twenty years shut up in an abandoned Roman fort.

The most celebrated Egyptian recluse was JOHN OF LYCOPOLIS, who is known from chapter 35 of the *Lausiac History* of PALLADIUS and the first chapter of the HISTORIA MONACHORUM IN AEGYPTO. He lived to a very advanced age in a three-room cave about five miles from Lycopolis (Asyūṭ). One room was reserved for prayer; in another room a window opened on a vestibule in which the numerous visitors waited to converse with John on Saturdays and Sundays. No one ever entered his cell, and he himself never left it. The *Historia monachorum* (chap. 6) mentions another recluse named Theonas, whose cell was in the neighborhood of Oxyrhynchus. He communicated with his visitors only in writing, for he had vowed perpetual silence. He came out only at night to gather the plants that were his food.

There also were some recluses in Lower Egypt. The APOPHTHEGMATA PATRUM mentions some among the monks of the deserts of NITRIA and SCETIS. Reclusion must be distinguished from the residence in the cell to which the monks in these deserts were constrained. They could leave their cells to visit one another, and above all to participate at the end of the week in the meal taken in common and in the liturgy celebrated in the church. But the recluse remained shut up in his cell and did not come out, even to go to church (cf. Nau, 1907, pp. 56–58). In certain cases, a priest came to celebrate the Eucharist in the recluse's cell. Since he never left his cell, the recluse used the services of a faithful layman to obtain what he required. It was not necessary to withdraw to the desert to practice reclusion. A young Alexandrian named Theodorus, who later became a disciple of PACHOMIUS, lived for twelve years in quarters that the patriarch ATHANASIUS had fitted up for him in the church, where he acted as a reader.

Reclusion was a form of solitary life better suited for women than anachoresis in the desert. The *Apophthegmata patrum* notes some cases of women recluses, such as the former prostitute converted by Serapion. Palladius heard in Alexandria of a young woman named Alexandra who, having left the town, shut herself in a tomb; she remained there until her death, ten years later, without seeing anyone, receiving what she required through an opening in the wall (Palladius, chap. 5).

This voluntary reclusion is evidently very different from the reclusion imposed upon monks guilty of serious faults. Some monasteries, like those of Pachomius and SHENUTE, had, in fact, prisons. Inspired by a purely religious motive, reclusion could appeal to the word of Jesus in Matthew 6:6: "When you pray, go to your private room and shut the door, and pray to your Father who is in secret."

Several historians (among them Bouché-Leclercq) have maintained, following H. Weingarten, that reclusion among the monks was a survival within Christianity of the way of life of men who lived in the Serapeum at Memphis, to whom the Greek papyri give the name *katochoi*, a term generally translated as "recluse." This thesis was refuted as early as 1920–1922 by P. Gobillot. Even retaining the meaning of "recluse," which has been contested by E. Preuschen, according to whom the *katochoi* were "possessed," the motives for this reclusion are not very clear and have been debated. K. Sethe saw recluses simply as prisoners, most often shut up for debt. For L. Delekat, they were people in difficulty who had taken refuge in the temple, claiming the right of asylum. According to these diverse hypotheses, the reclusion of the *katochoi* does not appear to be inspired by any religious motive, which is essential in monastic reclusion.

BIBLIOGRAPHY

Bouché-Leclercq, A. "Les reclus du Sérapéum de Memphis." In *Mélanges Perrot. Recueil de mémoires concernant l'archéologie classique, la littérature et l'histoire anciennes*, pp. 17–24. Paris, 1903.

Delekat, L. *Katoche, Hierodulie und Adoptionsfreilassung.* Münchener Beiträge zur Papyrusforschung und Antiken Rechtsgeschichte 47. Munich, 1964.

Gobillot, P. "Les origines du monachisme chrétien et l'ancienne religion de l'Egypte." *Recherches de science religieuse* 10 (1920):303–354; 11 (1921): 29–86, 168–213, 328–61; 12 (1922):46–68.

Lefort, L. T., ed. *Bohairic Life of St. Pachomius.* CSCO 89, p. 102. Louvain, 1953.

Nau, F. N. "Anonymous Apophthegms." *Revue de l'Orient chrétien* (1907):56–58; 181.

Preuschen, E. *Mönchtum und Sarapiskult. Eine religionsgeschichtliche Abhandlung.* Giessen, 1903.

Sethe, K. *Sarapis und die sogenannten κάτοχοι des Sarapis.* Abhandlungen der königlichen Gesellschaft der Wissenschaft zu Göttingen, Philologisch-historische Klasse n.s. 14, 5. Göttingen, 1913.

Weingarten, H. "Der Ursprung des Mönchtums im nachconstantinischen Zeitalter." *Zeitschrift für Kirchengeschichte* 1 (1877):1–35.

ANTOINE GUILLAUMONT

RED MONASTERY. *See* Dayr Anbā Bishoi.

REFECTORY, "table of the brethren," a standard element of monastery architecture, especially in cenobite monasticism, the room in which the monks took their common meals. According to the oldest examples so far identified in Egypt (Grossmann, 1982, pp. 162–63), the monks did not sit at long tables as is the custom today. Instead, they sat on benches arranged in the form of a circle, just as the Egyptian country folk still do during their work breaks in the fields. In the same way, the couches for the ancient meals for the dead, such as are found at al-Bagawāt (Grossmann, 1982, pp. 78–79), are arranged in a semicircle. The seating arrangement of the meal described in the Coptic life of Shenute of Atrīb during his stay in Constantinople (Amélineau, 1888, p. 43, fol. 48v) may not have been very different.

In order to accommodate as many such rings of seats as possible in one room, the refectories in Egypt were built with several aisles. The individual aisles were of equal width, and one ring of seats was provided for each of the bays formed by the columns. Most refectories contain two or three aisles. The largest examples so far identified in Egypt are the two refectories of DAYR AL-BALAY'ZAH, which both have three aisles. The refectories in the great Pachomian monasteries were probably similar. Very small refectories have only a single pillar standing in the middle of the room; the room is divided by arches thrown across to the four sides into four bays of roughly equal size (e.g., the present chapel of Mār Jirjis at DAYR ANBĀ BISHOI; cf. Evelyn-White, 1933, Vol. 3, pp. 161–62; DAYR AL-BARAMŪS, the actual "monastic henhouse"; and Qaṣr al-Wizz). In the late Fatimid period, a middle-sized type was developed with four pillars and nine symmetrically arranged bays (e.g., DAYR AL-FAKHŪRĪ at Isnā and Dayr Anbā Bishoi in Wādī al-Naṭrūn; cf. Evelyn-White, 1933, Vol. 3, p. 165, where this is described as "a large and nearly square building").

The rings of seats were in several cases built of bricks. In the refectory of DAYR ANBĀ HADRĀ, they were distributed remarkably irregularly. The equipment of the refectory also included a water jug stand and, in later times, a lectern. In addition, the kitchen and storerooms were logically accommodated in the neighborhood of the refectory.

BIBLIOGRAPHY

Amélineau, E. C., ed. *Monuments pour servir à l'histoire de l'Egypte chrétienne aux IVe et Ve siècles,* Vol. 1. Mémoires publiés par les membres de la Mission archéologique française au Caire 4. Paris, 1888.

Evelyn-White, H. G. *The Monasteries of the Wādī 'n Naṭrūn,* Vol. 3. New York, 1933; repr., 1973.

Grossmann, P. *Mittelalterliche Langhauskuppelkirchen und verwandte Typen in Oberägypten.* Glückstadt, 1982.

Grossmann, P., and H. G. Severin. "Reinigungsarbeiten im Jeremiaskloster bei Saqqāra." *Mitteilungen des Deutschen Archäologischen Instituts. Abteilung Kairo* 38 (1982):155–93.

Monneret de Villard, U. *Il Monastero di S. Simeone presso Aswan,* Vol. 1, pp. 105–108. Milan, 1927.
Scanlon, G. T. "Excavations at Kasr el-Wizz." *Journal of the American Research Center in Egypt* 58 (1972):7–41.

PETER GROSSMANN

REFORM PARTY ON CONSTITUTIONAL PRINCIPLES. *See* Political Parties.

REGULA, SAINT, a third-century missionary who, along with her brother, Saint FELIX, was a member of the THEBAN LEGION and was martyred near the fortress of Turicum (Zurich) (feast day: 1 Tūt). The massacre was at the hands of DECIUS, Roman governor of the region under Emperor Maximian. According to legend, during her martyrdom, Regula survived even after being dipped into boiling cobbler's wax and being forced to drink glowing lead. Like her comrades, she was beheaded, and with them she arose, carrying her head, and walked forty ells uphill to her resting place.

Along with Felix and Saint EXUPERANTIUS, also in the legion, Regula occupies a special place in the history of Zurich. Two great churches, the Grossmünster and the Wasserkirche, and a significant cloister beyond the river Limmat as well as the Frauenmünster, were erected to honor and house the relics of the saints. The headless figures of Felix, Regula, and Exuperantius, heads in hands, are depicted on the coats of arms of both the city and the canton of Zurich.

BIBLIOGRAPHY

Hottinger, J. H. "Divorum Felicis, Regulae et Exuperantii." In *Historia ecclesiastica,* Vol. 8. Tiguri, 1667.
Müller, J. *Geschichte der heiligen Märtyrer Felix und Regula.* Altdorf, 1904.
Schneider, G., and D. Gutscher. "Zürich in römischer Zeit." *Zeitschrift Turicum* 4 (1980–1981).
Ulrich, J. J. *Von dem alten wahrhaften catholischen Glauben St. Felix und St. Regula.* Bodmer, 1628.
Vögelin, S. "Der Grossmünster in Zürich." *Mitteilungen der Antiquarischen Gesellschaft in Zürich* 1 (1941).

SAMIR GIRGIS

RELIEFS. *See* Sculpture in Stone; Woodwork, Coptic.

RÉMONDON, ROGER (1923–1971), French papyrologist and historian. His specialties were Greek papyrology, with Coptic and Arabic on the side, and the history of Greco-Roman Egypt, especially Christian and Byzantine Egypt, with particular attention to economic, social, fiscal, military, administrative, and ecclesiastical questions. His works include "L'Acte de cautionnement byzantin P. Varsov. 30" (*Chronique d'Egypte* 48, 1973, pp. 140–44); "Situation présente de la papyrologie byzantine" (in *Akten des XIII. internationalen Papyrologenkongresses,* Munich, 1974, pp. 367–72); "Les Contradictions de la société égyptienne à l'époque byzantine" (*Journal of Juristic Papyrology* 18, 1974, pp. 17–32); and "Un Papyrus inédit des archives d'Abinnaeus" (*Journal of Juristic Papyrology* 18, 1974, pp. 33–37).

BIBLIOGRAPHY

Cadell, M. "Roger Rémondon." *Chronique d'Egypte* 47 (1972):292–98.
Montevecchi, O. "Roger Rémondon." *Aegyptus* 52 (1972):317–23.

JEAN GASCOU

RENAUDIN, PAUL (1864–1947), abbot of the Benedictine Abbey of Clervaux, Luxembourg, and French Coptologist. A list of his important works can be found in W. Kammerer's *A Coptic Bibliography.*

BIBLIOGRAPHY

Kammerer, W., comp. *A Coptic Bibliography.* Ann Arbor, Mich., 1950; repr. New York, 1969.

RENÉ-GEORGES COQUIN

RENAUDOT, EUSEBE (1646–1720), French Orientalist and liturgical writer. He was a member of the Académie française and the Académie des Inscriptions et Belles-Lettres. His published works are a history of the patriarchs of Alexandria, *Historia Patriarcharum Alexandrinorum Jacobitarum* (Paris, 1713), and a collection of Oriental liturgies, *Liturgiarum Orientalium Collectio: Accendunt Dissertationes Quatuor* (2 vols., Paris, 1716).

AZIZ S. ATIYA

REPUBLICAN PARTY. *See* Political Parties.

RESPONSES, MELODIES OF COPTIC. *See* Music, Coptic: Description.

RESPONSORY, a form of liturgical chant wherein a cantor says verses of the Psalms and the whole group of cantors or the congregation responds with a refrain. This refrain may take one of several forms: (1) it may be one fixed word, such as "Alleluia," in the psalmody of the Coptic month of Kiyahk; (2) it may be a fixed group of words, such as "For His mercy endures forever"; "O Lord Jesus Christ help me" in the Sunday psalmody; or "My Lord Jesus Christ, my good Savior" in the Saturday psalmody; (3) it may be a short petition, such as "Restore us, O God, and let Thy face shine, that we may be saved," which recurs three times in Psalm 80, or "Lord have mercy" (Kyrie Eleison), which is reiterated throughout the Divine Liturgy.

The choice of the appropriate category of liturgical chant—tractus (where a single cantor sings and the congregation listens), antiphon (where two alternating groups of singers take their turns), or responsory—depends primarily on the particular time of the day or night when it is to be used. Thus, at vespers, which is a comparatively short service, the tractus system is the one usually followed, whereas in long night vigils, the responsory proves to be more suitable.

It may be of particular interest to mention in this respect, that when in February 356 a military detachment invaded the church where Saint ATHANASIUS was celebrating a vigil service, the congregation was asked to join in a responsory. Here is the episode in full in the words of Athanasius, taken from his "Apologia de fuga" (Apology for Flight):

> It was night, and some of the people were keeping vigil, for a communion was expected. A body of soldiers suddenly advanced upon them, consisting of a general [Syrianus] and five thousand armed men with naked swords, bows and arrows and clubs. . . . I deemed that I ought not in such a time of confusion to leave the people, but that I ought rather to be the first to meet the danger; so I sat down on my throne and desired the deacon to read a psalm, and the people to respond "For His mercy endureth forever." Then I bade them all return to their own houses. But now the general with the soldiery forced his way into the church, and surrounded the sanctuary in order to arrest me. The clergy and the laity who had remained clamorously besought me to withdraw. This I firmly refused to do until all the others had retreated. I rose, had a prayer offered, and directed all the people to retire. "It is better," said I, "for me to meet the danger alone, than for any of you to be hurt." When the greater number of the people had left the church, and just as the rest were following, the monks and some of the clergy who had remained came up and drew me out. And so, may the truth be my witness, the Lord leading and protecting me, we passed through the midst of the soldiers, some of whom were stationed around the sanctuary, and others marching about the church.

BIBLIOGRAPHY

Iqlādiyūs Yūḥannā Labīb. *Al-Abṣalmūdiyyah al-Sanawiyyah al-Muqaddasah* (The Psalmody for the Whole Year). Cairo, 1908.

———. *Al-Abṣalmūdiyyah al-Muqaddasah al-Kiyahkiyyah* (The Psalmody for the Month of Kiyahk). Cairo, 1911.

Mattā al-Miskīn. *Al-Tasbīḥah al-Yawmiyyah wa-Mazāmīr al-Sawāʿī* (The Daily Psalmody and Canonical Hours Psalms), pp. 178–80. Cairo, 1968.

ARCHBISHOP BASILIOS

RESURRECTION, FEAST OF THE. *See* Feasts, Major: Easter.

RETURN AISLE. *See* Architectural Elements of Churches.

REVILLOUT, CHARLES EUGENE (1843–1913), French Egyptologist and Coptologist. He studied Oriental languages and Egyptology under J. de Rougé and later took up demotic. He was appointed professor of demotic, Coptic, and Egyptian Law at the Ecole du Louvre. With Heinrich Karl Brugsch and François Joseph Chabas, he founded the *Revue égyptologique* in 1880. He was made a chevalier of the Legion of Honor and was also for many years *conservateur-adjoint* in the Egyptian Department of the Louvre. He produced over seventy major books and studies as well as hundreds of articles. He died in Paris.

BIBLIOGRAPHY

Baille, C. "L'Egyptologue Eugène Revillout." *Procédés de l'Académie des sciences, belles-lettres et arts de Besançon* (1913):261–319.

Dawson, W. R., and E. P. Uphill. *Who Was Who in Egyptology,* pp. 246–47. London, 1972.
Kammerer, W., comp. *A Coptic Bibliography.* Ann Arbor, Mich., 1950; repr. New York, 1969.

AZIZ S. ATIYA

RICCI, SEYMOUR MONTEFIORE ROBERT ROSSO DE (1881–1942), English bibliographer and antiquary. He resided chiefly in Paris, and published many bibliographical works on rare books and manuscripts. He was Sandars Lecturer at Cambridge (1929–1930). He published a bibliography of Egyptology (*Revue archéologique* 5–8, 1917–1918) and of J.-F. Champollion, *Recueil d'etudes egyptologiques dédiées à la mémoire de Jean-François Champollion* (Paris, 1922).

BIBLIOGRAPHY

Kammerer, W., comp. *A Coptic Bibliography.* Ann Arbor, Mich., 1950; repr. New York, 1969.

AZIZ S. ATIYA

RIZQ AGHA (d. 1850), noted personality at the end of the Mamluk rule (1517–1798) and during the rise of MUḤAMMAD ALĪ dynasty at the beginning of the nineteenth century, he was nominated governor of the Sharqiyyah province in 1814 and was entrusted with the duties of policing the area and the levying of taxes. The term *Agha* in his name is a Turkish title granted by the viceroy to governors of provinces. Apparently he was active in repelling Arab marauders from the area east of the Damietta branch of the Delta and the establishment of security in that region. He founded a series of estates bearing his name in the district of Mīt Ghamr.

Muḥammad Alī's eldest son, Ibrahīm Pasha, was received by him as his honored guest together with Mu'allim GHĀLĪ in March 1822. After leaving Mīt Ghamr, Ghālī precipitated the wrath of the pasha, who murdered him and cast his body outside the district of Ziftā. On hearing what happened to his fellow Copt, Rizq hastened to the pasha's presence and pleaded for the recovery of Ghālī's body, which he took to the nearest Coptic church prior to burial. Rizq is one of the few Copts in the administration who happened to retain their position until their death. He left behind him a family of notable Copts and his name is still remembered in the district of Mīt Ghamr.

BIBLIOGRAPHY

Ramzī Tadrus. *Al-Aqbāṭ fī al-Qarn al-'Ishrīn,* 5 vols. Cairo, 1911–1919.

AZIZ S. ATIYA

ROMANCES. There are two Coptic romances: the *Alexander Romance* and the *Cambyses Romance.*

The Alexander Romance

All genres of literature—from history to poetry—include chronicles of the life of Alexander the Great of Macedonia (reigned 336–323 B.C.). The most widespread work, the *Alexander Romance,* is falsely ascribed to the Greek historian Callisthenes (c. 370–327 B.C.).

In different forms, whether varying recensions, synopses, or entirely new collections, the *Alexander Romance* filtered into the Middle East and later into the West. As a result, the history of the transmission of the work has become very complicated.

The Coptic version played an active role in that transmission. Probably during the sixth century, a text translated from Greek into Coptic was revised and perfected, and it gained an independent character that gave it a special place in the development of the romance. The fragmentary Coptic (Sahidic) version was taken from a book in the White Monastery (DAYR ANBĀ SHINŪDAH) of Apa Shenute the Great near Suhāj in Upper Egypt. Originally the 220-page manuscript consisted of about thirty-seven chapters. In all probability, each chapter had for its motto a verse from the Bible. The surviving recensions deal with Alexander among the Elamites, his rescue from the abyss (chaos) by Antilochos (Eurylochos in Gedrosia), how the disguised Alexander discovers the fidelity of the Macedonians and the disloyalty of the Persian King Agrikolaos, the legacy of the true Selpharios, Alexander's sojourn near the four streams of Paradise on the borders of the land of darkness, Alexander with the Brahmans, and finally Alexander's murder by poisoning. The last fragment closely resembles the text of Pseudo-Callisthenes.

The style of these Coptic versions of the *Alexander Romance* duplicates the literature of edification written by the monks. The narratives extend the stories of the martyrs and also of the apocalypses. Those who treat some Coptic literature as being "profane" err; Coptic literature is Christian. As a tool of God, Alexander could be considered a prophet; as a martyr, he foreshadowed Christ.

The Cambyses Romance

Of the *Cambyses Romance* there remains only a fragmentary version of six parchment leaves in poor condition at the Staatliches Museum in Berlin (P9009; probably eighth or ninth century). The text is written in Sahidic Coptic, and undoubtedly formed part of a larger manuscript of unknown origin.

The romance deals with the Persian King Cambyses II (reigned 529–522 B.C.). The epistle of Cambyses to the "Inhabitants of the East" attempts to incite them against Egypt and the pharaoh without success. Helped by the wise Bothros, the addressees stand firmly by Egypt, the pharaoh, and the holy bull Apis, god of Memphis. In their replies to his writings, the Egyptians express their animosity toward Cambyses and their loyalty to the safe stronghold of their country. At this point, the name of Cambyses changes to the Assyrian Nebuchadnezzar II (604–562 B.C.). One of the seven wise men of Nebuchadnezzar proposes that false messengers be sent to the Egyptians to assemble them for a feast—in the name of the pharoah and in the name of their god Apis. However, the Egyptians are not to be deceived. Soothsayers reveal the plan, and under the guise of accepting the invitation, the Egyptians assemble a strong army for the pharaoh Apries (588–568 B.C.). Here the text ends, but undoubtedly an Egyptian victory occurred, in spite of recorded history about the conquest of Egypt by Cambyses II.

The incomplete state of the manuscript makes it very difficult to judge the character of this romance. It can be compared to the *World Chronicle* of Bishop JOHN OF NIKIOU (C. A.D. 700). But, of course, this cannot be considered a source for the romance, although both works include the prophet Jeremiah. Otherwise, the *Cambyses Romance* echoes the reports of the Persian invasion of Egypt. The unusual geography, in which Egypt is presented as a land of the East, can be explained from the viewpoint of the Libyan oases and its robbers infiltrating into Egypt.

We cannot know for sure the extent of the work, nor the purpose of the author. We do know that the *Cambyses Romance* as it survived was revised by Christian Egyptians, and this would explain the name change from Cambyses to Nebuchadnezzar. The Coptic author seems to have been a monk of Upper Egypt who probably revised an older original for his own purposes. Biblical and Greek authors (including Herodotus) are the sources for the text. The form follows other examples of Coptic rhetoric. The fragments consist mainly of speeches and epistles. The romance was probably composed before the fifth or sixth century, or perhaps even as late as the eighth or ninth century, in response to the pressure of an Arabian invader. Jansen's hypothesis that an Aramaic-speaking Jew participated in the revision of the story (1950, p. 33) is also possible.

Without doubt, this Coptic romance connected the Bible—ending with the flight of the Holy Family to Egypt—to the history of Egypt for the monastic community.

BIBLIOGRAPHY

Alexander Romance

Bouriant, U. "Fragments d'un roman d'Alexandre en dialecte thébain." *Journal asiatique*, ser. 8, 9 (1887):1–38; 10 (1887):340–49.

Cramer, M. *Das christlich-koptische Ägypten einst und heute*, pp. 50–51, 53, 119–20. Weisbaden, 1959.

Lemm, O. E. von. *Der Alexanderroman bei den Kopten*. Saint Petersburg, 1903.

Maspero, G. *Les Contes Populaires de l'Egypte ancienne*, pp. 321–38. Paris, 1889.

Müller, C. D. G. "Alexanderroman 4. Koptische Version." In *Kindlers Literatur Lexikon*, Vol. 1, ed. W. von Einsiedel, cols. 394–95. Zürich, 1965.

Pietschmann, R. "Zu den Überbleibseln des koptischen 'Alexanderbuches.'" *Beiträge zur Bücherkunde und Philologie, August Wilmanns zum 25. März 1903 gewidmet*. Leipzig, 1903.

Cambyses Romance

Bilabel, F. "Bothros." *Philologus* 78 (1923):401–403.

Cramer, M. *Das christlich-koptische Ägypten einst und heute*, pp. 51–52, 118–19. Wiesbaden, 1959.

Grapow, H. "Untersuchungen über Stil und Sprache des koptischen Kambysesromans." *Zeitschrift für ägyptische Sprache und Altertumskunde* 74 (1938):55–68.

Jansen, H. L. *The Coptic Story of Cambyses' Invasion of Egypt*. Avhandlinger utgitt av Det Norske Videnskaps-Akademi i Oslo 2, Histisk-Filosofisk Klasse, 1950, no. 2. Oslo, 1950.

Lemm, O. von. "Kleine Koptische Studien XVIII: Bemerkungen zum Koptischen 'Kambysesroman.'" *Bulletin de l'Académie impériale des Sciences de Saint Pétersbourg* 13, 1 (1900):64–115.

Möller, G., and H. Schäfer. "Zu den Bruchstücken des koptischen 'Kambysesromans.'" *Zeitschrift für ägyptische Sprache und Altertumskunde* 39 (1901):113–16.

Müller, C. D. G. "Kambysesroman (kopt.)." *Kindlers Literatur Lexikon*, Vol. 4, ed. Wolfgang von Einsiedel, cols. 282–84. Zürich, 1965.

Schäfer, H. "Bruchstück eines koptischen Romans über die Eroberung Ägyptens durch Kambyses." *Sitzungsberichte der Königlichen Preussischen Akademie der Wissenschaften* 2 (1899):727–44.

Spiegelberg, W. "Arabische Einflüsse in dem koptischen 'Kambysesroman.'" *Zeitschrift für ägyptische Sprache und Altertumskunde* 45 (1908–1909):83–84.

C. DETLEF G. MÜLLER

ROMAN EMPERORS IN EGYPT. Although Alexandria never became a "Second Rome," the existence and, in some sense, the presence of the Roman emperor was a common and permanent experience for the inhabitants of Egypt.

The head of the provincial administration, the prefect of Egypt, was the direct representative of the emperor. The importance and power of the distant imperial overlord were constantly felt in everyday life. Documents from Augustus to DIOCLETIAN were dated by the regnal years of the emperor, often recalling his name and his victory titles. Annual official ceremonies commemorated the accession of the emperor and his anniversary. In their oaths, the subjects invoked the name and the fortune of the emperor, and they sacrificed to his divinity while performing the ruler-cult or to demonstrate that they were not Christians. Even the appearance of those emperors who never paid a visit to Egypt was well known to the inhabitants of the Nile Valley. The emperor's portrait figured on the coins they handled and his statues were omnipresent in official buildings, military camps, and temples (Kiss, 1984; Vogt, 1924). Well into the Roman period, the emperors were still represented on the walls of Egyptian-style sanctuaries in the traditional pharaonic attire (on the nomenclature of emperors in the Roman-Egyptian system, see Beckerath, 1984; Bureth, 1964; Grenier, 1988; and Saulnier, 1984; see, for example, the case of Nero, recently dealt with by Cesaretti, 1984, and Perrin, 1982).

Most intensely, of course, the power and prestige of the emperor were felt when he appeared personally in Egypt. The reasons for such visits were normally of a political or military order, but imperial journeys or expeditions were often combined with cultural or religious interests, leading not few of the emperors to the pyramids, the Serapeum of Memphis, the labyrinth in the Fayyūm, or the Memnonia on the West Bank near Thebes. This blend of political mission and educated sightseeing can already be observed with representatives of the Roman republic in Egypt: for example, the embassy of Scipio Aemilianus in 140–139 B.C., the visit of the Roman senator Lucius Memmius in 112 B.C. and, not least, Julius Caesar's journey on the Nile in 47 B.C., after the Alexandrian War and in the company of Cleopatra (see ROMAN TRAVELERS IN EGYPT).

Imperial visits or expeditions to Egypt not seldom marked crucial points in the history of both Egypt and the Roman Empire. The conquest of Egypt by Octavian and the fall of Alexandria in 30 B.C. brought an end not only to Ptolemaic rule in Egypt but also to the Roman Civil War and to the Roman republic. The beginning of the Roman imperial period and of the Julio-Claudian dynasty was thus closely tied up with the history of Egypt, as was, at the next stage of dynastic change, the accession of Vespasian and the Flavian dynasty, as Vespasian was proclaimed emperor by the prefect of Egypt, Tiberius Julius Alexander, in A.D. 69. Egypt played a significant role in the imperial ideology of another founder of a dynasty, Septimius Severus (r. 193–211), and in the early years of the Diocletianic tetrarchy (in 293–298).

When Octavian (Augustus since 27 B.C.) came to Egypt in 30 B.C., it was to conquer the country and to defeat his enemies, Mark Antony and Cleopatra. Entering Alexandria as victor, Octavian paid due respects to the memory of Alexander the Great, whose tomb and embalmed body he inspected and honored. But he declined to look at the remains of the Ptolemies and refused to offer a sacrifice to the divine Apis bull in Memphis. Octavian's attitude to Egyptian traditions was not wholly negative, as he readily assumed the role of pharaoh and gave fresh impulse to building activities in Egyptian sanctuaries. Egypt was now reorganized as a Roman province, its main role being to secure the food supply of Rome and to allow Augustus to be perceived as the great benefactor of the capital's population.

After the conquest, Augustus never returned to Egypt nor did his successor, Tiberius, ever visit that country. But the imperial prince Germanicus did in A.D. 19, traveling southward as far as Syene and Elephantine, admiring the monuments and besieged by an adulating population to whom he had opened the granaries in a time of dearth. Contrary to Augustus, Germanicus did not refrain from inspecting the Memphite Apis sanctuary and from feeding the sacred bull. Germanicus' attitude and dealings seem to have aroused the suspicion of the emperor Tiberius and were sharply criticized by him (imperial journeys from Augustus to Diocletian are treated comprehensively by Halfmann, 1986, with sources and bibliography).

The departure from the policies of Augustus is still more obvious in the case of the emperor Gaius, nicknamed Caligula (r. 37–41), who planned to go to Egypt but did not find the opportunity to do so. Having a strong propensity for things Egyptian and ardently wishing to enhance his divinity, he conceived the journey to Egypt as a means to realize his apotheosis.

Nero (r. 54–68) also intended to visit Egypt (in 64), and preparations for his impending tour were already under way, but the journey did not materialize. The splendor of Egypt and its traditions of ruler worship would have offered Nero the possibility to put on show his monarchical as well as his artistic ambitions.

When on 1 July 69 Tiberius Julius Alexander had his troops take the oath of allegiance to Vespasian, the latter was still in Judaea. At the end of 69, he went to Egypt and stayed there until the summer of 70. Vespasian's sojourn at Alexandria is famous for his visit to the Serapeum and for the healing wonders ascribed to him (cf. Barzano, 1988, with bibliography and detailed discussion of evidence). Wishing to obtain a divine confirmation of his newly won imperial dignity, to model himself on the role of Serapis, and to appear as a savior to the population, Vespasian was partly successful in increasing his own prestige and contributed much to the popularity of Serapis outside Egypt. That the presence of the emperor coincided with a felicitous rise of the Nile could be heralded as further proof of divine assent to Vespasian's accession. In 71, Titus, the son of Vespasian, also paid a visit to Egypt where the conqueror of Jerusalem offered a sacrifice to the bull-god Apis in Memphis.

Hadrian's sojourn in Egypt was surely among the most famous imperial visits to that country. Coming from Judaea and Gaza, the emperor paid his respects to the tomb of Pompei near Pelusium and arrived at Alexandria in the summer of 130. Hadrian and his wife Sabina there performed the traditional sacrifices, an homage duly advertised by the Alexandrian coinage. Traveling in the country and entering the Libyan desert, Hadrian made a demonstration of imperial *virtus* (excellence) by hunting a lion and killing it with his own hand. On the West Bank, near Thebes, several inscriptions record his visit to the colossus of Memnon in November 130. However, the best-known episode of Hadrian's stay in Egypt is the mysterious death of Antinous, the emperor's favorite. On the place where Antinous drowned in the Nile, the emperor founded in 130 a city perpetuating the name of the youth, Antinoopolis. It was to be one of the few Greek cities in Egypt, its constitution being modeled, with some exceptions, on that of Naucratis. Deified, Antinous was commemorated by cults and statues in many provinces of the empire.

The next ruler to visit Egypt was Marcus Aurelius in 175–176. His journey was prompted by the short-lived usurpation of Gaius Avidius Cassius, who had also been recognized in Egypt. Much more far-reaching were the consequences, a quarter-century later, of the stay of Lucius Septimius Severus in Egypt in 199–200. After the end of the Parthian War, the emperor did not immediately return to Rome, but stayed for some time in the Near East and proceeded first to Egypt via Pelusium, where he paid honors to the tomb of Pompei. If we may believe the author of the vita of Septimius Severus found in the late antique *Scriptores Historia Augusta* (17.3–4), the emperor wanted to visit Egypt because of his veneration for Serapis and his curiosity about antiquities and animals. Not content to inspect Alexandria, the pyramids, Memphis, and the labyrinth in the Fayyūm, he spent a whole year in Egypt, extending his journey to the Theban colossus of Memnon and to the southern frontier. Severus' veneration for Serapis went so far that he modeled himself on the appearance of this god, adopting the typical curls on the forehead and assuming, as a feature of imperial self-advertisement, the prestige of Serapis as a beneficent, patriarchal divinity. But this emperor's interest in religion was not free of fear and apprehension. That Septimius Severus went to see the embalmed body of Alexander the Great and then had the tomb sealed may be understood as a step to prevent dangerous imitation of Alexander by potential rivals. Already before entering Egypt, the emperor had sent instructions to the prefect enforcing strong measures against divination and magic. After all, Severus had just survived a string of wars against rival usurpers, and Egypt had supported his adversary, Pescennius Niger. Among the political and administrative measures taken by Severus in Egypt, one stands out as a major reform: the granting of a council to Alexandria and to the capitals of the nomes. Another decision, also designed to correct earlier discrimination and to enhance the status of Egypt, was the permission for Egyptians to enter the Roman senate.

Contrary to his father, Marcus Aurelius Antoninus, popularly called Caracalla, left an infamous record of his visit to Egypt in winter 215–216. He also paid his respects to the Alexandrian Serapis, even lodging in the sanctuary of the god, but the emperor's obsession with the imitation of Alexander sparked derision and raillery in Alexandria, a city well known for its propensity to mock even emperors and prefects. Caracalla took a terrible revenge, executing the dignitaries who had come to welcome him upon his entrance in Alexandria, killing the instigators of the troubles aroused by his arrival, prohibiting spectacles, and expelling strangers as well as Egyptian peasants from Alexandria.

That another Severan emperor, Severus Alexander (r. 222–235), intended to visit Egypt is clearly indicated by some texts mentioning preparations for the impending journey, but it is doubtful whether this visit ever took place.

With the end of the Severan dynasty began a troubled period of ephemeral emperors (235–284/285), characterized by external wars and constant usurpations. It came to an end only when Diocletian successfully established himself in 284/285 and stabilized the situation by creating a college of four emperors (with the first tetrarchy beginning in 293). These troubled decades were not propitious for imperial sightseeing in Egypt. When emperors of this crisis period visited Alexandria and the Nile Valley, they normally came to put down revolts and usurpations: for example, Aurelian in 273, Probus in 279, Galerius in 293–294, and Diocletian twice, in 298 with the siege of Alexandria, and probably in 301–302. Diocletian initiated reforms that reshaped the status of Egypt within the Roman Empire. He was the last emperor to visit that country. In 325, Constantine had planned a journey to Egypt, for which preparations are attested in the papyri, but the project was not carried out.

In the Byzantine period, the travels of the emperors followed a new and very different pattern. Though nearer to Alexandria and Egypt than the emperors coming from Rome, the rulers in Constantinople seldom troubled themselves to tour their empire as their predecessors had done, and they never went to Egypt. The endemic troubles of Alexandria and the tense climate of political and ecclesiastical relations, both within Egypt and between Constantinople and Alexandria, may partly account for the lack of imperial visits. But the progressive seclusion of the Byzantine emperor from his subjects and his realm also helps to explain the curtailed program of imperial visits. Nonetheless, the emperor's existence and power were still vividly perceived in Egypt: through his representatives and his laws, through his portrait on coins and his statues, and not least through the grain tax, which Egypt had to supply, year after year, for the maintenance of the emperor's administration and army in Egypt as well as for his residence, Constantinople (see ANNONA and TAXATION).

To imagine what an imperial visit meant for the regions and towns through which the emperor and his escort passed, nothing can compare with the papyri from Egypt for detail of administrative handling of such situations (see the excellent general survey by Millar, 1977, pp. 28–40). Impending visits of emperors led to a wide range of preparations, the nome leaders receiving instructions from the prefect of Egypt and passing them on to the officials of towns and villages. Food and fuel had to be supplied by the local population at prices fixed by the state or were doubtlessly often seized without compensation in times of crisis and civil war. Another regular feature of such visits and expeditions were liturgies, that is obligations and services to be fulfilled without salary, for instance, the supply of lodgings, draft animals, carriages, and ships. It was by no means always sure that the efforts of the local officials and population would be compensated by grants and privileges bestowed by the emperor, and one may doubt whether the prestige of an imperial visit was commonly prized by the local populace. When an emperor was on the move, he was not only accompanied by his court and his personal attendants, but also by the imperial chancery and a comprehensive section of the central administrative services as well as by an important military guard. This civil and military retinue alone could number four or five thousand persons, and might be still larger in times of war. One particularly well-documented example is the impending visit of Diocletian at Panopolis/Akhmīm at the end of September 298 (Skeat, 1964) with the accompanying collection of the *annona*, preparation of quarters, repair of ships, supply of sacrificial animals, et cetera. These papyri from Panopolis give clear evidence of the many problems generated by an imperial visit and attest a certain lack of enthusiasm on the side of the local administration.

[*See also:* Egypt, Roman and Byzantine Rule in.]

BIBLIOGRAPHY

Barnes, T. D. *The New Empire of Diocletian and Constantine*. Cambridge, Mass., and London, 1982.

Barzano, A. "Tiberio Giulio Alessandro, prefetto d'Egitto (66/70)." In *Aufstieg und Niedergang der römischen Welt,* ed. H. Temporini, pt. 2, Vol. 10.1, pp. 518–80, especially pp. 553–62. Berlin and New York, 1988.

Beckerath, J. von. *Handbuch der ägyptischen Königsnamen.* Münchner Ägyptologische Studien 20, pp. 296–306. Berlin, 1984.

Birley, A. R. *The African Emperor Septimius Severus,* 2nd ed. London, 1988.

Bowman, A. K. *Egypt After the Pharaohs: 332 B.C.–A.D. 642: From Alexander to the Arab Conquest.* London, 1986.

Bureth, P. *Les Titulatures impériales dans les papyrus, les ostraca et les inscriptions d'Egypte (30 a.C.–284 p.C.).* Papyrologica Bruxellensia 2. Brussels, 1964.

Cesaretti, M. P. "Nerone in Egitto." *Aegyptus* 64 (1984):3–25.

Gauthier, H. *Le Livre des rois d'Egypte,* 5 vols. Cairo, 1907–1917.

Geraci, G. *Genesi della provincia romana d'Egitto.* Studi di storia antica 9. Bologna, 1983.

Grenier, J.-C. "Notes sur l'Egypte romaine (I, 1–7)." *Chronique d'Egypte* 63 (1988):57–76 (concerned with hieroglyphic and demotic documentation for Roman emperors, it offers a series of corrections and observations).

Halfmann, H. *Itinera principum. Geschichte und Typologie der Kaiserreisen im Römischen Reich.* Heidelberger althistorische Beiträge und epigraphische Studien 2. Stuttgart, 1986.

Hennig, D. "Zur Ägyptenreise des Germanicus." *Chiron* 2 (1972):349–65.

Kiss, Z. *Etudes sur le portrait impérial romain en Egypte.* Travaux du Centre d'archéologie méditerranéenne de l'Académie polonaise des sciences 23. Warsaw, 1984 (covers the period from Julius Caesar to the tetrarchs).

Kolb, F. *Literarische Beziehungen zwischen Cassius Dio, Herodian und der Historia Augusta.* Antiquitas Series 4: Beiträge zur Historia-Augusta-Forschung 9, pp. 97–111. Bonn, 1972.

Martin, A. "La Dédicace impériale de Coptos I. *Portes* 84." *Chronique d'Egypte* 61 (1986):318–23.

McCann, A. M. *The Portraits of Septimius Severus (A.D. 193–211).* Memoirs of the American Academy in Rome 30. Rome, 1968.

Millar, F. *The Emperor in the Roman World, 31 B.C.–A.D. 337.* London, 1977.

Perrin, Y. "Néron et l'Egypte: une stèle de Coptos montrant Néron devant Min et Osiris (Musée de Lyon)." *Revue des études anciennes* 84 (1982): 117–31.

Saulnier, C. "Les Titulatures pharaoniques des empereurs romains." *Revue historique de droit français et étranger* 62 (1984):1–14.

Scriptores Historiae Augustae, with an English translation by D. Magie, 3 vols. Loeb Classical Library. London and New York, 1922–1932.

Skeat, T. C. *Papyri from Panopolis in the Chester Beatty Library Dublin.* Chester Beatty Monographs 10. Dublin, 1964.

Vogt, J. *Die alexandrinischen Münzen. Grundlegung einer alexandrinischen Kaisergeschichte,* 2 vols. Stuttgart, 1924.

Weingärtner, D. G. *Die Ägyptenreise des Germanicus.* Papyrologische Texte und Abhandlungen 11. Bonn, 1969.

HEINZ HEINEN

ROMAN TRAVELERS IN EGYPT. Egypt attracted visitors from Rome and Italy as early as Ptolemaic times. The initiation of diplomatic relations between the court of the Ptolemies and Rome in 273 B.C. was followed in the second century, especially after the Roman intervention against the Seleucid Antiochus IV in 168 B.C., by an increasing influence of Rome on Egyptian politics. In the first century B.C. the strong Roman pressure on Egypt so seriously eroded the independence of the country that in 55 B.C., Egypt was occupied by the Roman troops of Aulus Gabinius, and in 30 B.C. it was added to the Roman empire by Octavian (later Emperor Augustus; see Geraci, 1983). In addition to these political and military relations, there were Italian merchants in Egypt from the third century B.C. on. In connection with their diplomatic contacts, Roman politicians traveled the country, especially from the second century B.C. on, and thereby gained an impression of the economic potential of Egypt and visited its places of interest; examples are the mission of Scipio Aemilianus in 140/139 and the visit of the Roman senator L. Memmius in 112.

The Roman annexation of Egypt in 30 B.C. created a new situation for Roman journeys to and within Egypt. The chief posts in the administration and the army were to a considerable extent occupied by non-Egyptians from the rest of the Roman empire. Trade between Egypt and the empire, above all between Alexandria and Rome (or the harbors at Puteoli and Ostia) was extraordinarily intensive. What concerns us are the landscapes, the towns, and the places of interest that were especially sought out by travelers, as well as the reasons for their interest. Finally we consider from what groups the Roman visitors to Egypt derived. Here we leave aside the merchants from the West, who came and went in Egypt over longer or shorter periods. With regard to the many Roman politicians, government officials, and military men who traveled to Egypt on official missions, it should be emphasized that on these journeys they frequently also visited the places of interest in the country, and testified to their visits in numerous inscriptions and graffiti.

In Egypt not only the Romans but also the Greeks and the Orientals from the Near East encountered a world that to them was strange and stamped with a venerable antiquity. The very nature of the country aroused interest and a taste for inquiry. The regular Nile floods and the location of the sources of the Nile were already great subjects of investigation in the archaic and classical period (Herodotus, II.19–34). It was already almost a topos when the poet Lucan made Caesar meet with the Memphitic priest Akoreus during the Alexandrian War (48–47 B.C.) and converse about the sources of the Nile (Lucan *Pharsalia*, X.172–331). But neither such discussions nor isolated Roman advances into Nubia resolved the problem. In addition to the nature of the country, it was the monuments of Egypt that aroused the interest of visitors: the Pyramids, the so-called labyrinth at Hawara, the great temples, obelisks, and colossal statues (especially the colossuses of Memnon in West Thebes). Among the customs of the inhabitants, which had already evoked the astonishment of Herodotus, it was especially the Egyptian worship of animals that enticed the traveler to visit the sanctuaries concerned.

Although travelers reached Egypt by the land route via Gaza and Pelusium, most visitors from Rome and the West came by the sea route, and stepped on Egyptian soil for the first time in Alexandria (average duration of a favorable voyage from Puteoli to Alexandria, about twelve days). Alexandria was indeed the chief town of Egypt, but significantly it was officially called Alexandrea ad Aegyptum (Alexandria in Egypt). For the city founded by Alexander the Great was a Greek city that did indeed take on something from its Egyptian hinterland in the course of time but in terms of its character stood closer to the Greco-Syrian Antioch on the Orontes than to the much more clearly Egyptian towns of Memphis, Coptos, and Thebes. Yet for the visitor, Alexandria offered enough in the way of sights worth seeing, particularly the tomb of Alexander the Great and the Serapeum, which even in the fourth century ranked for the Roman historian Ammianus Marcellinus as the most noble monument in the world after the Capitol in Rome.

While the Roman governors of Egypt are said to have entered their office in Alexandria in fear and trembling—and not without reason—of the rebellious character of the population, most visitors must have enjoyed the flair of the city, which in size and population was surpassed only by Rome in the empire. The mild climate of Alexandria was particularly recommended to those seeking recovery of health. Important doctors had settled there and set up schools. The famous physician Galen (second century A.D.) studied in Alexandria. In addition to the medical colleges there were many other cultural centers and attractions in Alexandria, including the Museum and the Library. In the immediate vicinity of the city recreation grounds and bathing places offered their attractions, especially Kanobos (Canopus), somewhat to the west of Abūqīr; it was linked with Alexandria by a canal about 12.5 miles (20 km) long, the banks of which were bordered by a large number of hostelries.

If we sense in Alexandria the atmosphere of the Greco-Oriental harbor towns, the traveler, after crossing the Delta, had definitely left the Levant behind. In Memphis, the largest town in Roman Egypt after Alexandria, he was surrounded by the age-old past of the country: the living Apis bull was shown him by the priests, while quite nearby rose the Pyramids and the Sphinx, on whose paws many a visitor attested his veneration for this work, felt to be divine, in the form of a short commemorative inscription (*proskynemon*) or even a poem. From Memphis the Fayyūm was easily accessible. The feeding of the sacred crocodile Sobek/Suchos at Krokodilopolis/Arsinoë was part of the program of the travelers, who pushed forward as far as this realm of the crocodile god near Lake Moiris (Strabo *Geography*, XVII.1.38).

A journey into southern Egypt required a longer time. Although very largely stripped of its municipal significance, Thebes, with the temples on the east bank and the sanctuaries and tombs in West Thebes, still had a strong attraction for travelers. A quite special place was enjoyed by the colossuses of Memnon, the statues of Amenhotep III still standing in front of his mortuary temple, which in the interval has almost entirely disappeared. The northern of the two statues, of which the upper part was broken away, at sunrise emitted a dirgelike sound. Greeks and Romans recognized in it the voice of the mythical hero Memnon, who raised his mournful voice at the sight of his mother Eos, the goddess of the red morning sky. Over one hundred inscriptions by visitors, including that of Emperor Hadrian (A.D. 130), testify to the extraordinary veneration of the visitors for this monument, which by an *interpretatio graeca* could directly address the religious feelings of Greeks and Romans (Bernand and Bernand, 1960). When in the third century the broken-off upper part of the statue was restored to the lower part, the sound fell silent forever, and the visits ceased.

Numerous inscriptions from visitors in the Roman period have survived in the tombs of the kings driven deep into the rock in West Thebes, which because of their form were described by the Greeks as *syringes* (tubes). The grave of Ramses VI exercised the greatest power of attraction, since it was at that time assumed that Memnon was buried here. Of over 2,000 graffiti in the *syringes*, almost half are at this grave (Baillet, 1926). On the evidence of similar inscriptions, we can follow the further journeys of visitors into many places in Upper Egypt and sometimes also Lower Nubia.

After the conquest of Egypt in 30 B.C., it was forbidden for senators and leading members of the equestrian order (*equites illustres*) to visit the country without the permission of the emperor. This measure of Octavian/Augustus gives expression to the fear of possible usurpation. The demonstrations of the Alexandrians, which took place during the visit of the imperial prince Germanicus in A.D. 19, illustrate the unrest that could have originated in this province. A series of Roman emperors took up residence in Egypt for political or military reasons. Here an interest in Egyptian antiquities may have played a more or less large role, for example, with Titus (71), Marcus Aurelius (175–176), Septimius Severus (199–200), and Caracalla (215). Besides the journey of Germanicus to Egypt, the best-documented is the visit to the country by Hadrian (130–131), in the course of which the emperor's favorite Antinous was drowned in the Nile. Antinoopolis was founded at the time in honor of the deceased. The usurpations in the second half of the third century also convulsed Egypt and led to imperial expeditions into the country by Galerius (293–295?) and by DIOCLETIAN (297–298, 301–302). Thereafter no ruling emperor visited Egypt. The *Itinerarium Antonini* contains a detailed section on Egypt. It probably goes back in important elements to Caracalla, but is not a proper emperor's itinerary; it served in the first place for administrative purposes.

In the Christian empire of late antiquity, interest in the traditional places of interest and the pagan cults of Egypt died away. But as a prestigious center of monasticism, Egypt now drew quite new visitors: Christian men and women, above all from ascetic circles, sought out Egypt in order to become acquainted with the monastic life, either with individual desert fathers or in monasteries. Despite the ever stronger drifting apart of East and West after the fourth and fifth centuries, religiously motivated visitors also came from the Western empire to Egypt, often in the context of a pilgrim journey to the places of the Holy Land: Melania the Elder, Melania the Younger, Postumianus, Rufinus, Jerome, John Cassian, Egeria (frequently also cited under the name Etheria), Arsenius, and others. Apart from the monastic centers proper, the town of Menas (Karm Abū Mīnā), southwest of Alexandria, occupied the first place among the Christian pilgrim stations in Egypt. Here visitors from the West have been identified. East of Alexandria, in the immediate neighborhood of Canopus, another Christian place of pilgrimage, Menuthis/Abūqīr, came to be of great importance; Western pilgrims are attested at this site also.

BIBLIOGRAPHY

Baillet, J. *Inscriptions grecques et latines des tombeaux des rois ou syringes.* Mémoires publiés par les membres de l'Institut français d'Archéologie orientale du Caire 42. Cairo, 1926.

Bernand, A., and E. Bernand. *Les inscriptions grecques et latines du colosse de Memnon.* Institut français d'Archéologie orientale, Bibliothèque d'étude 31. Cairo, 1960.

______. *Les Inscriptions grecques de Philae,* 2 vols. Paris, 1969.

Bernand, E. *Inscriptions métriques de l'Egypte gréco-romaine. Recherches sur la poésie épigrammatique des grecs en Egypt.* Annales Littéraires de l'Université de Besançon 98. Paris, 1969.

Bowersock, G. W. "The Miracle of Memnon." *Bulletin of the American Society of Papyrologists* 21 (1984):21–32.

Casson, L. *Travel in the Ancient World.* London, 1974.

Friedländer, L. *Darstellungen aus der Sittengeschichte Roms in der Zeit von Augustus bis zum Ausgang der Antonine,* 10th ed., Vol. 1, pp. 423–46. Leipzig, 1922.

Geraci, G. "Ricerche sul proskynema." *Aegyptus* 51 (1971):3–211.

______. *Genesi della provincia romana d'Egitto.* Studi di Storia Antica 9. Bologna, 1983.

Hennig, D. "Zur Ägyptenreise des Germanicus." *Chiron* 2 (1972):349–65.

Kötting, B. *Peregrinatio religiosa. Wallfahrten in der Antike und das Pilgerwesen in der alten Kirche,* pp. 188–211. Forschungen zur Volkskunde 33–35. Münster, 1950.

Krause, M. "Karm Abū Mena." In *Reallexikon zur byzantinischen Kunst,* ed. K. Wessel and M. Restle, Vol. 3, cols. 1116–58. Stuttgart, 1978.

Reed, N. "Pattern and Purpose in the Antonine Itinerary." *American Journal of Philology* 99 (1978):228–54.

Van Berchem, D. "Les itinéraires de Caracalla et

l'*Itinéraire Antonin*." In *Actes du IXe Congrès international d'études sur les frontières romaines*, ed. D. M. Pippidi. Bucharest, Cologne, and Vienna, 1974.

Van't Dack, E. "Reizen, expedities en emigratie uit Italië naar Ptolemaeïsch Egypte." *Mededelingen van de Koninklijke akademie voor wetenschappen, letteren en schone kunsten van België, klasse der letteren* 42 (1980):no. 4.

Weingärtner, D. G. *Die Ägyptenreise des Germanicus*. Papyrologische Texte und Abhandlungen 11. Bonn, 1969.

HEINZ HEINEN

ROOF. *See* Architectural Elements of Churches.

RÖSCH, FRIEDRICH (1883–1914), German Coptologist. He worked in the Egyptian Department of the Berlin Museum and was also assistant at the German Archaeological Institute in Cairo, in which capacity he took part in the Amarna excavations. He was interested in Berber dialects as well as Coptic.

BIBLIOGRAPHY

Dawson, W. R., and E. P. Uphill. *Who Was Who in Egyptology*, p. 253. London, 1972.

Kammerer, W., comp. *A Coptic Bibliography*. Ann Arbor, Mich., 1950; repr. New York, 1969.

AZIZ S. ATIYA

ROSETTA. *See* Rashīd.

ROSSI, FRANCESCO (1827–1912), Italian Egyptologist and Coptologist. He became an assistant in the Egyptian Museum at Turin (1865) and then subdirector (1867), and he helped to compile the museum catalog. In addition to his contributions to Egyptology, he published numerous studies in Coptic. He died in Turin.

BIBLIOGRAPHY

Dawson, W. R., and E. P. Uphill. *Who Was Who in Egyptology*, p. 254. London, 1972.

Kammerer, W., comp. *A Coptic Bibliography*. Ann Arbor, Mich., 1950; repr. New York, 1969.

AZIZ S. ATIYA

RUBBAYTAH. *See* Provost.

RÜCKERT, FRIEDRICH (1788–1866), German poet and Orientalist. He was professor of Oriental languages in Erlangen and for a time in Berlin, to which he was called by King Friedrich Wilhelm IV. His chief contribution, aside from his poetry, is his translation of Arabic and Persian poetry into German. It is less well known that somewhere about 1851, while a teacher of Arabic and Persian, he was stimulated by his pupil P. de Lagarde to a study of the Coptic language. Evidently Rückert achieved excellence in Coptic. Lagarde (1867, p. vi) bears witness that in July 1864, Rückert conversed with him about the Coptic language and entrusted to him the perusal and publication of his coptological legacy. Lagarde, however, did not publish this orderly legacy (on many hundreds of sheets and slips of paper) of etymological investigations, explanations, and emendations to individual biblical books and researches into Bohairic grammar. It found its way to the Royal Library in Berlin, where L. Stern, at the instance of R. Lepsius, looked through it during the work on a catalog of Coptic manuscripts and also evaluated it for his *Koptische Grammatik* (1880, pp. xf.) and made it known through citations. In the dedication of his *Grammatik* to Rückert, Stern described him as a "grammarian of the Coptic language." The legacy is still unpublished.

BIBLIOGRAPHY

Engel, E. *Kurzgefasste deutsche Literaturgeschichte von den Anfängen bis zur Gegenwart*, 37th ed., pp. 270–72. Leipzig, 1929.

Lagarde, P. de. *Der koptische Pentateuch*, pp. v ff. Leipzig, 1867.

Prang, H., ed. *Rückert-Studien*. Schweinfurt, 1964.

Stern, L. *Koptische Grammatik*, pp. x ff. Leipzig, 1880; repr. Osnabrück, 1971.

MARTIN KRAUSE

RŪFĀ'ĪL AL-ṬŪKHĪ (1701–1787), Egyptian Coptic Catholic bishop; author, editor, lexicographer, and translator of various liturgical works. He was born at Jirjā, Upper Egypt, into an Orthodox family from Ṭūkh al-Naṣārā in the Delta province of Minufiyyah. When he was in his early twenties and had been converted to Roman Catholicism by Franciscan missionaries, he was sent to Rome to study at the Collegio Urbano di Propaganda Fide. This college was essentially for the training of missionaries but it also housed the missionary printing press for the Catholic church. (In 1671 the press had produced the earliest Bible printed in Arabic.) In 1735 Ṭūkhī obtained a doctorate in theology, thus becoming the first Egyptian to attain such a high degree. He was sent to Egypt for three years and returned to Rome, where he was appointed professor of Coptic language and church rite at the Collegio, a post that he occupied for over thirty-six years. He worked on liturgical books, in particular revising and edifying Coptic works. He was also a copyist of Arabic and Coptic manuscripts. In 1761 Pope Clement XIII consecrated Ṭūkhī bishop in recognition of his erudition and services. He died in 1787 and was buried at the Vatican.

Ṭūkhī always retained his innate affection for the Egyptian church. At Rome he was able to accomplish the prodigious task of editing a great number of works representing the various aspects of the Coptic liturgical heritage. The following is a selection of his most widely used publications:

ⲡⲓϫⲱⲙ ⲛ̀ⲧⲉ ⲡⲓϣⲟⲙϯ ⲛ̀ⲁⲛⲁⲫⲟⲣⲁ ⲉ̀ⲧⲉ ⲛⲁⲓ ⲛⲉⲙ ⲡⲓ ⲁⲅⲓⲟⲥ ⲃⲁⲥⲓⲗⲓⲟⲥ ⲛⲉⲙ ⲡⲓ ⲁⲅⲓⲟⲥ ⲅⲣⲏⲅⲟⲣⲓⲟⲥ ⲡⲓ ⲑⲉⲟⲗⲟⲅⲟⲥ ⲛⲉⲙ ⲡⲓ ⲁⲅⲓⲟⲥ ⲕⲩⲣⲓⲗⲗⲟⲥ ⲛⲉⲙ ⲛⲓⲕⲉ ⲉⲩⲭⲏ ⲉ̀ⲑⲟⲩⲁⲃ (Pijōm nte pishomti nanaphora ete nai nem pi agios Basilios nem pi agios Grēgorios pi theologos nem pi agios Kyrillos nem nike eukhē ethouab) (*Kitāb al-Thalāthat Quddāsāt ay Alladhī lil Qiddis Basīliyūs, wa-al-Ladhī lil Qiddīs Aghrīghūriyūs al-Thawlūghus, wa-al-Ladhī lil Qiddīs Kīrillus*) (The Euchologion, the three liturgies of Saint Basil, Saint Gregory, and Saint Cyril [Kyrillus]). Rome, 1736.

ⲡⲓϫⲱⲙ ⲛ̀ⲧⲉ ⲡⲓⲯⲁⲗⲧⲏⲣⲓⲟⲛ ⲛ̀ⲧⲉ ⲇⲁⲩⲓⲇ (Pijōm nte pipsaltērion nte David) (*Kitāb Zabūr Dawūd*) (The Psalms of David). Rome, 1744.

ⲡⲓϫⲱⲙ ⲛ̀ⲧⲉ ϯⲙⲉⲧⲣⲉϥϣⲉⲙϣⲓ ⲛ̀ⲛⲓⲙⲩⲥⲧⲏⲣⲓⲟⲛ ⲉⲑⲩ ⲛⲉⲙ ϩⲁⲛ ϫⲓⲛϩⲏⲃⲓ ⲛ̀ⲧⲉ ⲛⲓ ⲣⲉϥⲙⲱⲟⲧⲡ ⲛⲉⲙ ϩⲁⲛ ϫⲓⲛϩⲟⲥ ⲛⲉⲙ ⲡⲓ ⲕⲁⲧⲁ ⲙⲉⲣⲟⲥ ⲛ̀ⲁⲃⲟⲧ (Pijōm nte timetrefshemshi (e)nnimystērion ethouab nem han jinhēbi nte ni refmōotp nem han jinhōs nem pi kata meros nabot) (*Kitāb Khidmat al-Asrār al-Muqaddasah wa-Lajānīz al-Mawtā wa-al-Hūsāt wa-al-Qaṭamārus al-Shahrī*) (Sacramental services and monthly *qaṭamarus*). Rome, 1763.

ⲡⲓϫⲱⲙ ⲛ̀ⲧⲉ ⲛⲓⲑⲉⲟⲧⲟⲕⲓⲁ ⲛⲉⲙ ⲕⲁⲧⲁ ⲧⲁⲝⲓⲥ ⲛ̀ⲧⲉ ⲡⲓⲁⲃⲟⲧ ⲭⲟⲓⲁⲕ (Pijōm nte nitheotokia nem kata taksis nte piabot Khoiak) (*Kitāb al-Theyūtūkiyyāt wa-Tartīb Shahr Kiyahk*) (Theotokia and Ordo for the month of Kiyahk). Rome, 1764.

ⲡⲓϫⲱⲙ ⲉϥⲉⲣⲁⲡⲁⲛⲧⲟⲕⲧⲓⲛ ⲉϫⲉⲛ ⲛⲓ ⲉⲩⲕⲏ ⲉⲑⲟⲩⲁⲃ ⲡⲓ ⲙⲉⲣⲟⲥ ⲛ̀ϩⲟⲩⲓⲧ ⲉⲑⲃⲉ ⲛⲓϫⲓⲛⲫⲱϣ (Pijōm eferapantoktin ejen ni eukhē ethouab pi meros nhouit ethbe nijinphōsh) (*Kitāb Yashtamil ʿalā al-Ṣalawāt al-Muqaddasah, li-al Risāmāt al-Mukhtārīn li Darajāt ahl al-Iklīrus*) (Ordination services and consecration of the myron and churches). Rome, 1761.

Ghramatīq fī al-Lisān al-Qibṭī ay al-ʿMisrī (*Rudimenta linguae coptae sive aegyptiacae*) (Coptic-Arabic grammar). Rome, 1778.

RUSHDĪ AL-ṬŪKHĪ

RUFINUS (c. 345–410). Rufinus Tyrannius was born at Concordia in North Italy about 345 and in 371 was baptized at Aquileia, where he lived until he began his travels in the Middle East. He lived in Egypt for six years before going to Jerusalem for two years, after which he returned to Egypt for two more years. Part of his time in Egypt was spent in Alexandria, but most of it was with the Coptic monks in the monasteries of Wādī al-Naṭrūn. Rufinus then went to the Holy Land, where he stayed for eighteen years. During that time he became fully conversant with the Eastern churches and collected much material that he used in his writings. Back in Italy in 397, he spent most of his life at Aquileia until his death in 410.

Rufinus is best known in the West as the main translator of many works of Origen from Greek into Latin, but he also wrote numerous treatises of his own, based mainly on his Eastern experiences. He is one of the four contemporaries who continued writing church history after EUSEBIUS, the others being SOCRATES, SOZOMEN, and THEODORET.

His translations include the *Apology for Origen* of Pamphilus and Eusebius, the *Historia ecclesiastica* of Eusebius, the *Monastic Rule* of Saint Basil, the *De principiis* of Origen, the *Recognitions* of Clement, the *Sentences* of Xystus, the *Sentences* of Evagrius, the *Paschal canons* of Anatolius of Alexandria, and ten works by GREGORY OF NAZIANZUS.

Rufinus' own works include two historical works: an *Ecclesiastical History* continuing the work of Eusebius, and the HISTORIA MONACHORUM, which is a history of the Coptic hermits based on his experience among the monks of Wādī Habib in the Eastern Desert. A great admirer of Origen, he also wrote "A Dissertation on the Falsifications by Heretics of the Works of Origen." Later in life, when he fell out with Jerome, he wrote a special "apology" in two books, in which he tried to vindicate himself from the attacks launched against him by his old friend. The *Apology* was addressed to the Roman pope Anastasius. Rufinus also composed a commentary on the Apostles' Creed. This fourth-century version remains as that accepted by the Roman church.

It has been said that Rufinus' *Ecclesiastical History* was based on an original treatise composed by Gelasius, bishop of Caesarea (d. 393), but there is no solid basis for this assumption, and Rufinus must be accepted as its independent author. Although the work of Rufinus is sometimes described as uncritical, it is valuable as a source of church history after Eusebius in the fourth century.

BIBLIOGRAPHY

Murphy, F. X. *Rufinus of Aquileia, 345–411.* Washington, D.C., 1945.

Smith, W., and H. Wace. *Dictionary of Christian Biography,* Vol. 4, pp. 555–56. New York, 1974.

AZIZ S. ATIYA

RUTH. *See* Old Testament, Arabic Translations of the.

RUZAYQĀT, AL- (Armant), site of ruins near the modern Monastery of Saint George. Presumably these are the remains of a small monastery (popular designation: Dayr al-ʿAdhrā'), which was evidently already abandoned in early times. The potsherds lying around belong for the most part to the fifth and sixth centuries. The church is built of mud bricks, and is almost completely in ruins. We can recognize the position of the apse with a southern side room and a large part of the south wall, which contains several niches in close succession. An atrium appears to have been added on the west side at a later period.

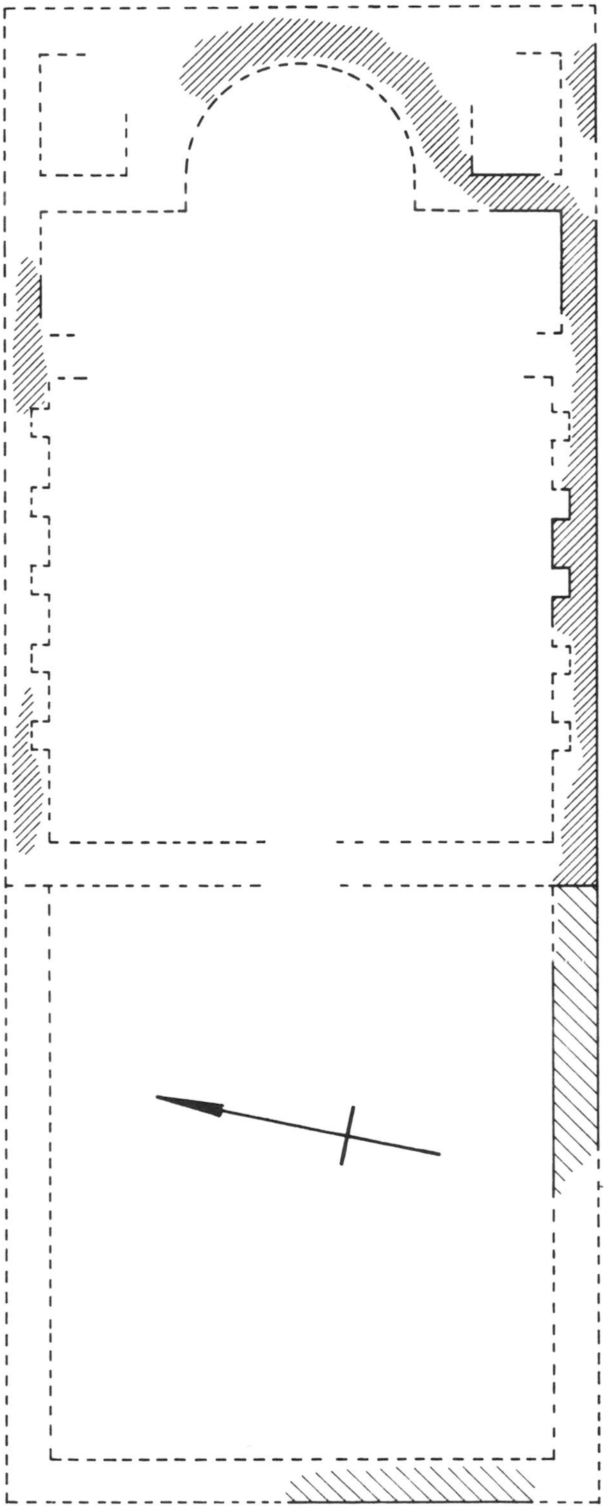

Plan of the church at the ancient monastery Dayr al-ʿAdhrā', the ruins of which are located at al-Ruzayqāt. *Courtesy Peter Grossmann.*

BIBLIOGRAPHY

Maspero, G. C. *Bibliothèque égyptologique,* p. 204. Paris, 1893.

PETER GROSSMANN

S

SAAD, ZAKI YUSEF (1901–1982), Egyptologist. He was one of the early graduates of the newly established Institute of Egyptology, Cairo (Fouad I) University, receiving his degree in 1930. In 1931 he was appointed a member of the Nubian expedition team to survey the archaeological excavations and Egyptian antiquities in that area before the second raising of the old Aswan Dam. Then he was transferred to Saqqara in 1934 where he worked with the archaeologist Walter Emery as assistant director in the excavations of the First Dynasty (2980 B.C.) and helped in the discovery of the tomb of Hemaka (published in 1938) and the tomb of Hor Aha (published in 1939). He remained in Saqqara until 1939 where he combined with his Memphis excavations those of Ḥilwān. As Director of the famous Royal Excavations sponsored by King Farouk I, he discovered and fully excavated more than 10,000 tombs of the First and Second Dynasties. Among his many publications is *The Ḥelwan Excavations* (Cairo, 1960), a work edited in English by J. Frank Autry (Norman, 1969). He is accredited with the excavation of DAYR ABŪ QARQŪRAH (St. Gregorios). He participated in the process of salvaging the Nubian monuments prior to the completion of the new High Dam.

LABIB HABACHI

SAB'AH WA-ARBA'AH, an Arabic ecclesiastical idiom commonly used by Copts in reference to the PSALMODIA for the month of Kiyahk. It literally means "seven and four." The seven refers to the seven Theotokias of the week, one for each day. The four refers to the four odes of the daily Psalmodia that follows the Office of Midnight Prayer.

As it is not easy to assemble a congregation every night for a month, the custom has arisen of using the whole consecutive series of Theotokias on Saturday night, breaking the monotony by inserting the odes and *psali* (metrical hymns) before the Monday, Wednesday, Friday, and Saturday Theotokias. Each Theotokia is preceded by its *psali,* one or more for each day, and is ended with its LOBSH and ṬARḤ. The *ṭubḥāt* (singular ṬUBḤ) and DOXOLOGIES are sung after the third ode and its *psali,* before the Friday Theotokia. Arabic *madā'iḥ* (songs of praise) are now sung after each part of the Psalmodia during Kiyahk.

BIBLIOGRAPHY

Kitāb al-Abṣalmūdiyyah al-Muqaddasah al-Kiyahkiyyah (The Book of the Holy Psalmodia for the Month of Kiyahk). Cairo, 1911.

O'Leary, De L. *The Coptic Theotokia.* London, 1923.

EMIL MAHER ISHAQ

SĀBĀ YĀSĀ (perhaps an alternative orthography for Yassā), a hierodeacon (that he was a monk is evident from his title Anbā) from the town of *Dr'*, which remains unidentified; Yāqūt al-Ḥamawī mentions nothing resembling it in his geographical encyclopedia called *Mu'jam al-Buldān.*

In 1320, he was in Cairo, where he lived in the residence of the Melchite patriarch of Alexandria, Gregory II (elected c. 1315 and d. before 1335). His residence was situated "at Miṣr the well-kept." It is there that he read the four gospels contained in today's Sinai Arabic 102, on Friday 20 June of the year 28 of the world, which must be corrected to read 6828, that is, A.D. 1320.

BIBLIOGRAPHY

Atiya, A. S., and J. N. Youssef. *Catalogue Raisonné of the Mount Sinai Manuscripts*, pp. 203–204. Alexandria, 1970.

Naṣrallah, J. *Histoire du mouvement littéraire dans l'église melchite*, Vol. 3, pt. 2, pp. 62 and 149 (both pages on the Melchite patriarch of Alexandria, Gregory II). Paris and Louvain, 1981.

KHALIL SAMIR, S.J.

SABELLIANISM, the most sophisticated form of modalist monarchian opinions concerning the godhead and named after its originator, Sabellius "the Libyan" (fl. c. 220). Nothing is known of Sabellius, except that he was in all probability a Christian from one of the cities of Cyrenaica, where his opinions continued to be supported throughout the third century, and that he is likely to have taught at Rome in the time of Pope Callixtus (217–222). (On Sabellianism in Cyrenaica, see Dionysius of Alexandria, quoted by Eusebius *Historia ecclesiastica* 7.6; Athanasius *De sententia Dionysii* 5.9).

Sabellius taught that in God there was one substance but three activities, while God was a unit, or Monad. He manifested Himself under three distinct aspects, in creation and giving the law, as Father; as Son in the work of redemption; and as Holy Spirit in the work of sanctification and grace. Sabellius thought of the Monad that was God as expanding and extending when carrying out the various phases of the divine life. These phases, however, did not constitute independent activities, but were the simple assumption of a fresh guise or outward appearance (*prosopon*) of the Godhead, just as an actor might assume a different mask in performing a different role while remaining himself.

Sabellius stressed the unity of God, and the indivisibility of God and Christ. In Cyrenaica around 260, during their defense against Bishop Dionysius of Alexandria, his disciples invented a new theological term, *Huiopator* (Son-Father) to demonstrate their beliefs (Athanasius *Epistula de synodis* 16), which continued to attract adherents in Egypt. The Melitians may have tended toward Sabellianism, and ARIUS seems to have thought Bishop ALEXANDER I of Alexandria (312–326) had Sabellian leanings when he challenged his views regarding the unity of the Godhead (Socrates Scholasticus *Historia ecclesiastica* 1.5). In the long controversy between Athanasius and his opponents among the Eastern episcopate, Sabellianism was a charge frequently urged against the bishop of Alexandria and his adherents, but one that ATHANASIUS repudiated vigorously (Athanasius *Tomus ad Antiochenos* 3 and 6, from the Council of Alexandria in 362).

The objection to Sabellius was that in asserting that there was in the Godhead a single substance but threefold operation, he was leading the church back to Judaism. As BASIL OF CAESAREA put the matter about 375, "Sabellianism is Judaism imported into the preaching of the Gospel," teaching "the same God transformed as the need of the moment required" (*Letter* 210; compare *Letters* 189 and 236). Despite formal condemnation at the Council of CONSTANTINOPLE in 381 (Canon 1), in Egypt the Sabellian tendencies of many ordinary Christians continued and pointed the way to MONOPHYSITISM in the fifth and later centuries.

BIBLIOGRAPHY

Bethune-Baker, J. H. *The Early History of Christian Doctrine*, 9th ed. London, 1951.

Kidd, B. J. *A History of the Church to A. D. 461*, Vol. 1. Oxford, 1922.

W. H. C. FREND

SACRAMENT. The Coptic church recognizes seven canonical sacraments: confirmation, the Eucharist, repentance, unction of the sick, Matrimony, and holy orders. These sacraments, which are rites ordained by Christ, are outward and visible signs of inward and spiritual grace. Though not enumerated together in the New Testament, they are mentioned separately in various passages.

From the apostolic age, the early fathers' writings conveyed testimonies of the practice of these sacraments in all Christian churches. Despite their own distinctive ritual, all apostolic churches are in full agreement regarding the number of sacraments. The Coptic church believes that sacraments are valid in themselves, irrespective of the condition of the recipient. Accordingly the church prescribes the administration of baptism, confirmation, and communion to children, in spite of their inability to profess their faith in accepting the sacraments.

BIBLIOGRAPHY

Habīb Jirjis. *Al-Ṣakhrah al-Urthūdhuksiyah* (The Orthodox Rock). Cairo, 1948.

———. *Asrār al-Kanīsah al-Sab'ah* (The Seven Sacraments of the Church), 2nd ed. Cairo, 1950.

Leeming, B. *Principles of Sacramental Theology*. London, 1956.

Mīkā'īl Mīnā. *'Ilm al-Lāhūt* (The Study of Theology), Vol. 2. Cairo, 1936.

ARCHBISHOP BASILIOS

SACRAMENT, RESERVATION OF THE BLESSED. The preservation of particles of the Holy Body and Precious Blood after Communion at the end of the liturgy is now not permitted in the Coptic church, except for communion of the sick and the prisoner in his cell. In this case, the priest takes the Holy Sacrament at the end of the Divine Liturgy and goes directly to the sick person or prisoner without delay. If, on arrival, the priest finds him dead or unfit to receive the Eucharist, he should not carry it back to the church but consume it forthwith himself. If a particle of the Holy Body is found unconsumed after the priest has drunk the water with which the paten has been washed, it should be given to a deacon or even to a layman who has not yet broken his fast. If none is available, the priest is directed to wrap it in a veil and place it between two burning candles, with the lamp in the eastern niche also burning, and the priest is to watch by it until the liturgy of the following day, to receive the particle fasting.

EMILE MAHER ISHAQ

SACRISTY. *See* Architectural Elements of Churches.

SACY, ANTOINE ISAAC SILVESTRE DE (1758–1838), French Orientalist. He was born in Paris. He studied Hebrew in order to verify the accuracy of the Latin and French versions of the Bible, and to this he later added many other Semitic languages. In 1785 he became one of the eight resident free Academicians in the Académie des Inscriptions et Belles-Lettres.

Arabic was not his special study until later in life. He was made professor of Arabic at the Ecole des Langues orientales vivantes at the National Library in Paris (1795–1796), to which Persian was afterward added. By 1805, de Sacy had completed his major work, the monumental *Grammaire arabe* (2 vols., Paris, 1810), and the great *Chrestomathie arabe* (3 vols., Paris, 1806). He was appointed royal censor by Louis XVIII (1814) and rector of the University of Paris (1815). He founded with Rémusat the Société asiatique and *Journal Asiatique* (1822) and was its first president. He also became administrator of the Collège de France (1823) and the School of Oriental Languages (1824).

De Sacy was the first person to read any ancient Egyptian words, albeit in a small way, for he recognized and translated three names in demotic, starting with Ptolemy (1802). Though his work had no direct bearing on the fields of Egyptology and Coptology, it would seem reasonable to consider his Arabic output as a natural background to both those disciplines. One of his students was J. F. CHAMPOLLION.

BIBLIOGRAPHY

Dehérain, H. *Silvestre de Sacy et ses correspondants, Extrait du Journal des savants, 1914–1919.* Paris, 1919.

Renouf, P. *The Life-work of Sir Peter Le Page Renouf,* Vol. 1, pp. 44, 88, 151, 167–69. Paris, 1902.

AZIZ S. ATIYA

SADAMANT. *See* Pilgrimages.

SADDLEBACK ROOF. *See* Architectural Elements of Churches.

SA'DIST PARTY. *See* Political Parties.

SA'D MĪKHĀ'ĪL 'ABDŪ (1831–1892), Egyptian government administrator. He was a contemporary of Basilius Bey in whose administration he worked. In the performance of his duties, he gained direct access to the khedive's court and was able to receive certain favors for the Coptic community from both Khedive Ismail (1803–1879) and his successor Tewfik (1879–1892).

He was a contemporary of four patriarchs: PETER VII (1809–1852), CYRIL IV (1854–1861), DEMETRIUS II (1862–1870), and CYRIL V (1874–1927). He consulted with them over all outstanding local problems of the day and participated in their solutions. He was responsible for securing the khedivial decree authorizing the construction of the church at Hārit al-Saqqāyīn. He took active part in supporting Cyril IV in his reform movement and in the foundation of Coptic schools.

Later he played a prominent role in the newly established COMMUNITY COUNCIL, where a great dispute was brewing between the patriarch Cyril V and the council members over the administration of Coptic religious property. Saʿd stood firm in support of the council whose activities were suspended by the patriarch, whom he consequently antagonized. In the circumstances of that misunderstanding, Saʿd withdrew from that debate in spite of his position as acting for BOUṬROS GHĀLĪ, who chaired the meetings. He remained silent on the problems of the community until his death.

MOUNIR SHOUCRI

SAʿD ZAGHLŪL (1858–1927), statesman and one of the best known leaders in the modern history of Egypt. Born at Ibyānah in the province of Gharbiyyah, he enrolled at al-Azhar University and became a disciple and follower of Shaykh Jamāl al-Din al-Afghānī, the Islamic polemical thinker. He was also in contact with Shaykh Muḥammad ʿAbdū, whose eloquence and oratory skills were an inspiration to him.

When Muḥammad ʿAbdū became editor of the official newspaper, *Al-Waqāʾiʿ al-Miṣriyyah,* in 1880, he asked Saʿd Zaghlūl to assist him. Saʿd Zaghlūl continued working for *Al-Waqāʾiʿ* until May 1882, when he transferred to the Ministry of Interior. In September of the same year, he was appointed director of the Legal Department of Giza Province. It was then that he cast off his Azharite cloak and started to wear European clothes.

He was an active supporter of the ʿUrābī revolt and wrote inflammatory articles, which resulted in his being dismissed from his government post in October 1882. Consequently he set up his own law practice. In 1892 the government appointed him judge alternate on the Court of Appeals, which set a precedent for the entire legal profession, as Zaghlūl was the first lawyer to be appointed to a juridical post.

In 1906, Zaghlūl was appointed minister of education. This marked a turning point in the policy of ministerial appointments, as appointment to such posts had previously been restricted to members of the Turkish aristocracy. That shift was in fact symbolic of the response of the British occupation authorities to the pressure exerted upon them by the Egyptian nationalist movement. In 1910, after the assassination of BOUTROS GHĀLĪ, he was appointed minister of justice in the Muḥammad Saʿid cabinet. But in March 1912 he resigned in protest against legal procedures taken by the prime minister in support of British occupation authorities against the leaders of the nationalist movement, without consulting with him.

In 1913 he was elected to the Legislative Assembly and at the end of World War I, together with ʿAlī Shaʿrāwī and ʿAbd al-ʿAzīz Fahmī, he presented the Egyptian demands to the British high commissioner in Cairo. His confrontation with British policy in Egypt resulted in his deportation to Malta on 9 March 1919. His forced exile ignited the most important popular and nationalistic revolution in the history of the country and resulted in the formation of the largest political party, the Wafd, led by Saʿd Zaghlūl. In response, the British authorities were compelled to release him, and allow him to go to Paris to present the patriotic movement's demands to the Peace Conference there.

Saʿd Zaghlūl's followers in Cairo succeeded in organizing a large-scale campaign to boycott the Milner Commission, sent by the British government to investigate the reasons behind the 1919 revolution. As a result the British Government agreed to hold negotiations in London between Saʿd Zaghlūl and Lord Milner, which failed.

In 1920 Saʿd Zaghlūl returned to Egypt and despite initial defeat he continued to mobilize Egyptian patriotic forces against the British presence and against moderate dissenters under the leadership of ʿAdly Yakan. He was again exiled in December 1921, this time to the Seychelles, where he suffered from a decline in his state of health resulting in his transfer to Gibraltar, where he remained until 1923. He returned home one year after Egypt had been granted a defective independence by the declaration of 28 February 1922 and the promulgation of the 1923 constitution, allowing the formation of a parliament by general and public election.

Saʿd Zaghlūl was intent throughout the struggle for independence on unifying both elements of the nation, Copts and Muslims. He had invited a number of Coptic leaders into the Wafd party, of whom the most distinguished was Wassef Ghālī, the son of the former prime minister Boutros Ghālī; Jurjī Khayyāṭ; and Sinot Ḥannā.

In January 1924, Saʿd Zaghlūl formed a cabinet. Despite King Fouad's opposition, he insisted on appointing two Coptic ministers, Murquṣ Ḥannā and Wassef Boutros Ghālī, out of the ten members of the cabinet. This set a precedent for the Wafd (see POLITICAL PARTIES) in all of its subsequent ministries.

The end of his term of office coincided with the assassination of Sir Lee Stack, *sirdar* (head) of the Egyptian army, governor-general of the Sudan, and one of the principal representatives of the British occupation in Egypt. As a result, a British ultimatum was addressed to Zaghlūl, which led to his resignation on 24 November 1924. Two years later, however, public elections were held and once again the Wafd was victorious under his leadership, winning by an overwhelming majority. Despite this, the British opposed his forming a new cabinet and Saʿd Zaghlūl accepted instead the chairmanship of the House of Representatives, which post he continued to occupy until his death on 23 August 1927.

BIBLIOGRAPHY

ʿAbbās Maḥmūd al-ʿAqqād. *Saʿd Zaghlūl, Sīrah wa Taḥiyyah.* Cairo, 1936.

ʿAbd al-ʿAẓim Ramaḍān. *Taṭawwur al-Ḥarakah al-Waṭaniyyah fī Miṣr (1918–1936).* Cairo, 1968.

ʿAbd al-Khāliq Muḥammad Lāshīn. *Sa'd Zaghlūl wa Dawruh fī al-Siyāsah al-Miṣriyyah.* Cairo, 1975.

Ahmad ʿAbd al-Raḥīm Muṣṭafā. *Tārīkh Miṣr al-Siyāsī min al-Iḥtilāl ilā al-Muʿāhadah.* Cairo, 1967.

Landau, J. *Parliaments and Parties in Egypt.* New York, 1954.

Lloyd, G. L., Baron. *Egypt Since Cromer.* 2 vols. London, 1933–1934; repr., New York, 1970.

Muḥammad Ibrāhīm al-Jazīrī. *Saʿd Zaghlūl.* Cairo, 1954.

Newman, P. *Great Britain and Egypt.* London, 1928.

YŪNĀN LABĪB RIZQ

ṢAFĪ IBN AL-ʿASSĀL, AL-, member of the great Coptic family of the AWLĀD AL-ʿASSĀL, who played an important role in the intellectual renaissance of the Coptic church in the thirteenth century. His complete name was al-Ṣafī Abū al-Faḍā'il Mājid. He is known by the name al-Ṣafī. He was the brother of al-ASʿAD ABŪ AL-FARAJ HIBAT ALLĀH, and the half-brother of ABŪ ISḤĀQ IBN FAḌLALLĀH. G. Graf considered al-Safī to be the eldest of the family, but no acceptable argument has been provided in support of this hypothesis.

Little is known of his life. He may have been born around 1205 and died around 1265. The dates thus far compiled of his literary activity are more certain.

In 1232, he summarized and revised the eighty-eight homilies of Saint JOHN CHRYSOSTOM on the Gospel of John, using the translation of the Melchite ʿAbdallāh ibn al-Faḍl al-Anṭākī (eleventh century). In 1235, he composed a discourse in honor of the election of the seventy-fifth patriarch, CYRIL III ibn Laqlaq. By 6 March 1236, he would have finished at Damascus the redaction of the first part (chaps. 1–32) of the *Great Nomocanon,* if he is the author. By 1237–1238, he had already written his summary and revision of the ninety homilies of Saint John Chrysostom on the Gospel of Matthew, after the translation of ʿAbdallah ibn al-Faḍl al-Anṭākī, for at this date al-Ṣafī's half-brother took a copy to Damascus in order to make a liturgical revision. During this same period, and in any case before 8 August 1239, al-Ṣafī composed a number of homilies in rhymed prose, among which is the homily of Good Friday that ends with a prayer for the patriarch Cyril.

In September 1238, al-Ṣafī completed the redaction of his *Nomocanon,* which justly brought him fame. On 3 September, he participated as a canonical counselor and secretary in the synod of Cairo demanded by the bishops to bring an end to the abuses of Cyril III. There he drafted a canonical compendium of twelve sections that was adopted by the synod, and ten days later, 13 September, he drew up a new compendium consisting of five chapters and nineteen sections, likewise adopted by the synod.

In July 1241 at Cairo, he finished the résumé of forty-one works of the Christian philosopher from Bagdad, Yaḥyā ibn ʿAdī (d. 974). In June 1242, he completed, also at Cairo, the redaction of his opuscule on the Trinity and the Incarnation. During the eight years of the reign of Cyril III, al-Ṣafī drafted eleven apologetical works in response to Muslim attacks against the Christians. His last dated work is the elegy that he pronounced on 11 March 1243 on the death of Cyril III.

There is nothing to indicate that al-Ṣafī was a priest. It is likely that he was a married layman, although the documents tell nothing of a wife or children.

His works fall into two broad categories: nonapologetic and apologetic.

Nonapologetic Works

Al-Ṣafī's literary output was considerable. Essentially religious, it presupposed a good knowledge of secular subjects such as Arabic language and literature, Greek and Arabic philosophy, and Muslim history and theology. All this erudition was used, however, either to defend the Christians against the repeated attacks of Muslim thinkers or to purify the church from within and place it upon the solid spiritual tradition of the church fathers.

On the basis of the dates mentioned above and from an examination of the contents of his literary production, al-Ṣafī's intellectual development can be traced through six chronological stages. The first five—during which he produced nonapologetic works—will be discussed briefly; the sixth is analyzed in greater detail in the discussion of his apologetic works below.

Epitomes (Mukhtaṣarāt) of Spiritual Patristic Works. The six works in this category probably belong to the beginning of his literary career; they may be dated before 1232. It does not appear that al-Ṣafī translated these epitomes directly from Greek, but rather that he based them on Arabic translations already in existence. His contribution consisted in selecting extracts from them to clarify the ideas, and in revising the language to make it more correct. These works may be arranged in the chronological order of the original Greek texts as follows: (1) epitome of the Arabic collection of fifty-two hymns attributed to Saint Ephraem Syrus; (2) epitome of a monastic ascetic compendium; (3) epitome of 100 chapters of Diadocus of Pholticea; (4) epitome of the *Ladder of Virtues* of John Climacus; (5) epitome of the thirty-five chapters on monastic life by Isaac of Nineveh; and (6) epitome of the *Spiritual Paradise,* in twelve chapters.

Epitomes of Homilies of Saint John Chrysostom. Al-Ṣafī began with the eighty-eight homilies on the Gospel of John, using the Arabic translation of the Melchite Anbā Anṭūniyūs of the Monastery of Saint Simeon near Antioch (tenth century). He finished the first forty-seven in March 1232; the others bear no date.

He then worked on the ninety homilies on the Gospel of Matthew, using the translation of the Melchite ʿAbdallah ibn al-Faḍl al-Anṭākī dated around 1050. However, al-Ṣafī avoided the theoretical part to concentrate on the moral part. The entire work was completed before 1237.

Liturgical Homilies in Rhymed Prose. The first two types of al-Ṣafī's works were a kind of exercise currently popular in the Arabo-Muslim world, which consisted in synthesizing the thoughts of the masters. Thereby, al-Ṣafī acquired a good command of the sacred art of writing and a profound spiritual foundation. Thereafter he turned to composing homilies in the pure Arabic style of rhymed prose, and fortunately succeeded in avoiding the vain pursuit of form at the expense of content. He divided his collection into six parts, of which approximately half have been published to date (parts two, four, and six); (1) the unity and trinity of God; (2) Christology (covering the eight festivals of the Lord); (3) morals (commandments of God and purification of the heart); (4) homilies on fasting (seven have been published); (5) spirituality (prayers to God, intercessions to the Virgin and saints); and (6) homilies for various circumstances (advice to newlyweds, letters of investiture of bishops, spiritual letters).

To this collection three writings of similar style may be added: (1) letter of congratulation upon the election of Cyril III (June 1235); (2) homily on the death of Cyril III (1243); and (3) Letter to his half-brother, consoling him upon the death of his wife.

Works on Canon Law. Al-Ṣafī's renown as a canonist has eclipsed other qualities that are no less evident. His great *Nomocanon* remains today the basis of ecclesiastical law for the Coptic church of Egypt, and even more so, for the church of Ethiopia (where it is entitled *Fetḥa Nagast*). This work also served as the basis for the Maronite ecclesiastical law, reformed in the eighteenth century by ʿAbdallāh Qaraʿalī. Four works on canon law by al-Ṣafī, dating from 1238 to 1243, are known: (1) a small canonical collection of twelve sections, regulating conflicts of a jurisdictional nature between bishops (September 1238); (2) a second canonical collection of five chapters and nineteen sections, treating baptism, marriage, wills, inheritance, and ordination (1238 September 13); (3) a compendium of the abstract of laws or *Nomocanon,* his renowned work of synthesis (*al-Majmūʿ al-Ṣafawī*)), also completed in September 1238; and (4) an abridgment of the canonical compendium, divided into forty-three chapters, and consisting of short decisions pertaining to ecclesiastical persons and matters and to certain questions of morals and discipline.

Epitomes of Arabic Apologetical Works. In this fifth stage of his intellectual development, which spanned the years 1239–1242, al-Ṣafī concerned himself with apologetical works written in Arabic, in direct contrast to his first two periods, in which he dealt with spiritual works written in Greek. However, he was not interested in the popular apologies (such as those of Baḥīrā or of Ibrāhīm al-Ṭabarānī of the ninth century), nor in historical and moral apologies (such as that of al-Kindī). Rather he worked only with apologies of a philosophical nature. Throughout these epitomes he scattered commentaries, sometimes lengthy, which were often subsequently cited in the *Theological Compendium* under the title of *al-Ḥawāshī al-Ṣafawiyyah* (commentaries of al-Ṣafī). It may be noted that all the writers upon whose works al-Ṣafī based these epitomes were Iraqi, of the Jacobite or Nestorian confession, dating from 825 to 1030.

Ten works summarized and discussed by al-Ṣafī have been thus far identified: (1) *Book of Questions and Answers* by ʿAmmār al-Baṣrī (c. 825); (2) *Book of The Proof* by ʿAmmār al-Baṣrī; (3) Forty-one opuscules of the great philosopher from Bagdad, YAḤYĀ IBN ʿADĪ (893–974); (4) the great refutation of Abū Īsā al-Warrāq by Yaḥyā ibn ʿAdī; (5) the great Christological controversy between Yaḥyā and al-Miṣrī; (6) the *Fundamentals of Law* (*Al-Uṣūl al-Sharʿiyyah*), or *Book of Guidance* (*al-Hidāyah*) by Ibn al-Athradī; (7) the Christological controversy among Quwayrī, Ibn al-Ṭayyib, and others; (8) conversations (*al-Majālis*) of Elias of Nisibis with the Vizier al-Maghribī; (9) *Book on the Virtue of Chastity* by Elias of Nisibis, in answer to al-Jāḥiẓ; and (10) opuscules on chastity by various spiritual authors.

Apologetic Works

All the foregoing works served to prepare al-Ṣafī for his great theologico-apologetic undertakings. Within three or four years, beginning in 1242, he drafted a number of works or tracts that were often written at the request of Christians troubled in their faith. These writings are characterized by clarity of content and exposition and a spirit of synthesis.

Brief Chapters on the Trinity and the Union. This theological tract, which is the jewel of his writings, was finished in Cairo in June 1242. It was inspired by various treatises of Yaḥyā ibn ʿAdī, but the synthesis is entirely al-Ṣafī's. It consists of one part on the Trinity (chaps. 1–16), another part on the Incarnation (chaps. 7–11), and ends with one chapter on the science of theology (chap. 12). A critical edition has recently been produced, with a French translation and an exhaustive lexical index. Chapter 8 is particularly noteworthy for its ecumenical tone, showing that the differences among the three Christian confessions (Nestorian, Melchite, and Monophysite) are of a philosophic, not dogmatic nature. Chapter 11, which discusses the Incarnation and its necessity, is one of the most powerful, being based on the idea that God is Love who must give Himself to the beloved, that is, to mankind.

Reply to al-Nāshi' al-Akbar. ʿAbdallah ibn Muḥammad al-Nāshi' al-Akbar, an Iraqi grammarian and poet who died in Cairo in 906, authored the book of *Opinions* (*al-Maqālāt*) in which he listed and refuted diverse philosophical and theological opinions, including those of the Christians. Al-Ṣafī, in turn, refuted the section on Christianity, basing his arguments on the Holy Scriptures and reason. He depended upon the *Refutation* of Abū ʿĪsā al-Warrāq made by Yaḥyā ibn Adī. Yaḥyā's work (as yet unpublished) consists of three parts: the Trinity (chaps. 1 and 4), the divine sonship of Christ (chap. 2), and the Incarnation (chap. 3). It is a work often cited by al-Ṣafī himself, as well as by al-Mu'taman ABŪ ISHAQ IBRĀHĪM IBN al-ʿAssāl and Abū al-Barakāt IBN KABAR. The section on the divine sonship of Christ, based upon the Gospel, is particularly suggestive, with Yaḥyā attesting a profound apologetic reflection upon the Gospels.

Reply to Rāzī on God's Inhabitation in Christ. Fakhr al-Dīn al-Rāzī was one of the most famous Muslim scholars of the twelfth century. He was born at Rayy (Teheran), and died at Herat, Afghanistan, in 1209. In the ninth question of the *Kitāb al-Arbaʿīn fī Uṣūl al-Dīn* (Book of the Forty about the Fundamentals of Religion), he affirmed that God cannot inhabit a creature, and that such inhabitation is neither necessary nor even optional.

Al-Ṣafī replied in eight chapters, establishing, first of all, the necessity of the inhabitation of God and its possibility, based on His love for the creature. He next established that this does not mean that God needs a dwelling, but rather that He becomes one with the dwelling by this union. In the second part, al-Ṣafī advanced proofs of the divinity of Christ that distinguish Him from Moses and all other prophets, and he rejected the objection that God may dwell not only in any man but even in a pismire. He then concluded by establishing the necessity of the Incarnation of God in Christ, basing his arguments on reason and tradition.

Reply to the Refutation of the Christians by Rāzī. In his work *Nihāyat al-ʿUqūl* (The Results of Reason), Rāzī claimed that there is no difference between Christ and the other prophets insofar as miracles are concerned. Al-Ṣafī began this reply by referring to his *Reply to al-Nāshi' al-Akbar* (above) and then adroitly moved to the *Book of the Forty* by Rāzī, in which Rāzī made a clear distinction between the prophet and the saint, though miracles are wrought equally through one or the other. Al-Ṣafī argued that the same distinction clearly exists between Christ and the prophets (although the prophets may have accomplished miracles), because Christ is the only one to claim divinity.

Three Christological Apologies No Longer Extant. In his *Reply to Jaʿfarī* (below) al-Ṣafī referred to three distinct apologies, whose argumentation may be traced by allusions to their context.

The first is the *Treatise on the Incarnation of Christ by the Holy Ghost and the Virgin Mary.* The Holy Ghost prepared Mary to conceive Christ without human intervention. The preposition "by" had various meanings: Mary is the material cause of the conception, whereas the Holy Ghost is the formal cause. Al-Ṣafī then wrote a philosophical commentary on the text from Proverbs 9:1, "Wisdom has built her house."

The second of these apologies is described by al-Ṣafī: "Herein I collected everything in the Gospels and Epistles which describes Christ with divine attributes, either explicitly, or in a manner that is by necessity deducible, or in a manner that is simply deducible." This corresponds to the second part of his *Reply to al-Nāshiʾ al-Akbar* (see above).

The third apology is an answer to the vulgar objection made by the Muslims: "Christ fulfilled his natural urge. Did he truly have to be incarnated for that!" Al-Ṣafī replied by showing that according to the Gospel, the purpose of the Incarnation was to teach man to master the powers of passion and anger in order to let himself be conquered by the rational soul.

Treatise of the Ten Fundamentals. This treatise was presented as a long introduction to the *Reply to Ṭabarī* (see below) and was constantly used thereafter by al-Ṣafī, for in his mind, these ten fundamentals formed the indispensable bases for every discussion with the Muslims. Each fundamental is usually accompanied by its own corollary. The fundamentals are: (1) the divine attributes and their varieties (the essential attributes are the hypostases); (2) simple and compound essences (the possibility of the union of divinity and humanity in Christ); (3) compound beings (Christ is composed of divinity and humanity); (4) real and metaphorical terms (these are essential in establishing the hermeneutic principles); (5) the meaning of "God" and of "Son" (understanding the difference between the filiation of Christ and that of other human beings); (6) the importance of typology (in order to explain the hypostatic union by natural and technical examples); (7) the conditions of contradiction (their absence excludes all contradiction); (8) faith goes beyond reason without contradicting it, as the philosophers attest; (9) proof of the divinity of Christ and of the Incarnation by three means: the Holy Scriptures, reason, and existence; and (10) the truth of the Gospel established by reason (in reply to the Muslim theory of the falsification of the Gospel).

Reply to Ṭabarī. ʿAlī ibn Rabbān al-Ṭabarī, born at Merv (c. 785–790), was a Nestorian Christian who became the secretary and physician of the amir of Ṭabaristān in 833. After several years in prison, he was freed and settled in Samarra'. Here he compiled his medical encyclopedia, dedicated to his patron, the caliph al-Mutawakkil (847–861), who frequently urged him to become a Muslim. Finally, after more than seventy years of age, Ṭabarī did convert to Islam, and thereupon wrote his *Refutation of the Christians*, which, as the first refutation written by an ex-Christian, quickly became famous. For this reason, al-Ṣafī was requested to write a reply to it, which he did in eighteen rather lengthy chapters, whose titles are: (1) introduction: Ṭabarī did not attain his goal; Islam is destined for the Arabs alone; an essay in Qur'anic Christology; (2) explanation of some embarrassing passages in the Gospel; (3) reply to the twelve points of agreement between the Muslims and Christians; (4) reply to the refutation of the creed; (5) reply to the four proofs concerning the divinity of Christ; (6) why call Christ God; (7) explanation of the agony of Christ; (8) the humanity and divinity of Christ; (9) the accord of the three Christian confessions as to Christology, and a call for an integral ecumenicism among all believers; (10) Christ destroyed both sin and death; (11) the royalty and divinity of Christ; (12) miracles wrought by Christians; (13) the meaning of the word "faith," and the belief of Christians; (14) Paul and the Council of Nicaea; (15) the Ascension of Christ and a comparison with certain prophets; (16) reply to the so-called contradictions of the Gospel; (17) the meaning of the veneration and glorification of the cross; and (18) motives for the conversion of Ṭabarī, and conclusion.

Reply to Jaʿfarī. Taqī al-Dīn Abū al-Baqā' Ṣāliḥ ibn al-Ḥusayn al-Jaʿfarī was a contemporary of al-Ṣafī who died after 1239. He wrote a refutation of the Christians entitled *Takhjīl Muḥarrifī al-Injīl* (The Corrupting Shame of the Gospel), a large volume filled with repetitions and based upon Ṭabarī's work (see above). A certain anonymous friend of the king made a résumé of it that spread throughout the area of Cairo. Patriarch Cyril III ibn Laqlaq asked al-Ṣafī to write a reply without, however, repeating anything he had already said in his *Reply to Ṭabarī*. Here again, al-Ṣafī depended upon the works of Yaḥyā ibn ʿAdī and of ʿAbdallāh ibn al-Ṭayyib (d. 1043), Ibrāhīm ibn ʿAwn, Ḥunayn ibn Isḥāq, and Qusṭā ibn Lūqā; he also referred to the *Commentary upon the Creed* by SAWĪRUS IBN AL-MUQAFFAʿ (the only Coptic writer to be mentioned). In addition, he cited Muslim authors, in particular Fakhr al-Dīn al-Rāzī (d. 1209) (see sections on replies to Razi, above).

Al-Ṣafī's reply, which is quite lengthy, consists of

five chapters: (1) defense of the hypostatic union in Christ; (2) defense of the text of the creed; (3) Christ is more than a prophet; (4) upon the real death, and the Resurrection of Christ; and (5) Muḥammad was not announced by the Holy Scriptures (Old and New Testament), contrary to what the Muslims proclaim.

In conclusion, al-Ṣafī demonstrated (by the Holy Scriptures and by reason) that there can be no prophet after Christ unless he is willing to call mankind to Christ.

Reply to Dimyāṭī. This is a reply to the *Refutation of the Christians,* written by a certain Abū al-Manṣūr ibn Fatḥ al-Dimyāṭī. Herein al-Ṣafī merely revised a reply already in existence.

The text is rather long, and as usual, follows the work being refuted, which explains a certain deficiency in structure. In his preparation of the critical edition of the text, Khalil Samir has divided the work into thirty-one small chapters that may be regrouped as follows: (1) Introduction (authenticity of the Gospels, the only means of bringing mankind to perfection); (2) divinity of Christ (man is incapable of attaining the essence of God; it is Christ who came to reveal the Father, being one with Him; the difference between Christ, on the one hand, and Adam, Beṣaleel, the prophets, and Israel, on the other; the trinitarian oneness of God; the names of Christ manifest His humanity, His divinity, and the union of the two, but Christ alone is the creative Spirit); (3) Muḥammad is not the Paraclete announced by Christ (the Paraclete is the Holy Spirit; the Gospel did not omit the name of Muḥammad; concerning the prophet announced in Dt. 18:15, this is Christ, not Muḥammad, as is also the case for other Old Testament prophecies; e.g., Dt. 32:2, Ps. 45:4); and (4) Conclusion (agreement among the three monotheistic religions; Christ brings the law to its completion; as for the Jews, they, like the Christians, refuse to believe in the divine origin of the Qur'ān and the mission of Muḥammad; Christianity and Judaism were not spread by the sword, in contrast to Islam).

Biblical Revelation and Qur'anic Revelation. The attribution of this opuscule to al-Ṣafī is not certain. Khalil Samir has published the text in the Lebanese journal *al-Manārah* beginning in 1983. There are two major parts, the first proving the truth of the known Gospels and of the Holy Scriptures in general (chaps. 1–7), and the second showing the needlessness for any new Holy Scripture or prophet (chaps. 8–10). It contains several points in common with the *Reply to Dimyāṭī* (see above).

Conclusion

From this rapid survey, the theologico-apologetic thought of al-Ṣafī ibn al-ʿAssāl may be distinguished. Incontestably, he was the greatest Coptic apologist of the Middle Ages, and one of the greatest Christian apologists in the Arabic language. This explains why he was the object of attacks even by the eighteenth-century Muslim apologist Ziyādah ibn Yaḥyā ibn al-Rāsī, author of two anti-Christian polemical works. Al-Rāsī directed his attacks primarily against ʿAbd al-Masīḥ ibn Isḥāq al-Kindī and al-Ṣafī ibn al-ʿAssāl.

BIBLIOGRAPHY

Samir, K. *Al-Ṣafī Ibn al-ʿAssāl, brefs chapitres sur la Trinité et l'Incarnation.* PO 42, fasc. 3, no. 192. Turnhout, 1985. With an exhaustive bibliography of al-Ṣafī of ninety-one titles.

KHALIL SAMIR, S.J.

SAHIDIC. *See Appendix.*

SAHLĀN IBN ʿUTHMĀN IBN KAYSĀN, a tenth-century Melchite physician of Miṣr (Old Cairo) and the brother of Abū Sahl KAYSĀN IBN ʿUTHMĀN. He served the Fatimid caliphs of Egypt, and reached the peak of his fame under the reign of al-ʿAzīz (975–996). He died at Old Cairo, very rich and highly respected, in 991.

Ibn Abī Uṣaybiʿah, the medical historian who died in 1269, mentions no work by Sahlān. Three were discovered by Paul Sbath, who spent dozens of years searching for manuscripts.

1. *Kitāb al-Aqrābādhīn* (Pharmacopoeia) survives in a single manuscript dated A.H. 472/A.D. 1079, in the possession of the family of Jurjī ʿAqqād, a Greek Catholic pharmacist of Aleppo. This work is still unpublished.

2. The Brief Account of Perfumes has been discovered in a single manuscript copied on 29 June 1093 by al-Rabbān Dāwūd, at the Monastery of the Mother of God, known as the Monastery of the Syrians (Dayr al-Suryān). It was in the possession of Anbā Īsīdhūrus, a Coptic bishop of Syrian origin who died in 1942. Sbath published this Arabic text in 1944. M. Ullmann writes concerning this treatise, "In his *Mukhtaṣar fī ṭ-ṭīb* Ibn Kaisān gives, in a highly condensed form, a wealth of extremely interesting information concerning perfumes" (p. 315).

3. *Mukhtaṣar fī al-adwiyah al-murakkabah fī*

akthar al-amrāḍ (Brief Account of the Mixed Medicines Used in Most Illnesses) was published in Cairo in 1953, with a French translation, by Sbath and C. D. Avierinos. According to Manfred Ullmann (p. 309), this work is actually no more than a résumé of *al-Dustūr al-Bīmāristānī*, composed by Ibn Abī al-Bayān al-Isrā'īlī (1161–1240) and published in 1933, again by Sbath; thus it would appear not to be the work of Sahlān. However, F. Sezgin expresses no doubts concerning its attribution to Sahlān.

BIBLIOGRAPHY

Sbath, P. "Le Formulaire des hôpitaux d'Ibn Abil Bayan médecin du bimaristan annacery au Caire au XIIIe siècle." *Bulletin de l'Institut d'Egypte* 15 (Cairo 1933):13–78.

______. "Abrégé sur les arômes par Sahlân Ibn Kaissân médecin chrétien melchite égyptien du Calife al-Aziz mort en 990." *Bulletin de l'Institut d'Egypte* 26 (1944):183–213.

Sbath, P., and C. D. Aviernos, eds. and trans. *Précis sur les médicaments composés employés dans la plupart des maladies par Sahlân Ibn Kaysan*. Publications de l'Institut français d'Archéologie orientale du Caire; Textes arabes et etudes islamiques 10. Cairo, 1953.

Sezgin, F. *Geschichte des arabischen Schrifttums*, Vol. 3, p. 310. Leiden, 1970.

Ullmann, M. "Die Medizin im Islam." *Handbuch der Orientalistik*. Leiden and Cologne, 1970.

KHALIL SAMIR, S.J.

ṢA'ĪD, designation for Upper Egypt. The division of Egypt into two parts, Lower and Upper Egypt, goes back to pharaonic antiquity. The term Miṣraim, used in some works, is a dual and hence betrays this duality founded on geography. For Lower Egypt, the Delta, the effective divisions were al-Qalyūbīyyah, al-Sharqiyyah, al-Daqhaliyyah, al-Gharbiyyah, al-Minūfiyyah, al-Beheira, and al-Jiziyyah. For the Ṣa'īd, which could not be presented as a block, it seems more practical to follow the tripartite division of the ancient Greek and Arabic geographers, such as Yāqūt (d. 1224), who distinguish (a) the lower Ṣa'īd (or Lower Thebaid), from Cairo (formerly Fusṭāṭ-Miṣr) to al-Bahnasā (Oxyrhynchus); (b) the middle Ṣa'īd (or Thebaid), from al-Bahnasā to Akhmīm; and (c) the Upper Ṣa'īd (or Upper Thebaid), from Akhmīm to Aswan. This forms three roughly equal parts (the third is a little larger).

The Fayyūm forms an entity apart, as do the oases.

A summary of the ancient statements and a setting out on the map of the positions adopted are in A. Grohmann (1959, pp. 22–33 and map 4, p. 21).

BIBLIOGRAPHY

Grohmann, A. *Studien zur historischen Geographie und Verwaltung des frühmittelalterlichen Ägypten*. Österreichischen Akademie der Wissenschaften, philosophisch-historische Klasse, Denkschriften 77, 2. Vienna, 1959.

RENÉ-GEORGES COQUIN

SA'ĪD IBN ṬUFAYL, Christian physician who worked at the court of the amir Aḥmad ibn Ṭūlūn (868–884), and used to accompany him on his travels. Later there was friction between them, as Aḥmad would consult other physicians when he disobeyed Sa'īd's instructions. Sa'īd died in the year 883 or 892. Isḥaq ibn 'Imrān dedicated to him his work, *Maqālah fī al-Istisqā'* (Treatise on the Dropsy).

BIBLIOGRAPHY

Sezgin, F. *Geschichte des arabischen Schrifttums*, 7 vols. Leiden, 1967–1979.

PENELOPE JOHNSTONE

SAI ISLAND, the largest permanent island along the course of the Nile. It is about 6 miles (10 km) long and 3 miles (5 km) wide, and is situated in northern Sudan a short distance downstream from the Third Cataract. A large, brick-walled fortress was built on the eastern shore of the island in the Eighteenth Dynasty, and the place was intermittently important as a religious and administrative center in many subsequent ages. Its name appears as Zah in medieval Christian inscriptions, as Shaye in a Meroitic text, and as Shaat in ancient Egyptian. According to J. Vercoutter (1958, p. 147), "the Christian period appears to have been a flourishing one for the island since at least up to the eleventh century it was the seat of a bishopric and Thābit Ḥassan was able to record, in 1954, five different churches along its banks." However, the cathedral has not been identified. After the Christian period, the fortress at Sai became one of the two principal Ottoman garrison points within NUBIA.

Archaeological excavations in the fortress of Sai were carried out by a French mission in 1955–1957, and again, intermittently, since 1967. The finds from the Christian period have not yet been systematically reported in print.

[*See also:* Nubian Church Organization.]

BIBLIOGRAPHY

Vercoutter, J. "Excavations at Sai 1955–7." *Kush* 6 (1958):144–69.

______. "La XVIIIe dynastie à Sai et en Haute-Nubie." *Cahiers de recherche de l'Institut de papyrologie et d'égyptologie de Lille* 2 (1973):7–38.

WILLIAM Y. ADAMS

SAINT-PAUL-GIRARD, LOUIS (1877–1935), French Coptologist. He was a member, and then secretary-librarian, of the Institut français d'Archéologie orientale du Caire. He studied with S. Gsell, P. Lejay, and L. Duchesne.

BIBLIOGRAPHY

Jouguet, P. "Louis Saint-Paul-Girard." *Bulletin de l'Institut français d'Archéologie orientale* 35 (1935):181–84.

Kammerer, W., comp. *A Coptic Bibliography*. Ann Arbor, Mich., 1950; repr. New York, 1969.

RENÉ-GEORGES COQUIN

SAINTS, COPTIC, holy men and women recognized in Egypt who died peacefully, as distinguished from MARTYRS, also saints, who met a violent end. The saints continued to reflect their faith throughout their lives, leaving behind them information that could help posterity record their labors for Christianity. Any listing of saints is an infinitesimal fraction of the true number, who were not concerned with what posterity would say about them. Prominent among them are members of the ecclesiastical hierarchy, whose history can be compiled from contemporary sources. They include PATRIARCHS of Alexandria, who bore the brunt of pressure from both Byzantine rulers and Islamic rulers after the Arab conquest in the seventh century. Below them ranked BISHOPS of cities and ABBOTS of monasteries. Lower than these were priests and then deacons.

In addition to these churchmen there is a tremendous number of self-denying holy persons who lived in remote monasteries in the Egyptian desert or who chose to live alone, secluded from the rest of the human race in concealed desert caves. When these solitary figures died, they left no trace of their religious existence.

The Coptic church, despite its antiquity and its major role in preserving the Christian faith in its early centuries, has suffered from the oblivion imposed on it after the Arab conquest and its consequent separation from the rest of the Christian world. Only recently has the Western world discovered the Copts and their church. A study of their saints, still in its infancy, offers unlimited possibilities for throwing light on this important area of the Christian heritage.

The following list is based essentially on De Lacy O'Leary's *The Saints of Egypt in the Coptic Calendar* (1937). It is an attempt to round up as many saints as the sources may yield. A considerable number do not figure in famous dictionaries of Christian saints, such as F. G. Holwek's *A Biographical Dictionary of the Saints* (1924), which appeared before the beginning of major inquiry into the realm of Coptic saints. Each saint is given an official commemoration day (feast day), if known. Many appear in the Copto-Arabic SYNAXARION but not all. The spelling is not necessarily that used by O'Leary, but alternatives are given. When a saint has a separate biography in the encyclopedia, the name is printed in small caps.

ABABIUS, a monk of Scetis.

ABILIUS, Auilius, Minius, Milius, or Milianos (feast day: 1 Tūt), first-century patriarch of Alexandria.

ABRAAM I, or Aphraam (feast day: 3 Ba'ūnah), nineteenth-century bishop of the Fayyūm noted for his devotion to the poor.

Abracas, or Abrākiyūs (feast day: 13 Kiyahk), a native of Upper Egypt who became a monk at twenty and lived until seventy.

ABRAHAM (feast day: 6 Kiyahk), tenth-century reforming patriarch of Alexandria.

ABRAHAM OF MINŪF (feast day: 30 Bābah), a monk and hermit.

ABRAHAM AND GEORGE OF SCETIS (feast days: 9 Ṭūbah and 18 Bashans respectively), monks who shared a cell at Dayr Anbā Maqqār for many years.

ACHILLAS (feast day 19 Ba'ūnah), fourth-century patriarch of Alexandria.

Agathon (feast day: 16 Bābah), seventh-century patriarch of Alexandria.

AGATHON, anchorite.

AGATHON THE STYLITE (feast day: 15 Tūt), an ascetic who lived on a pillar.

ALEXANDRA (feast day: 7 Amshīr), a fourth-century recluse.

AMMONAS, a disciple of Saint ANTONY OF EGYPT.

Ammonius of Aswan (feast day: 11 Hātūr), ascetic.

AMMONIUS OF KELLIA, a disciple of Saint PAMBO, a monk of Scetis.

AMMONIUS OF TŪNAH (feast day: 20 Bashans), a recluse.

AMUN, or Ammon (feast day: 20 Bashans), a fourth-century church father who lived chastely with his wife for eighteen years and then at her urging became a monk in Wādī al-Naṭrūn. Feeling too close to the well-traveled road, he went deeper into the desert to Niri or Nimone, or Kellia, where he lived alone for twenty-two years.

ANASTASIA (feast day: 26 Ṭūbah), a sixth-century ascetic virgin, born in Constantinople.

ANBĀ RUWAYS (Feast day: 32 Bābah), fourteenth-century monk.

ANDREW OF CRETE, seventh- to eighth-century hymn writer and theologian.

ANTONY OF EGYPT (feast day: 22 Ṭūbah), abbot.

APOLLINARIA (formally unrecognized by the Coptic church but recognized by the Orthodox church), a "woman monk" whose life seems to recapitulate that of Saint HILARIA. According to legend she was the elder daughter of the fifth-century Western emperor Anthemius who disguised herself as a monk, Father Dorotheus, at the Monastery of Saint Macarius in Wādī al-Naṭrūn. Her identity remained secret and she gained fame for her sanctity and miracles of healing. Her father sent her younger sister, possessed by a devil, to the monastery, where she was placed in Dorotheus' cell and healed. On returning to her father, he questioned Dorotheus and discovered "he" was his long-lost elder daughter. He allowed her to go to Scetis, where she died.

Apollo (feast day: 5 Amshīr) an ascetic who was a companion of Anbā Abīb.

Apollo of Bāwīṭ, a native of Akhmīn who was a monk at Mount Ablūj or Bāwīṭ. He is the namesake of a martyr commemorated 25 Bābah. He had many disciples and received a consolatory letter from Saint MACARIUS THE EGYPTIAN.

Apollonius, abbot of the Monastery at Monchosis, who helped produce a schism among the successors of Saint Pachomius over the handling of monastic properties.

Apollonius of Nitrea, an ascetic in Wādī al-Naṭrūn for twenty years, who subsequently was a peddlar to monks in Alexandria.

Archebius, an ascetic who was later bishop of Panephysis.

ARCHELLIDES (feast day: 14 Ṭūbah), a Roman noble who became a monk.

ARSENIUS OF SCETIS AND ṬURAH (feast day: 13 Bashans), fifth-century saint who was a tutor to royal children.

Athanasia of Mīnūf, or Bā'issah (feast day: 2 Misrā), rich woman who turned her big house into a shelter for traveling monks. Later it became known as a brothel and was investigated by Hegumenos John of Scetis. She received him in her bedroom but was persuaded by his preaching to spend the rest of her life as a solitary nun. She accompanied him to the desert, where one night as she slept, John saw a pillar of light descend from heaven to her body and heard a voice declare that she was forgiven.

ATHANASIUS I THE APOSTOLIC (feast day: 7 Bashans), fourth-century patriarch of Alexandria.

ATHANASIUS II (Feast day: 20 Tūt), fifth-century patriarch of Alexandria.

Barnabas (feast day: 22 Kiyahk) a native of Qifṭ, who was bishop of 'Aydhāb. He ministered to mariners and merchants sailing the Red Sea.

Barsūm the Naked, or Barsuma (feast day: 5 Nasī), saint.

BASIL THE GREAT, or Basil of Caesarea (feast day: 13 Tūt), one of the doctors of the Eastern church, who performed many miracles.

BENJAMIN I (feast day: 8 Ṭūbah), seventh-century patriarch of Alexandria.

BESSARION (feast day: 25 Misrā), disciple first of Saint ANTONY OF EGYPT and later of Saint MACARIUS THE EGYPTIAN.

Bessus, son of a slave who became *hegumenos* of the Monastery of Saint John Kāmā in Scetis in the eleventh century. He resisted al-Mustanṣir's black mercenaries and refused election as patriarch because of his lowly birth.

Bishoi (feast day: Abīb), monk.

Bishoi, see *Pshoi*, below.

CASSIAN, JOHN, fourth-century monk and author.

CELADION (feast day: 9 Abīb), second-century patriarch of Alexandria.

CERDON (feast day: 21 Ba'ūnah), first-century patriarch of Alexandria.

Christodorus, saint.

Christodoulus (feast day: 14 Kiyahk), a jeweler who became an ascetic in the desert.

Chrysostom, John, see *John Chrysostom,* below.

CLEMENT I, or Clement of Rome, bishop of Rome at the end of the first century.

CLEMENT OF ALEXANDRIA, second- to third-century writer.

Cleopas, saint.

Cornelius the Centurian (feast day: 23 Hātūr), saint.

Corpus, Apollo, and Peter, or Carpus, Papylus, and Peter (feast day: 16 Bābah), disciples of Anbā Isaiah.

COSMAS I (feast day: 30 Ba'ūnah), eighth-century patriarch of Alexandria.

COSMAS II (feast day: 21 Hātūr), ninth-century patriarch of Alexandria.

COSMAS III (feast day: 3 Baramhāt), tenth-century patriarch of Alexandria.

CRONIUS OF NITRIA, ascetic of Scetis who later served Saint ANTONY OF EGYPT and went to Alexandria, where he met PALLADIUS.

CYRIL I THE GREAT, or Cyril of Alexandria (feast day: 3 Abīb), fifth-century patriarch of Alexandria.

CYRIL II (feast day: 22 Baramhāt), eleventh-century patriarch of Alexandria.

CYRIL OF JERUSALEM (feast day: 18 March), fourth-century bishop of Jerusalem.

Cyrus (feast day: 8 Abīb), brother of Theodosius the Great, emperor of Constantinople. He lived many years in the desert of SCETIS, where PAMBO discovered him.

DAMIAN (feast day: 18 Ba'ūnah), sixth-century patriarch of Alexandria.

DANIEL OF SCETIS (feast day: 8 Bashans), sixth-century abbot of Dayr Anbā Maqār who was thrice seized in Berber raids. As a leader of the rejection of the Tome of Leo proposed by Justinian, he was driven from his monastery but returned after the emperor's death in 565. During another Berber invasion about 570 he was sold into slavery in Pentapolis.

DEMETRIUS I (feast day: 22 Bābah), third-century patriarch of Alexandria.

Dermataus of Pemje (feast day: 7 Kiyahk), ascetic.

Didymus of Tarshjebi, saint.

DIOSCURUS I (feast day: 7 Tūt), fifth-century patriarch of Alexandria.

Elias of Bishwāw (feast day: 17 Kiyahk), monk of exceptional austerity.

Elias of Jeme (feast day: 17 Kiyahk), a native of Iskhim who was a recluse on Mount Shamah. His disciple, John, wrote his biography.

ELIAS OF SAMHŪD (feast day: 13 Kiyahk), a sixth-century (?) monk whose birth was foretold by an angel.

EPHRAEM SYRUS, or the Syrian (feast day: 15 Abīb), an important religious writer of the fourth century.

Epiphania, or Euphemia (feast day: 12 Ba'ūnah), a devout and charitable widow.

Epiphanius of Salamis (feast day: 17 Bashans), bishop of Cyprus who spent most of his monastic life in Egypt and introduced Egyptian monasticism to Palestine. He supported the speculative theology of ORIGEN in opposition to Saints JEROME and RUFINUS.

EUMENIUS (feast day: 10 Bābah), second-century patriarch of Alexandria.

Euphrasia (feast day: 26 Baramhāt), the daughter of Emperor Honorius who went with her mother to Alexandria, stayed in a convent, and remained there as an ascetic.

EUPHROSYNA (feast day: 10 Bābah), a fifth-century holy woman of Alexandria who lived disguised as a monk.

Ezekiel of Armant (feast day: 14 Kiyahk), ascetic.

FĪS, monk.

GABRIEL I, tenth-century patriarch of Alexandria.

GABRIEL II IBN TURAYK (feast day: 10 Baramūdah), twelfth-century patriarch of Alexandria.

Gelasius (feast day: 12 Amshīr), saint.

GEORGE, or Jirjis al-Muzāhim.

George of Scetis, see *Abraham and George of Scetis,* above.

Gregory (feast day: 24 Tūt), a monk of Upper Egypt closely connected with Saint PACHOMIUS and Saint MACARIUS.

GREGORY OF NAZIANZUS, fourth-century writer. He is not commemorated with a feast day by the Coptic church.

GREGORY OF NYSSA, fourth-century theologian and younger brother of Saint BASIL THE GREAT.

HADRĀ OF ASWAN (feast day: 12 Kiyakh), a fifth-century bishop.

HADRĀ OF BENHADAB (feast day: 3 Amshīr), the first monk of the mountain of Benhadab.

HARMĪNĀ (feast day: 2 Kiyahk), a wandering monk.

HERACLAS, or Theoclas (feast day: 8 Kiyakh), third-century patriarch of Alexandria.

HILARIA (feast day: 21 Ṭūbah), a daughter of the fourth-century emperor Zeno, who lived disguised as a monk.

HILARION (feast day: 24 Baramhāt), fourth-century monk of Palestine.

HOP OF ṬŪKH, or Apa Hūb (feast day: 16 Hātūr), hermit.

HOR, APA (feast day: 4 Ba'ūnah), a native of Bahjūrah who was a hermit.

HOR, APA THE ASCETIC (feast day: 2 Kiyahk), a native of Nitrea who was a disciple of Saint Pachomius.

HOR OF ABRAḤAT (feast day: 2 Kiyahk), fifth to sixth-century monk.

HORSIESIOS, fourth-century monk who was the successor of Saint PACHOMIUS.

Irenaeus of Scetis, monk who fled from the Berbers to Gaza in 570.

ISAAC (feast day: 9 Hātūr), seventh-century patriarch of Alexandria whose life was recorded by Menas, bishop of Pshati.

ISAAC, or Isaac of al-Qalālī (feast day: 19 Bashans), a fourth- to fifth-century monk and priest of Kellia.

ISAAC OF HŪRĪN, or Isḥaq al-Hūrīnī (feast day: 22 Baramūdah), an ascetic in the desert who was not discovered till shortly before his death.

ISAAC OF SCETIS (feast day: 10 Baramūdah), hermit who was a disciple of Anbā Apollos for twenty-five years.

Isaac the Presbyter (feast day: 19 Bashans), an adherent of ORIGEN who was expelled by Theophilus, patriarch of Alexandria but returned in 408, the year of the Berber invasion of Scetis.

ISAIAH OF SCETIS, or Isaiah the Hermit (feast day: 11 Abīb), fifth-century anchorite whose writings influenced Eastern Christianity.

Isidorus of Hermopolis, a bishop who succeeded Dracontius and preceded Dioscorus. He met Saint Jerome, who mentioned him in epistles.

ISIDORUS OF PELUSIUM, fifth-century monk, priest, and author of a large body of letters.

ISIDORUS OF SCETIS, a fourth-century monk and priest credited with miraculous spiritual healing powers.

JACOB (feast day: 14 Amshīr), ninth-century patriarch of Alexandria.

JAMES (feast day: 3 Amshīr), an ascetic of Nitrea.

James of Antioch, or Jacob (feast day: 11 Bābah), patriarch of Antioch and opponent of Arianism.

James of Nisibis, or Jacob (feast day: 18 Ṭūbah), fourth-century bishop of Nisibis and teacher of Saint Ephraem Syrus. He attended the First Council of Nicaea in 325.

JAMES OF SCETIS, or Jacob (feast day: 5 Nasī), bishop of Miṣr.

JEREMIAH, fifth- to sixth-century monk.

JEROME, fourth- to fifth-century biblical scholar.

JOHN I (feast day: 4 Bashans), fifth-century patriarch of Alexandria.

JOHN II (feast day: 27 Bashans), sixth-century patriarch of Alexandria.

JOHN III THE MERCIFUL, seventh-century patriarch of Alexandria.

JOHN IV (feast day: 16 Ṭūbah), eighth-century patriarch of Alexandria.

JOHN VI (feast day: 11 Ṭūbah), twelfth-century patriarch of Alexandria.

JOHN IV THE FASTER, or John Jejunator, patriarch of Constantinople.

JOHN (feast day: 7 Kiyahk), bishop of Armant.

John (feast day: 11 Baramūdah), bishop of Gaza.

John (feast day: 13 Ba'ūnah), bishop of Jerusalem.

John (feast day: 3 Baramūdah), second-century bishop of Jerusalem under Emperor Hadrian.

JOHN CHRYSOSTOM (feast day: 12 Bashans), patriarch of Constantinople.

John Colobus, or John the Little (feast day: 20 Bābah).

JOHN KĀMĀ, or John the Black (feast day: 25 Kiyahk), monk of Scetis.

JOHN OF LYCOPOLIS (feast day: 21 Hātūr), a fourth-century saint in the time of Emperor Theodosius.

JOHN OF PARALLOS (feast day: 19 Kiyahk), bishop of Nikiou, called bishop of Parallos in the Synaxarion. He compiled the Synaxarion.

John of the Golden Gospel (feast day: 17 Ṭūbah), son of a Roman named Hadrian, he became a monk. He copied the Gospel of John in golden letters.

John the Confessor (feast day: 12 Kiyahk), saint.

JOSEPH THE CARPENTER (feast day: 26 Abīb), spouse of the Virgin Mary and foster father of Jesus Christ.

JOSEPH OF BISHWĀW (feast day: 5 Hātūr), monk who lived with Saint Elias of Bishwāw.

Joseph the Bishop, or Anbā Yusāb (feast day: 17 Baramhāt), bishop.

JUDAS CYRIACUS, second-century bishop of Jerusalem associated in legend with the discovery of the cross.

JULIAN (feast day: 8 Baramhāt), second-century patriarch of Alexandria.

JUSTUS, second-century patriarch of Alexandria.

Justus (feast day: 10 Ṭūbah), an ascetic.

Kha'īl I, or Michael (feast day: 16 Baramhāt), eighth-century patriarch of Alexandria.

Khā'īl II, or Michael II (feast day: 20 Baramhāt), ninth-century patriarch of Alexandria.

LATSON, or al-Bahnasāwī (feast day: 17 Ba'ūnah), a native of Oxyrhynchus (al-Bahnasā).

LEO I THE GREAT, fifth-century pope.

LONGINUS (feast day: 2 Amshīr), abbot of Enaton.

MACARIUS I, or Anbā Maqārah (feast day: 24 Baramhāt), tenth-century patriarch of Alexandria.

MACARIUS II, or Abbā Maqārah (feast day: 4 Tūt), twelfth-century patriarch of Alexandria.

MACARIUS ALEXANDRINUS (feast day: 6 Bashans).

Macarius of Tkow, saint.

MACARIUS THE EGYPTIAN, Macarius the Great, or Macarius of Scetis (feast day: 27 Baramhāt).

Macrobius (feast day: 7 Baramūdah), son of a governor of Tkow in the sixth-century who became a monk and abbot of Dayr al-Balyanā.

MANASSEH, sixth-century archimandrite.

Marcellus, an ascetic in Scetis who was seized in the Berber raid of 570 and sold into slavery in Pentapolis.

Marina, or Mary (feast day: 15 Misrā), a "woman monk" for forty years whose sex was revealed only at her death.

MARK I (feast day: 30 Baramūdah), one of the Twelve Apostles, traditionally regarded as author of the Gospel of Mark and first patriarch of the Coptic church.

MARK II (feast day: 22 Baramūdah), ninth-century patriarch of Alexandria. He was previously a monk of Dayr Anbā Maqār in Syria.

MARK III (feast day: 6 Ṭūbah), twelfth-century patriarch of Alexandria.

MARK (feast day: 10 Hātūr), ascetic who left the desert to live as a beggar in Alexandria.

MARK THE SIMPLE (feast day: 10 Hātūr), sixth-century monk who simulated madness as a penitence.

Martha the Egyptian (feast day: 3 Ba'ūnah), a dissolute woman who repented and lived in a convent for twenty-five years.

MARY OF ALEXANDRIA (feast day: 24 Ṭūbah), a recluse.

MARY THE EGYPTIAN (feast day: 6 Baramūdah), a saint.

MASIS (feast day: 11 Misrā), an ascetic of Scetis.

MATTHEW I THE POOR (feast day: 7 Kiyahk), an ascetic who was a fourteenth- to fifteenth-century patriarch of Alexandria.

MAURITIUS (feast day: 25 Tūt).

MAXIMUS (feast day: 14 Baramūdah), third-century patriarch of Alexandria.

MAXIMUS AND DOMITIUS (feast day: 17 Ṭūbah), ascetics of Scetis.

Menas, saint related to a monastery near Jeme.

MENAS (feast day: 7 Hātūr), bishop of Tmuis.

Menas of Pshati, bishop of Nikiou following John. He was inspector of the monasteries of Wādī al-Naṭrūn and the author of a Life of Anbā Isaac and a Eulogy of Saint Macrobius of Pshati.

Mercurius (feast day: 1 Baramhāt), an ascetic and a bishop.

MERCURIUS OF CAESAREA, or Abū Sayfayn (feast day: 25 Hātūr).

MICHAEL, archangel.

Michael I, see *Khā'īl I,* above.

Michael II, see *Khā'īl II,* above.

MICHAEL IV, or Mīkhā'īl IV (feast day: 30 Bashans), eleventh-century patriarch of Alexandria.

MICHAEL V, or Mīkhā'īl V (feast day: 3 Baramūdah), twelfth-century patriarch of Alexandria.

Michael (feast day: 22 Baramhāt), bishop of Naqādah.

Michael of Qamūlah, patron saint of Dayr al-ʿAyn at Jeme.

MĪNĀ I, or Menas I, eighth-century patriarch of Alexandria.

MIṢĀ'ĪL (feast day: 13 Kiyahk), an ascetic of Dayr al-Qalumūn.

Narcissus (feast day: 1 Baramhāt), third-century bishop of Jerusalem who retired to the desert but returned to Jerusalem to administer its diocese again before his death about 222.

Nathaniel, ascetic of Nitria.

ONOPHRIUS, or Abū Nofer or Naber (feast day: 16 Hatūr), ascetic in the inner desert.

PACHOMIUS (feast day: 14 Bashans, 14 May in the West, 15 May in the East), fourth-century abbot who established *Koinonia,* a community of many monasteries, which was the beginning of cenobitic monasticism.

PALAMON, fourth-century hermit in the Eastern Desert who was the mentor of Saint PACHOMIUS.

PALAMON (feast day: 30 Ṭūbah), hermit.

PAMBO, or Pamo or Pano (feast days: 1 July in the West, 18 July in the East), fourth-century anchorite who with Saint AMMON was among the first settlers in Wādī al-Naṭrūn.

Pambo, or Pamo or Bamfu, a fifth-century ascetic of Nitria who is often confused with the earlier Pambo.

PAPHNUTIUS OF PBOW, a fourth-century monk who was first steward of the Pachomian *Koinonia.*

Paphnutius, leader of a small community of ascetics at Heracleopolis.

PAPHNUTIUS THE HERMIT, or Paphnutius the Ascetic or Babnūda (feast day: 15 Amshīr), an anchorite in the Western Desert.

PAPHNUTIUS OF SCETIS, fourth-century disciple of Saint Macarius of Egypt. He is known by some authors as Paphnutius Kephalas.

Paphnutius of Tabennēse, saint.

PAPHNUTIUS (feast day: 11 Bashans), tenth-century monk and bishop.

Paphnutius Kephalas, fourth-century hermit, a disciple of Saint Antony, who later lived as a solitary at Scetis. Known by some authors as Paphnutius of Scetis.

Papohé, disciple of Apa Apollo and said to be the author of a Life of Apa Phib.

PATASIUS (feast day: 23 Ṭūbah), a hermit credited with many miracles.

PATERMUTHIUS, or Termoute (feast day: 7 Kiyahk), a desert father.

PAUL OF BENHADAB (feast day: 17 Hātūr).

PAUL OF THEBES, or Paul the Great or Anbā Būlā (feast day: 2 Amshīr), the first hermit in the Eastern Desert.

PAUL THE SIMPLE, an elderly peasant who became a monk and a follower of Saint Antony.

Paul the Solitary, see *Būlus al-Ḥabīs,* above.

Pelagia (feast day: 11 Bābah), a fifth- or sixth-century woman who dressed as a monk.

PETER II (feast day: 20 Amshīr), fourth-century patriarch of Alexandria.

PETER IV (feast day: 25 Ba'ūnah), sixth-century patriarch of Alexandria.

Peter (feast day: 6 Bābah), ascetic who was a disciple of Anbā Isaiah.

PETER OF SCETIS, or Peter the Ascetic (feast day: 25 Ṭūbah), a sixth-century tax collector who became a monk at Scetis.

Peter the Great, an unidentified saint whose tomb is on the Rock of Benhadab.

PETER OF THE PRESBYTER (feast day: 5 Baramhāt), a saint of Upper Egypt.

PETRONIUS (feast day: 27 Abīb), a fourth-century monk who was a disciple and successor of Saint Pachomius.

PHIB, or Abīb (feast day: 25 Bābah), a monk associated with Saint APOLLO OF BĀWĪṬ and Papohé.

Philas, or Philip (feast day: 14 Bābah), first-century saint, one of the seven deacons described in Acts.

PHIS, a hermit on the east bank of the Nile.

PIDJIMI (feast day: 11 Kiyahk), fifth-century ascetic and a recluse who was visited by Saint SHENUTE.

Pior, a fourth-century disciple of Saint Antony who was a solitary at Kellia for thirty years.

PISENTIUS (feast day: 20 Kiyahk), seventh-century monk and bishop of Armant.

PISENTIUS (feast day: 13 Abīb), seventh-century bishop of Coptos (Qifṭ) who was an outstanding preacher, administrator, letter writer, and servant of the poor.

PISENTIUS, fourth-to-fifth century bishop of Hermonthis.

Pitiryon, ascetic, who succeeded Saint Ammonius.

POEMEN, or Pamīn or Bīmīn (feast day: 4 Nasī), an anchorite of the fourth and fifth centuries who was famous for his spiritual counsel to other monks.

PROCLUS (feast day: 20 November in the East, 24 October in the West), fifth-century patriarch of Constantinople.

PSHOI, or Bishoi or Peter of Akhmīn (feast day: 5 Amshīr), a monk who founded a monastery.

PSHOI OF ṬŪD (feast day: 25 Kiyahk), ascetic of Upper Egypt.

Ptolemy (feast day: 24 Abīb), bishop of upper Minūf.

REGULA (feast day: 1 Tūt), third-century missionary who, along with her brother FELIX, was a member of the THEBAN LEGION.

Ruways, Anbā, see *Anbā Ruways,* above.

SAMUEL OF BENHADAB (feast day: 21 Kiyahk), bishop of Qifṭ.

SAMUEL OF QALAMUN, or Samuel (feast day: 8 Kiyahk), a monk.

Sansno, a saint to whom churches are dedicated at Ballaṣ and Fayyūm.

SARAH (feast day: 15 Baramhāt), an ascetic.

SARAPAMON OF SCETIS (feast day: 5 Baramhāt), an ascetic of the fourteenth century or later who was hegumenus, or presbyter, of Dayr Abū Yuḥannis.

SARAPION, or Serapion (feast day: 21 March), fourth-century bishop of Tmuis, disciple of Saint Antony, and friend of Saint Athanasius, who upheld the orthodox position in the Arian controversy.

SEVERIAN OF JABALAH, or Severianus (feast day: 7 Tūt), bishop of Jabalah who was a great orator.

SHENUTE (feast day: 7 Abīb), fourth to fifth-century abbot of Dayr Anbā Shinūdah, Suhāj, who was a writer and reformer.

SHENUTE I, or Sanutius (feast day: 24 Baramūdah), ninth-century patriarch of Alexandria.

SILVANUS OF SCETIS (feast day: 1 Baramūdah), ascetic who was a companion of Saint Macarius the Egyptian.

Simon, or Simeon the Stylite (feast day: 29 Bashans), pillar saint of Mount Antioch.

SIMON I (feast day: 24 Abīb), seventh-century patriarch of Alexandria.

SIMON II, ninth-century patriarch of Alexandria.

SOPHIA, see MARTYRS, COPTIC.

Stephen (feast day: 18 Tūt), presbyter.

Susinius (feast day: 21 Abīb), fourth- to fifth-century eunuch and tutor of Emperor Theodosius who lived at Scetis until the Berber raid of 408. He accompanied Saint CYRIL I to the Council of Ephesus in 431.

Syriacos (feast day: 29 Ṭūbah), saint.

Theoclas, see above "Heraclas."

THEODORA (feast day: 11 Tūt), a fifth-century woman who passed as a monk at Scetis until her death.

THEODORA (feast day: 11 Baramūdah), a third-century woman of Alexandria who passed as a monk.

Theodore, eighth-century patriarch of Alexandria.

THEODORUS, eighth-century patriarch of Alexandria.

Theodorus, disciple of Saint Amun and first colonizer of Nitria.

THEODORUS OF ALEXANDRIA, ascetic of Scetis who fled to Tabennēsē from the Berber invasion of 520.

THEODORUS OF TABENNĒSĒ, or Tādrus (feast day: 2 Bashans), ascetic in a Pachomian monastery.

THEODORUS OF PHERME, fourth- to fifth-century anchorite.

THEODOSIUS I (feast day: 28 Ba'ūnah), sixth-century patriarch of Alexandria.

THEOGNOSTA (feast day: 17 Tūt), fifth-century virgin who introduced Christianity to Georgia.

THEOPHILUS (feast day: 18 Bābah), fourth- to fifth-century patriarch of Alexandria.

THEOPHILUS (feast day: 14 Ṭūbah), a monk of Enaton.

TIMOTHEUS (feast day: 23 Kiyahk), anchorite.

TIMOTHY I (feast day: 26 Abīb), fourth-century patriarch of Alexandria.

TIMOTHY II AELURUS (feast day: 7 Misrā), fifth-century patriarch of Alexandria.

TIMOTHY II (feast day: 12 Amshīr), sixth-century patriarch of Alexandria.

VERENA, (feast day: 1 September and Easter Tuesday), fourth-century Egyptian holy woman associated with the THEBAN LEGION martyred in Switzerland.

VICTOR OF SHŪ, early fourth-century saint.

Warshenufe (feast day: 7 Ba'ūnah), saint.

Xene, fourth- to fifth-century Roman virgin who adopted monastic life in Alexandria.

Yūsāb (feast day: 5 Hātūr), a native of Qifṭ and a disciple of Anbā Isaiah at Mount Banhadah.

YŪSĀB I, or Joseph (feast day: 22 Bābah), ninth-century patriarch of Alexandria.

ZACHARIAS (feast day: 13 Hātūr and 9 Ṭūbah), eleventh-century patriarch of Alexandria.

Zacharias, seventh-century bishop of Ṣā.

ZACHARIAS (feast day: 21 Amshīr), eighth-century bishop of Sakhā.

Zanufius (feast day: 6 Bābah), ascetic who founded a convent for women at Akhmīm.

ZOSIMUS (feast day: 9 Baramūdah), a monk of Palestine who was closely acquainted with Saint Mary the Egyptian.

AZIZ S. ATIYA

SAKHĀ, town located in the northern Delta of Egypt about 1.5 miles (2 km) south of Kafr al-Shayk in the Gharbiyyah province. The town was known in Greek as Ξόις (Xois) and in Coptic as ⲤⲈⲔⲞⲞⲨ (Sekoou).

A reference in one of ATHANASIUS' letters to the bishop of Sakhā makes it clear that the town became a bishopric no later than the first half of the fourth century (Munier, 1943, p. 10).

Among the few references to Sakhā in Coptic martyrological literature for the period prior to 640 are the following: In its commemoration of JOHN COLOBOS on 20 Bābah the SYNAXARION mentions an Anbā Bamwayh from Sakhā. The festival calendar of Abū al-Barakāt IBN KABAR commemorates a Bishop Muna of Sakhā on 15 Abīb.

There is a Coptic church in Sakhā, the age of which is not known.

[*See also:* Zacharias, Bishop of Sakhā.]

BIBLIOGRAPHY

Abū al-Barakāt ibn Kabar. *Le calendrier d'Abou'l-Barakât,* ed. and trans. E. Tisserant. PO 10, pt. 3, no. 48. Paris, 1913.

Amélineau, E. *La Géographie de l'Egypte à l'époque copte,* p. 410. Paris, 1893.

Munier, H. *Recueil des listes épiscopales de l'église copte.* Cairo, 1943.

RANDALL STEWART

SALADIN. *See* Ayyubid Dynasty and the Copts.

SALAMA I. *See* Ethiopian Prelates.

SALAMA II. *See* Ethiopian Prelates.

SALAMA III. *See* Ethiopian Prelates.

SALĀMAH MŪSĀ (1887–1958), a writer who was one of the most influential Egyptian intellectuals in modern Egypt. For half a century, he was known as a popularizer of ideas in the fields of evolution, socialism, and sociology of religion. He left an enduring impact on his generation, whom he awakened to the significance of social criticism.

Born to a Coptic family in a small village near the city of Zagāzīg (al-Zaqāzīq) in the Sharqiyyah province in 1887, he received his primary and secondary education in local schools. In 1908 he began his higher education at first in Paris, where he attended courses in humanities, law, and literature at the University, and then in London, where he spent four years attending varied courses.

During that period, he joined the Fabian society, where he became acquainted with the ideas of evolution, socialism, and Russian literature. In 1912, he returned to Egypt and started a career of journalism by launching his first Egyptian weekly *Al-Mustaqbal* (The Future). In the 1920s, he edited a monthly periodical (*Al-Hilāl*), and in November 1929, he inaugurated his own monthly journal entitled *Al-Majallah al-Jadīdah* (The New Magazine), which he filled with his progressive ideas. In the meantime, he continued to publish a total of forty-six books and treatises of a novel character on issues of modernization and social change.

In his early youth, his writings betrayed an unreserved admiration for Western culture, in some instances bordering on extremism. In his first book, *Muqadimmat al-Sūbarmān,* published in 1910, he recommended the sterilization of the mentally retarded and encouraged younger males to marry Europeans to improve the quality of their offspring. He objected to religious traditions as a potential source of change for improvement. To him, Eastern culture was defunct and could no longer be revived. Although his basic ideas remained unchanged in later years, he tended to become less provocative in the expression of his principles. However, he aimed at the establishment of a new language, a new literature, and a new perspective of life and society.

Salāmah Mūsā advocated religious tolerance and believed that the essence of all religions was the same. In fact, religions reflected human progress in the sense that a given religion always represented an advance on the ethical and social levels beyond the other religion preceding it. As a secularist, he was prone to reject all sorts of theocracies and firmly promoted the doctrine of separation of religion and state on the political scene.

Under the influence of Darwin and George Bernard Shaw, he espoused the doctrine of evolution, which dubbed religion with a tint of mysticism aimed principally at the creation of a happy world. According to him, there was no real difference between the prophets and the philosophers, and consequently books of revelation became equivalent to important philosophical treatises such as Plato's *Republic* and G. B. Shaw's *Superman* or other works by Rousseau and Tolstoy.

Salāmah Mūsā pleaded for a secular culture based on scientific and artistic achievements of human civilization. In his zeal for European culture, he wanted to see a new Arabic language and literature capable of expressing the real feelings and aspirations of modern Egyptians. In 1939, he went so far as to advance the idea of the latinization of the Arabic script. The Latin alphabet, he believed, was easier to learn and would further bring Egypt within the pale of European thought and civilization. Symbolically the Egyptians would automatically begin to feel that they are part of the West and weaken their consciousness of being a part of a retrogressive African and Asiatic group of nations.

Turning to the field of economic relations, he became preoccupied with the problem of the underdevelopment of Egypt, ascribing this to the lack of democracy and freedom of thought as well as to the absence of socialist principles. Here he was influenced by Fabian thought, which aimed at the establishment of an egalitarian socialistic system of taxation and equal opportunities for all citizens. From the year 1930 onward he was further influenced by Marxist thought, though he was never an avowed communist.

In the realm of politics, Salāmah Mūsā considered freedom of thought to be the real basis of a new renaissance. He ascribed all the evils of Eastern nations to the degraded status of women in society, taking the freedom of women and their total equality with men to be the keystone of progress in society. Women should have full political rights and also the right to work, which would inevitably increase the productivity of the whole country.

Salāmah Mūsā's views brought about a confrontation with the British occupation of Egypt. British colonists were participants in the preservation of an underdeveloped agricultural society and the rejection of industrial progress.

Salāmah Mūsā was an innovative and controversial writer and thinker whose ideas constituted a serious challenge to the prevailing Egyptian system, sometimes exercising extremism. This led to his incarceration in 1946 as a communist enemy of the reigning monarchy.

BIBLIOGRAPHY

Abu Jaber, K. S. "Salāmah Mūsā: Precursor of Arab Socialism." *Middle East Journal* 20 (1966):196–206.

Dessouki, A. E. H. "The Views of Salama Musa on Religion and Secularism." *Islam in the Modern Age* 4 (1973):23–24.

Egger, V. *A Fabian in Egypt, Salāmah Mūsā and the Rise of the Professional Classes in Egypt: 1900–1939*. Lanham, 1986.

Haim, S. "Salama Musa: An Appreciation of His Autobiography." *Die Welt des Islams* 2 (1953):10–24.

Hanna, S. A., and G. H. Gardner. "Salama Musa, 1887–1958—A Pioneer of Arab Socialism." In *Arab Socialism, A Documentary Survey*, pp. 64–79. Leiden, 1969.

Ibrahim, I. I. "Salamah Musa, An Essay in Cultural Alienation." *Middle Eastern Studies* 15 (1979): 346–57.

Perlman, M. "The Education of Salama Musa". *Middle Eastern Affairs* 2 (1951):279–85.

Salāmah Mūsā. *The Education of Salama Musa*, trans. L. O. Schuman. Leiden, 1961.

ALI EL-DIN HILAL DISUQI

SALAMUNI, AL-. *See* Pilgrimages.

SALE. *See* Law, Coptic: Private Law.

SĀLIM IBN YŪSUF AL-SIBĀʿĪ AL-ITFĀWĪ, known only as the person donating fol. 286a of a manuscript (Sinai Arabic 136) containing the Gospels for the feasts of the year, copied by the hieromonk Elias and completed on 22 May 1685, to the Monastery of Sinai. The title *Ra'īs* in a note in the manuscript indicates a prominent citizen; his surname shows that the family was from Idfū in Upper Egypt, the Apollonopolis of ancient times. He must have lived at the end of the seventeenth century.

BIBLIOGRAPHY

Amélineau, E. *La Géographie de l'Egypte*. Paris, 1893.

Atiya, A. S., and J. N. Youssef. *Catalogue Raisonné of the Mount Sinai Manuscripts*, pp. 260–61. Alexandria, 1970.

KHALIL SAMIR, S.J.

SALIPPE, MIKARIUS (1780–1850), military man and interpreter, who joined the Coptic Legion at age twenty and emigrated to France in 1801 with the legionnaires who followed General YA'QŪB. He is supposed to have embarked for America with the Toulon Squadron in 1804 and to have spent two years there.

Salippe was with the Bataillon des Chasseurs d'Orient during the campaigns in Dalmatia, where he distinguished himself in the lifting of the blockade of Ragusa (Dubrovnik) in 1806, and in the Ionian Islands in 1807. Having been twice wounded in the head, he was put on half pay at Rome by General Miollis in 1813.

While working at the Dépôt des Refugiés égyptiens at Marseilles, Salippe was recalled to the army in 1830, at the time of the French expedition to Algiers, to serve as guide and interpreter. Named auxiliary interpreter in 1846, he served in that capacity at Fort Mers-el-Kébir.

BIBLIOGRAPHY

Féraud, L.-C. *Les Interprètes de l'armée d'Afrique,* p. 220. Algiers, 1876.

ANOUAR LOUCA

SAMANNŪD, city in the middle of the Egyptian Delta some 5 miles (8 km) east of al-Maḥallah al-Kubrā in the Gharbiyyah province. Greek documents give the name of the city as Sebennytos and in Coptic it was known as ϫⲉⲙⲛⲟⲩϯ (Djemnouti).

Sebennytos/Samannūd has a very old Christian tradition. ATHANASIUS I reported that the city had a Melitian bishop in 325 (Munier, 1943, p. 3) and the name of the city appears often in early martyrological literature. The martyr Saint ANUB, for instance, was said to have passed through Samannūd on his way from Atrīb. Anub found that the churches in the city had been destroyed and that a temple had been built in their place. In the fourteenth century, when the SYNAXARION was composed, Anub's body was in Samannūd. There is still a church of Anub in the city.

The earliest attested bishop of Samannūd after the ARAB CONQUEST OF EGYPT in the seventh century was not in office until the early eighth century. The increased activity of the Gaianites (see GAIANUS) and BARSANUPHIANS at the end of the seventh and the beginning of the eighth century may be responsible for the absence of Samannūd in Coptic orthodox literature for this period.

One of the most famous bishops of Samannūd was John, who was in office between 1235 and 1257. A literary man, John wrote grammatical works, copied manuscripts, and composed hymns.

BIBLIOGRAPHY

Amélineau, E. *La Géographie de l'Egypte à l'époque copte,* pp. 411–12. Paris, 1893.
Munier, H. *Recueil des listes épiscopales de l'église copte.* Cairo, 1943.

RANDALL STEWART

SĀMĪ GABRĀ (1893–1979), Egyptian archaeologist. After studying at the American College at Asyūṭ, he decided to embark on a legal career and obtained bachelor and doctoral degrees from Bordeaux University. He then taught law at the old Egyptian University.

In 1926 he obtained the diploma of archaeology from Liverpool University, and in 1929, a Sorbonne doctorate in archaeology. On his return to Egypt, he started his archaeological career as a curator of the Egyptian Museum. He was appointed professor of ancient Egyptian history at the newly established Egyptian University and was the first Egyptian to head the Institute of Egyptian Archaeology.

He combined his teaching activities with excavations at Upper Egyptian sites, especially prehistoric sites near Asyūṭ, at Dayr Tāsā. But his name will always be linked with Tūnah al-Jabal, the necropolis of Hermopolis Magna, where he worked for over twenty years. There, he uncovered a funerary city of over twenty-eight acres that had been in constant development for six centuries, from the time of Alexander the Great up to the third century A.D.

After his retirement in 1953, he taught for two years at the University of Chicago. Upon his return to Egypt, he took an active part in establishing the Mallawī Museum, one of the best provincial museums in Egypt. With Aziz S. Atiya, he collaborated in founding the Institute of Coptic Studies, where he was active for many years as its director. He was also a founding member of the SOCIETY OF COPTIC ARCHAEOLOGY in 1934. Gabrā produced numerous excavation reports, lectures, and articles in Arabic, English, and French. Some of the most important are: *Peintures et fresques de Touna-al-Gabal,* with the collaboration of E. Drioton (Cairo, 1941); and *Chez les derniers adorateurs du Trismégiste: La Nécropole d'Hermopolis* (Cairo, 1971).

BIBLIOGRAPHY

Ghali, M. B. "Sami Gabra (1893–1979)." *Bulletin de la Société d'archéologie copte* 24 (1979–1982): 128–30.

MIRRIT BOUTROS GHALI

SAMUEL, Coptic bishop (1920–1981). He was born Sa'd 'Azīz on 8 December 1920, to a pious middle-class family. From his early youth, he associated himself with the Sunday School movement, where he became a staunch supporter known for his immense piety and unassuming humility, two qualities that he retained throughout his later distinguished career.

After his secondary education, he studied law at Cairo University, graduating in 1942. Later, he joined the Clerical College, where he obtained a diploma in divinity in 1944 while simultaneously working for the bachelor's degree at the American University in Cairo. In 1955, he was granted a scholarship by Princeton Theological Seminary, where he obtained a master's degree in religious education.

In 1944 he was called to serve in Ethiopia as a lecturer in the Theological Seminary at Addis Ababa. Here he combined a voluntary lectureship at the Teachers College with his official position, and helped to establish the Sunday School movement. Upon his return to Egypt in 1946, Emperor Haile Selassie decorated him with the order of the Star of Ethiopia.

At this point, he decided to take the monastic vows under the name of Makārī at the hands of Abūnā Mīnā, a well-known solitary in Old Cairo who later became CYRIL VI (1959–1971). He remained for three years with his mentor before moving to the Monastery of Saint Samuel in the Fayyūm and later to the Monastery of Our Lady, known as DAYR AL-SURYĀN in Wādī al-Naṭrūn.

In 1954, Father Makārī al-Suryānī was commissioned by Pope Yūsāb II to go to Evanston, Illinois, together with Abūnā Ṣalīb Suryal and Dr. Aziz S. Atiya as the first delegation of the Coptic church to the World Council of Churches. This proved to be an important milestone in his international career, for he became a permanent deputy of the Coptic church in several committees of the World Council.

From 1955 to 1962, Father Makārī al-Suryānī taught pastoral theology in the Clerical College, and he saw it move from its dilapidated old quarters at Mahmashah to a new modern establishment at Anbā Ruways. With the foundation of the Higher Institute of Coptic Studies in 1954, he was chosen to lead its department of social studies. Later, he founded the Saint Didymus Institute for the Blind and equipped it with a specialized printing press where he published a magazine for the blind cantors of the community.

In 1959, he launched a major program called the Rural Diaconate for the service of Coptic families in isolated villages who had not received the sacrament of baptism and were without the slightest notion about their religion. He recruited a battalion of volunteers who were called upon from the nearest towns to go to those secluded hamlets in order to acquaint villagers with the rudiments of their faith. Movable altars to celebrate the liturgy and administer the sacrament of Holy Communion and baptism were used by itinerant priests.

When his old mentor Mīnā the Solitary became Pope Cyril VI, one of his first acts was the elevation of a number of eminent monks to the rank of the episcopate. These included Father Makārī al-Suryānī, who became bishop of public, social, and ecumenical services. In this capacity, he fostered the Diaconate of the *Rīf* (countryside) and sponsored social and educational movements in the church, notably the Sunday School movement and the creation of centers for the training of young men and women in the varied technical handicrafts. He played an important part in the completion of the huge edifice of the new Saint Mark's Cathedral on the grounds of Anbā Ruways. He worked hard with the Coptic communities overseas for the establishment of Coptic churches in Europe, America, and Australia. In his administrative capacity, he became instrumental in dealing with national problems, continuously moving between ministerial offices to heal wounds inflicted on the community by misguided bigots.

Beyond the Egyptian frontiers, he proved himself to be a force in ecumenical movements. As a permanent member of the Central Committee of the World Council of Churches, he participated in the solution of most religious disputes of his day and became an eloquent representative of his church in that universal forum. On the African scene, he became vice-president of the All Africa Conference of Churches, of which he was a cofounder. He continued his vigorous service to the church and the whole of Coptic society, including both rich and poor, until his death, together with President Anwar al-Sadat, at the hand of assassins. In compliance with his will, his body was later buried beside his mentor, Cyril VI, in the new monastery of Abū Mīnā in the district of Mareotis.

GABRIEL ABDELSAYYED
MAURICE AS'AD

SAMUEL OF BENHADAB, SAINT, a native of the province of Qifṭ and a monk on the mountain of Benhadab. He was ordained a priest by Anbā Timotheus, bishop of Qifṭ, who named him the superior of the monks who lived on this mountain. This nomination by the bishop of the town, and not by election by the other monks, as was the case elsewhere, is notable. Samuel never wished to distinguish himself from his brothers in diet or in clothing, but sought to be the least of all. He ate no animal flesh, but contented himself with bread and salt. He was priest and head of the monks for seventeen years. When an angel warned him of his approaching death, he gathered the brethren together to urge them to observe the monastic canons. His body was buried in the church of Anbā Peter the Elder in the town of Qifṭ.

Samuel appears only in the notice in the recension of the SYNAXARION of the Copts from Upper Egypt at 21 Kiyahk.

RENÉ-GEORGES COQUIN

SAMŪ'ĪL OF QALAMŪN, SAINT (c. 597–695). Samū'īl was born in the village of Tkello near the city of Pelhip in the northwest Delta. The SYNAXARION records that he came from the diocese of Maṣīl. Coptic-Arabic geographical lists give Maṣīl as Fuwwah. His parents were Silas, a presbyter, and Kosmiane. At the age of twelve Samū'īl became a subdeacon. In spite of his parents' wish that he should marry, he insisted on becoming a monk. Shortly after the death of Kosmiane, when Samū'īl was eighteen, Silas had a vision in which it was revealed to him that his son would one day be a great monk. Silas therefore built a beautiful church and made Samū'īl a deacon of it. Four years later Silas died, and Samū'īl went to SCETIS to become a monk at the age of twenty-two. In a synopsis given toward the end of his Life, it is recorded that Samū'īl became a monk when he was eighteen. This probably refers to his age when his father had his vision.

On his arrival at Scetis, Samū'īl became the disciple of Agathon, whose cave was situated "on a high peak" between those of Apa MACARIUS and Apa John. H. G. Evelyn-White (1922, p. 252, n. 5) thinks it was probably "one of two or three conical knolls" in this area that do not exceed 48–65 feet (15–20 m) in height. He stayed there until Agathon died three years later, and he was expelled by order of the agent (*magistrianus*) of Cyrus, the Melchite patriarch of Alexandria appointed by Emperor Heraclius in 631. Cyrus had been sent to Egypt with a recently formulated Christological doctrine, which the emperor hoped would prove acceptable to the Monophysite Egyptians. It laid stress on the "one energy" and the "one will" of Christ. Heraclius was not the first emperor since the Council of CHALCEDON to try to reconcile the dissident Egyptians to official doctrine and, having driven the Persians out of Egypt only two years before, he must have been acutely aware of the need for unity within the empire. But Cyrus, who had been invested with civil and ecclesiastical authority, was not particularly subtle in his methods of winning the Egyptians over. He sent his rather brutal agent to Scetis with the new doctrine (referred to anachronistically in the Life of Samū'īl as the "Tome of Leo"). When the monks, led by Samū'īl, refused to accept it, and Samū'īl actually tore up the document, the *magistrianus* flogged him mercilessly, stopping only when the whip dislodged Samū'īl's eye. The description of this incident is very similar to what one might find in a martyrology. In fact Samū'īl is referred to several times as a "martyr who does not lose his life."

After his expulsion from Scetis, Samū'īl made his way south to Neklone (al-Naqlūn) in the Fayyūm, accompanied by four monks. Within three and a half years he had established a community of 200 *kosmikoi* (an uncertain term, perhaps meaning "lay brothers") and 120 monks. About this time Cyrus came to the Fayyūm, where he was warmly received by Bishop Victor, who was clearly regarded as a traitor by the Monophysites. Mueller (1968, p. 84) describes him as the "bishop who bears the sins of his city." He was also reviled in the Life and elsewhere in Coptic literature as a traitor. Samū'īl told his community to leave Neklone to avoid meeting Cyrus. For this "crime" Samū'īl was arrested and brought before Cyrus. The exchange between them resembles a typical martyrological interview between a Christian martyr and a pagan governor. Once again Samū'īl was beaten severely; he was rescued from death only by the timely intervention of local magistrates.

Driven out of Neklone, Samū'īl went south to Takinash, where he spent six months. From there he went into the desert "like Abraham" until he came upon a small church covered in sand, which had been abandoned "for a long time," at al-Qalamūn. It had probably been built by the Christian community known to have existed there in the fifth century. Here Samū'īl was twice captured by Berber raiders. The first captivity was brief, for the camel on which he was placed refused to move. The second captivity lasted three years. He was taken to the oasis of Siwa where he met John the Hegumenos of Scetis, who had fled from Cyrus. Samū'īl was released by his captors after performing several miracles, including two for the benefit of the wife of one of them, thereby acquiring the reputation of a powerful magician. In gratitude they presented him with some handsome camels and escorted him back to Qalamūn.

Soon after his return to Qalamūn, Samū'īl was joined by monks from Neklone and Takinash. Qalamūn began to prosper, both from the labors of the monks and from donations by generous benefactors. One such was Gregory, bishop of Kois (al-

Qays), an ill-tempered prelate whom Samū'īl had cured of an illness according to Ziadeh. He gave Samū'īl a hundred solidi, twenty measures of oil, thirty artabas of wheat, and a hundred jars of wine.

Gradually Samū'īl began to hand over the administration of the monastery, which was dedicated to the Virgin Mary, to his deacon, Apollo, who appears to have been responsible for collecting the donations for the construction of a new church at al-Qalamūn. A large benefactor to the church was Mena, eparch of Pelhip and a relative of Samū'īl. With the monastery in such a thriving condition, Samū'īl felt able to spend more time in solitude in the desert or marshes. He visited the monastery only once every three months. Once during his absence there was a shortage of grain because all the camels belonging to the monastery had been requisitioned to transport grain to Clysma (Suez). This may be the only reference in the Life to the ARAB CONQUEST OF EGYPT. It is known from the Arab historian Balādhurī that in A.H. 21/A.D. 643/644 the caliph 'Umar sent a letter to 'Amr, his general in Egypt, saying that there was a food shortage in Medina and that he should gather all the grain he had collected as KHARAJ (tax) and transport it by sea to the Arabian capital. Suez is an obvious point of departure for traveling to Arabia. Whether the event in the Life is the same as that in Balādhurī or a subsequent one cannot be determined.

It is recorded that Stephen the Presbyter, an extremely ascetic disciple of Samū'īl, was consecrated bishop of OXYRHYNCHUS, but the date is uncertain. In a fragment of a homily on Samū'īl the author speaks of ". . . the orthodox bishops which came out of the holy monastery. . . ." Stephen may have been the first of these. In the life (p. 117) he is said to have spent eighteen years in ascetic practices. Assuming he spent all these years at Qalamūn and that he was one of the first monks there, one might estimate the date of his transfer to the see of Oxyrhynchus to have occurred in the late 650s or early 660s.

Samū'īl spent fifty-seven years at Qalamūn and died at the age of ninety-eight.

BIBLIOGRAPHY

There are four versions of the life: three in Coptic, one in Ethiopic.

1. The only complete Coptic version, in Pierpont Morgan Library MS 578, is Sahidic with traces of Fayyumic dialect (probably 9th/10th century). A facsimile edition of the original has been published by H. Hyvernat in Bibliothecae Pierpont Morgan codices coptici. . . . 31. Rome, 1922.
2. Nine fragments of a pure Sahidic version were published by E. Amélineau in *Monuments pour servir à la histoire de l'Egypte chrétienne.* Paris, 1895.
3. Two fragments of a Bohairic version: one published by W. E. Crum in *Catalogue of Coptic MSS in the British Museum* (London, 1905), no. 917, the other an unpublished text in the Staatsbibliothek, Hamburg.
4. A complete Ethiopic version, published (with translation) by F. M. Esteves Pereira: *Vida do Abba Samuel do mosteiro do Kalamon.* Lisbon, 1894. Jean Simon has discussed the origin of the Ethiopic version in "Saint Samuel de Kalmon et son monastère dans la littérature éthiopienne." *Aethiopica* 1 (1933):36–40. Ethiopic translations are often made from Arabic versions, but no Arabic text of the life has survived.

Aḥmad ibn Yaḥyā Al Balādhurī. *Kitāb Futūḥ al Buldān,* trans. Philip Khuri Hitti. New York, 1916.

Alcock, A. ed. and trans. *The Life of Samuel of Kalamun by Isaac the Presbyter.* Warminster, England, 1983.

Evelyn-White, H. G. *The Monasteries of the Wadi'n Natrūn.* Pt. 2, *The History of the Monasteries of Nitria and Scetis.* New York, 1932.

Müller, C. D. G. *Die Homilie über die Hochzeit zu Kana* . . . . Heidelberg, 1968.

Munier, H. "La géographie de l'Egypte d'après les listes coptes-arabes." *Bulletin de la Société d'archéologie copte* 5 (1939):201–243.

Simon, J. "Fragment d'une homélie copte en l'honneur de Samuel de Kalamon." *Miscellanea biblica* 2 (1934).

Ziadeh, J. "Apocalypse of Samuel." *Revue de l'Orient chrétien* 10 (1915–1917):374–407.

ANTHONY ALCOCK

ṢANABŪ (Minya), according to al-MAQRĪZĪ, site of two monasteries: to the north is one dedicated to the Holy Virgin; to the south is one dedicated to Saint Theodorus, said to be in ruins. ABŪ ṢĀLIḤ THE ARMENIAN (early thirteenth century) does not mention any monastery at or near Ṣanabū, but only a church dedicated to the Virgin Mary.

The *Description d'Egypte* (Jomard, Vol. 4, pp. 302–303) says that to the northwest of Ṣanabū is DAYR ABŪ MINĀ; to the southeast, a monastery dedicated to Saint Theodorus, under reconstruction; and in the village, a third, dedicated to Saint

George. It survives in the form of a church (Clarke, 1912, p. 208, nos. 4–6).

BIBLIOGRAPHY

Clarke, S. *Christian Antiquities in the Nile Valley.* London, 1912.

Jomard, E. F. *Description de l'Egypte.* Paris, 1821–1829.

RENÉ-GEORGES COQUIN
MAURICE MARTIN, S.J.

SANCTUARY. *See* Architectural Elements of Churches.

SANDALS. *See* Costume, Civil.

SANQŪRIYYAH. *See* Pilgrimages.

SANUTIOS. *See* Shenute, Saint.

SAQQARA. *See* Dayr Apa Jeremiah (Saqqara).

SARA, SAINT, ascetic (feast day: 15 Baramhāt). According to the SYNAXARION, Sara was born in Upper Egypt of rich and pious parents. She lived for fifteen years in a monastery of virgins, then for sixty years she dwelt in a cell provided with a terrace that dominated the valley of the Nile. It is related that she never lowered her eyes to look at the river. She acquired a great reputation for asceticism. The alphabetic recension of the APOPHTHEGMATA PATRUM has preserved eight apothegms under her name; we learn from it that monks came to visit her—sometimes from afar, from Scetis, or even from the region of Pelusium. She died at the age of eighty. In an unpublished apothegm (Guy, 1962, p. 31), she appears to have been a contemporary of an abbot Paphnutius, seemingly the one at Scetis, nicknamed the Bubal.

ANTOINE GUILLAUMONT

SARAPAMON OF SCETIS, SAINT, an ascetic who was hegumenos of SCETIS (feast day: 5 Baramhāt). All that we know of him is supplied by the notice in the SYNAXARION from Lower Egypt. The passage offers no means of learning, even approximately, when this saint lived. However, since the Synaxarion mentions Saint BARSŪM THE NAKED, who died in 1317, it must have been composed after that date, which at least provides us with a *terminus post quem.* The ancient documents that describe sectis do not speak of Sarapamon. The Synaxarion tells us nothing of his family, nor of his place of birth, although it is probable, given the recruitment patterns of the monks of the Wādī al-Naṭrūn, that he was a native of the Delta. It can be deduced that he embraced the monastic life fairly young. The text tells us that Sarapamon entered the Dayr Abū Yuḥannis John (which designates John Colobos [the Little; the other John is explicitly named as Kama]) "in his youth," which is rather vague. He showed himself zealous from the beginning, both in asceticism and in the service of the "elders." We are told that this fervor endured for thirty-two years. Sarapamon was then elected HEGUMENOS of his monastery, and held this office for twenty years. He then lived as a recluse for ten years, eating only on Saturdays and Sundays. At the approach of his death (he must have died at a fairly advanced age, since he lived for sixty-two years at Scetis), he had a vision of an angel who brought him a cross of fire.

RENÉ-GEORGES COQUIN

SARAPION, or Serapion, the name of several monks, who appear in the monastic sources of the fourth and fifth centuries. The name derives from that of the god Sarapis. It is not easy to distinguish the various Sarapions. The attempt was first made by Lenain de Tillemont (Vol. 10, pp. 56–62) and later by Butler (Vol. 2, pp. 213–15).

PALLADIUS (*Historia lausiaca,* chaps. 7, 46; Butler, pp. 25, 134) mentions (1) a Sarapion the Great among the principal monks who lived in NITRIA when Melania visited this desert in 372–373. We must probably distinguish from this Sarapion of Nitria (2) an abbot Sarapion, whom John CASSIAN knew at SCETIS toward the end of the fourth century and to whom he ascribes his fifth *Conference,* in which he sets out an Evagrius-inspired theory on the eight principal vices (Vol. 42, pp. 188–217). This Sarapion was then a very aged monk who was distinguished, according to Cassian, by the grace of discernment that he had received. This remark of Cassian's, it seems, rules out identifying this monk with (3) another Sarapion who also lived at Scetis at this time, "surpassing almost all the others by his age and by his merits"; from what Cassian reports of him (Vol. 54, pp. 76–77), he was not conspicuous for his discernment. In fact, like many monks of Scetis, he remained attached to a literal interpretation of Genesis 1:26 ("Let us make man in our image and likeness"), believing in his simplicity that God has a human form, and he accepted only with great difficulty the synodical letter of 399, in which the patriarch THEOPHILUS condemned the opinions of the Anthropomorphites. It is difficult to say with which of these two monks we should identify an abbot Sarapion of whom Cassian further on in his *Conferences* (Vol. 64, pp. 23–24) reports the manner in which he taught a young monk true humility—or whether the latter is a namesake.

The alphabetic recension of the APOPHTHEGMATA PATRUM has four apothegms under the name of Sarapion (413D–417A). The last is an extract from Cassian's *Conference* 18. In apothegm 2, (4) a monk named Sarapion criticizes a brother in whose cell he sees a cupboard full of books, saying to him, "What shall I say to you? You have taken the goods of the widows and orphans, and put them in this cupboard"—the reflection of an unlettered monk who could well be the Anthropomorphite Sarapion. As for (5) the Sarapion who (in apothegm 1) converts a prostitute while pretending to be a client, he is probably the Sarapion nicknamed Sindonita.

Palladius devotes chapter 37 of his *Historia lausiaca* to this Sarapion, called Sindonita because he wore as his only garment a *sindonion,* a piece of light linen in which he wrapped himself. An Egyptian by birth, he led an itinerant life of asceticism. In the course of his wanderings, he sold himself as a slave to a couple of actors, then to some Manichaeans for the sole purpose of converting them. After traveling in various countries, he ended his life in Rome. According to some witnesses, he returned to Egypt and was buried "in the desert." R. Reitzenstein saw in the story of Sarapion Sindonita a pure romance adapted from a cynical aretalogy (1906, p. 64), and conjectured the existence of a "Sarapion corpus" used by Palladius and by the author of a more developed life preserved in a Syriac version and published by Bedjan (Vol. 5, pp. 263–341). Relying on the latter, F. Nau showed that this Sarapion is the monk called Paphnutius in the legendary life of Thaïs, a converted prostitute. The story has striking resemblances to the Sarapion of apothegm 1. A. Gayet claimed to have discovered, in the course of his excavations at Antinoopolis, the tombs of Thaïs and Sarapion, buried side by side.

This Sarapion is probably the hero of an anecdote, widely circulated in ancient monastic literature as "the story of the little Gospel," from the *Practical Treatise* of Evagrius (chap. 97, pp. 704–705, in an anonymous form) to the *Life of Saint John the Almoner* (p. 48), of whom the different recensions have been cataloged by C. Butler (Vol. 1, 1898, pp. 98–99). Sarapion's only possession was a Gospel. He sold it and gave the money to the starving, saying, "I have sold the book which said to me: 'Sell what you possess and give the price to the poor.'" In a long recension of the *Historia lausiaca,* the name of Bessarion is substituted for that of Sarapion, a substitution that seems also to have occurred in the apopthegm Bessarion 12 in the alphabetic recension of the *Apophthegmata Patrum.*

There was also (6) an abbot Sarapion who was head of numerous monasteries in the region of Arsinoë and is mentioned by the author of the HISTORIA MONACHORUM. Also distinct is (7) Sarapion, a disciple of Saint ANTONY, to whom is incorrectly attributed the Coptic Life of Macarius of Scetis published by E. Amélineau (p. 46); it is, in fact, much later (see MACARIUS THE EGYPTIAN). This Sarapion is, in fact, the bishop of Tmuis (see SARAPION OF TMUIS).

BIBLIOGRAPHY

Amélineau, E. C. *Histoire des monastères de la Basse-Egypte.* Paris, 1894.

Apophthegmata Patrum, ed. J. B. Cotelier. PG 65. Paris, 1864.

Bedjan, P. *Acta martyrum et sanctorum,* 7 vols. Paris and Leipzig, 1890–1897.

Butler, C., ed. *The Lausiac History of Palladius,* 2 vols. Cambridge, 1898–1904.

Cassian, John. *Conferences,* ed. E. Pichery. Sources chrétiennes 42, 54, and 64. Paris, 1955–1959.

Evagrius Ponticus. *Traité pratique ou Le Moine,* ed. A. Guillaumont and C. Guillaumont. Sources chrétiennes 170–171. Paris, 1971.

Gayet, A. *Antinoë et les sépultures de Thaïs et Sérapion.* Paris, 1902.

Lenain de Tillemont, L.S. *Mémoires pour servir à l'histoire ecclésiastique des six premiers siècles,* Vol. 10. Paris, 1705.

Leontius von Neapolis. *Das Leben das heiligen Iohannes des barmherzigen Erzbischofs von Alexandrien.* Freiburg and Leipzig, 1893.

Nau, F. *"Histoire de Thaïs." Annales du Musée Guimet* 30, (1902):51–114.

Reitzenstein, R. *Hellenistische Wundererzählungen.* Leipzig, 1906; 2nd ed., 1963.

ANTOINE GUILLAUMONT

SARAPION OF TMUIS, SAINT, or Serapion, fourth-century bishop of Tmuis who supported the orthodox patriarch Saint ATHANASIUS I THE APOSTOLIC in the Arian controversy (feast day, 21 March). Apparently he received a good education because Saint Jerome claims that the epithet *Scholasticus* was added to his name because of his eloquence and erudition. He was a monk and an abbot and was bishop of Tmuis in the Delta by 339, for Athanasius addressed his festal letter for that year to Sarapion as bishop. Sarapion was a disciple of Saint ANTONY OF EGYPT, who, on his death in 356, left Sarapion one of his two sheepskins.

Sarapion directed questions about the Holy Spirit to Athanasius, who in 359–360 wrote him at least four letters on that subject. Athanasius also wrote an account (356–358) of the death of the heretical theologian ARIUS, which he sent to Sarapion. At about the same time, or slightly earlier, Athanasius, then in exile, sent an embassy, including Sarapion, to represent him before Emperor Constantius II. From this evidence it appears that Sarapion was Athanasius' closest ally and colleague among the bishops of Egypt, although from the style of Athanasius' letters, Sarapion was probably the junior partner.

Far from conciliating the emperor to Athanasius, Sarapion was deposed by Constantius and became known as a "confessor." When Epiphanius (*Panarion* 73.26) states that Ptolemaeus went to the Synod of Seleucia in 359 as the bishop of Tmuis, one cannot be certain whether Sarapion was still in exile (making Ptolemaeus an Arian replacement) or had died.

Sarapion wrote numerous works, most of which have not survived. Jerome states that he wrote a commentary on the titles of the Psalms and a number of epistles to various people. There was once a collection of at least twenty-three of his letters in circulation, but few of them are extant, the longest being one written to some monks at Alexandria. Sarapion wrote a brief letter to an ailing bishop, Eudoxius, and one to the disciples of Antony on the occasion of their leader's death in 356. Sarapion's best-known work, an attack against MANICHAEANISM, is a good example of polemic biblical argumentation, even if it suffers from some ignorance of Manichaean theology. In this work it is noteworthy that Sarapion in discussing the nature of Christ uses the term *homoios* ("of like substance") not *homoousius* ("of one substance"), as Athanasius would undoubtedly have preferred.

A sacramentary (technically, an euchologion) in a manuscript from the Monastery of Mount Athos is comprised of thirty prayers, followed by a treatise on the Father and Son. Sarapion's name is found in two of the prayers, and many assume that he is responsible for the entire collection, which is dated to the middle of the fourth century. This sacramentary contains the first definite use of the Sanctus in eucharistic liturgy.

Other writings of doubtful authenticity have been ascribed to Sarapion, but none with the certainty of those mentioned above.

BIBLIOGRAPHY

Brightman, F. E. "The Sacramentary of Serapion of Thmuis." *Journal of Theological Studies* 1 (1900):88–113, 247–77.

Casey, R. P. *Serapion of Thmuis Against the Manichees.* Harvard Theological Studies 15. Cambridge, Mass., 1931.

Quasten, J. *Patrology,* Vol. 3. *The Golden Age of Greek Patristic Literature.* Utrecht, 1960.

C. WILFRED GRIGGS

SARJIYŪS, MALAṬĪ (1883–1964), Egyptian clergyman better known as Qummuṣ Sarjiyūs. He was born in Jirjā, in Upper Egypt, with a long line of clerical ancestors behind him. Sarjiyūs joined the CLERICAL COLLEGE in 1899 and graduated with a distinguished record that qualified him to teach in the same college. His revolutionary tendencies, which characterized his entire career, had their beginnings at an early age. Feeling the need for radical reforms at the Clerical College, Sarjiyūs provoked students to go on strike.

In an attempt to discipline Sarjiyūs, Patriarch CYRIL V (1874–1927) summoned him, ordered him to get married as a prerequisite to joining the clergy, and ordained him priest for Mallawī's church in Upper Egypt in 1904. His new assignment as clergyman did not prevent him from pursuing his campaign for reforming the Coptic church. Only three months after his ordination, Sarjiyūs was tried by a clerical board and sent into retirement. Penniless, he returned to his native town of Jirjā.

Three years later, Bishop Macarius of Asyūṭ (later Patriarch MACARIUS III) summoned Sarjiyūs and appointed him priest for the Asyūṭ church. In 1912 the bishop of Khartoum and the Coptic Society in the Sudan expressed a desire to profit from the services of Sarjiyūs. While in Khartoum (1912–1914), Sarjiyūs edited a weekly organ. His critical editorials were full of revolutionary views. Whereas Bishop Abraam of the Fayyūm hailed the magazine and backed Sarjiyūs, the patriarchate in Cairo put him on trial on sixty counts, all revolving around his editorials. When the Clerical Council failed to induce Sarjiyūs to plead guilty, the whole trial was called off, and he was allowed to return to the

Sudan, where his popularity increased, not only among Copts but also among Muslims.

Sarjiyūs' popularity in the Sudan was resented by the British, who decided to deport him. He thus returned in May 1915 to his native town once again, but he had no church there. His devoted Sudanese congregation did not fail him and continued to remit his salary until he built his own church in the popular quarter of Qulalī in Cairo. Multitudes of Copts and Muslims crowded the church and nearby streets to listen to his revolutionary sermons.

When the Egyptian national leader SA'D ZAGHLŪL was arrested by the British, Sarjiyūs headed toward al-Azhar Mosque, where he was given a tumultuous welcome by the grand *shaykh* and Muslim worshippers. The first non-Muslim ever to mount the pulpit of the thousand-year-old mosque, Sarjiyūs continued for fifty-nine consecutive days to deliver speeches in which he championed national unity behind the leader and the national cause of independence. His caustic speeches at the Mosque of Ibn Ṭūlūn and the Coptic church of Fajjālah, a popular quarter of Cairo, resulted in his banishment by the British to Rafaḥ in the Sinai Peninsula. His orations won him the epithets Orator of al-Azhar, Orator of the Revolution, and Orator of Egypt, the last bestowed by Sa'd Zaghlūl.

In 1920, Sarjiyūs resumed his bid for reforming the church and challenged the patriarch. This prompted a new trial before the Holy Synod that ended in a judgment rendered in absentia that defrocked, excommunicated, and banished Sarjiyūs to his native town.

In flagrant defiance of the judgment, Sarjiyūs proceeded to his favorite church in Qulalī. He continued to preach until late August 1921, when the church was forcibly appropriated by the patriarchate, and Sarjiyūs was expelled. Six months later, Sarjiyūs managed to rent a hall in the nearby quarter of Fajjālah, and forthwith, multitudes filled the entire hall.

Following a reconciliation with the new patriarch, JOHN XIX (1928–1942), Sarjiyūs was appointed religious guide by the Coptic COMMUNITY COUNCIL in 1935. During the years 1930–1942, he edited a weekly newspaper published in Cairo.

In 1944, Sarjiyūs was chosen by Patriarch Macarius III (1944–1945) to act as deputy to the patriarchate. In this capacity, he convened a conference for all heads of Christian denominations in a bid for unity. This was one of his greatest achievements.

In 1952, following a rift between Patriarch YŪSĀB II (1946–1956) and Sarjiyūs, the latter was again defrocked and excommunicated. Between then and 1956, he was subjected to confinement at home by the state.

At the time of his death in 1964, Sarjiyūs was still banned by the Coptic church. At an impressive funeral, mourners forced their way to Saint Mark's Cathedral for memorial prayers. In the face of this massive demonstration, Pope CYRIL VI (1959–1971) rescinded the excommunication order as an act of rehabilitation to this dedicated reformer.

BIBLIOGRAPHY

Jamā'at al-Ummah al-Qibtiyyah. *Al-Wa'y al-Qibṭī.* Cairo, 1965.

IBRĀHĪM HILĀL

SASSANID INFLUENCES ON COPTIC ART.

In addition to the traditional influences mentioned as contributing to the formation of Coptic art—Hellenistic, ancient Egyptian, Roman, and Christian—some more distant influences must be explored. Indeed, it has been argued that the art of India, and even Central Asia, bore some relationship with Coptic art (Zaloscer, 1947).

A no less important source for Coptic art was the Sassanid art that influenced practically all medieval civilizations as illustrated in the respective arts of the Middle Ages. In the case of Coptic art, the natural flux of artistic influences encountered in other areas is here even more concrete, probably due to the fact that, in the first half of the seventh century, Egypt was conquered by Khosrow II (590–628) and was under direct Sassanid influence.

Through Sassanid art, Coptic art incorporated two layers of influence; the first was the ancient Oriental artistic legacy that Sassanid art had already adopted, and the second was the motifs peculiar to Sassanid art itself. Examples of the first influence include the traditional motifs of "the Woman at the Window," as seen on a fragment of textile from Antinoë (ANTINOOPOLIS), and the repeated *eads,* or masks, reproduced on Antinoë textiles as well as on a Saqqara fresco. Examples in Coptic art of typical Sassanids motifs include roundels with rams or winged horses on various textiles, accompanied by the traditional details of beaded frames, flying ribbons, or pairs of birds facing each other. All these can be seen on textiles found in Egypt. The culmination of the Sassanid influence may be found on the famous Khosrow textile, found at Antinoë, and preserved in the Textile Museum of Lyons. The piece represents a seated personality, suggested to be Khosrow, against a background scene of fighting cavaliers and archers. A very similar interpretation of the majestic personality can be seen on a Coptic plaque of ivory, conserved at the Walters Art Gallery, Baltimore.

BIBLIOGRAPHY

Ghirshman, R. *Persian Art: The Parthian and Sasanian Dynasties, 249 B.C.–651 A.D.* New York, 1964.

Shepherd, D. G. *Iran: Between East and West*, pp. 84–105. Offprint of *East-West in Art*. Bloomington, Ind., 1966.

Zaloscer, H. *Quelques considérations sur les rapports entre l'art copte et les Indes*. Cairo, 1947.

MYRIAM ROSEN-AYALON

SATURDAY, seventh day of the week, the day on which Christ's body rested in the tomb. The early Christians of Jewish origin continued to observe Saturday as the Sabbath, a day of rest and prayer. But the fact that the Resurrection and descent of the Holy Ghost on the apostles had taken place on the first day of the week soon led to the observance of that day (see SUNDAY). Soon the observance of Saturday was regarded as a sign of imparting a Jewish character to Christianity (Col. 2:16; Epistle of Ignatius to the Magnesians 9 and Epistle to Diognetus 4, in Jurgens, 1970, pp. 62, 26). This motivated the Council of Laodicea (343–381) to legislate Canon 29, saying, "Christians must not Judaize by resting on the Sabbath, but must work on that day, rather honoring the Lord's Day, and if they can, resting then as Christians. But if any shall be found to be Judaizers, let them be anathema from Christ."

Fasting Day

In the East, Saturday is still, as in early times, treated as a festal day, except in regard to the cessation of work, and is characterized by the absence of fasting and by standing in prayer.

The West, on the contrary, especially Rome, in protest against the Judaization of Christianity, observed the seventh day of the week as a fast day, like Friday. This is noted by Socrates, who said, "At Rome they fast every Saturday." And from Saint Augustine's letter 36, it appears that he fasted on Saturday and regarded this the regular and proper course to be pursued.

It appears from a remark of Saint Jerome that the Saturday fast was known in Rome as early as the beginning of the third century, for he said that Hippolytus discussed the question of the Saturday fast and of a daily reception of the Eucharist. Tertullian (c. 160–225), however, writing on fasting condemned this practice, calling the Sabbath "a day never to be kept as fast except at the Passover Season." In more recent times, the Saturday fast in the West became restricted to Italy, where it was eventually abolished in 1918.

The Eastern tradition agrees with Apostolic Canon 66, which decrees, "If any of the clergy be found fasting on the Lord's day, or on the Sabbath, excepting the one only, let him be deposed. If a layman, let him be excommunicated."

Similarly the APOSTOLIC CONSTITUTIONS state, "But keep the Sabbath and the Lord's day festival, because the former is the memorial of the creation, and the latter of the resurrection. But there is one only Sabbath to be observed by you in the whole year, which is that of our Lord's burial, on which men ought to keep a fast, but not a festival." They also say, "He appointed us to break our fast on the seventh day at the cock-crowing, but to fast on the Sabbath-day. Not that the Sabbath-day is a day of fasting, being the rest from the creation, but because we ought to fast on this one Sabbath only, while on this day the Creator was under the earth." Pope CHRISTODOULUS (1046–1077) affirmed the same rule in Canon 19: "And it is not allowed to any of the faithful to fast on a Saturday, except on one Saturday in the whole year, and this is the Great Saturday which is the end of the fast."

A Day of Worship

The Constitutions of the Holy Apostles (Book 5, Section 3) give an injunction: "Every Sabbath-day excepting one, and every Lord's day, hold your solemn assemblies and rejoice."

Similarly, the Arabic Didascalia (William S. Qelādah, 1979, chap. 10) commands, "Assemble ye each day in the Church especially on Saturday and the Resurrection day which is Sunday." It also says (chap. 38), "The Holy Bread shall be offered on Saturday and Sunday." Likewise, the ninety-third of the canons attributed to Saint Athanasius says, "O my beloved. None of the priests or the Christians shall be neglected of the Sacraments [anaphoras] on the Sabbath and Sunday" (Riedel and Crum, 1904, p. 60).

The Saturday service, however, was not universally liturgical. Down to the fifth century, the Divine

Liturgy was not celebrated on Saturday at Rome or Alexandria. This was noted by Socrates: "For although almost all churches throughout the world celebrate the sacred mysteries on the Sabbath of every week, yet the Christians of Alexandria and at Rome, on account of some ancient tradition, have ceased to do this." But he added, "The Egyptians in the neighborhood of Alexandria, and the inhabitants of Thebais, hold their religious assemblies on the Sabbath, but do not participate of the mysteries in the manner usual among Christians in general, for after having eaten and satisfied themselves with food of all kinds, in the evening making the offerings [celebrating the Eucharist] they partake of the mysteries" (1979, p. 132).

Certain instructions were given as to the observance of Saturday and the manner of conducting its service, whether liturgical or nonliturgical. "The Gospels are to be read on the Sabbath with the other scriptures" (Canons of the Synod Held in the City of Laodicea). Hence, the Constitutions of the Holy Apostles say, "Let slaves work five days; but on the Sabbath-day and the Lord's day let them have leisure to go to church for instruction in piety. We have said that the Sabbath is an account of the creation, and the Lord's day of the resurrection."

The biographies of Coptic monks, anchorites, and bishops often record the custom of assembling on Saturdays and Sundays for the synaxes and Holy Communion. Saint PAPHNUTIUS the hermit said that Saint Onophrius and the anchorites in the desert used to "partake of the Sacrament on the Sabbath Day and on the First day of the week, through an angel of God who cometh and administereth the Sacrament to every one who is in the desert, and who liveth there for God's sake and who seeth no man" (Budge, 1914, pp. 464, 470).

Saturday During Lent

Canon 49 of the Council of Laodicea decrees, "During Lent, the Bread must not be offered except on the Sabbath Day and on the Lord's Day only." This rule is still observed by the Syrians, Armenians, and Greeks, but not the Copts. Also "The Nativities of the Martyrs are not to be celebrated in Lent, but commemorations of the holy Martyrs are to be made on the Sabbaths and Lord's days" (Canon 51).

In view of the eucharistic character of Saturday, Patriarch Timothy of Alexandria (380–385) stated that it is a day of abstention from the conjugal act.

Similarly SĀWĪRUS IBN AL-MUQAFFA', bishop of Ashmūnayn (tenth century), in the eighth treatise of his *Al-Durr al-Thamin,* condemned those who think that Saturday and Sundays of Lent are not counted among the forty holy days that the Lord fasted and accordingly abstain from the conjugal act on all the days of the fast except Saturdays and Sundays.

Ritual Notes

The Coptic church nowadays observes Saturday as a festal day on which fasts and prostrations are prohibited all the year round except Holy Saturday, which is to be fasted. But the Divine Liturgy on Holy Saturday is celebrated early in the morning, and not at noon as it should be according to the ritual rule. Hence, most communicants do break the fast by taking a drink of water immediately after communion.

During fasting seasons, Saturdays and Sundays are not to be observed with complete abstinence but only from animal products, according to the rules and customs of fasting. Fish is allowed in some fasts, namely the Fast of Advent, the Fast of the Apostles, and the Fast of the Virgin. Hence, fish is also allowed on Saturday and Sundays that fall in the above three fasts. But it is not allowed on Saturdays and Sundays included in other fasts, namely, the PARAMONE day of Christmas and Epiphany, and the fifty-five days of Lent. In Ethiopia, however, fish is not to be eaten on any of the fast days of the year.

Although few cathedrals and large churches have a daily celebration of the Divine Liturgy, the usual practice in most churches is to avoid celebrating it on Saturday except on rare occasions, such as feasts of particular importance in the calendar and funerals.

Even during Lent most churches in Egypt have a daily celebration of the liturgy (at noon), except on Saturday. In case of necessity, the liturgy is to be celebrated on Saturdays of Lent early in the morning, and some of the hymns and prayers of the PSALMODIA and the liturgy are to be sung to a special tone for Saturdays and Sundays of Lent.

The evening being an end to the work of the day, and Saturday being an end to the cycle of the week, both symbolize the end of earthly life. Thus, the Intercession for the Dead is to be said at the evening raising of incense every day, while the prayers for the sick, for travelers, or for the sacrifices are to be said at the morning raising of incense. But on Saturday, being the day on which the Lord rested in the tomb, the prayer for the faithful departed is to be said at both the evening and morning services of raising of incense. At present, there are exceptions to this rule during the Paschaltide and the feasts of the Lord (and Sunday evening according to a variant tradition), where the prayer of the dead is not to be said in the evening raising of incense nor on Saturday in the morning raising of incense. Hence, the prayer for the sick is to be said instead.

BIBLIOGRAPHY

Amélineau, E. "Un Evêque de Keft au VIIe siècle." *Mémoires de l'Institut égyptien* 2 (1887):149.

Budge, E. A. T. Wallis. *Coptic Martyrdom, etc., in the Dialect of Upper Egypt.* London, 1914.

Carleton, J. G. "Festivals and Fasts (Christian)." In *Encyclopaedia of Religion and Ethics,* Vol. 5, p. 844. New York, 1925.

Jurgens, W. A. *The Faith of the Early Fathers,* 3 vols. Collegeville, Minn., 1970.

Maclean, A. J. "Fasting (Christian)." In *Encyclopaedia of Religion and Ethics,* Vol. 5, p. 767. New York, 1925.

Muyser, J. "Le Samedi et le dimanche dans l'église et la littérature coptes." In *Le Martyre d'apa Epima,* ed. Togo Mina, pp. 89–111. Cairo, 1937.

Riedel, W., and W. E. Crum. *The Canons of Athanasius.* London, 1904; repr. 1973.

EMILE MAHER ISHAQ

SAUNERON, SERGE (d. 1976), French Egyptologist. He studied at the Ecole Normale Supérieure and received the *doctorat d'état* at the Sorbonne. He was member, librarian, associate director, and finally director of the Institut francais d'Archéologie orientale in Cairo from 1969 until the accident that caused his death. Sauneron studied Coptic at the Institut Catholique, Paris, in 1949. From 1950, at long intervals down to 1970, he published pharaonic etymologies of Coptic terms. After his excavations of the temple of Isnā, he published (with the collaboration of Jean Jacquet) *Les Ermitages chrétiens du désert d'Esna* (1972). It was on his initiative and on behalf of the French Institute in Cairo that Jules Leroy undertook his work on several large Coptic monasteries, continued by Paul van Moorsel.

PIERRE DU BOURGUET, S.J.

SAWADAH. *See* Pilgrimages.

SAWIROS. *See* Ethiopian Prelates.

SĀWĪRUS IBN AL-MUQAFFA‘, earliest great Coptic writer in the Arabic language. Sāwīrus was born early in the tenth century to a pious family that provided him with a thorough Christian education. His dates of birth and death are not known with precision, but his life must have covered most of the tenth century. His name as a layman was Abū al-Bishr, and his father was called al-Muqaffa‘ (the Bent-Backed), an indication of a physical infirmity. He was brought up at a time when the Copts diligently learned Arabic as the language of their rulers and seriously began its use in parallel with Coptic, in order to retain their places in the Arab administration of the country. He started his career as a scribe in that administration, where he remained for a few years until he decided to resign all worldly positions and retire to monastic life. It is possible that he then changed his Arabian secular name to Sāwīrus.

We do not know how long he was a simple monk, nor do we know the monastery where he resided. It is probable, however, that he had enrolled at DAYR NAHYĀ near Cairo, though a stronger possibility is that it was at DAYR ANBĀ MAQĀR, with its fabulous library, that he spent most of these years, studying and reading the lives of the great fathers. Undoubtedly this period was long enough for him to complete his religious education and biblical scholarship. He may even have started writing some of his immense contributions in Arabic during that period. So profound had his knowledge of Coptic tradition, exegetic science, and even Greek philosophy become, that he was destined to become the official champion of the Coptic faith and his own church during the remaining years of his life.

Though he was somewhat secluded in his monastic life, Sāwīrus' fame began to spread, and the archons of the city of al-Ashmūnayn selected him to fill their vacant bishopric. We do not know the patriarch who consecrated him or the date of his consecration. We do know that he became bishop of al-Ashmūnayn under the name of Sāwīrus, a name he may have adopted during his time as a monk, though this is uncertain. Al-Ashmūnayn is, of course, the ancient Hermopolis Magna in the district of Antinoopolis. Then situated in a rich area of arable land on the bank of the Nile, al-Ashmūnayn is now reduced to a small village in the district of al-Roḍah in the province of Asyūṭ, and the Nile has receded from it by a few miles. It has been suggested that the patriarch responsible for Sāwīrus' consecration could have been THEOPHANES (952–956) or MĪNĀ II (956–974), the sixtieth and sixty-first occupants of the throne of Saint Mark (Samir, 1978). But he may have been consecrated during the patriarchate of Macarius I (932–952), since we know that he defended his Coptic church against the destructive attacks eloquently launched by Saʻīd IBN AL-BIṬRĪQ, Melchite patriarch Eutychius (935–940), who was supported by the Ikhshid Muḥammad ibn Tughj (935–946).

During the early Fatimid period, Sāwīrus seems to have been popular with Caliph al-Muʻiz (972–975), during whose reign he participated in a number of religious discussions with Muslim imams and Jewish rabbis. These were conducted in the presence of the caliph, who was greatly affected by Sāwīrus' defense of the Coptic faith and tradition.

An amusing account is often quoted of one of his disputations with the Muslim chief justice (*qāḍi al-quḍāt*), who asked Sāwīrus whether a passing dog was Muslim or Christian. To avoid an incriminating answer, Sāwīrus replied, "Ask him." The judge said, "The dog does not talk." It was Friday, a fast day for the Copts, so Sāwīrus said that fasting Copts on that day eat no meat, and break the fast by sipping sacramental wine (*abārkah*). He suggested offering the dog meat and wine, so that if he ate the meat, he was a Muslim, and if he drank the wine, he must be a Christian. In this manner he gave an answer that the chief justice could not refute.

Few specific dates are established in the life of Sāwīrus, and we have to deduce most of his chronology from the dates of the reigning patriarchs. However, two dates are known with precision. He mentions 955 as the date of the completion of his second book on the councils. And at the age of eighty he was the first signatory of a synodal letter of the sixty-third Coptic patriarch, PHILOTHEUS (979–1003), addressed to Athanasius V, patriarch of Antioch (987–1003), defining the answer to certain theological problems. This letter was dated either 987 or 988, and Sāwīrus was the foremost exponent among the bishops in the patriarchal reply.

At that time he must have composed most of his numerous works said by the fourteenth-century Coptic encyclopedist Abū al-Barakāt IBN KABAR (d. 1324) to total twenty-six books, all in the classical Arabic of the period. More recently Kamil Ṣāliḥ Nakhlah compiled a list of thirty-eight works, some of which had been declared lost until they were found in manuscript repositories.

First, in his works on theological science, Sāwīrus discussed all manner of problems from the Coptic viewpoint. Second, he wrote a number of items on Coptic traditions and liturgical practices. Third, he displayed an extraordinary knowledge of exegetical and biblical studies. Samir (1978, p. 11) states that in one of his works Sāwīrus quoted 1,161 written sources in support of his arguments: 307 references to the Old Testament and 854 to the New Testament. We may legitimately assume that Sāwīrus must have memorized the whole Bible and that he was able to quote it freely in his disputation with Rabbi Moses in the presence of the Fatimid caliph al-Muʻizz in 975. Fourth, he proved himself to be the great champion of Coptic Christianity in works defending its doctrines against the vehement attacks of the Melchite patriarch Eutychius (also known as Saʻīd ibn Biṭrīq), a favorite of the Fatimid caliphs. In 950 Sāwīrus composed his book on the councils in reply to an abusive treatise by Eutychius. Fifth, he composed a miscellaneous body of treatises encompassing varied subjects from moralistic works to child guidance and his own disputations comprising answers to problems posed by a certain Ibn Jārūd.

Sixth were his historical works, of which the *History of the Patriarchs* stands as a permanent monument to his erudition and critical mind (for a different opinion, refer to HISTORY OF THE PATRIARCHS OF ALEXANDRIA). He was probably the most eminent among a growing school of historians in the Coptic monasteries who wrote mainly in Coptic. For the first time in history, he worked on the unique compilation in the Arabic language of the biographies of the patriarchs from Saint Mark to the tenth century. He based his accounts on all available manuscripts in Greek and in Coptic in the various monasteries, notably DAYR NAHYĀ near Cairo and DAYR ANBĀ MAQĀR in Wādī al-Naṭrūn. In a difficult pursuit of the original sources, he availed himself of assistance from contemporary figures who showed great competence in their knowledge of Greek and Coptic as they scanned monastic libraries for manuscripts that they translated for him into Arabic. These were the deacon Mīkhā'īl ibn Bidayr al-Damanhūrī (later bishop of Tanis); Shaykh Buqayrah al-Rashīdī, known as the bearer of the cross; the presbyter Yū'annis ibn Zakīr, abbot of the Nahyā monastery; and the deacon Tidra or Tadros ibn Mīnā of Minūf.

Sāwīrus did not compile his work by accepting a single manuscript for each of his subjects, but compared various manuscripts in search of the historical facts. This, of course, did not prevent him from recording popular legends and superhuman miracles associated with his saintly martyrs and holy figures. In this way he started the record of the patriarchs that was continued by a number of authors until modern times.

Sāwīrus was highly venerated by contemporary patriarchs, respected by the Fatimid caliphs, and beloved and appreciated by noted figures of his own day, among whom was the noted saint al-WĀḌIḤ IBN RAJĀ', a convert from Islam to Coptic Christianity whom Sāwīrus sponsored and with whom he studied the lives of the saints and martyrs of the church. Throughout his life Sāwīrus championed the cause of his church. He pioneered the recording of its heritage in the Arabic language, and since the tenth century he has remained one of its greatest historians. He lived to a ripe old age, definitely beyond the eighties, though the exact year of his death is unknown. He probably died during the reign of the sixty-third patriarch, PHILOTHEUS (979–1003).

BIBLIOGRAPHY

Cheikho, L. *Kitāb al-Muntakhabāt al-'Arabiyyah li-Katabat al-Nasrāniyyah.* Beirut, 1924.

Samir, K., ed. *Kitāb Miṣbāh al-'Aql.* Cairo, 1978. Contains a detailed biography of Sāwīrus in the introduction.

AZIZ S. ATIYA

SAYCE, ARCHIBALD HENRY (1845–1933), English Assyriologist. He was educated at Grosvenor College, Bath, and Queen's College, Oxford. His main field was Assyrian and West Asian archaeology and philology; nevertheless, he was intimately connected with Egypt for over half a century, traveling there extensively. He spent many winters in his own boat on the Nile, copying inscriptions and the like. He also studied early Christianity. A listing of what he published in the field of Coptic studies can be found in Kammerer's *A Coptic Bibliography* (1950; 1969). He also edited *Murray's Handbook to Egypt* (1896).

BIBLIOGRAPHY

Dawson, W. R., and E. P. Uphill. *Who Was Who in Egyptology.* London, 1972.

Kammerer, W., comp. *A Coptic Bibliography,* p. 261. Ann Arbor, Mich., 1950; repr. New York, 1969.

AZIZ S. ATIYA

SCARVES. *See* Costume, Civil.

SCETIS, name that historically designated the area of monastic settlement extending about 19 miles (30 km) through the shallow valley known in the medieval period as Wādī Habīb, now called Wādī al-Naṭrūn, which runs southeast to northwest through the Western or Libyan Desert, about 40 miles (65 km) southwest of the Nile Delta. In a very broad sense, "Scetis" or the "Desert of Scetis" also designated the ensemble of monastic colonies in the wilderness or on the edge of the desert southwest of the Delta, thus including NITRIA or the "Mountain of Nitria" (not to be confused with Wādī al-Naṭrūn); KELLIA, in the desert south of Nitria; and Scetis in the narrower and more proper sense, still farther into the desert, south of Kellia. This article is concerned with Scetis in the more proper sense.

The district of Scetis, far enough from the inhabited regions of Egypt to satisfy the monastic search for solitude in the desert but not too far away to make transportation a serious problem, a district in which brackish water is available from the marshes and lakes along the north side of the valley and fresh water can be obtained from wells, lent itself well to the establishment of monastic cells, in isolation or in clusters. Its development as a monastic colony began when MACARIUS THE EGYPTIAN moved into the valley about 330 and set up a cell near the site of the present DAYR AL-BARAMŪS; soon, however, there were neighboring cells of monastic admirers who wished to learn from him.

Some of the first monks in Scetis had doubtlessly lived the monastic life in Nitria and elsewhere. Macarius himself had had contact with Nitria, although he had not lived there. He had visited Saint ANTONY OF EGYPT but there is no evidence that he lived near Antony for any length of time. In any case, the monastic style of the settlement established around Macarius and of the other early monastic settlements in Scetis was certainly not a tightly organized cenobitic one like that of the monasteries founded in Upper Egypt by PACHOMIUS. It was the semianchoritic style characteristic of Nitria in its earliest period, with monks guided by an experienced father or elder but living essentially as solitaries. Although Rufinus, repeated by Socrates and Sozomen, wrote that Macarius of Egypt, like MACARIUS ALEXANDRINUS, was exiled briefly by the Arian patriarch Lucius about 374, that statement is of dubious accuracy, as far as the involvement of Macarius of Egypt is concerned. There is no reason to think that the growth of monastic life in the extreme isolation of Scetis was disrupted by events in the Arian controversy.

Probably by the time Macarius died (c. 390), and

certainly by the end of the century, there were in Scetis four monastic settlements, each clearly defined by a nucleus with a central church to which the collection of scattered cells was related. These were the four settlements that became the monasteries of Baramūs, of Saint Macarius (DAYR ANBĀ MAQĀR), of DAYR ANBĀ BISHOI, and of Saint John the Short (JOHN COLOBOS), the first three of which still exist.

With details that can be gleaned from the *Lausiac History* of PALLADIUS, from John CASSIAN'S *Institutes* and *Conferences*, and from the APOPHTHEGMATA PATRUM we can form a fairly good idea of how the monks of Scetis lived in the late fourth and early fifth centuries, and of how their settlements were organized. From the literary evidence, it has been inferred that the growth of cenobitic houses originally meant as training establishments for new monks was giving Nitria a semicenobitic character by this time. Life in Kellia, in contrast, was still strongly anchoritic, while in Scetis the semicenobitic and the anchoritic forms of life were perhaps less sharply distinguished (Evelyn-White, Vol. 2, p. 169).

From a reading of the texts in the light of what French and Swiss archaeologists have more recently found at the site of Kellia (see the two reports by A. Guillaumont and R. Kasser in Wilson, pp. 203–208, 209–219), one suspects that the evolution of life and organization in Kellia at this time was similar to that in Scetis. The monks lived in cells that often were a considerable distance apart. In his cell a monk performed all his labors with his own hands, prepared and ate his meals, tried to pray constantly, and recited the formal prayers enjoined upon him at fixed times on ordinary days. His solitude did not prevent him from receiving visits and extending generous hospitality according to his frugal means. The larger clusters of cells centered on the church of one of the four settlements formed what may properly be called a laura. On Saturday the monks went to the center of their particular laura, in order to be present for Vespers, the Night Office, and the eucharistic offering in the church, and to take a Sunday meal in common. To this central place they also took the products of their week's work, and from it carried supplies back to their cells on Sunday.

In Scetis there was no common written rule to be followed by all. The norms of life were those of the Gospels, supplemented by custom and by the wisdom of any experienced monastic father to whom a newly arrived monk apprenticed himself. Such a father might live with one or two monastic apprentices who were his close disciples in a single cell comprising several small rooms, while other disciples lived in smaller individual cells nearby.

Each of the four monasteries or lauras that existed by the end of the fourth century had a central church as its focal point. Each was presided over by a priest-monk who was in charge of the church and who also exercised certain powers and had certain duties as the religious superior, the father of the monastery. Each monastery had a council, at least some of whose members were clerical monks. The maintenance of general order and discipline was the responsibility of the father of the monastery, acting with the council. The father of the monastery of Saint Macarius was also the "father of Scetis." Of all the monks in Scetis he was the one highest in dignity, the monastic superior who represented all Scetis in relations with the patriarchate and with the civil authorities. The position of the superior of Dayr Anbā Maqār as "father of Scetis" lasted for a very long time, although the title was changed eventually to "HEGUMENOS of Scetis"; a *hegumenos* of Scetis still called upon the Coptic patriarch annually to report on the conditions of the monasteries in the eleventh century.

When the Origenist controversy became acute in Egypt in the last years of the fourth century, for reasons of ecclesiastical politics as well as of theological principle, the partisans of ORIGEN were found almost exclusively among educated men whose intellectual culture was Hellenistic. To most of the Egyptian monks the only issue in the controversy that mattered was that some of the more speculative Hellenists insisted on the spirituality and immateriality of God. This offended and pained the more literal, relatively uneducated, monastic majority, who were accused of an unacceptable ANTHROPOMORPHISM for their attachment to concepts of God with human shape, form, and emotions. There were noteworthy Hellenists among the monks of Nitria and of Kellia, but not among those of Scetis. Of the four presbyters presiding over the four monastic settlements of Scetis, PAPHNUTIUS alone, and with reluctance, accepted the condemnation of anthropomorphism by Patriarch THEOPHILUS (385–412) in his paschal letter of 399; the whole controversy probably caused little trouble in Scetis. When Theophilus turned against the Origenists, the monks of Scetis and their leaders found themselves automatically on the politically safe side of the controversy, whereas Nitria and Kellia lost some of their leading figures in the turmoil.

Scetis was raided by barbarians, with destruction of buildings and temporary dispersal of the monks, in 407, 434, and 444. When Egypt was divided ecclesiastically into Melchite and Monophysite parties in the aftermath of the Council of Chalcedon, the majority of the monks in Scetis sided with the Monophysite party, which quickly prevailed there. They managed to win the goodwill of Emperor Zeno, whose endowment of their monastic establishments assured their economic well-being for generations to come.

During the reign of Patriarch TIMOTHY III (517–535), monastic adherents of the "Aphthartodocetist" Christology of Julian of Halicarnassus began to gain power in the monasteries of Scetis. Those who held to the opposing doctrine of SEVERUS OF ANTIOCH were eventually dispossessed. There is good reason to see these dispossessed followers of Severus as the founders of four new monasteries, three of which are known to have been dedicated to the Virgin Mother of God, which came into being around this time as counterparts of the four existing monasteries. This division of the four communities probably took place after 535, the year in which the Monophysite church in Egypt was divided into a Severan or Theodosian faction led by Patriarch THEODOSIUS I (535–567, by right) and a Julianist or Gaianite faction led by GAIANUS, antipatriarch for a few months in 535.

Of the new monasteries, presumably founded by the dispossessed Theodosians, little is known of the history of the counterpart of Dayr Anbā Maqār other than that it was known as the Cell of the Forty-nine after the relics of the FORTY-NINE MARTYRS OF SCETIS were removed to it in the reign of Patriarch BENJAMIN I (622–661). The counterpart monasteries of the Virgin of Baramūs and of the Virgin of JOHN COLOBOS are known to have survived at least until the fourteenth and fifteenth centuries, respectively. Anbā Bishoi's counterpart monastery, originally called the monastery of the Virgin of Anbā Bishoi but known later as DAYR AL-SURYĀN, still exists. There were Gaianites at Scetis as late as 710, but it is not likely that the four original monasteries remained in their hands very long after the monastic communities were divided. If Dayr Anbā Maqār was once the residence of the Coptic patriarch (a fact first stated in texts of a much later period), and if this was the case shortly after the middle of the sixth century (Evelyn-White, Vol. 2, pp. 236–40), it would be difficult to reconcile this with Dayr Anbā Maqār's being in the control of the Gaianite party at that time. In any case, Scetis was again raided by barbarians toward the end of the sixth century, and for many years afterward few monks resided anywhere in Scetis.

As Egypt adjusted to the ARAB CONQUEST OF EGYPT, completed in 641, monastic life in Scetis rose again. The monasteries were little affected by the change from rule by the Chalcedonian Byzantines to rule by the Muslim Arabs, but they shared in the general rise of the non-Chalcedonian Coptic church to unfettered predominance in the Christian society of Egypt, which the political change had made possible. The monasteries also, from time to time, were in conflict with Muslim authorities over taxes to be paid by non-Muslim subjects, despite the exemption that could in principle be claimed by Christian monastic establishments. The first of these conflicts, lasting from 705 to 717, entailed physical violence to the monks and was aimed at the reduction of their numbers, if not their total extinction. Bishops and patriarchs were frequently chosen from the desert monasteries, a fact that brought to their gates many men whose vocation was motivated not so much by genuine monastic ideals as by interest in an ecclesiastical career, a condition noticed during a visit to Scetis made in 829/830 by the Jacobite patriarch of Antioch, DIONYSIUS I. He also observed that manual labor and psalmody, but not study, were still in evidence.

After further destruction of churches and cells by foreigners about 817, a general reconstruction began from which some architectural and decorative elements survive today. At the same time, a new monastery, that of JOHN KAMA, was organized, and the monastery of the Virgin of Anbā Bishoi had become a Syrian monastery. Experience had at last led the monks to fortify the walls surrounding the nuclei of their monasteries, a measure that provided them with far better protection from marauders than had the fortified towers on which they had previously relied. In the centuries that followed, monks began to abandon the scattered, isolated cells and to live within the compounds of the fortified nuclei, where the large medieval refectories show that the life was becoming somewhat more cenobitic. When the process was complete, perhaps by the fourteenth century, the monasteries had completely lost the appearance of primitive lauras, but that does not necessarily mean that the monastic life within their walls had become strongly cenobitic. Meanwhile, outside the fortified nuclei, by the seventh century the primitive clusters of detached cells in which monks lived either alone or with one or two close disciples tended to give way to a larger, more complex type of cell called a dwelling, which, to judge both from the texts and from examples uncovered in the French and Swiss excavations of Kellia, was a compact assemblage of individual living units with some common rooms, all arranged around a courtyard and surrounded by an unfortified wall. In the medieval period, most of these dwellings seem to have been dependent upon either the monastery of Anbā Maqār or that of John Colobos.

Numerically, the monastic establishment of the Wādī Habīb, as Scetis was called in medieval times, held up well until the end of the fourteenth century. By far the most important monastery was Dayr Anbā Maqār, whose patriarchal ceremonies, visits, and vicissitudes are almost the only monastic events in the Wādī Habīb that were chronicled in medieval narrative sources. Of the 712 monks in the Wādi Habīb counted by the historiographer MAWHŪB IBN MANṢŪR when he was there in 1088, 400 were of Dayr Anbā Maqār and 165 of the Monastery of John Colobos; in interpreting such statistics, however, one must reckon with the fact that those were the two monasteries to which the cells and dwellings still existing outside the fortified walls of the regular monasteries were then attached.

Copts were not the only inhabitants of the monastic houses. At one time or another in the medieval period each of the other non-Chalcedonian Oriental churches was represented by a monastic community in the Wādī Habīb. Dayr al-Suryān was occupied by Syrian monks until their gradual replacement by Copts in the sixteenth and seventeenth centuries. There was an Armenian community near the Monastery of John Colobos, but the dates of Armenian occupation are unknown. Unmentioned in the monastic listings of the fourteenth century (which are incomplete), that monastery was already in ruins when al-MAQRĪZĪ wrote his *History of the Copts* about 1440. There were Ethiopian monks in the Monastery of John Colobos and cells attached to it when Patriarch BENJAMIN II visited the Wādī in 1330. Pehōout, a large cell or dwelling with a church dedicated to Saint Elias, seems to have had Copts as its occupants in 1199, however, and if that is correct, it must have become Ethiopian after that date. Its occupants were Ethiopian in 1419, but when al-Maqrīzī wrote about twenty years later, it was abandoned and in ruins, the Ethiopians having moved to the Monastery of the Virgin of John Colobos. There have often been Ethiopians in the Wādī throughout its history as a monastic colony, even when they had no house to call their own.

By the time of al-Maqrīzī's account, the entire monastic population of the Wādī had declined, and many of the monastic buildings had fallen into ruinous condition. There were only a few monks in the great Monastery of Anbā Maqār when al-Maqrīzī wrote, only three in the Monastery of John Colobos, and in its counterpart Monastery of the Virgin of John Colobos, the Coptic community had been replaced by the Ethiopians who had abandoned Pehōout. Other dwellings and cells, and the Monastery of John Kama, were abandoned and in ruins. Among the reasons for this drastic decline, which set in after 1346, were surely the Black Death, which raged in Egypt in 1348 and 1349; the great famine of 1374, followed by a new pestilence; and the serious depreciation of the monasteries' endowments. By about 1493 the monastery of John Colobos was extinct. The Monastery of the Virgin of John Colobos, and all the communities of the outlying dwellings, ceased to exist in their turn. Close examination of the evidence makes it difficult to decide whether it is the original Monastery of Baramūs or its counterpart, the Monastery of the Virgin of Baramūs, that has survived as the present Dayr al-Baramūs. The only other monasteries to survive are the present Dayr Anbā Maqār, Dayr Anbā Bishoi, and Dayr al-Suryān.

By the end of the fifteenth century, candidates for the religious life arriving from Lebanon and Syria brought some new life to Dayr al-Suryān. Reconstruction of buildings in Dayr Anbā Maqār indicates some vitality there around 1517, but the reports of visitors in the seventeenth century indicate that the monastery, which for more than a millennium had been the greatest and the most influential of them all, was more dilapidated than any of the other three surviving monasteries in the Wādī. In 1712 only four monks were reported there, and only four in Dayr Anbā Bishoi, while Dayr al-Suryān and Dayr al-Baramūs each had twelve or fifteen. By the end of the eighteenth century numbers had risen slightly in all four of the monasteries, but during the nineteenth century they were still poor in human and economic resources. In more recent years these monasteries in the Wādī al-Naṭrūn have experienced a strong monastic and cultural renewal. The study of monastic and patristic texts has led to new vitality of monastic ideals and observance, first in Dayr al-Suryān particularly, and then in the other monasteries. Since 1969 Dayr Anbā Maqār has experienced rapid expansion. In 1976 the number of monks attached to each of the four monasteries was reported thus: Dayr Anbā Maqār, fifty-five; Dayr al-Baramūs, thirty-five; Dayr Anbā Bishoi, thirty-two; Dayr al-Suryān, forty (Meinardus, 1977, pp. 67–69). The majority of the monks live in the monastery to which they belong. Others reside in the dependent house that their monastery maintains in the cultivated land of the Delta, and still others work elsewhere for the church or live the strictly eremitical life.

BIBLIOGRAPHY

Cauwenbergh, P. van. *Etude sur les moines d'Egypte depuis le Concile de Chalcédoine (451) jusqu'à l'invasion arabe (640)*. Louvain, 1914.

Evelyn-White, H. G. *The Monasteries of the Wādi'n Natrûn*, Vols. 2 and 3. New York, 1932–1933.

Guy, J. C. "Le Centre monastique de Scété dans la littérature du Ve siècle." *Orientalia Christiana periodica* 30 (1964):129–47.

Meinardus, O. F. A. *Monks and Monasteries of the Egyptian Deserts*. Cairo, 1961.

———. "Recent Developments in Egyptian Monasticism 1960–1964." *Oriens Christianus* 49 (1965):79–89.

———. "Zur monastischen Erneuerung in der koptischen Kirche." *Oriens Christianus* 61 (1977):59–70.

Toussoun, O. *Etude sur le Wadi Natroun, ses moines et ses couvents*. Alexandria, 1931.

Wilson, R. McL., ed. *The Future of Coptic Studies*. Leiden, 1978.

AELRED CODY, O.S.B.

SCEVOPHILACION. *See* Architectural Elements of Churches: Pastophorium.

SCHÄFER, HEINRICH (1868–1957), German Egyptologist. He studied Egyptology under A. Erman (1887). He was appointed to a post in the Berlin Egyptian Museum, becoming director in 1907. He was also professor at Berlin University. From this time on, Schäfer was responsible for a great amount of reorganization and cataloging of this great collection. On his first visit to Egypt with Ulrich Wilcken, they found a papyrus at Ahnas. Schäfer assisted at the excavation of Niuserre's sun temple and with H. Junker's survey of Philae, collecting Nubian texts. On the philological side, he worked on texts of the Ethiopian period and those in the Berlin Museum and, with Junker, on texts in the Kenzi dialect. He also published the Coptic Cambyses story. His bibliography is a very large one, covering the fields of Egyptian art, archaeology, and philology.

BIBLIOGRAPHY

Dawson, W. R., and E. P. Uphill. *Who Was Who in Egyptology*, pp. 261–62. London, 1972.

Kammerer, W., comp. *A Coptic Bibliography*. Ann Arbor, Mich., 1950; repr. New York, 1969.

AZIZ S. ATIYA

SCHERMANN, THEODOR (1878–1922), German Catholic theologian. He studied the Coptic liturgy. Among his significant works are *Ägyptische Abendmahlsliturgien des ersten Jahrtausends in ihrer Überlieferung* (Paderborn, 1912); "Der Aufbau der ägyptischen Abendmahlsliturgien vom 6. Jahrhundert an" (*Katholik* 92, 1912, pp. 229–54, 325–54, 396–417); "Rubrizistische Vorschriften für die Kirche und Messe nach ägyptischen Quellen vom 3.–6. Jahrhundert" (*Theologie und Glaube* 4, 1912, pp. 817–30); "Der ägyptische Festkalender vom 2.–7. Jahrhundert" (*Theologie und Glaube* 5, 1913, pp. 89–102); and "Agapen in Ägypten und die Liturgie der vorgeheiligten Elemente" (*Theologie und Glaube* 5, 1913, pp. 177–87).

MARTIN KRAUSE

SCHILLER, A. ARTHUR (1902–1977), American specialist in Coptic law. He was appointed lecturer at Columbia University in 1929, assistant professor of law in 1930, associate professor of law in 1937, professor of law in 1949, and professor emeritus in 1971. He published Coptic documents and many outstanding contributions to Coptic law.

BIBLIOGRAPHY

Bagnall, R. S., and W. V. Harris, eds. *Studies in Roman Law in Memory of A. Arthur Schiller*. Leiden, 1986.

MARTIN KRAUSE

SCHMIDT, CARL (1868–1938), German Coptologist. He was born in Hagenow, Mecklenburg, and studied at the universities of Leipzig and Berlin (1887–1894). He became a privatdocent in Berlin (1899), honorary professor extraordinary (1909), honorary professor (1921), and professor ordinary (1928), retiring in 1935. He edited and published many important Coptic texts and in 1930 discovered the famous Manichaean papyri. He visited Egypt several times to obtain Coptic manuscripts. Some of his manuscripts went to Louvain and were edited by L. T. Lefort, but most of them were destroyed by enemy action during World War II. The rest were sold to the University of Michigan after his death (see Kammerer, 1950, 1969, pp. 196–97). A list of his important works is found in Kammerer.

BIBLIOGRAPHY

Dawson, W. R., and E. P. Uphill. *Who Was Who in Egyptology*, p. 264. London, 1972.

Kammerer, W., comp. *A Coptic Bibliography*. Ann Arbor, Mich., 1950; repr. New York, 1969.

AZIZ S. ATIYA

SCHOLTZ, CHRISTIAN (1697–1777), German clergyman and Coptologist. He was a preacher at the Prussian court and engaged in Coptic studies, influenced by P. E. Jablonski, his brother-in-law. From 1746 to 1751, Scholtz corresponded about Coptic studies with Jablonski, who gave him copies of Coptic manuscripts. In addition, Scholtz studied the Coptic manuscripts of the Berlin Library. He also owned a copy of La Croze's *Coptic Dictionary*. His edition of this dictionary was published in 1775 by his pupil C. G. Woide (Kammerer, 1950, 1969, no. 289), who also published in 1778 Scholtz's *Coptic Grammar*. (Kammerer, Nr. 451).

BIBLIOGRAPHY

Kammerer, W., comp. *A Coptic Bibliography*. Ann Arbor, Mich., 1950; repr. New York, 1969.

Quatremère, E. *Recherches critiques et historiques sur la langue et la littérature de l'Egypte*, pp. 94–103. Paris, 1808.

Siegfried, C. *Allgemeine deutsche Bibliographie*, Vol. 32, pp. 228–29. Berlin, 1881.

MARTIN KRAUSE

SCHOOLS, COPTIC. *See* Education.

SCHUBART, WILHELM (1873–1960), German papyrologist. He was a pupil of Ulrich Wilcken and worked from 1898 until 1937 at the Papyrusabteilung of the State Museum at Berlin. After his retirement from the museum, he was professor of ancient history at Leipzig University (1945–1952). Among his numerous publications (cf. Morenz, 1950, pp. 7–24) there are important books about Christian Egypt, including *Ägypten von Alexander dem Grossen bis auf Mohammed* (Berlin, 1922) and *Justinian und Theodora* (Munich, 1943), and many publications of Christian papyri, such as "Ein lateinisch-griechisch-koptisches Gesprächsbuch" (*Klio*, 13, 1913, pp. 27–38) and "Christliche Predigten aus Ägypten" (*Mitteilungen des archäologischen Instituts Kairo* 1, 1930, pp. 93–105). He published some texts with C. Schmidt (*Berliner Klassiker-Texte, Vol. 6, Altchristliche Texte*, Berlin, 1910; *Acta Pauli*, Glückstadt and Hamburg, 1936) and with H. Junker ("Ein griechisch-koptisches Kirchengebet," *Zeitschrift für ägyptische Sprache und Altertumskunde* 40, 1902, pp. 1–31).

BIBLIOGRAPHY

Morenz, S. "Wilhelm Schubart." *Zeitschrift für ägyptische Sprache und Altertumskunde* 86 (1961):i–ii.

______, ed. *Aus Antike und Orient: Festschrift Wilhelm Schubart zum 75. Geburtstag*. Leipzig, 1950.

MARTIN KRAUSE

SCHWARTZE, MORITZ GOTTHILF (1802–1848), German Coptologist. He earned his doctorate at Halle in 1829 with "De Jove Ammone et Osiride." In 1843 he published two works, the two-volume *Das alte Ägypten* and an edition of the Bohairic text of the Psalter (*Psalterium*).

In 1845 he was named professor extraordinary of Coptic language and literature at Berlin University. Of his planned edition of the Bohairic New Testament, only the four Gospels appeared in his lifetime (*Quattuor Evangelia*, 1846). The intended edition of Acts was instigated by Alexander von Humboldt and published by P. de Lagarde after Schwartze's death, using Schwartze's preliminary work.

From the Coptic manuscripts (biblical and Gnostic) transcribed by him in England, two works were posthumously published: *Pistis Sophia* (1851) and "Bruchstücke der oberägyptischen Übersetzung des alten Testaments" (*Nachrichten von der königlichen Gesellschaft der Wissenschaften*, Göttingen, 1880, no. 12, pp. 401–440). After his death there also appeared his *Koptische Grammatik* (ed. H. Steinthal, Berlin, 1850).

BIBLIOGRAPHY

Endesfelder, E. "Moritz Gotthilf Schwartze (1802–1848), erster Professor für koptische Sprache und Literatur an der Berliner Universität." In *Carl-Schmidt-Colloquiam an der Martin-Luther-Universität Halle-Wittenberg* 1988, ed. P. Nagel, pp. 105–117. Halle, 1990.

Harnack, A. *Geschichte der Königlich preussischen Akademie der Wissenschaften zu Berlin*, Vol. 1, pt. 2. Berlin, 1900.

Krause, M. "Die Disziplin Koptologie." In *The Future of Coptic Studies*, ed. R. M. Wilson. Leiden, 1978.
Siegfried, C. "Schwartze: Moritz Gotthilf S." *Allgemeine deutsche Biographie*, Vol. 33, pp. 215–16.

MARTIN KRAUSE

SCREEN. *See* Architectural Elements of Churches: Cancelli; Woodwork, Coptic.

SCRIPTORIUM, the room in which copyists transcribed manuscripts (later, also the writing school that developed around it). An archdeacon instructed the scribes, who carried out their work in the scriptorium. The alphabet was taught both in the business hand (cursive) and in the book script (uncial). On the evidence of literary reports (Athanasius *Apology to Constantius,* 4), there must have been a large scriptorium at Alexandria. Here, among other things, many Bibles were transcribed for Christian communities in Italy, by order of Emperor Constans. Although most of the manuscripts written in the scriptoria have not survived, the existence of scriptoria can be deduced from the colophons of extant manuscripts. On the evidence of surviving colophons, we know that scriptoria were especially numerous in the monasteries of Upper Egypt (Isnā, Thebes, Atrīb), in the Fayyūm, and in the monastery of Saint Anthony (DAYR ANBĀ ANṬŪNIYŪS). In the monasteries of the Wādī al-Naṭrūn manuscripts were copied in the library or in the great hall of the keep (Evelyn-White, 1926, Vol. 1, p. xlv).

[*See also:* Libraries.]

BIBLIOGRAPHY

Crum, W. E. *Catalogue of the Coptic Manuscripts in the British Museum.* London, 1905.
Crum, W. E., and H. E. Winlock. *The Monastery of Epiphanius at Thebes,* Vol. 1. New York, 1926.
Evelyn-White, H. G. *The Monasteries of the Wadi 'n Naṭrūn,* Vol. 1, *New Coptic Texts from the Monastery of Saint Macarius.* New York, 1926.

MARTIN KRAUSE

SCRIPTURE, CANON OF THE. There are two basic uses of the word "canon." The one refers to the shape of a limited body of literature held sacred by a believing community. The other refers to the function in such a community of texts and traditions held sacred by it. Traditional terms used to designate these distinct uses are *norma normata,* in reference to a limited and authoritative list of sacred books, and *norma normans* in reference to literature and/or traditions that function authoritatively in the community, which finds in them its identity and indications for its lifestyle. But the terms "shape" and "function" are broader and include pre- and protocanonical literary and historical factors as well as factors resulting from the eventual stabilization of text and canon.

Some (though not all) of the great religions of the world are scriptured, such as Judaism, the Samaritan religion, Christianity, Islam, Confucianism, Taoism, Buddhism, Hinduism, and Zoroastrianism. When one speaks of a canon of sacred literature, one must relate it to a community of faith (Sanders, 1984a). In antiquity there were differing canons within Judaism and Christianity, and to a lesser extent the situation persists. The Sadducees, like the Samaritans, accepted only the Pentateuch as canon, and the extent of the canon of the Jewish sect at Qumrān is not certain. The word "canon" is used by J. Neusner to refer to the rabbinic corpus in addition to the Jewish Bible or even instead of the Bible (Neusner, 1987, pp. 43–51).

Within Christianity the so-called Apocrypha were included in printed editions of the Bible until the late nineteenth century when some Protestant groups began to omit them; the Roman Catholic Bible has always included them as deuterocanonical. The Orthodox churches sometimes include more than the Apocrypha. The Ethiopian Orthodox Church has eighty-one books in its canon. The Church of Jesus Christ of Latter-day Saints is perhaps the latest to claim the Christian canon to be open-ended (Davies, 1986). The discovery at Nag Hammadi of documents dating from the second and following centuries has brought the number of known noncanonical gospels to about twenty-five. This has raised the issue in scholarly discussion of whether there should be a clear distinction between canonical and noncanonical.

The word "canon" is derived from the Greek *kanon,* which itself came from a Semitic root (Hebrew *qaneh,* Assyrian *qan u,* [Sumerian-] Akkadian *qin,* Ugaritic *gn*). The original meaning was "reed," as in the English "cannon," something firm and straight. It came to designate a stick used for drawing a straight line or for measuring, such as a "ruler." Metaphoric uses included meanings like "model," "standard" (Phil. 3:16 in some manuscripts), "limit" (2 Cor. 10:13) or "paradigm." ATHA-

NASIUS was the first (367) clearly known to use the word to designate the twenty-seven books of the New Testament: "Let no one add to these; let nothing be taken away from them."

Jews did not apparently use the word until after the Enlightenment. The canon of the early churches was the so-called Old Testament, or what was included in the term "Scripture" (e.g., Jn. 2:22 and Acts 8:32) or "the Scriptures" (Mk. 12:24; 1 Cor. 15:3–4) at that time. Other terms were "Holy Scriptures," "the writings," "the sacred scriptures," "the Law and the Prophets," "the Law and the Prophets and other writings," or ". . . and Psalms" as in Luke 24:44. In Judaism, other terms used were "holy books," "reading," "holy writings," "that which is written," and "those [books] that soil the hands." The most precise term used in Judaism for the tripartite Jewish canon is TaNaK—an acrostic designating *Torah, Neb i im* (Prophets), and *Ket ub im* (Hagiographa, or Writings)—but it is not certain when the term began to be used, perhaps not until Talmudic times.

Rabbinic disputes between the fall of Jerusalem in A.D. 70 and the Second Jewish Revolt in 132 indicate that five books in the Jewish canon were focuses of debate about whether they soiled the hands: Ezekiel, Proverbs, the Song of Songs, Ecclesiastes, and Esther. There is disagreement as to whether these were in doubt (the majority view) or whether questions about them were raised only in academic debate. There is, however, general agreement that the gathering of rabbis (c. 90) at the Palestinian coastal town of Yabneh (Jamnia) did not constitute an official canonizing council. This is largely taken to mean that the canonical process was the result of sociopolitical factors and community needs over a period of time and that such gatherings only ratified what had already happened in the communities in the historical process. A few take it to mean that canonization had already taken place by the end of the second century B.C., either de facto or de jure.

The Jewish Bible, or canon, was stabilized in stages beginning with the Torah, or Pentateuch, which was edited in the large Babylonian Jewish community in the sixth and fifth centuries B.C. and brought to Jerusalem in the middle of the fifth by Ezra (Neh. 8). The Early Prophets, the section including Joshua, Judges, the two Samuels, and the two Kings, was accepted about the same time, the salient observation being that a firm distinction was made in the story that runs from Genesis through 2 Kings between Torah (Pentateuch) and Early Prophets (Joshua to Kings). The text of the Early Prophets was not stabilized until later. The Later Prophets, the section including the three Major Prophets (Isaiah, Jeremiah, and Ezekiel) and the twelve Minor Prophets (Hosea to Malachi) was probably also set in its basic present contours about the same time, but the stabilization of the order of the various books of the Later Prophets and of their texts came considerably later. While the texts were stabilized in surviving Pharisaic-rabbinic Judaism soon after the fall of Jerusalem toward the end of the first century A.D., the order has varied down through the centuries to a limited extent.

The third section, called the Hagiographa, or the Writings, also was not stabilized for all Judaism until the Pharisaic-rabbinic denomination prevailed as the Judaism that continues until today. Some scholars hold that this section was stabilized or canonized by the end of the second century B.C., and others, that it did not attain such stability until early in the second century A.D. Those that hold the former position see the Jewish library at Qumrān and the Septuagint as benign aberrations of a canon already officially set. Those that hold the latter position deny clarity of evidence in such extrabiblical witnesses as Sirach, 2 Maccabees, Philo, and the New Testament for a pre-Christian closing of the Writings. Rather, they emphasize the value of the actual extant manuscripts from Qumrān and the evidence of the Septuagint as clearer witnesses to the more traditional view that the Hagiographa was closed by the end of the first century A.D. (the twenty-four books mentioned in 4 Esd. 14:44–46; cf. Josephus *Against Apion* 1.37–43) for surviving Judaism but remained open for Christianity for some time to come.

While Athanasius, bishop of Alexandria, was very clear about the canon of twenty-seven New Testament books to which none should be added or subtracted, the rest of the church in the East was not so clear. No fewer than six different lists of the contents of the two testaments were officially received in the Greek church in the tenth century. The Coptic church, like others in the East, has included two epistles of Clement. The Ethiopian Orthodox Church has thirty-five books in its New Testament. The testimony of actual extant manuscripts of the Greek New Testament is telling. While there are some 2,328 manuscripts of the Gospels, there are only 287 of the Book of Revelation. Only three uncials and fifty-six minuscules contain the whole of the New Testament. "It is obvious that the conception of the canon of the New Testament was not essentially a dogmatic issue whereby all parts of the text were regarded as equally necessary" (Metzger, 1987).

While the church in the West sought greater uniformity by sanction of high authority, it, too, has an interesting history in terms of closure of the canon of the New Testament. Augustine was very clear in his *De doctrina christiana* (completed 426) that there were twenty-seven books in the New Testament. While he questioned Pauline authorship of the Epistle to the Hebrews, he nonetheless accepted its canonicity. Augustine cast his considerable weight behind church synods held in the fourth and fifth centuries to limit the New Testament canon to the twenty-seven books (Metzger, 1987). But it was not until the Council of FLORENCE in 1439–1443 that the Roman church issued a categorical opinion on the issue of canon.

Luther had considerable trouble with Hebrews, James, Jude, and Revelation, and Lutherans generally thereafter had questions about them, sometimes creating a tripartite New Testament: the Gospels and Acts, Epistles of Holy Apostles, and the Aprocryphal New Testament. Calvin would not accept Roman authority as valid for determining the canon but rather the interior witness of the Holy Spirit. He denied Pauline authorship of Hebrews and questioned Petrine authorship of 2 Peter, though he accepted them as canonical. He failed to write commentaries on 2 and 3 John and Revelation, though he occasionally quoted them as he did non-Masoretic books of the Old Testament.

It was not until 1546 at the Council of Trent, prompted by such opinions of the reformers and of some in the Roman Catholic church itself, that the church issued an absolute article of faith (*De Canonicis Scripturis*), sealed by anathema, concerning the canon of the Christian Bible, Old and New Testaments. Reformed confessions of the end of the sixteenth and beginning of the seventeenth centuries list the twenty-seven books of the New Testament; and the sixth of the Thirty-nine Articles of the Church of England, issued in 1563, lists the books of the Old Testament and concludes that the books of the New Testament commonly received are canonical. None of the Lutheran confessional statements includes such lists.

The concept of the shape of a canon also includes the observation that a canon of scripture is a compressed literature written by many different authors over a long period of time. It has been rightly observed that in contrast to the Qur'ān, the Bible is made up of human responses to divine revelations rather than being a record of divine revelation to one person. Canon in this sense creates a context in which to read the parts. Each literary unit may be read in its original historical context by means of historical, formal, and redactional criticism, but it may also be read in the light of the whole. If the New Testament, for instance, is read only in the synchronic context of the Hellenistic-Roman period, it is in effect decanonized. For Christians, the same is true of the Old Testament. To read the Old and New Testaments canonically is to read them in the light of the theocentric-monotheizing hermeneutics of their canonical context.

The community of faith that adheres to a canon finds in it the community's ongoing identity in the ever-changing situations and ambiguity of reality and finds in it clues for its lifestyle and obedience. There is an ongoing dialogue between the community and its canon. A compressed canon includes both pluralism between its parts and multivalency within the richness of its literary units. This constitutes what may be called the canon's built-in self-corrective, or prophetic, apparatus. "What is written in Torah and how do you read it?" Jesus asked an interlocutor (Lk. 10:26). Both the choice of text and the hermeneutics by which it then is read in the new historical context and in which it is repeated or reread are important.

Three factors in community dialogue with scripture as *norma normans* must always be kept in mind: the text read; the sociopolitical contexts from which it arose and in which it is reread; and the hermeneutics by which it is reread. Authoritative oral traditions functioned in this way in ancient Israel and Judah and in the early church well before they were written down; and they were written well before they became scripture or canon. Study of how they functioned on their route to becoming canon as *norma normata* is the study of canonical hermeneutics.

Such study has shown that the "mid term" (Sanders, 1987, pp. 9–39) between a canon's stability as canon (shape) and its adaptability as canon (function) is theocentric-monotheizing hermeneutics. The God that emerges from the canon as a whole is a compressed concept made up of many different views of God along the path of formation of canon. God is made up of high gods and local deities, tutelary gods and personal gods, national and international gods, male and female deities. God is, however, One God: creator, sustainer-nurturer, judge, and redeemer. The surviving names of these gods in the compressed text become epithets or occasional names. There is a tradition that God has seventy names, but God is above all One, the integrity of Reality. Ancient Israel and the early church learned from others of God's creatures and from international wisdom, and adapted what they learned into its monotheizing mode. The Bible is a record of many struggles against the polytheisms of the five culture eras and many idioms and mores through which it passed in its formation. It is a paradigm for how believing communities may go and do likewise, in order to pursue and affirm the integrity of Reality and thus become integrated themselves into that Reality, which is the One God of All.

It has been recognized that "inspired" and "canonical" are not synonymous terms. Whether inspired noncanonical literature can be called scripture is disputed. In any case, the concept of inspiration is a broader one than that of canon. Taking a clue from Augustine, Luther, and Calvin, one should broaden the traditional concept of inspiration of individual authors to include the work of God or God's Holy Spirit all along the path of formation of the canon. The new concept would be inclusive in several senses: it would include the work of editors, redactors, and scribes; it would include the pseudepigraphic writings that pervade both testaments; it would include recognition of Israel's, Judaism's, and the early church's learning from international wisdom. It would provide a way for present-day believing communities to work toward an understanding of their canons as paradigms wrought over many ancient centuries and thus of how to continue to benefit from those canons.

BIBLIOGRAPHY

Aicher, G. *Das Alte Testament in der Mischna*. Freiburg im Breisgau, 1906.

Aland, K., and B. Aland. *The Text of the New Testament*, trans. E. Rhodes. Grand Rapids, Mich., and Leiden, 1987.

Barr, J. *The Bible and the Modern World*. San Francisco, 1973.

Barthelemy, D. "L'Etat de la Bible juive depuis le début de notre ère jusqu'à la deuxième révolte contre Rome (131–135)." In *Le Canon de L'Ancien Testament: Sa formation et son histoire*, ed. J.-D. Kaestli and O. Wermelinger, pp. 9–45. Geneva, 1984.

Beckwith, R. *The Old Testament Canon of the New Testament Church and Its Background in Early Judaism*. Grand Rapids, Mich., 1985.

Brown, R. E. "The Gospel of Peter and Canonical Gospel Priority." *New Testament Studies* 33 (1987):321–43.

Buhl, F. *Canon and Text of the Old Testament*, trans. J. Macpherson. Edinburgh, 1982.

Childs, B. *Introduction to the Old Testament as Scripture*. Philadelphia, 1979.

Cowley, R. W. "The Biblical Canon of the Ethiopian Orthodox Church Today." *Ostkirchliche Studien* 23 (1974):318–23.

Crossan, J. D. *Four Other Gospels: Shadows on the Contours of the Canon*. Philadelphia, 1985.

Davies, W. D. "Reflections on the Mormon Canon." *Harvard Theological Review* 79 (1986):44–66.

Freedman, D. N. "Canon of the Old Testament." In *Interpreters Dictionary of the Bible* Supplement (1976):130–36.

Gottwald, N. "Social Matrix and Canonical Shape." *Theology Today* 42 (1985):307–321.

Jepsen, A. "Zur Kanonsgeschichte des Alten Testaments." *Zeitschrift für die alttestamentliche Wissenschaft* 71 (1959):114–36.

Kaestli, J.-D. "Le Récit de IV Esdras 14 et sa valeur pour l'histoire du canon de l'Ancien Testament." In *Le Canon de l'Ancien Testament: Sa formation et son histoire*, ed. J.-D. Kaestli and O. Wermelinger. Geneva, 1984.

Kealy, S. P. "The Canon: An African Contribution." *Biblical Theological Review* 9 (1979):13–26.

Koester, H. "Apocryphal and Canonical Gospels." *Harvard Theological Review* 73 (1980):105–130.

Leiman, S. *The Canonization of Hebrew Scripture: The Talmudic and Midrashic Evidence*. Hamden, Conn., 1976.

Lewis, J. P. "What Do We Mean by Jabneh?" *Journal of Bible and Religion* 32 (1964):125–32.

Metzger, B. *The Canon of the New Testament: Its Origin, Development and Significance*. Oxford, 1987.

Neusner, J. *The Oral Torah: The Sacred Books of Judaism—An Introduction*. San Francisco, 1986.

———. *What Is Midrash?* Philadelphia, 1987.

Ostborn, F. *Cult and Canon: A Study in the Canonization of the Old Testament*. Uppsala, 1950.

Pfeiffer, R. "Canon of the Old Testament." In *Interpreters Dictionary of the Bible* 1 (1962):498–520.

Pokorny, P. "Das theologische Problem der neutestamentlichen Pseudepigraphie." *Evangelische Theologie* 44 (1984):486–96.

Robinson, J., and H. Koester. *Trajectories Through Early Christianity*. Philadelphia, 1971.

Sanders, J. A. "Cave 11 Surprises and the Question of Canon." *McCormick Quarterly* 21 (1968):284–98.

———. *Torah and Canon*. Philadelphia, 1972.

———. *Canon and Community: A Guide to Canonical Criticism*. Philadelphia, 1984a.

———. "Canonical Criticism: An Introduction." In *Le Canon de l'Ancien Testament: Sa formation et son histoire*, ed. J.-D. Kaestli and O. Wermelinger, pp. 341–62. Geneva, 1984b.

———. *From Sacred Story to Sacred Text: Canon as Paradigm*. Philadelphia, 1987.

Sandmel, S. "On Canon." *Catholic Biblical Quarterly* 28 (1966):207.
Sundberg, A. *The Old Testament of the Early Church.* Harvard Theological Studies 20. Cambridge, Mass., 1964.
———. "Canon of the New Testament." *Interpreters Dictionary of the Bible* Supplement (1976):136–40.
Talmon, S. "Heiliges Schrifttum und kanonische Bücher aus jüdischer Sicht—Überlegungen zur Ausbildung der Grösse 'Die Schrift' im Judentum." In *Die Mitte der Schrift,* ed. M. Klopfenstein et al., pp. 45–79. Bern and New York, 1987.
Tov, E. "Hebrew Biblical Manuscripts from the Judaean Desert: Their Contribution to Textual Criticism." *Journal of Jewish Studies* 39 (1988):5–37.
Westcott, B. F. *The Bible in the Church.* London, 1864; repr., 1980.
Yeivin, I. *Introduction to the Tiberian Masorah,* trans. and ed. E. J. Revell. Atlanta, 1980.

JAMES A. SANDERS

SCULPTURE. *See* Ceramics, Coptic: Terra-cotta Figurines; Metalwork, Coptic; Sculpture in Stone, Coptic; Statuary; Woodwork, Coptic.

SCULPTURE IN STONE, COPTIC, figures in the round and especially architectural ornament carved in stone and stucco in Egypt from the fourth to the seventh century.

State of Research

In comparison with studies on the sculpture of the late classical and early Byzantine periods in other Roman provinces (e.g., Italy, the Balkans, Greece, Asia Minor, Syria), assessments of Coptic sculpture in Egypt are still remarkably controversial; the technical literature presents an extremely confused picture. This state of affairs is due chiefly to the effect of mistakes in earlier research.

In many old excavations yielding the best-known complexes of sculpture, such as those at Ahnās, Bahnasā, Bāwīṭ and Saqqara, faulty evaluations of the architecture have led to misunderstanding of the sculpture. Thus, for example, the sepulchral character of certain buildings and their stone decoration was not recognized, and the complexes were wrongly interpreted as Christian ecclesiastical constructions (e.g., in E. Naville's excavation at Ahnās; in J. E. Quibell's excavation at Saqqara, particularly in mausoleum no. 1823; in E. Breccia's excavation at al-Bahnasā). Furthermore, numerous sculptures produced for pagan clients, especially the mythical representations in tomb decorations at Ahnās and al-Bahnasā, were claimed as Christian works, with the result that a screen of sham problems has blocked further inquiry. Finally, too little allowance has been made for the time-honored practice, especially in Egypt, of reusing older buildings or parts of buildings as well as their decorative elements for other structures of identical, similar, or even different functions. Hence, many buildings with architectural decoration, especially churches, were wrongly regarded as homogeneous (e.g., the south and north churches at Bāwīṭ, the main church at Saqqara, the transept basilica at al-Ashmūnayn). Older, reused pieces led to a too early dating of the buildings, as in the main church of Dayr Apa Jeremiah, Saqqara, and the Great Basilica of Abū Mīnā. Thus research has been seriously impeded through ideas of alleged Christian and alleged ecclesiastical decoration, not to mention alleged fixed points of dating.

Since sculptures of Egyptian provenance acquired through the art trade are almost without exception provided with false statements on the place of discovery, any connection with the original location is destroyed; any clues as to the topography, genre, and chronology as well as the iconographic and formal context are suppressed. These uncertain circumstances generate mystification and make it easy for the forgers to dispose of their goods. The field of figurative sculpture in particular has been grievously confused by the large number of modern or counterfeit works purported to be authentic. Particularly noteworthy in this regard are the reliefs allegedly deriving from Shaykh Abādah, which since the early 1960s have been thrown on the market on a huge scale and have given rise to a wave of illusory problems on the question of "pagan or Christian." The authentic models, that is, the pagan tomb reliefs, come from Bahnasā. The information on the old excavations may be meager or ambiguous. In any case, it is wise to base judgments on the old discoveries of sculpture of assured provenance.

The most significant collections of sculptures are located in the Coptic Museum, Cairo; the Greco-Roman Museum, Alexandria; the Louvre in Paris (particularly from Dayr Apa Apollo, Bāwīṭ); and the State Museum of Berlin (cf. Wulff, 1909, pp. 24–47, 65–78, 309–15; Effenberger, 1976).

The stock of sculptures on archaeological sites and in the late classical and early Christian buildings still extant in Egypt has thus far received attention and been documented only in particular cases.

Some of the papers dealing with the stone sculpture of this period give little or no attention to the output of Alexandria or dependent workshops, or indeed to marble sculpture generally. This self-restriction entails a penalty. Decisive factors in the repertoire of form and type and in development are overlooked; clues for dating and the opportunity for synthesis are missed. It is not only important to establish when, where, and to what extent marble sculpture was extant, known, or representative. For the complete picture, it is also instructive to know what types and forms of marble sculpture were not adopted further inland.

Materials

The materials of sculptured works in Egypt in the late classical and early Byzantine period were porphyry, granite, marble, limestone, sandstone, and stucco. In the Middle Ages, the materials were limestone, sandstone, and stucco.

Porphyry. The indigenous porphyry from Mons Porpyrites was worked in special workshops, probably located in Alexandria; it appears to have been exported in the third to the fifth centuries in the form of finished products essentially for imperial requirements. Imperial burials in porphyry sarcophagi came to an end with Marcian about 450, but production could have continued in other types of products. The latest surviving imperial portrait in porphyry is a sixth-century head probably of JUSTINIAN in the Church of Saint Mark, Venice. Whether the great porphyry column shafts in the conchs of the sixth-century Hagia Sophia in Istanbul were expressly prepared for this building is uncertain.

Granite. Granite appears to have been scarcely worked into building elements at all after the fourth century. Most of the granite components in late classical and early Byzantine building in Egypt, may be instances of reused materials from the ancient Egyptian, Ptolemaic, and imperial Roman periods.

Marble. Marble, which was much sought after, was not found in Egypt (apart from a very inferior kind) and had to be imported by sea. This means of transport was considerably cheaper than land transport. Nonetheless, the immense quantity of marble material brought to Egypt is astonishing. Late classical and early Byzantine marble artifacts are today to be found primarily in Alexandria, at Abū Mīnā, and in the Coptic Museum in Cairo. However, many hundreds of marble pedestals and bases, column shafts, and capitals were reused in Islamic buildings, especially of the Fatimid and Mamluk periods. This occurred particularly in Cairo but also in Middle Egypt. The marble must also have been taken from buildings of the fourth to sixth centuries.

This rich store allows us to conclude that the kind of marble used was, as a rule, Proconnesian marble, from the island of Proconnesos in the Sea of Marmara near Constantinople. Securely datable artifacts of the third century, especially capitals, are extremely rare, and assured works of the sixth century, such as impost capitals, are attested only in small numbers. The great mass of the marble artifacts in Egypt comes from the fourth and fifth centuries. The conclusion is natural that the extensive importation of marble was connected with the newly founded eastern Roman capital of Constantinople. It is an attractive conjecture, but as yet unattested in terms of sources, that here the Egyptian grain fleet played an essential role. It had to deliver large consignments of grain annually to Constantinople, and it could have loaded marble among other things as ballast and cargo for the return journey. Expensive finished imports from Constantinople seem to have been relatively scarce but can be attested at least up to the second quarter of the sixth century. Essentially, the rough-cut forms imported were probably fashioned or decorated in Alexandria and from there marketed in the country. The Corinthian marble capitals with a central, wreathed cross on the abacus are quite certainly local works that are found neither in Constantinople nor in other provinces. Whether there were qualified marble workshops outside Alexandria in the fourth to sixth centuries is not known.

Limestone. The cheap, common, and easily worked stone in the interior was limestone and, in Upper Egypt, sandstone. It was in these types of stone that the extensive local stone sculpture production of Egypt, commonly described as Coptic sculpture, was wrought.

Stucco. Large capitals ornamented in stucco—such as, for example, the imperial exemplars in Tūnah al-Jabal—appear to have been rare in late antiquity (for example, various types on the church of Akhbariyyah and a beautiful single piece in the church of the Dayr al-Baramūs, Wādī al-Naṭrūn). Stucco was also used for the keystones in cupolas and conchs and for the detailed decoration of the plain surfaces of limestone works (such as the cornice fragment in the transept basilica, at al-Ashmūnayn). The attempt in the Tulunid period to introduce the stucco style, originating in Samarra, into the wall decoration of a church such as that of Dayr al-Suryān, Wādī al-Naṭrūn, appears rather restrained and in its general effect unassuming.

Basket capital with cross from al-Fusṭāṭ. *Courtesy Aziz S. Atiya collection.*

Forms

Freestanding figures, chiefly portrait statues and busts of emperors and officials, were made in porphyry down to the sixth century. There may have been some extremely rare examples in marble or local stone, for example, a portrait in the State Museum of Berlin, probably of a pagan priest from the Roman period. Recumbent lions in the round were not intended as freestanding objects but to guard doorways. Some furniture, such as decorative stands for water jars and table supports with figured decoration were made of marble. The largest category of sculpture was architectural: door jambs, lunettes, door lintels, gables for niches, cornices and friezes, pedestals and bases, columns and pilasters, capitals, latticework screens and windows, and posts. Most tomb reliefs were for architectural decoration. Most of this architectural work was in marble or local stone, but imperial buildings had decorations in porphyry.

Characteristics and Influences

Porphyry. A special if not unique status was accorded to the imperial likenesses in porphyry. They appear to be provincial productions, in that they modified the formal complexity characteristic of works made in major centers. The shape and content of the original models were reproduced in a simplified form, heightening the expression of individual elements. As the dissemination of these Egyptian works over wide areas of the Roman empire shows, they were officially accepted by the emperors and were considered appropriate for conveying clearly the desired message, that is, the soldierly qualities and the harmoniousness of the emperors, to people who would be unresponsive to the traditional images. From the historical and aesthetic point of view, this was a step that had implications reaching beyond the ancient world: the use of portraits of unmistakably provincial character as vehicles of imperial propaganda, probably directed especially to the lower classes of the empire. In the period from Constantine to Justinian, when other images and ideas were created, porphyry portraits seem to have been preferred but were brought into line with the style of work produced at the imperial court. Provincial simplification and exaggeration were evidently no longer in demand for imperial likenesses, but the polished sheen of the expensive stone symbolized austerity and detachment.

The huge porphyry sarcophagi delivered to Rome and Constantinople, undoubtedly special commissions, show no specifically Egyptian characteristics in the overall design of their decoration, which after the mid-fourth century was nonfigurative, ex-

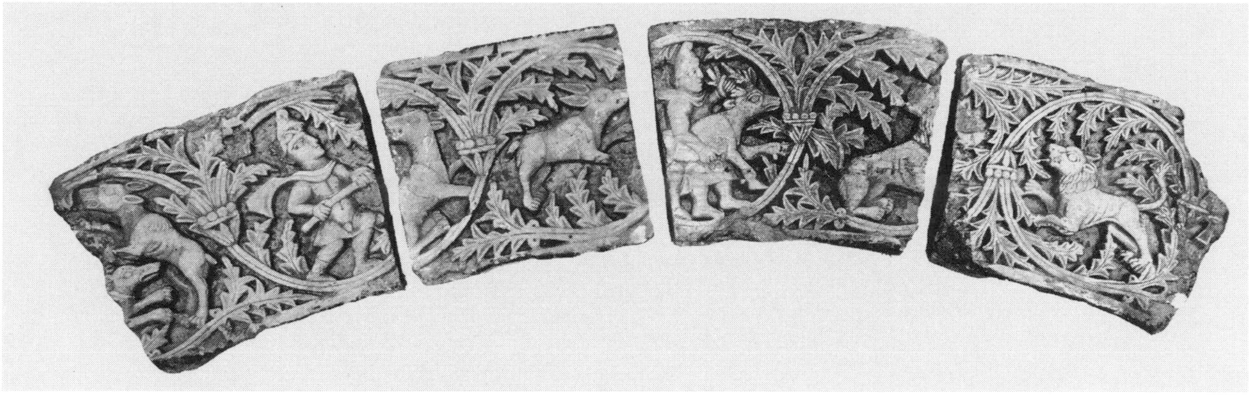

Sculptured lintel. Provenance unknown. Seventh–eighth centuries. *Courtesy Coptic Museum, Cairo.*

cept occasionally for an Egyptian motif such as the ankh. The gigantic block of porphyry used for a sarcophagus was enough to convince everyone that the province of Egypt was at the service of the emperor.

Marble. Sculpture in marble, in keeping with the origin of the stone, was subject to continual foreign influence. Its forms and motifs were based on prototypes produced in the eastern Roman empire, especially Constantinople. This association was so close, as, for example, in the case of column capitals, that pieces from imported, rough-cut marble clearly made in Egypt, probably in Alexandria, as a rule betray Egyptian workmanship not by their type and form but only through some iconographical detail, or occasionally through a lower level of quality. The marble pilaster capitals, however, were less closely connected with eastern models and reveal rather local forms and motifs. As a rule, these pieces must have been prepared for special architectural positions, were therefore less often brought into the country as finished imports, and may thus have offered a better starting point for local taste and local traditional forms than did the standardized column capitals.

Limestone and Sandstone. In sculpture in local limestone and sandstone, direct eastern Roman influences are rare and limited in time and place. Also, there were scarcely any direct connections with the Alexandrian sculpture in marble. On the one hand, fashionable models of the type produced in Constantinople could be completely absent in limestone or sandstone sculpture for generations, as, for example, in the second half of the fifth century the basic motif of the fine-toothed acanthus with its corresponding types and motifs. On the other hand, correct copies, or imitations of them, in local stone are evidence that a specific choice of eastern Roman models could have been standard practice. If the criteria for this choice could be determined, important insights would be gained. In the first half of the sixth century, the most current models from Constantinople were accepted, primarily the impost capital in the special form of the impost capital of the fold type, as well as ornamental and figurative configurations with typical relief techniques. These influences, however, appear to have remained so much locally restricted (particularly at Bāwīṭ, Saqqara, and the Fayyūm) that one might wonder whether this limited selection of Constantinople models was determined by the personal needs and tastes of a particular class of client.

The rich treasury of motifs in sculpture in local limestone and sandstone drew on imperial models from the eastern Mediterranean and often continued local traditional motifs for centuries. The character of this production is late antique and provincial, with easily recognizable peculiarities that are clearly contrasted with non-Egyptian sculpture. Especially typical are "broken" gables over niches, cornices and friezes with scrolls and leaf-work, cornices with console friezes and coffer fillings, Corinthian capitals decorated in fantastic detail, and tomb reliefs with diversified architectural motifs.

The individuality of the local Egyptian sculpture of the late classical and early Byzantine period has always been recognized by the specialists but very differently interpreted. Extreme views that seek to trace the stock of models and style directly to the pharaonic heritage, with no consideration of the cultural environment of the Byzantine empire from the third to the sixth centuries, have miscarried just as much as views that the individuality reflects an

Triumphal cross flanked by two angels. Frieze above decorated with plants and animals. *Courtesy Coptic Museum, Cairo.*

artistic aspiration of nationalist Egypt, which developed in opposition to the culture of the Greek ruling class or to the government and church of the Byzantine empire.

A sober view that takes into account the historical and archaeological facts, social conditions, and the strong survival of paganism will stress the following facts.

High expenditure for tomb construction and decoration was an age-old tradition for property owners in Egypt. The information so far available shows that a very large part of the late classical sculptural complexes known to us, Ahnās, Bahnasā, and Saqqara, was fashioned for tomb constructions. A considerable number belonged to pagan clients. Thus the iconography of the much-cited gables over niches, decorated with Leda and the Swan, Aphrodite, Daphne, Dionysus, fauns and maenads, and Nereids and sea creatures, matches admirably with the themes of pagan imperial sepulchral art from other regions such as in Rome (Torp, 1969, pp. 106–112). The same workshops built and decorated mausoleums for Christian clients; Christian and pagan tombs adjoined one another in the necropolis. The decoration of their tombs was both publicly representational and privately symbolic.

Late classical Egyptian tomb architecture and decoration scarcely corresponded to any mortuary work in other regions. It was highly prized and was produced in local stonemason's workshops, which can be called necropolis workshops. This connection of the local workshops with tomb architecture explains clearly the limited range of essential types, the concomitant display of splendor, the independence from foreign models, and finally the traditionalism and a certain introversion in Egyptian sculpture. When the completely novel task of church decoration presented itself, people evidently turned to the practiced local necropolis workshops.

Local styles can indeed be detected, but more cosmopolitan stylistic movements were also present. Thus, about the middle of the fifth century, types and forms of similar character are attested in the decoration of the tomb constructions of al-

Bahnasā and the church of Dayr Anbā Shinūdah, Suhāj. At the end of the fifth century and in the first half of the sixth, corresponding types and forms are present at Dayr Apa Jeremiah and Dayr Apa Apollo.

Building decoration in the ancient sense came to an end at latest with the Arab conquest in the seventh century. Even before that, the reusing of older pieces was everywhere becoming the order of the day. Thereafter, if there was any work that was fashioned and decorated to order, it belonged almost exclusively to the realm of tomb reliefs.

Problems of Dating and Fixed Points

There is no evidence to date precisely the figurative reliefs and architectural decoration from the period before the Arab conquest. For particular types of capitals the eastern Roman prototypes provide criteria for dating. The chronology of architectural sculpture in marble, especially of the fourth century, is still uncertain. From this period an extraordinary amount of material has survived in Egypt, although not in its original architectural context but reused in Christian and Islamic buildings. In Constantinople, conversely, capitals of the fourth century have survived only in relatively small numbers, and there are no firmly dated buildings before the end of the century.

The chronology and development of local sculpture in limestone and sandstone still cannot be outlined with certainty. It therefore seems useful to adduce here three complexes of architectural decoration that can be dated with confidence within the fifth century: (1) from the first half of the century, the relatively few pieces originally fashioned for the transept basilica in al-Ashmūnayn, (2) from the middle of the century, the remains of the pieces originally fashioned for the church Dayr Anbā Shinūdah; and (3) from the second half of the century, the uniquely preserved decoration in the triconch of the church of Dayr Anbā Bishoi, Suhāj.

BIBLIOGRAPHY

Beckwith, J. *Coptic Sculpture 300–1300*. London, 1963.

Bourguet, P. du. *Die Kopten*. Baden-Baden, 1967.

Crum, W. E. *Coptic Monuments*. Catalogue général des antiquités égyptiennes du Musée du Caire, Nos. 8001–8741. Cairo, 1902.

Duthuit, G. *La Sculpture copte*. Paris, 1931.

Effenberger, A. *Koptische Kunst. Ägypten in spätantiker, byzantinischer und frühislamischer Zeit*. Vienna, 1976.

______. "Scultura e arte minore copta." *Felix Ravenna* 1 and 2, 4th ser. (1981):65–102, 121–22.

Kitzinger, E. "Notes on Early Coptic Sculpture." *Archaeologia* 87 (1938):181–215.

Parlasca, K. "Der Übergang von spätrömischen zur frühkoptischen Kunst im Lichte der Grabreliefs von Oxyrhynchos." *Enchoria* (Sonderband) 8 (1978):115–120.

Perkins, J. B. W. "The Shrine of St. Menas in the Maryut." *Papers of the British School at Rome* 17 (1949):60–71.

Severin, H.-G. "Frühchristliche Skulptur und Malerei in Ägypten." In *Spätantike und frühes Christentum*, ed. Beat Brenk. Propyläen Kunstgeschichte, Supplement 1, pp. 243–53. Frankfurt, Berlin, and Vienna, 1977.

______. "Problemi di scultura tardoantica in Egitto XXVIII." *Corso di Cultura sull'arte Ravennate e Bizantina*, pp. 299–314. Ravenna, 1981.

Strzygowski, J. *Koptische Kunst*. Catalogue général des antiquités égyptiennes du Musée du Caire, Nos. 7001–7394, 8742–9200. Vienna, 1904.

Torp, H. "Leda Christiana. The Problem of the Interpretation of Coptic Sculpture with Mythological Motifs." *Acta ad archaeologiam et artium historiam pertinentia* 4 (1969):101–12.

Wessel, K. *Koptische Kunst. Die Spätantike in Ägypten*. Recklinghausen, 1963.

Wulff, O. *Altchristliche und mittelalterliche byzantinische und italienische Bildwerke*. Part 1: *Altchristliche Bildwerke*. Beschreibung der Bildwerke der christlichen Epochen 2. Berlin, 1909. Vol. 3, 2nd edition, describes the sculpture of the Christian period.

HANS-GEORG SEVERIN

SEALS. *See* Ceramics, Coptic; Woodwork, Coptic.

SEASONS. *See* Mythological Subjects in Coptic Art.

SECOND TREATISE OF THE GREAT SETH. This—the second treatise of Codex VII of the NAG HAMMADI LIBRARY—presents a familiar theme to readers of Gnostic literature: Christ teaches his disciples about creation, the origin of souls, and the future blessedness of believers. Christ describes his role in the council of the incorruptible gods "before the foundation of the world when the whole multitude of the Assembly came together," and "the whole house of the father of truth rejoiced" that Christ would descend and reveal the truth "to my kindred and my fellow spirits." Christ briefly describes the creation of the physical universe by Sophia and then offers a docetic interpretation of his incarnation and crucifixion. According to this document, the incorruptible Christ descended from above and appropriated his physical form from the mortal who had first inhabited it. But he vacated his borrowed body just before the Passion (as in the APOCALYPSE OF PETER and elsewhere), thus remaining totally undefiled: "I did not die in reality but (only) in appearance."

Christ then explains how all this affects the disciples, those whose souls originated in the upper world where "the wedding of the wedding garment" and "the bridal chamber of the heavens" are. They will be freed from the world below and endowed with nobility. "They will pass by every gate without fear and will be made perfect in the third glory" (cf. 2 Cor. 12:2).

In common with much other Gnostic literature, *The Second Treatise of the Great Seth* teaches the doctrine of preexistence of souls. According to this document, the souls of believers originated in the world above ("our home") and descended into this world to inhabit physical bodies. Believers do not remember their preexistent state because "the fleshly cloud overshadows" them. In the material world, these spiritual beings from above are subjected to the enmity of ignorant mortals and of the malicious and ignorant archons whom most mortals serve. However, as a result of the ministry of Christ, in some unspecified way, the souls of believers are released from this world and rise again to the realm above. Thus, Resurrection is interpreted in this document in terms of souls trapped in the material world "rising" to the spiritual realm.

The supreme God of the incorruptible world is repeatedly referred to as "the Man," thus facilitating a Gnostic interpretation of the Jewish title "Son of Man" as applied to Christ, that he is the son of the heavenly Man, the supreme God of the upper, incorruptible world. *The Second Treatise of the Great Seth* also rejects the moral perspective of Judaism and "orthodox" Christianity. As elsewhere in gnosticism, the God of the Old Testament is here identified with an inferior being, and those who serve him or observe his Law, including Adam, Abraham, Isaac, Jacob, David, Moses, and the other prophets and John the Baptist, are called laughingstocks.

It is likely that *The Second Treatise of the Great Seth* was written early in the third century, perhaps in Alexandria. The original language would have been Greek (Painchaud, 1982). The composition polemicizes against the "orthodox" Christian view of the origin of the soul; the Incarnation, Crucifixion, and Resurrection of Christ; and the nature of the church (Painchaud, 1981).

BIBLIOGRAPHY

Bethge, H.-G. "'Zweiter Logos des grossen Seth': Die zweite Schrift aus Nag-Hammadi-Codex VII eingeleitet und übersetzt vom Berliner Arbeitskreis für koptisch-gnostische Schriften." *Theologische Literaturzeitung* 100 (1975):97–110.

———. "Anthropologie und Soteriologie im 2 Log-Seth (NHC VII, 2)." In *Studien zum Menschenbild in Gnosis und Manichäismus,* ed. P. Nagel, pp. 268–76. Halle, 1979.

Gibbons, J. A. (intro.); R. A. Bullard (trans.); and F. Wisse (ed.). "The Second Treatise of the Great Seth." In *The Nag Hammadi Library,* ed. J. M. Robinson, pp. 329–38. New York, 1978.

Painchaud, L. "La Polémique anti-ecclésiale et exégèse de la passion dans le *Deuxième traité du grand Seth* (NH VII, 2). In *Colloque international sur les textes de Nag Hammadi,* ed. B. Barc, pp. 340–51. Bibliothèque copte de Nag Hammadi, Section "Etudes." Quebec, 1981.

———. *Le Deuxième traité du grand Seth (NH VII, 2).* Bibliothèque copte de Nag Hammadi, Section "Textes" 6. Quebec, 1982.

Tröger, K.-W. "Der zweite Logos des grossen Seth: Gedanken zur Christologie in der zweiten Schrift des Codex VII (p. 49, 10–70, 12)." In *Essays on the Nag Hammadi Texts: In Honor of Pahor Labib,* ed. M. Krause. Leiden, 1975.

STEPHEN E. ROBINSON

SECRET GOSPEL OF SAINT MARK. In 1958, Morton Smith of Columbia University discovered two and a half pages of a letter purportedly written by CLEMENT OF ALEXANDRIA to an unknown Theodorus. The contents of this late copy of the original relate that Mark, after writing his Gospel in Rome with Peter, left that city after the apostle's martyrdom and journeyed to Alexandria. From both his and Peter's notes, which he had brought with him, Mark then wrote a secret gospel, the purpose of which was to be a ritual text for Christians "being initiated into the great mysteries." According to the letter, Clement's purpose in writing to Theodorus was to warn him that CARPOCRATES had purloined a copy of the secret gospel and had both corrupted and misinterpreted the text. Answering Theodorus' questions concerning the text, which was still kept under guard in Alexandria, Clement is giving a commentary on some passages when the fragment ends.

In the decade following his publication of the text, Smith cataloged publications and responses relating to the authenticity of the letter of Clement and the Secret Gospel of Mark. Acceptance of the letter's authenticity was overwhelming, but not one publication defended the authenticity of the Secret Gospel of Mark that Clement mentioned and quoted to Theodorus.

BIBLIOGRAPHY

Smith, M. *Clement of Alexandria and a Secret Gospel of Mark.* Cambridge, 1973.

______. "Clement of Alexandria and Secret Mark: The Score at the End of the First Decade." *Harvard Theological Review* 75, no. 4 (1982):449–61.

C. WILFRED GRIGGS

SEMI-ARIANS, A group drawn from among Arian theologians that was founded by Basil of Ancyra around 356. Its members espoused a doctrine of the sonship of Jesus that stood somewhere between the orthodox and the Arian (see ARIANISM) principles. They adopted the HOMOIOUSION theology and leaned toward orthodoxy. Saint ATHANASIUS returned to Alexandria in 362 and held a council that reconciled many moderate views, causing semi-Arians to reaffirm their orthodoxy at the Council of CONSTANTINOPLE in 381.

[*See also:* Arius; Homoeans; Homoiousion.]

BIBLIOGRAPHY

Gummerus, J. "Die homöusianische Partei bis zum Tode des Konstantius." *Beitrag zur Geschichte des arianischen Streites in 356–61* (1900).

Gwatkin, H. M. *Studies of Arianism.* London, 1902.

SUBHI Y. LABIB

SEM'ON. *See* Ethiopian Prelates.

SENOUTHIOS. *See* Shenute.

SENTENCES OF MENANDROS, a group of proverbial sayings written down at an unknown date (perhaps first century A.D.), probably to be attributed to the great comic poet Menandros. It seems to have enjoyed a fair popularity, comparable to that of similar collections (gnomologies) that were widespread in late antiquity; like these it seems to have been subjected to frequent manipulations.

The original redaction, now lost, was in Greek; it is not easy, therefore, to form a precise idea of the original content. It seems that the main components were the imitation of various verses actually by Menandros, the influence of biblical wisdom literature, and a group of sayings on the usefulness of learning to read and to write. This last component indicates that the text was produced and preserved in scholastic circles. However, the first author, who made an effort at writing in iambic trimeters, totally lacked concepts of prosody and classical metrical rules.

The complete Syriac translation (ed. Land, 1975, Vol. 1, pp. 64–73) and a Slavonic translation are extant, as well as a number of fragments in a Greek and Coptic bilingual version (ed. Hagedorn and Weber, 1968). It is clear that the *Sentences of Menandros,* which had been used for practice in Greek circles, were also used later in Coptic circles, probably for learning to write in Coptic and for learning rudimentary notions of Greek.

BIBLIOGRAPHY

Baumstark, A. *Geschichte der syrischen Literatur; mit Ausschluss der christlich-palestinischen Texte.* Bonn, 1922.

Hagedorn, D., and M. Weber, eds. "Die griechisch-koptische Rezension der Menandersentenzen." *Zeitschrift für Papyrologie und Epigraphik* 3 (1968):15–50.

Land, J. P. N. *Anecdota syriaca.* Leiden, 1875. Repr. Jerusalem, 1975.

TITO ORLANDI

SENTENCES OF SEXTUS. About one-quarter of a Coptic version of the *Sentences of Sextus,* a collection of almost 500 wisdom sayings drawn largely from pagan sources and thinly Christianized by a second-century editor, appears in the scattered folios of Codex XII of the NAG HAMMADI LIBRARY (NHC XII, 1.15–16 and 27–34; *Sextus* 158–80 and 307–397). James M. Robinson (1972, 1973, 1977) believes that this codex once contained the whole of the *Sentences* and that the missing segments were lost or destroyed shortly after their discovery in 1945.

What survives of the Coptic version is typical of the entire collection and indicates why the *Sentences* held a special attraction for Christian monks during the patristic period and later. The ideal person is the "wise man" or "philosopher" (equated by the Christian editor with the person of true faith, *Sextus* 171a, etc.). Such an individual possesses what God possesses (310) and acts to do good as God does good (176). It is this person who is free (309), self-sufficient (334), in harmony with life's circumstances (385), and disturbed neither by thoughts of death (323) nor by onslaughts of tyrants (363b–64).

This emphasis on wisdom leads readily to the very Hellenic viewpoint that reason is "the essence of humanity" (315). Indeed, to know this inner self is to know God (394). Allied with this is a pervasive body-soul dichotomy; the body is the soul's "garment" (346) or even its "fetters" (322). Yet suicide is forbidden (321). The wise man will neither cling to his body nor consider it a disability (320), but will learn to make proper use of it (335). This principle underlies both the "mild asceticism" characteristic of the *Sentences* (e.g., marriage and the possession of goods are allowed if used properly) and the pervasive concern found in it for correct ethical behavior in this world (Edwards and Wild, 1981). The surviving Coptic portions, for example, emphasize care for the needy (330, etc.); the careful use of speech (157–71b), especially speech about God (350–68); and the necessity of conforming actions to words (172–80).

The moderate dualism of the *Sentences* makes it clear that this was not a Gnostic composition. In fact, the presence of this document (and certain others) in the Nag Hammadi corpus may indicate that these manuscripts were not a "Coptic Gnostic library" as such but were the possession of Egyptian monks, perhaps followers of PACHOMIUS, who valued them for their emphasis on asceticism (Wisse, 1978; cf. Krause, 1978). The discovery of this Coptic version of the *Sentences*, now the earliest known of the versions, provides further evidence for the close association of this wisdom text with Egypt and, possibly, the monastic movement, an association previously attested by ORIGEN's use of the work in the early third century and by the interest in it evinced by Jerome and Rufinus, Latin churchmen deeply involved with Egyptian MONASTICISM.

Textually the Coptic manuscript supports the traditional ordering of the sayings found in the Vatican Greek manuscript and in the translation by Rufinus and adopted by modern editors. Redactional additions are rare and the number of textual variants is not large. Interestingly, many of these show agreement with the chief Syriac witness. Despite much redactional overlay and a different order for the sayings in the Syriac, the two versions probably derive from closely related Greek sources (Edwards and Wild, 1981).

BIBLIOGRAPHY

Chadwick, H. *The Sentences of Sextus.* Texts and Studies 5. Cambridge, 1959.

Delling, G. "Zur Hellenisierung des Christentums in den 'Sprüchen des Sextus,'" *Studien zum Neuen Testament und zur Patristik. Festschrift für Erich Klostermann.* Text und Untersuchungen 77, pp. 208–241. Berlin, 1961.

Edwards, R., and R. Wild, eds. *The Sentences of Sextus.* Society of Biblical Literature Texts and Translations, 22. *Early Christian Literature,* Vol. 5. Chico, Cal., 1981.

Krause, M. "Die Texte von Nag Hammadi." In *Gnosis: Festschrift für Hans Jonas,* ed. B. Aland. Göttingen, 1978.

Poirier, P.-H. "Le Texte de la version copte des *Sentences de Sextus.*" *Colloque international sur les textes de Nag Hammadi (Québec, 22–25 août 1978).* Bibliothèque copte de Nag Hammadi, Section "Etudes" 1, pp. 383–89. Quebec, 1981.

______. *Les Sentences de Sextus.* Bibliothèque copte de Nag Hammadi, Section "Textes" 11. Quebec, 1983.

Robinson, James M. *Introduction to the Facsimile Edition of the Nag Hammadi Codices,* pp. 2–3. Leiden, 1972.

______, ed. *The Facsimile Edition of the Nag Hammadi Codices: Codices XI, XII and XIII.* Leiden, 1973.

Wisse, F. "Die Sextus-Sprüche und das Problem der gnostischen Ethik." In *Zum Hallenismus in den Schriften von Nag Hammadi,* ed. A. Böhlig and F. Wisse. Wiesbaden, 1975.

______. "The Sentences of Sextus (XII,1)." In *The Nag Hammadi Library in English,* ed. James M. Robinson, pp. 454–59. San Francisco, 1977.

______. "Gnosticism and Early Monasticism in Egypt." In *Gnosis: Festschrift für Hans Jonas,* ed. B. Aland. Göttingen, 1978.

ROBERT A. WILD, S.J.

SERAPION, SAINT, a martyr from Lower Egypt (feast day: 27 Ṭūbah). The legend that tells of the martyrdom of Serapion (*Bibliotheca Hagiographica Orientalis* 1048, ed. Balestri and Hyvernat, 1955,

1960) belongs to the type of martyrologies predominant in Egypt. There are rescues among a multitude of tortures, miracles, and promises for the cult center in Panephosi in the eastern Delta, from which the saint came. The entry in the Arabic *Synaxarion Alexandrinum* presupposes another version of the martyrdom of Serapion.

BIBLIOGRAPHY

Balestri, I, and H. Hyvernat. *Acta Martyrum I.* CSCO 43, *Scriptores Coptici,* Vol. 3, pp. 63–88. Louvain, 1955. CSCO 44, *Scriptores Coptici,* Vol. 4, pp. 47–60. Louvain, 1960. Latin translation in Bibliotheca Hagiographica Orientalium 1048.

Baumeister, T. *Martyr invictus,* pp. 128, 129. Münster, 1972.

Crum, W. E. Review of *Serapion.* In *Journal of Theological Studies* 10 (1909):461.

Delehaye, H. "Les martyrs d'Egypte." *Analecta Bollandiana* 40 (1922):5–154; 299–364.

O'Leary, De L. *The Saints of Egypt,* p. 245. London and New York, 1937.

THEOFRIED BAUMEISTER

SERAPION SINDONITA. *See* Sarapion.

SETH,

eighth-century archimandrite of Apa Shenute. Both the HISTORY OF THE PATRIARCHS and the SYNAXARION of the Copts tell us very little about Seth. We know only that he was archimandrite of the White Monastery (DAYR ANBĀ SHINŪDAH) at the beginning of the eighth century. The Synaxarion calls him "the greatest of the abbots of the monasteries of Egypt." He was celebrated for the cures that he effected and the miracles that occurred at his tomb.

This Seth is mentioned in the typika of the White Monastery (Leiden, Insinger 36^{c-d}, ed. Pleyte and Boeser, p. 195; Mingarelli, pp. 51–55; Vienna, Staatsbibliothek K9731, Wessely, no. 264). He is also mentioned in a fragment of a lectionary preserved in Cairo, Coptic Museum, no. 9225 (Munier, p. 13).

The *History of the Patriarchs* mentions him in the notice devoted to the patriarch ALEXANDER II (705–730), with MATTHEW THE POOR, JOHN HEGUMENOS OF SCETIS, and ABRAHAM AND GEORGE OF SCETIS, as one of the saints who lived in the time of Alexander.

In a Coptic manuscript in van Lantschoot's collection there is mention of a church, situated south of the White Monastery, dedicated to Seth and to CLAUDIUS, the anchorite.

The Luxor manuscript of the Upper Egyptian recension of the Synaxarion of the Copts gives a very short report of his life at 29 Ṭūbah (Coquin, 1978, p. 361).

BIBLIOGRAPHY

Coquin, R.-G. "Le Synaxaire des Coptes: Un nouveau témoin de la recension de Haute-Egypte." *Analecta Bollandiana* 96 (1978):351–65.

Lantschoot, A. van. *Recueil des colophons des manuscrits chrétiens d'Egypte.* Bibliothèque du Muséon 1. Louvain, 1929.

Mingarelli, L. G. *Aegyptiorum codicum reliquiae Venetiis in Bibliotheca Naniana asservatae,* Vol. 2. Bologna, 1785.

Munier, H. *Catalogue général des antiquités égyptiennes du Musée du Caire. Manuscrits coptes.* Cairo, 1916.

Pleyte, Willem, and Pieter A. A. Boeser. *Manuscrits coptes du Musée d'antiquités des Pays-Bas à Leide.* Leiden, 1897.

Wessely, C. *Studien zur Palaeographie und Papyruskunde,* Vol. 18. Leipzig, 1917.

RENÉ-GEORGES COQUIN

SETHE, KURT HEINRICH

(1869–1934), German Egyptologist. He studied Egyptology under Adolf Erman at Berlin University and was appointed professor of Egyptology at the University of Göttingen (1900), later succeeding Erman at Berlin (1923). He was a member of the British Academy. Sethe was, with Erman, one of the two greatest figures in Egyptian philology in the twentieth century. He worked with texts ranging from those of the early dynastic period to demotic and Coptic, making important discoveries in each. Of his many grammatical works, the great *Das Ägyptische Verbum* (3 vols. Leipzig, 1899–1903) was the most important. Though his principal works are in the field of Egyptology, he made notable contributions in the area of Coptic language and culture. His publications are listed in Kammerer, *A Coptic Bibliography* (1950, 1969).

BIBLIOGRAPHY

Dawson, W. R., and E. P. Uphill. *Who Was Who in Egyptology,* pp. 266–67. London, 1972.

Kammerer, W., comp. *A Coptic Bibliography*. Ann Arbor, Mich., 1950; repr. New York, 1969.

AZIZ S. ATIYA

SEVEN ASCETICS OF TŪNAH. This is a classic story concerning martyr hermits. No details are given about their ascetic life except that they lived near Tūnah. It seems, moreover, that only five of them were ascetics, and that Anbā Psate (or Basidi) and Anbā Kutilus, who was a priest, joined the ascetics in their confession of Christ. The governor (it is not said where he resided) tortured and imprisoned them but, achieving nothing, sent them to Alexandria, where they were tortured again. Then, as a last resort, six of them were beheaded when they refused to worship the idol of Apollo. Kutilus (the priest, apparently) was consigned to the flames.

These seven martyred ascetics are known only from a brief notice in the recension of the SYNAXARION of the Copts from Lower Egypt.

This text presents two problems for the reader. First is the question of the place called "the mountain of Tūnah." It could be the town that disappeared in the floods of Lake al-Manzalah or the mountain called in Middle Egypt Tūnah al-Jabal, in the district of Mallawī. E. Amélineau inclines to the second site (1893, pp. 525–26), but it seems that in fact it is the town of this name that is meant. In fact, if that were the case, it is more natural that the governor should send them to Alexandria.

Second, the names of these martyr ascetics are not certain, for the spelling varies greatly from one manuscript to another. What seems certain is that two of them had a foreign name—they are said to have called themselves "Kutilus" (the transcription credited to a Syrian saint "Gawbdalahu" [22 Tūt]). It may therefore be that these two ascetics were of Syrian origin. The other names appear to be Egyptian. In any case, they all seem thoroughly "pagan," and hence guarantee their antiquity. The Ethiopic version of the Synaxarion renders *jabal* (mountain) as "monastery," and precedes the name Tūnah by the word "town." It therefore interprets "al-jabal Tūnah" as designating "the monastery of the town of Tūnah" (without doubt an anachronism), and places it in the Delta rather than in Middle Egypt.

BIBLIOGRAPHY

Amélineau, E. *La Géographie de l'Egypte à l'époque copte*. Paris, 1893.

Budge, E. A. W. *The Book of the Saints of the Ethiopian Church*, 4 vols. Cambridge, 1928.

RENÉ-GEORGES COQUIN

SEVERIAN OF JABALAH, SAINT, or Severianus, one of the great orators of the fourth century (feast day: 7 Tūt). Known for numerous homilies, he died after 408.

Severian had been invited to court at Constantinople, where he must have known Saint JOHN CHRYSOSTOM, with whom he did not sympathize. Indeed, the bishop of Jabalah was among Chrysostom's opponents in the long affair of his lawsuit and exile. Ironically, many of Severian's homilies later passed under the name of Chrysostom: about thirty out of thirty-five Greek texts counted in *Clavis Patrum Graecorum* (1974, pp. 468–482, nos. 4185–4272). By identifying quotations in the CATENAE, and by comparisons with the five undoubted works, J. Zellinger (1974) was able to rediscover several of Severian's works. The use of Armenian versions has also been of great help. Almost all of Severian's sermons speak of the Trinity. Many turns of phrase in Greek are peculiarly his own.

Coptic Tradition

In Coptic, there remains a eulogy of Saint Michael in Sahidic (Pierpont Morgan codex 602, preceding fol. 198), part of which is a fragment of another manuscript published by J. Leipoldt in 1904. Specialists do not acknowledge its authenticity (see *Clavis Patrum Graecorum* 4278). There is a homily on Matthew 25:13 (fols. 14–30), of which a Bohairic fragment was published by H. O. Burmester in 1932, according to fragments of homilies used for Holy Week (*Clavis Patrum Graecorum* 4279). Another homily, on Matthew 25:31, immediately follows (*Clavis Patrum Graecorum* 4280) in the same Hamūlī codex, dating from the ninth century (fols. 31–52). Besides these three texts, another codex from the Pierpont Morgan collection (M 606, pp. 1–56) has preserved a homily on the twelve apostles. Fifth, there is a homily on the Nativity, which exists in fragmentary form under the name of Proclus of Constantinople (Saint PROCLUS) in the Turin collection of papyri. The Paris fragments of this homily were identified and published by E. Lucchesi (1979). They correspond to those analyzed in 1933 by E. Porcher (1933; *Clavis Patrum Graecorum* 4282). Sixth, there is a homily on penitence, expressly attributed to Severian but found among the pseudo-Chrysostomica (PG 60, pp. 765–68). H. G. Evelyn-White (1926, pp. 178–180) found fragments from the same codex, Vatican Coptic 68, in Cairo, giving other passages from the homily.

Finally, in the theological texts on papyrus published by W. E. CRUM in 1913, G. Mercati (1916–1917) identified a passage from the same homily. But here again, the specialists in the style of Severian deny him the authorship of the pseudo-Chrysostomicum to which J. A. de Aldama (1965) gave the number 462. The seventh and only work that all regard as being authentic in both Coptic and Greek is the set of sermons on Genesis (*Clavis Patrum Graecorum* 4194). A series of Coptic fragments from these sermons, obtained from DAYR ANBĀ SHINŪDAH, Suhāj, is in Paris (MS Copte 129.13, fols. 96–103, and 131.6, fol. 46). Finally, there is an extract in the Coptic catena of Saint Matthew, published by P. de Lagarde (1886). This extract explains the meaning of the expression "Son of Man," but it is not possible to state its origin precisely (*Clavis Patrum Graecorum* 4295).

Arabic Tradition

Few works of Severian of Jabalah have come down to us in Arabic. The main details have been given by G. Graf (1944). There are, first, the homilies on Genesis (*Clavis Patrum Graecorum* 4194), which, in Paris Arabe 68 (1339), fols. 36–67, include one homily more than in the Greek version, although this homily, number 7, dealing with Adam's expulsion from Paradise, exists in part in Greek (*Clavis Patrum Graecorum* 4217).

Second, there is a homily on the Annunciation preserved in the manuscript Sinai 423 (1626), fols. 353–58, and in Beirut manuscript 510, pp. 500–509. This homily corresponds with neither *Clavis Patrum Graecorum* 4204, although the Greek incipit appears at first sight to be somewhat similar, nor the Syriac homily on the Nativity published by C. Moss (1947–1948) (*Clavis Patrum Graecorum* 4260). According to the title, it was translated from Syriac into Arabic by Gregory of the Black Mountain. Its style corresponds perfectly with the rather prolix manner of Severian.

Third, there is a homily on the twelve apostles, preserved in the fifteenth-century manuscript Vatican Arabic 536, fols. 1–32, and Cairo, Graf 717, fols. 115–30 (1358).

Fourth, an Arabic translation of the extract from a homily already in existence in Coptic as a lectionary for Holy Week is preserved in Borgia Arabic 57, fols. 135–36; Cairo, Graf 170 fols., 53–54 (fifteenth century).

BIBLIOGRAPHY

Aldama, J. A. de. *Repertorium Chrysostomicum*. Paris, 1965.

Burmester, O. H. E. "The Homilies or Exhortations of the Holy Week Lectionary." Le Muséon 45 (1932):21–70.

Evelyn-White, H. G. *The Monasteries of the Wādi 'n Natrūn*, pt. 1. *New Coptic Texts from the Monastery of Saint Macarius*. New York, 1926.

Hyvernat, H. *Bibliothecae Pierpont Morgan codices coptici photographice expressi . . .*, 56 vols. in 63 facsimilies. Rome, 1922.

Lagarde, P. de. *Catenae in evangelia quae supersunt*. Göttingen, 1886.

Leipoldt, J. *Ägyptische Urkunden aus den Königlichen Museen zu Berlin. Koptische Urkunden* 1, 6. Bibliotheca Hagiographica Orientalis 761. Berlin, 1904.

Lucchesi, E. "Proclus of Constantinople." *Analecta Bollandiana* 97 (1979):111–27.

Mercati, G. "A Parallel to a Coptic Sermon on the Nativity." *Journal of Theological Studies* 18 (1917):315–17.

Migne, J.-P. *Patrologia Cursus Completus, Series Graeca*, Vol. 60. Montrouge and Paris, 1859.

Moss, C. "Homily on the Nativity of our Lord by Severian, Bishop of Gabala." *Bulletin of the School of Oriental and African Studies* (1947–1948):555.

Porcher, E. "Analyse des manuscrits coptes 131^{1-8} de la Bibliothèque Nationale, avec indication des textes bibliques." *Revue d'Egyptologie* 1 (1933):124.

Vis, H. de. *Homélies coptes de la Vaticane*. Copenhagen, 1922.

Zellinger, J. *Studien zu Severian von Gabala*. Münsterische Beiträge zur Theologie 8, Münster, 1926.

MICHEL VAN ESBROECK

SEVERUS. *See* Sāwīrus Ibn al-Muqaffa'.

SEVERUS OF ANTIOCH (c. 465–538), the most famous of Monophysite leaders. Evagrius (*Historia ecclesiastica*, 3.33) said that he was born and brought up in Sozopolis in Pisidia. It is also known that he studied law and was trained in grammar and rhetoric at Beirut. Much of what is known of his career comes down through the distorted views of his theological opponents.

Upon completion of his legal training, Severus became a Monophysite and went to live in a monastery. The first community where he lived was situated between Maiuma and Gaza. He then became acquainted with Peter the Iberian, who had been ordained bishop of Gaza by Theodosius, the fiery Monophysite monk. Soon he joined a Eutychian monastery near Eleutheropolis under the archimandrite Mamas, and he continued to further his spiritual development in monophysitism.

He strongly rejected the HENOTICON of Zeno and called it by various negative epithets such as *diaireticon* (disuniting edict). At the same time, he anathematized PETER MONGUS, the Monophysite patriarch of Alexandria, for having accepted it.

Later Severus lived in a monastery in Egypt under the direction of the abbot Nephalius. Nephalius had fallen away from the Monophysite view, and Severus made an unsuccessful attempt to reconvince him. This action resulted in his being expelled from the monastery. Then Severus stirred up mobs in Alexandria, which led to violence and bloodshed there.

At the beginning of the reign of the emperor Anastasius (491), the patriarch of Antioch had been Palladius. He accepted the Henoticon in the company of other bishops in northern Syria and attempted to put it into effect. At this time the mood of Antioch was turning toward monophysitism under the influence of PHILOXENUS OF MABBUG (Hierapolis), who was becoming the spokesman for the extreme Monophysite viewpoint.

At the time of the accession of Severus to the patriarchate of Antioch, the feelings between the parties were becoming very bitter. Anastasius must have been familiar with conditions in the city in regard to the relations between the parties, since he had been living in Antioch at the time of Peter the Fuller (488).

The religious troubles between the factions in Syria abated somewhat when war broke out between the Persian empire and Rome in 502. The energies of Philoxenus were then diverted to the difficulties of his own people (Le Bon, 1909).

After the war ended, Anastasius attempted to deal with the religious question. From 505, the actual date of the cessation of hostilities, it is possible to see a trend in his religious activities. He began to take covert action to assist the Monophysite party.

Anastasius had always been favorably disposed toward the Monophysites. The attempt now to strengthen the party may have represented an effort to fight the Nestorians, who were obtaining support from the Persian government. Following the episode of violence at Alexandria, Severus went to Constantinople, accompanied by 200 monks, to try and win imperial favor. He was successful in this to the extent that the emperor would have liked to make him patriarch there, but the orthodox party was too strong.

Severus remained in Constantinople from 508 to 511, a period during which Syrian monks, particularly those who lived around Antioch, revolted. The emperor charged Severus with writing a new formula that would be satisfactory. Severus then took up the dispute with John of Claudiopolis, bishop of Isauria, who tried in vain to win him over to the opinion of Flavian. Severus wrote a unitarian formula, and the bishops of Isauria rallied behind it.

The events of the patriarchate of Severus are difficult to date with precision, because of the state of the sources. But it is known that on 16 November 512, Severus was consecrated patriarch of Antioch in the presence of twelve bishops. According to the Synodicon, Anastasius made him swear that he would never speak or act against the Council of CHALCEDON. Yet Severus, on the very day he became bishop, pronounced an anathema upon Chalcedon and accepted the Henoticon, which he had previously repudiated. Confident of the emperor's protection, Severus dispatched his synodal letters to the other prelates and demanded their communion. In these missives, he anathematized Chalcedon and all who held to belief in the two natures.

Severus had a zealous supporter in Peter of Apamea. Severus was charged with abetting Peter in setting up an ambush of some pilgrims on the way to the Monastery of Saint Simeon. A contingent of Jewish mercenaries were said to have attacked the pilgrims and slain 250 people, leaving them unburied by the side of the road. They were also charged with having burned the monasteries in which the fleeing pilgrims had taken refuge and slaughtered the monks who protected them. The monasteries of Palestine remained steadfast with the orthodox faith.

In his era, Severus was regarded as the champion of monophysitism, which was in the ascendancy during his patriarchate. His triumph was to be a short one.

His strong position could not be maintained without the support of the emperor Anastasius. The successor of Anastasius, the orthodox JUSTIN I, came to the throne in 518. As soon as Justin became emperor, Monophysite patriarchs were deposed in favor of orthodox. Irenaeus, the Comes Orientis, was ordered to arrest Severus and to cut out his tongue as a punishment for his blasphemies. Severus, however, managed to evade this edict. He escaped from Antioch and in September 518 boarded a boat bound for Alexandria. Paul was ordained in his stead.

Severus was enthusiastically received in Alexandria by both the people of Alexandria and its bishop, TIMOTHY III. He was a recognized leader in the battle against Nestorianism. Alexandria soon became a refuge for Monophysites.

A dispute arose between Severus and JULIAN OF HALICARNASSUS as to the corruptibility of the Lord's human body before his Resurrection. Julian maintained that not only was Christ's body not subject to corruption, but it was free from the temporary character of ordinary human bodies. There was no settlement in this controversy. Severus was summoned to Constantinople and then condemned at a synod in 536. The sentence was later ratified by JUSTINIAN.

Severus wrote a great number of Greek works, but only a few of them are extant. Chiefly fragments survive. Much of his Syriac writing is extant, such as a letter in which he refutes 244 chapters culled by a Chalcedonian opponent from the work of CYRIL OF ALEXANDRIA. He also wrote treatises against Julian of Halicarnassus, four letters against the extreme Monophysite Sergius, and a great number of hymns in Syriac.

BIBLIOGRAPHY

Baumstark, A. *Geschichte der syrischen Literatur.* Bonn, 1922.

Chestnut, R. *Three Monophysite Christologies.* Oxford, 1976.

Downey, G. *History of Antioch in Syria.* Princeton, 1961.

Duchesne, L. *L'Eglise au VI siècle.* Paris, 1925.

Frend, W. H. C. *The Rise of the Monophysite Movement.* Cambridge, 1972. See especially for the early life.

______. *The Rise of Christianity.* London, 1984.

Grillmeier, A., and H. Bacht. *Das Konzil von Chalkedon,* 3 vols. Würzburg, 1954.

Hefele, C. *History of the Christian Councils.* Edinburgh, 1906.

Honigman, E. *Evêques et évêchés monophysites d'Asie antérieure au VI siècle.* Louvain, 1951.

Le Bon, A. *Le Monophysisme syrien.* Louvain, 1909.

Nau, F. N., ed. and trans. *Vie de Sevère.* In *Opuscules maronites,* Pt. 2, pp. 26–98. Paris, 1900.

LINDA KNEZEVICH

SEYFFARTH, GUSTAVUS

SEYFFARTH, GUSTAVUS (1796–1885) German-American Orientalist, archaeologist, and theologian. He studied classics at the University of Leipzig (1815–1819). He was later appointed docent and was given the task of completing the two volumes of Friedrich August Wilhelm Spohn's *De Lingua et Literis Veterum Aegyptiorum . . .* (1825–1831). To do this, he visited many European collections from 1826 to 1828 and made over ten thousand copies of Coptic manuscripts and impressions from Egyptian monuments. This vast corpus of material, Bibliotheca Aegyptiaca Manuscripta, filled fourteen royal folio volumes, not including an index in quarto, bequeathed by him at his death to the New-York Historical Society. In 1830 he was appointed to the first professorship in archaeology at Leipzig University.

Seyffarth had controversial ideas that aliented his colleagues, especially Champollion and his followers. He finally left Germany in 1854 and settled in the United States. After teaching for five years in St. Louis at Concordia College, he moved to New York to work at the Astor Library.

Seyyfarth was a prolific writer. Many of his works were published, while others remained in manuscript form. Among his contributions to Coptic studies are *Thesaurus Copticus* (4 vols., 1829), "Inschriften aus Ägypten," *Zeitschrift der deutschen morgenländischen Gesellschaft* 4 (1850):254–62, and "Coptische Klosterurkunde aus dem IV. Jahrhundert auf einem Pariser papyrus" (article included in his *Theologische Schriften der alten Ägypter nach dem Turiner Papyrus zum ersten Male übersetzt,* Gotha, 1855, pp. 109–117).

Seyffarth did have a certain following; Knortz, his biographer, went so far as to state that the translation of the Rosetta Stone was only made possible through his system. The arrangement of the papyrus fragments of the Canon of Kings at Turin is mainly due to him. He died in New York, and his papers are now in the Brooklyn Museum.

BIBLIOGRAPHY

Dawson, W. R., and E. P. Uphill. *Who Was Who in Egyptology,* pp. 267–68. London, 1972.

Kammerer, W., comp. *A Coptic Bibliography.* Ann Arbor, Mich., 1950; repr. New York, 1969.

AZIZ S. ATIYA

SHABEHMŌT, an Arabic ecclesiastical term, literally meaning "receiving grace." *Shabehmōt* is the title of the Prayer of Thanksgiving, beginning, "Let us give thanks to the Doer of Good and the Merciful, God the Father of our Lord and our God and our *Savior* Jesus Christ, for He hath sheltered us, He hath helped us, He hath guarded us, He hath purchased us, He hath spared us, He hath aided us, He hath brought us unto this hour."

The Lord's Prayer and the Shabehmōt are both introductory prayers to almost all church services, except the Hours of the Holy Week, which have a special arrangement.

BIBLIOGRAPHY

For the text of the prayer in Coptic and Arabic, see *Kitāb al-Khulājī al-Muqaddas* (Cairo, 1902); for the English translation, see O. H. E. Burmester, *The Egyptian or Coptic Church* (Cairo, 1967).

EMILE MAHER ISHAQ

SHAFT. *See* Architectural Elements of Churches: Column.

SHAMM AL-NASIM, literally, "sniffing the breeze." It signifies the rising of the Egyptian people, Coptic as well as Muslim, at dawn to go to fields and gardens to inhale the pure air of the first day of spring, when the new vegetation is green and the Nile flood starts swelling. This is one of the most popular feast days in Egypt, and its beginnings are rooted in remote antiquity. Though it has no religious significance for the Copts, it is always associated with Easter, on the second day of which it is celebrated every year. It is the beginning of the period known as Khamasīn (Fifty Days), a special season recognized from ancient times for the occasional hot winds from the desert, sometimes accompanied by sandstorms.

On the eve of Shamm al-Nasīm, people hang green onions on their doors and place them under their pillows, to ward off disease and epidemics. Food on that day traditionally includes onions and pickled fish. The place of onions in the Shamm al-Nasīm festivities as healing ingredient and as food must be related to dynastic habits; onion bunches are seen in the temple and tomb paintings and have been found with mummies. To this day the farmers of Egypt believe in the medicinal effects of the onion. As food it is nourishing, appetizing, soothing, healing, and even aphrodisiac. Herodotus made a special mention of the enormous amounts of onions consumed by the Egyptians. In modern times onions remain a chief staple on Shamm al-Nasīm for all Egyptians.

BIBLIOGRAPHY

Blackman, W. S. *The Fellaheen of Upper Egypt, Their Religious, Social, and Industrial Life Today, with Special Reference to Survivals from Ancient Egypt.* London, 1927.

Nerval, G. de. *Voyage en Orient,* 2 vols. Paris, 1958.

Wassef, Cérès Wissa. *Pratiques rituelles et alimentaires des coptes,* pp. 220–25. Cairo, 1971.

AZIZ S. ATIYA

SHAMS AL-DĪN (Munisis), small Romano-Byzantine village a little more than one mile to the north of Barīs in the south of the oasis of Khargah and at the fork of the great track heading from Hibis toward the southwest in the direction of Dūsh and the valley. This village contains a small church with columns that was cleared by the Institut français d'Archéologie orientale in 1976. This building of modest dimensions consists of a choir, a nave and two transepts, a side entrance, a vestibule, an access corridor, and a *kathesterion* (room for welcoming passing strangers) leading to the principal entrance of the church. Almost seventy Greek graffiti and mural drawings adorn its walls providing abundant information about the faith and worship of the time. They date from the middle or second half of the fourth century and, together with a few Greek ostraca found in situ, they raise the possibility of tracing its origin in all probability to the Constantinian period.

The faithful, who did not leave their name or their function, concentrated rather on imploring help and solace from God and Christ. Thus the most common type of graffito is "N, slave of Jesus Christ," or "N, slave of God." The writers of the graffiti oftentimes refer to the oneness of godhead in such statements as "one God" or "1 God." Invocations are made to God as savior and to Jesus as

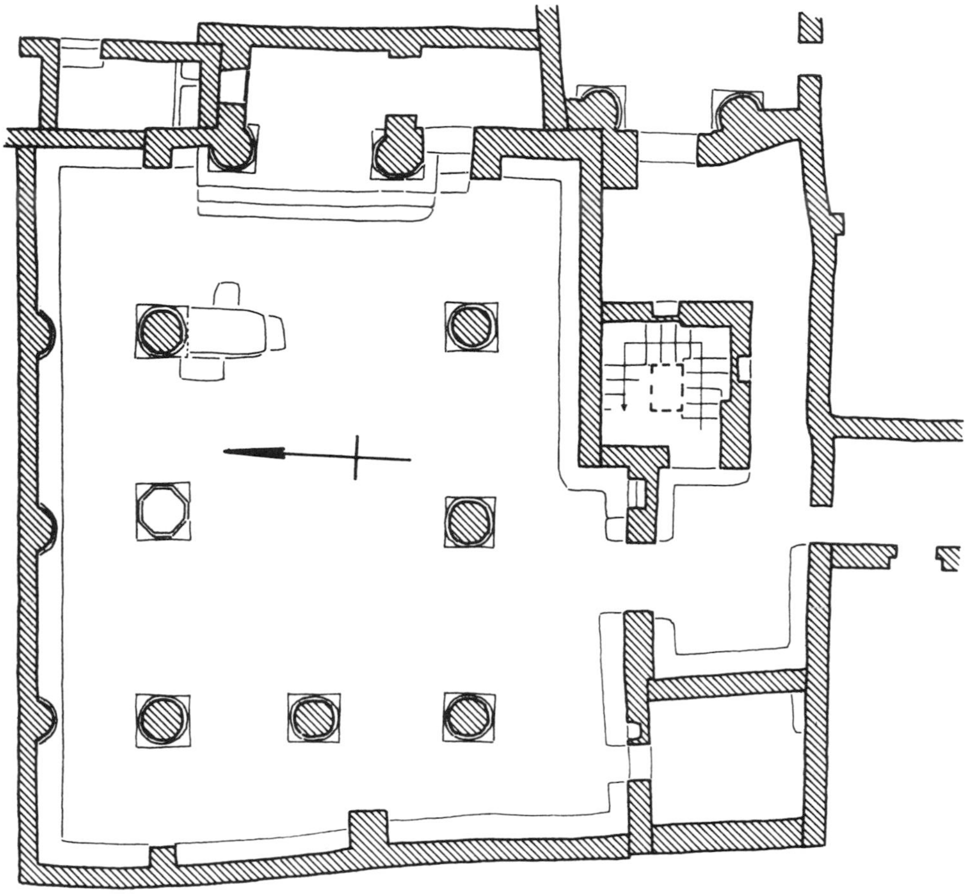

Plan of the church unearthed at Shams al-Dīn. *Courtesy Peter Grossmann.*

protector. Occasionally we read the inscription "Christ shall conquer." Twice the epithet "lord" is used to qualify Christ, while the church is described as "the house of God," seconded by a formula reading "one God, Jesus Christ the saviour of souls." From this collection of inscriptions one has the sense of a great simplicity and antiquity. The absence of any reference to the Virgin and the saints confirms that we are at the very beginning of what came to be known as the Peace of the Church, when Constantine legalized its status through the edict of Milan.

The church of Shams al-Dīn is presumably one of the oldest churches of Egypt, and its construction fits perfectly into the prodigious extension of church construction in Egypt at the beginning of the age of Constantine. The ancient name of Shams al-Dīn, Munisis, as the graffiti inform us, literally signifies "water of Isis," which is a reminder of the cult of Isis that had flourished in the oasis in the Roman period.

BIBLIOGRAPHY

Wagner, G. "Inscriptions et graffiti inédits grecs de la Grande Oasis." *Bulletin de l'Institut français d'Archéologie orientale* 76 (1976):283–88. For the texts from Shams al-Dīn, see pp. 285–86; cf. *Supplementum Epigraphicum Graecum,* vol. 26 (1976–1977), nos. 1783–1791, ed. H. W. Pleket and R. S. Stroud. Alphen aan den Rijn, Netherlands, 1979.

GUY WAGNER

SHANASHĀ, town in the Delta province of Daqahliyyah.

PSHOI OF SCETIS was born in Shanashā in the second half of the fourth century. The place was a bishopric from the middle of the thirteenth century at the latest until at least the beginning of the fourteenth century. The patriarch GABRIEL III (1268–1271) ordained a man named Peter as bishop of Shanashā and later this Peter, as the oldest bishop in northern Egypt, ordained Patriarch Theodosius II

(1294–1300). Peter was present as bishop of Shanashā, Sandūb, Ṭandatā, and Samannūd in 1299 and again in 1305 at the consecration of the holy chrism (see CHRISM) in Cairo.

There are no other references to Shanashā in Coptic-Arabic Christian literature, but the Coptic life of Patriarch ISAAC (686–689) relates that Isaac baptized a number of men and women in a place called in Coptic Psanasho. The account, however, provides no information about the location of the town (Porcher, 1915, p. 357). Nonetheless, the similarity of the names led E. Amélineau to identify this Psanasho with Shanashā (1893, pp. 373–74). While there is nothing that counts against this identification, the evidence that would verify it is also wanting.

BIBLIOGRAPHY

Amélineau, E. *La Géographie de l'Egypte à l'époque copte,* pp. 373–74. Paris, 1893.

Graf, G. "Die Rangordnung der Bischöfe Ägyptens nach einem protokollarischen Bericht des Patriarchen Kyrillos ibn Laklak." *Oriens Christianus* 24 (1927):299–337.

Munier, H. *Recueil des listes épiscopales de l'église copte.* Cairo, 1943.

Porcher, E., ed. *Vie d'Isaac, patriarche d'Alexandrie de 686 à 689.* PO 11, pt. 3. Paris, 1915.

Timm, S. *Das christlich-koptische Ägypten in arabischer Zeit,* pt. 5, Wiesbaden, 1988.

RANDALL STEWART

SHAQALQIL. *See* Pilgrimages.

SHĀQ AL-HAYKAL. *See* Orientation Toward the East.

SHARŪNAH, site of a Christian community at the time of the Arab conquest. The *Futuḥ al-Bahnasā* (Galtier, 1909, p. 131) says explicitly that the Christians of Sharūnah allied themselves with those of Ahrīt (see DAYR AL-ḤADĪD).

There were two monasteries close at hand, according to the *Livre des perles enfouies,* the date of which is unknown but the most ancient manuscript of which appears to be from the fifteenth century (Daressy, 1917, p. 203).

The first monastery was called Dayr al-Kilāb (monastery of the dogs), a name frequently given by the Muslims to Christian monasteries. Daressy remarks that there is still a church of Saint Michael at Sharūnah. This is perhaps what remains of the monastery that the *Livre des perles enfouies* calls "pretty, and built of stone." The second monastery was called DAYR AL-ZAYTŪN by the same author (Daressy, p. 206).

BIBLIOGRAPHY

Daressy, G. "Indicateur topographique du *Livre des perles enfouies et du mystère précieux.*" *Bulletin de l'Institut français d'Archéologie orientale* 13 (1917):175–230.

Galtier, E., trans. *Foutouḥ al-Bahnasa.* Mémoires publiés par les Membres de l'Institut français d'Archéologie orientale du Caire 22. Cairo, 1909.

RENÉ-GEORGES COQUIN

SHAWL. *See* Costume, Civil.

SHAYKH ABADAH. *See* Antinoopolis.

SHAYKH ʿABD AL-QURNAH, a small church in the courtyard of Amenemhat that evidently belonged to the federation of the monastery of DAYR EPIPHANIUS at West Thebes. It was found during excavations in 1926 and is now preserved only fragmentarily. It was divided into three aisles and had a three-room sanctuary with a rectangular altar chamber. A sill at the entrance to the altar chamber is to be interpreted as the substructure of cancelli. Of the columns only a few very heavy bases of the north row were found, sunk into the soil without any further foundation. By reason of their arrangement, the existence of a return aisle cannot be excluded. The possible date is the seventh century.

BIBLIOGRAPHY

Gardiner, A. H. "The Tomb of Amenemhet, High Priest of Amon." *Zeitschrift für ägyptische Sprache und Altertumskunde* 47 (1910):87–99.

Mond, R., and W. B. Emery. "The Burial Shaft of the Tomb of Amenemhāt." *Liverpool Annals of Archaeology and Anthropology* 16 (1929):49f., pl. 81.

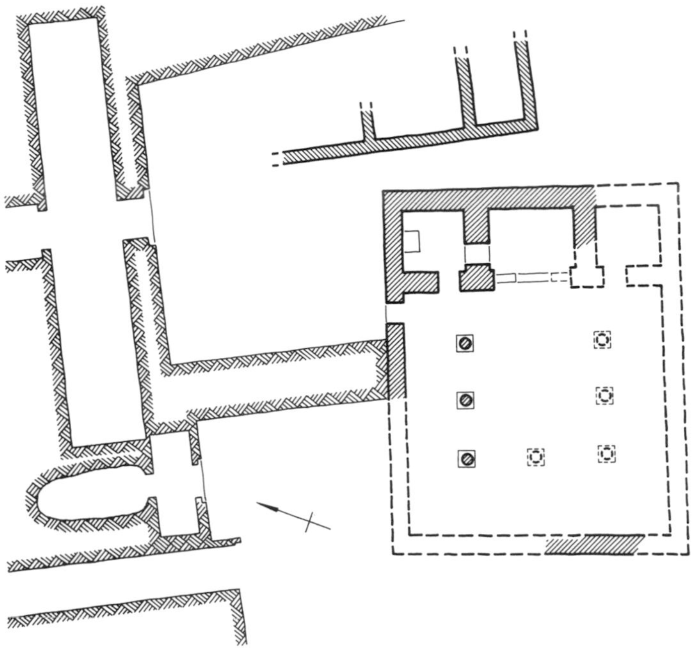

Plan of Shaykh ʿAbd al-Qurnah. *Courtesy Peter Grossmann.*

Monneret de Villard, U. *Les Couvents près de Sohâg,* Vol. 2, p. 115, pl. 137. Milan, 1926.

Porter, B., and R. L. B. Moss. *Topographical Bibliography of Ancient Egyptian Hieroglyphic Texts, Reliefs, and Paintings,* 2nd ed., Vol. 1, Pt. 2, pp. 669ff. Oxford, 1964.

PETER GROSSMANN

SHAYKH ḤASAN, AL-, ancient quarries situated on the right bank of the Nile, opposite and a little to the south of the town of Maṭāy. The Greek inscriptions with their lists of fathers were first mentioned by G. Wilkinson (1843, Vol. 2, pp. 24–31), then by travel guides (Murray, Isambert, Johanne), and incompletely published by G. Lefebvre (1907, nos. 114–16).

In addition to these inscriptions, the site includes some arrangements and symbols that reveal occupation by Christian hermits: niches on eastern walls for prayer, mortises for hanging lamps, engraved ankhs, graffiti representing barks like those that have been found at Abydos (Piankoff, 1960, pp. 37–144), at Isnā (Sauneron and Jacquet, 1972, Vol. 1, p. 79), or at the KELLIA (Mission suisse, p. 21).

BIBLIOGRAPHY

Isambert, E. *Itinéraire descriptif historique et archéologique de l'Orient,* pt. 2. 2nd ed., Paris, 1878; 3rd ed., Paris 1881; repr. ed., Paris, 1890.

Johanne, A. L., and E. Isambert. *Itinéraire descriptif historique et archéologique de l'Orient.* Paris, 1861.

Lefebvre, G. *Recueil des inscriptions grecques chrétiennes d'Egypte.* Cairo, 1907.

Mission suisse d'Archéologie Copte de l'Université de Genève. *Le site monastique des Kellia-Basse-Egypte.* Louvain, 1984.

Murray, J. *A Handbook of Travels in Egypt, Including of the Course of the Nile, to the Second Cataract.* London, 1867, 1873, 1875.

______. *A Handbook for Travellers in Lower and Upper Egypt.* London, 1890, 1891.

Piankoff, A. "The Osireion of Seti I at Abydos During the Graeco-Roman Period and the Christian Occupation." *Bulletin de la Société d'archéologie copte* 15 (1960):125–49.

Sauneron, S., and J. Jacquet. *Les Ermitages chrétiens du désert d'Esna,* Vol. 1. Fouilles de l'Institut français d'Archéologie orientale 29/1. Cairo, 1972.

Wilkinson, G. *Egypt and Thebes,* 2 vols. London, 1843.

RENÉ-GEORGES COQUIN
MAURICE MARTIN, S.J.

SHAYKH ṢAʿID, AL-. Less than 2 miles (about 3 km) south of the village of al-Barshā, on the right bank of the Nile, are some tombs from ancient Egypt, known as the tombs of al-Shaykh Ṣaʿīd. They were later fitted up as dwellings, like those of Banī Ḥasan, and one of them served as a chapel. Others were transformed into cells, and sometimes a door was cut to connect two tombs.

The complex is described by Davies (1901, esp. pls. VII, 7, 11, 13, 14, 33), by Badawy (1953), and by Meinardus (1965, 1977).

The tombs are called Dayr Abū Fām by the inhabitants of the region, and are described by that name by Nestor L'Hôte, Davies, and Meinardus. This perhaps indicates that the painting in the chapel, said to be of Saint George, is in reality that of PHOIBAMMON. Four graffiti are reproduced by Sayce (1885–1886, p. 186, 1886–1887, p. 192).

BIBLIOGRAPHY

Badawy, A. "Les Premiers établissements chrétiens dans les anciennes tombes d'Egypte." In *Tome commémoratif du millinaire de la Bibliothèque patriarcale d'Alexandrie.* Publications de l'Institut d'Etudes orientales de la Bibliothèque patriarchal d'Alexandrie 2. Alexandria, 1953.

Crum, W. E. "Christian Egypt." In *Archaeological Report* 11, ed. F. Ll. Griffith (1901–1902):48–58.

Davies, N. de Garis. "Archaelogical Survey." In *Archaeological Report* 8, ed. F. Ll. Griffith (1899–1900):4–7.

______. *The Rock Tombs of Sheikh Saʿid.* London, 1901.

L'Hôte, N. *Lettres écrites d'Egypte en 1838 et 1839.* Paris, 1840.

Meinardus, O. *Christian Egypt, Ancient and Modern.* Cairo, 1965; 2nd ed., 1977.

Sayce, A. H. "Coptic and Early Christian Inscriptions in Upper Egypt." *Proceedings of the Society of Biblical Archaeology* 4 (1885–1886):175–91.

______. "Dated Inscriptions of Amenophis III." *Proceedings of the Society of Biblical Archaeology* 9 (1886–1887):195–97.

RENÉ-GEORGES COQUIN
MAURICE MARTIN, S.J.

SHENOUDA III, 117th patriarch of the See of Saint Mark (1971–). Born Naẓīr Jayyid, he graduated from Cairo University in 1947 and from the CLERICAL COLLEGE in 1949. He taught theology in a Coptic seminary in Ḥilwān while participating in many activities of the church. In 1952, he was elected member of the Egyptian Journalists' Syndicate, while editing the Sunday School Monthly Magazine.

In 1954, he took the monastic vow at DAYR AL-SURYĀN in Wādī al-Naṭrūn where, for a time, he retired to a cave in the western desert, and was ultimately ordained HEGUMENOS by the name of Anṭūniyus al-Suryānī. In 1962, Patriarch CYRIL VI elevated him to the rank of bishop in charge of theological education.

In 1971, he was selected for the patriarchate. Immediately afterward in the same year, he was consecrated patriarch of the Coptic Church.

GABRIEL ABDELSAYYED

SHENOUTE. *See* Shenute.

SHENUFE, SAINT, a fourth-century martyr under DIOCLETIAN (feast day: 7 Bābah). His Passion has survived complete in a codex (Pierpont Morgan Library, New York, M 583, fols. 103–138; ed. Reymond and Barns, 1973, pp. 83–127) and in fragments of another codex (Coptic Museum, Cairo, Sottas, 1919).

At the beginning of the text there is an interesting and unusual list of prefects of Egypt at the time of Diocletian. This is followed by the usual promulgation of the edict of persecution and the sending of letters to the prefect ARIANUS in Egypt. Shenufe and his family (his brothers were martyred with him) from Empaiat, near Alexandria, are then presented.

After seeing a vision of Jesus, Shenufe presents himself to Arianus in Alexandria and confesses his faith. He is brought first to Memphis, where he is tried and where he performs miracles, and then to the Fayyūm, where various miraculous episodes take place—the dead being raised, healings, etcetera. After this there is the list of magistrates of the Fayyūm. After various moves within the Fayyūm, the final sentence, and a last vision of the Savior, he is martyred in the presence of Julius of Aqfahs.

In this version, the text represents a contamination of the Cycles of Basilides and the Cycle of Julius of Aqfahs; however, the break in the narrative clearly shows that the elements taken from the

Cycle of Basilides are extraneous to a preceding narrative, whether written or oral is uncertain.

BIBLIOGRAPHY

Baumeister, T. *Martyre Invictus. Der Märtyrer als Sinnbild der Erlösung in der Legende und im Kult der frühen koptischen Kirche,* p. 129. Münster, 1972.

Horn, J. "Der erste Märtyrer. Zu einem Topos der koptischen Märtyrerliteratur (mit zwei Anhängen)." In *Studien zur Spätantik und frühchristlichen Kunst und Kultur des Orients,* ed. G. Koch. Weisbaden, 1982.

Munier, H. "Fragments des actes du martyre de l'apa Chnoubi." *Annales du Service des Antiquités* 17 (1917):145–59.

Reymond, E. A. E., and J. W. B. Barnes. *Four Martyrdoms from the Pierpont Morgan Coptic Codices.* Oxford, 1973.

Sethe, K. In *Zeitschrift für ägyptische Sprache und Altertumskunde* 57 (1922):139–40.

Sottas, E. *Revue Egyptologique* n.s. (1919):264–67.

TITO ORLANDI

SHENUTE, SAINT, fourth–fifth-century reforming abbot of DAYR ANBĀ SHINŪDAH (the White Monastery) situated near the ancient village of Atrīb, near Suhāj, in the region of Akhmīm (feast day: 7 Abīb). The source material that makes it possible to reconstruct his life and work consists mainly of the literary remains of his own writings and of the Life composed by his disciple BESA, who succeeded him as abbot of the White Monastery. The Life, although doubtless originally written in Sahidic, has survived in its entirety only in Bohairic and in several other Oriental versions (Arabic, Syriac, Ethiopic). In spite of its hagiological nature—it abounds in miracle stories—it contains valuable historical information.

Shenute's dates are not certain. He probably died in 466 and, if he really reached the age of 118 as reported by Besa, he was born in 348. His place of birth was the village of Shenalolet in the region of Akhmīm, where his parents owned a small holding and some sheep. As a youth, Shenute worked as a shepherd. He soon seems to have come under the influence of his maternal uncle, PJOL, the founder of the White Monastery, which he entered in about 371. When Pjol died, in about 385, Shenute became abbot.

His life's work was the running of the White Monastery, which grew significantly under his rule and contained houses for nuns as well as houses for monks. The Arabic version of the Life speaks of 2,200 monks and 1,800 nuns. Those who wished to enter the monastery had to renounce all their belongings and to make a vow, which was introduced by Shenute, to lead a pure life. Before they were finally accepted, they had to spend a trial period at the gate house, which was also the place where visitors were received, and which was supervised by a trusted monk. Once in the monastery, they were expected to take part in the work and worship of the community. Precise rules regulated all activities, including eating and drinking in the refectory, which was, of course, severely ascetic. Only in the infirmary were the dietary rules relaxed. All responsible positions within the monastery were occupied by older, trusted monks.

Shenute was a strict disciplinarian. He administered the monastery in accordance with the rule introduced by Pjol, which was itself a good deal harsher than the rule of Saint PACHOMIUS, and he supplemented it by innumerable detailed instructions contained in his many epistles. Obedience for him was the keystone of the monastic life. He waged a constant war against the sins and failings of his monks and nuns. The punishments that he imposed on them could be fierce and included corporal punishment and, in extreme cases, expulsion from the monastery.

His passionate and violent nature is revealed in his writings and found expression in his dealings with his monks and nuns. It sometimes turned into depression and despair when his authority was not instantly accepted and obeyed. But it must be remembered that in all his activities he saw himself as God's obedient servant. Indeed, it is clear that he considered himself to be inspired by God and to be the vessel of prophetic enthusiasm. In spite of his heavy responsibilities in the monastery, he withdrew from time to time to a retreat in the desert in order to pray and enjoy a closer communion with God, and it is reported that he was vouchsafed visions there. The high spiritual claims of the monastic movement, which saw itself as a spiritual elite and was accepted as such by many, sometimes caused tensions with the episcopal hierarchy, but it seems that Shenute managed to avoid any serious clash.

One event in Shenute's life is of special importance. In 431, he, with CYRIL, archbishop of Alexandria, attended the Council of EPHESUS. The story in Besa's Life of Shenute's violent clash with NESTORIUS may be open to doubt, but that he attended the council can be accepted as historical fact, and it is

Stone relief of Saint Shenute. *Courtesy State Museum of Berlin.*

quite possible that it was on this occasion that he was given the rank of an ARCHIMANDRITE in recognition of his services. Cyril, no doubt, had invited Shenute to accompany him to Ephesus because he had heard of his reputation as a reliable defender of the Alexandrian cause. But, although on this occasion Shenute supported Cyril, it must be doubted whether he fully appreciated the theological complexities of the doctrinal controversies of his time. In spite of his knowledge of the Greek language and some acquaintance with Greek philosophy and classical mythology, Shenute was at heart a true Copt whose religion and piety were practical rather than theoretical.

In his writings, he was predominantly concerned with the practical affairs of his monastery and the moral issues affecting his charges. He knew the Bible well and his writings abound in references to it, but he was not a thinker who was able to develop a coherent theology. He was aware of some of the heresies of his time and attacked, for instance, the Arians, the Melitians, and the Manichaeans, but he did not examine theological questions in any depth. His discussions of Christological problems revealed him as a follower of Cyril of Alexandria, but here again his emphasis was on the practical concerns of monasticism. In this connection it is interesting to see how little he has to say on the veneration of the Virgin MARY (cf. Weiss, 1969–1970). He also wrote a polemical treatise against Origenist gnosticism (cf. Orlandi, 1982). But none of this affects the overall picture. Shenute is not famous as a theologian.

His influence was not confined to the White Monastery. His work brought him into contact with the population of the surrounding region, and thus his popularity grew in a wider field. A constant stream of visitors came to consult him and to receive his blessing. These included bishops and ascetics, as, for example, monks from SCETIS and from the Pachomian monasteries, as well as secular dignitaries. The monastic services were open to laymen who would attend and listen to Shenute's sermons, many of which are preserved among his writings. Often visitors came to ask for advice on both secular and spiritual matters. Even military commanders would seek his guidance and receive his blessing before going into battle against nomadic tribes, which from time to time made incursions into Upper Egypt from the south. Shenute seems to have made himself accessible to all who wished to approach him, and there are many references in the sources to his pastoral activities. He had a lively concern for the welfare of the whole region. He offered up special prayers for the flooding of the Nile, which ensured the country's prosperity.

His charitable acts were many. The poor received alms, and in times of famine special relief was mounted and the distribution of bread was organized. On one occasion, when invading tribes devastated the country, Shenute reports that 20,000 men, women, and children sought refuge behind the walls of the White Monastery. They were fed and clothed by the monks and all their needs were taken care of. Their sick were tended and their dead buried. Shenute was obviously very proud of this achievement, for he described the incident in great detail. He was careful, however, not to claim any credit for himself, but rather to praise God who had made this feat possible. Incidentally, his account throws some light on the economic strength of the White Monastery and on his own organizational ability. It also illustrates his active involvement in the affairs of his country.

On many occasions, Shenute appeared as the champion of the poor and oppressed. He upbraided the rich for exploiting their workers and for their cruelty in their dealings with the poor. The moral failings of the rich were often singled out for opprobrium. But his very special hatred was reserved for pagan religion, which he opposed in word and deed. In his writings there are many passages which heap scorn and insult on pagan superstitions and beliefs. In many instances his fanatical hatred of paganism and pagans was translated into action. He himself led attacks against pagan temples and his admirers followed his example. Temples were burned down and cult objects were carried off or destroyed. Even the houses belonging to pagans were not safe from his attention. All attempts of the pagans to restrain Shenute by law were frustrated by the militant popular support he enjoyed.

Shenute's writings, which have come down to us in a fragmented state, are not yet completely assembled and edited. Their importance for the history of indigenous Coptic literature is considerable. Their popularity is attested by their having been copied over and over again and by their having been read in the White Monastery for many generations. Shenute's literary style, especially in his letters, mirrors his character. It is highly individualistic and very powerful. Often the speed and passion of his thinking affected the clarity of his expression. He liked to repeat an idea by means of synonymous expressions, and he used many biblical quotations and allusions. His style is a vehicle for conveying his emotions and his strength of character. His influence on the development of the Sahidic literary language is not yet fully explored.

Shenute's prominent position in the history of the Coptic church is assured. He was not only a famous monk held in high esteem by his contemporaries as a man of God but also an important leader of the church and an author whose influence extended far beyond his own monastery.

BIBLIOGRAPHY

Amélineau, E. *Oeuvres de Schenoudi: Texte copte et traduction française,* Vols. 1 and 2. Paris, 1907–1914.

Bell, D. N. *Besa: The Life of Shenoute.* Kalamazoo, Mich., 1983.

Colin, G., ed. and trans. *La version éthiopienne de la vie de Schenoudi.* CSCO 444–45: *Scriptores Aethiopici,* Vols. 75–76. Louvain, 1982.

Leipoldt, J. *Schenute von Atripe und die Entstehung des national ägyptischen Christentums.* Leipzig, 1903.

Leipoldt, J., ed. *Sinuthii Vita* (Bohairic). CSCO 41, *Scriptores Coptici,* Vol. 1. Louvain, 1951. Translated into Latin by H. Wiesmann in CSCO 129, *Scriptores Coptici,* Vol. 16. Louvain, 1951.

Leipoldt, J., and W. E. Crum, eds. *Sinuthii Archimandritae Vita et Opera Omnia.* CSCO 42, 73, *Scriptores Coptici,* Vols. 2 and 5. Louvain, 1954–1955. Translated into Latin by H. Wiesman in CSCO 96, *Scriptores Coptici,* Vol. 8 (Louvain, 1953) and 108, *Scriptores Coptici,* Vol. 12 (Louvain, 1952).

Orlandi, T. "A Catechesis against Apocryphal Texts by Shenoute and the Gnostic Texts of Nag Hammadi." *Harvard Theological Review* 75 (1982):85–95.

Weiss, H. F. "Zur Christologie des Schenute von Atripe." *Bulletin de la société d'archéologie copte* 20 (1969–1970):177–209.

For fuller bibliographical information, see P. J. Frandsen and E. Richter-Aerøe, "Shenoute: A Bibliography." In *Studies Presented to Hans Jakob Polotsky,* ed. D. W. Young. East Gloucester, Mass. 1981.

K. H. KUHN

SHENUTE I, fifty-fifth patriarch of the See of Saint Mark (858–880). Shenute, or Sanutios in Coptic and Shinūdah in modern Arabic, was a native of the village of al-Batanūn, today a village in the governorate of Shibīn al-Kom, the capital city of the Minūfiyyah province in Lower Egypt. Little is known about his early secular life, and even his date of birth is unknown. However, he could have taken the monastic vow at the monastery of Saint Macarius (DAYR ANBĀ MAQĀR) during the patriarchate of YŪSĀB I (830–849), which would make him a contemporary of three patriarchs, Yūsāb, KHĀ'ĪL II (849–851), and COSMAS II (851–858). In his monastery, he was elevated to the rank of HEGUMENOS, or archpriest, in recognition of his sanctity, Christian humility, and the devotion with which he served his brotherhood.

His fame must have extended beyond the walls of his convent, for when his predecessor, Cosmas II, died, the bishops, the clergy, and the leading Coptic archons automatically and unanimously thought of him as a worthy successor to the throne of Saint Mark. At a meeting in Miṣr (al-Fusṭāṭ) they decided to hasten to his monastery to bring him to the valley for his nomination. But one archon, Abraham, knowing that he would be unwilling to accept their call, suggested that he himself should go and ask Shenute to come only to help them in finding the right candidate for that dignity. Once he was present, the council would force him to go to Alexandria with them for consecration, even against his will. And this is exactly what happened. Ultimately the bishops laid their hands on him on 13 Ṭūbah, and he had to face the heavy responsibilities of his office.

He began his reign with the usual attempt to secure good relations with the sister church of Antioch by the issuance of a synodical epistle to its patriarch, John (Yuḥannā). He dispatched his epistle with a delegation of two bishops, Malunulas of Dawikh and John (Yuḥanna) of Diusia, together with some Coptic clergymen.

Having performed this international function, Shenute began to devote his energy to local matters in need of special attention. One of his first acts was to forbid the use of simony (CHEIROTONIA), which his predecessors were prone to practice in order to help them in meeting the financial imposts of the Muslim administration. Then he directed his attention toward helping the monasteries of Upper Egypt, which were situated too far from Alexandria to claim papal care. He also gave much of his time in the early years of his patriarchate to the improvement of the material welfare of his flock. Within the region of Alexandria, he dug a special canal to bring Nile water within reach of the inhabitants. This was a new branch of the canal known as the *Khalīj*, which had been established by Caliph al-Mutawakkil (847–861) and which poured in the Mediterranean outside the city limits. He was also responsible for building a subterranean sewage system in the city to ensure sanitation and constructing fountains of drinking water in public squares.

All this did not stop him from watching over the religious orthodoxy of his flock. In Upper Egypt he managed to stifle a heretical movement that had arisen in the district of al-Balyanā, in which some people said that the divinity of Christ could be considered dead with the death of his humanity. He rectified the theology of others, such as the bishop of Samannūd and the bishop of Minyat Tānah, who resided in the monastery of Saint Macarius.

The HISTORY OF THE PATRIARCHS (Vol. 2, pt. 1, p. 23) states that the children of Ilyās (Ibn Yazīd), who was the governor of Alexandria during the patriarchate of Jacob (819–830), rendered to Shenute money that their father had extorted from Jacob, and that this must have made Shenute's reform projects possible. However, this atmosphere of peace and security did not last long. With the murder of Caliph al-Mutawakkil in 861 and the accession of al-Muntaṣir (861–862), the situation changed drastically, for the new caliph dismissed all his predecessor's governors and replaced them with others from his realm. The new governor of Egypt was Aḥmad ibn Muḥammad al-Mudabbir, a man known for his greed and brutality from when he was posted in Palestine. In Egypt, Ibn al-Mudabbir laid a heavy hand on its population—Muslims, Christians, and Jews alike, without discrimination. But the condition of the Christians was probably the worst, for he tripled the poll tax (JIZYAH) to three dinars and imposed it on both laymen and clergy alike, including the monks, who were numbered and registered for strict payment of the imposts. He imposed the KHARAJ tax on all possessions, including not only cattle but also beehives and fruit trees on private lots. He gave his agents explicit orders to spare nobody and to arrest and chain any defaulter.

Thus, it may be assumed that the year 861 began a period of great trials for Shenute, who was pursued by the governor's representatives and ultimately took to flight from his new persecutor for a period of six months. When he saw no means of escape from his oppresser, however, accompanied by his assistant, Mīnā, he decided to plead for justice and mercy. The harsh governor told the patriarch that he owed him 2,300 dinars for the monasteries, 7,000 dinars for the *kharaj* tax, and 6,000 dinars poll tax. When the Coptic archons heard that the pope was held responsible for payment of these tremendous sums of money at the risk of his freedom, they started allotting these debts to all the people. Many Copts apostatized to Islam to save themselves from rendering money they did not possess.

A breathing space, however, came when al-Muntaṣir died and Caliph al-Mustaʿīn (862–866) succeeded him. With the blessings of the patriarch, two Coptic archons, Ibrāhīm and Sawīrus, decided to go to Baghdad to complain to the new caliph about the injustices and cruelty of Ibn al-Mudabbir, such as his excessive financial imposts and the abuse of Coptic religious institutions. The result was a decree of relief from injustice for the oppressed Copts, which allowed them to start restoration of their ruined churches. But ensuing warfare between caliphal pretenders, al-Muʿtazz (866–869) and al-Muhtadī (869–870), plagued the later Abbasid period, and Egypt became easy prey to bedouin marauders who stormed some of the monasteries in the desert and descended on the valley in Upper Egypt, pillaging and burning churches throughout a defenseless countryside. Even the replacement of the fierce Ibn al-Mudabbir by more lenient governors, such as one named Muzāḥim, did not help very much. One of them was Yaḥyā ibn ʿAbdallāh, who seems to have been aided by collaborators from within the Christian community, such as a certain Stephen (Uṣṭufān) ibn Andūnah.

This state of confusion seems to have persisted until the caliphate of Aḥmad ibn Ṭūlūn (870–881), during whose reign Shenute died after a tempestuous reign lasting twenty-one years and three months.

BIBLIOGRAPHY

Lane-Poole, S. *History of Egypt in the Middle Ages.* London, 1901.

Weil, G. *Geschichte der Chalifen,* 5 vols. Mannheim, 1846–1862.

SUBHI Y. LABIB

SHENUTE II, sixty-fifth patriarch of the See of Saint Mark (1032–1046). Shenute was a native of the town of Tilbānat-ʿAdiy, but the date of his birth is unknown. He joined the Monastery of Saint Macarius (DAYR ANBĀ MAQĀR) at the youthful age of fourteen. The HISTORY OF THE PATRIARCHS records that he was an ambitious monk, and that he coveted the episcopate of Miṣr (al-Fusṭāṭ), but he could not attain it because he had no funds to offer for his investiture. He was a contemporary of the Fatimid caliphs al-Ẓāhir Abū al-Ḥasan ʿAli (1021–1035) and al-Mustanṣir Abū Tamīm Mʿadd (1035–1094). When Shenute was selected to become patriarch a delegation headed by Buqayrah al-Rashidī, the bearer of the cross in al-ḤĀKIM's reign and a member of the Coptic delegation, went to the vizier, Najīb al-Dawlah Abū al-Qāsim ʿAli ibn Aḥmad al-Jurjāni, to get the permission to elect him. The vizier advised Buqayrah to use a system known as *al-qurʿah al-haykāliyyah,* or the sanctuary lottery, as practiced in Baghdad by the church of Antioch (see PATRIARCHAL ELECTION). Though the delegation departed with the vizier's approval, they refrained from applying his advice. They chose the monk of Saint Macarius, Shenute, but they procrastinated in his consecration until they secured his written approval of their conditions; in the meantime they raised him to the position of archpriest or HEGUMENOS. Their conditions included the payment of 500 dinars annually to the people of Alexandria for the benefit of their churches, and the suppression of simony (CHEIROTONIA) levied on the bishops and the clergy at their investiture. The ambitious Shenute approved their conditions, although he had no intention of following them after his consecration. He later explained to Buqayrah, the bearer of the cross, that by obeying the conditions he would not be able to pay the 3,000 dinars due to the state on the occasion of his accession, nor meet the heavy expenses of his office. He requested 600 dinars for investing the new bishop of Asyūṭ and even confiscated the religious property of Īliyyā, bishop of Bishnānah, after his death, while deposing Yuḥannā, bishop of al-Faramā, for his inability to pay his simony. Such events recurred throughout his reign.

However, a number of events worthy of recording took place during Shenute's patriarchate. Contrary to Islamic tradition, Caliph al-Ẓāhir permitted the Copts, who had been forced to apostatize to Islam during the reign of al-Ḥākim, to return to their Christian faith without incrimination or decapitation. Also, in the year 1040, the Nile was low, and the land was desiccated. The meager crops were further attacked by rats, which exterminated the corn from the fields and the grapes from the vineyards.

The biographer of the *History of the Patriarchs* adds an interesting supplement to his account, ascribed to MAWHŪB IBN MANṢŪR IBN MUFARRIJ, the deacon from Alexandria. He records the total number of monks in the area of Wādī Habīb in 1088 as 712: 400 in Dayr Anbā Maqār, 165 in DAYR YUḤANNIS AL-QAṢĪR, 25 in DAYR YUHANNIS KAMA, 20 in DAYR AL-BARĀMŪS, 40 in DAYR ANBĀ BISHOI, 60 in DAYR AL-SURYĀN, and 2 in the cave of Abū Mūsa—one Syriac and another Coptic. The number of itinerant monks was unknown. The caliph at this time was al-Mustanṣir Billāh, who succeeded his predecessor at the age of seven and occupied the throne of Egypt for fifty-nine years. His minister was Badr al-Jamālī.

BIBLIOGRAPHY

Lane-Poole, S. *The Mohammadan Dynasties.* London, 1894.

______. *History of Egypt in the Middle Ages.* London, 1901.

Prise, F. *The Book of Calendars.* New York, 1974.

SUBHI Y. LABIB

SHENUTEAN IDIOM. *See Appendix.*

SHIBĀB AL-DĪN AḤMAD NUWAYRĪ. Shibāb al-Dīn Aḥmad ʿAbd al-Wahhāb al- Nuwayrī (d. 1332) wrote an encyclopedia called *Nihāyat al-Arab fī funūn al-adab* (The Limits of Desires in the Arts of Literature). Among other things, it is an important source of information about the Nubian campaigns of the Mamluk sultan Qalawun, which contributed greatly to the final dissolution of the Christian kingdom of MAKOURIA. Nuwayrī's account provides the most detailed surviving information about events and conditions in Nubia toward the close of the Middle Ages. Much of this material was subsequently copied in the *Kitāb al-sulūk* (Book of Behavior) of al-MAQRĪZĪ.

BIBLIOGRAPHY

Nuwayrī, Aḥmad ibn ʿAbd al-Wahhāb al-. *Nihāyat al-arab fī funūn al-adab.* Cairo, 1923–.

Vantini, G. *The Excavations at Faras: A Contribution to the History of Christian Nubia,* p. 103, Bologna, 1970.

______. *Oriental Sources Concerning Nubia,* pp. 467–92, Heidelberg and Warsaw, 1975.

WILLIAM Y. ADAMS

SHIRT. *See* Liturgical Vestments.

SHOTEP. *See* Shuṭb.

SHUBRA. *See* Toponymy.

SHUKRALLĀH JIRJIS (Muʿallim), Coptic contemporary of the French Expedition to Egypt and a close friend and colleague of General YAʿQŪB. Though the particulars of his early life are unknown, we must assume that he was born in the first half of the eighteenth century. During French rule in Egypt, he is known to have headed the finance department and to have devised a taxation system. The system met all the needs of the state without undue pressures on the taxpayers, who were accustomed to the extortionate and erratic impositions of the Mamluks. Apparently he earned the respect and admiration of General Ménou, who wrote to Napoleon praising him and commending him as a person who took the interests of his country to heart. It is said that Napoleon sent General Yaʿqūb a missive in his own hand in which Shukrallāh was cited.

AZIZ S. ATIYA

SHUṬB, town situated on the west bank of the Nile about 5 miles (8 km) southeast of Asyūṭ in the province of the same name. In Coptic the town was known as Shotep. It was a bishopric by the end of the thirteenth century, as evidenced by the name of Yu'annis, bishop of Shuṭb and Ṭaḥā, in the list of those who attended the preparation of the CHRISM in Cairo in 1299 (Munier, 1943, p. 36).

BIBLIOGRAPHY

Munier, H. *Recueil de listes épiscopales de l'église copte.* Cairo, 1943.

RANDALL STEWART

SHUTTLE. *See* Textiles, Coptic: Manufacturing Techniques.

SIBIRBĀY, small village east of Ṭanṭā in the province of Gharbiyyah. Its Coptic name was ⲯⲉⲙⲉⲣⲫⲉⲓ, Psemerphei, and in older Arabic sources the village was called Simirbāyah. Sibirbāy has an old church dedicated to the archangel Michael whose anniversary is celebrated by faithful pilgrims on 12 Ba'ūnah.

BIBLIOGRAPHY

Amélineau, E. *La Geógraphie de l'Egypte à l'époque copte,* pp. 376–77. Paris, 1893.

Viaud, G. *Les Pèlerinages coptes en Egypte.* From the notes of Jacob Muyser. Cairo, 1979.

RANDALL STEWART

SICARD, CLAUDE (1676–1726), French Jesuit missionary in Egypt (1712–1726), where he was dedicated to the service of lepers. He was particularly interested in the monasteries of Wādī al-Naṭrūn as well as those of Saint Antony and Saint Paul on the Red Sea. On account of his apostolic mission, which took him all over the country, he was able to accomplish considerable archaeological work in the regions of Thebes, Abydos, Idfū, and Philae. In 1718 he founded in Akhmīm the first Coptic Catholic community. He refused to separate the practice of the sacraments by Catholics from that of their original Coptic community and fought long with the Roman authorities in defense of his view.

Sicard's works were reproduced in the Lettres édifiantes et curieuses, Vol. 5 (Paris, 1905). A critical edition of his writings was published by the Institut français d'Archéologie orientale: *Oeuvres* (3 vols., Cairo, 1982).

BIBLIOGRAPHY

Honigmann, E. *Trois mémoires posthumes d'histoire et de géographie de l'Orient chrétien préparés pour l'impression par Paul Devos*, pp. 127–207. Brussels, 1961.

Sommervogel, C. *Bibliothèque de la Compagnie de Jesus*, 2nd ed., Vol. 7, pp. 1185–89. Brussels, 1896.

Streit, R., and J. Dindinger. *Bibliotheca Missionum*, Vol. 17, pp. 9–141. Münster, 1916–1955.

MAURICE MARTIN, S.J.

SĪDĀRŪS, GABRIEL (1768–1851), also called Sidarious, Sidarous, Sidarousse, or Sidarosse, military man born in Cairo. He was better known by his given name, spelled Gabrielle. He himself signed Gabriel S. He was a nephew of General YA'QŪB on both sides of his family.

Sīdārūs started his adult life as intendant on the estates of the Mamluk amir Ibrāhīm Bey, who ruled with Murād Bey, and before the arrival of Napoleon in Cairo conducted the affairs of Muḥammad Bey al-Alfī for two years. After September 1798 he assisted YA'QŪB, who was nominated intendant under General Louis Desaix de Veygoux, during the campaign against the Mamluks in Upper Egypt. In spite of his being a Copt, a condition that in principle forbade him to carry arms or to ride a horse, he distinguished himself in the battles against the bedouins and the Mamluks in Jirjā and especially at Abū Mannā', where on 17 February 1799 he received a sword wound in his head.

Sīdārūs held the rank of colonel in the Coptic Legion. After his retirement from the French Army of Egypt, Sīdārūs, followed by a number of legionnaires, went with General Ya'qūb to France. He became the main officer in the Coptic Legion following the death of General Ya'qūb in 1801.

BIBLIOGRAPHY

Homsy, Gaston. *Le Général Jacob et l'expédition de Bonaparte en Egypte, 1798–1801*, pp. 64–67. Marseilles, 1921.

______. "Un Egyptien, colonel dans les armées de Napoléon Ier." *Bulletin de l'Institut d'Egypte* (1927–1928):83–96.

"L'Orient des Provençaux dans l'histoire." In *Catalogue des expositions des Archives départementales, de la Chambre de commerce et des Archives de la ville*, pp. 96–98. Marseilles, 1982.

ANOUAR LOUCA

SIDFI. *See* Pilgrimages.

SILK. *See* Textiles, Coptic: Yarns.

SILVANUS OF SCETIS, SAINT, a native of Palestine who was a monk at SCETIS in the late fourth century (feast day: 1 Baramūdah). He was looked upon as one of the old men and had twelve disciples, among whom, according to the APOPHTHEGMATA PATRUM (PG. 65, cols. 408–412; cf. col. 176), were Zeno (Zeno 1), Zacharias (Silvanus 1. 3. 8), Nitras, and Mark. The latter worked as a calligrapher and was particularly beloved by his master because of his obedience. Abba Moses doubtless was not one of his disciples but did interview him. Silvanus left Scetis in all probability on the occasion of a barbarian raid and went into Sinai and then to Palestine, where "having built himself a cell near the river he spent the rest of his life in it, just as at Scetis." This "monastery of the abba Silvanus" was located at Gerara, the modern Oum-Djerar (Vailhé, pp. 281–282).

Silvanus appears in the *Apophthegmata* as a great contemplative, the favored recipient of visions and ecstasies, but also as someone who did not always go about with his eyes shut and who worked to gain his daily bread. His mortification of the flesh was carried to great lengths, but he was also able to reconcile strict asceticism with the demands of charity. He is mentioned in the Copto-Arabic SYNAXANON as a disciple of Saint MACARIUS THE EGYPTIAN, who was also at Scetis, but there is no reference to his departure for Sinai and Palestine.

BIBLIOGRAPHY

Chitty, D. J. *The Desert a City*, pp. 71–74. Oxford, 1966.

Evelyn-White, H. G. *The Monasteries of the Wadi'n Natrûn,* Part II, pp. 181–183. New York, 1932.
Parys, M. van. "Abba Silvain et ses disciples." *Irenikon* 61 (1988):315–31; 451–80.
Vaihlé, S. "Répertoire alphabétique des monastères de Palestine." *Revue de l'Orient chrétien* 5 (1900):281–82.

LUCIEN REGNAULT

SIMAIKAH, MARCOS. *See* Murqus Simaykah.

SIMʿĀN IBN ABĪ NAṢR AL-ṬAMADĀʾĪ, thirteenth-century copier of a manuscript now in the Coptic Museum, Cairo. It is a text of the four Gospels in Bohairic Coptic, beautifully decorated in black, red, and gold, with numerous miniature letters of pharaonic inspiration. The manuscript (Bible 92) contains 327 large-format sheets (34 × 25 cm), with twenty-three lines to the page. The first two sheets are missing. The colophon (fol. 327b) gives some interesting information, which is translated in Horner (p. 104).

Simʿān was a priest from Ṭamadā. He copied the manuscript when he was living in Cairo in the quarter of Qaṣr al-Shamʿ. He probably lived in the residence of the donor of the manuscript, the *shaykh* al-Raʾīs al-Amjad Abū al-Majd, son of the *shaykh* al-Akram Abu al-Muffaḍḍal. Al-Amjad donated this manuscript to the Church of the Muʿallaqah, situated in the Qaṣr al-Shamʿ in Old Cairo.

BIBLIOGRAPHY

Graf, G. *Catalogue de manuscripts arabes chrétiens conservés au Caire,* p. 65, no. 152. Vatican City, 1934.
Horner, G. W. *The Coptic Version of the New Testament in the Northern Dialect,* pp. 102–104. London, 1898–1905.

KHALIL SAMIR, S.J.

SIMEONSTIFT COPTIC COLLECTION. *See* Museums, Coptic Collections in.

SIMON I, saint and forty-second patriarch of the See of Saint Mark (689–701). His nomination came at a difficult time. His predecessor, ISAAC, had died in the midst of the fury arising from his meddling in the conflict between Ethiopia and Nubia without consulting the Umayyad governor of Egypt, ʿAbd al-ʿAzīz ibn Marwān. In addition, there was local strife in Alexandria between the clergy of Saint Mark's Cathedral and those of the formidable Angelion church, whose clergy numbered 140. Whereas the former supported the nomination as patriarch of a certain Yuḥannā from the ENATON monastery for his learning, the latter promoted another monk by the name of Victor (Buqṭur) from Dayr Taposiris, for his sanctity rather than his scholarship. In the end, the balance was tipped in favor of Yuḥannā by the archon Tadrus, secretary of the *diwan* in Alexandria. Tadrus wrote to ʿAbd al-ʿAzīz. The amir requested the presence of the nominee, who came with his favorite disciple Simon, a Syrian from the DAYR AL-SURYĀN in Wādī al-Naṭrūn. In an audience with Yuḥannā and the bishops, a voice was raised proposing Simon for the patriarchate, and curiously the others applauded him. Thus Simon was brought before the governor. When asked about Yuḥannā, Simon meekly declared that Yuḥannā was the fittest for the position of patriarch. Nevertheless ʿAbd al-ʿAzīz gave his approval of Simon's candidacy.

Simon's parents had brought him to Egypt when he was a child, during the patriarchate of AGATHON, and he ultimately joined Dayr al-Suryān, where he received intensive religious training in the Coptic tradition. He displayed unusual talents, and he was elevated from deacon to the position of presbyter. After his consecration as patriarch, his mentor Yuḥannā died, and Simon transported the body to Dayr al-Suryān where he also built his own tomb beside that of his spiritual father.

Returning to Alexandria, he had to face the difficult task of his new office. But instead of attending to the daily requirements and responsibilities of his office, he retired to a life of strict asceticism and secluded prayer. The clergy, whose routine affairs were neglected, were exasperated by this behavior and began to contemplate the elimination of the patriarch from the scene. It is recorded that four members of the clergy in conjunction with a magician poisoned the patriarch's food, which caused him much suffering but miraculously did not kill him. ʿAbd al-ʿAzīz, who happened to visit Alexandria at the time, was informed about the conspiracy and at once issued an order for burning the four clerical conspirators and the magician who had participated in the preparation of the poisoned food. As a good Christian, the patriarch appealed for the release of the guilty priests, who recovered their freedom, but the magician suffered death.

Simon decided afterward to confide the affairs of

the monasteries to the more experienced JOHN OF NIKIOU. Although John administered satisfactorily for a short period, a group of monks from Wādī al-Naṭrūn were disenchanted with his governance and organized a plot for disgracing the community under his surveillance and embarrassing the church by means of secretly seducing a nun for intercourse with one of the monks. The story reached John of Nikiou, who consequently brought that monk for correction and beat him so severely that he died after ten days. The other bishops, on hearing the news of the death of the monk, held a synod and decided that the bishop of Nikiou had gone beyond reason in his corrective methods and suspended him from his office. They then chose a successor by the name of Menas from DAYR ANBĀ MAQĀR.

A more calamitous issue was brewing in the whole church when a general movement arose among men who wanted to obtain the right to leave their legal wives in favor of taking concubines and still adhering to the church as Christians. They appealed to the governor to legalize this behavior, and consequently ʿAbd al-ʿAzīz convened a special council, which was attended by sixty-four bishops in Alexandria, to look into this strange matter. This council included the orthodox Coptic bishops as well as the Melchite bishops Theophylact, the Chalcedonian; Theodore, the Gaianite follower of Eutychius; and George, the Barsanuphian, who were not recognized by Simon. Apparently no concrete result was reached from that meeting, although the Coptic church adhered to the principle of the sanctity of its matrimonial policies.

Public attention was distracted from this local movement by the news of developments in the international realm. In the Byzantine empire, Justinian II was murdered and Leontius (695–698) followed him on the throne of Constantinople, thus threatening more trouble by inciting unrest within Egypt. ʿAbd al-ʿAzīz ibn Marwān wanted to be assured about the loyalty of the Egyptians. He called for the reunion of Coptic and Muslim leaders to declare their loyal views, at the same time forbidding the practice of church offices to avoid doubtful conglomerations under the cover of religion. The governor was reassured about Coptic loyalty to Arab rule when Simon announced that he anathematized the Chalcedonians, the Gaianites, and the Barsanuphians as heretics, since these were the doubtful elements who harbored Byzantine leanings.

The last important episode in Simon's patriarchate was the advent of a delegate from the Indian church of Saint Thomas on the Malabar coast to request the consecration of a bishop for that church. Simon refused to answer this request without the explicit authorization of the Umayyad authorities. Therefore, the Indian delegate went to the Gaianite enemies of the patriarch, who took him to the heretical sects in Alexandria. His request was fulfilled there by the consecration of a bishop and two priests from Mareotis for him, and the group departed in secret from Egypt only to be intercepted by the caliph's bodyguard in the Eastern Desert. They were returned to ʿAbd al-ʿAzīz in Egypt with a caliphal verdict to punish the patriarch Simon for his indiscretion. The patriarch's innocence was not hard to prove when the Indian delegate confessed his actions to the governor.

ʿAbd al-ʿAzīz continued his friendly relations with Simon, to whom he granted land in Ḥilwān to build two churches and the monastery of Saint Gregorius (DAYR ABŪ QARQŪRAH).

Simon spent the remainder of his life in peace with the Umayyad administration of the country. He managed throughout his reign to steer out of trouble with the Muslim government, as he aimed at the establishment of a peaceful coexistence between the Copts and their Muslim neighbors.

Simon was buried in the church of the Angelion in Alexandria instead of the tomb he had prepared for himself beside that of Bishop Yuḥannā in Dayr al-Suryān.

BIBLIOGRAPHY

Atiya, A. S. *History of Eastern Christianity.* London, 1968.

Lane-Poole, S. *History of Egypt in the Middle Ages.* London, 1901.

______. *The Mohammadan Dynasties.* Paris, 1925.

SUBHI Y. LABIB

SIMON II, Saint and fifty-first patriarch of the See of Saint Mark (830). Simon was a deacon and monk from Alexandria. His life is briefly recorded in the HISTORY OF THE PATRIARCHS. He was a close disciple of JACOB, his predecessor, and his sanctity was known to the clergy and archons of the city. He also was a contemporary of MARK II, a fact that indicates that he must have been an elderly person at the time of his consecration, although his date of birth is unknown and there is no significant record of his very short reign. His patriarchate lasted only five months and sixteen days.

SUBHI Y. LABIB

SIMON, JEAN (1897–1968), Belgian Coptologist and Ethiopic scholar. A member of the Society of Jesus, he was ordained priest in 1928. At first a Bollandist (1930), he had for reasons of health to be assigned to less demanding work. Simon was professor of the Coptic and Ethiopic languages at the Pontifical Biblical Institute (Rome) from 1932 to 1966. He published texts in both languages and took an interest in the continuance of the Coptic dialects for a linguistic congress (1936). In 1938 Simon accompanied L. T. Lefort in his exploration of the Pachomian monastic sites in Egypt. Besides his courses, his most extensive activity, and the one that earned him the recognition of Coptologists, was the annual publication in *Orientalia* from 1948 to 1965 of a "Bibliographie copte," which took up in a different form the work of W. Kammerer.

PIERRE DU BOURGUET, S.J.

SIMONY. *See* Cheirotonia.

SINHIRA. *See* Pilgrimages.

SINJĀR, an important Christian center and episcopal see in Lower Egypt, especially from the eleventh to the thirteenth century. Sinjār is mentioned in the Coptic SYNAXARION, under 4 Misrā, as the place where David and his brothers suffered martyrdom during the DIOCLETIAN persecution. By the eighth century, Sinjār had become an episcopal see.

At the time of the patriarchate of CHRISTODOULUS (1047–1077), Sinjār had increased in importance, partly because of the monks there and partly because of the relics of Saint Philotheus and Saint Thecla the Apostolic that had been transferred from the hermitage of Nafūh at Nastarūh to the hermitage of Sinjār. In 1086, Jirgis ibn Madkūr, the chronicler of the HISTORY OF THE PATRIARCHS, visited Sinjār and the saints' relics. During the middle of the eleventh century, the hermitage of Sinjār gained importance through its monks: Buṭrus al-Sinjārī, who was known for many miracles he wrought; Yustus al-Sinjārī, priest of the Church of Saint Mercurius in Old Cairo; and Kāyīl al-Sinjārī, priest of the Church of the Holy Virgin at al-Jidiyyah.

At the time of CYRIL II (1078–1092), Theodorus of Sinjār was among the forty-seven bishops who participated in the episcopal council at Cairo in 1086. After the death of Cyril II, Michael, the anchorite and *hegumenos* of the hermitage of Sinjār, was elected his successor.

The bishopric of Sinjār continued to exist until the thirteenth century, for during the patriarchate of CYRIL III Ibn Laqlaq (1235–1243), Mark, bishop of Sinjār, had joined the other bishops in their accusations against Cyril; and Buṭrus, bishop of Sinjār, was present at the ceremony of the concoction of the holy chrism in 1257.

One of the last references to Sinjār is by the Arab historian and geographer Abū al-Fidā Ismā'īl ibn 'Alī 'Imad al-Dīn (1273–1331), who is quoted by Qalqashandī (d. 1418). The fourteenth-century list of episcopal sees of Coptic MS 53 of the John Rylands Library also mentions Sinjār.

Sinjār ceased to exist as an inhabited site, because of the rising water level of Lake Burullus, sometime in the sixteenth or seventeenth century. Its ruins are on the northwestern part of the island of Sinjār in Lake Burullus, just over 11 miles (18 km) southwest of Burj al-Burullus. The uninhabited island is about 800 yards (700 m) long and from about 220 to 440 yards (200 m to 400 m) wide. The northwestern part of the island, known as Kom al-Aḥmar, is about 195 by about 130 yards (180 by 120 m), and is covered with a thick layer of broken pottery, burned bricks, broken glass, broken green ceramics, and oxidized coins. A considerable part of ancient Sinjār is submerged. With the rising of the water level, more and more of the island will disappear beneath the waters of Lake Burullus.

BIBLIOGRAPHY

Amélineau, E. *La Géographie de l'Egypte à l'époque copte,* p. 275. Paris, 1893.

Maspero, J., and G. Wiet. *Matériaux pour servir à la géographie de l'Egypte,* Vol. 1, p. 211. Cairo, 1914.

Meinardus, O. "Singar, an Historical and Geographical Study." *Bulletin de la Société d'archéologie copte* 18 (1966):175–79.

Munier, H. *Recueil des listes épiscopales de l'église copte,* p. 35. Cairo, 1943.

Muyser, J. "Contribution à l'étude des listes épiscopales de l'église copte." *Bulletin de la Société d'archéologie copte* 10 (1944):148.

Quatremère, E. M. *Mémoires géographiques et historiques sur l'Egypte,* Vol. 1, p. 280. Paris, 1811.

Villecourt, L. "Les observances liturgiques et la discipline du jeûne dans l'église copte." *Le Muséon* 36 (1923):263.

OTTO MEINARDUS

SINODA. *See* Ethiopian Prelates.

SIRYAQUS. *See* Pilgrimages.

SISOĒS (Jijōi), anchorite (fourth–fifth century). In the APOPHTHEGMATA PATRUM some fifty items mention Sisoēs or Tithoēs, which is another form of the same word. But it is proper to distinguish at least two if not three persons with this name. The earliest and most renowned lived with Ōr and MACARIUS at Scetis; he left there shortly after the death of Saint ANTONY (c. 356) to settle at the hermitage of this saint with his own disciple Abraham. Later he withdrew to Clysma. It is not impossible that this Sisoēs is identical with the person called Sisoēs the Theban in several apothegms, but there is also a Sisoēs of Petra who is definitely different from the Theban one, since there is an account of a brother asking Sisoēs of Petra about something that Sisoēs the Theban had said to him.

Despite some possible confusions, the majority of these apothegms certainly refer to the Sisoēs from Scetis and Clysma, and a good number relate to the long period spent "in Abba Antony's mountain"—more than seventy-two years if the figure given in the apothegm Sisoēs 28 is correct. In all these texts Sisoēs appears as a great lover of solitude and silence, and as a paragon of simplicity and humility, but also as intimate with God and often sunk in contemplation to the point of forgetting bodily needs (Sisoēs 4.27; Tithoēs 1). He brought a dead child back to life (Sisoēs 18). His prayer for his disciple was of astonishing boldness (Sisoēs 12). He had unlimited confidence in the divine mercy, though this did not prevent him, on his deathbed, from asking the angels who came for him to grant him time "to be penitent for a little." His face then shone like the sun, and apostles and prophets came to meet him, and the Lord said of him, "Bring me the chosen vessel of the desert." It is understandable that Sisoēs should have left an indelible memory in the minds of all who knew him. He was valued "like pure gold in a balance" (Tithoēs 2). When old men began talking about Sisoēs, POEMEN would say: "Leave aside Abbā Sisoēs' affairs, for they range far beyond what we could speak of" (Poemen 187).

BIBLIOGRAPHY

Cotelier, J. B., ed. *Apophthegmata patrum*. PG 65, pp. 392–408; 428f. Paris, 1864.

LUCIEN REGNAULT

SITT DIMYANAH. *See* Pilgrimages.

SITT RIFQAH. *See* Pilgrimages.

SIWA (Western Desert), oasis about 190 miles (300 km) from Marsā Maṭrūh, to the west of Alexandria, the most westerly of the Egyptian oases and the most easterly point at which people still speak a Berber dialect. C. Belgrave states that at Balad al-Rumi, near Khamīsah, he saw Christian ruins with a Coptic cross engraved on a stone, perhaps the remains of a monastery (p. 88).

BIBLIOGRAPHY

Belgrave, C. D. *Siwa, the Oasis of Jupiter Ammon.* London, 1923.

RENÉ-GEORGES COQUIN
MAURICE MARTIN, S.J.

SLEEVES. *See* Liturgical Vestments.

SLIPPERS. *See* Liturgical Vestments.

SOBA, the capital city of the medieval Nubian kingdom of ʿALWĀ. It was situated on the east bank of the Blue Nile, a short distance upstream from the confluence with the White Nile. The city is not mentioned by name in any text before the early Middle Ages, but it must have been founded at a much earlier date, for various Meroitic antiquities have been found there. Soba is probably to be identified with the "city of ʿAlwā," conquest of which is claimed by the Axumite emperor Aezana (see AXUM) on a stela of 350. This text gives the impression that Soba was the principal city of the NOBA people, who overran much of the territory of the empire of KUSH in the fourth century.

The earliest mention of Soba by name is in the *Taʾrīkh* (History) of al-Yaʿqūbī (fl. 872–891). This merely states that ʿAlwā is a large kingdom to the south of MAKOURIA, and that Soba is its capital. More detailed information is given a century later by IBN SALĪM AL-ASWĀNĪ: "In the town are fine buildings, spacious houses, churches with much gold, and gardens. There is a quarter in it inhabited by the Muslims" (Burckhardt, 1819, p. 500). ABŪ ṢĀLIḤ THE ARMENIAN repeats much the same information, adding: "All its inhabitants are Jacobite Christians. Around [the town] there are monasteries, some at a distance from the stream and some upon its banks. In the town there is a very large and spacious church, skillfully planned and constructed, and larger than all the other churches in the country; it is called the church of Manbali" (p. 264).

After the time of Abū Ṣāliḥ there is almost no further mention of Soba by name. The kingdom of ʿAlwā is mentioned in a number of documents, but none of them makes specific reference to Soba, and one or two of them imply that the royal capital may have been shifted to another locality. Nevertheless, the Sudanese folk tradition that is known as the Funj Chronicle clearly indicates that Soba was still the capital at the time it was overrun and conquered by Arab nomads, near the beginning of the sixteenth century. At that time the Christian kingdom of ʿAlwā came to an end, but there were still some inhabitants at Soba when the intrepid traveler David Reubeni passed through in 1523. The town was apparently in ruins, but some people were still living in wooden houses. Reubeni's is the last mention of Soba as an inhabited community. Something of the mystique of the place evidently lingered on in oral tradition, for as late as the nineteenth century members of the Sudanese Hamej tribe were known to swear oaths on "Soba the home of my grandfathers, and grandmothers, that can make the stone float and the cotton boll sink."

One of the ruined churches at Soba, a relatively modest affair with four columns, was excavated in the early years of the twentieth century. Additional archaeological work on the townsite was undertaken by the Sudan Antiquities Service in 1950–1952, and by the British Institute in Eastern Africa since 1982. These excavations have shown that the town in its heyday was a large one, but they have not revealed many specific details of its layout or nature.

BIBLIOGRAPHY

Adams, W. Y. *Nubia, Corridor to Africa*, pp. 470–71, 537–39. Princeton, N.J., 1977.

Burckhardt, J. L. *Travels in Nubia*, p. 500. London, 1819.

Griffith, F. L. *Meroitic Inscriptions*, Part I, pp. 51–53. Archaeological Survey of Egypt, Nineteenth Memoir. London, 1911.

Shinnie, P. L. *Excavations at Soba*. Sudan Antiquities Service, Occasional Papers, no. 3. Khartoum, 1955.

Vantini, G. *Christianity in the Sudan*, pp. 132–36, 200–01. Bologna, 1981.

Yaʿqūbī, Aḥmad ibn Abī Yaʿqūb. *Taʾrīkh al-Yaʿqūbī*. 3 vols. al-Najaf, Iraq, 1939.

WILLIAM Y. ADAMS

SOCIALIST PARTY. *See* Political Parties.

SOCIETY OF COPTIC ARCHAEOLOGY, scholarly institution founded in Cairo in 1934. The society is a scientific body, with no religious aims or affiliations. It is mainly concerned with publishing, but it has also conducted excavations on Coptic sites. Its main publications are the *Bulletin, Excavation Reports, Texts and Documents, Art and Archaeology*, and *MSS Catalogues*. Articles in the *Bulletin* are printed in their original languages. The Bulletin has two title pages, one in French and one in Arabic. The society's library has some thirteen thousand volumes.

MIRRIT BOUTROS GHALI

SOCKS. *See* Costume, Civil.

SOCRATES (c. 380–456), church historian. Socrates was a native of Constantinople, where he lived and obtained his education. He ultimately became a lawyer and earned the title Scholasticus. He is best known as a church historian and seems to have started where EUSEBIUS OF CAESAREA left off. Thus his history is probably the most important compendium after Eusebius', though it has been said that he made use of the historical work of RUFINUS, which must have appeared only a short time before. His work was planned in seven books, each dealing with an imperial reign, beginning with DIOCLETIAN in 305 and covering the period to 439. After writing its first version, Socrates became better acquainted with the works of Saint ATHANASIUS, whom he admired, and this led him to produce a second and definitive version, which is the one extant today.

On the whole, Socrates' history is lucidly written, and his objectivity of judgment is uncontested. His accounts of the ecumenical councils are based on the documentary collection of Sabinus of Heraclea, and he is more versed in events connected with Constantinople. Though a good historian of the church, he displays no special interest in the theological controversies of his time. His history attracted attention from the earliest days of printing, its first edition appearing at Paris in 1544, by Stephanus; later versions were by Valesius at Paris in 1688 and by W. Reading at Cambridge in 1720. It was reproduced by J. P. Migne at Paris in 1859 and by W. Bright at Oxford in 1878. It appeared in English translation by A. C. Zenos, in the Nicene and Post-Nicene Series, in 1890.

BIBLIOGRAPHY

Milligan, W. "Socrates." In DCB 4. New York, 1974.

AZIZ S. ATIYA

SOPHIA, SAINT. [*A holy woman of the fourth century or later whose remains are interred in the Church of Santa Sophia (Hagia Sophia) in Constantinople (feast day: 5 Tūt). There are several versions of her story.*]

The Jacobite Tradition

The Jacobite-Arabic SYNAXARION, preserved in a seventeenth-century copy (restored in the nineteenth century) in the National Library, Paris (Arabe 4869), tells the story of a Saint Sophia of Jerusalem, which at first seems to lack chronological references. An earlier account had certainly existed in Coptic. According to the Jacobite account, a patrician named Theognostus and his wife, Theodora, were attached to the court of the emperor Arcadius in Constantinople in the late fourth and early fifth centuries. They were rich but had no children. The emperor, who was related to them, referred them to Saint JOHN CHRYSOSTOM, patriarch of Constantinople, who anointed them with oil from the sanctuary. Nine months later the child Sophia ("Wisdom") was born. When she was five years old, her parents built for her a lofty golden chamber, full of precious stones, with a gold cross in the middle so that she could pray. Later, she married the patrician Castor, and they had three children, Stephen, Mark, and Paul.

Then her husband and her parents died, and Sophia, left with the three children, did not know what to do: "If I remain a widow, I shall be remarried because of my three children. God will hate me and I shall be humiliated before my parents and my husband. But if I go to the convent the children will come and burn down the convent because of me." So she took counsel from John Chrysostom, who quoted the gospel to her. At night as Sophia prayed, the Virgin appeared to her and said, "I am Mary, mother of Light. If you wish to please God, he will call you no more in this town. Arise and follow me, I shall cause you to speak to my Son." The next day, Sophia found herself miraculously transported near the Mount of Olives in Jerusalem. The children, deprived of their mother, went to John Chrysostom, who could only sympathize.

Theodore, patriarch of Jerusalem, for his part, sent a letter to the emperor, explaining the circumstances of Sophia, but it took three months to reach him. When the letter arrived, the children left for Jerusalem, a journey requiring six months. Meanwhile Sophia was imposing the harshest penances on herself. On 11 Ṭūbah, the exhausted Sophia fell ill. The Virgin appeared to her saying, "You will come and rest with me, but you will see your three sons before you die. They will bear your body to Constantinople and place it in the golden pavilion. They will turn your house into a church, dedicated to my Son, and it will be the emperor's principal church forever." At dawn on 21 Ṭūbah, surrounded by soldiers, the sons arrived and Sophia died. Her venerated body was brought back to Constantinople and placed in a golden pavilion, which was consecrated by John Chrysostom. It was called the Church of Saint Sophia, the name that it still bears.

This legend is significant in several respects, when examined in relation to the denial of the monophysite doctrine after the time of John Chrysostom. The patriarch Theodore of Jerusalem is certainly the adversary of Juvenal, patriarch of Jerusalem after Chalcedon. The date of 21 Ṭūbah is that of the Dormition of Mary, which, according to the Panegyric by Saint MACARIUS OF TKOW, served as a rallying point for the MONOPHYSITES, gathered at Gethsemane against Juvenal.

Nor is that all. At the beginning of the former cycle of the Dormition, on 8 August, there was inaugurated in Jerusalem a Church of Wisdom, of Saint Sophia, on the site of Pilate's house, between Mount Zion and the Temple (Garitte, 1958, pp. 296–98). Wisdom is thus placed at both dates of the Coptic cycle of the Dormition, and topographically, in both holy places of the Dormition that served as symbols in the dissidents' liturgy—Gethsemane and Mount Zion. As one reads it today, the legend supposes a restoration at Constantinople at a time when monophysitism was triumphant, from about 512 to 518.

But the greatest interest lies in the fact that this Jacobite legend in no way constitutes the fruit of the unbridled "imagination" which often can be assumed about Coptic literature. In fact, the Greek Passion of Saint Sophia and her three daughters, Agape, Pistis, and Elpis (the theological virtues of charity, faith, and hope), attests that well before the Copts, the Byzantines had used a similar type of literature. A Syriac version dates from the fifth century. The Greek legend of Saint Sophia is a Passion intended to provide Constantinople with credentials in competition with those of ancient Rome. This Passion takes place in the second century under Hadrian. The Latins placed the Passion of Sophia, mother of the three Virtues, on 1 August, one of the most stable dates in the history of the calendars, for it was always dedicated to the seven Maccabaean brothers and their mother, Shamounit. There are versions of this legend where the mother—Shamounit, the eighth, or Ogdoad—exhorts each of her sons to sacrifice himself by invoking them as the seven days of the creation. This gnosticizing structure, then, took its historical character from the Passion of the Maccabees. To avoid ambiguity, the Passion of Wisdom and the three theological Virtues were added, incorporated in a harsh story of persecution.

By adopting the same symbolic style, the Coptic legend of Sophia of Jerusalem affirms that at the time of Arcadius, under John Chrysostom, the faith had not yet been injured by the odious denial of the Virgin's title "Theotokos" because of subtle distinctions of two different natures in Christ. In Jerusalem Sophia loses her anguish and wins eternal life. Sophia's sons are naturally called to continue the work of Arcadius in the shadow of the imperial throne. But the death of their parents makes it difficult to continue those beautiful days of Byzantine orthodoxy.

Far from being a strange fabrication of Coptic imagination, the legend of Sophia is the direct extension of a language already familiar in Byzantium for the famous Saint Sophia. Moreover, through this little Coptic tale, we can understand better why Justinian wanted to rebuild Saint Sophia. As in the case of so many churches enumerated in the *Peri Ktismaton* of Procopius, the problem was not to build new things, but, under cover of an enterprise of consolidation, to supplant certain links in a doctrinal chain and thus break the connection with theological interpretations that would be unacceptable in the future.

BIBLIOGRAPHY

Esbroeck, M. van. "Le Saint comme symbole." In *The Byzantine Saint,* ed. S. Hackel. Chester, 1981.

Garitte, G. *Le Calendrier palestino-géorgien du sinaiticus 34.* Brussels, 1958.

MICHEL VAN ESBROECK

The Arabic Tradition

According to the Copto-Arabic Synaxarion, Sophia was one of the most famous martyrs of Upper Egypt. Attracted to Christianity by her neighbors, she was baptized by the bishop of Memphis and later denounced for her conversion to the Roman governor Claudius, who questioned her. When she fearlessly defended her faith, Claudius had her body flogged, her joints burned, and her tongue cut out. Then he put her in prison and sent his wife to coax her to recant with promises of reward. Eventually he had her decapitated. Christians bribed the imperial guards to save her body, which they wrapped in precious shrouds and placed in her home. There it was reported to be the occasion of miraculous healings, to emit the scent of incense, and to be enveloped in a halo of light. When Constantine became the first Christian emperor in 312, he had her body removed to Constantinople and placed under the altar of the Church of Santa Sophia, which he built for it.

BIBLIOGRAPHY

Holweck, F. G. *A Biographical Dictionary of the Saints.* London, 1924.

O'Leary, De L. *The Coptic Saints of Egypt in the Coptic Calendar.* London, 1937.

AZIZ S. ATIYA

SOPHIA OF JESUS CHRIST. *See* Eugnostos the Blessed and the Sophia of Jesus Christ.

SOUROS (fourth century), with Pshentaēse and Pshoi, one of the first three disciples of PACHOMIUS. He also appears in various lists of the "ancient brothers" who seem to have constituted a very clearly defined group within the organization of the *koinonia.* Pachomius appointed him father of Phnoum, in the south, the last Pachomian foundation. Like so many other ancient brothers, he died during the plague of 346. He was the recipient of Pachomius' first, fourth, and sixth letters. With Cornelius he was one of the two persons with whom Pachomius exchanged letters in code.

[*See also:* Monasticism, Pachomian; Pachomius, Saint: Letters of Pachomius.]

ARMAND VEILLEUX

SOZOMEN (fifth century), church historian. His full name was Hermias Sozomenus Salamanes (or Salaminius), which has misled some to associate him with the town of Salamis in Cyprus. This is a mistake, since he is known to have been born in the village of Bethelia near the town of Gaza in Palestine. His grandfather was the first convert to Christianity in his family. Thus Sozomen was born to Christian parents, and he was given his early education by a Christian monk named Hilarion, to whom the family owed its conversion. Beyond that, his early life is obscure and his dates are uncertain. He probably was born in 400 but the date of his death is unknown, though he must have died in Constantinople, to which he moved for the completion of his education as a lawyer. There Sozomen became interested in church history and decided to write a continuation of the Eusebian *Historia ecclesiastica*. He was a contemporary of SOCRATES, who may have preceded him by two decades. It is possible that he profited from the work of Socrates, according to Valesius, the first editor of both of their works. Sozomen's *History of the Church* appeared in nine books covering the period from 323 to 425. Though his work displays no major contributions to Christianity as a whole, his accounts stand out in relation to the Armenians, the Saracens, and the Goths. In style he is superior to Socrates, but he shares with him the failure to comprehend the theological and dogmatic issues of his day. He dedicated his work to Emperor Theodosius the Younger.

Sozomen's work, like that of Socrates, attracted the attention of Western scholars from the earliest days of publishing. His first edition appeared in Greek at Paris in 1544, and another in Greek, with a Latin translation by Christophorsonos and Suffridus Petrus, at Cologne in 1612. An edition by Valesius appeared in 1668, followed by another at Cambridge in 1720. The revised and annotated edition in three volumes by R. Hassy appeared at Oxford in 1860. Migne included it in Patrologia Graeca (Vol. 67).

BIBLIOGRAPHY

Bidez, J. "Le texte du prologue de Sozomène et de ses chapitres (VI. 28–34) sur les moines d'Egypte et de Palestine." *Akademie der Wissenschaften, Berlin, Sitzungsberichte* 18 (1935):399–427.

Milligan, W. "Sozomen." In DCB, Vol. 4, pp. 722–23.

Schaff, P., and H. Wace, eds. *The Ecclesiastical History of Sozomen*. A Select Library of Nicene and Post-Nicene Fathers of the Christian Church, 2nd ser., Vol. 2, pp. 179–454. Grand Rapids, Mich., 1952.

AZIZ S. ATIYA

SPEOS ARTEMIDOS. *See* Banī Ḥasan and Speos Artemidos.

SPIEGELBERG, WILHELM (1870–1930), German Egyptologist and demoticist. He was educated at the universities of Strasbourg and Paris. He was appointed professor of Egyptology successively at the universities of Strasbourg (1898), Heidelberg (1918), and Munich (1923). His earlier work was mainly on hieratic papyri, and he made a special study of juristic texts, on which he did valuable research. Later he turned chiefly to Coptic and demotic studies, becoming the leading exponent of the latter in Germany and, with F. L. Griffith, the foremost in Europe. He published a useful demotic grammar and a great many important literary texts hitherto overlooked in collections all over Europe. In 1921 he brought out his *Coptic Dictionary*, a work of great value superseded only by the great Coptic dictionary of W. E. Crum. Spiegelberg was also interested in archaeology and art, writing works in these fields as well as philology. He made several visits to Egypt. A master of the short article, Spiegelberg wrote hundreds for all the leading journals of his day and contributed more to the *Zeitschrift für ägyptische Sprache und Altertumskunde* than any other author—159 in all.

BIBLIOGRAPHY

Dawson, W. R., and E. P. Uphill. *Who Was Who in Egyptology*, pp. 278–79. London, 1972.

Kammerer, W., comp. *A Coptic Bibliography*. Ann Arbor, Mich., 1950; repr. New York, 1969.

AZIZ S. ATIYA

SPINDLES AND SPINDLE WHORLS. *See* Woodwork, Coptic.

SPINNING. *See* Textiles, Coptic: Manufacturing Techniques.

SPOON. *See* Eucharistic Vessels.

STAFF, PASTORAL. *See* Liturgical Insignia.

STAMPS, COPTIC. *See* Ceramics, Coptic.

STATE MUSEUM OF BERLIN. The Coptic collection of the Staatliche Museen in East Berlin is one of the most extensive and most important outside Egypt. It contains some 2,000 works of all kinds.

Its origin is closely connected with the building up of a section for Early Christian and Byzantine works of art; from about 1895, this collection was systematically bought by Wilhelm Bode for the Kaiser Friedrich Museum, opened in 1904 and called today the Bode Museum. In the winter of 1901–1902 he commissioned J. Strzygowski, at that time probably the best judge of Byzantine and Early Christian art in the Orient, to purchase Coptic works of art in Egypt for the Berlin Museum. By far the greatest part of the Coptic works were bought at that time (cf. the catalog in Wulff, 1909, pp. 332–34): sculptures and figures in relief, funerary stelae, small carvings in stone, architectural sculptures, wood-carvings, stamps, clay lamps, earthenware, stoppers for jars, statuettes, funerary boards, bone carvings for furniture decorations, glassware, leather work, bronze vessels or utensils and parts thereof, pieces of jewelry, gold, silver or bronze, lead ornaments, textiles. Places of purchase are given chiefly as Akhmīm, Alexandria, (Old) Cairo, al-Ashmūnayn, Bāwīṭ, Idfū, Armant, the Fayyūm, Giza, Ḥilwān, Qinā, Luxor, and other places, but that tells us nothing about the actual origin of the pieces.

From 1901 numerous minor works of Coptic art were added as well as some pieces passed on from the Egyptian Museum. From 1903 important purchases repeatedly appear in the inventory with the statement of origin "Egypt," occasionally also "Bāwīt," but the circumstances of purchase and the agents concerned are not made known. In 1902 a large number of lamps and ampullae from ABŪ MĪNĀ were added (among them a number donated by Bode), as well as terra-cotta and architectural sculptures from Abu Mīnā and Cairo (some of them allegedly again from Bāwīṭ). The Coptic collection in this way steadily grew until 1912. The holdings of Coptic textiles were considerably expanded by the collection of the German consul in Cairo, C. Reinhardt, purchased in 1900 by Bode and given by him to the Museum. In 1905 parts of the collection of T. Graf (Vienna) were added, and also valuable private donations, such as some of the large tapestries. The textiles purchased by C. Schmidt in Antinoopolis, G. Schweinfurth in Arsinoë (the Fayyūm), and others in the 1930s were also handed over to the textile collection of the early Christian and Byzantine collection. The collection today comprises about 1,500 pieces.

The Coptic collection was badly affected by the great losses that the early Christian and Byzantine collection suffered in World War II. Almost all the small works of art in wood, bone, leather, and metal depicted in Wulff, 1909 (pls. 8–58), have been destroyed. From the textiles only the large multicolored tapestries (e.g., pls. 2, 4, 5, 10, 39, 43–48, and others) perished. As a result of the separation of the Berlin museums, some pieces are today preserved in West Berlin (Wulff, 1909, no. 42, 243). For most of the works destroyed, the old negative plates are still in existence.

Among the works in the plastic arts, architectural reliefs of the third to fifth centuries predominate, such as the top part of a round niche with the head of Aphrodite in the conch (Wulff, 1909, no. 58), a bust of Tyche (Wulff, no. 55), frieze blocks with mythological themes and figures (Leda and the swan, Wulff, no. 64; sea creatures, Wulff, no. 59; putti, Wulff, nos. 60–62). Among the Christian exhibits of the fourth to seventh centuries the important panel in relief with the Entry of Christ, allegedly deriving from Suhāj (Wulff, no. 72), stands out, as does a tympanum, though badly worn, with the presentation of Apa PHOIBAMMON before the enthroned Christ (Wulff, 1911, no. 2240). The group of the funerary reliefs includes a remarkable selection of all the current local types of the third to eighth centuries, among them the stela of Apa SHENUTE, readily connected with the founder of the White and Red monasteries, which is alleged to derive from Suhāj (Wulff, 1909, no. 73). Of special significance for the history of iconography is a colored picture of a poised lactating mother (Wulff, 1909, no. 79), which on the basis of recently analyzed inscriptional remains could be recognized as a Christian adaptation of a pagan model (Effenberger, 1977). The stela with figures (Wulff, 1909, no. 77) is firmly dated by inscription 703, but with this late date little is gained for the chronology of Coptic reliefs.

The Berlin collection also possesses an outstanding selection of Coptic architectural moldings: a two-tier capital bought in Cairo in 1909 (Wulff,

1909, no. 1656), which imitates contemporary Constantinopolitan models of the period of Justinian and attests the high artistic level of Coptic architectural sculpture at the time; and a wall fragment from Bāwīṭ with a circular design and Christogram (Wulff, no. 237), two wainscoting panels of the sixth/seventh century, probably from the same source, adorned with geometrical and ornamental designs (Wulff, nos. 1641–42), as well as a frieze originating in the fifth century consisting of five blocks with slender fronds, animals, and a head of Tyche in laurel wreaths borne aloft by putti (Wulff, no. 208). Capitals of different types, sometimes carved after imported models, frieze fragments with decorative, pagan, or symbolic Christian designs, conchs, sometimes filled with crosses (Wulff, no. 233), and other motifs also appear. Among the wood-carvings, adorned with figures or ornaments, door jambs and frieze boards predominate. Unique pieces are the pilaster cornice with "relief of a besieged town" (Wulff, no. 342, today in West Berlin) and the console with a representation of Daniel between lions (Wulff, no. 242, with doubtful derivation from Bāwīṭ). The beams with their inscriptions and ornamental reliefs of figures provide important stylistic and iconographical clues, still not fully evaluated, for the chronology of Coptic plastic arts of the sixth to eighth centuries.

Also of value for cultural history is the extant stock of wooden bread stamps (Wulff, 1909, pl. 12).

Among the paintings on wooden boards, the three most important have fortunately survived: the icon of Bishop ABRAHAM of Hermonthis (Wulff, 1909, no. 1607), the panel of a coffer ceiling with busts (Wulff, no. 1608), and the casket with Christ the Redeemer and busts of angels and saints (Wulff, no. 1604). The icon of Abraham could be identified with the bishop of Hermonthis of the same name, and dated to the period about 600 (Krause, 1971).

The collection of Coptic textiles is in essentials identical with the stock cataloged by Wulff and Volbach in 1926. The most important fragments have been carefully restored in recent years. The most important works of the Berlin collection have repeatedly been the subject of research and publication (cf. Wessel, 1963; Effenberger, 1974; Badawy, 1978), but a fundamental new treatment is urgently needed.

BIBLIOGRAPHY

Badawy, A. *Coptic Art and Archaeology. The Art of the Christian Egyptians from the Late Antique to the Middle Ages.* Cambridge, Mass., and London, 1978.

Effenberger, A. *Koptische Kunst. Ägypten in spätantiker, byzantinischer und frühislamischer Zeit.* Leipzig and Vienna, 1975.

______. "Die Grabstele aus Medinet el-Fajum. Zum Bild der stillenden Gottesmutter in der koptischen Kunst." *Forschungen und Berichte* 18 (1977):158–68.

______. "Ein spätantikes Noppengewebe mit Puttengenre und seine Wiederherstellung." In *Textilkunst im Orient und in Europa,* ed. Burchard Brentjes. Martin-Luther-Universität Halle-Wittenberg. Halle, 1981.

Effenberger, A. and E. Rasemowitz. "Der Pfau im Blütengezweig." *Forschungen und Berichte* 16 (1975):241–44.

Krause, M. "Zur Lokalisierung und Datierung koptischer Denkmäler. Das Tafelbild des Bischofs Abraham." *Zeitschrift für ägyptische Sprache* 97 (1971):106–111.

Wessel, K. *Koptische Kunst. Die Spätantike in Ägypten.* Recklinghausen, 1963.

Wulff, O. *Altchristliche und mittelalterliche byzantinische und italienische Bildwerke,* Vol. 1, *Altchristliche Bildwerke,* Vol. 2, *Mittelalterliche Bildwerke christlichen Epochen,* 2nd ed., Berlin, 1909 and 1911.

Wulff, O., and W. F. Volbach. *Die altchristlichen und mittelalterlichen byzantinischen und italienischen Bildwerke,* Vol. 3, *Ergänzungsband.* Berlin and Leipzig, 1923.

______. *Spätantike und koptische Stoffe aus ägyptischen Grabfunden in den Staatlichen Museen.* Berlin, 1926.

ARNE EFFENBERGER

STATUARY. If the statue is defined as a complete figure in full relief, Coptic art did not cultivate the technique. On this point it conformed to the taste of the time. The carving of statues had diminished considerably from the beginning of the second century of the Roman empire. As generals who no longer belonged to the Roman aristorcracy acceded to the throne, they were influenced by the simplified perspective of the middle and popular levels of society. Later, by the end of the second century A.D., the Neoplatonic philosophy of sacrificing form for idea spread throughout the Mediterranean basin. Two-dimensional arts were to be prevalent for centuries in Egypt as in the rest of the empire.

Thus, the only known works in stone in Coptic art are: the statuette of an Egyptian soldier of the

Roman army (18 inches [45cm], Louvre); an eagle perched on a *crux immissa* (Staatliches Museum, Berlin, 6th century); and, frequently enough, mouthpieces of WATER JUGS (*zirs*) in the form of lions in high relief which are more akin to statuary.

Wood, ivory, and bone have yielded chiefly magic dolls.

In modeling clay there is a statuette, designed as a magical charm, executed in the Alexandrian style (Louvre).

Ceramics can count a fairly large number of terracotta statuettes of pharaonic gods and goddesses. These belong more to Alexandrian than to Coptic art and are chiefly objects of the transition from one style to the other. An example from the ninth century, originating from Middle Egypt in painted clay, is a woman in the posture of an orant (Museum of Icons, Recklinghausen) (see CHRISTIAN SUBJECTS IN COPTIC ART).

There are a few statuettes in bronze, among them one of a dancer with sistra (Louvre).

One may suggest that, in the domain of contemporary art, statuary, already extremely rare in Coptic art, practically disappeared in the course of the fourth century.

BIBLIOGRAPHY

Badawy, A. *Coptic Art and Archaeology*, pp. 117–225. Cambridge, Mass., 1978.

Bourguet, P. du. *L'Art copte*. Paris, 1968. See especially pp. 90–99, 118–29.

PIERRE DU BOURGUET, S.J.

STEGEMANN, VIKTOR (1902–1948), German philologist. Stegemann was a specialist in religious antiquity, mainly in astrology. Stegemann won lasting merit in two areas of Coptology, paleography and texts on magic and witchcraft. His works in these areas include *Die Gestalt Christi in den koptischen Zaubertexten* (Heidelberg, 1934); *Die koptischen Zaubertexte der Sammlung Papyrus Erzherzog Rainer* (Heidelberg, 1934); "Zur Textgestaltung und zum Textverständnis koptischer Zaubertexte" (*Zeitschrift für ägyptische Sprache und Altertumskunde* 70, 1934, pp. 125–31); "Über Astronomisches in den koptischen Zaubertexten" (*Orientalia* n.s. 4, 1935, pp. 391–410); *Koptische Paläographie* (Heidelberg, 1936); and "Neue Zaube und Gebetstexte aus koptischer Zeit in Heidelberg und Wien" (*Le Muséon* 51, 1938, pp. 73–87).

BIBLIOGRAPHY

Kürschners deutscher Gelehrten-Kalender 1940–41, 6th ed., p. 840. Berlin, 1941.

MARTIN KRAUSE

STEINDORFF, GEORG (1861–1951), German Egyptologist and Coptologist. He was educated at the universities of Berlin and Göttingen, and was Adolf Erman's first student. From 1885 to 1893 he occupied the post of assistant curator of the Berlin Museum. He was professor of Egyptology at Leipzig from 1893 until 1938. There he founded the Egyptian Institute and filled it with objects from his excavations in Egypt and Nubia. Steindorff made a special study of Coptic, and was, with W. E. Crum, one of the two leading authorities in his field. He explored the Libyan Desert and excavated at Giza and in Nubia. He edited the *Zeitschrift für ägyptische Sprache und Altertumskunde* for forty years and contributed many articles to it. His studies in Coptic were of the utmost importance, and his *Coptic Grammar* (Berlin, 1894) still remains a standard work of reference and perhaps the most popular ever written in this field. In philology as a whole, he was in the first rank and established the rules that are generally accepted for the vocalization of Egyptian.

In 1939 he was forced to leave Nazi Germany and emigrate to America, where he started another career at the age of nearly eighty. He continued his studies in the museums of New York, Boston, and Baltimore and at the Oriental Institute at the University of Chicago. He became an honorary member of the American Oriental Society. At Baltimore he compiled a twelve-volume manuscript catalog of Egyptian antiquities in the Walters Art Gallery. Both his seventieth and eightieth birthdays were the subject of tributes. His published works are numerous and his bibliography lists about 250 books, articles, and reviews, the first of which appeared in 1883, the last in the year of his death, nearly seventy years later. Apart from a great multitude of articles, his Coptic bibliography can be found in Kammerer, *A Coptic Bibliography* (1950, 1969). He also edited many editions of Baedeker's *Egypt*, making it a standard work for all travelers and the best general guide available. He died in Hollywood, California.

BIBLIOGRAPHY

Dawson, W. R., and E. P. Uphill. *Who Was Who in Egyptology*, p. 281. London, 1972.

Kammerer, W., comp. *A Coptic Bibliography*. Ann Arbor, Mich., 1950; repr. New York, 1969.

AZIZ S. ATIYA

STEINWENTER, ARTUR (1888–1959), Austrian legal historian. He was a pupil of Leopold Wenger, a professor at the University of Graz, a member of the Austrian Academy of Sciences, and, with A. A. Schiller, one of only two historians of law who then worked also with Coptic Law. He published two books about Coptic law, *Studien zu den koptischen Rechtsurkunden aus Oberägypten* (Leipzig, 1920; repr. Amsterdam, 1967) and *Das Recht der koptischen Urkunden* (Munich, 1955), and many articles.

BIBLIOGRAPHY

Kaser, M. "In memoriam Artur Steinwenter." *Zeitschrift der Savigny-Stiftung für Rechtsgeschichte* 76 (1959):670–77.

MARTIN KRAUSE

STELA, upright stone slab or pillar. Today some 1,100 ornamented Christian funerary stelae from Egypt (excluding Nubia) are known, most of them distributed over many museums. The most important collections are those of the Coptic Museum in Cairo, the Greco-Roman Museum in Alexandria, the British Museum in London, the Staatlichen Museen in Berlin, and the Metropolitan Museum of Art in New York. There are many other minor but interesting collections.

Probably a great part of the original production of decorated stelae has been lost by natural or human action, such as reuse for other purposes or destruction by Muslims. What remains has not always been published in a careful manner. Therefore, the importance of these sculptures as a type of funerary monument in Christian Egypt and, more generally, as one of the artistic expressions of the Copts, is still not clear.

Excluding Nubia with its relatively unimportant production of decorated stelae, we may say that only some 330 stelae have a more or less firmly established origin. This result contrasts sharply with all the original specifications given by museum catalogs, exhibitions, and auctions. Very few traces come from the north, with the exception of the gravestones from DAYR APA JEREMIAH in Saqqara. There are dispersed finds from the Fayyūm, mainly Madīnat al-Fayyūm, and some concentrations around Antinoopolis, Matmar, Dayr al-Balāyzah, Badāri, Qāw, and Akhmīm. The most important series surely comes from the Thebaid region, more precisely Luxor and Armant, and from Isnā and its surroundings.

Of all the decorated stelae only fourteen can be exactly dated from their epitaphs. These dates vary from the beginning of the seventh century until about 1100. Unfortunately, these examples do not belong to one of the more important types or centers of production. Other elements, such as the content of the texts (formulas, dates, titles, names of persons and places), the stylistic and technical treatment, the iconography, and the archaeological context allow us to situate the main types between 350 and 750.

Funerary stela decorated with an orant beneath a pediment containing a cross. Limestone. Fourth century. *Courtesy Coptic Museum, Cairo.*

Christian funerary stela in the name of Sabek with a pediment upon columns surmounted by two peacocks facing each other. Limestone. Ninth century. Height: 47 cm; width: 35 cm; thickness: 5 cm. *Courtesy Louvre Museum, Paris.*

The material for these monuments is mostly limestone, but sandstone is also used (Armant, Nubia). More rarely, marble, terra-cotta, schist, alabaster, and wood are used. The stones are either triangular or rounded on top, or they are rectangular. Gravestones were laid upon the grave, or were placed against or inside the tomb wall, or they stood independently.

The sculptural techniques show a wide variation from the simple pattern engravings to the nearly full statues. The ornamentation was often plastered and then painted over, or, sometimes, the whole surface was plastered and the ornamentation subsequently painted upon it. This painting can be polychrome, although not always very logical or naturalistic, or monochrome, mostly red or black, possibly with a symbolic meaning.

Distinctions must be made when reviewing the compositorial elements of the stela decoration. The surface-organizing elements are either decorated or nondecorated architecture and frames. Frames are mostly combined with an architectural pediment. Other elements function as real and more or less meaningful representations. They include: crosses and monograms (e.g., staurogram, chrismon, I-and-X, cross-and-X, staurogram-and-X, whether encircled/wreathed or not); life signs; human figures (e.g., orant; persons with crosses, birds, wreaths, or grapes in their hands; horseman; reading man; a lactans-woman); animals (single or heraldic including: gazelles, dogs, lions, hares, fishes, dolphins, doves, eagles, peacocks, griffins); rosettes; wreaths; vegetation (mostly a filler ornament including: leaves of acanthus or ivy, corner leaves, twigs, tendrils with grapes, leaf buds); vessels; *tabulae ansatae;* and geometrical patterns (mostly filled up with vegetation). Some of these elements, or types of them, are geographically confined.

Among the architectural schemes is the simple pediment, triangular or arched on top and with an architrave, without supporting columns or resting upon a simple frame. These function as the stylization of a real portal and are typical for the south, especially in Thebes and Armant. Schemes like a triangular pediment resting without an architrave upon two columns and the arched pediment resting with an architrave upon two or two pairs of columns come from the south in general. The more complex architecture, with more than one portal and more than one floor, is also typical for the Thebaid region, including Isnā. The doubled or tripled and the interrupted decorated frames are also a southern phenomenon.

Among the representational elements, a geographically limited use can be discerned for the staurogram (Thebes and Armant), the wreathed monogram (mostly Isnā), the life sign (Theban region, especially al-Badāri, al-Maṭmar, and Armant), and the animal elements (generally the south). The compositions upon the Coptic funerary stelae, although based on interactions between this rather limited number of organizing and representational elements, show a great variation. Representational elements can be doubled or tripled or combined with others; they can be situated free upon the surface, or inside an architecture or a decorated frame, or inside a combination of various organizing elements. The compositions with the elements free upon the surface or inside an architecture are amply the most common, followed, at a long distance, by compositions with decorated frames or with the frame and the architecture combined.

The most common compositions are: the empty

or text-filled architecture, the cross and the wreathed cross free upon the surface, the wreathed monogram free upon the surface (mainly Isnā), the free life sign (especially al-Badāri), the free human person, the cross inside the architecture, and the bird inside the architecture (especially Isnā). All these elements can be worked out or ornamented in a highly decorative manner. The architraves and the triangular or arched roofs show linear ornaments (lines and zigzags), interlaces, and vegetal patterns (twigs, undulating twigs). Above the front there are often two heraldic peacocks, inside the front we see mostly a shell (pecten, cardium or heart-shaped shell), a disk or button, a cross, a leaf (acanthus), and the birds flanking a vessel or cross. The acroteria as well as the capitals of the columns are mostly vegetal—acanthus, a stylization of voluted Corinthian capitals, or designs of vegetal origin. The columnar shafts have a wide perpendicular channeling (e.g., Armant), oblique lines, a feather design (especially Isnā), or a combination of these patterns. Other shafts are vegetally decorated. Most of the decorated frames are vegetally conceived with undulating tendrils and eventually with bunches of grapes, simple twigs, and rows of separate leaves, or show a geometrical design with interlacings, zigzags, or various types of the meander. Crosses, monograms, and life signs often have their arms hollowed out or widened to their extremities, or even display a vegetal shape. Frequently the crosses are transformed into *cruces gemmatae* (crosses ornated with precious stones). The loops of the life signs are mostly filled in with little human heads, eventually with a shell-shaped background, with buttons, or with vegetal motifs (rosettes). The wreaths are usually vegetal (stylized tendrils of ivy or laurel), but other types exist, such as the wreath of interlacings or with a row of pearls. Some human figures show classical characteristics, thus joining the official trends of the early Byzantine imperial art. Others look more provincial or markedly primitive. Different currents can be discerned in the treatment of the animals. For example, a robust, even coarse, but plastic style for birds alternates with and probably has been replaced by a more delicate, linear, and vegetally inspired style. The iconographic and stylistic evidence shows that the Coptic funerary stelae share the general existing currents of late antique and medieval art as development and modification—often called deformation—of the Hellenistic-Roman cultural basis, and shows the typical antinomy of that roughly five-century period of endurance (fourth to eighth centuries). The conflict was between provincialism and

Funerary stela inscribed in the name of Saint Theodore. Limestone. Height: 35 cm. *Courtesy Louvre Museum, Paris.*

popular spontaneity on the one hand (these two currents, although with different origins, converge to such an extent that it is very difficult to distinguish them), and the more official classicizing "revivals," on the other. Among the meaningful representational themes, the nearly total absence of pagan subjects, in contrast to the dominating Christian or Christianized "neutral" motifs, is very striking. Even the Coptic life sign is often very differently shaped from its pagan prototype and is clearly impressed by an elaborated Christian symbolism. Evidently this is due to the limited possibilities of this artistic genre, where narrative scenes, even if converted into ideological or ethical examples, can hardly be realized, and where representations have to be concentrated around a few items. The absence of pagan themes is also due to the relatively late appearance of the Coptic funerary stelae in the

Funerary stela with one face (*top*) depicting two holy personages in orant pose, the other face (*bottom*) depicting columns, conch, vegetal motifs, and two peacocks. Limestone. *Courtesy Coptic Museum, Cairo.*

late antique cultural world, a sharp contrast with the early prosperity of the CATECHETICAL SCHOOL in Alexandria and the traditions about the early founding of the Egyptian church by Saint MARK.

Besides the statement that Coptic funerary stelae form part of the general evolution of the late Hellenistic artistic language, the question arises whether they have any relationship to other sculptural groups of late antique Egypt, for example, the Kom Abū Billū stelae and the sculptures of the Bahnasā and Ahnās types. The Kom Abū Billū stelae, although basically Hellenistic in character, occasionally show survivals of the pharaonic past. Linguistically, we find some demotic inscriptions. Stylistically they use sunken relief, and the treatment of hair, hands, and feet survives from the past. Ideologically and iconographically, the jackal and falcon are used. The relation of this group to the real Coptic gravestones is not yet established. An eventually Christian character of the Kom Abū Billū type cannot be proved and seems improbable, first because of the lack of any indication in that direction. Second, the dates of those stelae, which were originally believed to be somewhere in the third to fourth centuries, are now more and more situated from the second to the eleventh century and even earlier. An immediate evolution from Kom Abū Billū to Coptic funerary art could hold only for the orant figure. But the nonexistence of most of the Abū Billū iconography in the Coptic group arouses the question whether the Abū Billū orants were really the ideological and significant precursors of the Christian ones. Indirectly, however, Abū Billū stelae can be linked with the Coptic gravestones for some of their stylistic and iconographic connections with the so-called Bahnasā group that in its latest production is at least partly Christian. The Ahnās sculptures, too, provide us with a link between the pagan and the Christian funerary art in late antique Egypt. As for the meaning of the iconography of the Coptic gravestones, we refer to the many studies dealing with themes like the orant, the cross, the peacock, the eagle, the fish, and the Heaven's Gate. In general, Coptic stelae represent the deceased or the apparition of God or His power (e.g., cross, monogram, eagle). Their presence has to be considered as an expression of faith and hope for protection against evil powers.

BIBLIOGRAPHY

Badawy, A. *Coptic Art and Archaeology. The Art of the Christian Egyptians from the Late Antiquity to the Middle Ages.* Cambridge, Mass., and London, 1978.

Crum, W. E. *Coptic Monuments—Catalogue général des antiquités égyptiennes du Musée du Caire,* Nos. 8001–8741. Cairo, 1902.

Hall, H. R. *Coptic and Greek Texts of the Christian Period from Ostraca, Stelae, etc. . . . in the British Museum.* London, 1905.

Mond, R., and O. Myers. *Cemeteries of Armant 1.* London, 1937.

Pelsmaekers, J. "The Funerary Stelae with Crux Ansata from Esna." *Bulletin van het Belgisch Historisch Instituut te Rome* 57 (1987):23–29.

JOHNNY PELSMAEKERS

STEPHEN, SAINT, the first of the followers of Jesus to suffer martyrdom, and therefore called the protomartyr (feast day: 1 Ṭūbah). His personality, activity, and death are described in the Acts of the Apostles, chapters 6–7.

As the number of Christians grew, there were increasing difficulties in attending to the needs of all of them, and the Greek-speaking converts protested that their widows were neglected in favor of the Hebrews'. The Twelve put seven men in charge of ministering to the needs of the Hellenists, that is, the converts to Christianity from among the Greek-speaking Jews resident in Jerusalem. These seven men are sometimes assumed to be deacons and ministers.

Stephen is the first of the seven mentioned in Acts and is described as "a man full of faith and of the Holy Spirit," indicating the excellent reputation he enjoyed among the Christians of Jerusalem. Because of his Greek name (Stefanos, "crowned"), he is considered to be of the same Hellenist origin as the other six. Stephen's activity was directed toward the conversion of the Hellenist Jews resident in Jerusalem and was accompanied by extraordinary or miraculous phenomena (Acts 6:8). This provoked the reaction of a group of Hellenist Jews from the Synagogue of the Freedmen, so called because it was apparently the place of worship of Jews from Rome, descendants of those led away as captives by Pompey, 63 B.C. This group provoked the arrest of Stephen and his trial before the Jewish authorities. During the trial the extraordinary incident described in Acts 6:15 occurred: "Those who sat there in the Council saw his face looking like the face of an angel." Stephen defended himself during the trial in the speech related in Acts 7:11–54. The accused presented a synthesis of the history of salvation and accused the Jews of having murdered Christ. This provoked the wrath of those present, who on hearing Stephen declare that he was contemplating Christ in glory, stoned him. The narration in Acts ends by relating the presence and cooperation of Saul, and the attitude of Stephen, who commended his spirit to Christ, and also forgave his executioners.

The martyrdom of Stephen took place in Jerusalem in all probability in the winter of the year 36–37. In the autumn of 36 Pontius Pilate had left Judea for Rome, on the orders of Vitelius, in order to account for his administration of the area. The death of Stephen initiated a persecution of the Christians, causing their dispersal to other cities of Palestine. At a later date further legendary narratives of the life and martyrdom of Stephen were produced. They follow the story of Acts. The Georgian version of an original Greek text of a *Martyrium Stephani* is preserved in a tenth-century codex found in Mount Athos (PO 19, ed. N. Marr, pp. 689–99). In Coptic there is a *Life of Saint Stephen Protomartyr* transmitted in a codex in the Pierpont Morgan Library, New York (ed. Hyvernat, 1922) and some fragments in the Borgia collection (ed. Guidi [1888], trans. *Giornale della Societa Asiatica Italiana* 2), which contain the *Acts of Stephen* together with those of some apostles.

The legendary tales of the martyrdom of Stephen were probably developed in the fifth or sixth century, following the supposed discovery of the relics of the saint in 415 by the priest Lucianus of Kĕfar-Gamlá. Lucianus' Greek account of his discovery was soon translated into Latin by Avitus of Braga, and this is the oldest version still extant (PL 61, cols. 807–18). There are Syriac and Armenian versions of the narration, and a longer recension in Greek. Everything would seem to indicate that it was a popular tale throughout Christendom and that it gave a considerable stimulus to the cult of Saint Stephen, although this cult already existed, as can be seen from numerous sermons in honor of Saint Stephen from earlier times (cf., e.g., *Gregory of Nyssa*, PG 56, cols. 701–36; Asterius of Amasea, PG 40, cols. 337–52). There is no known evidence to substantiate either the account of Lucianus or the authenticity of the relics.

The Coptic church celebrates the feast of the Invention of the relics of Saint Stephen on 1 Ṭubāh, coinciding with other Eastern churches, such as that of Constantinople. In the Syriac martyrology, however, it is celebrated on 26 December. A further celebration was the feast of the translation of the relics on 15 Tūt. There are indications that in the middle of the sixth century, under the direction of Bishop Theodorus, the pronaos of the Temple of Isis at Philae was transformed into a sanctuary dedicated to Saint Stephen (cf. Revillout, 1874).

BIBLIOGRAPHY

Asterius of Amasa. *Laudatio sancti promartyris Stephani.* In PG 40, cols. 337–52. Paris and Montrouge, 1863.

Gordini, G. D. "Stefano protomartire." *Bibliotheca Sanctorum,* Vol. 11, pp. 1376–87. Rome, 1968.
Guidi, I. "Frammenti Copti." *Rendiconti Accademia dei Lincei* ser. 4, 3/1 (1887):47–63.
______. "Gli atti apocrifi degli apostoli nei testi copti, arabi ed etiopici." *Societa asiatica italiana* [Florence], *Giornale* 2, (1888):19–35.
Hyvernat, H., ed. *Life of St. Stephen Protomartyr.* Bibliothecae Pierpont Morgan Codices . . . 53. Rome, 1922.
Leclercq, H. *"Etienne."* In *Dictionnaire d'archéologie chrétienne et de liturgie,* Vol. 5, pp. 624–71. Paris, 1922.
Marr, N., ed. *Le Synaxaire géorgien.* In PO 19, pp. 689–699. Turnhout, 1947.
Meinardus, O. F. A. *Christian Egypt Faith and Life,* pp. 150, 404. Cairo, 1970.
Revillout, E. "Mémoires sur les Blemmyes." *Mémoires presentés à l'Académie des Inscriptions et Belles Lettres* 1, 17 (1874):5.

GONZALO ARANDA PÉREZ

STEPHEN OF HNĒS, sixth-century bishop of Hnēs (Herakleopolis). Stephen is known to us only from two Coptic literary works that are attributed to him, the *Panegyric on the Martyr Saint Elijah* and the *Panegyric on Apollo, Archimandrite of the Monastery of Isaac.* An unedited Arabic manuscript (Cairo 712, fols. 330v–338v) contains a panegyric by the same author on the occasion of the dedication of a church (cf. Graf, 1944, p. 535). Stephen's dates are unknown. As he refers in the *Panegyric on Apollo* to events that took place in the reign of JUSTINIAN I (A.D. 527–565), it may be conjectured that he lived in the sixth century, or at any rate not much later.

In the *Panegyric on Saint Elijah,* Stephen eulogizes the martyr, who was both soldier and physician. Although Stephen was not an eyewitness of the martyrdoms, the greatness of the martyrs is proved for him by the many miracles that occur in the oratories dedicated to them. Elijah's name is likened to the sun (*hēlias, hēlios*) and his virtues shine. His career as soldier and physician is described and he is compared to the prophet Elijah, to Daniel, and to the evangelist Luke. As he refused to worship idols, his fate was sealed. He was tortured and executed, but his final victory was assured. Stephen refers to healings at the martyr's shrine and exhorts his audience to lead a moral life.

In the other panegyric, Apollo, the founder of the Monastery of Isaac, who died on 20 Ba'ūnah, is celebrated on his day of commemoration. Apollo's virtues are compared to those of his biblical predecessors, Moses, David, Joshua, and Elijah, and those of the prophets, apostles, and martyrs. As a young man, Apollo entered the Pachomian monastery of PBOW. His ascetic way of life and his virtues are extolled. He was vouchsafed visions, which included a vision of Christ. During the reign of Justinian I, the Monophysite "orthodoxy," which had ruled in the Coptic church, came once more under attack. This gave rise to some polemic against the Council of CHALCEDON. The monastery of Pbow became Chalcedonian, and its abbot, ABRAHAM OF FARSHŪṬ, was expelled. Apollo, too, left and eventually founded the Monastery of Isaac. There, Apollo encountered the hostility of a Melitian community. Apollo's pastoral work is recalled and his ordination to the priesthood is mentioned. He built a small church. Many miracles are attributed to him. Mention is made of a monastery and a nearby convent, both clearly foundations of Apollo. During his final illness, when near death, he comforted and exhorted his grieving brethren. The panegyric ends with a prayer and a doxology.

BIBLIOGRAPHY

Cauwenberg, P. van. *Etude sur les moines d'Egypte depuis le Concile de Chalcédoine (451) jusqu'à l'invasion arabe (640),* pp. 158f. Paris and Louvain, 1914.
Grillmeier, A., and H. Bacht, eds. *Das Konzil von Chalkedon,* Vol. 2, pp. 335f. Würzburg, 1953.
Kuhn, K. H., ed. and trans. *A Panegyric on Apollo, Archimandrite of the Monastery of Isaac, by Stephen, Bishop of Heracleopolis Magna.* CSCO 394–95; *Scriptores Coptici,* Vols. 39–40. Louvain, 1978.
Orlandi, T. *Elementi di lingua e letteratura copta,* p. 114. Milan, 1970.
Sobhy, G. P. G., ed. *Le Martyre de Saint Hélias et l'encomium de l'évêque Stéphanos de Hnès sur Saint Hélias.* Bibliothèque d'études coptes 1, pp. 67–94; French translation, pp. 113–20. Cairo, 1919.

K. H. KUHN

STEPHEN THE THEBAN, monk. Nothing is known about Stephen the Theban other than that he was a monk. His literary heritage has been transmitted to us in Greek, Arabic, and Georgian, and not in Coptic or any other language. The Greek tradition, according to the research carried out by Jean Darrouzès, attributes three works to him: *Logos Askētikos, Entolai,* and *Diataxis.* The latter two texts were edited by K. I. Dyobouniotis in 1913 under the name of Stephen the Sabaite. In fact, the *Diataxis* is composed of extracts from Sermons 3 and 4 of Isaiah of Gaza. As for the *Entolai,* they seem to be no more than extracts from the *Precepts* of Saint Antony the Great and Abbot Isaiah.

It would appear that Stephen can claim authorship of only the *Ascetic Sermon,* the Greek text of which was edited in 1969 by Etienne des Places on the basis of an eleventh–twelfth-century manuscript in the National Library, Paris (Greek 1066; not collated with Lavra Greek 248) with a French translation. The Georgian text was published in 1970 by Gérard Garitte, on the basis of a tenth-century manuscript (Sinai Georgian 35; this version corresponds sometimes with the Greek against the Arabic, and sometimes with the Arabic against the Greek).

Darrouzès observes of the content, "[This] work is a rather loose collection of counsels addressed to the author's spiritual son who is being initiated into monastic life: he must renounce the world, practice the ascetic life by developing the virtues, stay in his cell, and dismiss bad thoughts" (Darrouzès, 1961, col. 1525, bottom).

The *Ascetic Sermon* is well attested in Arabic at an early date in several South Palestinian and Egyptian manuscripts (Vatican Library, Arabic 71, parchment, copied at the monastery of Saint Saba in A.D. 885, fols. 226b–34a, A in J.-M. Sauget's edition; Sinai Arabic 571, copied on Sinai in the twelfth century, fols. 216a–22b, C in Sauget; Sinai Arabic 236, copied on Sinai in 1298, fols. 208a–15b, *logoi* 57–109 are missing, B in Sauget; and National Library, Paris, Arabic 253, copied in Egypt in the fourteenth century, fols. 246a–50v, D in Sauget). Vatican Arabic 695 is a copy of Vatican Arabic 71 made in Rome in the eighteenth century. Thus the Arabic manuscript tradition is older and far better attested than the Greek or Georgian traditions.

In Arabic this collection is divided into 109 sections. It was published by J.-M. Sauget in 1964 on the basis of the four manuscripts mentioned above, with a French translation and a Greek-Arabic index of the spiritual terminology. This Arabic text is translated directly from the Greek, without an intermediary translation. The translator does not always render the same Greek term with the same Arabic equivalent; his language is rather rough and his syntax is excessively reminiscent of the Greek original.

Sinai Arabic 235 (copied on Sinai in 1570) also contains (fols. 37b–38b) a brief text attributed to Stephen the Theban with the following incipit: "If you [pl.] wish to enter into life, and rejoice [sing., sic] with all the saints. . . ." This incipit recalls *logos* 78 that begins: "My son, if you wish to enter the kingdom of heaven . . ." (Sauget, 1964, p. 392), although the content is quite different. It is also quite different in the Greek text, and also in the Georgian, both of which are occasionally different from the Arabic. These two pages of the Sinai manuscript have not yet been edited.

The *Ascetic Sermon* was certainly known to the Copts at the beginning of the thirteenth century. Around 1230, al-Ṣafī ibn al-ʿAssāl summarized it in an epitome (*mukhtaṣar*). This epitome has not yet been edited, but it is attested in two fifteenth-century manuscripts (Vatican Library, Arabic 398, Egypt, fols. 102a–4a; and the Paris Syriac 239, fols. 137b–39b).

Concerning the text, Sauget writes (p. 371): "Comparison of the two manuscripts demonstrates that the text is one and the same, despite what Graf says, and that far from being extracts from the recension witnessed by the above-mentioned manuscripts this text offers in a decidedly more 'literary' style a very abbreviated and summarized version of the 'normal recension.'"

In conclusion, Graf (1944, Vol. 1, p. 413) attributes to Stephen the Theban texts that actually belong to another Stephen.

BIBLIOGRAPHY

Atiya, A. S., and J. N. Youssef. *Catalogue raisonné of the Mount Sinai Arabic Manuscripts* (in Arabic). Alexandria, 1970.

Darrouzès, J. "Etienne le Thébain." In *Dictionnaire de Spiritualité,* Vol. 4. cols. 1525–26 (with bibliography). Paris, 1961.

Des Places, E. "Le 'Discours Ascétique' d'Etienne de Thèbes. Texte grec inédit et traduction." *Le Muséon* 82 (1969):35–59.

Garitte, G. "Le 'Discours ascétique' d'Etienne le Thébain en géorgien." *Le Muséon* 83 (1970):73–93.

Sauget, J.-M. "Une Version arabe du 'sermon ascétique' d'Etiènne le Thébain." *Le Muséon* 77 (1964):367–406.

KHALIL SAMIR, S.J.

STERN, LUDWIG (1846–1911), German Egyptologist, Orientalist, and Celtic scholar. He specialized in Oriental languages, mastering Hebrew, Arabic, and Ethiopic. He turned to Egyptology under H. K. Brugsch in 1868 and continued his studies in the Egyptian Department of the Berlin Museum. In

1872 he was appointed librarian of the Khedivial Library at Cairo. In 1874 he was appointed to the staff of the Egyptian Department of the Berlin Museum. His best-known Coptic work was his valuable *Koptische Grammatik* (1880). His Coptic bibliography may be found in W. Kammerer, *A Coptic Bibliography* (1950, 1969).

BIBLIOGRAPHY

Dawson, W. R., and E. P. Uphill. *Who Was Who in Egyptology,* p. 282. London, 1972.

Kammerer, W., comp. *A Coptic Bibliography*. Ann Arbor, Mich., 1950; repr. New York, 1969.

AZIZ S. ATIYA

STICHARION. *See* Liturgical Vestments.

STOPPERS. *See* Ceramics, Coptic.

STROTHMANN, RUDOLPH (1877–1966), German Islamic scholar. His most important work on the Copts is *Die koptische Kirche in der Neuzeit* (Tübingen, 1932).

MARTIN KRAUSE

STRZYGOWSKI, JOSEF (1862–1941), Austrian art historian and professor at the University of Vienna. At the beginning of his career Strzygowski was interested in the sources of late antique and early Christian art, and he pointed out the importance of the Orient for the evolution of Western art. Between 1898 and 1906 he published the following important works on Coptic art: "Die christlichen Denkmäler Ägyptens," *Römische Quartalschrift* 12 (1898):1–41; *Orient oder Rom?* (Leipzig, 1901); "Der Schmuck der älteren el-Hadrakirche im syrischen Kloster der sketischen Wüste," *Oriens Christianus* 1 (1901):356–72; *Hellenistische und koptische Kunst in Alexandria* (Vienna, 1902); "Der koptische Reiterheilige und der hl. Georg," *Zeitschrift für ägyptische Sprache und Altertumskunde* 40 (1902–1903):49–60; "Seidenstoffe aus Ägypten im Kaiser Friedrich-Museum," *Jahrbücher der preussischen Kunstsammlungen* 24 (1903):147–78; *Koptische Kunst* (Vienna, 1904); and *Eine alexandrinische Weltchronik. Text und Miniaturen eines griechischen Papyrus der Sammlung W. Goleniscev* (Vienna, 1906), with Adolf Bauer.

BIBLIOGRAPHY

Dimand, M. S. "In memoriam Josef Strzygowski (1862–1941)." *Ars Islamica* 7 (1940):177.

Ginhart, K. "Josef Strzygowski." *Forschungen und Fortschritte* 17 (1941):87–88.

Zaloscer, H. "Strzygowski, sa méthode et ses recherches sur l'art copte." *Bulletin de la Société d'archéologie copte* 6 (1940):1–17.

MARTIN KRAUSE

SUBAKHMIMIC. *See Appendix.*

SUBDEACON, a novice deacon at the first stage of his diaconate. His duty is to look after the sacred vessels of the divine liturgy. In the early days of the church he was required to watch over the doors and make sure that no stranger or heretic entered. After he has acquired sufficient experience, a subdeacon may be elevated to a deacon.

BIBLIOGRAPHY

Burmester, O. H. E. *The Egyptian or Coptic Church.* Cairo, 1967.

ARCHBISHOP BASILIOS

SUBDIALECTS. *See Appendix.*

SUBORDINATIONISM, the inferiority of the Son to the Father, a doctrine explicitly maintained by ARIUS and later Arians. The term "of one substance" was designed to meet this claim. Another form of subordinationism maintains the inferiority of the Spirit to both Father and Son.

Arius, in the opinion of Archbishop Alexander I of Alexandria, taught that the Word did not always exist but was made by God out of what did not exist. The Son was a creature and a work of the Father, unlike in essence and not the true Word and Wisdom of the Father. He was subject to change like other rational creatures, alien and separate from the Father's essence. He had less than perfect knowledge of the Father; indeed, He had no knowledge of His own essence, for He was a mere instrument of God, made for the purpose of man's creation.

The Nicene Creed met these points by insisting that the Son was begotten from the essence of the Father—begotten, not made, of the same substance as the Father. Yet subordinationism persisted in finding a clear statement in the so-called blasphemy of Sirmium, which denied the propriety of the terms "substance," "same substance," and "like substance," since they referred to what was beyond human knowledge and were not found in Scripture: "It is certain that there is one God, all-ruling and Father. There is no uncertainty that the Father is greater: It cannot be doubtful to anyone that the Father is greater than the Son in honor and dignity and renown and majesty, and in the very name of Father, since he himself bears witness. 'He who sent me is greater than I.'"

Macedonius, bishop of Constantinople until his deposition in 360, was credited with the belief that while the Son was in essence like the Father, the Holy Spirit was merely an angelic servant. He argued that if the Spirit is unbegotten, then there must be two unbegotten beings. If the Spirit be begotten of the Father, then there are two sons and brothers in the Trinity; if he be begotten of the Son, then he would be God's grandson. All of this is absurd; therefore the Spirit is a creature.

Terms and propositions that appear to support subordinationism have been found earlier than Arius, notably in ORIGEN. There is no greater and lesser among the divine triad, although the scope of activity varies from person to person (*On First Principles* 1.3.7). Yet the Father transcends the Son, at least as much as the Son and the Spirit transcend the best of other beings (*Commentaria in Evangelium Joannis* 13.25.151). Further, Origen's view on this point is affected by opposition to the Gnostic subordination of the Father or creator to the Son or redeemer (*Contra Celsum* 8.15). The coherence of Origen on this point has been defended by his interpreters; but the tensions are evident. The generation of the Son is eternal, as brightness from light (*On First Principles* 1.2.4), and there never was a time when the Son did not exist (4.4.28). He is distinct both numerically (*Commentaria in Evangelium Joannis* 10.37.246) and substantially (*On First Principles* 1.2.2) from the Father. Yet he is begotten of the substance of God and is of the same substance (*Fragmenta in epistolam ad Hebreos*). For Origen the Father is *agennetos*, "ungenerated" (*Commentaria in Evangelium Joannis* 2.10.75), while the Son is a *ktisma*, "creature" (*On First Principles* 4.4.1) and *theos*, "god," rather than *ho theos*, "the God" (*Commentaria in Evangelium Joannis* 2.2.16). The Savior is in the middle, between the *agenetos*, "uncreated," and the nature of all *geneta*, "created things" (*Contra Celsum* 3.34). He differs from *genneta*, "begotten things," in his immediacy to God but stands over against the *agennetos* in the chain of *genneta* (*On Prayer* 15.1).

Yet the mystery of God is perhaps to be grasped among *geneta* only by Christ and the Holy Spirit (*Commentaria in Evangelium Joannis* 2.28.172). The Son and Holy Spirit, however, are both *genetos* and *agenetos*. The Arian controversy underlined the confusion that had existed between *agennetos* and *agenetos*. Eusebius of Caesarea develops the concept of a Second God (*Demonstratio evangelica* 5.4.9–14), a term that indicates the problem of preserving the pure unity of the Father in contrast with the universality of the Son.

Confusing as the evidence is, there is a reasonable explanation. Origen was concerned with the dialectic of God becoming man, that man might become divine with the negation of negation, a Johannine theme developed by Irenaeus and others. The Arians were concerned with a hierarchy of being and exhibited the more wooden approach of some later Platonists in this area.

BIBLIOGRAPHY

Pollard, T. E. *Johannine Christology and the Early Church*. Cambridge, 1970.

Prestige, G. L. *God in Patristic Thought*. London, 1936.

ERIC F. OSBORNE

SUDAN, CATHOLIC COPTS IN THE. Catholics of the Coptic rite have been present in the Sudan since the Anglo-Egyptian conquest of 1898. Some of the soldiers of the expeditionary force settled in Omdurman and Khartoum and worked in private business or in government service. A greater number came from Egypt to be employed, especially in the Post and Telegraph Service. The total number of Catholic Copts increased to about one hundred families. They never formed an organized community along confessional lines. Socially they joined the Coptic Orthodox community.

Local priests of the Latin rite have ministered to the Catholic Copts in their parishes. Copts who lived in the provincial towns of the northern Sudan where no resident priest was to be found were regularly visited by a Latin missionary on camel-back.

Catholic Copts were brought by the Latin vicar apostolic from Egypt to staff the Catholic schools in Khartoum and Omdurman from 1902. In 1951 a Latin priest took the Coptic rite in order to give the

Copts pastoral care in a more appealing way, but the initiative met with no success and was abandoned. From 1970, a bishop or a priest from Egypt visits the Coptic Catholics in Khartoum and Omdurman.

GIOVANNI VANTINI

SUDAN, COPTIC EVANGELICAL CHURCH IN THE. The establishment of the Coptic Evangelical Church in the Sudan goes back to the beginning of the twentieth century as an offshoot of the Evangelical Church of Egypt.

After the fall of the Mahdist rule in the Sudan in 1898 and the establishment of the Anglo-Egyptian Condominium, many Egyptians were enrolled in the service of the Sudan government. As there were among them about seventy Evangelicals, Jabrā Ḥannā was delegated by the mother church of Egypt to give them pastoral care (1900).

The Evangelical Church in Khartoum was officially organized in December 1907, and elders were ordained. This was, and still is, the mother of all the other Egyptian churches in the Sudan—that is, the churches of ʿAṭbarah, Port Sudan, Kuraymah, Wādī Ḥalfā, Wād Madanī, al-Qaḍārif, and al-Ubayyiḍ. All services in these churches are conducted in Arabic. As Southern Sudanese began migrating to the north in large numbers (as from 1960), new churches were opened in Kustī, al-Duwaym, Shandī, and Huṣayḥiṣah, where services are conducted in Arabic or in tribal languages of the Southern Sudan.

In 1932, owing to financial difficulties, many Egyptians left the Sudan. The churches of ʿAṭbarah, Wādī Halfā, Kuraymah, and Port Sudan were closed. Later on those in ʿAṭbarah and Port Sudan were reopened.

In 1946 the Synod of the Nile of the Evangelical Church of Egypt, in response to a petition from the Sudan Presbytery, gave permission for the organization of the Upper Nile Presbytery, which included the congregations of Doleib Hill and Nāṣir.

In March 1956 the Church of Christ in the Upper Nile was officially recognized by the Sudan Presbytery and later also by the United Presbyterian Church in the USA.

In March 1964 all the foreign missionaries were expelled from southern Sudan by order of the government. The local pastors (about 100) took over all the church administration in the South. The total number of Evangelicals of Coptic (Egyptian) origin is about 2,000; those of African origin (southern Sudan) is estimated at about 150,000.

In 1970 the Church of Christ in the Upper Nile merged with the Evangelical Church in the northern Sudan, under the official name of Presbyterian Church in the Sudan.

GIOVANNI VANTINI

SUDAN, COPTS IN THE. The presence of Copts in the Sudan goes back to the early nineteenth century, when Muḥammad ʿAlī pasha sent out an expedition to annex the Sudan to Egypt. Copts were sent along as superintendents of accounting and finance and were given the task of mapping the land and assessing taxation.

These Copts remained in the service of the Egyptian administration in the Sudan until 1881, when a wave of persecution against the Copts forced them to leave the country.

They were recalled in 1898 to occupy posts as assistants in the supreme command of the army as interpreters, accountants, and clerks. Soon they spread into other administrations after the dual agreement of the Anglo-Egyptian Sudan. The British employed Copts on a provisional basis, that is, until a generation of educated Sudanese loyal to Britain could assume the responsibilities of management within the limits laid down by the British. After that, Egyptians were to be gradually eliminated; this eventually took place in the 1920s. The Copts, however, were the last to be dismissed from the Egyptian administration in the Sudan, in view of their higher level of education and their particular expertise in the use of foreign languages.

After the Egyptian rule was established in 1899, the Sudan was administratively divided into provinces and districts. The number of Copts working in the provinces, particularly the distant ones, kept growing. They constituted more than half of the total number of employees in the country. Their integration into their new environment was consolidated through intermarriage with Sudanese families. They gradually came to be employed in senior positions in the departments of administration of finance and legal affairs, as well as in the office of the governor general.

According to an approximate statistic, there were 600 Coptic families in Kartoum in 1960 and another 500 in other parts of the Sudan.

YUWĀKĪM RIZQ MURQUS

SUHĀJ. *See* Dayr Anbā Bishoi (Suhāj); Monasteries of the Fayyūm.

SUNBĀṬ, modern name of a town in the Egyptian Delta known in Coptic as ⲧⲁⲥⲉⲙⲡⲟϯ (Tasempoti) and in Arabic as Sanbāṭ, Sambūṭiyyah, or Sanmūṭiyyah. The town is located in the middle of the Delta in the province of Gharbiyyah about 12 miles (19 km) east of Tanta, halfway between Abūsīr Banā and Zifta.

Tasempoti/Sunbāṭ was an important town in martyrdom literature for the period prior to 640. For example, the town figures prominently in the Coptic martyrdom of Piroou and Athom (see MARTYRS, COPTIC). In Tasempoti/Sunbāṭ Piroou and Athom buried the martyr Anoua, and after they themselves had been martyred, they were buried in the same place.

The SYNAXARION relates that Samnūtiyyah/Sunbāṭ was the burial place of the remains of the martyrs Agathon, Peter, John, Amun, Amuna, and Rebecca.

The HISTORY OF THE PATRIARCHS mentions Sunbāṭ (spelled Sanbūṭ in this instance) as a geographical reference for a place called Shubra where a group of Bashmurites successfully battled against the troops of ʿAbd al-Malik in 751. From the fact that the text says that Shubrā is near Sanbūṭ one can deduce that Sanbūt was the more important of the two towns.

Around 1186 there was a strong Greek Orthodox minority in Sunbāṭ with its own metropolitan. Markus ibn al-Qanbar demanded one of Sunbāṭ's churches from the metropolitan, but the demand went unheeded. Although this report implies that there was more than one church in Sunbāṭ around 1190, al-MAQRĪZĪ mentions for the town only one Coptic church, a Church of the Apostles, at the end of the fourteenth or the beginning of the fifteenth century.

Each year in the Church of Saint Rebecca (Sitt Rifqah) in Sunbāṭ a feast is held on 17 September in honor of the saint and the martyrs who died with her (Meinardus, 1965, p. 176).

BIBLIOGRAPHY

Meinardus, Otto. *Christian Egypt, Ancient and Modern.* Cairo, 1965.

RANDALL STEWART

SUNDAY, the weekly commemoration of the Resurrection and appearance of the Lord to His disciples (Jn. 20:19, 26). It falls on the first day of every week.

Sunday has been kept by Christians since apostolic times as a day of joyful worship. Saint Paul and the Christians of Troas gathered on the first day of the week "to break bread" (Acts 20:7), and the apostle, writing to the Corinthians, asked his converts to save their alms on this day (1 Cor. 16:2).

In opposition to Gnostic Manichaean asceticism, the Coptic church condemned the practice of fasting on Sunday. Apostolical Canon 66 decrees, "If any of the clergy be found fasting on the Lord's day or on the Sabbath, excepting the one only, let him be deposed. If a layman, let him be excommunicated." The "Constitutions of the Holy Apostles" declares that "he will be guilty of sin who fasts on the Lord's day, being the day of the Resurrection." Canon 18 of the Council of Gangra (325–381) anathematizes the Eustathians for teaching fasting on the Lord's day.

Although kneeling was the common posture of prayer in the early church, prostration is not allowed at prayer on the Lord's Day and the fifty days between Easter and Pentecost. Peter I of Alexandria (300–311) said in Canon 15, "We keep the Lord's Day as a day of joy, because then our Lord rose. Our tradition is, not to kneel on that day" ("Apostolical Canons," 1956, p. 601).

In the Coptic church, marriages are now contracted on any nonfasting day, especially Sundays and Saturdays. The usual hour for celebration of marriages in the church is from five o'clock onward into the evening. The couple to be married normally receive Holy Communion either two or three days or even one week before the marriage service.

The Commemorations and the Intercessions of the Martyrs and Saints form a consistent part of the PSALMODIA, the liturgy, and the Synaxarion of the Coptic church, and are to be sung or read every day, including Sunday. This does not contradict canon 51 of the Council of Laodicea (343–381), which states, "The nativities of Martyrs are not to be celebrated in Lent, but commemorations of the Holy Martyrs are to be made on the Sabbaths and the Lord's days." This is because the Divine Liturgy was not to be celebrated in Lent, except on Saturday and Sunday, a practice still observed by the Syrians, Armenians, and Greeks.

On Sundays all the year round, burial and memorial services for the dead are to be performed without using the mourning melody. Hymns are to be sung only to the BIKAWARNIDĀS, called *al-laḥn al-sanawī* (i.e., the ordinary melody; see LAḤN).

This is in accordance with canon 11 of Pope CHRISTODOULUS (1046–1077), which says, "And there shall not be allowed on Sundays weeping or lamentation or speeches, and it is not allowed to a Christian to do this or anything of it for the dead, except the Intercession and the Eucharist and the prayer for the dead and alms, in the measure of his (the Christian's) ability, that the Lord may have mercy upon the souls of your dead."

BIBLIOGRAPHY

Muyser, J. "Le Samedi et le Dimanche dans l'eglise et la littérature coptes." In *Le Martyre d'apa Epima,* ed. Togo Mina. Cairo, 1937.

Riedel, W., and W. E. Crum. *The Canons of Athanasius.* London, 1904; repr. 1973.

Ṣafī ibn al-ʿAssāl, al-. *Al-Kitāb al-Qawānīn* (Book of Canons), ed. Murqus Jirjis. Cairo, 1927.

EMILE MAHER ISHAQ

ṢUQĀʿI FAḌL ALLĀH IBN FAKHR, AL-, thirteenth-century historian and biographer, a Christian resident of the city of Damascus. He was a scribe in the *diwan* (government office). He died a centenarian in 1326. In Christian literature, he was noted for his compilation of the four Gospels in a unified work in numerous languages including Hebrew, Syriac, Coptic, and Greek. Presumably, he also memorized the whole Bible, including the Psalms and the Gospels. He was also a famous biographer responsible for a summary of Ibn Khallikān's obituaries (*Wāfayāt al-Aʿyān*) to which he appended a supplement dealing with celebrated personalities of Egypt and Syria between 1261 and 1324. His other works include a few religious studies, which show that he was familiar with Egyptian Christianity and the Copts.

AZIZ S. ATIYA

SURETY. *See* Law, Coptic: Private Law.

SURIEL, ARCHANGEL (Arabic, Suryāl). Ranking fourth among the archangels, Suriel's name is derived from Hebrew, meaning "my rock is God," and occurs once in the Old Testament (Nm. 3:35). His feast is celebrated by the Coptic church on 27 Ṭūbah.

In the Coptic psalmody, there is a special doxology in honor of Suriel: "Let us venerate Suriel the fourth archangel. Great is the joy brought by Suriel, which surpasses the joys of the vanishing world, the joys that pass away, while Suriel's joy lasts forever. Intercede for us, O holy Archangel Suriel the trumpeter, so that the Lord may forgive us our sins."

Citing his feast day on 27 Ṭūbah, the SYNAXARION adds that "Suriel is he that brought the good news of salvation to Adam, the one that saved Joseph from the snares of the Egyptian woman, the one that appeared to Esdras the prophet and aquainted him with the sacred mysteries. He is also the comforter of hearts, the intercessor on behalf of sinners."

Again, under 9 Amshīr, the Synaxarion gives the story of a certain Paul, a Coptic martyr who was comforted and encouraged by the archangel Suriel at Ashmūnayn, in Upper Egypt, while being tortured by the governor, and was eventually sent to Alexandria where he was executed, winning the crown of martyrdom.

On both dates, 27 Ṭūbah and 9 Amshīr, the DIFNĀR (antiphonarium of the Coptic church) celebrates the memory of Archangel Suriel the Trumpeter.

BISHOP GREGORIUS

SWITZERLAND, COPTIC MISSIONARIES IN. *See* Theban Legion.

SYLLABICATION. *See Appendix.*

SYMBOLS IN COPTIC ART. [*This entry consists of a number of short articles by various authors:*
Alpha and Omega
Conch Shell
The Cross
Dolphins
Eagle
Fish
Nimbus]

Alpha and Omega

Alpha and omega (Α and Ω) are the first and last letters of the Greek alphabet. In Middle Eastern astrology, they are related to the cosmos, the signs of the zodiac, and the twenty-four hours of the day. In Egyptian alchemy they are linked to the good genius, Agathodaimon. During the Greco-Roman period, these letters, loaded with this mystique, were transferred to Christianity to symbolize Christ as the beginning and end of life. Christ as *Logos* ("the Word") was the creator, and Christ will be the judge at the end of the world. The Book of Revelation alludes to this theme in three passages (1:8; 21:6; 22:13) of which the last is the most complete: "I am the Alpha and the Omega, the first and the last, the beginning and the end."

Among literary sources, the alpha and omega are mentioned in a treatise by Zosimus Alexandrinus. The theologians Irenaeus and Tertullian both mention the Gnostic interpretation of alpha and omega by Mark, a disciple of the Gnostic philosopher VALENTINUS. According to Mark, the letters, given a numerical value, form the number 801, which corresponds to the dove.

In art the alpha and omega appear at the beginning of the fourth century in connection with Christological debates that were settled at the Council of NICAEA. The council sanctioned their use as an expression of the dogma that Christ is of like substance (HOMOIOUSION) with the Father. From the time of Constantine in the early fourth century, the alpha and omega were associated with words or symbols signifying victory for which one may presume several meanings. The symbol enjoyed an exceptional diffusion in Egypt in nearly every medium and for a very long time. Its presence is particularly significant in funerary objects, where it represents life in its entirety and above all signifies eternal life.

The letters are most often found on funerary stelae, which the Egyptians adorned with completely original design concepts and figural representations. On one of the most ancient stelae, dating from the fourth century, an aged man in a toga is crouched in a chapel while the two letters are carefully painted in red on the stela's triangular crown on either side of an ANKH (a cross with a loop above the cross bar, which is the Egyptian sign of eternal life) whose loop or handle encloses a chrismon (the Greek letters *chi* and *rho,* forming the monogram of Christ). The most consistent groups of stelae bearing an engraved alpha and omega come from Armant and Akhīm. At Armant a popular motif is a chapel with a triangular pediment, with the letters either at the sides of or within the pediment or else inside the chapel. In a stela in the British Museum, London (Cramer, 1955, figs. 8, 10; ill. 10), the chapel encloses a great chrismon having an open *rho.* This is the type most common in Egypt after the beginning of the sixth century; the earlier type was a closed *rho.* The letters are engraved in the sides and upper part, while two ankhs appear in the lower part. In another stela from the same museum (Cramer, 1955, ill. 17), the alpha and omega occupy

Stela decorated with a cross, two ansate crosses (*crux ansata*), alpha and omega. *Courtesy Coptic Museum, Cairo.*

both the exterior and the interior of the pediment, where they flank a chrismon. In the space below two engraved ankhs are separated by an element that M. Cramer recognized as the hieroglyphic *sm* ꜣ, that is, "unite."

Such a layout takes on strong characteristics of originality and assumes a significance that has not been sufficiently emphasized. It is, in fact, difficult to interpret this symbol in any other way than as referring to Christ, the beginning and end of life, who unites the two lives, that is, who by His sacrifice enables humanity to achieve a union of mortal and immortal life. Here the sign *sm* ꜣ maintains its primitive Egyptian meaning and legibility though transposed into a Christian context. Moreover, the same may be said for alpha and omega, which have the same significance at present, even for those who do not know Greek, precisely because of their union as a widely used Christian symbol.

Another category of stelae from Armant (dated probably to the seventh century) shows the letters at the sides of a bird wearing a necklace and bulla (hollow pendant). Its outspread wings support a crown that encloses a chrismon (Crum, 1902, no. 8656).

In stelae from Akhmīm, alpha and omega appear in the pediment of the chapel, either inserted between the arms of a chrismon (Crum, 1902, no. 8602) or under the arms of an ankh (Crum, no. 8575), with the handle of the ankh sometimes being filled with a rosace (circle enclosing a rosette) or a face.

In the stelae of Isnā, the two letters are suspended from a cross (the alpha is reversed) in the interior of a small chapel flanked by two large bunches of grapes and two ankhs with pointed arms crowned by a cross (Cramer, 1955, ill. 40).

An important vine motif fills the open space of a stela of unknown provenance dating from the seventh or eighth century. In this example the letters are suspended from an ankh and are repeated below, alongside the ribbons of a crown enclosing a chrismon.

Stelae from the Fayyūm often portray a figure praying in a chapel with a triangular pediment. The alpha and omega appear in the pediment either at the sides of an ankh (Cramer, 1955, ill. 34) or else suspended from the arms (Cramer, ill. 33). This position must have been the actual custom as is attested in later times by processional ankhs from which alpha and omega were suspended by small chains (Cabrol, 1907, col. 4).

The letters are often present in the architecture of churches and monasteries. At Oxyrhynchus, the archeologist E. Breccia mentions them as flanking some ankhs beside the apse of a church. In a stone relief, likely of the same provenance, they appear at the sides of an ankh in a medallion surrounded by acanthus scrolls. It may be assumed that these date from the fourth to the sixth century (Cramer, 1955, ill. 44). In wooden lintels from Dayr Apa Apollo at BĀWĪṬ dating from the sixth century, conserved at the Louvre Museum, Paris, the letters are incised or encrusted here and there in lead in an aedicula (shrine) that encloses a cross in a shell (Rutschowscaya, 1977, pp. 181–84). In an unusual piece of sculpture the letters are framed by inscriptions bearing the names of the fathers of the monastery; there are also haloed figures, among whom Saint MENAS may be recognized (Rutschowscaya, p. 185). The alpha and omega also appear on a wooden pyx from Akhmīm (Forrer, 1893, pl. XI, no. 5). It is known that in the Christian world generally these letters were also depicted on the hosts.

In ceramics the letters appear on a seal of Egyptian manufacture. Sometimes they accompany the chrismon in a few plates and goblets for which a liturgical use may legitimately be proposed. Two examples dating from the fourth or fifth century have been brought to light in the excavations of the University of Rome at ANTINOOPOLIS (Guerrini in Donadoni, *Antinoë*, 1974, p. 74). One other, very similar, has been conserved at the Louvre.

The documentation in textiles is very rich, consisting for the most part of sizable pieces destined for liturgical or funerary furnishings. For example, a hanging at the Victoria and Albert Museum, London (Kendrick, 1921, no. 317) dating from the fourth or fifth century, has the alpha and omega lodged beside a bejeweled cross in a crown carried in flight by two winged victories. In another tapestry at the Coptic Museum in Cairo (Ḥabīb, 1967, no. 111), the letters appear under arcades flanking the ankh, together with peacocks and doves; the whole ensemble indicates a funerary purpose. Other examples of large dimensions, the first dating from the fifth century, are conserved at the Louvre. Their presence is rarer in tunics, as in an unpublished example of the Archeological Museum in Florence,

Lintel decorated with an aedicula having a pediment showing a cross and flanked by an alpha and omega. Wood. Bāwīṭ, south church. Sixth century. Length: 2.5 m; width: 35 cm; thickness: 15 cm. *Courtesy Louvre Museum, Paris.*

where they flank the staff of a chrismon enclosed in a small oval medallion. The decorative arrangement of this tunic—which evidences great care and quality—depicts animals from the hunting theme and vegetal motifs usually found in connection with the Dionysiac repertoire (see MYTHOLOGICAL SUBJECTS IN COPTIC ART); a funerary destination would hence be probable.

In painting, the alpha and omega appear at times, but more rarely, in company with the chrismon, as in a painting brought to light in the southern necropolis of Antinoopolis probably dating from the fourth or fifth century (Donadoni, in *Antinoë*, 1974, p. 153, table 80, 1); or they are found until a very late period near the cross-inscribed halo of Christ or of the Infant Jesus, as is attested by an icon at the Coptic Museum in Cairo (Ḥabīb, 1967, no. 135).

In the art of bookmaking, they are incorporated into a chrismon on the plates of silver binding conserved in the Coptic Museum (Strzygowski, 1904, nos. 7202, 7204). Manuscripts constitute important documentation that is constant across the centuries. One of the most ancient is a Sahidic Gnostic one in the Bodleian Library, Oxford (Bruciamus 96), which depicts an ankh with the handle enclosing a cross with alpha and omega. Under the arms of the cross is the inscription *heis theos* ("one God") with the alpha and omega repeated in major dimensions (Cramer, 1964, ill. 31). In a Bohairic-Arabic manuscript dating from 1362 at the Coptic Museum in Cairo, the letters appear below an arrangement of the Cross and the chrismon. Here the alpha shows a tendency to be transformed into a bird, a tendency that will increase (Cramer, 1964, ill. 39; see also the table of the transformations of the initial alphas in Coptic manuscripts in Cramer, 1959, ill. 127). A Bohairic-Arabic manuscript in Cairo dating from 1486 (Cramer, 1964, figs. 14, 42) has the letters above and below a large rosette of geometric motifs whose prototype probably goes back to the ankh with the handle filled with a starred chrismon. A comparable arrangement appears in the Arabic-Bohairic manuscript Borgia 70 in the Vatican Library, which dates from 1699. In two similar copies of the same manuscript, the alpha keeps its normal form in the one; in the other, it is transformed into a bird (Cramer, 1964, ills. 44, 45).

Finally, these letters have certain peculiarities in Egypt, as in other countries of the Christian world. In several examples, the letters are shown reversed both in order and direction. Sometimes one of the letters is missing, and at times, the alpha is repeated in place of the omega, as for example, on both sides of Christ in a textile from Panopolis (Gerspach, 1890, no. 108).

BIBLIOGRAPHY

Bourguet, P. du. *Catalogue des étoffes coptes*, Vol. 1. Musée National du Louvre. Paris, 1964.

Cabrol, F. "Alpha et Omega." In *Dictionnaire d'archéologie chrétienne et de liturgie*. Paris, 1907.

Cecchelli, C. "Alpha e Omega." In *Enciclopedia Italiana*. Rome, 1929.

Cramer, M. *Das altägyptische Lebenszeichen im christlichen (koptischen) Ägypten*. Wiesbaden, 1955.

———. *Das christlich-koptische Ägypten einst und heute, eine Orientierung*. Wiesbaden, 1959.

———. *Koptische Buchmalerei*. Recklinghausen, 1964.

Crum, W. E. *Coptic Monuments*. Catalogue général des antiquités égyptiennes du Musée du Caire. Cairo, 1902.

Deneuve, G. *L'arte copta*. Florence, 1970.

Donadoni, S., et al. *Antinoe (1965–1968)*. Missione Archeologica in Egitto dell' Università di Roma. Rome, 1974.

Dornseiff, F. *Das Alphabet in Mystik und Magie*. Berlin, 1925.

Forrer, R. *Die frühchristlichen Alterthümer aus dem Gräberfelde von Achmim-Panopolis*. Strasbourg, 1893.

Gerspach, E. *Les Tapisseries coptes*. Paris, 1890.

Ḥabīb, R. *The Coptic Museum: A General Guide*. Cairo, 1967.

Kendrick, A. F. *Catalogue of Textiles from Burying-Grounds in Egypt*, 3 vols. London, 1920, 1921, 1922.

Romeo, A., and A. Ferrua. "Alpha e Omega." In *Enciclopedia Italiana*. Rome, 1929.

Rutschowscaya, M.-H. "Linteaux en bois d'époque copte." *Bulletin de l'Institut français d'Archéologie orientale* 77 (1977):181–91.

Strzygowski, J. *Koptische Kunst*. Catalogue géneral des antiquités égyptiennes du Musée du Caire. Vienna, 1904.

LORETTA DEL FRANCIA

Conch Shell

The Greeks associated the conch shell with Aphrodite, the Nereid Thetis, and sea divinities generally. Coptic artists inherited it from the Greeks by way of Alexandria. They used it sometimes in connection with Aphrodite Anadyomene ("rising from the waters") and sometimes for its own sake. It

Niche decorated with a conch. *Courtesy Coptic Museum, Cairo.*

appears in abundance in stone reliefs and decorative tapestry panels on fabrics.

In both media the conch underwent a development in style from naturalistic to schematic or distorted. In sculpture the alveoli (furrows) in the shell, still close to their original form even in the sixth century, became progressively elongated, resulting in parallel sunken lines in the seventh and eighth centuries. Examples may be seen at DAYR APA JEREMIAH at Saqqara. In tapestry, the conch was distorted to the point where it took the shape of a vase, from which Aphrodite emerges.

BIBLIOGRAPHY

Beckwith, J. *Coptic Sculpture.* London, 1963.

Bourguet, P. du. *Catalogue des étoffes coptes I.* Musée du Louvre, Paris, 1964.

Duthuit, G. *La Sculpture copte.* Paris, 1931.

PIERRE DU BOURGUET, S.J.

The Cross

It is difficult to determine the moment at which the cross appears in Christian Coptic art. The simplest and most common form in the earliest times at which we can find it, the fourth century, is the crossing at right angles of two lines of equal length, which appears to be inspired by the Greek cross. It seems to have served as a convenient sign of Christian belief rather than as an ornament. One may suppose this usage from its presence in the mausoleum of the Exodus at Khargah, although, in fact, this mausoleum, without having any well-defined character, must be under Byzantine influence. But the symbolic use of this simplified form of the cross may, without too much error, be regarded as the most common, for it is often repeated later in Christian Coptic art.

Near the Greek-inspired cross in the same mausoleum is a distinctive form of the *crux ansata,* or ankh. Where the upper element of the Egyptian ankh is elongated, that of the Coptic *crux ansata* is a circle. According to Rufinus (Doresse, 1960, pp. 24–26), the Copts availed themselves of the distant resemblance between the Egyptian ankh, signifying "life" in hieroglyphics, and the cross, replacing the upper element of the cross by the crown worn by Roman victors. This development took place in the fifth century at the time of the destruction of the temples of Serapis. The Coptic *crux ansata* is more and more frequently found in later Coptic art.

From the fourth to the thirteenth century these two crosses (the simplified Greek cross and the Coptic *crux ansata*) were dominant in Coptic representations. One will also find occasionally, however, the Byzantine cross with eight branches, for example, in the sixth-century church of DAYR ABŪ FĀNĀ at Mallawī in Middle Egypt and later on Coptic fabrics of the twelfth century (du Bourguet, 1964, no. I, 30 and index p. 566).

Broken pediment above a conch. Limestone. Bāwīṭ. Seventh century. Height: 60 cm; width: 87 cm; thickness: 22 cm. *Courtesy Louvre Museum, Paris.*

Series of five ansate crosses (*crux ansata*) between two rows of interlacings above another fragmentary *crux ansata* between an alpha and omega. Tapestry on linen background. Seventh century. Length: 30 cm; width: 46 cm. *Courtesy Louvre Museum, Paris.*

Textile square with indigo background containing a square that is itself divided into four squares, each with a red cross in the center. Tapestry. Twelfth century. Each side: 19 cm. *Courtesy Louvre Museum, Paris.*

Another form of cross during this period has slightly bell-shaped extremities. It exists only in rare examples. The most typical is on a limestone panel that was collected in the church of Armant near Luxor and now belongs to the Louvre. It stands on the head of a dolphin, both carved in relief (du Bourguet, 1968, p. 14).

After the thirteenth century, another form of cross tends to dominate. Similar to a moline cross, it terminates at each extremity in two folioles (small leaf shapes), which part company. This is the "Coptic" cross. It has practically supplanted the others in the liturgical usages of the Coptic community.

BIBLIOGRAPHY

Bourguet, P. du. *'Art copte.* Collection L'Art dans le Monde. Paris, 1968.

______. *Catalogue des étoffes coptes I.* Musée du Louvre. Paris, 1964.

Dinkler, E. *Signum Crucis.* Tübingen, 1965.

Doresse, J. *Les hiéroglyphes à la croix.* Publications de l'Institut historique et archéologique néerlandais. Istanbul, 1960.

PIERRE DU BOURGUET, S.J.

Dolphins

Having but little concern with the sea, Egypt in the pharaonic period did not portray the dolphin. It was Greco-Roman iconography that brought it to the country. This likable animal, which appears in the legend of Dionysus (see MYTHOLOGICAL SUBJECTS IN COPTIC ART), was considered as a savior of the shipwrecked. On Roman mosaics it accompanies the Nereids (sea nymphs) or the putti (cupids), who sometimes ride on its back. These figures were copied in Coptic bas-reliefs: for example, ones in limestone in the Coptic Museum, Cairo, or in the Civic Museum of History and Art, Trieste; a bone plaque in Cairo and a pin surmounted by a dolphin, in the Egyptian Museum, Berlin. The marine setting is then transformed into Nilotic decoration. The dolphin keeps company with a crocodile on a relief in the British Museum. In the numerous tapestry decorations that illustrate the same theme, the dolphin, if it appears, is hardly distinguishable from the stylized fish or sea monsters. We may note, however, a very fine example on a fragment preserved in the Pushkin Museum of Fine Arts, Moscow.

A fourth-century bronze lamp in the Louvre shows a dolphin ridden by a cupid. Others, in the Louvre, the Egyptian Museum in Turin, and the Egyptian Museum in Berlin, have the shape of a dolphin holding the spout. A stela in Berlin displays two of these lamps, one on each side of an orant (praying figure), which points to a religious use. Other objects set the motif in a Christian context, where the dolphin symbolizes salvation from sin. A lamp in the State Hermitage Museum, Leningrad, shows a cross on a dolphin's forehead. A church candelabrum is adorned with twelve dolphins. Two paterae (saucers), one in Cairo, one in the Louvre, have a handle in the form of a woman brandishing a cross, the whole framed by two dolphins. Two sixth-century reliefs from Armant in the Louvre and in the National Museum, Warsaw, clearly depict the Savior Christ in the form of a dolphin bearing a cross.

Capital decorated with the ram symbol of Christ, a peacock, and a cross. *Courtesy Coptic Museum, Cairo.*

The idea of the dolphin as a symbol of salvation appears also on a series of Coptic funerary stelae of the Islamic period, in which the dolphin, duplicated, contributes admirably to the symmetrical decoration, filling the corners or plunging in a rounded movement around a garland containing the cross.

BIBLIOGRAPHY

Badawy, A. *Coptic Art and Archaeology*. Cambridge, Mass., and London, 1978.

Crum, W. E. *Coptic Monuments*. Catalogue général des antiquités égyptiennes du Musée du Caire. Cairo, 1902.

Strzygowski, J. *Koptische Kunst*. Catalogue général des antiquités égyptiennes du Musée du Caire. Vienna, 1904.

DOMINIQUE BENAZETH

Eagle

The eagle played a very small role in religion and art under the pharaohs. Its importance began with the influence of Hellenistic and Roman art and grew in the Coptic period.

The symbolic interpretations given to the eagle, especially in funerary art, are various and controversial. For some scholars it is a symbol of Christ or of Christ's resurrection. Their arguments are based mainly on Latin sources and on the Greek letters alpha and omega (see above) that sometimes accompany the eagle (Clédat, 1904, p. 150; Leclercq, 1934, cols. 1425ff.; Pelsmaekers, 1982, p. 160). The Oriental texts do not confirm these interpretations. Beginning with the Old Testament, they emphasize the eagle's miraculous and protective qualities. In Deuteronomy 31:11, the eagle's wings offer protection. In Psalm 102:5, the eagle is shown as capable of rejuvenation. Magic texts mention the protection granted by the eagle's wings and the power to overcome demons and all kinds of evil (Kropp, 1930/1931, Vol. 2, pp. 19, 178; Vol. 3, p. 72). Further, the eagle is compared to archangels and to clericals (Papyrus 9, Pierpont Morgan Library, New York).

The eagle's ability to soar high and approach the sun enables it in popular imagination to be a messenger between earth and heaven. Considering that

Cross from Apocryphal Acts manuscript in the library of Dayr Anbā Maqār. *Photography by Egyptian Expedition, The Metropolitan Museum of Art.*

fact and the Oriental texts, it seems probable that the fear of demons threatening the dead made the Copts choose for their funerary stelae the eagle with its protective qualities, reinforced by amulets, as a safe attendant for the dead. In profane art the eagle with an amulet probably also had a protective and apotropaic role, especially above entrances. But there were certainly also examples of merely decorative eagle figures, as on capitals.

In the paintings in chapels in Dayr Apa Apollo, eagles are depicted several times. The accompanying inscriptions also refer to eagles. For example, in chapel 27 some eagles are flanking a pediment, with the inscription ΑΕΤΟΣ ("eagle"); in chapel 32 eagles ornament four lunettes, while in chapel 38 there is the inscription—ΑΪΤΟΣ. They may carry crosses in their beaks or wear different amulets on their necks such as bullae or lunulae (crescent ornaments) with a cross, and in room 27 they are found with laurel wreaths surrounding the alpha and omega (Clédat, 1904, 150; 1916, 11 pl. 6,1. 9; Maspero-Drioton, 1931–1943, graffito 480). Only in Nubia do eagles occur in church apses; they are, for example, in paintings and reliefs at Faras and reliefs at Qaṣr Ibrīm (Gartkiewicz, 1978, p. 88).

The old motif of eagle and serpent reappears on an eighth-century bronze censer in the Louvre (du Bourguet, 1967, pp. 160ff.).

Although the identification of the bird on Coptic funerary stelae has often been discussed, there is little doubt that it is meant to be an eagle. The reasons are the resemblance to Roman stelae that show eagles in gables in a frontal position with outstretched wings, and the similarity to the eagle paintings of Bāwīṭ (cf. Leclercq, 1934, col. 1426) in that both sets of eagles have identical attributes—amulets, crosses in beak, and laurel wreaths. In the early Middle Ages the strong stylization and the prevalence of decorative elements cause the bird to lose its natural aspect (e.g., stela, Crum, n. 1902, 8659). Several groups of stelae can be distinguished: a small group shows the eagle within a pointed gable (Lucchesi-Palli, 1981); a group from Armant represents the eagle with a cross in a wreath over its upstretched wings (Crum, 1902, pls. 41–44); a group from Isnā places eagles, sometimes more than one, in aediculae or under round arches (Crum, nos. 8665, 8671; du Bourguet, 1970, pp. 179ff., designates the bird as a dove; Sauneron-Coquin, (1980, pls. 39–44). Some stelae do not belong to specific groups. In one example, in the British Museum the eagle is under the bust of the deceased. On another stela, in the Victoria and Albert Museum, the eagle is framed by quadrupeds with an ankh above it (*Enchoria* 8 [1978]: pl. 23; Beckwith, 1963, fig. 130).

A clear separation of profane art from religious art is often impossible. Eagles appear on keystones, doors, and lintels as found in the Coptic Museum, Cairo (Strzygowski, 1904, figs. 75, 184; Zaloscer, 1948, pls. 4, 7). They appear on various other objects, such as a box for weights in the Louvre; a container for cosmetics in the Roman-German Central Museum for Prehistory and Early History, Mainz; and decorative carvings, perhaps for furniture, in the German National Museum, Nuremberg (Kötzsche, 1979, 158; Pelka 1906, pp. 35ff.). Eagles

Stone frieze depicting two nymphs riding dolphins. Third–fourth centuries. *Courtesy Coptic Museum, Cairo.*

are also frequent motifs on textiles, as on a seventh-century hanging with an eagle and a peacock from Akhmīm in the Abegg Foundation, Bern, and a fifth-century fragment from Antinoë, showing an eagle with a wreath in its beak in the Louvre (du Bourguet, 1967). Eagles are also found on pottery. In the Bode Museum, Berlin, there is a clay lamp from Akhmīm with an eagle relief and a stamped seventh- or eighth-century roundel from Qenā, which shows an eagle with four crosses (*Dictionnaire d'archéologie chrétienne et de liturgie,* Vol. 1, p. 1051; Effenberger, 1975, p. 100, fig. 97).

Dolphin-shaped lamp on a stand. Bronze. Stand—Height: 70.2 cm; width: 21.5 cm; lamp—Height: 12.8 cm; width: 21.5 cm; thickness: 9.8 cm. *Courtesy Louvre Museum, Paris.*

BIBLIOGRAPHY

Beckwith, J. *Coptic Sculpture, 300–1300.* London, 1963.

Bourguet, P. du. *Die Kopten.* Baden-Baden, 1967.

Clédat, J. "Le monastère et la nécropole de Baouît." *Mémoires de l'Institut français d'Archéologie orientale* 12 (1904); 39 (1916).

Crum, W. E. *Coptic Monuments.* Catalogue général des antiquités égyptiennes du Musée du Caire, Vol. 4. Cairo, 1902.

Effenberger, A. *Koptische Kunst: Ägypten in spätantike, byzantinischer und frühislamischer Zeit.* Leipzig, 1975.

Gartkiewicz, M. In *Nubian Studies,* ed. J. M. Plumley. Cambridge, 1978.

Kötzsche, L. "Reliquienbehälter. . . ." *Gesta* 18 (1979):158.

Eagle in a pediment. Limestone. *Courtesy Pushkin Museum, Moscow.*

Krause, M., and P. Labib. *Gnostische und heremetische Schriften aus Codex II und Codex VI.* Glückstadt, 1971.

Kropp, A. M. *Ausgewählte koptische Zaubertexte.* Brussels, 1930–1931.

Leclercq, H. "Miroirs et miroitiers." In *Dictionnaire d'archéologie chrétienne et de Liturgie,* 11, 2, cols. 1415–1431. Paris, 1934.

Lucchesi-Palli, E. "Observations sur l'iconographie de l'aigle funéraire dans l'art copte et nubien." In *Etudes nubiennes, Colloque de Chantilly 1975,* pp. 175–91. Cairo, 1978.

______. "Eine Gruppe koptischer Stelen und die Herkunft ihrer figürlichen Motive und Ornamente." In *Jahrbuch für Antike und Christentum 24,* pp. 114–30. Münster, 1981.

Maspero, J., and E. Drioton. "Fouilles exécutées à Baouît." In *Mémoires de l'Institut français d'Archéologie orientale* 59 (1931–1943).

Pelsmaekers, J. "The Coptic Funerary Bird-Stelae: A New Investigation." In *Orientalia Lovaniensia Periodica* 13, pp. 143–184. Leuven, 1982.

Sauneron, S., and R.-G. Coquin. In *Mémoires de l'Institut français d'Archéologie orientale* 104 (1980):pls. 39–40.

Strzygowski, J. *Koptische Kunst.* Vienna, 1904.

Zaloscer, H. *Une Collection de pierres sculptées au Musée Copte de Vieux Caire.* Cairo, 1948.

ELISABETTA LUCCHESI-PALLI

Fish

From predynastic times, the fish was an esteemed theme in Egypt. Artists knew how to use its form, its movement, and its natural milieu for decorative purposes. Linked with the Nile and with thc legend of Osiris, it also symbolized regeneration. The fish also appeared in Greco-Roman iconography and passed readily into Coptic art, where fishes appear in abundance.

Coming from a long and manifold tradition, the fish seems to have inspired Coptic artists by its shape, already schematic: a rounded mass stamped with a round eye and expanded fins. The arrangement of several fish, head-to-tail, chasing one another or linked by some plant, lent itself admirably to decoration.

At first the Copts undoubtedly saw biblical allusions in the fish. Thus, on a fresco from the catacomb of Karmūz of the Miracle of the Loaves, Saint Andrew carries two fish. Later, at Dayr Apa Apollo fish appear in the scene of the Baptism of Christ. A potsherd from Alexandria and a papyrus from Antinoë present the acrostic Jesus Christ in a Coptic abbreviation, which associates the fish with the person of the Lord.

But the religious significance of the fish is not

always made explicit in Coptic art. As early as the second century a tapestry from Antinoë, sprinkled with fish, recalls the decoration of some Greco-Roman mosaics (Louvre; Historic Museum of Textiles, Lyons). In a sixth-century relief of Jonah in the Louvre; a fishing scene on a relief in the Coptic Museum in Cairo; and numerous Nilotic scenes on reliefs and tapestries, fishes simply evoke water. The fish appears also alone or in a group sometimes within a scroll, in tapestry braids, wooden friezes, and a fragment of painted wood (in the Louvre). It stands out in relief on a lamp of baked earth from Akhmīm, a seal preserved in the Egyptian Museum in Berlin, and the bottom of a fourth-century stone vase in the Louvre. The fish was a particularly effective motif on painted ceramics. Finally, it lent its form to a sixth-century bronze censer (in the Walters Art Gallery, Baltimore), and to an ampulla of baked earth from Idfū in the Egyptian Museum, Berlin.

BIBLIOGRAPHY

Wulff, O. *Beschreibung der Bildwerke der christlichen Epochen,* nos. 1358, 1410, 1411, 1510, 1565. Berlin, 1909.

DOMINIQUE BENAZETH

Fish painted on a ceramic plate. Diameter: 30 cm. *Courtesy Louvre Museum, Paris.*

Nimbus

A circle of light, called a nimbus or halo, surrounding the head of Christ, the Virgin, the angels, and the saints is a well-known iconographical feature throughout Christian art. It originated in the luminous crown of certain pagan divinities—particularly solar gods, and signifies holiness.

In Coptic painting the nimbus surrounding the heads of the Virgin and the saints is of a single color, mostly yellow or light green, with a black or dark brown line around the edge, as for example in the apse of the church of Dayr Apa Apollo at Bāwīṭ. The nimbus of Christ always has a cross on it; the three equal branches of the cross are in dark brown or black on a background of yellow or light green, as for example on an icon from Bāwīṭ in the Louvre. In medieval Coptic painting, the arms are geometrically drawn on the nimbus and the dark edge of the nimbus is often further set off by a row of pearls.

On the bas-reliefs the nimbus is less frequently found, and often figures of the Virgin, angels, and saints lack it altogether. It takes the form of a self-colored disk behind the person's head. Christ's nimbus is still cruciferous, with the three branches of the cross shown in relief, as, for example, on the wooden panels of the door of the Al-Mu'allaqah Church in Old Cairo.

On Coptic fabrics, such as decorative tapestry squares in the Austrian Museum of Applied Art, Vienna, mythological personages such as Dionysus or Ariadne, or stylized personages, have their heads surrounded by a nimbus. It is of a light hue against a darker background. Here the symbolism of light is less in evidence, and the decorative function prevails. In religious scenes, for example, the story of Joseph, the nimbus is very much reduced and simply distinguishes the holy personage.

ZSOLT KISS

SYNAXARION, COPTO-ARABIC, list of saints used in the Coptic church. [*This entry consists of two articles,* Editions of the Synaxarion *and* The List of Saints.]

Editions of the Synaxarion

This book, which has become a liturgical book, is very important for the history of the Coptic church. It appears in two forms: the recension from Lower Egypt, which is the quasi-official book of the Coptic church from Alexandria to Aswan, and the recension from Upper Egypt. Egypt has long preserved this separation into two Egypts, Upper and Lower, and this division was translated into daily life through different usages, and in particular through different religious books.

This book is the result of various endeavors, of which the Synaxarion itself speaks, for it mentions different usages here or there. It poses several questions that we cannot answer with any certainty: Who compiled the Synaxarion, and who was the first to take the initiative? Who made the final revision, and where was it done? It seems evident that the intention was to compile this book for the Coptic church in imitation of the Greek list of saints, and that the author or authors drew their inspiration from that work, for several notices are obviously taken from the Synaxarion called that of Constantinople.

The reader may have recourse to several editions or translations, each of which has its advantages and its disadvantages. Let us take them in chronological order.

The oldest translation (German) is that of the great German Arabist F. Wüstenfeld, who produced the edition with a German translation of part of al-Maqrīzī's *Khiṭaṭ*, concerning the Coptic church, under the title *Macrizi's Geschichte der Copten* (Göttingen, 1845). He also translated the Synaxarion (without including the Arabic text), but only the first half-year appeared, under the title *Synaxarium, das ist Heiligen-Kalender der coptischen Christen* (2 vols., Gotha, 1879). He had prepared the second part of the year, but the manuscript remained in the library in Göttingen. Wüstenfeld translated only a single Arabic manuscript in Gotha, dating from 1826 and representing only the recension from Lower Egypt.

R. Graffin's Patrologia Orientalis published the Synaxarion in several fascicles with a French translation, under the title *Le Synaxaire arabe-jacobite (rédaction copte)*. Begun in 1904, it was completed in 1929, after the death of its author, R. Basset. It represents a great step forward for our knowledge of the history of the Coptic community, but unfortunately the author, well versed in the Arabic language of the Muslims, was completely unaware of the peculiarities of the language of the Christians of Egypt. Also, misinterpretations are not lacking, to the point that the reader may wonder if Basset had employed a ghost writer. In 1905 the Corpus Scriptorum Christianorum Orientalium collection—at that time in competition—brought out the *Synaxarium alexandrinum*, with a Latin translation.

While the Patrologia Orientalis edition was based on two manuscripts from the Bibliothèque nationale in Paris, one dated by codicologists to the fourteenth century and the other to the seventeenth (restored in the nineteenth), the Corpus Scriptorum Christianorum Orientalium edition had the great fault of taking as its base a late manuscript, and relegating to notes the variants of six other manuscripts, including those used by Basset. The latter published two manuscripts—especially for the first half-year—amalgamating them without taking account of the fact that they represented two different recensions—so much so that the finished product is a Synaxarion that never existed! In the Corpus Scriptorum Christianorum Orientalium Forget was more fortunate, for when he began his edition, he noted that the text of Paris Bibliothèque nationale 4869 gave a different recension. He therefore published it separately (vols. 47–48, pp. 291ff). Unfortunately his translation mingled the two recensions; and it, too, fabricated a hybrid Synaxarion that never existed in the manuscripts. We can at least separate the two recensions, for he indicates in the margin the pages of the Arabic text. If the page is 291 or beyond, the reader who has been warned will know that it is the Sahidic recension. The translation errors are less frequent, and the number of manuscripts used is greater; but here, as in Basset's edition, there was no serious analysis of the manuscripts of the Synaxarion beforehand. In particular, the manuscripts deposited in Egypt had not been consulted.

In 1935–1937 there was an edition at Cairo, without a translation into a European language, made by two *qummus* (a special rank in the Coptic Church, superior to the simple priest, and a title given also to the abbots of monasteries, deriving from the Greek HEGUMENOS), ʿAbd al-Masīḥ Mīkhā'īl and Armāniyūs Ḥabashī Shitā al-Birmāwī. This was based—according to the preface—on several Egyptian manuscripts, enumerated below, and on the Paris edition. It has the advantage of adding to the manuscripts of the Synaxarion some notices, taken from other sources that are not named, concerning certain recent patriarchs or saints who are not found in the manuscripts of the Synaxarion—for example, saints Dimyanah, Macrobius, Pshoi, and Petrus, whose relics are still the object of a pilgrimage to Ṣidfā. The authors suppressed what appeared to them worthless or unseemly. Although this edition is precious because it uses manuscripts unknown in Europe, one cannot trust it completely, since its choice remains arbitrary. There is, thus, no totally reliable edition, and each has its advantages and its limitations.

These editions ignore the true calendar indicating which saint is to be celebrated on each day. Such a calendar was found in most of the manuscripts of the *Qatamarus*. The 1900–1902 edition of the annual *Qatamarus*, completed later for Lent, Holy Week, and the Pentecostal season (the period between Easter and Pentecost), gives this calendar, indicating by a rubric which saint or which New Testament event is to be commemorated, whereas the Synaxarion offered the faithful all the saints known to the authors. If the development of the printing press caused these printed editions of both the Synaxarion and the Lectionary to become the quasi-official editions in use everywhere in Egypt, this diffusion does not put an end to possible contradictions. Through their formation, local usage, which has become that of all Egypt, may retain a saint or event in the Lectionary that is unknown in the Synaxarion and vice versa.

The reader who wishes information about the cult of a saint of the Coptic church therefore must have recourse to several editions, each with its lacunae and its unique information. One must also take account of the fact that some local or ancient saints have not found a place in the Synaxarion or the Lectionary. Some Egyptian saints retained as such by the Greek books, liturgical or historical, are unknown to the Coptic books.

BIBLIOGRAPHY

'Abd al-Masīḥ Mikhā'il and Armanīyus Ḥabashī Shitā al-Birmāwi. *Al-Sinaksār*, 2 vols. Cairo 1935–1937.

Malan, S. C. *The Calendar of the Coptic Church.* Original Documents of the Coptic Church, 2. London, 1873.

Wüstenfeld, H. F. *Macrizi's Geschichte der Copten.* Göttingen, 1845.

RENÉ-GEORGES COQUIN

The List of Saints

Synaxarion is the Coptic and Greek term for the Latin *synaxarium*, and is a formal compilation of the lives of the martyrs, saints, and religious heroes of the Coptic church. These biographies are sometimes reduced to a mere citation of each martyr or saint read in the course of the liturgy, after excerpts from the Acts (ABRAXOS) during the morning service on the day of the passion of each. This is usually presented in the form of an encomium or homily for the edification of the congregation.

The development of the martyr cult in the Coptic church dates from the early centuries, when those encomiums were read in both Sahidic and Bohairic (from the beginning of the Middle Ages), and in Arabic (after the ARAB CONQUEST OF EGYPT). In most cases, these biographies were translated into Arabic from Greek and Coptic originals. Furthermore, the current Arabic text includes a limited number of extraneous entries besides these biographies, in which certain notable events are commemorated on given dates, such as the Crucifixion, the feasts and fasts of the church, the apparition of an archangel or the Virgin Mary, the Coptic New Year, the dedication of a historic church, and so on. But the bulk of the work remains dedicated to the saints and martyrs whose cult became embedded in church traditions.

Until the fourteenth century, the lives of these holy men and women were read separately, in independent encomiums, on their passion days. Ultimately they were assembled in a single book, an operation primarily associated with Anbā Buṭrus al-Jamīl, bishop of Malīj, though others are known to have participated in this task, including Anbā Mīkhā'īl, bishop of Atrīb, and Anbā Yuḥannā, bishop of Parallos (Burullus). At later dates, however, names of other holy men appeared in the fourteenth-century Arabic text, such as Anbā Abraham, bishop of Fayyūm, in modern times. The present recension of the Arabic Synaxarion, approved by the church authority and read throughout the Coptic church, has been compiled from a number of older manuscripts, of which some are directly ascribed to Anbā Buṭrus, bishop of Malīj. They are the following:

1. Three manuscripts in the patriarchal library, the oldest of which is dated 1114 A.M./A.D. 1398, which could be contemporary with Anbā Buṭrus.

2. Two copies in the Coptic Museum Library, one of which is dated 1056 A.M./A.D. 1340 and must have been from the time of Anbā Buṭrus. The other is dated 1450 A.M./A.D. 1734 and is supposed to have been rendered into Arabic from an older Ethiopic translation by Christodoulos, the Coptic primate of Ethiopia at the time.

3. Two copies in the Baramūs Monastery Library in Wādī al-Naṭrūn: one dated 1360 A.M./A.D. 1644, and the other dated 1496 A.M./A.D. 1780. The second copy is said to have been restored by IBRAHIM AL-JAWHARĪ.

Other, older, printed editions of the Arabic text are extant. The first publication was started by J. Forget (see above). The text of ʿAbd-al-Masīh Mikhā'īl and Armāniyus Ḥabashī Shitā al-Birmāwī has been reproduced several times and is still in print. In the following pages, we have reproduced a summary of its contents under each date of the Coptic calendar. It is undoubtedly the most complete formal register of all known names of martyrs and saints to be cited in the church liturgies, and it must remain the primary source of Coptic HAGIOGRAPHY, even though it may occasionally be uncritical and apocryphal. Side by side with the Synaxarion, mention must be made of the DIFNĀR or Antiphonarium, consisting of two alternative hymns for each day of the year to commemorate a saint or saints included in the liturgy on that date according to the authority of the Synaxarion.

Inasmuch as the formula to convert Coptic calendar dates into their Gregorian equivalents varies from century to century, the corresponding Julian calendar date, which remains constant through time, is given for each Coptic day in the list below. To convert the Julian date into its Gregorian equivalent add thirteen to the Julian day for the years 1900–2100. For example, in the years 1900–2100 the Julian date 1 September takes 14 September (1+13=14) as its Gregorian equivalent. The Coptic New Year, listed as 29 August in the Julian calendar, is on 11 September in the Gregorian reckoning and the Coptic celebration of Christmas, which comes on 25 December in the Julian year, falls on 7 January in the Gregorian calendar. For the years 2101–2200, fourteen must be added to the Julian date to give the Gregorian equivalent. Thus, in the twenty-second century, Copts who follow the Gregorian calendar will celebrate the New Year on 12 September and Christmas on 8 January, though from the standpoint of the Coptic and Julian calendars the dates will not have changed. (For other conversions and for more information on the interconnections between the various calendars, see Calendar, Coptic; Calendar, Gregorian; Calendar, Julian.)

Table 1. Coptic Church Calendar (Synaxarion) with Corresponding Julian Dates

	MONTH OF TŪT (AUGUST–SEPTEMBER)
1 Tūt—29 Aug.	Coptic New Year (*Nawrūz*) Bartholomew the Apostle Abilius, 3rd patriarch of Alexandria
2—30	Martyrdom of John the Baptist Dāsyah of Tanda martyred
3—31	Holy Synod convened at Alexandria in A.D. 242
4 Tūt—1 Sept.	Macarius II, 69th patriarch of Alexandria
5—2	Martyrdom of Saint Sophia
6—3	Isaiah the Prophet Martyrdom of Bashilīliyah (Basilissa)
7—4	Dioscorus I, 25th patriarch of Alexandria Martyrdom of Agathon, Peter, John, Amūn, Ammūnah, and Rifqah, their mother Severianus, bishop of Jabalah
8—5	Martyrdom of the prophet Zacharias The prophet Moses Martyrdom of Dayumīdis (Diomede)
9—6	Martyrdom of Pisura the Bishop
10—7	Martyrdom of Saint Maṭrūnah Commemoration of Bāsīn and her children
11—8	Martyrdom of Saint Wāsīlīdas (Basilidas)
12—9	Holy Synod of Ephesus to try Nestorius (A.D. 431) Interment of Saint Iqlīmus and his company
13—10	Matthew II, 90th patriarch of Alexandria Miracle of Saint Basil of Caesarea in Cappadocia
14—11	Saint Agathon the Stylite
15—12	Translation of the body of Saint Stephen the Archdeacon

Table 1. *Coptic Church Calendar (Synaxarion) with Corresponding Julian Dates (continued)*

	MONTH OF TŪT (AUGUST–SEPTEMBER) (CONTINUED)
16—13	Dedication of the Church of the Resurrection Translation of the body of Saint John Chrysostom
17—14	Exaltation of the Holy Cross Saint Theognosta who introduced Christianity to India [Georgia]
18—15	Martyrdom of Saint Porphyrius (Porphyry) Commemoration of Stephen the Priest and Nakīṭā (Nicetas) the Martyr
19—16	Commemoration of Gregory the Armenian patriarch
20—17	Athanasius II, 28th patriarch of Alexandria Martyrdom of Saint Melitina the Virgin Theopista the Ascetic Nun
21—18	Commemoration of the Virgin Mary Martyrdom of Saints Cyprian and Justin
22—19	Martyrdom of Saints Cotylas and Axuwā, children of Shapur, king of Persia, and their friend Tatus Martyrdom of Julius of Aqfahs, recorder of martyrs' biographies
23—20	Martyrdom of Eunapius and Andrew Martyrdom of Saint Thecla Dedication of the Church of the Virgin in Ḥārit al-Rūm, after its closure
24—21	Gregory, Pachomian monk Commemoration of *quadratus* of the seventy disciples
25—22	Jonah the Prophet
26—23	Annunciation of John the Baptist's birth to his father, Zacharias
27—24	Martyrdom of Eustathius and his wife and two sons
28—25	Martyrdom of Abadīr (Apater) and his ster Īrā'ī (Herai or Erai)
29—26	Martyrdom of Repsima and her sisters, all virgins, by Diocletian
30—27	Athanasius the Apostolic, 20th patriarch of Alexandria
	MONTH OF BĀBAH (SEPTEMBER–OCTOBER)
1 Bābah—28 Sept.	Martyrdom of Saint Anastasia
2—29	Advent of Severus, patriarch of Antioch, to Egypt
3—30	Simon II, 51st patriarch of Alexandria Martyrdom of Saint John the Soldier
4 Bābah—1 Oct.	Martyrdom of Wākhus (Bacchus)
5—2	Martyrdom of Paul, patriarch of Constantinople
6—3	Commemoration of Ḥinnah, mother of Prophet Samuel
7—4	Paul of Ṭammah, Martyr
8—5	Martyrdom of Saint Matra by Decius Martyrdom of Apa Hor, Tūsyā (Susanna) and her children, and Agathon the Hermit
9—6	Eumenius, 7th patriarch of Alexandria Eclipse of the sun in A.M. 958 Commemoration of Simon the Bishop
10—7	Martyrdom of Saint Sergius, companion of Saint Bacchus (Wākhus)

Table 1. *Coptic Church Calendar (Synaxarion) with Corresponding Julian Dates (continued)*

	MONTH OF BĀBAH (SEPTEMBER–OCTOBER) (CONTINUED)
11—8	Jacob, patriarch of Antioch Commemoration of Saint Pelagia
12—9	Demetrius II, 12th patriarch of Alexandria Martyrdom of Matthew the Evangelist Commemoration of Archangel Michael
13—10	Commemoration of Saint Zacharias the Monk
14—11	Commemoration of Philip or Philas, one of the seven deacons
15—12	Martyrdom of Pantaleon the Physician
16—13	Agathon, 39th patriarch of Alexandria Commemoration of Saints Carpus, Papylus, and Peter
17—14	Dioscorus II, 31st patriarch of Alexandria
18—15	Theophilus, 23rd patriarch of Alexandria
19—16	Holy Synod of Antioch against Paul of Samosata Martyrdom of Saint Theophilus and his wife
20—17	Saint John Colobos
21—18	Commemoration of the Mother of God Translation of body of Lazarus Joel the Prophet Saint Evagrius
22—19	Saint Luke the Evangelist
23—20	Yūsāb I, 52nd patriarch of Alexandria Martyrdom of Dionysius the Bishop
24—21	Hilarion the Hermit Martyrdom of Saints Paul, Longinus, and Zena
25—22	Saints Apollo and Abīb Dedication of the Church of Saint Julius of Aqfahṣ
26—23	Martyrdom of Saint Timon, one of the seventy disciples Commemoration of the seven martyrs in the mountain of Saint Antony
27—24	Martyrdom of Saint Macarius, bishop of Tkow (Idkū)
28—25	Martyrdom of Saints Marcianus and Mercurius
29—26	Martyrdom of Saint Demetrius of Thessalonica
30—27	Dedication of Saint Mark's Church and apparition of his decapitated head Saint Abraham the Hermit of Minūf
	MONTH OF HĀTŪR (OCTOBER–NOVEMBER)
1 Hātūr—28 Oct.	Martyrdom of Saints Maximus, Numitius, Victor, and Philip Commemoration of Saint Cleopas and his companion
2—29	Peter III (Mongus), 27th patriarch of Alexandria
3—30	Saint Cyriacus Saint Athanasius and his sister Irene
4—31	Martyrdom of Saints John and Jacob, bishops of Persia Martyrdom of Saints Epimachus and ʿAzāryanūs
5 Hātūr—1 Nov.	Apparition of Saint Longinus' head Martyrdom of Saint Timothy and translation of the body of al-Amīr Tadrus (Theodorus) of Shotep
6—2	Saint Felix, pope of Rome Dedication of the Church of Our Lady in Dayr al-Muḥarraq at Qusqām

Table 1. *Coptic Church Calendar (Synaxarion) with Corresponding Julian Dates (continued)*

	MONTH OF HĀTŪR (OCTOBER–NOVEMBER) (CONTINUED)
7—3	Martyrdom of Saint Georgius of Alexandria Martyrdom of Saint Naharua Menas, bishop of Tmuis Dedication of the Church of Saint Georgius the Cappadocian
8—4	Commemoration of the Four Bodiless Beasts (Rev. 4:6–7)
9—5	Isaac, 41st patriarch of Alexandria Ecumenical Council of Nicaea (A.D. 325)
10—6	Martyrdom of the fifty virgins and their mother, Sophia Holy Synod of Rome to decide the dates of Epiphany and the fasts during the papacy of Demetrius I of Alexandria and Victor, pope of Rome
11—7	Saint Ḥinnah (Anna), mother of Our Lady Martyrdom of Saint Archelaus and Saint Elijah the *Qummuṣ*
12—8	Commemoration of Michael the Archangel
13—9	Saint Timothy, bishop of Antinoopolis Zacharias, 64th patriarch of Alexandria
14—10	Saint Martinus, bishop of Tours
15—11	Martyrdom of Saint Menas the Miracle Maker
16—12	Fast of the Nativity in the Coptic Church Dedication of the Church of Onophrius (Abū Nofer)
17—13	Saint John Chrysostom
18—14	Martyrdom of Saints Adrūsīs and Yu'annā (Junia) Martyrdom of Saint Philip the Apostle
19—15	Dedication of the Church of Saints Sergius and Bacchus Commemoration of Saint Bartholomew
20—16	Anianus, 2nd patriarch of Alexandria Dedication of the churches of al-Amīr Tadrus ibn Yuḥannā of Shotep and al-Amīr Tadrus al-Mashriqī
21—17	Commemoration of the Virgin Mary, Mother of God Saint Gregory the Miracle Maker Cosmas II, 54th patriarch of Alexandria Commemoration of Ḥalfa (Alphaeus), Zakkā (Zacharias), Romanus, and John, all martyrs Saints Thomas, Victor, and Isaac of al-Ashmūnayn
22—18	Martyrdom of Saints Cosmas and Damian, their brothers, and their mother
23—19	Cornelius the Centurion Dedication of the Church of Saint Marina
24—20	Commemoration of the twenty-four elders (Rev 4:4, 10–11)
25—21	Martyrdom of Saint Mercurius (Abū Sayfayn)
26—22	Martyrdom of Valerianus and his brother Tibarcius Commemoration of Gregory, bishop of Nyssa
27—23	Martyrdom of Saint James Intercisus (Jacob the Sawn)
28—24	Martyrdom of Saint Sarapamon, bishop of Nikiou
29—25	Martyrdom of Saint Peter, 17th patriarch of Alexandria Martyrdom of Saint Clement, pope of Rome
30—26	Acacius, patriarch of Constantinople Martyrdom of Saint Macarius Dedication of the Church of Saints Cosmas and Damian, their Brother, and their Mother

Table 1. *Coptic Church Calendar (Synaxarion) with Corresponding Julian Dates (continued)*

	MONTH OF KIYAHK (NOVEMBER–DECEMBER)
1 Kiyahk—27 Nov.	Saint Peter al-Rahāwi, bishop of Ghazza Dedication of Saint Shenute's Church
2—28	Saint Apa Hor the Ascetic
3—29	Commemoration of the entry of the Virgin into the Jerusalem sanctuary
4—30	Martyrdom of Saint Andrew the Apostle, brother of Peter
5 Kiyahk—1 Dec.	Nahum the Prophet Martyrdom of Victor of Asyūṭ Martyrdom of Saint Isidore
6—2	Martyrdom of Saint Bāṭlas (Anatole) the Priest Abraham, 62nd pope of Alexandria
7—3	Matthew the Poor, ascetic
8—4	Heraclas, 13th pope of Alexandria Martyrdom of Saints Barbara and Juliana Martyrdom of Saints Paese and Thecla Commemoration of Saint Samuel of Dayr al-Qalamūn
9—5	Saint Bīmīn (Pamin) the Confessor, bloodless martyr
10—6	Translation of the body of Saint Severus, patriarch of Antioch, to the Enaton Monastery west of Alexandria Saint Nicolas, bishop of Myra, bloodless martyr
11—7	Anbā Pidjimi, ascetic in the wilderness of Shihāt, from the city of Fīshah
12—8	Commemoration of Archangel Michael Anbā Hadra of Aswan Saint John the Confessor Council of Rome against Novatus
13—9	Martyrdom of Saint Barsanuphius Father Abrākiyūs (Abracas), ascetic Dedication of the Church of Saint Miṣā'īl
14—10	Martyrdom of Saints Bahnām and his sister Sarah Martyrdom of Saint Christodoulus Martyrdom of Saints Simeon of Minūf, Apa Hor, and Apa Mena the Elder Martyrdom of Saint Ammonius, bishop of Isnā
15—11	Saint Gregory, patriarch of the Armenians
16—12	Gideon, Old Testament judge of the Israelites Martyrdom of Saints Harwāj, Ananius, and Khūzī Dedication of the Church of Saint Jacob the Persian
17—13	Commemoration of Saint Luke the Stylite and translation of his remains
18—14	Translation of the body of Saint Titus to Constantinople Commemoration of the martyr Heracleas and the priest Philemon
19—15	Saint John, bishop of Parallos, compiler of the Synaxarion
20—16	Haggai the Prophet
21—17	Commemoration of Mary, Mother of God Martyrdom of Saint Barnabas, one of the seventy elders
22—18	Commemoration of Archangel Gabriel Anastasius, 36th patriarch of Alexandria
23—19	David the Prophet Saint Timotheus the Wanderer

Table 1. *Coptic Church Calendar (Synaxarion) with Corresponding Julian Dates (continued)*

	MONTH OF KIYAHK (NOVEMBER–DECEMBER) (CONTINUED)
24—20	Martyrdom of Saint Ignatius, patriarch of Constantinople Saint Philogonius, patriarch of Antioch Birth of Saint Takla Hāymānot the Abyssinian
25—21	Saint John Kāmā (the Black) of Scetis
26—22	Martyrdom of Saint Anastasia Martyrdom of Saint Juliana
27—23	Martyrdom of Saint Bisādā the Bishop
28—24	Martyrdom of 150 men and 24 women from Antinoopolis
29—25	Feast of the Nativity of Our Lord
30—26	Commemoration date of Anbā Yu'annis, Hegumenos of Scetis
	MONTH OF ṬŪBAH (DECEMBER–JANUARY)
1 Ṭūbah—27 Dec.	Martyrdom of Saint Stephen the Archdeacon Martyrdom of Saint Leontianus
2—28	Theonas, 16th patriarch of Alexandria Martyrdom of Saint Callinicus, bishop of Awsīm
3—29	Murder of the Innocents of Bethlehem by King Herod
4—30	Saint John the Evangelist
5—31	Martyrdom of Saint Eusignius, general in Constantine's army
6 Ṭūbah—1 Jan.	Circumcision of Jesus Christ Commemoration of Elijah the Prophet Marcianus, 8th patriarch of Alexandria Saint Basil the Great, bishop of Caesarea
7—2	Sylvester, pope of Rome
8—3	Dedication of the Church of Saint Macarius Andronicus, 37th patriarch of Alexandria Benjamin, 38th patriarch of Alexandria
9—4	Saint Abraam, ascetic of Scetis and companion of Anbā Jawirjah (George)
10—5	Paramone of the Epiphany (Christ's baptism)
11—6	Theophany (apparition of Our Lord) Epiphany
12—7	Commemoration of the Archangel Michael Martyrdom of Saint Theodorus the Oriental Martyrdom of Saint Anatolius
13—8	Feast of Cana in Galilee Theophilus the Ascetic Martyrdom of Saint Dimyānah
14—9	Saint Archellides, ascetic of Saint Romanos Monastery Saint Maximus, brother of Saint Domitius, both sons of the king of the Romans
15—10	Obadiah the Prophet
16—11	Martyrdom of Saint Philotheus John IV, 48th patriarch of Alexandria
17—12	Saints Maximus and Domitius, ascetics of Scetis Anbā Yusāb, bishop of Jirjā, known as al-Abaḥḥ
18—13	Saint Jacob, bishop of Nisibis
19—14	Discovery of the remains of Saints Apa Hor and Pisura and their mother, Empira, all martyrs

Table 1. *Coptic Church Calendar (Synaxarion) with Corresponding Julian Dates (continued)*

	MONTH OF ṬŪBAH (DECEMBER–JANUARY) (CONTINUED)
20—15	Saint Prochorus, one of the seventy elders Dedication of the Church of Saint John of the Golden Gospel and translation of his remains to it Martyrdom of Saint Bahnā and Anbā Kalūj the Presbyter
21—16	Commemoration of Our Lady's death Saint Hilaria, daughter of Emperor Zeno Saint Gregory, brother of Basil the Great
22—17	Commemoration of Saint Antony the Great
23—18	Martyrdom of Saint Timotheus the Elder Cyril IV, 110th patriarch of Alexandria
24—19	Saint Mary, ascetic recluse Anbā Bisādah the Presbyter
25—20	Saint Peter the Ascetic Saint Ascla (Askirla) the Martyr
26—21	Martyrdom of the 49 saints and elders of Scetis Saint Anastasia, ascetic of the reign of Justinian
27—22	Martyrdom of Saint Sarapion Commemoration of the angel Suryāl (Sūrī'īl) Translation of the body of Saint Timotheus the Elder Martyrdom of Saint Abī Fām (Epiphanius), a soldier
28—23	Martyrdom of Saint Clement Martyrdom of Saint Kā'ū (Kaou) from the town of Bamwayh in the Fayyūm
29—24	Commemoration of Saint Aksānī (Xene) Commemoration of Saint Cyriacus
30—25	Martyrdom of Saints Pistis, Helpis, and Agape, virgins, and their mother, Sophia
	MONTH OF AMSHĪR (JANUARY–FEBRUARY)
1 Amshīr—26 Jan.	Ecumenical Council of Constantinople (A.D. 381) Dedication of the first church built in commemoration of Saint Peter the "Seal of the Martyrs"
2—27	Saint Paul the Great, first of the wanderer saints Saint Longinus, abbot of the Enaton (Dayr al-Zujāj)
3—28	Saint Jacob the Ascetic
4—29	Saint Agapius, one of the seventy elders
5—30	Agrippinus, 10th patriarch of Alexandria Anbā Bishoi, abbot of Dayr Akhmīm and Anbā Abānūb (Nob) Saint Apollo, companion of Anbā Abīb Translation of the bodies of the forty-nine elders of the Shihāt wilderness
6—31	Apparition of Saint Hippolytus of Rome Martyrdom of Saint Apa Kīr (Cyrus) and Saint John and three virgins—Theodora, Theopista, Theodoxia—and their mother, Athanasia
7 Amshīr—1 Feb.	Alexander II, 43rd patriarch of Alexandria Theodore, 45th patriarch of Alexandria
8—2	Feast of the entry of Jesus Christ into the Temple
9—3	Saint Barsuma, father of the Syrian monks Martyrdom of Saint Paul the Syrian

Table 1. *Coptic Church Calendar (Synaxarion) with Corresponding Julian Dates (continued)*

	MONTH OF AMSHĪR (JANUARY–FEBRUARY) (CONTINUED)
10—4	Martyrdom of Jacob the Elder, son of Ḥalfā (Alphaeus) Martyrdom of Saint Justus, son of Emperor Numerianus Saint Isidorus of Pelusium (al-Faramā) Martyrdom of Philo, bishop of Persia
11—5	Martyrdom of Fabianus, pope of Rome
12—6	Commemoration of Archangel Michael Saint Gelasius
13—7	Martyrdom of Saint Sergius of Atrīb, his father, and his mother Timothy III, 32nd patriarch of Alexandria
14—8	Severus, patriarch of Antioch Jacob, 50th patriarch of Alexandria
15—9	Zechariah the Prophet Dedication of the first Church of the Forty Martyrs of Sebaste Saint Paphnutius the Ascetic
16—10	Saint Elizabeth, mother of John the Baptist
17—11	Martyrdom of Saint Menas the Ascetic from Akhmīm
18—12	Malatius, patriarch of Antioch
19—13	Translation of the body of Saint Martinianus from Athens to Antioch
20—14	Peter II, 21st patriarch of Alexandria Martyrdom of Saints Basil, Theodore, and Timothy
21—15	Commemoration of the Virgin Mary Martyrdom of Saint Onesimus, Saint Paul the Apostle's pupil Gabriel I, 57th patriarch of Alexandria Saint Zacharias, bishop of Sakhā
22—16	Martyrdom of Mārūtā, bishop of Mayāfirqīn
23—17	Martyrdom of Eusebius, son of Basilidas, minister of Diocletian
24—18	Saint Agapitus the Bishop Martyrdom of Timotheus and Matthias, priests
25—19	Martyrdom of Archippus, Philemon, and Abfiyyah the Virgin Martyrdom of Saints Qūnā (Conon) of Rome and Menas of Cyprus
26—20	Hosea the Prophet Martyrdom of Saint Zadok and his 118 companions
27—21	Saint Eustathius, patriarch of Antioch
28—22	Martyrdom of Saint Theodorus the Roman
29—23	Martyrdom of Saint Polycarpus, bishop of Smyrna (A.D. 167)
30—24	Discovery of John the Baptist's head
	MONTH OF BARAMHĀT (FEBRUARY–MARCH)
1 Baramhāt—25 Feb.	Saint Narcissus, bishop of Jerusalem (A.D. 222) Martyrdom of Saint Alexandrus, bishop of Cappadocia Saint Mercurius the Bishop
2—26	Martyrdom of Saint Makrāwī (Macrobius), bishop of Nikiou

Table 1. *Coptic Church Calendar (Synaxarion) with Corresponding Julian Dates (continued)*

	MONTH OF BARAMHĀT (FEBRUARY–MARCH) (CONTINUED)
3—27	Cosmas III, 58th patriarch of Alexandria Martyrdom of Saint Porphyrius (Porphyry) Anbā Ḥadīd the Presbyter
4—28	Holy synod of the Island of Banī ʿAmr for deciding the date of Easter Martyrdom of Saint Hanulius, prince of Perga
5 Baramhāt—1 Mar.	Anbā Sarapamon, presbyter of Dayr Abū Yuḥannis Martyrdom of Saint Eudoxia Saint Peter the Presbyter
6—2	Martyrdom of Saint Dioscorus Saint Theodotus the Bishop
7—3	Martyrdom of Saints Philemon and Apollonius Martyrdom of Saint Mary the Israelite
8—4	Martyrdom of Saint Matthias the Elder Julian, 11th patriarch of Alexandria Martyrdom of Arianus, governor of Antinoopolis
9—5	Saint Conon Martyrdom of Saints Andrianus and Martha, his wife, Eusebius, Armāniyūs, and the forty martyrs
10—6	Commemoration of the apparition of the Holy Cross
11—7	Martyrdom of Saint Basilios the Bishop (A.D. 298)
12—8	Commemoration of Archangel Michael Apparition of Saint Demetrius, 12th patriarch of Alexandria Martyrdom of Saint Malachias in Palestine Martyrdom of Saint Gelasinus in Damascus
13—9	Saint Dionysius, 14th patriarch of Alexandria Return of Saints Macarius the Great and Macarius Alexandrinus from exile Martyrdom of the forty martyrs of Sebaste
14—10	Anbā Kyrillos (Cyril), 75th patriarch of Alexandria Martyrdom of Saint Shenute of Bahnasā Martyrdom of Saints Eugenius, Agathodorus, and Elpidius
15—11	Saint Sarah the Ascetic Martyrdom of Saint Helias of Hnes (Ahnās)
16—12	Anbā Khā'īl, 46th patriarch of Alexandria
17—13	Lazarus, friend of Our Lord George the Ascetic, Belasius the Martyr, and Anbā Yusāb the Bishop Anbā Basilios, archbishop of Jerusalem Martyrdom of Sidhom Bishāy in Damietta
18—14	Martyrdom of Isidorus, companion of Sina the Soldier
19—15	Saint Aristobulus the Elder Martyrdom of the seven saints, Alexandrus, Agapius, and their companions
20—16	Anbā Khā'īl III, 56th patriarch of Alexandria Raising of Lazarus from the dead
21—17	Commemoration of Our Lady, the Virgin Mother of God Commemoration of the advent of Our Lord Jesus Christ to the house of ʿAnyā Consultation of the chief priests for killing Lazarus, whom the Lord raised from the dead

Table 1. *Coptic Church Calendar (Synaxarion) with Corresponding Julian Dates (continued)*

	MONTH OF BARAMHĀT (FEBRUARY–MARCH) (CONTINUED)
22—18	Saint Cyril, bishop of Jerusalem Saint Michael, bishop of Naqadah
23—19	Daniel the Prophet
24—20	Apparition of Our Lady at the Church of Zaytūn Anbā Macarius, 59th patriarch of Alexandria
25—21	Saint Fresca, one of the seventy disciples (elders) Matthew IV, 102nd patriarch of Alexandria
26—22	Saint Euphrasia, virgin Peter VI, 104th patriarch of Alexandria
27—23	Crucifixion of Our Lord Jesus Christ Saint Macarius the Great Martyrdom of Saint Domicius
28—24	Emperor Constantine the Great Peter VII, 109th patriarch of Alexandria Anbā Sarapamon, surnamed Abū Ṭarḥah, bishop of Minūfiyyah Province
29—25	The Annunciation The Resurrection of Our Lord
30—26	Commemoration of Archangel Gabriel Translation of the body of Saint Jacob the Sawn (James Intercisus) Samson, judge of the Israelites
	MONTH OF BARAMŪDAH (MARCH–APRIL)
1 Baramūdah—27 Mar.	Silvanus, ascetic of Scetis Raid of Arabs of Upper Egypt on the wilderness of Shihāt (Scetis) Aaron the Priest, brother of Moses
2—28	Martyrdom of Saint Christophorus Anbā Yu'annis (John IX), 81st patriarch of Alexandria
3—29	Saint John, bishop of Jerusalem Michael V, 71st patriarch of Alexandria
4—30	Martyrdom of Saints Victor, Decius, Irene the Virgin, and their companions
5—31	Ezekiel the Prophet Martyrdom of Hībātyūs, bishop of Gangra
6 Baramūdah—1 Apr.	Apparition of Our Lord to Thomas after His resurrection Saint Mary the Egyptian
7—2	Joachim, Christ's grandfather Saint Macrobius Saints Agapius, Theodora, and Macrobius (Abū Maqrūfah)
8—3	Martyrdom of the saintly virgins Agapia, Irene, and Siyunyah Martyrdom of the 150 believers at the hands of the king of Persia
9—4	Saint Zosimus Commemoration of the miracle performed by Shenute I, 55th patriarch of Alexandria
10—5	Anbā Isaac, disciple of Anbā Apollos Gabriel II, 70th patriarch of Alexandria
11—6	Saint Theodora Saint John, bishop of Ghazza

Table 1. *Coptic Church Calendar (Synaxarion) with Corresponding Julian Dates (continued)*

	MONTH OF BARAMŪDAH (MARCH–APRIL) (CONTINUED)
12—7	Saint Alexandrus, bishop of Jerusalem Saint Anṭūniyūs, bishop of Thmuis
13—8	Martyrdom of Saints Yashuʿ and Joseph Martyrdom of Dayūnīsyah the Deaconess and Mīdyūs Anbā Yu'annis (John XVII), 105th patriarch of Alexandria
14—9	Maximus, 15th patriarch of Alexandria
15—10	Dedication of the first altar of Saint Nicholas, bishop of Myra, for the Jacobite Christians Dedication of the Church of Saint Agapius the Disciple Saint Alexandra the Queen Mark VI, 101st patriarch of Alexandria
16—11	Martyrdom of Saint Antipas, bishop of Pergamon
17—12	Martyrdom of Saint Jacob the Disciple, brother of Saint John the Evangelist
18—13	Martyrdom of Saint Arsenius, follower of Saint Susinius
19—14	Martyrdom of Saint Simeon the Armenian, bishop of Persia, together with 150 companions Martyrdom of Saint John (Yūḥannā Abū Najāḥ) the Great Martyrdom of Abū al-ʿAlā' Fahd ibn Ibrāhim and his companions Martyrdom of David the Ascetic
20—15	Martyrdom of Saint Paphnutius of Dandarah
21—16	Commemoration of Our Lady, Mother of God Saint Protheus the Latin
22—17	Saint Isḥaq al-Hūrīnī Anbā Alexandros I, 19th patriarch of Alexandria Mark II, 49th patriarch of Alexandria Khā'īl II, 53rd patriarch of Alexandria
23—18	Martyrdom of Saint George the Great (A.D. 307)
24—19	Shenute I, 55th patriarch of Alexandria Martyrdom of Saint Sina, soldier
25—20	Martyrdom of Saint Sarah and her two sons Commemoration of Saint Paphnutius the Hermit and Saint Theodorus the Ascetic and 120 Martyrs
26—21	Martyrdom of Saint Susinius John VII, 77th patriarch of Alexandria
27—22	Martyrdom of Victor, son of Romanus
28—23	Martyrdom of Saint Milius the Ascetic
29—24	Erastus, one of seventy disciples Saint Acacius, bishop of Jerusalem
30—25	Martyrdom of Saint Mark the Evangelist
	MONTH OF BASHANS (APRIL–MAY)
1 Bashans—26 Apr.	Nativity of the Virgin Mary, Mother of God
2—27	Job the Prophet Saint Tādrus (Theodorus), disciple of Saint Pachomius Martyrdom of Saint Philotheus
3—28	Saint Jason, one of the seventy elders Saint Utīmūs, priest from Fuwwah Gabriel IV, 86th patriarch of Alexandria
4—29	John I, 29th patriarch of Alexandria John V, 72nd patriarch of Alexandria

Table 1. *Coptic Church Calendar (Synaxarion) with Corresponding Julian Dates (continued)*

	MONTH OF BASHANS (APRIL–MAY) (CONTINUED)
5—30	Martyrdom of Jeremiah the Prophet
6 Bashans—1 May	Martyrdom of Saint Isaac of Difrah Saint Macarius the Alexandrian Saint Babnūdah (Paphnutius) of al-Bandarah
7—2	Saint Athanasius I the Apostolic, 20th patriarch of Alexandria
8—3	Martyrdom of Saint John of Sanhūt Saint Daniel, *qummuṣ* of Shihāt
9—4	Saint Helena the Queen (A.D. 327) John XI, 89th patriarch of Alexandria Gabriel VIII, 97th patriarch of Alexandria
10—5	The Three Youths in the Furnace: Ananias, Azarias, and Misael
11—6	Martyrdom of Saint Theoclia, wife of Saint Justus Saint Paphnutius the Bishop
12—7	Dedication of the Church of Saint Dimyanah Translation of the remains of Saint John Chrysostom Apparition of a cross of light on Golgotha Mark VII, 106th patriarch of Alexandria Martyrdom of Muʿallim Malaṭī, scribe of the Mamluk Ayyūb Bey al-Defterdar in A.M. 1519/A.D. 1811
13—8	Saint Arsenius, mentor of the royal children (A.D. 445)
14—9	Saint Pachomius of Tabennēsē, father of the cenobitic rule Martyrdom of Saint Epimachus of Pelusium (al-Faramā)
15—10	Martyrdom of Simʿān al-Ghayyūr (Simon Zelotes) Four hundred martyrs of Dandarah Saint Mena the Deacon
16—11	Saint John the Evangelist
17—12	Saint Epiphanius, bishop of Cyprus
18—13	Saint George, companion of Saint Abraam Pentecost (Whitsuntide)
19—14	Saint Isaac, priest of the cells (al-Qalālī) Martyrdom of Saint Isidor of Antioch
20—15	Saint Ammonius the Recluse
21—16	Commemoration of the Virgin Mary Saint Martinianus (Motianus)
22—17	Saint Andronicus, one of the seventy disciples
23—18	Saint Yūnyās (Julius), one of the seventy disciples Martyrdom of Julian and his mother at Alexandria
24—19	Commemoration of the advent of Christ into Egypt Habakkuk the Prophet Martyrdom of Bashnūnah, monk of Dayr Anbā Maqār
25—20	Martyrdom of Saint Colluthus of Antinoopolis (surnamed Abū Qultah) Commemoration of Muʿallim Ibrāhīm al-Jawharī
26—21	Saint Thomas the Apostle
27—22	John II, 30th patriarch of Alexandria Lazarus, brother of Mary and bishop of Cyprus
28—23	Translation of the body of Saint Epiphanius to Cyprus (A.D. 403)
29—24	Saint Simeon Stylite

Table 1. *Coptic Church Calendar (Synaxarion) with Corresponding Julian Dates (continued)*

	MONTH OF BASHANS (APRIL–MAY) (CONTINUED)
30—25	Michael IV, 68th patriarch of Alexandria
	Saint Phorus, one of the seventy disciples
	MONTH OF BA'ŪNAH (MAY–JUNE)
1 Ba'ūnah—26 May	Dedication of the Church of Saint Leontius the Syrian
	Martyrdom of Saint Cosmas of Ṭaḥā and his companions
	Martyrdom of Saint Epiphanius the Soldier
2—27	Finding of the bodies of John the Baptist and the Prophet Elijah in Alexandria
	John XVIII, 107th patriarch of Alexandria
3—28	Dedication of Church of Mār Jirjis at Birmā and another at Bīr Mā' in the Oases
	Saint Martha the Egyptian
	Martyrdom of Saint Allādyūs the Bishop
	Cosmas I, 44th patriarch of Alexandria
	Anbā Abraam, bishop of Fayyūm (A.D. 1914)
4—29	Martyrdom of Saint Sīnūsyus
	Martyrdom of Saint Ammon and Saint Sophia
	Martyrdom of Saint Yuḥanna al-Hiraqlī (John of Heraclea)
	Saint Apa Hor
	John VIII, 80th patriarch of Alexandria
5—30	Saint Jacob the Oriental (al-Mashriqī)
	Martyrdom of Anbā Bishoi and Anbā Buṭrus
	Dedication of Saint Victor's Church at Shū
6—31	Martyrdom of Saint Theodorus the Ascetic
7 Ba'ūnah—1 June	Martyrdom of Saint Abiskhīrūn the Soldier
8—2	Dedication of the Church of the Virgin at al-Miḥmah
	Saint Tamada and her children, and Saint Armanus and his mother
	Martyrdom of Jirjis al-Jadīd (the Isma'ilite) (A.D. 1387)
9—3	Saint Samuel the Prophet
	Martyrdom of Saint Lucilianus and four companions
	Translation of the remains of Saint Mercurius to Egypt
10—4	Martyrdom of Saint Dabamon
	Closure of the pagan temples and opening of churches
	John XVI, 103rd patriarch of Alexandria
	Demetrius II, 111th patriarch of Alexandria
11—5	Martyrdom of Saint Claudius
	Dedication of the Altar of the Forty Martyrs in the Church of the Resurrection
12—6	Justus, 6th patriarch of Alexandria
	Cyril II, 67th patriarch of Alexandria
	Commemoration of Archangel Michael
	Saint Euphemia
13—7	Saint John, bishop of Jerusalem
	Archangel Gabriel and Daniel the Prophet
14—8	John XIX, 113th patriarch of Alexandria
	Martyrdom of Saints Apa Kīr (Cyrus), John, Ptolemeus, and Philip
15—9	Transfer of the remains of Saint Mark the Apostle (from Italy to Cairo) by Paul VI, pope of Rome
	Dedication of the Church of Saint Mena in Mareotis

Table 1. *Coptic Church Calendar (Synaxarion) with Corresponding Julian Dates (continued)*

	MONTH OF BA'ŪNAH (MAY–JUNE) (CONTINUED)
16—10	Saint Onophrius (Apa Nofer) the Wanderer
17—11	Depositing of the remains of Saint Mark in the new Saint Mark's Cathedral (in Cairo) Saint Latson of Bahnasā (al-Bahnasāwī)
18—12	Dedication of Saint Mark's Cathedral in Dayr Anbā Ruways Damian, 35th patriarch of Alexandria
19—13	Celebration of the first liturgy in the new Saint Mark's Cathedral (June 1968) Achillas, 18th patriarch of Alexandria Martyrdom of Saint George, known as Jirjis al-Muzāḥim (A.D. 959) Martyrdom of Saint Bishāy Anūb at ʿAyn Shams (Heliopolis)
20—14	Elijah the Prophet
21—15	Dedication of the first Church of the Virgin Mary in Philippi Martyrdom of Saint Timotheus the Egyptian Cerdon, 4th patriarch of Alexandria
22—16	Dedication of the Church of Saints Cosmas and Damian, Their Brothers, and Their Mother in a city of the land of the Arabs
23—17	Saint Apa Nob the Confessor
24—18	Saint Moses the Black
25—19	Martyrdom of Judas, one of the seventy disciples Peter IV, 34th patriarch of Alexandria
26—20	The Prophet Yashūʿ (Joshua) ibn Nūn Dedication of the Church of the Archangel Gabriel
27—21	Martyrdom of Saint Ananias the Disciple Martyrdom of Saint Tūmas (Thomas) al-Shandalātī
28—22	Theodosius I, 33rd patriarch of Alexandria Dedication of the Church of Anbā Sarapamon, bishop of Nikiou
29—23	Martyrdom of the seven ascetics on the mountain of Tūnah Martyrdom of Saints Apa Hor, Anbā Bishoi (Bishāy), and their mother, Diodora (Theodora)
30—24	Nativity of Saint John the Baptist
	MONTH OF ABĪB (JUNE–JULY)
1 Abīb—25 June	Martyrdom of Saint Afrūnyah (Febronia) the Ascetic Saints Biyūkhah and Bināyin, priests
2—26	Saint Thaddaeus the Disciple
3—27	Cyril I, 24th patriarch of Alexandria Saint Celestine, pope of Rome
4—28	Translation of the remains of Saints Apa Kīr (Cyrus) and Yuḥannā (John)
5—29	Martyrdom of the Apostles Peter and Paul
6—30	Martyrdom of Saints Olimpas the Disciple and Theodosia and her companions
7 Abīb—1 July	Saint Shenute, Father of the Hermits Martyrdom of Saint Ignatius, bishop of Antioch, at Rome

Table 1. *Coptic Church Calendar (Synaxarion) with Corresponding Julian Dates (continued)*

	MONTH OF ABĪB (JUNE–JULY) (CONTINUED)
8—2	Anbā Bishoi the Saint Martyrdom of Abīruh (Piru) and Atom Martyrdom of Saint Balānā the presbyter Martyrdom of Anbā Bīmānun (Epima) Saint Kārās (Cyrus), brother of Emperor Theodosius
9—3	Martyrdom of Saint Simeon (son of) Klūbā the Disciple Celadion, 9th patriarch of Alexandria
10—4	Martyrdom of Saint Theodorus, bishop of the Five Towns Martyrdom of Saint Theodorus, bishop of Corinthos, and his companions Gabriel VII, 95th patriarch of Alexandria
11—5	Martyrdom of Saints John and Simeon, his cousin Saint Isaiah the Hermit
12—6	Commemoration of Archangel Michael Martyrdom of Saint Apa-Hor of Siryāqūs
13—7	Saint Pisentius, bishop of Qifṭ Martyrdom of Saint Abāmūn of Ṭūkh Martyrdom of Anbā Shinūdah, at the beginning of the Arab period
14—8	Martyrdom of Saint Procopius of Jerusalem Peter V, 83rd patriarch of Alexandria
15—9	Saint Ephraem the Syrian (A.D. 379) Martyrdom of Saint Cyriacus and Julita, his mother Martyrdom of Saint Hursiyūs (Horsiesios)
16—10	Saint John of the Golden Gospel Translation of the body of the martyr Saint George to Old Cairo
17—11	Martyrdom of Saint Euphemia
18—12	Martyrdom of Saint Jacob the Apostle, bishop of Jerusalem
19—13	Martyrdom of Saints Bidaba, bishop of Qifṭ, and Anbā Andrew and Christodoulus Martyrdom of Saint Baṭlān (Pantaleon) the Physican John X, 85th patriarch of Alexandria
20—14	Martyrdom of Saint Theodorus of Shotep (A.D. 220)
21—15	Saint Susinius the Eunuch
22—16	Martyrdom of Saint Macarius, son of Basilides, minister of Diocletian Martyrdom of Saint Leontius of Tripoli
23—17	Martyrdom of Saint Longinus the General Martyrdom of Saint Marina
24—18	Martyrdom of Saint Apa-Nob Simon I, 42nd patriarch of Alexandria
25—19	Saint Thecla, follower of the Apostle Paul Martyrdom of Saint Isaac Martyrdom of Saint Hilaria Martyrdom of Saints Thecla and Mūjī Martyrdom of Saint Antoninus (Andūrā) Martyrdom of Saint Abā Krajon Martyrdom of Saint Domadius the Syrian Dedication of the Church of Abū Sayfayn Saint Palamon, Father of the Monks (A.D. 316)

Table 1. *Coptic Church Calendar (Synaxarion) with Corresponding Julian Dates (continued)*

	MONTH OF ABĪB (JUNE–JULY) (CONTINUED)
26—20	Saint Joseph the Carpenter Timothy I, 22nd patriarch of Alexandria
27—21	Dedication of the Church of Epiphanius Martyrdom of Saint Abāmūn of Tarnūṭ in Upper Egypt
28—22	Saint Mary Magdalene
29—23	Translation of the remains of Saint Andrew the Apostle Martyrdom of Saint Barsanuphius
30—24	Martyrdom of Saints Mercurius and Ephraem
	MONTH OF MISRĀ OR MESORE (JULY–AUGUST)
1 Misrā—25 July	Martyrdom of Saint Apoli, son of Justus Cyril V, 112th patriarch of Alexandria
2—26	Commemoration of Saint Bā'issah of Minūf
3—27	Translation of the body of Saint Simeon Stylite to Antioch Primus, 5th patriarch of Alexandria
4—28	Ezekiel the King Dedication of the Church of Saint Anthony
5—29	Saint John, the general of Julian the Apostate
6—30	Martyrdom of Saint Julita
7—31	Annunciation of the birth of the Virgin Mary to Saint Joachim Timothy II, 26th patriarch of Alexandria
8 Misrā—1 Aug.	Martyrdom of Saint Lazarus, his wife Salome, and their children The Apostle Peter's confession that Christ is the Son of God
9—2	Martyrdom of Saint Ūrī of Shatānūf
10—3	Martyrdom of Saint Bīkhībis (Bikabes) of Ashmūn Ṭanaḥ
11—4	Anba Moses, bishop of Awsīm
12—5	Commemoration of the archangel Michael Accession of Constantine the Great
13—6	Transfiguration of Our Lord on Ṭūr Ṭabūr
14—7	Theodosius, 33rd patriarch of Alexandria
15—8	Saint Mary, better known as Marina the Ascetic
16—9	Ascension of the body of Mary the Virgin Matthew IV, 102nd patriarch of Alexandria
17—10	Martyrdom of Saint Jacob the Soldier
18—11	Alexandros, patriarch of Constantinople Martyrdom of Saint Eudamon of Armant
19—12	Return of the body of Saint Macarius to his monastery in Shihāt
20—13	Martyrdom of the seven youths of Ephesus
21—14	Commemoration of Our Lady, Mother of God Saint Irene, daughter of King Licinius
22—15	Micah the Prophet Martyrdom of Saint Ḥadīd of Giza (A.D. 1387)
23—16	Martyrdom of thirty thousand Christians in Alexandria Martyrdom of Saint Damian of Antioch
24—17	Saint Thecla Haymanot the Abyssinian Saint Thomas, bishop of Mar'ash in Syria

Table 1. *Coptic Church Calendar (Synaxarion) with Corresponding Julian Dates (continued)*

	MONTH OF MISRĀ OR MESORE (JULY–AUGUST) (CONTINUED)
25—18	Saint Bessarion the Great Macarius III, 114th patriarch of Alexandria
26—19	Martyrdom of Saint Moses and his sister, Sarah Martyrdom of Saint Agapius the Soldier and his sister, Thecla
27—20	Martyrdom of Saint Benjamin and his sister, Eudoxia Martyrdom of Saint Mary the Armenian
28—21	Commemoration of the saintly fathers Abraham, Jacob, and Isaac
29—22	Martyrdom of Saint Athanasius the Bishop, and Saints Jerasimus and Theodotus Advent of the body of Saint John Colobus into the Shihāt wilderness
30—23	Malachi the Prophet
	INTERCALARY DAYS OF NASI (AUGUST)
1 Nasi—24 Aug.	Saint Eutychius, disciple of Saint John the Evangelist Martyrdom of Saint Bishoi of Antioch
2—25	Saint Titus, disciple of Saint Paul
3—26	Commemoration of Archangel Raphael Martyrdom of Saint Andrianus John XIV, 96th patriarch of Alexandria
4—27	Saint Liberius, bishop of Rome Anbā Bīmīn (Poemen) the Hermit
5—28	Father Jacob, bishop of Miṣr Amos the Prophet Saint Barsūm the Naked John XV, 99th patriarch of Alexandria
6—29	Thanks be to God the High

LIST OF THE MOVABLE FEASTS

Easter
Holy Thursday
Pentecost

BIBLIOGRAPHY

Balestri, J., and H. Hyvernat. *Acta martyrum,* 2 vols. CSCO, *Scriptores Coptici.* Paris, 1907–1924.

Budge, E. A. W. *Coptic Martyrdoms in the Dialect of Upper Egypt.* London, 1914.

Holweck, F. G. *A Biographical Dictionary of the Saints.* London, 1924.

O'Leary, De L. *The Saints of Egypt.* New York, 1937; Amsterdam, 1974.

Till, W. *Koptische Heiligen- und Märtyrerlegenden,* 2 vols. Orientalia Christiana Analecta 102 and 108. Rome, 1935–1936.

AZIZ S. ATIYA

SYNAXARION, ETHIOPIAN. There are two reasons for an article on the Ethiopic Synaxarion to be in a Coptic encyclopedia: first, the Ethiopic Synaxarion contains historical notices about Egypt—for example, the patriarchs or the churches of Old Cairo, based on lost documents; and, second, the Egyptian edition of the Coptic SYNAXARION by the *qummuṣ* ʿAbd al-Masīḥ Mīkhā'īl and Armāniyus Ḥabashī Shaṭā al-Birmāwī (1935–1937) has become the semiofficial edition of the Coptic church. For this edition its authors used an Arabic version of the Ethiopic Synaxarion (Coptic Museum, MS Lit. 155 a–c). Certain notices complete the ancient recension of the Synaxarion of the Copts. It is therefore important to say a few words about the genesis of the Ethiopic Synaxarion.

Until 1951 the ABUN, the religious head of Ethiopia, was an Egyptian monk chosen by the patriarch of Alexandria. It was therefore entirely natural that Ethiopia should turn to Egypt when it desired to acquire a Synaxarion for its use. In the first effort a very literal translation was made (there are only two manuscripts of this first recension, both in the Ethiopian section of the Bibliothèque nationale in Paris: Abbadie 66–66bis and Ethiopien 677 [formerly Trocadero Museum, no. 5], the latter half burned and containing only the first half of the year). The first manuscript is provided with a valuable colophon that has been studied and published by I. Guidi and by Conti Rossini; it states that the Arabic Synaxarion had been translated at the monastery of Saint Antony, in the desert called Wādī al-'Arabah, near the Red Sea. This is what is conventionally called the first recension. The date is not given, but the translator, Sim'on, is known from other works, and it can be inferred that the colophon was translated at the end of the fourteenth century or the beginning of the fifteenth. (See Guidi, 1911, and Conti Rossini, 1912.)

With time, however, this first recension was judged by the Ethiopians to be too literal, and not to give enough place to Ethiopian saints. A second recension was therefore made, today represented in a large number of manuscripts, that was translated back into Arabic. We cannot say exactly how far back this new Ethiopic version of the Synaxarion goes. However, since the oldest known manuscript is dated to A.D. 1581, the revision was prior to that date.

There is still no critical edition of the Ethiopic Synaxarion. In 1897, R. Graffin wished to include one in his Patrologia Orientalis, and he entrusted R. Basset with the publishing of an edition of the Arabic Synaxarion of the Copts with French translation. Graffin divided the task among four Ethiopic scholars: I. Guidi, C. Conti Rossini, J. Perruchon, and Basset. Only Guidi completed his work, and between 1905 and 1912 published the last third of the year, from the month of Sanē (Coptic: Ba'ūnah) to the month of Pāguemēn (which has no Coptic equivalent). Later, S. Grébaut presented the month of Takhśāś (Kiyahk) in two fascicles (1926, 1946). More recently G. Colin has set himself to complete the work, and has edited, with a French translation, the months of Maskaram (1986), Ṭeqemt (1987), and Khedār (1988). Unfortunately, thus far no comparison has been made with the Synaxarion of the Copts.

We have, then, a critical edition of seven months of the year. Regrettably, this work was not preceded by any detailed study or precise classification of the manuscripts. In particular, no account was taken of the fact that the manuscript Abbadie 66–66bis had arrived in Europe in disorder, and had been paginated by a European without the pages being restored to order. The Ethiopian copyists were not in the habit of paginating their books, or of writing at the bottom of the page the word or words with which the following page begins. The pages that the editors note as missing are, in fact, in the manuscript but incorrectly placed. This is of some importance, for certain notices are sometimes marked as belonging to the "revision" although they are, in fact, in the first recension.

The second recension includes notices of Egyptian saints for whom the author(s) of the recension from Lower Egypt did not have a Coptic text from which a summary could be made in Arabic. This is the case for patriarchs who lived after the compilation of the Synaxarion of the Copts and of saints from Upper Egypt. The author summarized Arabic lives (for several patriarchs and Sahidic saints) and even used sermons (this is the case with the panegyric of John, bishop of Asyūṭ, on the holy martyrs of Isnā, which he divided over several days). He also used texts translated from Syriac. It is not known where this second recension was made, but it is clear that it must have been in an Egyptian monastery that had a rich library. Ethiopians could reside in Egypt where they had dependencies: at DAYR AL-MUḤARRAQ, also in the Wādī al-Naṭrūn, and at Saint Antony (DAYR ANBĀ ANṬŪNIYŪS) on the Red Sea. There they could have met Syrian monks, which would explain the presence of typically Syrian texts in their Synaxarion, which is a very eclectic document.

E. A. W. Budge had begun an edition of the Ethiopic Synaxarion but gave it up when Graffin announced his project at the Congress of Orientalists in Paris in 1897. He did not wish to be in competition with Patrologia Orientalis. However, perhaps because of the delays with the project, in 1928 he published a translation of the whole work based on manuscripts preserved in London (hence of the second recension), a publication that is still valuable despite its inadequacies.

BIBLIOGRAPHY

'Abd al-Masīḥ, Mīkhā'īl, and Armāniyūs Ḥabashī Shaṭā al-Birmāwī. *Al-Sinaksār,* 2 vols. Cairo,1935–1937.

Budge, E. A. W. *The Book of the Saints of the Ethiopian Church,* 4 vols. Cambridge, 1928.

Colin, G. *Le Synaxaire éthiopien. Mois de Maskaram,* PO 43, fasc. 3; *Mois de Ṭeqemt,* PO 44, fasc. 1; *Mois de Hedār,* PO 44, fasc. 3.

Conti Rossini, C. "Piccoli studi etiopici. 4. Sull' età della versione abissina del Sinassario." *Zeitschrift für Assyriologie* 27 (1912):371–72.
Coquin, R.-G. "Le Synaxaire éthiopien. Note codicologique." *Analecta Bollandiana* 102 (1984):49–59.
Dillmann, A. *Chrestomathia aethiopica*. Leipzig, 1866.
Grébaut, S. *Le Synaxaire éthiopien. IV. Mois de Taḫschasch*. PO 15, fasc. 5, and 26, fasc. 1.
Guidi, I. *Le Synaxaire éthiopien. I. Mois de Sane; II. Mois de Hamlé; III. Mois de Nahasé et de Paguemen*. PO 1, fasc. 5; 7, fasc. 3; 9, fasc. 4.
______. "The Ethiopic Senkassar." *Journal of the Royal Asiatic Society* n.s. 43 (1911):739–58 and 44 (1912):261–62.
Simon, J. "Notes bibliographiques sur les textes de la 'Chrestomathia aethiopica' de A. Dillmann." *Orientalia* n.s. 10 (1941):285–311, esp. 287–91.

RENÉ-GEORGES COQUIN

SYNCLETICA (fourth century?), nun. The little that is known about Syncletica is furnished by a *Vita sanctae Syncleticae,* transmitted by numerous Greek manuscripts, that at a late date was arbitrarily attributed to Athanasius of Alexandria. It is modeled on the *Vita sancti Antonii,* which probably explains this incorrect attribution. It is in the main a treatise on asceticism in which the biographical data occupy little space. Of Syncletica we learn only that she belonged to a family from Macedonia that had settled in Alexandria. Her parents were Christians. After their death, she renounced the world, as a sign of which she cut off her hair, distributed all her goods, and withdrew to a tomb near the town with her blind sister, to live there in virginity and asceticism. She died there at the age of eighty, after long and terrible sufferings due to a malady that the biographer describes with precision, and that seems to have been a purulent osteitis. The most important part of the *Vita* reports the teaching that she gave to the virgins who came to visit her or, as it seems, lived beside her.

The alphabetic recension of the APOPHTHEGMATA PATRUM has collected eighteen apothegms under her name, which are extracts from the *Vita.* The latter is probably from the fifth century, for it exhibits the influence of the teaching of EVAGRIUS. I. Hausherr thought that it could be earlier than Evagrius, and detected in it the influence of Methodius of Olympus. In this case, if we are to accord any historical value to the *Vita,* Syncletica would have lived in the fourth century. A French translation has been published in the collection *Spiritualité orientale.*

BIBLIOGRAPHY

Bernard, O. B. "Vie de sainte Synclétique." Presentation of Dom Lucien Regnault. *Spiritualité orientale,* no. 9. Bellefontaine, 1972.
Cotelier, J. B., ed. *Apophthegmata patrum.* PG 65, pp. 421A–428A. Paris, 1864.
Hausherr, I. "De doctrina spirituali christianorum orientalium." *Orientalia Christiana* 30, no. 3 (1933):173–75.
Vita et gesta sanctae beataeque magistrae Syncleticae. PG 28, pp. 1487–1558. Paris, 1887.

ANTOINE GUILLAUMONT

SYNESIUS (c. 370–c. 414), bishop of Ptolemais. Born at Cyrene in the Pentapolis to a wealthy pagan family, he was brought up as a pagan and sent by his parents to complete his higher education in Alexandria under HYPATIA, the famous Neoplatonist Greek philosopher, to whom he became attached and remained loyal despite the growing hostility of the Christian hierarchy to Hypatia, culminating in her murder in 415. In 403 Synesius married a Christian and became closely acquainted with Archbishop Theophilus (385–412), under whose influence he was converted to Christianity and led a successful embassy to the imperial court at Constantinople. In 410 his fame spread over his native country, where his Christian coreligionists selected him to succeed the deceased bishop of Ptolemais; the choice was submitted to Theophilus, who decided to accept his nomination in spite of certain irregularities: Synesius was a married man, and although a convert, he was not yet formally baptized.

Since Synesius was a Neoplatonist follower of Hypatia, most of his principal writings before his conversion were philosophical but imbued with spirituality. They included a set of Egyptian tales entitled *De providentia, De regno,* and *De dona astrolabii.* Most of his letters, sermons, and a collection of Christian hymns belong to his episcopal period.

BIBLIOGRAPHY

Altaner, B. *Patrology.* Edinburgh and London, 1960.
Tando, J. C. *The Life and Times of Synesius of Cyrene.* Washington, D.C., 1940.

AZIZ S. ATIYA

SYNOD, HOLY, the supreme ecclesiastical authority of the Coptic church, under the presidency of the patriarch of Alexandria. Ever since the foundation of the church by Saint Mark in the first century, there has existed such an authority to protect the faith, preserve tradition, and ensure the welfare of the church. Membership is vested in all metropolitans and bishops ex officio, whose number varies from time to time, the modern average being fifty.

The latest constitution of the Holy Synod, as ratified on 2 June 1985, consists of ten sections that may be summed up as follows:

1. *Introduction and definition.* The Coptic Orthodox Church of Alexandria is an apostolic church, affiliated to other Oriental Orthodox churches through faith, sacraments, and ecclesiastical tradition.

2. *Membership.* The Holy Synod consists of the pope of Alexandria as president, with all metropolitans, bishops, abbots of monasteries, chorepiscopi, and patriarchal deputies (vicars-general) as members.

Membership is for life, and may be withdrawn from those who deviate from the Orthodox Christian faith, fall into heresy, lose their mental faculty, or become excommunicated. This withdrawal shall follow a trial in which the member in question is given an opportunity to vindicate himself.

3. *Jurisprudence.* The Holy Synod is the highest legislative body in the church, empowered to make ecclesiastical laws and issue statues governing all ranks of the clergy. It is entitled to pass judgment in all cases of infringement of church doctrine. It also considers appeals against its judgments.

It is the highest authority responsible for safeguarding faith and doctrine, interpreting this faith in the light of established ecclesiastical tradition. In this capacity, it may examine publications dealing with church doctrine and give relevant decisions.

It is the primary source of church ritual.

Its decisions are final, but may be reviewed in the light of changing circumstances. It may pardon repentant offenders and heretics.

It supervises the entire process of papal election, from nomination to enthronement.

4. *Chairmanship.* The pope is the head of the Holy Synod, without whom it may not be convened, except in the following cases: his physical inability to speak or think, as attested by competent doctors and certified by more than half the number of members; and his refusal to convene the Holy Synod, despite his ability to attend, providing the majority of members request it be convened. In the event of the patriarchal throne becoming vacant, the locum tenens acts as chairman.

5. *Secretariat.* The secretary shall be chosen by secret ballot for a period of three years; his tenure may be extended for a similar period in a subsequent election. He is assisted by three members, two to be elected and the third appointed by the pope.

6. *Committees.* The Holy Synod incorporates the following committees: Doctrine and Ecclesiastical Education; Legislative; Diocesan Affairs; Church Ritual; Ecclesiastical Relations; Public Relations; Pastoral Work; and Ecclesiastical Development and Planning. An additional committee, consisting of the secretariat and rapporteurs of all other committees, is responsible for the implementation of the synodal decisions.

7. *Sessions.* The Holy Synod shall hold two sessions every year, at the beginning of the Great Lent and at the Coptic New Year. Extraordinary sessions may be convened to deal with an emergency, providing reasonable notice is given to all members residing in Egypt. It may also be convened at the request of the majority of members.

The quorum for ordinary sessions is two-thirds of all members. For emergency sessions, the quorum is two-thirds of those members residing in Egypt.

Decisions must be agreed upon by at least three-quarters of the members attending; the chairman's vote counts as two. Synodal decisions are binding on all.

8. *President and members.* The president of the Holy Synod is the pope, who is the patriarch of Alexandria, successor to Saint Mark; he is also the bishop of the cities of Alexandria and Cairo and, as such, is the archbishop of the See of Saint Mark, in accordance with the decrees of the Council of Nicaea (see NICAEA, COUNCIL OF).

The successor to Saint Mark must be an orthodox Egyptian Copt. The locum tenens must also be an orthodox Egyptian Copt.

The pope is the bishop responsible for vacant dioceses or new dioceses established abroad until such bishops are duly ordained or appointed. He may delegate a papal representative or appoint a synodal committee to assist him in running dioceses outside Egypt.

He may appoint general (suffragan) bishops and preside over their ordination to the episcopacy. The pope, together with member bishops, may ordain new bishops and raise them to the rank of metropolitan or catholicos.

He represents the church vis-à-vis the state and other churches and official and religious organizations.

Coptic monasteries are under the pope's supervision. The pope supervises the Coptic monasteries, to which he appoints abbots.

All possessions left by the pope after his death shall be the sole property of the patriarchate, and not his locum tenens or his own relatives by blood.

9. *Metropolitans and bishops.* Priests and deacons are ordained by bishops, who also consecrate churches, altars, baptismal fonts, icons, and sacramental vessels. New bishops are to be first recommended by people of the diocese, and their candidacy must be approved by the pope. Applications for ordination must also be approved by the majority of synod members.

Bishops may not be inherited by the patriarchate but by their diocese, with the pope acting as trustee until their belongings have been received by the diocese.

10. *General (suffragan) bishops.* The pope may ordain general bishops to assist him in his diocese, other church services, or pastoral work. No recommendation is required by the candidate, other than that of the pope or the bishop in whose diocese he will assist. A general bishop may be promoted to the bishopric, subject to the recommendation of his diocese and the approval of the pope.

11. *Amendments.* Any amendment application to articles of this constitution must conform with canonical laws and traditions, subject to the approval of at least three-quarters of the total number of all members, giving them a month's notice. No amendment may be introduced in the absence of the pope.

BIBLIOGRAPHY

Lā'iḥah al-Asāsiyyah lil Majma' al-Muqaddas, al-. Cairo, 1985.

FUAD MEGALLY

SYNODS, LETTERS OF. By this name two types of documents are generally described.

1. The letters addressed either to other bishops or to some other contemporary personage, preserved in Greek or Coptic. These have been conveniently indexed by M. Geerard in his *Clavis Patrum Graecorum* (*CPG*). They derive from the synods held in the ancient period at Alexandria, which was the seat of the Coptic patriarchate down to the tenth century. These synods, with their letters, are:

Synod of A.D. 320: *CPG* 2000 and 2002
Synod of 338: *CPG* 2123, sec. 1
Synod of 362: *CPG* 2134
Synod of 363: *CPG* 2135
Synod of 400: *CPG* 2595 and 2596

2. The letters called "synodical letters" designating the letters which the patriarchs of Alexandria exchanged with those of the see of Antioch after their election; they thus bore witness to their community in faith. The majority are preserved in Arabic in the dogmatic florilegium entitled *Confession of the Fathers* (I'tirāf al-Abā'). This work, important for the history of the patriarchate of Alexandria, has been analyzed and almost all the pieces in it identified by G. Graf (1937, pp. 345–402). There are some data in this article that Graf did not include in his treatment of the text in *Geschichte der christlichen arabischen Literatur* (Vol. 2, pp. 321–23). We may add here and to the pages of Graf's *Geschichte* the notes by Khalil Samir (1979, pp. 64–67).

Graf in his *Geschichte* (Vol. 1, pp. 443–44) gives in detail the synodical letters, the Arabic translation of which is found in the work entitled *Al-Kharīdah al-Nafīsah fī Tārīkh al-Kanīsah* (ed. 'Aṭā Allāh Arsānīyūs, Cairo, 1924); they stretch from the eighth to the eleventh century. Graf also indicates the letters that are preserved in the *Bibliotheca Orientalis* of J. S. Assemani or in the *Nomocanon* of Mīkhā'īl of Damietta.

The letters mentioned above were addressed by the patriarchs of Antioch to the patriarchs of Alexandria. The letters of the patriarchs of Alexandria—at least what has been preserved of them—are noted by G. Graf (1944–1953, Vol. 1, pp. 480–81), who indicates their locations.

BIBLIOGRAPHY

Graf, G. "Zwei dogmatischen Florilegien der Kopten." *Orientalia Christiana Periodica* 3 (1937):345–402.

Riedel, W. *Die Kirchenrechtsquellen des Patriarchats Alexandrien*. Leipzig, 1900; repr. Aalen, 1968.

Samir, K. "Le Kitāb I'tirāf al-Aba' [inv. 10781]." *Bulletin d'Arabe chrétien* 3 (1979):64–67.

RENÉ-GEORGES COQUIN

SYNOPTIC GOSPELS, the Gospels of Matthew, Mark, and Luke. The similarity of considerable segments of their subject matter and even their phraseology may be explained by one of two theories. The Gospel of Saint Mark is supposed to be the earliest of the three Gospels and could have been utilized by the other two. This interdependence and the pooling of knowledge in that era is a common trait of that age. Saint Mark was the most highly educated of the evangelists. Another possibility advanced by some theological scholars is that the three Gospels drew upon a fourth source, one lost and unknown.

In the meantime, one must bear in mind that Matthew and Luke used some material peculiar to each and without parallel in Mark's Gospel. Whether each evangelist had his own independent source on certain matters, in addition to their common knowledge, is debatable. In this situation of uncertainties and multiple probabilities, the Coptic theologians insist on the seniority and superiority of the Gospel according to Saint Mark the Evangelist, the founder of Egyptian Christianity and the first pope and patriarch of their church.

BIBLIOGRAPHY

Taylor, V. *The Gospels: A Short Introduction.* London, 1938.

Thompson, J. M. *The Synoptic Gospels.* Oxford, 1910.

AZIZ S. ATIYA

SYNTHRONON. *See* Architectural Elements of Churches.

SYRIAN INFLUENCES ON COPTIC ART. Numerous factors were favorable to an influence from Christian Syria upon Coptic art: relative proximity, a common tendency to the eremitic life and to monasticism, the accentuation of the relationship through being cut off from the rest of the Christian world after the Muslim conquest, and more particularly the foundation in the fifth century of the monastery of the Syrians (DAYR AL-SURYĀN) in the heart of the monastic complex in Wādī al-Naṭrūn (see SCETIS).

Syrian influence made itself felt to some extent on the level of iconography. It is possible that illuminated manuscripts penetrated Egypt into the monasteries to the point of introducing some new themes. This could be the case for the Triumph of Christ, the most ancient version of which appears to be the illumination of the gospel of Rabbula in Syria (sixth century), and the exploitation of which in Egypt resulted notably in several wall paintings in the chapels of the monastery at BĀWĪṬ. It is necessary to note, however, that Coptic figurative illumination does not seem to begin until the twelfth century. A Mediterranean legend of Syrian origin, that of Saint Pelagia, seems to have passed into the motif of the conch with the cross, the latter being a derivative from the myth of *Aphroditē anadyomenē*. The scenes (dated to the tenth and eleventh centuries) from the Infancy Gospel of Christ (James, 1983) located on the vault of the choir in the al-ʿAdhrā' church of the monastery of the Syrians in the Wādī al-Naṭrūn are consistent with the contemporary iconography of these themes in Byzantine art as a whole.

On the other hand, the style of Syrian art, which with a certain liberty and joie de vivre all its own remained in the Byzantine domain, does not seem to have exercised any influence on the Coptic style. The difference of perspective between the two is too glaring. One may even ask whether the thick-set appearance of the figures and the square composition of the pupils of their eyes in the Sinope Codex (National Library, Paris) are not due to a Coptic influence on the style of the illumination of this manuscript, practically the only one of its kind in the Byzantine area.

BIBLIOGRAPHY

Bourguet, P. du. *L'Art copte,* pp. 9, 129. Collection L'Art dans le monde. Paris, 1968.

______. *Peintures chrétiennes: Couleurs paléochrétiennes, coptes et byzantines,* pp. 210–11. Geneva, 1980.

James M. R., ed. *The Infancy Gospel.* In *The Apocryphal New Testament.* Oxford, 1983. First ed., 1924. Corrected ed., 1953.

PIERRE DU BOURGUET, S.J.

T

TABENNĒSĒ, location of the first monastery of Saint PACHOMIUS, and though he and his successors soon lived in the second house established at PBOW, it still gives its name to the type of monasticism that he inaugurated. His monks were called Tabennesiotes, and the superior general was called either "archimandrite of Pbow" or "archimandrite of the Tabennesiotes." The etymology of this Egyptian place-name was established by W. E. Crum (Vol. 2, no. 163, n. 8). The name means "sanctuary of Isis," and this interpretation has been adopted by all Egyptologists (see, for example, Černý, p. 353). The name survives elsewhere among Egyptian place-names under the form Tafnīs.

Since the site disappeared very early, carried away by the floods of the Nile, to which it was very close, no ancient evidence remains. The first to investigate the Tabennēsē of Saint Pachomius on the spot appears to have been M. JULLIEN, who thought he would find its remains in the neighboring town of Dishnā, a name that he ingeniously made the equivalent of Tabennēsē (1901, p. 251). This town is almost 20 miles (30 km) downstream from Qinā. In 1904 H. Gauthier proposed the same identification (pp. 86–87), but in 1912 he rejected it, both from a linguistic point of view and because the town of Dishnā is too distant from Faw al-Qiblī and thus does not agree with the texts (pp. 122–27). Finally, in 1939, L. T. Lefort, after setting out the solutions of his predecessors, showed that Tabennēsē must have been carried away by the Nile and must have been situated southwest of Pbow (pp. 393–97).

BIBLIOGRAPHY

Černý, J. *Coptic Etymological Dictionary.* Cambridge, 1976.

Crum, W. E. *The Monastery of Epiphanius at Thebes,* 2 vols. New York, 1926.

Gauthier, H. "Notes géographiques sur le nome panopolite." *Bulletin de l'Institut français d'Archéologie orientale* 4 (1904):39–101.

______. "Nouvelles notes géographiques sur le nome panopolite." *Bulletin de l'Institut français d'Archéologie orientale* 10 (1912):89–130.

Jullien, M. "A la recherche de Tabenne et des autres monastères fondés par saint Pachôme." *Etudes* 89 (1901):238–58.

Lefort, L. T. "Les Premiers monastères pachômiens. Exploration topographique." *Le Muséon* 52 (1939):379–407.

Sauneron, S. *Villes et légendes d'Egypte.* Cairo, 1974.

RENÉ-GEORGES COQUIN

TĀDRUS AL-MASHRIQĪ, recorder of the history of the three Coptic patriarchs who governed in his lifetime, PETER VII (1809–1852), CYRIL IV (1854–1861), and DEMETRIUS II (1862–1870), in a manuscript of miscellanies, written by him in 1868.

VINCENT FREDERICK

TĀDRUS SHINUDAH AL-MANQABĀDĪ (1859–1932), newspaper editor. He was born in Asyūṭ. When he was six years old, he was enrolled in a Coptic school, where he spent three years learning the elements of both Coptic and Arabic, as well as penmanship and arithmetic, the normal subjects of study in the native Coptic schools of the day. In 1862, Patriarch DEMETRIUS (1862–1870) visited the city of Asyūṭ where he was able to prevail upon the rich natives, along with the support of the authorities, to establish a Coptic school. Al-Manqabādī was educated in that Coptic school.

Beginning in 1873 he held various administrative capacities in government service. In 1895 al-Manqabādī resigned his government post and moved to Cairo to start the daily paper, *Miṣr,* with which his name became associated. However, his social and economic activities extended far beyond journalism. In 1884 he had founded a society for the preservation of Coptic history (*Jam'iyyat Ḥifẓ al-Tārīkh al-Qibṭī*) in Asyūṭ, which became responsible for reinstating the celebration of the Coptic New Year's Day on a national basis. The society also introduced the Coptic calendar to all organs of the press, both Coptic and Muslim. On the economic front, he devised the idea of a Coptic Trading Corporation. One-tenth of the income of the new company was devoted to the purchase of land for the support of the Coptic College in Asyūṭ.

Al-Manqabādī was a founding member of the Tawfīq Coptic Society. He was a great supporter of the COMMUNITY COUNCIL and used his newspaper as a means of strengthening its position vis-à-vis the patriarchal party, whose aim was to monopolize the administration of all religious property. In 1897 he participated in the reform of the Clerical College and the convening of the Holy Synod, after centuries of lethargy. In support of his reform programs, he started a new periodical called *al-Nūr* to help societies and organizations serving the Coptic community.

His life ended with a false accusation of his illegitimately appropriating lands. His arrest and incarceration for a period proved without foundation. His accuser was dismissed from Egyptian justice, and the khedive granted Al-Manqabādī the title of bey as consolation and appeasement.

BIBLIOGRAPHY

Ramzī Tadrus. *Al-Aqbāṭ fī al-Qarn al-'Ishrin,* 5 vols. Cairo, 1910–1919.

MIRRIT BOUTROS GHALI

TĀDRUS AL-SHUTBI. *See* Pilgrimages.

TAFA, or Taifa, in both ancient and modern times a settlement in Lower Nubia, about 30 miles (50 km) south of Aswan. In a number of classical texts it is called Taphis. Two small temples were built here in pharaonic times, and the place later became the main center of Roman military administration in Lower Nubia. At the beginning of the eighth century the more northerly of the pharaonic temples was converted into a church, an event that is commemorated in an Old Nubian inscription carved in one of the walls. Tafa must still have been an important place at that time, for it was designated as one of the seven or eight original Coptic bishoprics in the kingdom of MAKOURIA. However, the importance of the settlement apparently soon declined, and the episcopal seat was removed to the nearby settlement of TALMĪS. Excavations revealed few important remains of the later medieval period in and around Tafa, although ABŪ ṢĀLIḤ THE ARMENIAN spoke of it as an important place, with a church and a monastery, in the twelfth century.

[*See also:* Nubian Church Organization.]

BIBLIOGRAPHY

Monneret de Villard, U. *La Nubia medioevale,* Vol. 1, pp. 26–27. Cairo, 1935.

Roeder, G. *Debod bis Bab Kalabsche,* Vol. 1, pp. 189–209. Cairo, 1911.

Vantini, G. *Christianity in the Sudan,* pp. 51–52. Bologna, 1981.

WILLIAM Y. ADAMS

TAFSĪR, an Arabic term (pl., *tafāsīr*) for explanation or interpretation. This is a metrical Coptic composition inspired by a THEOTOKION; though called an "explanation" or "paraphrase" of an original text, it is in fact a more or less free composition on the themes contained in the original.

A *tafsīr* paraphrase is divided into a number of sections equal to that of the theotokion. Each section of a *tafsīr* is intended to be used liturgically immediately after the section of the theotokion that it interprets, although some are private compositions that perhaps never attained the dignity of recitation in church. Thus, the paraphrases form a body of popular hymnody that is approved, but not officially authorized, by the church. Their use is optional; those who use them are at liberty to select whichever they please.

Abū al-Barakāt IBN KABAR (fourteenth century), in his *Misbāḥ al-Ẓulmah* (The Luminary of Church Services), expressed the opinion that the best of these paraphrases are the older and shorter ones. The shorter paraphrases that occur in combination with the text were thought at one time to be confined to the Sunday and Saturday theotokia, but the discoveries at DAYR ANBĀ MAQĀR suggest that at some period there was a full liturgical series of all the seven theotokias, each with its own *tafsīr.*

Some of these paraphrases (especially those of Saturday and Sunday) are now sung only as part of the SAB'AH WA-ARBA'AH in the month of Kiyahk. But the manuscript of *Tartīb al-Bī'ah* (The Order of the Church) says that they are to be sung not only on the eve of Sundays (Saturday evening) of the month of Kiyahk but also optionally on the eve of Sundays of Lent and the whole year.

Some of the *tafāsīr* found in the manuscripts collected by De Lacy O'Leary in *The Coptic Theotokia* (1923) appear in the *Kitāb al-Abṣalmūdiyyāt al-Muqaddasāt al-Kihyāhkiyyah,* for the month of Kiyahk 1911, under the title LOBSH (e.g., pp. 289–329).

In the Saturday theotokia are nine sections called SHĀRĀT, followed by a LOBSH. Each of these nine sections has three *tafāsīr* called respectively *rūmī,* or Greek; MU'AQQAB (i.e., repeated); and Bohairic. These are found in the relatively older manuscripts published by De Lacy O'Leary. The *Kitāb al-Abṣalmūdiyyāt* adds some (probably later) *tafāsīr* that are Bohairic, *Miṣrī* (i.e., Cairene), or Sahidic (Upper Egyptian), as well as a series of six Arabic *tafāsīr.*

BIBLIOGRAPHY

Kitāb al-Abṣalmūdiyāt al-Muqaddasāt al-Kiyahkiyyah. Cairo, 1911.

O'Leary, De L. *The Coptic Theotokia.* London, 1923.

______. "The Coptic Theotokia." In *Coptic Studies in Honor of Walter Ewing Crum.* Boston, 1950.

EMILE MAHER ISHAQ

TAKINASH (Banī Suef), a monastery mentioned several times in the Life of SAMŪ'ĪL OF QALAMŪN. Driven from Scetis by the envoy of Cyrus, the Chalcedonian archbishop of Alexandria, Samū'īl withdrew with his disciples to the south, to the mountain of Takinash. After being delivered from the bedouin who had taken him prisoner, he founded Qalamūn with some brothers who had come from the mountain (monastery) "of Takinash" (see Alcock, 1983, index).

A Coptic papyrus from the Fayyūm mentions "the expenses from the feast of Takinash" (Crum, 1893, no. 45v).

At the entrance of a track leading to al-Qalamūn, G. Daressy noted a *ḥoḍ* (basin) called Diqnash, west of the village of Mazūrah, 7.5 miles (12 km) south of Dashāshah.

The present dependency of the monastery of Saint Samuel is near the village of al-Zawarah, west of Maghāgha (Meinardus, 1st ed., pp. 255–56; 2nd ed., p. 359; see Amélineau, 1895, p. 121).

BIBLIOGRAPHY

Alcock, A., ed. *The Life of Samuel of Qalamūn.* Warminster, England, 1983.

Amélineau, E. *La Géographie de l'Egypte à l'époque copte.* Paris, 1895.

Crum, W. E. *Coptic Manuscripts Brought from the Fayyūm by W. M. Flinders Petrie.* London, 1893.

Daressy, G. "Position de la ville de Takinash." *Annales du Service des antiquités d'Egypte* 18 (1918):26–28.

Meinardus, O. *Christian Egypt, Ancient and Modern.* Cairo, 1965; 2nd ed., 1977.

RENÉ-GEORGES COQUIN
MAURICE MARTIN, S.J.

TALL AL-'AMARNAH, also known as Tall Banī 'Imrān, from the name of the bedouin tribe that established itself in the neighborhood, site famous for the ruins of the capital founded by Amenophis IV, the pharaoh who wished to impose the cult of one god. Several tombs in the necropolis, north of the town, were fitted up by the hermits. Attention is drawn to them by N. Davies. One also may consult Badawy's "Les Premiers établissements."

It appears that the inscriptions have not been published. Two tombs are of particular interest: tomb no. 4, of Merire, for its inscriptions; and tomb no. 6, of Panehsi, for its transformation into a chapel. A niche was enlarged to form a baptistery.

A description of the entire site is given in O. Meinardus.

BIBLIOGRAPHY

Badawy, A. "Les Premiers établissements chrétiens dans les anciennes tombes d'Egypte." *Tome commémoratif du millénaire de la Bibliothèque patriarcale d'Alexandrie,* pp. 66–69. Alexandria, 1953.

Davies, N. de Garis. *The Rock Tombs of el-Amarna,* Vols. 1 and 2. London, 1903–1908.

Meinardus, O. *Christian Egypt Ancient and Modern.* Cairo, 1965; 2nd ed., 1977.

RENÉ-GEORGES COQUIN
MAURICE MARTIN, S.J.

TALL ATRĪB (Province of al-Qalyūbiyyah), monastery dedicated to the Virgin. It was situated at Atrīb, on the northern boundary of Banhā al-'Asal. The fifteenth-century writer states that the monastery had been destroyed and that there were only three monks there.

The account of a miracle of the Virgin at Atrīb during the caliphate of al-Ma'mūn (813–833) describes the church. This text has been published in Graf (1944, Vol. 1, p. 255; Vol. 2, p. 489), and in *al-La'ālī' al-Saniyyah fī al-Mayāmir wa-al-'Ajā'ib al-Maryamiyyah* (pp. 168–75).

The monastery, dependent on the see of Jerusalem, was destroyed by bedouin tribes about 866, at the same time as Saint Menas in the region of Mareotis, according to the HISTORY OF THE PATRIARCHS, in the patriarchate of SHENUTE I (858–880).

The festival of the Virgin took place on 21 Ba'ūnah.

In 1967–1968 Polish archaeologists discovered the ruins of a church of the Virgin destroyed in the thirteenth century (Leclant, 1969, p. 251).

BIBLIOGRAPHY

Atiya, A. S., ed. "Some Egyptian Monasteries According to the Unpublished MS of Al-Shābushtī's 'Kitāb al-Diyārāt.'" *Bulletin de la Société d'archéologie copte* 5 (1939):1–28.

Al-La'ālī' al-Saniyyah fī al-Mayāmir wa-al-'Ajā'ib al-Maryamiyyah. Cairo, 1966.

Leclant, J. "Fouilles et travaux en Egypte et au Soudan." *Orientalia* 38 (1969):240–307.

Miṣā'īl Baḥr. *Kanīsat Atrīb-Banhā fī Jamī' al-'Uṣūr,* pp. 34–55. Alexandria, 1974.

RENÉ-GEORGES COQUIN
MAURICE MARTIN, S.J.

TALL BROTHERS.

See Ammonius of Kellia; Theophilus.

TALMĪS,

an important Roman fortress and caravansary in Lower Nubia, and the site of a major temple of Augustus. Its location corresponded approximately to that of the modern Nubian village of Kalabsha, about 40 miles (60 km) south of Aswan. After the Roman withdrawal from Nubia, Talmīs remained an important commercial and religious center in the time of the BALLANA KINGDOM. With the coming of Christianity the temple of Augustus was converted into a church, and in the eighth century the place became an episcopal seat, replacing the earlier episcopate of TAFA. However, in the later Middle Ages, Talmīs seems to have lost most of its importance, to judge by the archaeological remains that have been found there. In the twelfth century ABŪ ṢĀLIḤ THE ARMENIAN mentioned "Darmus" (Talmīs) as the site of an "elegantly proportioned church" but not as an episcopal see. There is no mention of Darmus or Talmīs in any other medieval Arabic document.

[*See also:* Nubian Church Organization.]

BIBLIOGRAPHY

Curto, S., et al. *Kalabsha.* Orientis Antiqui Collectio 5. Rome, 1965.

Monneret de Villard, U. *La Nubia medioevale,* Vol. 1, pp. 32–40. Cairo, 1935.

______. *Storia della Nubia cristiana,* pp. 160–65. Orientalia Christiana Analecta 118. Rome, 1938.

WILLIAM Y. ADAMS

TAMBUQ.

See Monasteries of the Province of Daqahliyyah.

TAMĪT,

the name given in modern times to the ruins of a medieval Nubian village situated on the west bank of the Nile a few miles north of the Abu Simbel temples. The ancient name of the place is nowhere recorded, for it was not large or important enough to figure in any written accounts. Our knowledge of Tamīt therefore comes entirely from archaeology.

The main ruins at Tamīt were those of about twenty mud brick houses that were tightly clustered along the top of a hill or ridge beside the Nile. A short distance inland was a single large building enclosed within a walled compound. This was presumed by U. MONNERET DE VILLARD to have been the residence of a local dignitary, but it was never excavated and nothing is known specifically about its history or function.

The most interesting feature of medieval Tamīt was the presence of no fewer than eight churches. There were clusters of three churches close together at the eastern and at the western extremities of the settlement. A single church was located more or less in the middle of the village, and another was close to the cemeteries west of the town. Most of the buildings were of the classic Christian Nubian type (see NUBIAN CHURCH ARCHITECTURE), but the most westerly church had an extraordinary cruciform plan that was very rare in Nubia. On its walls were fragments of about fifty paintings, of which some of the best preserved were depictions of angels. As a result, it was designated by the excavators as the Church of the Angels. Fairly well preserved wall paintings were also found in the nearby

Church of Saint Raphael, and traces of decoration survived in a number of the other Tamīt churches as well. Many of the paintings were accompanied by legends in Old Nubian.

The number of churches found at Tamīt exceeds that at any other Nubian settlement, large or small. The surviving archaeological remains provide no real explanation for such a concentration. Apart from the unusual walled compound and "palace," the nonecclesiastical remains at Tamīt are those of a typical Nubian hamlet of the late medieval period, similar to dozens of others up and down the Nile. Excavations revealed that the settlement had been occupied only between about 1100 and 1400. The churches were probably built at various times during that period, but in the last century of occupation they may all have been in use simultaneously.

The remains at Tamīt were first observed and recorded by Monneret de Villard in 1932–1933 and were partly excavated by an expedition from the University of Rome in 1964. They have since been inundated by the filling of Lake Nasser.

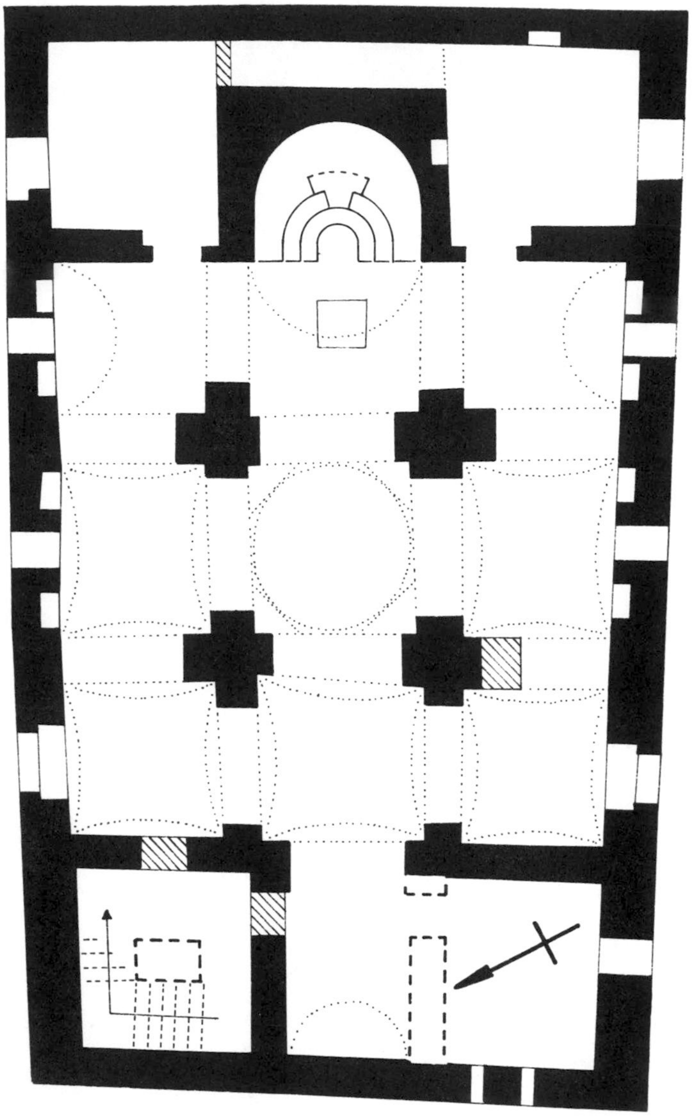

Plan of the Church of Saint Raphael at Tamīt. *Courtesy Peter Grossmann.*

BIBLIOGRAPHY

Missione Archeologica in Egitto dell'Università di Roma. *Tamīt (1964)*. Università di Roma, Istituto di Studi del Vicino Oriente, Serie Archeologica, 14. Rome, 1967.

Monneret de Villard, U. *La Nubia medioevale*. Vol. 1, pp. 146–66. Cairo, 1935.

WILLIAM Y. ADAMS

TAMNŪH, monastery called by this name (probably a place-name) in the Life of the patriarch THEODORUS (731–743) in the HISTORY OF THE PATRIARCHS. The name also appears in the recension of the SYNAXARION from Lower Egypt. Nothing further is known about this monastery.

RENÉ-GEORGES COQUIN

ṬANBIDĀ (Maghāghah), monastery mentioned at the beginning of the thirteenth century. The church of the monastery was dedicated to Saint Tarnima, whose body was buried in the church. We cannot be certain whether it was the monastery or another church that was outside the town.

The HISTORY OF THE PATRIARCHS OF THE EGYPTIAN CHURCH, under the patriarch CYRIL II (1078–1092), mentions the body of the martyr Apa Bīmā (Epima) in his monastery at Ṭanbidā.

A colophon in a Coptic manuscript of the twelfth century locates Ṭanbidā in the nome of Pemje (van Lantschoot, 1929, no. 102, l. 15).

AL-MAQRĪZĪ (d. 1441) mentions a church of the Virgin outside Ṭanbidā. One may consult E. Amélineau (p. 479) on Ṭanbidā and its etymology.

Ṭanbidā should not be confused with its namesake in the Delta, in the *markaz* (district) of Shibīn al-Kom.

BIBLIOGRAPHY

Amélineau, E. *La Géographie de l'Egypte à l'époque copte*. Paris, 1893.

Lantschoot, A. van. *Recueil des colophons des manuscrits chrétiens d'Egypte.* Bibliothèque du Muséon 1. Louvain, 1929.

RENÉ-GEORGES COQUIN
MAURICE MARTIN, S.J.

TAPOSIRIS MAGNA. *See* Abūṣīr (Taposiris Magna).

TARNŪṬ, town located on the western edge of the Egyptian Delta some 12 miles (19 km) west of Minūf in the province of Minufiyyah. The site of the town is now known as Kom Abū Billū.

Tarnūṭ was a bishopric at least as early as the end of the fourth century when Bishop John administered in the city (Munier, 1943, p. 11). At the beginning of the fifth century a man named Arsinthius appears to have been bishop and Eulogius of Tarnūṭ appears in the lists of bishops who attended the Council of EPHESUS in 431 (Munier, 1943, pp. 12, 14).

Stela from Kom Abū Billū (Tarnūṭ). *Courtesy Ikonen-Museum, Recklinghausen.*

BIBLIOGRAPHY

Kosach, W. *Historisches Kartenwerk Ägyptens.* Bonn, 1971.
Munier, H. *Recueil des listes épiscopales de l'église copte.* Cairo, 1943.

RANDALL STEWART

TATTAM, HENRY (1789–1868), English Coptologist. He visited Egypt and Syria in 1838–1839 to obtain Oriental manuscripts and brought back a considerable number of Coptic manuscripts and antiquities. He was one of the pioneers of Coptic studies in England and probably the most distinguished figure in the field at that time. He published many important works, especially *A Compendious Grammar of the Egyptian Language as Contained in the Coptic and Sahidic Dialects* (London, 1830).

BIBLIOGRAPHY

Dawson, W. R., and E. P. Uphill. *Who Was Who in Egyptology,* p. 285. London, 1972.
Kammerer, W., comp. *A Coptic Bibliography.* Ann Arbor, Mich., 1950; repr. New York, 1969.

AZIZ S. ATIYA

TAWFĪQ. *See* Muḥammad ʿAlī Dynasty.

TAXATION IN ROMAN EGYPT. A leading authority on taxes and "liturgies" (unpaid obligations) in Roman Egypt summarized very aptly, "No ancient government and few modern ones have had a tax structure rivalling in intricacy that of Roman Egypt. There we confront a staggering array of charges and surcharges assessed upon the person, the land, occupations and services, sales and transfers, movement of goods and people, and real and personal property—a bewildering patchwork of staples and accretions. If we add up the taxes and imposts, regular and occasional, that we encounter during the centuries of Roman rule, their number comes to something considerably in excess of a hundred" (Lewis, 1983). There is a considerable wealth of sources, especially papyri and ostraca, providing numerous details of tax collection and financial administration, but texts lending themselves to generalizations are rare. No document has survived that might provide a survey of Egyptian tax revenues or a tableau of the financial administration of that province in Roman or Byzantine times.

Hence, it is necessary to draw conclusions from thousands of single, often small documents abounding with concrete details but isolated from the general framework that would permit the assessment of their overall relevance for the budget of Egypt and the tax burden of its inhabitants.

Nevertheless, the sources available offer the materials for a survey of taxation that no other province of the Roman and Byzantine empires could rival, in respect both of details and of comprehensiveness. Much work has been done in editing and interpreting relevant papyri, and many valuable articles and books have been written on particular and general features of taxation in Roman and Byzantine Egypt, but there exists no up-to-date monograph covering the complete range of that subject. The studies of Rouillard (1928), Wallace (1938), Johnson and West (1949), and Lallemand (1964), precious as they are, need in certain respects a revision that takes account both of the wealth of papyri and ostraca that have been published in the meantime and of new approaches elaborated in the recent past.

Taxation in Roman Egypt Before Diocletian

Along with the proverbially rich province of Gaul, Egypt was one of the most productive domains of the empire and provided the city of Rome with grain for four months (Josephus *Bell. Jud.* 2.386; Hopkins, 1980). *Sitologoi,* local officials serving without salary and performing their duty as "liturgists," collected the grain from all over Egypt. Other liturgists brought it to the granaries in Alexandria, where Roman procurators supervised its collection and shipment to Rome. The grain tax was surely the most important of Egypt's fiscal contributions to the ruling city. Taxes in kind (that is, foodstuffs) provided for the maintenance of the Roman troops stationed in Egypt (see ANNONA; ARMY, ROMAN). Agricultural products such as wine, oil, and vegetables were also taxed, many in money rather than in kind, as they could not be exported to Rome. Taxes were also levied on animals, pastures, and buildings. Capitation taxes in cash were imposed to pay for certain services, such as the maintenance of dikes and baths. But the most important per capita charge was the poll tax (*epikephalaion, laographia*) that was paid by all male inhabitants, presumably from the age of fourteen to the age of sixty, the rate varying from nome to nome (at reduced rate in the nome capitals). However, Roman citizens in Egypt as well as the citizens of the Greek towns, notably Alexandria, Antinoopolis, Naucratis, and Ptolemais, were exempted from the poll tax. From the reign of Vespasian to that of Hadrian, Jews were obligated to pay a special poll tax, the *Ioudaion telesma.*

Taxes were imposed also on the exercise of trades and professions. Thus, Egyptian priests had not only to pay taxes for certain activities and revenues of the temples but also upon entrance into their profession (*eiskritikon*). On the other hand, a given number of priests were exempted from the poll tax, the rate differing from temple to temple (Hobson, 1984). Requisitions of food, equipment, and transport had to be supported by the population not only for the maintenance of the army but also for inspection tours of higher officials and the occasional visits of the emperors, with their entourages and escorts.

A further source of tax revenue comprised the customs imposed on the import to, and export from, Egypt as well as on transit in the interior of the country, on the road from Koptos (QIFṬ) to the Red Sea (cf. the "tariff of Coptus" in Bernand, 1984, no. 67, A.D. 90). Transfer of real property and certain other types of property was also taxed (*enkyklion*). Roman citizens had to pay a 5 percent tax on the manumission of slaves (*vicesima libertatis*) and on entering upon an inheritance (*vicesima hereditatum*).

The system of financial administration and taxation just described was typical of Roman Egypt, but many of its aspects had their roots in the Ptolemaic period. One important change concerns the gradual replacement in Roman Egypt of salaried officials and of tax collectors by a system of liturgies, which reached its full development in the second and third centuries A.D. About a hundred separate liturgies are known, each with its own appointee or group of appointees serving one to three years (Lewis, 1982). At the end of their period of service, liturgists were generally entitled to a respite of some years, but such considerations were often outweighed by the shortage of eligible nominees and the wide range of liturgies. There is not sufficient general or statistical data to assess properly the effects of taxes and liturgies on the population of Egypt.

Naturally enough, papyri are full of complaints by taxpayers and state officials. Indeed, their grievances are precisely what caused many of the documents to be written. But how far are these complaints typical of the overall situation in Egypt? Diverging from some previous evaluations, recent research sometimes tends to represent the tax burden as less oppressive, because the rate of taxation was indeed low and was effectively reduced in the course of the Roman and Byzantine periods (cf. Johnson and West, 1949; Hopkins, 1980; Oates, 1988). These figures need, however, to be confronted with the changing rate of productivity in Egypt. As Bagnall (1985) has shown for some Fayyumic villages, the decline in taxes might be paralleled and caused by a decline in productivity, so that the burden of taxation and liturgies may in fact have been resented as oppressive. But Bagnall was right to warn that even in the case of the relatively well-known Fayyumic villages, generalizations must be carefully weighed, and this circumspection is still more imperative for Egypt as a whole and for a period stretching from Augustus to the ARAB CONQUEST OF EGYPT. Anyway, it would seem rash to conclude that fiscal oppression, tax evasion, and flight (*anachoresis*) played a decisive role in the emergence of Egyptian MONASTICISM (Rousseau, 1985, pp. 9–11).

Taxation in Byzantine Egypt

As a consequence of the reforms of Diocletian (284–305), Egypt lost much of its special status, and its administration was adapted to that of other provinces of the Roman and Byzantine empires. The Alexandrian mint ceased its production of specifically Alexandrian coinage and was absorbed into the overall imperial monetary program. The financial administration comprehended two sections: the Egyptian fisc (*sacrae largitiones, hierotaton tamieion*) and the imperial treasury (*res privatae, despotika pragmata*). Beginning in the third century A.D., the fisc was headed by a *rationalis* (*katholikos*) residing in Alexandria and responsible for all of Egypt. Later, Alexandria also became the seat of the *praefectus annonae*, who supervised the transport of corn formerly destined for Rome and now directed to Constantinople.

The fiscal reform of Egypt is attested for 297 by the edict of Aristius Opatus, the prefect of Egypt (P. Cairo Isid. 1; cf. Boak and Youtie, 1960). It introduces and summarizes the imperial edict promulgating the fiscal reform, but unfortunately, the accompanying schedule of taxes has been lost. The professed intention of this reform was to assure a more even distribution of the tax burden. In accordance with the imperial edict, the prefect of Egypt set forth the quota of each *aroura* (one hundred cubits square) in proportion to its quality. He also fixed a per capita tax to be paid by all males of the rural population (*agroikoi*), presumably in cash. The prefect ordered the provincials to meet their obligations promptly under threat of punishment, whereas he warned the tax collectors that their lives were at risk if they did not abide by the regulations of this new "salutary rule" (*typos sōtērios*). Possibly the above-mentioned capitation applied not only to the rural population but also to those inhabitants of provincial towns who had no full citizenship rights in their local metropolis.

Annual declarations of landed property were to specify the status of the land (whether public or private) and its condition after inundation. The fiscal assignations (*epigraphai*) took place yearly within a five-year *annona* cycle. This cycle functioned from 287 to 302, the series of earlier census declarations having been interrupted in the turmoil of the second half of the third century. The five-year cycle was replaced in 314 by the fifteen-year indiction cycle, the first indiction of this new system to be reckoned retroactively from 312/313. The system of land taxes instituted by Diocletian was abandoned toward the middle of the fourth century and replaced by the *capitatio–iugatio* already prevailing in other provinces of the empire. This new system was based on the evaluation of all landed property according to abstract units (*capita, iuga*). Taxes were paid in kind or in cash (listed by Lallemand, 1964, pp. 191–205). Taxes in kind could be replaced, or arrears made up, by an equivalent amount of money. In some cases, taxes were paid in gold or silver bullion, such as the *pragmateutikon chrysargyron*, which was imposed on commercial activities. As in the preceding centuries, the actual business of tax collection remained very much liturgical work (cf., for instance, the roster of liturgical officials in a fourth-century tax roll of Philadelphia in the Fayyūm, in Bagnall and Worp, 1984, p. 59).

The fifth century is marked by a conspicuous scarcity of papyrological documentation. This situation has often been explained by deep changes in economic and social conditions, especially by the impoverishment of the curial class (which, however, persisted into the early Arab period) and by a different assessment of taxes. According to a widespread theory, many small landowners, under the pressure of liturgies and taxes, gave up their land and placed themselves under the protection of big landowners. This development, already perceptible in the fourth century, spurred the rise of a powerful class of patrons, notwithstanding the endeavors of the state to diminish the strong relationship between patrons and farmers (*coloni*). That relationship was indeed considered damaging to the authority of the central government, which feared losing its direct control of small farmers and taxpayers.

Finally, in 415, a constitution of Honorius and Theodosius II, especially concerning Egypt, recognized the *patrocinium* as a fait accompli; the patrons would be held responsible to the state for the payment of taxes and for the implementation of liturgies by their *coloni* (Codex Theodosianus 11.24.6). There has been, however, considerable debate about the real significance of this development. Was the emergence and strengthening of the *patrocinium* (service of a patron) a prelude to a feudal structuring of society, or did the powerful houses (*oikoi*) of Byzantine Egypt, such as the well-known house of the Apions, still function within the solid framework of the traditional administration and in full conformity with the interests of the central government? There is no doubt, however, that a certain amount of fiscal mediation had by now taken root in Egypt (see Gascou, 1985). Concerning the *coloni*, Carrié (1984) has strongly advocated the view that through the succession of the terms *coloni originales, homologoi* (persons admittedly liable to taxation), and *enapographoi* (*adscripticii*, that is, registered farmers), a continuous development can be discerned from the fourth to the sixth century. However, one may evaluate the development of *patrocinium* in a larger perspective, for there have been, since the fifth century, evident changes in the traditional way of tax collection and fiscal administration. It was long a common opinion that some of these new features were reflected by the evolution of *autopragia*, that is, the authorization for a village or for big landowners to raise and pay taxes independently of the local or even provincial administration. In the sixth century, the *autopragia* of villages was thought to have come under attack from big landowners determined to eradicate the fiscal autonomy of the villages.

One famous, because disputed, case is the *autopragia* of the village of APHRODITO in the Thebaid. Recent research has offered an important reevaluation of the conflict opposing Aphrodito to the PAGARCHS of Antaeopolis and has emphasized the fact that the latter were not only big landowners but also and at the same time liturgists bound to fulfill their obligations (*munus*) within the fiscal administration (Geraci, 1979; Gascou, 1985, pp. 38–52, the latter with an overall reexamination of the evidence concerning *autopragia*). Another document concerning Aphrodito is a long extract of a land register compiled in 524 by the *scholasticus* and *censitor* Joannes (edition by Gascou and MacCoull, 1987). It is relevant for the present context because it gives a comprehensive survey of the different categories of land in Aphrodito, showing an overwhelming predominance of land for the growing of cereals and a much smaller area for gardens and vineyards. Another interesting feature of this register is the landed property of ecclesiastical institutions (churches, monasteries), which amount in Aphrodito to one-third of the total of registered land.

The Reforms of Justinian

Relations between Egypt and Constantinople had been strained since 451, when the council of CHALCEDON sharpened the hostility between Monophysites and Melchites. These tensions and conflicts persisted down to the very end of Byzantine rule in Egypt. The troubles of the first decennium of JUSTINIAN's reign led, probably in 538–539, to the promulgation of the well-known Edict 13. It was intended to put an end to the administrative disorder in Egypt and to secure the collection of taxes and the shipment of grain to Constantinople. The responsibility for conveying grain to the Byzantine capital was incumbent on the *dux augustalis* (imperial general) of Egypt and Alexandria. Egypt was divided into several duchies (*ducatus*) dependent on the *praefectus praetorio Orientis* (Pretorian prefect of the East). The duchies were themselves subdivided into provinces (see EPARCHY) and the latter into pagarchies. The pagarchs, responsible for tax collection in their respective *pagi* (districts), were supported by different aides of their office. On the local level, citizens with administrative duties assisted the pagarch in collecting taxes. These taxes were fundamentally the same as in the fourth and fifth centuries. They were paid in money or in kind. The tax in grain to be contributed by Egypt was set at 8 million units (presumably *artabas*), whereas the amount of taxes collected in gold is more difficult to determine (Johnson and West, 1949, p. 288). Referring to Egyptian revenues, Johnson (1951, p. 126) wrote that "it is not impossible to estimate the total income of the Byzantine rulers at 2,000,000 solidi annually." The salaries of the state officials were provided for by the population, which had also to maintain the army, whose duty consisted of, among other things, supporting the tax collectors with force if other means failed (Edict 13.9, 11). Had the burden of taxation thus become unbearably oppressive? One would think so, but on the basis of the tax register of Antaeopolis, Johnson (1951, p. 123) calculated that an Egyptian peasant under Justinian paid less than half the tax his ancestor would have paid under Augustus. However, this estimate is probably not the complete picture, as it does not take into account the decline of productivity in later Roman Egypt.

As for the period between Diocletian and the early years of Arab rule, no really significant changes appear in the overall rate of taxation, except for some adaptations to special circumstances and contributions that varied because of the military situation inside and outside of Egypt.

For the first decades of Arab rule, widely diverging numbers have been given for the tribute of Egypt. M. al-Abbadi (1981) made some interesting suggestions concerning the methods of calculating and converting the amounts given in Arab sources. Seeming at first glance mutually exclusive, these amounts can be brought, according to this scholar, into a relatively consistent pattern. In his opinion, the total tax income of Egypt would have run to 2 million solidi annually, about 25 percent thereof going to the caliph in Medina. The same amount having been estimated by Johnson as being the total income of Justinian's Egypt if converted in cash, the Arab conquest seems not to have led to an aggravation of the fiscal burden of Egypt. But taking into account the effects of war and the requirements of an occupying army and allowing for regional differences, it is not easy to assess the real weight of taxation in the years of Arab conquest.

BIBLIOGRAPHY

Abbadi, M. al-. "Historians and the Papyri on the Finances of Egypt at the Arab Conquest." In *Proceedings of the Sixteenth International Congress of Papyrology*, ed. R. S. Bagnall et al., American Studies in Papyrology 23. Chico, Ca., 1981.

Bagnall, R. S. "Agricultural Productivity and Taxation in Later Roman Egypt." *Transactions of the American Philological Association* 115 (1985):289–308.

Bagnall, R. S., and K. A. Worp. "The Fourth-Century Tax Roll in the Princeton Collection." *Archiv für Papyrusforschung* 30 (1984):53–82.

Bernand, A. *Les Portes du désert: Recueil des inscriptions grecques d'Antinooupolis, Tentyris, Koptos, Apollonopolis Parva et Apollonopolis Magna*. Paris, 1984.

Boak, A. E. R., and H. C. Youtie. *The Archive of Aurelius Isidorus in the Egyptian Museum, Cairo, and the University of Michigan*. Ann Arbor, Mich., 1960.

Bowman, A. K. "The Economy of Egypt in the Earlier Fourth Century." In *Imperial Revenue, Expenditure and Monetary Policy in the Fourth Century* A.D.: *The Fifth Oxford Symposium on Coinage and Monetary History*, ed. C. E. King, pp. 23–40. Bar International Series 76. Oxford, 1980.

Carrié, J.-M. "Figures du 'colonat' dans les papyrus d'Egypte: Lexique, contextes." In *Atti del XVII Congresso Internazionale di Papirologia* 3. Naples, 1984.

Gascou, J. "Les Grands Domaines, la cité et l'état en Egypte byzantine (Recherches d'histoire agraire, fiscale et administrative)." *Travaux et mémoires* 9 (1985):1–90.

Gascou, J., and L. MacCoull. "Le Cadastre d'Aphrodito." *Travaux et mémoires* 10 (1987):103–158.

Geraci, G. "Per una storia dell'amministrazione fiscale nell'Egitto del VI secolo d. C.: Dioskoros e l'autopragia di Aphrodito." In *Actes du XVe Congrès International de Papyrologie* 4. Papyrologica Bruxellensia 19. Brussels, 1979.

Hobson, D. W. "P. VINDOB, GR. 24951 + 24556: New Evidence for Tax-Exempt Status in Roman Egypt." In *Atti del XVII Congresso Internazionale di Papirologia* 3. Naples, 1984.

Hopkins, K. "Taxes and Trade in the Roman Empire (200 B.C.–A.D. 400)." *Journal of Roman Studies* 70 (1980):100–125.

Hussein, F. *Das Steuersystem in Ägypten von der arabischen Eroberung bis zur Machtergreifung der Ṭūlūniden 19–254/639–868 mit besonderer Berücksichtigung der Papyrusurkunden*. Heidelberger orientalistische Studien 3. Frankfurt and Bern, 1982.

Johnson, A. C. "Roman Egypt to the Reign of Diocletian." In *An Economic Survey of Ancient Rome*, Vol. 2, ed. T. Frank. Baltimore, 1936.

———. *Egypt and the Roman Empire*. Jerome Lectures, ser. 2. Ann Arbor, Mich., 1951.

Johnson, A. C., and L. C. West. *Byzantine Egypt: Economic Studies*. Princeton University Studies in Papyrology 6. Princeton, N.J., 1949.

Lallemand, J. *L'Administration civile de l'Egypte de l'avènement de Dioclétien à la création du diocèse (284–382): Contribution à l'étude des rapports entre l'Egypte et l'Empire à la fin du IIIe et au IVe siècle*. Brussels, 1964.

Lewis, N. *The Compulsory Public Services of Roman Egypt*. Papyrologica Florentina 11. Florence, 1982.

———. *Life in Egypt Under Roman Rule*. Oxford, 1983.

Morimoto, K. *The Fiscal Administration of Egypt in the Early Islamic Period*. Asian Historical Monographs 1. Kyoto, 1981.

Neesen, L. *Untersuchungen zu den direkten Staatsabgaben der römischen Kaiserzeit (27 v. Chr.–284 n. Chr.)* Antiquitas Reihe 1: Abhandlungen zur

alten Geschichte 32. Bonn, 1980. Detailed discussion of Egyptian evidence within the general frame of Roman taxation.
Oates, J. F. "The Quality of Life in Roman Egypt." In *Aufstieg und Niedergang der römischen Welt*, Vol. 10.1, ed. H. Temporini. Berlin and New York, 1988.
Rea, J. R. *The Oxyrhynchus Papyri*, Vol. 51. London, 1984 Nos. 3628–3636 concern commodity prices and tax accounts of the fifth century; no. 3637 refers to a tax or levy of gold coin during the last Persian occupation of Egypt, A.D. 623.
Rouillard, G. *L'Administration civile de l'Egypte byzantine*, 2nd ed. Paris, 1928.
Rousseau, P. *Pachomius: The Making of a Community in Fourth-Century Egypt*. Berkeley and Los Angeles, 1985.
Thomas, J. D. "Epigraphai and Indictions in the Reign of Diocletian." *Bulletin of the American Society of Papyrologists* 15 (1978):133–45.
Wallace, S. L. *Taxation in Egypt from Augustus to Diocletian*. Princeton, N.J., 1938.
Wilcken, U. *Griechische Ostraka aus Ägypten und Nubien. Ein Beitrag zur antiken Wirtschaftsgeschichte*. 2 vols. 1899; repr. Amsterdam, 1970. The pioneering work on the subject.

HEINZ HEINEN

TBOW (District of Nag Hammadi). In the Lives of PACHOMIUS it is related that a certain Petronius, a native of Pjōj, founded a monastery on an estate belonging to his parents at Tbow, then attached himself to the Pachomian community. The text specifies that Pjōj was in the nome of Hou (today Hiw), on the left bank of the Nile. It is more than probable that Tbow was not far from Pjōj; it was certainly a farm or small hamlet of which there is no trace.

The precise location of Pjōj is difficult to establish. W. E. Crum (1939, p. 799a) advances the hypothesis that it was the present village of Abū Ṭisht, 8 miles (13 km) northwest of Farshūṭ, but L. T. Lefort (1943, pp. 402–403) thinks that it is the village of Abū Shūshah, almost 4 miles (6 km) north of Abū Ṭisht; J. Černý puts forward the same opinion (1976, p. 351).

Unfortunately, no archaeological traces survive.

BIBLIOGRAPHY

Amélineau, E. *Géographie de l'Egypte à l'époque Copte*, pp. 498–99. Paris, 1893.
Černý, J. *Coptic Etymological Dictionary*. Oxford, 1976.
Coquin, R.-G. "Un Complément aux vies sahidiques de Pachôme, le manuscrit Institut français d'Archéologie orientale copte 3." *Bulletin de l'Institut français d'Archéologie orientale* 79 (1979):209–247.
Crum, W. E. *A Coptic Dictionary*. Oxford, 1939.
Lefort, L. T. "Les premiers monastères pachômiens. Exploration topographique." *Le Muséon* 52 (1939):379–407.
______. *Les Vies coptes de saint Pachôme*. Bibliothèque du Muséon 16. Louvain, 1943.

RENÉ-GEORGES COQUIN

TEACHINGS OF SILVANUS. The fourth of five works in the Nag Hammadi Codex VII (4:84.15–118.7), it was entered into the Coptic Museum at Old Cairo on 9 June 1952, was declared national property in 1956, and received inventory number 10546 in 1959. Its state of preservation is excellent, there being only small lacunae mostly at the bottom of the pages. Codex VII consists of only one quire, containing 127 written pages, so that the fourth tractate belongs entirely to the second half of the codex. The pages measure 29.2 cm in height and 17.5 cm in width at most. The fibers of the pages of the fourth tractate run horizontally on the odd pages. The average number of the lines per page is 32 to 33. The title appears at the beginning of the tractate and is marked by indentation, by some horizontal strokes above and underneath, by a koronis to the left and a colon with a set of diple signs to the right, so that there is a decorated title. Dated documents used for the cartonnage of the binding make dating the codex to the third quarter of the fourth century A.D. probable.

The contents of this tractate point to some connection with monastic life, as does the site of the find, not far from a monastery of Pachomius. Another link with anchorite life arises from the passage 97.3–98.22 (which also occurs on a sheet of parchment in the British Museum, BM 979), dating from the tenth or eleventh century and ascribed to Saint ANTONY, the father of monasticism in Egypt. The Greek original could perhaps be dated as early as 200 A.D. The contents are certainly not Gnostic (although some ideas could be combined with gnosticism) but resemble Hellenized Alexandrian theology, so that they are compatible with ideas of CLEMENT OF ALEXANDRIA and ORIGEN, although the author is less philosophic than they. The name of the author is almost certainly pseudepigraphic and possibly derived from Paul's companion. The author was influenced by current popular philosophy, which was a blend of middle Platonism and Stoicism. Like Clement and Origen, he is Platonic in his conception of the transcendent God and Stoic in his ethics.

The tractate has the literary form of wisdom literature. The author addresses the reader as his "son" (85.1–2), asking him to accept his education and teaching (87.5). The fool is opposed to the wise men (88.35–89.1; 89.26; 97.7–9). Wisdom is personified (89.5; cf. Prv. 1:20; 8:1). As in Stoic ethics, rational conduct is opposed to a life in passions and desires (84.20; 90.4; 105.23). Man shall follow the mind as his guiding principle (*hegemonikon*, 85.1; 108.24), an idea inspired by middle Platonism and late Stoicism. Mind and reason are man's guide and teacher (85.24–26), a "pair of friends" (86.14–15), "divine" faculties in man (88.4; 91.24–25). The mind is divine because man was created in conformity with the image of God (92.23–26). This conception concurs with Hellenistic Alexandrian theology and resembles the Stoic idea of the *logos spermatikos*. Mind and reason steer man as a helmsman or a rider, a notion that agrees with Plato's imagery of the mind as a charioteer (90.12–17). Although mind and reason may give man a certain natural knowledge of God, he needs the inspiration of the Holy Spirit (107.35) and God's revelation through Christ (100.24–25) in order to receive full knowledge of God. Christ is the Savior, "the Tree of Life" (106.21–22), "the good Shepherd" (106.28) who died "as a ransom" for man's "sin" (104.13). This is a biblical point of view. There are many cases in which "Silvanus" refers to biblical passages. Christ is the true vine (107.26–27; cf. Jn. 15:1). "Do not give sleep to your eyes nor slumber to your eyelids, that you may be saved like a gazelle from snares and like a bird from a trap" is an almost literal quote from Proverbs 6:1.

The tractate is certainly not Gnostic. Some passages contain perhaps anti-Gnostic polemics. "Strange kinds of knowledge" (94.32) and "spurious knowledge" (96.3) are rejected. The world was not made by a fallible demiurge but by the Father, who used Christ as his hand (115.3–6); thus the Creator is not ignorant (116.5–9). On the other hand, there are passages in which a Gnostic could recognize himself. The essence of sin is ignorance (87.20), which is characterized as "death" (89.13–14) or "drunkenness" (94.20–22). The "bridal chamber" is the place of origin of the Christian (94.27–28). Sometimes the visible world is evaluated negatively (98.1–2). The lower faculties in man are female, the mind is male (93.12). God's transcendence is described in a Platonic way when it is said that God is not at a place and that nothing can contain God (99.29–100.4). "For that which contains is more exalted than that which is contained" (100.3–4). We find the same idea with Clement of Alexandria. Christ's incarnation is pictured as his descent into Hades (103.34–104.5; 110.18–29). In doing so Christ showed humility (110.32), which is also a basic Christian virtue (104.19). Humility was also a monastic ideal. Christ humiliated himself in order that man might be exalted and become like God (111.1–13). "He who guards himself . . . makes himself like God [108.21–27] . . . according to the statement of Paul who has become like Christ" (108.30–32; cf. Gal. 2:20). This idea of becoming equal to God is also familiar to Clement of Alexandria who refers to Plato, *Theaetetus* 176ab.

In summary, "Silvanus" was a biblical Christian, influenced by contemporary philosophy, a popular thinker of the Alexandrian type, and not a Gnostic.

BIBLIOGRAPHY

Zandee, J. "Die Lehren Silvanus, Stoischer Rationalismus und Christentum im Zeitalter der frühkatholischen Kirche." In *Essays on the Nag Hammadi Texts in Honour of Alexander Böhlig.* Nag Hammadi Studies 3, ed. Martin Krause. Leiden, 1972.

______. "'The Teachings of Silvanus' from the Library of Nag Hammadi (Nag Hammadi Codex CG VII: 84, 15–118,7)," in cooperation with M. L. Peel. *Novum Testamentum* 14 (1972):294–311.

______. "Les Enseignements de Silvanos et Philon d'Alexandrie." In *Mélanges d'histoire des religions offerts à Henri-Charles Puech,* pp. 337–45. Paris, 1974.

______. "Die Lehren des Silvanus als Teil der Schriften von Nag Hammadi und der Gnostizismus." In *Essays on the Nag Hammadi Text in Honour of Pahor Labib.* Nag Hammadi Studies 6, ed. Martin Krause. Leiden, 1975.

______. *"The Teachings of Silvanus" and Clement of Alexandria: A New Document of Alexandrian Theology.* Leiden, 1977.

______. "Die Lehren des Silvanus (Nag Hammadi Codex VII,4) im Vergleich mit anderen Schriften aus Nag Hammadi und verwandter Literatur. Bemerkungen zur religiösen Sprache im Zeitalter des Frühkatholizismus." In *Aufstieg und Niedergang der römischen Welt,* ed. W. Haase. Principally Vol. 2, pt. 2, 22 (Gnostizismus und Verwandtes).

JAN ZANDEE

TEBTUNIS. *See* Monasteries of the Fayyūm; Umm al-Barakat.

TENTYRA. *See* Dandarah.

TER AND ERAI, SAINTS, or Abadir or Apater and Herai or Īrā'i, brother and sister of Antioch who were martyred in Egypt under DIOCLETIAN (feast day: 28 Tūt). The text of their Passion is extant, both in a Sahidic redaction (fragments from two codices: National Library, Vienna, Wiener Papyrussammlung, K2563 a-l, ed. Orlandi, 1974, and National Library, Paris, Copte 129.16.104) and in a Bohairic redaction (Vatican Library, Rome, Copti 63, fols. 1–65, ed. Hyvernat, 1886–1887). The Copto-Arabic SYNAXARION gives a summary of their lives. The two Coptic versions are different in form but, as far as can be judged from the fragmentary state of the Sahidic text, they agree on content.

This text belongs to the hagiographical cycle of BASILIDES the General (see LITERATURE, COPTIC, and HAGIOGRAPHY) and at the very beginning it mentions many of the same characters. Ter and Erai are children of Basilides (other texts give a different genealogy) and have another sister, Calonia. Mention is made of Diocletian's apostasy, the first Antiochene martyr, the bishop Theopemptos, and Sokrator, a comrade of Ter, who also desires martyrdom. Ter's mother tries to stop him from going and confessing his faith, but (after a few visions) his sister Erai persuades him to flee Egypt. At this point there begins an independent episode narrating the young Constantine's marriage with Calonia.

Meanwhile, Ter and Erai leave Alexandria, their first port of call, to seek the relics of the martyr Erai, the namesake of Ter's sister. They find them at Tamma, and then move on to Shmun, the village of Tshinla, on instructions from heaven. From here they continue to ANTINOOPOLIS, where they confess their faith before the tribunal of the prefect. There now follow the customary episodes of tortures, altercations, miracles, and visions. Mention is also made of the famous martyr Paphnutius and of Colluthus, who do not usually figure in the cycle of Basilides. Finally, ARIANUS has the two martyrs beheaded. At this point JUSTUS, the brother of Basilides, also makes an appearance.

BIBLIOGRAPHY

Baumeister, T. *Martyr Invictus. Der Märtyrer als Sinnbild der Erlösung in der Legende und im Kult der frühen koptischen Kirche.* Münster, 1972.

Hyvernat, H. *Les Actes des martyrs de l'Egypte tirés des manuscrits coptes de la Bibliothèque Vaticane et du Musée Borgia.* Paris, 1886–1887.

Orlandi, T. *Papiri copti di contenuto teologico.* Mitteilungen aus der Papyrussammlung der österreichischen Nationalbibliothek, n. s., 9. Vienna, 1974.

TITO ORLANDI

TERRA-COTTA. *See* Ceramics, Coptic.

TESMINE. *See* Akhmīm.

TESTIMONY OF TRUTH (Nag Hammadi Codex IX, 3). The *Testimony of Truth* is a Christian Gnostic tractate whose purpose is to define and uphold the "truth" against other versions of Christian faith deemed by its author to be false and heretical. The title of the work has been editorially assigned on the basis of content ("the word of truth," 31.8; "the true testimony," 45.1). A title may have occurred at the end, but the last pages (75–76) are lost. The tractate is preserved in fragmentary condition; the best-preserved material is from the first half of the document (pp. 29–45).

The first part of the tractate (29.6–45.6) consists of a homily in which a number of themes are addressed, with polemical attacks against those who hold "false" doctrines: (1) rejection of the "Law," understood as summarized in the command to marry and procreate (Gn.1:28; 2:24; etc.), in favor of a strict encratism (29.6–31.22); (2) polemics against those who willingly embrace martyrdom for the faith (31.22–34.26); (3) a "spiritual" interpretation of the resurrection centered upon "knowledge" (*gnosis*), and polemics against those who uphold the doctrine of the corporeal resurrection (34.26–38.27); (4) reiteration of emphasis on strict encratism and virginity (38.27–41.4); and (5) an account of the paradigmatic career of the gnostic man, who is saved by his knowledge of himself and God (41.5–45.6). It is clear that the doctrines opposed in this section of the document are those of emergent ecclesiastical orthodoxy.

The second part of the tractate (45.6–74.30 . . .) consists of miscellaneous blocks of material: (1) the "mystery" of Jesus' virginal birth (45.6–22); (2) a Midrash on the serpent of the paradise story in Genesis 3, wherein the serpent is credited with saving knowledge and "God" is regarded as a villain

(45.23–49.10); (3) contrasts between life in Christ and death in Adam (49.10–50.28 . . .; very fragmentary material); and (4) polemics against schismatics and heretics, of whom (surprising for a Gnostic document) Valentinus, Basilides, Isidorus, and others are mentioned by name (55.1–74.30 . . .), but among whom are also representatives of ecclesiastical Christianity, especially in a section denouncing those who observe water baptism (69.7–32).

The *Testimony of Truth* contains numerous references to the person and work of Christ; its use of a (Johannine) "Son of Man" Christology is especially noteworthy. The author makes liberal use of the New Testament canon, but also of noncanonical apocryphal traditions. The most noteworthy examples of its use of the Old Testament are the aforementioned Midrash on the serpent, a similar Midrash on David and Solomon's consorting with demons (70.1–23), and an allegory on the sawing asunder of Isaiah the prophet (40.21–41.4).

The Gnostic character of the *Testimony of Truth* is evident from beginning to end. Despite its anti-Valentinian polemics, it exhibits numerous points of contact with Valentinian doctrines. This, coupled with its radical encratism, has been taken (Pearson, 1981, pp. 118–20) to suggest the possibility that the document was written by an ex-Valentinian encratite known to CLEMENT OF ALEXANDRIA, namely, Julius Cassianus (cf. Clement of Alexandria, *Stromata* I.101; III.91, 93, 95, 102). A time and place for the tractate might accordingly be suggested: Alexandria or its environs, around the turn of the third century. An alternative suggestion for the authorship of the *Testimony of Truth* has also been proposed, namely, HIERACAS OF LEONTOPOLIS, a contemporary of PACHOMIUS (Wisse, 1978, pp. 439–40).

BIBLIOGRAPHY

Giversen, S. "Solomon und die Dämonen." In *Essays on the Nag Hammadi Texts in Honour of Pahor Labib;* ed. M. Krause, pp. 16–21. Nag Hammadi Studies 6. Leiden, 1975.

Koschorke, K. "Die Polemik der Gnostiker gegen das kirchliche Christentum: Skizziert am Beispiel des Nag-Hammadi-Tractates Testimonium Veritatis." In *Gnosis and Gnosticism: Papers Read at the Seventh International Conference on Patristic Studies*. ed. M. Krause. Nag Hammadi Studies 8. Leiden, 1977.

______. "Der gnostische Traktat 'Testimonium Veritatis' aus dem Nag-Hammadi-Codex IX: Eine Übersetzung." *Zeitschrift für die neutestamentliche Wissenschaft* 69 (1978):91–117.

______. *Die Polemik der Gnostiker gegen das kirchliche Christentum: Unter besonderer Berücksichtigung der Nag-Hammadi-Traktate 'Apokalypse des Petrus' (Nag Hammadi Codex VII,5) und 'Testimonium Veritatis' (Nag Hammadi Codex IX,3)*, pp. 91–174. Nag Hammadi Studies 12. Leiden, 1978.

Pearson, B. A. "Jewish Haggadic Traditions in *The Testimony of Truth* from Nag Hammadi (CG IX,3)." In *Ex Orbe Religionum: Studia Geo. Widengren*, Vol. 1, ed. J. Bergman et al. Leiden, 1972.

______. "Anti-Heretical Warnings in Codex IX from Nag Hammadi." In *Essays on the Nag Hammadi Texts in Honour of Pahor Labib*, ed. M. Krause. Nag Hammadi Studies 6. Leiden, 1975.

______. "Gnostic Interpretation of the Old Testament in the *Testimony of Truth (NHC IX,3).*" *Harvard Theological Review* 73 (1980):311–19.

______, ed. *Nag Hammadi Codices IX and X (The Coptic Gnostic Library)*, pp. 101–203. Nag Hammadi Studies 15, Leiden, 1981. This is a critical edition, with introduction, Coptic transcription, English translation, and notes.

Pearson, B. A., introduction; S. Giverson and B. A. Pearson, trans. "The Testimony of Truth (IX, 3)." In *The Nag Hammadi Library*, ed. J. M. Robinson. San Francisco, 1977.

Tröger, K.-W., ed. *Gnosis und Neues Testament*, pp. 70–72.

Wisse, F. "Die Sextus-Sprüche und das Problem der gnostischen Ethik." In *Zum Hellenismus in den Schriften von Nag Hammadi*, ed. A. Böhlig and F. Wisse. Göttinger Orientforschungen 6. Reihe Hellenistica, Vol. 3. Wiesbaden, 1975.

______. "Gnosticism and Early Monasticism in Egypt." In *Gnosis: Festschrift für Hans Jonas*, ed. B. Aland. Göttingen, 1978.

BIRGER A. PEARSON

TETRACONCH. *See* Architectural Elements of Churches.

TETRAMORPH. *See* Christian Subjects in Coptic Art.

TEXTILES, COPTIC. [*Throughout their long history, Egyptians have practiced the art of weaving. The Coptic period has yielded enormous numbers of textiles displayed in many museums and private collections all over the world. These textiles have come mainly from archaeological excavations of burial grounds and* ākwam *(mounds containing antique objects). The pieces attest a variety of uses, functional as well as ornamental (see* COSTUME, CIVIL; COSTUME, MILITARY*). Coptic textiles are rich in iconographic images (see* BIBLICAL SUBJECTS IN COPTIC ART; CHRIS-

TIAN SUBJECTS IN COPTIC ART; MYTHOLOGICAL SUBJECTS IN COPTIC ART). *To the present day, certain towns in Egypt such as Naqadah, Isnā, Akhmīm, and others, are still known for unique kinds of textiles. Some of the weavers still keep their looms in their homes. This entry is composed of five articles by various authors:*

Types of Fibers
Manufacturing Techniques
Organization of Production
Iconography of Woven Textiles
Iconography of Resist-Dyed Textiles]

Types of Fibers

Coptic weavers used yarn made from four types of fibers all known from the pharaonic period or the Greco-Roman era. They were linen, wool, silk, and cotton.

Linen

Wild flax, the source of linen, grows all around the Mediterranean, but no trace of it has been found in Egypt. Nevertheless, it was cultivated there from the most remote periods; it was probably introduced from western Asia. Flax became and remained the characteristic Egyptian textile fiber during the whole of the pharaonic period. Beginning from the time of the Ptolemies, it was rivaled by wool, but it remained widely used for linen cloth or for the warp for textiles woven in wool.

Since the techniques of harvesting and treating the fibers underwent practically no development during these periods, we can easily reconstruct the different operations on the basis of the numerous representations painted in Egyptian tombs and on the testimony of ancient authors such as Pliny in his *Natural History*.

Flax seeds were sown in the middle of November, when the Nile floodwaters had receded. The plant was harvested in different stages of its growth according to the use that was to be made of it. When still in flower it yielded green stalks, whose soft fibers were utilized in the manufacture of *byssos*, a Greek term for linen that was applied to the fine linen cloths of very high quality that clothed important persons and wrapped mummies. Yellowed

Linen cloth with design woven in loops of colored wool (bouclé technique). *Courtesy The Metropolitan Museum of Art, New York. Gift of Miss Helen Miller Gould, 1910.*

stalks furnished stronger fibers but made the weaving less fine. Very mature and tough stalks served for the making of cordage and matting.

The stalks were gathered by hand and bound together according to size to form bundles, which were then exposed to the sun. After they were dried, they were put through a process of dressing. The seeds were separated from the stalks by means of a wooden comb with long, fine teeth. To isolate the fibers, the bundles were untied and steeped (retted) in water for some ten days. The fibers were then pounded with a mallet and thereafter combed (carded) to separate the fibers and remove those that were too short or parts that were too tough. Damaged fibers could be used for making cheap clothes, wicks for lamps, or cordage. The fibers ready for spinning were made up into bundles or balls and kept in earthenware pots or in baskets. The distaff, a stick holding the quantity of fibers intended for spinning, seems only to have appeared in the Roman period.

Wool

Although many classical authors such as Herodotus, Pliny, Apuleius, and Plutarch report that the Egyptians felt an aversion for wool, because they considered it unclean, it is probable that it was employed in very ancient times. In any event, samples of wool have been discovered from as early as the predynastic period, and the walls of tombs present again and again pictures of flocks of sheep, whose fleeces were undoubtedly not disdained. In the Roman and Christian period, however, wool was widely appreciated. Egypt has not yielded any information on the preparation of wool, but it is easy to describe the operations in the light of what took place in other countries. Shearing was accomplished either by pulling the wool off the sheep with a comb or with a metal tool in the form of scissors. The wool was washed and beaten with clubs to remove the impurities. This process at the same time separated the fibers and allowed the wool to be carded more easily.

Silk

The use of silk probably spread in the Roman world at the period when Rome conquered Syria and a part of western Asia. The Greeks knew of the existence of the silkworm, which eats mulberry leaves and spins itself a cocoon, in which it metamorphoses into a moth. They also knew of the simple process of immersing the cocoons in hot water and unwinding their long silk thread and then joining several together and winding them on a spool (Forbes, 1956, Vol. 4, pp. 50–58). But Greek production of silk was never so significant as the importing of silk thread and fabric from the Far East. For a long time the silk trade was the monopoly of Sassanid Persia, which imported silk from China and sold it in the Roman Empire in the form of thread or fabric at exorbitant prices. That is why many people resorted to smuggling in order to obtain the precious thread at a lower price. For its part, China jealously guarded the secret of the manufacture of silk. According to a legend, perhaps partly true, a Chinese princess at the beginning of the fifth century smuggled into Chotan some silkworm eggs and some mulberry seeds hidden in her headdress. In 557 two monks brought silkworm eggs to Constantinople, thus beginning a celebrated and flourishing industry. It was, no doubt, Byzantine military officers and high officials who introduced silk into Egypt. From the fifth century, there was an imperial *gynaikeion* (factory) at Alexandria that wove silk for the court of Byzantium. Other large cities with a Greek population, such as Akhmīm or Antinoopolis, may have had workshops weaving silk. Nevertheless, it is very probable that numerous items must have been imported that were already woven.

It would even seem that people in Alexandria developed the practice of importing silk fabric in order to unravel the threads to use them in making new articles to fit the taste of the day. This was certainly a long process that called for great dexterity.

However that may be, the tombs of this period have yielded a quantity of silks with typically Sassanid decorations—horsemen placed face-to-face, animals enclosed in geometrical tracery, the tree of life, palmettes, and hearts. Embroideries in silk on linen, presenting scenes from the New Testament, such as a Nativity in the Louvre Museum, Paris, or an Annunciation and the holy women at the tomb, in the Victoria and Albert Museum, London, witness to a clearly Byzantine influence. At Akhmīm there have been discovered *clavi* (vertical, ornamental bands) woven in silk and appliquéd down the front of linen or wool tunics, no doubt of local production. It appears, further, that the iconography of the silk fabrics strongly influenced the weavers in linen and wool, for we frequently find compositions or themes drawn from the Sassanid repertoire. In addition, this fashion for Persian mo-

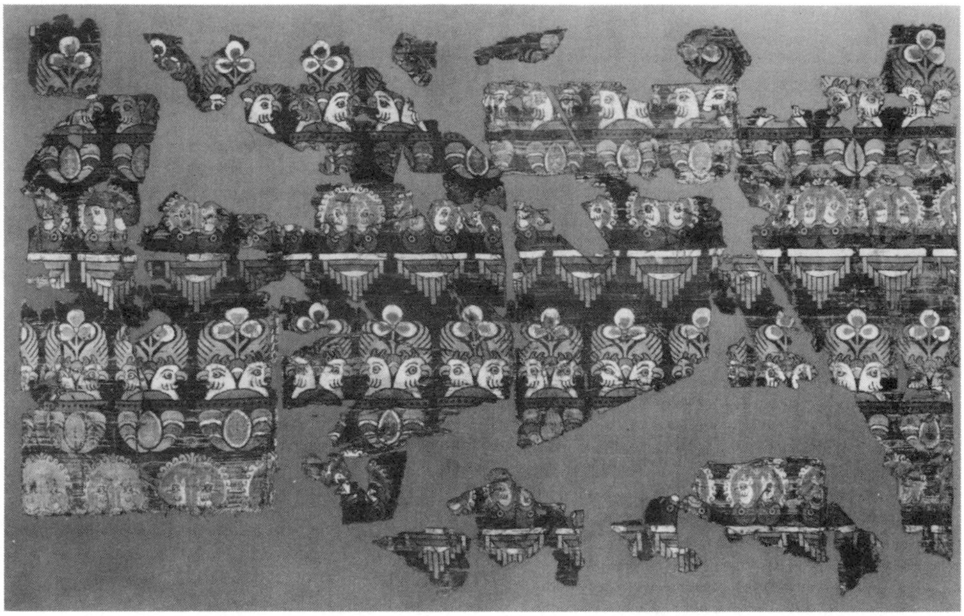

Silk. Fragment. *Courtesy Louvre Museum, Paris.*

tifs was no doubt in part stimulated by the Persian occupation of Egypt from 615 to 618.

Cotton

Cotton is the down adhering to the seeds enclosed in the pods of the cotton plant, and its production requires shelling, beating, and carding.

Native to India, Abyssinia, and Senegal, cotton was known in Egypt from the Greek period on. Herodotus mentions a "cuirass" of Amasis of the twenty-sixth dynasty, the decoration of which was made in part from "wool from a tree." Pliny reports that Egyptian priests wore cotton garments. The oldest known cotton goods, dated at the beginning of the first century A.D., were found at Meroë in the Sudan and at Karanog in Nubia. It was perhaps from there that cotton fabrics were exported to Egypt, although no trace of them now remains. We must, in fact, await the Arab conquest in the seventh century for the actual cultivation of cotton to be introduced into the country. Nevertheless, if the Arabs preferred cotton, the Copts continued the traditional manufacture of fabrics in linen and wool. It is possible, however, that they employed cotton for some as yet undetermined purposes.

BIBLIOGRAPHY

Forbes, R. J. *Studies in Ancient Technology.* Leiden, 1956.

MARIE-HÉLÈNE RUTSCHOWSCAYA

Manufacturing Techniques

Textile manufacture consists of a number of techniques—spinning, dyeing, and weaving. These may be quite simple or of considerable sophistication.

Spinning

Spinning is the general term for three operations by which the fibers are joined together to form a thread—drawing, twisting, and winding. Linen, wool, and cotton must of necessity be spun, but silk, already in long threads, can be woven without spinning.

Spinning Without Implements. Fibers can be spun without implements by rolling the fibers between the fingers, between the palms, or more commonly between palm and thigh to leave one hand free for drawing out the threads before twisting them.

Spinning with Implements. For spinning with implements, a mass of fibers is attached to a spindle, a tapered wooden stick that is notched or hooked at one end and weighted by a whorl (disk) of wood, stone, bronze, or ivory at the other. The weaver can allow the spindle to hang free at the end of the fibers, turning of its own weight, or she can hold it in one hand, rolling it on her thigh. As the spindle turns it draws out the fibers with a torsion that makes a thread, or yarn. When the thread becomes inconveniently long, it is wound on

Embroidery in silk on linen. *Courtesy Louvre Museum, Paris.*

the spindle's notch or hook. The most skilled spinners handle several spindles at one time. Even today in the Egyptian countryside women can be seen spinning on their doorsteps while carrying on a conversation. It is not known when the spindle first appeared. Although most shafts have vanished, a quantity of whorls dating from 5000 B.C. have been discovered in countries on the shores of the Mediterranean.

There has been much discussion of the direction of the torsion of the fibers, Z or S; that is, to the right or to the left. R. Pfister had established that the Z torsion was peculiar to India and the Middle East, while the S torsion was characteristic of Egypt. It has subsequently been ascertained that these two ways of spinning were common to both geographical areas. In fact, it seems rather that the direction is to be attributed not to geography but to the natural torsion of the fiber when it is steeped or simply to the technique peculiar to each spinner.

Dyeing

Dyeing took place at different stages of manufacture depending on the fiber. Linen was dyed after it was spun, wool before. Finished clothes were rarely dyed, although white garments were bleached as a final operation.

Three documents, containing recipes for dyeing wool, provide valuable information on the coloring materials and the techniques of dyeing used in the ancient world: a papyrus preserved in the National Museum of Antiquities, Leiden; another at the Royal Academy of Letters, History, and Antiquities, in Stockholm, dated at the end of the third or beginning of the fourth century; and a collection attributed to Bolos Democritos of Mendes, who lived at Alexandria toward 200 B.C., the oldest copy of which, dated from the end of the tenth century, is in the National Marcan Library, Venice (MS 299).

To this information may be added the fruits of archaeological research and chemical analysis. At Athribis (Atrīb) in the Delta, for example, a dyer's establishment has been discovered, one room of which was occupied by nineteen pits still covered with traces of dyes. The analyses of Coptic textiles in the Louvre deriving from Antinoopolis, made in the 1930s by R. Pfister, have made it possible to determine the nature of a number of dyes, and his results in large measure confirm the ancient writings.

Coptic textiles in general consist of a weft of wool on a warp of linen. Since linen is difficult to dye, it remained untreated. Only the wool was dyed.

The actual operation of dyeing was preceded by two stages essential for the dye to take proper hold of the thread.

The first was washing to remove the fatty substances naturally contained in the wool. Dyers used a detergent (soda, potassium, asphodel or some other alkaline plant, soapwort, or urine fermented to release ammonia).

The second stage was mordanting, or treating with an appropriate salt or caustic, in order that the dye might adhere to the fibers. The caustic most often used was an aluminum salt, alum, employed with an acid auxiliary. But salts of iron, such as acetate or sulphate, were also used.

The final stage consisted of plunging the skeins of thread or fibers into the dyeing vats.

The coloring materials, of vegetable or animal

origin, offer an extremely rich chromatic palette. The most resistant reds were obtained from madder, the root of *Rubia tinctorum.* In weaker proportion it yielded rose. Archil, a lichen originating from the eastern Mediterranean, was also used for a range of red to violet. Although little employed in Egypt because of their high price, the eggs of the female Kermes, an insect of Oriental origin, afforded scarlet dyes, brilliant and very stable, used for dyeing precious garments. Cochineal, an insect related to the Kermes and imported from Armenia, produced red. Another source was lac, a sort of resin secreted by the lac insect and harvested from trees. The insect was imported from India into Egypt when relations with Armenia, Byzantium, and the north were interrupted by the Arab invasions in the middle of the seventh century. Because of this fact, it is important for the dating of Coptic textiles.

Blue came from woad (*Isatis tinctoria*), which was cultivated in the Fayyūm in the Christian period. The majority of blues, however, were obtained by macerating the leaves of the indigo plant: *Indigofera tinctoria,* imported from India, and *Indigofera argentea,* which grows wild in Nubia, at Kordofan, at Sennar, and in Abyssinia. Purples, ranging from lilac to violet-blue and from blue-black to black, were achieved by the use of indigo over a base color of madder, or conversely, in varying proportions. In the same way, yellows, which were obtained from Persian berries (from a *Rhamnus* plant), were transmuted on an indigo base into various shades of green.

The famous true purple deriving from the Murex, a shellfish of the eastern Mediterranean, was perhaps employed by the Egyptians. Nevertheless, Pfister found no trace of it at the time of his analyses, no doubt owing to the fact that this extremely costly coloring would have considerably increased the price of Egyptian fabrics (Pfister, 1935, pp. 16, 28, 31, 36, 41).

By playing on variations in the proportions of the dyestuffs or by utilizing one caustic or another it was possible to obtain all these colors, of manifold shades and sumptuous hues, which are characteristic of Coptic textiles.

Looms

A loom is an apparatus for holding a set of parallel threads, the warp, through which other threads, the weft, are interlaced at right angles. The origin of weaving on a loom in Egypt is extremely old. Specimens of textiles and woven basket work from Neolithic times have been found at the same time and on the same sites, such as al-ʿImārah and al-Badārī. A dish from al-Badārī in red earthenware with a white pattern shows skeins hanging from a thread, waiting to be used on the loom represented lower down.

The warp is prepared by stretching the threads either on pegs fixed to the walls or on posts driven into the ground. These bundles of thread can then be attached to the loom.

Horizontal Loom. The horizontal (low-warp) loom is the oldest known in Egypt. It was used exclusively until the end of the Middle Empire and sporadically thereafter. It reappeared in the Roman period, with many improvements added. The warp was stretched between two beams, fixed to four pegs on the ground. The threads of the warp were divided into two layers formed by the odd threads being attached to one stick or bar (the heddle rod) by small loops and the even threads being attached to another stick (the shed rod). When the heddle rod was raised, a space (shed) was made between the two layers of warp through which the weft thread, often attached to a shuttle, was passed. Before the weft was returned, the shed rod was raised to create another shed, thus locking the weft in place. While the shed was changing the weft was beaten in, or beaten up, against the previous weft with the help of a wooden comb. The separation of the layers of warp threads (shedding) could be regulated by means of wooden pins.

Vertical Loom. The vertical (high warp) loom was used during the New Empire. It was probably introduced by the Hyksos invaders from the east at the end of the Middle Empire, which is why it is thought to have been invented in Syria or Palestine. It offered the same characteristics as the horizontal loom, but the parts were placed vertically, which made it more manageable for the weaver, who did not need help in order to operate the heddle and shed rods. It practically displaced the horizontal loom and was used until the present time.

Warp-Weighted Loom. The warp-weighted loom was a vertical loom in which the warp was kept taut, thanks to a series of weights made of stone or hardened clay. Weights that must have belonged to this kind of loom have been discovered in Egypt since the time of the New Empire. It is to be noted that a modern loom with weights, adapted as a horizontal loom, was still in use recently in the village of Maḥarraqah in Middle Egypt.

Treadle Loom. The treadle loom was a horizontal loom, in which the layers of warp threads, hanging through a harness, were moved by pedals (treadles). Each time a pedal was pressed, a layer of warp threads was moved up or down, opening a shed for the shuttle to pass. Spanning arms regulated the spacing and tension of the threads, while a more efficient batten (instead of a comb) allowed the threads to be beaten up each time the shuttle passed. Such looms permitted the use of more layers of warp and thus more intricate patterns.

It was perhaps this kind of loom that occupied the eight loompits found at Dayr Epiphanius in Thebes in the sixth century. We do not know whether such techniques existed in pharaonic times. In any case, this system seems to have been adopted in Alexandria about the first century.

Drawloom. The drawloom was a horizontal loom which had in addition to treadles a second method of raising the layers of warp threads, operated by means of a system of cords hanging at one side of the frame and forming the "simple" or "draw." Helpers (drawboys) were responsible for pulling the cords, which were previously selected. The cords to be operated at the same time were bound together by a fine cord to form a large loop. The loop so formed was attached to another cord that itself was looped round a vertical cord. The background of the fabric depended on the action of the drawboy, while the weaver seated at the loom made the pattern using treadles. The pattern was virtually in existence when the set of the loops was completed.

It was on this type of loom that the figured materials that required the use of many layers of warp threads were made. This technique was probably invented in China for the manufacture of the richly patterned silks for which the Chinese were famous. Alexandria seems to have been the first great textile center in the West to have used the drawloom. In fact, classical writers mention the "figured Alexandrian materials" that were particularly appreciated in Rome: "But weaving with a very great number of warp threads, what is called damask, was undertaken by Alexandria" (Pliny, *Natural History* 8. 74. 2). On these looms one could weave either a continuous pattern or repeated motifs over the whole surface of the fabric. Damasks have no "wrong side"; that is, the colors of background and pattern are interchangeable. A series of fabrics in linen and wool, with a complex geometrical, plant, or figured pattern, found at Antinoopolis, seem to witness to the use of the drawloom, no doubt at Antinoopolis itself.

Tablet loom. A tablet loom used from ten to a hundred square tablets, or plaques, of bone, wood, leather or cardboard, pierced with holes. The holes might be in the four corners of the tablet or more numerous. The warp threads (of dyed wool) passed through the holes and were gathered and tied together at each end. Each time the tablets were twisted, to create a shed, a weft thread (of natural linen) was passed through, holding the twisted warp threads in position. The weft thread would thus be entirely covered by the twisted warps, which made the pattern. This loom, slow but simple to use, permitted the making of decorative braids, which could be sewn on to the edges of garments.

The oldest known example of braiding is a geometrically patterned border found in Thebes dating from the time of Hatshepsut in the Eighteenth Dynasty. A sizeable number of braided strips and a number of tablets used in such braiding have been discovered at Coptic sites. A. Gayet wrote of an embroidery kit he discovered in Antinoopolis at the end of the nineteenth century: "This kit includes . . . a complete set of square tablets in sycamore wood, pierced by a hold at each of four corners, the purpose of which is hard to specify at

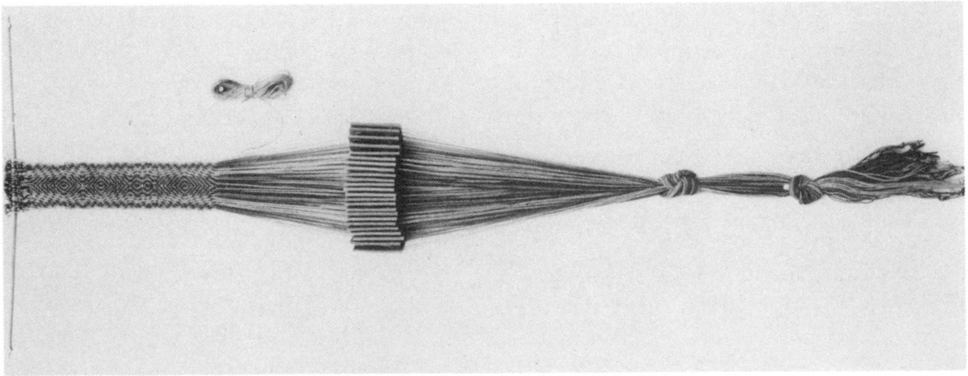

Example of tablet weaving. Modern mounting. *Courtesy Louvre Museum, Paris.*

present" (Gayet, 1900, p. 6). The Royal Museums of Art and History, Brussels, have twenty-five tablets of the embroidress Euphemiaan from a tomb excavated by Gayet in Antinoopolis. The Louvre has seventeen tablets probably found in Antinoopolis.

Weaving Techniques

A vast number of Coptic fabrics have come to light, and a mass of documentation has been discovered. These sources make possible a precise study of the weaving processes used in the manufacture and decoration of Coptic textiles. Coptic weavers used a variety of techniques.

Plain weaving. Plain, or tabby, weaving is the simple weave described above in which the weft passes over and under alternate warps the full width of the piece of fabric. It was used for linen, wool, and cotton and could produce cloth varying from very fine to coarse.

Tapestry Weaving. Tapestry weaving is a kind of plain weaving on a high-warp or low-warp loom in which many colored wefts, usually wool, are interlaced with undyed warps (wool, linen, or silk) according to the requirements of the design to produce a fairly heavy fabric. Most tapestry was executed in *louisine*, a taffeta weave (a variety of plain weave) in which fine warp threads and heavier weft threads present a corded or ribbed effect. The technique made it possible to produce motifs or whole scenes in monochrome or multicolor.

Fine detail and an illusion of three-dimensionality could be achieved by means of the flying shuttle, which laid additional threads over the basic tapestry-woven motif.

Tapestry could be used for decorative panels to be appliquéd on a plain woven fabric, or canvas, or for a whole fabric. When the first Coptic fabrics came to light, their relationship to the technique of French Gobelin tapestries led to their being called Coptic Gobelins.

Tablet Weaving. In tablet weaving, as described above, colored warp threads passed through pierced tablets are twisted and then held in place with a natural weft thread to produce strips of braid, ribbon, or belting. A famous example of this technique is the girdle of Ramses II, from the New Empire (length: 5.7 yards [5.20 m]; width: 4.9 inches [12.7 cm] to 1.9 inches [4.8 cm]) preserved in the Merseyside County Museum, Liverpool.

Bouclé Weaving. In bouclé (looped-pile) weaving, the weft thread passes at regular intervals around little rods to form loops. Once these loops have been stabilized by the gathering together of the weft threads, it is possible to withdraw the little rods and start the operation over again. The result is a heavy, shaggy fabric such as a ninth-century example showing the Triumph of the Cross, in the Louvre, and a fourth-century example showing cupids in a boat, in the British Museum, London.

This type of rough-textured fabric could be of Mesopotamian origin and suggests the *kaunakēs*

Example of bouclé technique. Triumph of the Cross. Ninth century. *Courtesy Louvre Museum, Paris.*

cloth resembling fleece worn by Ebih-il the Steward, dating about 3000 B.C., now in the Louvre. According to E. Cherblanc (1937), the technique of bouclé fabrics was an Egyptian invention, which was later adapted in the East for the manufacture of carpets. Nevertheless, in Egypt the most ancient example dates from the Eleventh Dynasty and comes from Dayr al-Baḥrī.

Embroidery. Needle-embroidered fabrics are much rarer in Egypt. In the Brooklyn Museum, there are four fragments, of unknown origin, dating from the fifth to sixth centuries. One shows an angel front on, holding a goblet and a palm; the others have birds and a vase. These embroideries in flax and wool are executed with chain stitching. Examples preserved in the Victoria and Albert Museum, London, and the Louvre in silk on a linen canvas show a Christian iconography: the Last Supper, what appears to be the Adoration of the Magi, what appears to be the Adoration of the Shepherds, the appearance of Christ to Mary Magdalene, the Annunciation and Visitation, angels (Victoria and Albert Museum), and the Nativity (Louvre). The composition and style of these fabrics are clearly Byzantine (fifth to sixth centuries), and therefore they are not, properly speaking, Coptic art. Moreover, their restricted number in Egypt tends to confirm the foreign origin of this technique.

Sprang. Sprang, a word of Scandinavian origin, originally described any loose-textured fabric but now is specifically restricted to the technique of plaiting (braiding) tensioned threads. Fabric is made by crossing manually or with a needle the tensioned threads of a chain fixed at both extremities, each row being temporarily kept in position by a rod. This technique, which is similar to that for lace making, can be recognized in a significant batch of bags and hair nets found in Egypt.

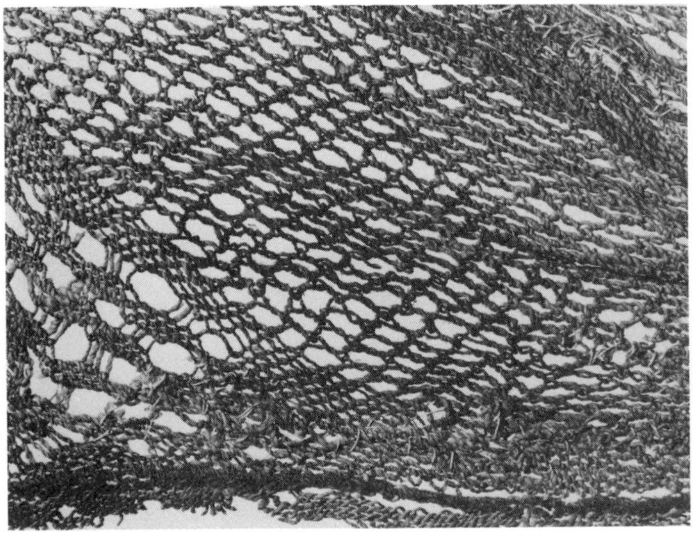

Example of sprang. Detail. *Courtesy Louvre Museum, Paris.*

BIBLIOGRAPHY

Burnham, H. B. "Bolton 'Quilts' or 'Caddows.'" *Bulletin de liaison du CIETA* (Lyons) 41–42 (1975):22–29.

Cherblanc, E. *Le Kaunakes.* Paris, 1937.

Du Bourguet, P. *Catalogue des étoffes coptes,* Vol. 1. Paris, 1964.

Forbes, R. J. *Studies in Ancient Technology,* Vol. 4. Leiden, 1956.

Gayet, A. *Notice relative aux objets recueillis à Antinoé pendant les fouilles exécutés en 1899–1900.* Paris, 1900.

Kendrick, A. F. *Catalogue of Textiles from Burying-Grounds in Egypt.* London, 1922.

Pfister, R. "Teinture et alchimie dans l'orient hellénistique." In *Seminarium Rondakovianum,* Vol. 7. Prague, 1935.

Staudigel, O. "Tablet-Weaving and the Technique of the Rameses-Girdle." *Bulletin de liaison du CIETA* (Lyons) 41–42 (1975):71–100.

MARIE-HÉLÈNE RUTSCHOWSCAYA

Organization of Production

The study of the organization of Coptic textile production is based on Greek and Coptic documents, public and private, written on papyri or ostraca. Literary texts contain some useful pieces of information but are decidedly less helpful than the documents. The remains of ancient fabrics, which are of basic importance in other respects, cannot tell us much about the organization of production.

Stages of Production

Textiles in Coptic Egypt, as in earlier periods, were made at home by women and their servants mainly for household needs and in shops by professional craftsmen working for the market. Either way, there were several stages of production, which were more or less specialized.

First came the treating of the raw linen or wool, the dyeing, and the spinning of the thread. Treating of fibers and spinning were generally carried on by women at home, along with their other chores. Sometimes highly specialized workmen took part in this stage of production, but it was rather rare and concerned only linen. Silk thread was imported during the Byzantine epoch and not produced until the introduction of sericulture in the Arab period. Cotton was rare. It was unusual to have wool or linen dyed at home, even for home-woven fabrics. Dyeing was usually done by specialists who had properly equipped workshops, dyes purchased from merchants, and a good knowledge of techniques.

Second came the actual weaving process. The weaver produced fabric in the size of the clothes or other articles to be made from it.

Third was finishing. Various processes such as fulling (working wool to give it a tight, smooth texture), bleaching (lightening), shearing, and embroidering were used depending on the raw material and type of fabric. These tasks were carried out by professionals.

Finally, garments, hangings, cushions, or other articles were sewn. Sometimes sewing was entrusted to tailors, but usually that was not necessary.

Craftsmen

The proportional shares of domestic and commercial manufacture cannot be defined. Home production is rarely described in the sources and therefore is insufficiently known, although it certainly played a significant role in production. It may be presumed that fine-quality, decorative fabrics—luxury goods—such as those now in museums were made by professionals in specialized crafts, although home production cannot be excluded.

The majority of people professionally manufacturing fabrics were the craftsmen working on their own and at their own risk. They owned their tools and had easy contact with their customers. Usually all members of the family were engaged in the work. Of great help were the apprentices, whose wages most probably increased with their years of service. There is evidence of this practice in earlier periods, and there is no reason to suppose the custom was changed. Hired workers were employed very rarely, for only an exceptionally difficult situation (most frequently debts) could force an adult specialist to give up his independence. This did not apply to fulling and dyeing, which required appropriately equipped workshops and qualified craftsmen. Most individuals did not have the qualifications or equipment to work on their own. Slaves were rarely engaged in workshops in the Roman period and only sporadically in the Coptic period.

Thus, the Coptic production structure, inherited from the past, was maintained despite significant economic and social changes. In the Coptic period there were a certain number of craftsmen dependent on great landowners, but it was a rare phenomenon. The Egyptian elite purchased textiles from craftsmen, just like other inhabitants. There is no information about the existence of the imperial weaving workshops, either in rural areas or in Alexandria. There is a lack of evidence on the activities of larger workshops employing many specialists. The church did not play any significant role in the production of textiles. In some monasteries and hermitages weaving was common but on a limited scale.

In all the specialized crafts, their practice was hereditary. This was not the result of the state's intervention but rather the effect of the general character of economic life, such as little territorial and social mobility, the convenience of inheriting tools and customers from one's father, and the ease in acquiring the necessary professional training. Skills were either passed by father to son or were acquired during apprenticeships lasting two to three years but sometimes even eight years. During the Coptic times the custom of sending one's son away for several years to another specialist in the same branch of production was probably common. A man's professional capabilities were thus expanded by the experience gained in another family. It seems that a craftsman having once acquired his profession could not abandon it. Nothing indicates that the state would in any way determine the number of specialists in a given branch in a given locality, but such a possibility cannot be excluded.

Craftsmen belonging to the same specialization and living in the same area would establish a guild. There was no compulsion to join, but in practice everybody joined. Guilds were established not only in cities but also in villages, where they constituted a significant proof of the development of a given specialization. Such corporations of craftsmen in Byzantine times did not resemble medieval guilds in Europe. They were not engaged in regulating the size of production, prices, or access to the profession. They were, above all, associations assembling craftsmen to face the state. They were engaged in paying taxes and fulfilling the orders and other services imposed on them by the authorities. They also organized social and religious life; their members could expect their comrades' help in difficult situations.

Such craftsmen must have belonged chiefly to the Coptic-speaking population of Egypt. Greeks, no doubt numerous in Alexandria, could have also inhabited the towns in the rural areas. There was probably no difference between the living standards and methods of work between the Greeks and the Copts. Although the country's elite was mainly Greek in Byzantine times, the division into Greeks and Copts did not coincide with the division into rich and poor. One wonders if the fabrics made by Greek weavers differ from those manufactured by Copts, or if they bore any signs of ties with the Hellenistic tradition. The answer to the question, always hypothetical because of the lack of reliable sources, depends on the evaluation of both the character and function of Coptic art in times when the Greeks were still living in Egypt. Such differences probably did not exist. One has to remember that the form of fabrics depended also, and maybe above all, on the customers' taste.

Customers

According to the papyri, most textiles were made to order for a particular customer, who specified the size, color, and ornamentation of the item. One may presume that cartoons (drawings) of ornaments were in use as samples. Their use is taken for granted by all researchers, although not even one such sample has been preserved, and written sources are silent on the subject. Attempts to find this information in papyrus collections have not brought any results so far. Frequently the customer brought his own thread to the weaver. Most probably the system of placing orders pertained mainly to the more costly, luxurious fabrics, for a craftsman could not waste manufacturing time and consume expensive materials for items he was not sure of selling. With his small stock of material resources, many unsold goods meant catastrophe.

That contacts between craftsman and customer were common is also indicated by scanty mention of garment merchants, whereas information about yarn merchants is more frequent. The fact that spinners worked at home instead of in a few large workshops meant that weavers in larger cities could not have had direct contact with them. Because weavers sold their products on their own, merchants could act only as intermediaries in transactions with distant customers, namely the inhabitants of larger cities or even other countries. Export of Egyptian fabrics, quite considerable during the Roman period, largely diminished later due to general impoverishment and the difficulties of navigating the Mediterranean.

The Roman state became an important customer; it required above all garments for the army. (It is not known if these garments were only for detachments stationed in Egypt.) The state owned textile workshops and it required some craftsmen, in the shops or at home, to fill orders according to the quantity of textiles planned by state authorities. They were provided with raw materials obtained partly from taxes in kind, collected from private craftsmen, and partly by purchase with money taxes from the general population. Such tax money also paid for their labor. In principle, craftsmen were not more burdened than other taxpayers, but in practice they were paid little and payment was delayed. Some of the in-kind taxes were in the form of fine-quality linen goods, which were probably offered as presents to favored individuals and institutions, such as the church, or were sold.

Centers of Textile Production

Those people who are under the impression that a great number of fabrics originated mainly from two ancient centers, Panopolis (Akhmīm) and Antinoopolis, will be surprised by the statement, well documented in written sources, mainly papyri, that various branches of the textile craft existed in all localities known today. These include not only capitals of nomes (metropolises) but also villages. Most probably the production of luxury fabrics was concentrated in cities, where richer, more sophisticated customers lived, and where craftsmen could specialize more narrowly and thus produce fabrics that were technically and artistically superior. But there is no sure evidence that the village craftsmen did not also participate in luxury production.

Although direct evidence is largely lacking, the great city of Alexandria may be presumed to be among the outstanding cities in textile production (M. A. Marzoul, 1948–1949, pp. 111–35).

The necropolises of Panopolis and Antinoopolis have supplied a considerable part of the fabrics that are conserved in museums.

In the first century A.D., Panopolis had the reputation of being an old production center of linen fabrics (Strabo *The Geography* 4. 913). Papyri, mainly the text published by Z. Borkowski in 1975, confirm considerable concentration of various specialists there in the fourth century. In the Byzantine era it was a medium-sized city, in which the Greek elite developed a rich and intensive cultural life. At the same time, it happened to be one of the more important centers of Coptic culture.

Antinoopolis was established in 130 A.D. as a Greek *polis* (city) and became a provincial capital, but during Byzantine times, its Greek character was blurred due to the influx of Coptic population—there the weavers were surely Copts—and the consolidation of the Coptic elite. In general, historians of art tend to overestimate its size and the importance of its ties with Greek culture, but it did not differ from other cities of administrative rank, such as Arsinoë in the Fayyūm. Written sources do not confirm that Antinoopolis played a more significant role than other cities in the production of textiles. The richness of textiles found in its necropolises reflects the wealth of its inhabitants, and if there are significant stylistic differences between fabrics found there and those from Panopolis, a subject of discussion, then one should not consider them a reflection of cultural differences between the two cities.

Terminology

The complexity and degree of specialization of Coptic textile production may be indicated by the special terms found in the sources, some of which are borrowed from Latin.

Weaving Proper

γέρδιος (gérdios), general term signifying the weaver (*ὑφάντης* [hyphantēs] is very rare)

λινούφος (linoúphos), linen fabrics weaver, a term that declined in favor of *στιππουργός* (stippourgós) (*στίππιον, σίππιον*, which previously meant tow, in the Byzantine era became a synonym for *λίνον*)

λανάριος, λαναπουργός (lanários, lanapourgós), specialist in wool fabrics

βαρβαρικάριος (barbarikários), manufacturer of brocade

βρακάριος (brakários), manufacturer of trousers

ταρσικάριος (tarsikários), manufacturer of fabrics that were a specialty of Tarsus

καυνακοποιός, καυνακοπλόκος (kaunakopoiós, kaunakoplókos), manufacturer of fabrics with projecting long locks and thread tufts

οὐηλάριος (ouēlários), manufacturer of gauzes, such as for curtains

ταπητάριος, ταπῆτας (tapētários, tapētas), manufacturer of rugs

τριμιτάριος (trimitários), manufacturer of fabrics with a three-thread warp

τυλοπλόκος, τυλοφάντης (tyloplókos, tylophántēs), manufacturer of pillows.

Other Aspects of Textile Production.

βαφεύς, κογχιστής (bapheús, konkhistēs), dyer

γναφεύς (gnapheūs), fuller

ἐριοκάρτης (eriokártēs), person who sheared off the surface of material

ἡπητής, ῥάπτης (ēpētēs, rháptēs), tailor

λινοπλυγτής (linoplygtēs), specialist in treating raw linen

ποικιλτής, πλουμάριος (poikiltēs, ploumários), embroiderer

ⲥⲁϩⲧ (saht), ⲥⲁϣⲧ (sasht), weave

ϣϯⲧ (shtit) and ⲩⲡⲁⲛⲧⲏⲥ (ypantēs), weaver

BIBLIOGRAPHY

T. Reil's older book, *Beiträge zur Kenntnis des Gewerbes im hellenistischen Aegypten*, Borna-Leipzig, 1913, is not sufficient today because of the influx of new sources. It is replaced by works of F. Dunand, "L'Artisanat du textile dans l'Egypte Lagide," *Ktema* 4, 1979; E. Wipszycka, *L'Industrie textile dans l'Egypte Romaine*, Wroclaw, 1965; I. F. Fikhman, "Egipiet na rubieze dwuch epoch," *Remieslenniki i riemieslennyj trud w IV-seriedinie VII*, Moscow, 1965. The basic theses of Fikhman's book were presented in an article by the same author, "Grundfragen der handwerklichen Produktion in Ägypten," *Jahrbuch für Wirtschaftsgeschichte* 4, 1969. Cf. also E. Wipszycka's extensive review of that book in *Journal of Juristic Papyrology* 16–17 (1971). Further sources include Z. Borkowski, *Une Description topographique des immeubles à Panapolis*, Warsaw, 1975; and M. A. Marzoul, "Alexandria as a Textile Centre," *Bulletin de la société d'archéologie copte* 13 (1948–1949):111–35.

EWA WIPSZYCKA

Iconography of Woven Textiles

Coptic textiles are rich in iconography, but that richness is less the result of the number of themes presented than of the variety of detail, brilliant color, and iridescent effect. Most decorated textiles were produced by the tapestry weaving of brightly dyed wools, although tablet weaving and bouclé weaving were also used. The survey of subjects offered here does not claim to be exhaustive.

Like all complicated movements spread over a period of time, this iconography evolved in different ways during the approximately ten centuries (third to twelfth) that it lasted. Some subjects have the advantage of being depicted many times; others make only an occasional if not a single appearance. Among those subjects present at the beginning, some, prominent for a period, later disappeared, while new subjects came forward. But others, among the oldest, were used throughout the period.

All those that lasted, whether a short or long time, were altered in either external appearance or meaning. This survey will follow a chronological development.

The subjects of this iconography varied according to the kind of article they adorned. Scenes depicting people commonly appeared on the hangings or panels for walls and the *orbicula* (roundels) and square panels that decorated tunics and shawls.

Busts are shown in small panels along with some animal or bird; at the end of the last period some even appeared on tunic cuffs between two decorative motifs. Ornamental themes generally appeared on neck openings, plastrons (biblike trimmings), *clavi* (vertical bands), tunic or coat cuffs, cushion covers, and shawls.

Proto-Coptic Period (Third through Mid-Fifth Centuries)

In the Hellenistic and early Roman periods, the Egyptians substituted the forms of Greek and Roman gods for those of their own pharaonic gods. There is no trace of the pharaonic heritage other than the evocation of the Nile god, seen from an Alexandrian and Roman angle. Christian themes were virtually nonexistent. Greco-Roman and decorative themes were predominant, especially as developed in the Greek city of Alexandria. To this preliminary period belong Dionysiac characters such as Dionysus himself in the State Museum, Berlin (Staatliche Museen, Berlin) and the Abegg Foundation, Riggisberg; the bust of the goddess Gaea, in

Bust of Dionysus in a square with a border of heart-shaped leaves. Tapestry. Fifth century. Length: 26 cm; width: 23 cm. *Courtesy Louvre Museum, Paris.*

the State Hermitage Museum, Leningrad; the Nile god, in the State Pushkin Museum of Fine Arts, Moscow; and the fish and other important fragments originally from ANTINOOPOLIS that are now in the Guimet Museum, Paris, and the Louvre.

The Proto-Coptic period picks up some of the characters in its own more stylized way, as well as many others of very varied appearance. They include the Parthian horseman, the centaur, the Three Graces, Victory, Eros the archer, Nereids riding a sea creature, the four seasons, and even the Mesopotamian hero Gilgamesh. One of the most important is Dionysus. He is found either face-to-face with Ariadne, each as a bust on a separate panel as in the fifth-century group in the Louvre, or in bacchic scenes with whirling dancing girls, some holding castanets. Square panels are occupied by mythological scenes with several characters. Scenes of farm work enliven a series of *orbicula* belonging to the Brooklyn Museum. The country scenes in which the shepherd predominates are found on *clavi* and wide ornamental bands found in the Louvre.

Shawl decorated with leafy vine-branches. Linen and tapestry. Fourth century. Length: 1.20 m; width: .70 m. *Courtesy Louvre Museum, Paris.*

Polychrome woven in embroidery with figure of musician, horsemen, and group of dancers in animated postures. Fourth century. *Courtesy Coptic Museum, Cairo.*

The putti (cupids), deriving from the Roman art of Pompeii, are represented in different activities, such as a small group of steersmen on bouclé material in the British Museum. They are more often used for decorative purposes, as in an important fragment of a fourth-century hanging in the Louvre, where they are grouped like grape pickers or musicians in scroll patterns.

Certain animals and plants are associated with mythological characters: we find a dog and a panther with the huntsman; a clump of grass in the country where the Parthian horseman rides; a fish in the water cleft by a boatload of putti or crossed by a Nereid on a sea creature; and a lamb or a ewe with the shepherd. However, animals and plants may be treated for their own sake. Examples on *clavi* include chasing of animals, evocative of a hunt (a dog after a lion, or a panther tracking down an antelope); multicolored vine branches or scrolls containing figures; interlaced alternating stems; intersecting squares; and panels with an open flower or a leaf in vertical position shown in full and generally in a reddish purple color that is extensively used in this period. Finally, entwined or alternating plant stems, as well as geometric motifs (meanders, interlacing swastikas, intersecting squares, broken lines in the Greek style) form the outer or inner border of the field that these subjects occupy.

For the most part, the characters conform to their Alexandrian models, as much in their attitudes as in the emblems appropriate to them. They are placed in their traditional relationships to one another. The Parthian horseman, with his body sideways and his head full-face, rides his rearing horse above a small desert animal (usually a hare) or a dog, and makes the gesture of blessing, except in those cases in which he is confused with the hunting horseman. The dancers—either in a group of a man and a woman, or singly, especially the dancing girls—are shown facing front. The gods are most often in the form of a bust, the head turned slightly three-quarters. Each appears with his or her special attributes: Dionysus is crowned with myrtles; the Three Graces are in their habitual grouping; a hovering Victory is shown with laurel wreath; and a Season is treated as chubby-headed.

Dionysus and an Isis-like personage. Tapestry. Antinoë (?). Seventh century. Length: 58 cm; width: 55 cm. *Courtesy Louvre Museum, Paris.*

Already in this period, the realistic or naturalistic aspect characteristic of Alexandrian style is rivaled by a simplification—sometimes partial, sometimes complete—of subject and composition, as well as of form. This new style replaces, more or less, the illusion of sculpture created by the hatching (fine criss-crossed lines) produced by the flying shuttle. It is satisfied with indicating outlines, whether in the features of the face, or in the contours of muscles or limbs. It separates surfaces by color or line, creating a two-dimensional effect. The subject becomes impersonal and tends to be decorative rather than realistic. Details such as clothes, furniture, plants, and animals increasingly fill the empty spaces.

Coptic Period (Mid-Fifth through Seventh Centuries)

The Coptic period is marked by a greater richness of both subject and detail, and consequently of variations on the same subject. Exploitation of the weaving technique flourishes. The reddish-purple color, while still used extensively, is now augmented by other colors.

It is strange that in this period when Christianity became more and more predominant in Egypt, so that it reached almost the whole population, Christian subjects are rare, to the point of being limited almost entirely to symbols (the Alpha and Omega, the *crux ansata* [ankh], the labarum [a Roman imperial standard], and the Byzantine cross), which are often lined up on one piece of cloth. There are very few examples of pieces with a Christian figurative subject. The explanation may be wear and tear, which usually ends in disappearance, or the fact that so many surviving Coptic materials, generally the garments serving as shrouds for the dead in Coptic cemeteries, have suffered damage. One beautiful hanging from the sixth to seventh centuries in the Cleveland Museum of Art represents Mary with the Child, enthroned between two angels and with a border of a series of apostles' heads. It is one of the rare examples of a genre that may have been rich in the most varied subjects. Some Christian hangings apparently decorated surviving pagan sanctuaries, for example the fifth-century Judgment of Paris in the Hermitage or those scattered with horsemen and plants in the Field Museum of Natural History, Chicago, and the Coptic Museum, Cairo. Seventh-century panels show Dionysus with a figure suggesting Isis in the Louvre and a Nereid in the Cleveland Museum of Art.

The clothes, or decorative elements originating from them (tunics and shawls and sometimes cushion covers), form the great mass of Coptic materials that have come down to us. The Greco-Roman mythological motifs that decorate them are a remnant from the preceding period, but the profusion and variety of detail are peculiar to this new stage. Nonetheless, there are fewer scenes with persons, while single characters of allegorical or symbolic importance predominate. The constant themes include the Parthian horseman, the huntsman, and the centaur (who tend to become confused); the seasons, with details of dress adapted to each one; the Three Graces; and especially the cycles of Aphrodite, Dionysus, and the Nile god. To be exact, the divinities themselves are seldom represented; characters from their trains—sea nymphs and tritons, dancing girls and putti—are multiplied. Characters are often changed from one category to another. Thus the Nereid may appear with arms uplifted, as if at prayer, or outstretched, shaking castanets or holding a piece of fruit or a bird; or extended above a Triton; or holding a sea creature by the tail. The putti provide the greatest variety of figures: winged or not, crouching, sitting, running, swimming, dancing; arms stretched out, holding cymbals, a plant, a piece of fruit, a goblet, a bird, a *pedum* (shepherd's crook), a stone, three balls, a vase; chasing an animal, swimming after a duck whose feet they are holding, or swimming and pushing a medallion bearing a head. The dancing girls and the busts offer a comely variety in the portraits. The female dancers are treated singly or are placed beside a male dancer; they are used so often that they count among the most common subjects.

The decorative themes—geometric, architectural, vegetal, and animal—are not any fewer. As in the preceding period, they may be used to decorate *clavi* and occasionally cushion covers, sometimes forming a border surrounding a field occupied by the figurative subject.

The predominance of pagan themes raises a question. The clothes found in Coptic tombs are for the

Ritual theme of the hunt (in this case, a lion hunt), with a border depicting lions and hares. Tapestry. Sixth century. Each side: 22 cm. *Courtesy Louvre Museum, Paris.*

Aphrodite Anadyomene in a Nilotic decor. Tapestry. Sixth century. Length: 27 cm; width: 26 cm. *Courtesy Louvre Museum, Paris.*

Dancers within a square framed by another square ornamented with a row of vases and stylized flowers. Sixth century. Each side: 42 cm. *Courtesy Louvre Museum, Paris.*

most part those of Christians. The Egyptians who used them as shrouds (i.e., the Copts) would undoubtedly have been sensitive to the anathemas of the fifth-century Bishop Asterius of Amaseia in Pontus against the ornamentation of the clothes of Christians with subjects borrowed from pagan mythology. We have to understand the turn of mind typical of the period. During Greco-Roman times, when gods of Greek, and then of Roman, origin were substituted for the Egyptian gods, the pagan Egyptians saw a new outward appearance for their native gods, Osiris and Isis-Hathor. The substitution was duly established in the seventh-century tapestry in the Louvre (cited above) that includes Dionysus and an Isiac character. There is every possibility that a similar substitution was made by the Christians in the persons composing the train of Dionysus and Aphrodite: putti, Nereids, and dancing girls. Proof seems to be offered in a fabric in the Louvre representing a Nereid whose nimbus (a frequent attribute of characters in pagan mythology) bears a cross. The sixth-century Shawl of Sabine in the Louvre, originating from Antinoopolis, provides an excellent example. Beside a square panel and an *orbiculum* with subjects from pagan mythology (Artemis the huntress and Bellerophon's victory over the Chimera, respectively), another square shows Daphne sinking into a tree to escape pursuit from Apollo, and holding out toward him, like a defensive weapon, a cruciform plant.

Therefore, the ornamental motifs, animal and vegetal, as well as those of the hunt, in their turn take on a new meaning, which could no longer be the evocation of the Elysian Fields and the "blessing" of the Parthian horseman to the Beyond, but rather of Paradise.

Coptic Period Under Islamic Rule (Eighth Through Twelfth Centuries)

As the times of the pharaohs withdrew still further into the past, a revival of their themes could not be anticipated. And so, on a fabric in the Louvre, the form of an ancient Egyptian eye (Udjat) near the stem and bulb of a plant shows simply the decorative adaptation of a subject met among ancient and abandoned monuments. It occurs only once.

Figurative Christian subjects are always a feature of hangings in churches or the homes of the pious.

Those that have survived date from the ninth century, a period of relative well-being for the Coptic community. The Triumph of the Cross, conserved in the Louvre, is outstanding. It is of bouclé material, with a glorious cross potent issuing from an ankh, flanked on the right by what seems to be Balaam's Prophecy and, on the left, by Jonah rising from the *kētos* (sea monster), which hangs directly above the Iranian tree of life in an Eden of plants and playing animals.

Some Christian subjects of the same period appear on other pieces, particularly on panels. One such panel in the Detroit Institute of Arts shows the bust of a holy person. Saint George and the dragon decorate a tunic in the Louvre. On a cuff in the Victoria and Albert Museum Christ is depicted in the center of a circle, flanked by the Annunciation and the Adoration of the Magi. In several examples, dispersed among different museums, we find the theme of Joseph sold by his brothers, in its various episodes, either as groups on imposing *orbicula,* no doubt from shawls, or singly on *clavi* or cuffs.

But the immense mass of ornamental pieces from garments continue to display the range of examples of Alexandrian origin. There one always finds elements taken from the cycles of Dionysus and Aphrodite, although in the course of these four centuries, their style became purely decorative at the expense of the figurative. The iconography remained Christianized, as much because of the episodic acceptance of Christian subjects as of the presence of small crosses on subjects of pagan origin. But there is no lack of persons—notably dancing girls—of plants, open flowers, fourfooted animals, and birds. Details of clothing reflect the new cultural influences. In the ninth and tenth centuries, a period of much contact with Constantinople, these influences resulted in reproductions of richly ornamented Byzantine vestments. In the tenth century, dancers wearing Oriental Islamic clothes appear on textiles.

It is noteworthy that during the ninth century, Coptic weavers, who had the monopoly of this craft, put heads with Alexandrian features on fabrics intended for Muslims. In the tenth century, on pieces made in the Fayyūm, they used characters and subjects of their own patterns.

If it is true that the word *qabāṭ* (the plural of "Copt") was applied to fabrics woven in a certain technique by Copts, then the iconography, with all its original characteristics, was Coptic. The influence of that iconography went beyond the Muslim world, even as far as India.

Bust of a woman surrounded by Nereids within a square. Tapestry. Sixth century. Antinoë (?). Length: 31 cm; width: 29 cm. *Courtesy Louvre Museum, Paris.*

BIBLIOGRAPHY

Beckwith, J. "Les Tissus coptes." *Les Cahiers Ciba* 7 (1959):2–27.

Bourguet, P. du. *Catalogue des étoffes coptes,* Vol. 1. Musée National du Louvre. Paris, 1964.

Kendrick, A. F. *Catalogue of Textiles from Burying Grounds in Egypt,* 3 vols. London, 1920–1922.

Wulff, O. K., and W. F. Volbach. *Spätantike und koptische Stoffe aus ägyptischen Grabfunden in dem Staatlichen Museum.* Berlin, 1926.

PIERRE DU BOURGUET, S.J.

Iconography of Resist-Dyed Textiles

Another technique of producing a motif in a textile, perhaps of Alexandrian origin, was resist-dyeing. Parts of the textile were treated to resist the subsequent dye so that they remained in their natural color. The images on all these resist-dyed textiles bear names and sometimes even inscriptions.

Pagan subjects are treated in a number of resist-dyed textiles: the Veil of Antinoë, which has Dionys-

Portrait of a woman in a frame of lozenges. Ninth century. Tapestry. Length: 21 cm; width: 19 cm. *Courtesy Louvre Museum, Paris.*

iac motifs, in the Louvre; the Tapestry of Artemis from al-Ashmūnayn at the Abegg Foundation; and a fragment of a hunting scene in the Hermitage Museum. A rather important group of tapestry fragments with Christian subjects belongs to the Victoria and Albert Museum. These fragments measure between 10 inches (25 cm) and 3 feet (1 m) on a height of about 12 inches (30 cm). A number of subjects are treated. In the Annunciation, Mary is seated in profile, busy with her spinning. In the Nativity, Mary is lying on a bed as was Semele in an Alexandrian fabric, which may have served as its prototype. The Child is lying in a manger, with an ox at one side. An Old Testament subject is the law being given to Moses at Sinai, in which Christ, in the bush, follows Moses with his gaze. In the same fragment, the woman with the issue of blood is being healed. It also treats the resurrection of Lazarus; he appears with his wrappings at the entrance of the tomb. Another theme is Christ in the Garden of Olives, though this identification is conjectural,

Dancer beneath a pediment between two zones, each depicting a group of two dancers. Tapestry. Twelfth century. Length: 24 cm; width: 10 cm. *Courtesy Louvre Museum, Paris.*

since it is based on the reading of Judas' name. Above a group of apostles appear the names of Thomas and Mark; the names cause this scene to be interpreted as the Communion of the Apostles.

Without creating an exhaustive list, we may add two very beautiful fragments of tapestry belonging

An elongated putto chasing a quadruped across three superposed levels; at the side: a cruciform motif in a square surmounted by a vase. Tapestry. Decoration for a "cuff." Tenth century. Length: 4 cm; width: 14 cm. *Courtesy Louvre Museum, Paris.*

Three personages (an imperial group?) in a disk. Tapestry. Tenth century. Length: 18 cm; width: 20 cm. *Courtesy Louvre Museum, Paris.*

Two dancers reduced to two busts at one end, and in the opposite direction, three superposed putti holding a duck. Tapestry. Wide shoulder-band. Eleventh century. Length: 16 cm; width: 10 cm. *Courtesy Louvre Museum, Paris.*

to the State Museum, Berlin. Both are remarkable for the richness of the garments and the decoration. One represents Daniel among the lions. The other shows Saint Peter bowing.

Finally, in the Cleveland Museum of Art, we find a fragment divided into registers, in which, starting from the top, are set the Adoration of the Magi and the Multiplication of the Loaves. In the lowest register Jonah appears under the castar-oil plant near the *kētos* (sea monster). He is followed by Moses, and each personage is isolated by two columns.

All appear to have originated in Egypt, although the genre is not Coptic. The form of the names and letters inscribed is exclusively Greek.

The examples described seem to belong to two different social classes in respect to the quality of the work and desired requirements. They should be attributed to a Greek or Byzantine milieu during the period of coexistence between pagans and Christians, possibly the middle of the fifth century. The disappearance of the genre was due to the effects of the ARAB CONQUEST OF EGYPT.

BIBLIOGRAPHY

Baratte, F. "Héros et chasseurs: la tenture d'Artémis." *Fondation Eugène Piot. Monuments et Mémoires* 67 (1987):31–76.

Boreux, C. "Département des antiquités égyptiennes du Musée National du Louvre." *Guide, Catalogue sommaire,* Vol. 1. Paris, 1932.

Illgen, V. *Zweifarbige reservetechnisch eingefärbte Leinenstoffe mit grossfiguren biblischen Darstellungen aus Ägypten.* Ph.D. diss. Mainz, 1968.

Kendrick, A. F. *Catalogue of Textiles from Burying Grounds in Egypt,* Vol. 3. London, 1920–1922.

Strzygowski, J. "Einfarbige Stoffe mit biblischen Darstellungen aus Ägypten." In *Orient oder Rom.* Leipzig, 1901.

Weitzmann, K., ed. *Age of Spirituality.* Catalog of the Exhibition, Metropolitan Museum of Art. New York, 1977–1978.

PIERRE DU BOURGUET, S.J.

TEXTILES, ICONOGRAPHY OF COPTIC. *See* Textiles, Coptic.

TEXTILES PRESERVATION. *See* Art Preservation.

TEZA, EMILIO, Italian philologist born at Venice in 1831 and died at Padua in 1912. He worked in the National Marcan Library, Venice, and in the Medici-Laurentian Library, Florence. He taught Sanskrit, classical languages, and Romance languages in Bologna, Pisa, and Padua. His contributions to Coptic studies include the following: *Inscrizioni cristiane d'Egitto; due in copto e una in graeco* (Pisa, 1878): "Dei manoscritti copti del Mingarelli nella Biblioteca dell'Università di Bologna," *Atti della R. accademia dei Lincei, Rendiconti,* ser. 5, no. 1 (1892):488–502; and "Frammenti inediti di un sermone di Scenuti in dialetto sahidico," *Rendiconti della R. accademia dei Lincei* 5, no. 1 (1892):682–97.

TITO ORLANDI

THAIS. *See* Sarapion.

THEBAID, THE. *See* Ṣa'īd.

THEBAN HERMITAGES. *See* Hermitages, Theban.

THEBAN LEGION, according to Saint Eucherius, legion consisting of 6,600 Christian soldiers who had been recruited in Thebes (the Thebaid) in Upper Egypt as part of the Roman army.

Three detailed manuscripts tell of the martyrdom of the Theban Legion, mainly at Agaunum (Saint Maurice-en-Valais), during the reign of Emperor DIOCLETIAN (284–305) and his co-emperor Maximian (286–305). The first account, *Passio Agaunensium martyrum* (Paris, National Library, no. 9550), is by Bishop Eucherius, who was elected to the see of Lyons in 434 (d. c. 449). The second account is anonymous, but we know it was written between 475 and 500 by a canon of the grave chapel that Bishop Theodorus (370–393) of Octodurum (Martigny) had erected on the site of the Theban martyrdom. This second account survives in two manuscripts: (1) the "Version X2," or *Passio sancti Mauritii et sociorum ejus . . .*, dating from the ninth century (library of the monastery of Einsiedeln, Switzerland, no. 256, fols. 357–380); and (2) a later manuscript (Paris, National Library, no. 5301, fols. 204^{v}–207^{r}), which contains many alterations.

In addition to these three manuscripts, there are other very early medieval narratives specifically dedicated to the lives and activities of certain legionnaires, and many later martyrologies and writings, such as the *Wahrhafte christli Histori* (1594) of Peter Canisius, in which the names of the Theban martyrs and the locations of their martyrdom are perpetuated. Also, in many towns and villages in northern Italy, parts of Switzerland, and down the Rhine Valley as far as Cologne, as well as in various parts of France, local traditions have given rise to many monuments and churches where relics are preserved and works of art are dedicated to saints from the legion. Cologne, with its numerous churches throughout the city commemorating Saint Gereon, is an outstanding example of local tradition related to the Theban legionnaires. Furthermore, a great number of religious foundations in this vast region commemorate members of the legion. Among them are Saint Maurice-en-Valais, Saint Moritz in the Engadine, the Monastery of Einsiedeln, Solothurn, Zurzach, and Zurich.

Actually there were two legions bearing the name "Theban," both of them formed by Diocletian sometime after the organization of the original Egyptian legion, stationed at Alexandria. One of these two legions from Thebes was transferred from Egypt to Europe in order to assist Maximian in Gaul, and although we cannot be certain which legion was chosen, we do know that the titles and names of the principal officers were as follows: the commander (*primicerius*), Mauritius; the chief instructor (*campidoctor*), Exuperius (according to Version X2, he is called *signifer,* bearer of the banner); and the military senator (*senator militum*), Candidus (in Version X2, he is also called *princeps vel campidoctor,* commander of the middle-aged soldiers of the first cohort). Saint Eucherius further mentions Saint Ursus and Saint Victor as members of this legion, and the anonymous account adds Innocentius (Innozentius) and Vitalis (Vital).

At Agaunum, during Maximian's campaign against the Bagaudae (c. 285–286), when the Theban troops disobeyed imperial commands to worship heathen gods (version X2), Maximian himself, stationed nearby at Octodurum, ordered the slaughter of every tenth soldier. According to Saint Eucherius, the cause of the decimation was their refusal to take part in shedding the blood of innocent fellow Christians. As the legionnaires, persisting in a resolute and constant confession of the Christian faith, steadfastly refused to obey Maximian's directives, the latter angrily called for a second decimation. However, the commander, Mauritius, strengthened by Exuperius and Candidus, continued to exhort the soldiers to be true to the faith and to follow the example of the Theban leaders rather than the Romans. Ultimately, after a public confession, in which Mauritius reiterated his loyalty to the emperor but also stoutly proclaimed his belief in Christ, Maximian became so enraged that he commanded all the Christian troops to be martyred.

Although the early date of this Roman persecution of Christian soldiers has been rejected by some renowned scholars who have insisted that 302 is the first time for such violence, their opinions do not seem valid in the face of extant evidence concerning other early martyrdoms, such as those of Saint Maximilian of Tebessa (Algeria) in 295 and of Saint Marcellus, centurion of Tingis (Tangier) in 298.

As to the number of Theban legionnaires actually martyred at Agaunum, we have no definite figure. However, Johan Mösch, after comparing information from the various chronicles on the events and geography of the martyrdoms of the legionnaires, concluded that only a cohort was martyred at Agaunum. The remainder of the battalions were either on the march or already stationed along the Roman

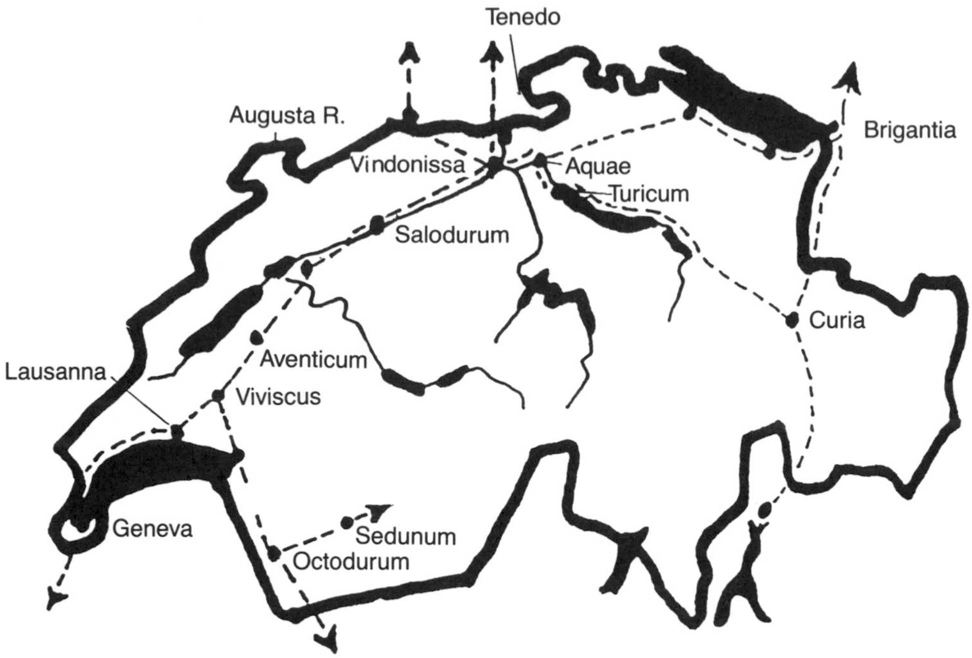

Map of Switzerland during the Roman era. *Courtesy Samir F. Girgis.*

road that ran from Liguria to Turin and Milan, then across the Lepontine Alps to Agaunum, on to Salodurum (Solothurn), and down the Rhine to old Verona (Bonn) and Colonia Agrippinensis (Cologne). Other scholars, who have studied this question from totally different approaches, have reached the same conclusion. For example, L. Dupraz and Paul Müller, by carefully examining the military titles and ranks of the legionnaires and thereby determining the total number of soldiers involved, estimated that the Thebans martyred at Agaunum consisted of but one battalion whose number did not exceed 520 men.

As for the other battalions of the legions posted along the military highway, large numbers were progressively and methodically massacred, mainly in Switzerland, Germany, and Italy.

Some of the most celebrated names of Theban legionnaires and saints associated with Swiss cantons are the following: saints Mauritius, Exuperius, Candidus, Innocentius, Vitalis, and the rest of their cohort, martyred at Saint Maurice-en-Valais; saints FELIX, REGULA, and EXUPERANTIUS, at Zurich; saints Ursus, Victor, and sixty-six companions at Solothurn; and VERENA OF ZURZACH.

In Germany, we can trace among the Theban saints Tyrsus (or Thirsus), Palmatius, and Bonifatius at Trier; saints Cassius, Florentinus, and their cohort at Bonn; Saint Gereon and 318 others at Cologne; and saints Victor, Mallosus (or Mallosius), and 330 companions at Xanten.

In Italy we find these Theban saints: Saint Alexander of Bergamo, Saint Antonius of Piacenza; saints Constantius, Alverius, Sebastianus, and Magius from the Cottian Alps; Saints Maurilius, Georgius, and Tiberius at Pinerolo; saints Maximius, Cassius, Secundus, Severinus, and Licinius at Milan; Saint Secundus of Ventimiglia; and saints Octavius, Solutor, and Adventor at Turin. There are many lesser saints as well.

Saint Maurice, Mauritius, or Moritz of Agaunum is the most popular, with more than 650 places bearing his name in Western Europe, notably in France and Switzerland. He is the patron saint of the diocese of Sitten (Sion) and of the town that bears his name in the region of Valais, as well as of Saint Moritz in the Engadine. In Canton Appenzell Inner Rhodes, his feast is a cantonal holiday. Several European orders were established in his name. Foremost among them were the Order of Saint Maurice, established by Amadaeus VIII of Savoy in 1434, and the Order of the Golden Fleece, by Duke Philip the Good of Burgundy in 1429.

Throughout the Middle Ages, Mauritius was the

patron saint of many communities and kingdoms: the Longobardi (Lombards), the Merovingians, the Carolingians, the Burgundians, and, at a later, the Savoyards. Some emperors are known to have been crowned at the altar of Saint Maurice in Saint Peter's Cathedral at Rome. In spite of his wide renown, Saint Maurice and his companions of the Theban Legion remained unknown to the Copts in the land of their origin, and the Coptic Synaxarion includes no reference to their names.

Nevertheless, the Coptic descent of the legion appears to be proven by several pieces of evidence. First, early Coptic sources confirm several specific details related to Egypt in the local European repositories. Second, some personal names are not only of Coptic-Ptolemaic, but even of ancient Egyptian, origin. Maurice or Mauritius appears in the Greco-Coptic papyri as Maurikios and the derivative feminine as Maurikia. Maurikios is identical with the Roman name Mauritius, according to Heuser. P. Müller suggests that the name may have been derived from Moeris, which is associated with the ancient lake existing in the Fayyūm; indeed, this name appears in epitaphs of the Ptolemaic and Coptic periods, and it is identical with the name of this lake, which is still used as a personal name among the Copts. The name Chaeremon is ancient Egyptian and means Son of Amon. Verena could be identified as the popular Coptic short form of the Ptolemaic Berenice after replacing the suffix *ice* with *a*, a phenomenon often encountered among Coptic personal names. The name could also be of ancient Egyptian origin, a compound of the Coptic and ancient Egyptian words *vre* (seed), and *ne* (town, or *the* town, which meant Thebes), thus "seed of Thebes." The name Victor is identical with the Arabic Coptic Buktor (the *B* in Coptic reads *V* when followed by a vowel, and *u* is pronounced *i*). Ursus is found in the Greco-Coptic papyri as Orsos, Orseus, and Orsis, the last of which means Horus, son of Isis. These are only a few examples of a subject that calls for further exploration.

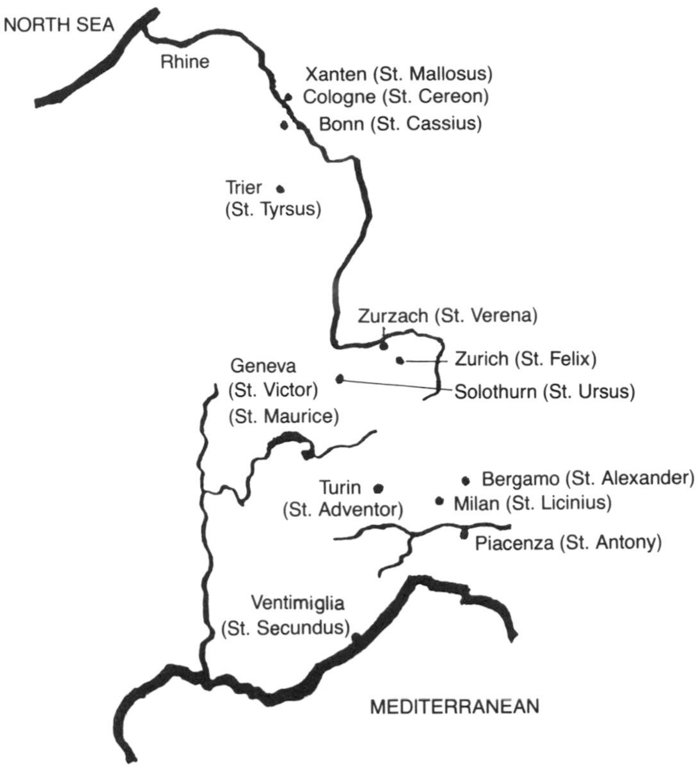

Map showing places of martyrdom of some of the well-known saints of the Theban Legion. *Courtesy Samir F. Girgis.*

BIBLIOGRAPHY

Balthasar, J. A. F. *Schutzschrift für die thebäische Legion oder den heiligen Mauritius und seine Gesellschaft wider Prof. Sprengen.* Lucerne, 1760.

Baulacre, L. "Du martyre de la légion thébaine." In *Journal helvétique.* Neuchâtel, 1746.

Berchem, D. von. *Le martyre de la légion thébaine.* Basel, 1956.

Braun, J. W. J. *Zur Geschichte der thebäischen Legion.* Bonn, 1855.

Bütler, J. *Die thebäische Legion.* Lucerne, 1951.

Canisius, P. *Wahrhafte christli Histori.* Freiburg im Uchtland, 1594.

Crum, W. E. *Short Texts from Coptic Ostraca and Papyri.* Oxford, 1921.

Crum, W. E., and G. Steindorff. *Koptische Rechtsurkunden des 8. Jahrhunderts aus Djeme.* Leipzig, 1971.

De Bochat, C. G. L. *Mémoires critiques pour servir d'éclaircissement sur divers points de l'histoire ancienne de la Suisse,* Vol. 1. Lausanne, 1747.

Dupraz, L. *Les Passions de Saint Maurice d'Agaune.* Fribourg, 1961.

Egli, E. *Kirchengeschichte der Schweiz.* Zurich, 1893.

Fox, J. R., and E. Sillem. *Saint Maurice—the Martyr and His Abbey,* Abbaye St. Maurice en Valais, n.d.

Gelpke, E. F. *Kirchengeschichte der Schweiz.* Bern, 1856.

Girgis, S. F. *Der koptische Beitrag zur Frühchristianisierung der Schweiz.* Zurich, 1984.

______. *The Theban Legion in the Light of the Early Coptic Sources as Well as the Greco-Coptic and Ancient Egyptian Etymology.* Zurich, 1984.

Graffin, R., and F. Nau. "Martyrologes et ménologes orientaux." *PO* 10, fasc. 1, no. 47, and fasc. 3, no. 48. Turnhout, 1973.
Grenfell, B. P., and A. S. Hunt. *The Tebtunis Papyri.* Berkeley, Calif., and London, 1907.
Herzberg, A. J. *Der heilige Mauritius.* Düsseldorf, 1936.
Heuser, G. *Die Personennamen der Kopten.* Studien zur Epigraphik und Papyruskunde 1. Leipzig, 1929.
Hyvernat, H., and I. Balestri. *Acta martyrum, scriptores coptici.* Louvain, 1950.
Lütolf, A. *Glaubensboten der Schweiz vor St. Gallus.* Lucerne, 1871.
Meinardus, O. F. A. "An Examination of the Traditions of the Theban Legion." *Bulletin de la Société d'archéologie copte* 23 (1976–1978):5–32.
Mösche, J. "Um den historischen Kern der Legende vom Martyrium der thebäische Legion." In *Zeitschrift für Schweizerische Kirchengeschichte.* Stans, 1949.
Preisigke, F. *Sammelbuch griechischer Urkunden aus Ägypten.* Strasbourg, 1913.
———. *Namenbuch.* Heidelberg, 1922.
Rettberg, F. W. *Kirchengeschichte Deutschlands.* Göttingen, 1846.
Spiegelberg, W. *Ägyptische und griechische Eigennamen aus Mumienetiketten der römischen Kaiserzeit.* Leipzig, 1901.
Stolle, F. *Das Martyrium der thebäischen Legion.* Münster, 1891.
Till, W. *Datierung und Prosopographie der koptischen Urkunden aus Theben.* Vienna, 1962.

SAMIR F. GIRGIS

THECLA, SAINT. *See* Christian Subjects in Coptic Art.

THEODORA, wife of JUSTINIAN I (527–565), empress of Byzantium from 4 April 527 until her death on 28 June 548 (Malalas, 1831, pp. 422, 484). A woman of great personal influence, especially in ecclesiastical matters, she favored the Monophysites and is remembered as their saintly protector.

Her reputation, however, is tainted by a shady past as an entertainer of the Hippodrome performing in shows of extreme sexual explicitness (Procopius, 1961, p. 9) and as a member of a brothel, a fact attested by the otherwise trustworthy witness John of Ephesus (*Lives of the Eastern Saints,* p. 189). After various adventures, including a trip to Alexandria, and several abortions and illegitimate children, she caught the attention of the patrician Justinian, who married her after the death (523) of the existing empress, who had opposed the match, and after securing a relaxation of the law forbidding senators to marry actresses. The new law rehabilitated reformed actresses and any children of subsequent marriages. However, the marriage of Theodora and Justinian was childless, despite attempts to enlist divine aid through the prayers of Saint Sabas.

The general view of Procopius concerning Theodora is very hostile, and the details of his account of her early life are no doubt exaggerated but not totally false, since Theodora made no attempt to conceal her background. On the contrary, she founded in Constantinople a famous convent to house reformed women like herself, and the contemporary monophysite tradition was proud to see her as its supporter. Only much later was an expurgated version of her life put forward excluding mention of her origins.

Theodora clearly exercised a great influence over Justinian and public affairs, and is named with Justinian in some official sources; but her power was wielded behind the scenes by virtue of her personality rather than by right. She is accused by Procopius of interfering in public affairs at all levels, especially to further or protect her favorites. She is alleged by him to have been a close friend of Antonina, the forceful wife of the general Belisarius, and to have acted with her to promote or to hinder his career at various times—implying that she exercised an influence over the conduct of Justinian's war policy. Her most famous secular intervention was during the Nika Revolt (532), when she is said by Procopius to have urged the wavering Justinian to stand firm with the words "The empire is a fair winding sheet" (Bridge, 1978, p. 76). She is also said to have secured the final disgrace of the minister John the Cappadocian.

Theodora's main influence, however, was in the ecclesiastical sphere and particularly in support of monophysitism. She gave shelter to many monophysite clergy in the palace of Hormisdas, including some exiles reportedly hidden without Justinian's knowledge until her death. She also encouraged the mission of Jacob Baradaeus to ordain monophysite priests in Syria. She sponsored missions in the monophysite interest to Nubia, with important long-term consequences for the development of Christianity in that area. For these activities she was much revered by the Monophysite church, as is most clearly shown in the *Lives of the Eastern Saints* by her contemporary, John, bishop of Ephesus. Procopius, another main source for Theodora, is totally out of sympathy with these actions and represents them as designed to cause maximum trouble in the empire.

Theodora is said to have been small and pale and, though not beautiful, very much concerned with her appearance. Only one certain portrait survives, in the famous mosaic from San Vitale at Ravenna, where she is shown in imperial dress; it bears out Procopius' description. Though she could bear no heir for Justinian, she had at least two children by previous liaisons; through one of them, a daughter, she allied herself to the highest aristocratic circles, probably to the surviving family of Emperor Anastasius. Her sister, Comito, married Sittas, one of Justinian's leading generals, and Theodora's niece, Sophia, perhaps the daughter of this marriage, was married to Justin the *curopalates* (administrator of imperial palace), nephew of Justinian. She became empress when he succeeded to the throne. Theodora was thus able to promote the interests of her family, aided by the large endowments given her by Justinian. She died of cancer in 548 while probably still in her forties, leaving Justinian a lonely man to reign for seventeen more years.

BIBLIOGRAPHY

Bury, J. B. *History of the Later Roman Empire*, 2nd ed., Vol. 2, pp. 27–35. London, 1923.

Cameron, A. "The House of Anastasius." *Greek, Roman and Byzantine Studies* 19 (1978):269ff.

Daube, D. "The Marriage of Justinian and Theodora. Legal and Theological Reflections." *Catholic University Law Review* 16 (1967):380ff.

John of Ephesus. *Lives of the Eastern Saints* 13. Patrologia Orientalis 17. Louvain, 1923.

Malalas, J. *Chronographia*. Bonn, 1831.

Procopius of Caesarea. *Secret History*. Ann Arbor, Mich., 1961.

Stein, E. *Histoire du Bas-Empire*, ed. J.-R. Palanque, Vol. 2, pp. 235–39. Amsterdam, 1949.

Popular books about Theodora include the following:

Bridge, A. *Theodora: Portrait in a Byzantine Landscape*. London, 1978. Less sensational, concentrates on the ecclesiastical side.

Vandercook, J. W. *Empress of the Dusk*. New York, 1940.

The romanticized view of Theodora comes from the influential works of Charles Diehl, *Theodora, impératrice de Byzance* (Paris, 1904) and *Figures byzantines* (Paris, 1920).

AVERIL CAMERON

THEODORA, SAINT

THEODORA, SAINT (feast day: 11 Tūt). The life of Saint Theodora illustrates a theme dear to the Byzantine hagiographers: the woman monk wearing men's clothing and living in a monastery of men (Patlagean, pp. 602, 612). Saint Theodora, who lived during the reign of Emperor Zeno (474–491), was courted by a man other than her husband and yielded to him. Then, filled with remorse, she cut off her hair, put on men's clothing, took the name Theodore, and allowed herself to be taken for a servant. She entered a monastery of men, where she received the angelic habit. Accused of having sinned with a woman, she was driven from the monastery with the child of whom she was accused of being the father. She remained in the desert with her supposed son for seven years. Edified by her conduct, the abbot readmitted her to the monastery, where she died shortly afterward. Her sex then became known, and her patience and sanctity were revealed.

Theodora is commemorated in the SYNAXARION on 11 Tūt. This notice appears to be borrowed from the Greek Synaxarion.

The Life preserved in Greek has been published by K. Wessely. Several Arabic manuscripts contain an unpublished Life that appears to be of Syrian origin.

BIBLIOGRAPHY

Patlagean, E. "L'histoire de la femme déguisée en moine et l'évoluvtion de la sainteté feminine à Byzance." *Studi medievali* 17 (1976):597–623.

Wessely, K. *Die vita s. Theodorae, fünfzehnter Jahresbericht des K. K. Staatgymnasiums in Hernals*. Vienna, 1889.

RENÉ-GEORGES COQUIN

THEODORE. *See* Theodorus.

THEODORET

THEODORET (c. 393–458), writer of exegetical and historical works. A native of Antioch, he was born into a pious Christian family of great wealth and received his education in a monastic school. After the death of his parents while he was in his twenties, he decided to distribute his inherited wealth to the poor and the needy, and then retire to the Monastery of Nicerte (c. 416). There he devoted all his time to prayers and intensive study of church history and the sacred traditions of the church. Ultimately Theodoret's fame for chastity, piety, and saintly life spread widely in the region of Antioch and, against his will, he was forced by the congregation to be consecrated as bishop of Cyrrhus in Syria in 423. He conducted the affairs of his ecclesiastical office with great sagacity, and he was firm in fighting paganism and all manner of heresy as he saw it.

Gradually Theodoret became involved in the Christological conflicts between the two giants of the church, NESTORIUS, archbishop of Constantinople, and Pope CYRIL I of Alexandria. His close friendship with and admiration for Nestorius swung him to the side of the patriarch of Constantinople and placed him against Cyril, who accused him of confusion of the orthodox Christology with APOLLINARIANISM and the maintenance of the duality of Christ's nature. The THEOTOKOS was accepted by Theodoret only as a figurative term. The rising tide of polemics over these conceptions led to the convening by Emperor Theodosius of the First Council of EPHESUS in 431. As chairman of the council, Cyril opened the meeting of the council before the arrival of the Syrian delegation, which included Theodoret. The council accepted the formula of Cyril and deposed and anathematized Nestorius. When the Syrian bishops under the leadership of Theodoret arrived, they held a rival council, which in turn excommunicated Cyril and confirmed Nestorius.

The polemical disputes between Alexandria and Constantinople kept flaring up until Theodosius II decided tc summon another council, also at Ephesus, in 449. Cyril had died, and his successor, DIOSCORUS I, came to the council with a firm commitment to uphold the principle of MONOPHYSITISM that EUTYCHES professed at Constantinople. The council reversed the decisions made at Constantinople and reinstated Eutyches before the arrival of the Roman delegation with Pope Leo's "Tome," which was not read at the meeting. Dioscorus accused Theodoret of making Christ two sons, and had Theodoret deposed and anathematized. Ephesus II was dubbed by the rival party "Robber Council" or Latrocinium, a term used by Leo in his "Tome." The succession of Marcian and Pulcheria, following the death of Theodosius II, imposed a new policy hostile to Alexandria and Dioscorus, whom they summoned to another council at CHALCEDON in 451. The decisions of the Latrocinium were reversed; Theodoret was confirmed, and Dioscorus was anathematized, deposed, and exiled to Gangra in Paphlagonia. The Copts never recognized Chalcedon as an ecumenical council, and to this day repudiate its decisions as heretical.

Theodoret spent his remaining years peacefully completing his literary works, which may be roughly divided into four categories. First are his exegetical works, which rank among the best on record. They include a vast number of treatises dealing with Old Testament books such as Psalms and the Song of Songs, the Octateuch, Kings, Chronicles, Major Prophets, and Minor Prophets. On the New Testament, Theodoret left commentaries on the fourteen epistles of Saint Paul, including that to the Hebrews, that are considered among the best specimens of religious writings.

Second, the works of controversial character that appear to have occupied his latter years deal with his conflicts with Cyril I and Dioscorus I over the problem of monophysitism. In them he discussed heresies in general in five books composed at the request of Sporacius, an imperial commissioner present at Chalcedon.

Third, his theological works include his *Graecarum affectionum curatio*, a fine work of Christian apologetics, in which he compiled statements of the pagan philosophers in twelve discourses, with the Christian answers in elegant style and forceful expression.

The fourth category includes his historical works. The first is his *Ecclesiastical History*, which was intended to be a continuation of the *Historia ecclesiastica* of Eusebius and covers the period from the rise of ARIANISM to the death of THEODORUS OF MOPSUESTIA in 429. In this work, he supplements the works of SOCRATES and SOZOMEN while correcting some of their errors. He uses original documents, but one must be cautious of his chronology. The second, *Religious History*, is a biographical treatise on thirty hermits and ascetics of his day, in which he displays his personal knowledge of or acquaintance with these persons.

To the above categories may be added Theodoret's accumulation of letters written to contemporary personalities on the outstanding theological problems of his time, as well as his sermons and orations.

The works of Theodoret that are lost number at least ten, with the following titles traceable: (1) *Pentalogus*, on the Incarnation, written against Cyril I; (2) *Opus mysticum;* (3) *De theologia et incarnatione*, consisting of three dialogues against the Macedonians and Apollinarians, wrongly attributed to Saint Athanasius; (4) *Opus adversus Marcionem;* (5) *Opus adversus Judaeos;* (6) *Responsiones ad quasita majorum Chrysostomi;* (7) "Allocations Against Cyril" at Chalcedon; (8) "Fragments Against Sabellius";

(9–10) two sermons, one at Antioch and the other on JOHN CHRYSOSTOM.

BIBLIOGRAPHY

Altaner, B. *Patrology,* trans. H. C. Graef. Edinburgh and London, 1960.

Bardenhewer, O. *Patrology: Lives and Works of the Fathers of the Church,* trans. T. J. Shahan. St. Louis, 1908.

Quasten, J. *Patrology,* 3 vols. Westminster, Md., 1951–1960.

Venables, E. "Theodoretus (2)." In DCB 4, pp. 904–919.

AZIZ S. ATIYA

THEODORUS, forty-fifth patriarch of the See of Saint Mark (731–743). Theodorus (Tawadrūs) was a monk at Dayr Tamnūrah on the fringe of Mareotis, west of Alexandria. The sources are silent about his early secular life as well as on the date and place of his birth and his activities before he took the monastic vow. However, the HISTORY OF THE PATRIARCHS is explicit about his saintly character and his humility, as well as his love of serving others throughout his life. He aimed always at the execution of Christ's words to his disciples: "Whoever would be great among you must be your servant, and whoever would be first among you must be your slave" (Mt. 20:26–27). He literally carried out the Lord's words by serving his fellow monks, and as patriarch he continued to serve the whole community in the same way.

His fame spread through Alexandria, and its notables and archons as well as its clergy nominated him for the patriarchal dignity. It is said in the *History of the Patriarchs* that his spiritual father, ALEXANDER II, had prophesied that Theodorus would succeed to the throne of Saint Mark.

His reign was marked on the whole by an atmosphere of peace and serenity, though for a short time at the beginning this was not so. ʿUbayd Allāh, the governor of Egypt at Theodorus' accession, proved to be a tough extortionist who doubled the capitation tax (JIZYAH) from one to two dinars and even imposed heavier taxation on his fellow Muslims. It is said that the Muslims, not the Copts, were the first to protest against his imposts to the lenient caliph Hishām, who listened to their complaint and removed ʿUbayd Allāh from Egypt to the Maghreb, where he met his end in Morocco. With ʿUbayd Allāh's disappearance from the country, peaceful coexistence prevailed and the people, both Muslims and Copts, lived together harmoniously with no fear of excessive and illegal taxation. The Covenant of ʿUmar ibn al-Khaṭṭab was observed by the new governors in relation to the Coptic people.

The Coptic community kept growing under Theodorus owing to the return of many Chalcedonians to the mother church.

BIBLIOGRAPHY

Atiya, A. S. *History of Eastern Christianity.* London, 1968.

Cambridge History of Islam, 2 vols. ed. P. M. Holt, Ann K. S. Lambton, and Bernard Lewis. Cambridge, 1970.

Hitti, P. K. *History of the Arabs.* London, 1946.

Lane-Poole, S. *History of Egypt in the Middle Ages.* London, 1901.

SUBHI Y. LABIB

THEODORUS, SAINT, the name of two Coptic martyrs. One is surnamed Stratelates ("the General") and the other "Anatolius" (though, as we shall see, understanding this as equivalent to "Eastern" is not correct). The sources concerning them are sometimes common to both, so that we shall deal with them together, while pointing out the distinction between them.

The Coptic tradition on Theodorus Stratelates is directly derived from the Greek tradition, which in turn had a complex development (Delehaye, 1922). The relatively ancient, invented text of the Passion of a Theodorus, a soldier who refused to offer sacrifice and who set fire to a pagan temple, was expanded until Theodorus became a general and battled a dragon near the city of Eucaita.

The Coptic tradition took up this last version, perhaps adding other details of its own, especially concerning the events leading up to the dragon episode. The basic text is that of the Passion, which is found in at least three codices, two in Bohairic (National Library, Turin, now lost; Vatican Library, Rome, Copti 66, fols. 172–98, ed. Hyvernat, 1886–1887, part 1, 157–81) and one in Sahidic (Pierpont Morgan Library, New York, M 586), and consists simply of the story of his encounter with the dragon and his martyrdom. An Encomium attributed to ANASTASIUS OF EUCAITA adds a story concerning the saint's family before describing the battle with the dragon. An Encomium attributed to one Theodorus, bishop of Antioch, adds not only the story of the saint's family but also that of a journey he made to

Egypt, where he apparently met Theodorus Anatolius before his martyrdom.

Last, we have two texts describing miracles performed by the relics of the saint in his shrines; one is attributed to Theodorus of Antioch and the other is anonymous (Vatican Library, Rome, Copti 66, fols. 199–210, ed. Hyvernat, pt. 1, pp. 182ff.).

Theodorus Anatolius is a character from the hagiographico-fictitious Cycle of the family of BASILIDES the General. It is difficult to say whether he was in some way suggested by the existence of the other Theodorus; it is certain that the actions attributed to him are quite different. Theodorus is described as the son of one Sotericus, a royal prince, and he apparently received the surname ANATOLIUS from an uncle of this name.

His Passion has come down in a number of codices (Vatican Library, Rome, Copti 63, fols. 28–54, ed. Hyvernat, Vol. 1, pp. 34ff.; Pierpont Morgan Library, New York, M 583, 584, 613) and includes the stories of Diocletianus-Agrippida and of Bishop Gaius of Antioch, the traitor, as well as the description of his martyrdom. This text is the basis of the Encomium attributed to Theodorus of Antioch found in a Sahidic codex (British Library, London, Or. 7030).

BIBLIOGRAPHY

Balestri, I., and H. Hyvernat. *Acta Martyrum,* 2 vols. CSCO 43, 44. Paris, 1908.

Baumeister, T. *Martyr Invictus. Der Märtyrer als Sinnibild der Erlösung in der Legende und im Kult der frühen koptischen Kirche,* pp. 145–48. Münster, 1972.

Delahaye, H. "Les Martyrs d'Egypte." *Analecta Bollandiana* 40 (1922):5–154; 299–364.

Hyvernat, H. *Les Actes des martyrs de l'Egypte tirés des manuscrits coptes de la Bibliothèque Vaticane et du Musée Borgia.* Paris and Leroux, 1886–1887.

Rossi, F. *I Papiri copti del Museo Egizio di Torino,* 2 vols., 10 issues. Turin, 1887–1892.

Winstedt, E. O. *Coptic Texts on Saint Theodore the General, St. Theodore the Eastern, Chamoul and Justus.* London and Oxford, 1910.

TITO ORLANDI

THEODORUS OF ALEXANDRIA, SAINT, Greek-speaking disciple of Saint PACHOMIUS. He must be distinguished from THEODORUS OF TABENNĒSĒ (the Egyptian), an assistant of Pachomius who eventually succeeded him. The vocation of Theodorus of Alexandria is narrated in the Coptic and Greek Lives of Pachomius, and he is mentioned several times in the LETTER OF AMMON.

Born of pagan parents in Alexandria, Theodorus was converted to Christianity, probably at the age of seventeen, and became a lector in the church of Alexandria under Patriarch ATHANASIUS I (326–373). Having received Athanasius' permission to become a monk, he approached Pachomius, who first assigned him to the "house" of the Greek brothers. Acknowledging Theodorus' charisma as a spiritual leader, Pachomius entrusted him with the care of souls and appointed him father of the house of the Greek and other foreign brothers. But the most important occupation of Theodorus was in the office of interpreter, which he fulfilled under Pachomius, HORSIESIOS, and Theodorus of Tabennēsē, translating their instructions into Greek for all the brothers who could not understand Coptic. In this capacity Theodorus was not merely an interpreter but also a comforter of his brothers, concerned about the purity of their heart at prayer. The Lives mention him as one of the pillars of the Pachomian community until the first tenure of Horsiesios as superior of the *koinonia.*

ARMAND VEILLEUX

THEODORUS OF MOPSUESTIA (c. 350–428), theologian and biblical exegete. Born into a wealthy family at Antioch, Theodorus enjoyed opportunities for education and intellectual advancement. He was a lifelong friend of JOHN CHRYSOSTOM, and as young men together, they attended the lectures of the sophist Libanius. Chrysostom, who had become converted to the spiritual life, exerted his influence on Theodorus, and they entered the monastic school of Carterius and Diodorus. Theodorus was ordained a priest at Antioch, probably in 383. It is likely that he left Antioch for Tarsus in 386 or shortly thereafter. In 392 he became bishop of Mopsuestia, a free town 12 miles (19 km) from the sea on the Pyramus River, midway between Tarsus and Issus. He held this position until his death in 428.

Theodorus was an accomplished orator, as evidenced by the fact that the emperor Theodosius I had learned of his fame and desired to hear him speak. Afterward, impressed by what he had heard, Theodosius said he had never met with such a teacher. Theodorus was a zealous laborer both within and beyond his diocese. It is said that he converted the city of Mopsuestia, driving out Arianism and other heresies. He was known in all the churches of the East as the herald of truth and a doctor of the church. But his enemies, heretics whom he had attacked, exploited his fame by altering some of his writings to make him appear guilty of heterodoxy.

After Theodorus' death in 428, opinion about him was split. In the East, where he had lived and worked, his former adherents continued to revere him, but elsewhere he came under condemnation because of his connection with the heterodox Nestorians, who had adopted his writings as the best exposition of their beliefs. Sometime between 543 and 546, the emperor JUSTINIAN issued an edict in which he condemned the Three Chapters—that is, the writings of Theodorus, the *Christological Letter* of Ibas of Edessa, and THEODORET's work against the *Twelve Anathemas* of Cyril. This edict was ratified, though with some reluctance, by the (Fifth Ecumenical) Council of CONSTANTINOPLE in 553.

Theodorus was a prolific writer. Among his literary remains are fragments of exegetical works on most books of the Old and New Testaments (the commentaries on Galatians and the nine following epistles are extant in Latin translation); fragments of a treatise, originally in fifteen books, on the Incarnation; fragments of works against APOLLINARIANISM; a fragment of a work against Eunomius; an outline (preserved in Photius) of a work against those who assert that men sin by nature, not by conscious act; a fragment of a work on miracles; fragments of a work on the mysteries; and Syriac and Latin translations of a liturgy. References in other authors reveal that Theodorus also wrote two tomes on the Holy Spirit, three books on "Persian Magic," a treatise on the priesthood, and various hermeneutical works such as *On Obscure Language*, *On the Giving of the Law*, and *Against the Allegorizers*. His letters, which have not survived, were known to the Nestorians of Syria as the *Book of Pearls*.

That many of Theodorus' writings were preserved in Latin translation is attributable to the fact that many bishops in the West and particularly in Africa were not sympathetic to the edict of Justinian that anathematized him. They argued that the edict tampered with the decisions of the Councils of EPHESUS and CHALCEDON and violated the sanctity of the dead. In an attempt to become better acquainted with the works that had been condemned, Justinian's opponents read Theodorus' writings and translated them into Latin for wider circulation in the West. To avoid recriminations, they often published these works under the name of Saint Ambrose.

Though Theodorus' style is unwieldy and devoid of both warmth and vivacity, his writings are the best surviving representatives of the middle Antiochian school of interpretation and thought.

BIBLIOGRAPHY

Dewart, J. M. *The Theology of Grace of Theodore of Mopsuestia*. Studies in Christian Antiquity 16. Washington, D.C., 1971.

Swete, H. B. "Theodorus (26), Bishop of Mopsuestia." In DCB 4, pp. 934–48. Repr. New York, 1974.

RANDALL STEWART

THEODORUS OF PHERME, SAINT, an anchorite of the fourth–fifth century. Several persons named Theodorus are mentioned in the APOPHTHEGMATA PATRUM, but the only one of whom much is said is the Theodorus customarily described as "of Pherme" because he lived there for the greater part of his life. He had been a monk at Scetis and withdrew to Pherme, some 20 miles (30 km) to the northwest, when SCETIS was devastated by the Mazices in 407. He had known MACARIUS, Theonas, ACHILLAS, and several monks of the Kellia, among them John the Eunuch. Ordained a deacon against his will, Theodorus never wished, for reasons of humility, to exercise the functions of that office. He and ARSENIUS were particularly renowned for their disdain of any human glory, and for this reason they often fled from their fellow men. Like Arsenius, Theodorus did, however, have disciples, particularly one called Isaac, but he was loath to govern them. When he became old and infirm, he had no lack of visitors, who constantly brought him food. He distributed almost all of it and likewise disposed even of his books. For six years he struggled against impurity, and subjected himself to a very strict rule. The Lord finally delivered him, and as an old man he became a terror to the demons.

BIBLIOGRAPHY

Arras, V., ed. *Collectio monastica*, 13, 15; 14, 5; 14, 48. CSCO 238, pp. 87, 110, 122.

Cotelier, J. B., ed. *Apophthegmata Patrum*. PG 65, pp. 188–96. Paris, 1864.

LUCIEN REGNAULT

THEODORUS OF TABENNĒSĒ, SAINT, fourth-century head of Pachomian community of PBOW. Theodorus was born of a prominent family and received a good education. As a youth, he joined a monastery in the diocese of Snē. As soon as he heard of PACHOMIUS and his community, however, he wanted to become one of his disciples; he arrived at Tabennēsē around 328. Theodorus was one of the group known as the "ancient brothers," those who entered Tabennēsē before the great movement of expansion started with the foundation of Pbow in 329.

He made rapid progress in virtue. Pachomius appointed him father of the community of Tabennēsē and then as his assistant at Pbow, when he established the central administration of all the monasteries of the *koinonia* there. He was a great comforter of souls and was highly esteemed by the brothers. However, although the Life of Pachomius (written by followers of Theodorus) states in a passage inserted by a later scribe that Theodorus "had great grace" while Pachomius was "fearful and always mournful," it appears from the whole of the Life that Theodorus was often more rigid and less understanding than Pachomius.

When Pachomius appointed PETRONIUS, in whom he had recognized exceptional gifts of discernment, as superior of Tsmine and as supervisor of all the monasteries of the region of Shmin, he was paving the way for him as a potential successor for the headship of the *koinonia.* However, when Pachomius fell ill some time later, the ancient brothers came to Theodorus and asked him to promise that he would be their father after the death of Pachomius. He agreed. When Pachomius recovered from his illness and learned about this, he reprimanded Theodorus severely and discharged him from all his responsibilities.

Before his final illness, Pachomius appointed the ailing Petronius as his successor. On his deathbed a few months later, Petronius nominated HORSIESIOS as his successor. The latter was a holy man who won the esteem of all the brothers during his first five years as superior. But Theodorus always remained the man trusted by the ancient brothers. When Horsiesios sent him to Phnoum, the newest and most remote foundation, to assume the humble office of housemaster of the bakers, this proved to be too much, and the time became ripe for the smallest pretext to spark a revolt. In the circumstances, Horsiesios, a humble man, decided to step down and let Theodorus take command of the *koinonia.* Although the biographers awkwardly try to give the impression that Theodorus acted simply as the vicar of Horsiesios, it is clear that Horsiesios was forced to resign. In his first address as head of the *koinonia,* Theodorus says to the brotherhood: "You have risen against our blessed and holy father, Apa Horsiesios. You have removed a truly good man from this position. . . . a man whom God and our father installed in this holy place. . . ."

In spite of the rather questionable circumstances under which Theodorus assumed the leadership of the *koinonia,* he retained his position for eighteen years. With the death of the majority of the "ancient brothers" in the plague of 367, he began to sense a growing opposition to his rule and decided to summon Horsiesios to take over as superior. Theodorus died in the following year, after the reinstatement of Horsiesios.

The personality of Theodorus combined with holiness and spirituality certain qualities that made Pachomius, in spite of his love for him, regard him as second choice for the office of superior. His sensitivity, which retained the affection and support of the "ancient brothers" for him, also made him vulnerable in the ensuing power struggle with Horsiesios, whose extraordinary humility saved the *koinonia* from imminent disaster. The acute sensitivity of Theodorus' feelings is illustrated by his reaction when Pachomius deposed him from his principal position. He cried constantly, to the extent that the brothers became apprehensive that he might lose his vision.

Though Theodorus is known to have entered the Pachomian movement at a very early age, it remains uncertain whether he joined the *koinonia* at the age of thirteen, fourteen, or twenty. Thirteen seems to be the most likely, according to the sources. However, two dates in his biography are relatively certain: about 328 for his arrival at Tabennēsē and 368 as the year of his death.

There are two letters by Theodorus. One of them is preserved in Jerome's Latin translation, and the other, in Coptic, has been published by H. Quecke.

[*See also:* Monasticism, Pachomian.]

BIBLIOGRAPHY

Quecke, H. "Ein Brief von einem Nachfolger Pachoms." *Orientalia* 44 (1975):426–33.

Steidle, B. "Der heilige Abt. Theodor von Tabennesi. Zur 1600. Wiederkehr des Todesjahres (368–1968)." *Erbe und Auftrag* 44 (1968):91–103.

______. "Der Osterbrief unseres Vaters Theodor an alle Klöster. Zur 1600. Wiederkehr des Todesjahres (368–1968)." *Erbe und Auftrag* 44 (1968):104–19.

Veilleux, A. "Teodoro di Tabennesi." *Bibliotheca sanctorum* 12 (1969):270–72.

ARMAND VEILLEUX

THEODOSIANS, followers of THEODOSIUS I (d. c. 567), the Jacobite patriarch of Alexandria. They comprised the section of the Monophysite party known as Severians. Their adherence to Severus' belief in the corruptibility of the body of Christ earned them the name Corrupticolae ("worshipers of the corruptible") and the blood-spilling enmity of the followers of Gaianus, the Phantasiastae, who believed the body of Christ was incorruptible. The Theodosians also clashed with the agnoetae, a Severian faction that asserted that the incarnate Christ was not omniscient. On 3 June 633, Cyrus of Phasis managed to effect a union of the Theodosians and the Gaianites.

BIBLIOGRAPHY

Hefele, C. J. *A History of the Councils of the Church from the Original Documents,* Vol. 3, pp. 459–60, trans. editor of Hagenbach's *History of Doctrines.* Edinburgh, 1883. Vol. 5, pp. 18–21, trans. W. R. Clark. Edinburgh, 1896.

Neale, J. M. *A History of the Holy Eastern Church: The Patriarchate of Alexandria,* Vol. 2, pp. 33–35. London, 1847.

Wigram, W. A. *The Separation of the Monophysites,* pp. 122–24, 156. London, 1923.

RANDALL STEWART

THEODOSIUS I, saint and thirty-third patriarch of the See of Saint Mark (535–567). Theodosius was the secretary of TIMOTHY III and was chosen to succeed him. This occurred with the support of the Empress THEODORA's chamberlain, Calotychius, and official circles at Alexandria. When he appeared for his enthronement, a popular uprising swept a rival candidate into his place, Archdeacon Gaianus, a supporter of the Julianist theology. Julian, bishop of Halicarnarsus (d. 518), attested that the body of Christ was incapable of corruption while the Monophysites believed that was true only after Christ's resurrection. Theodosius was driven from the city for several months, but was restored by military forces under the Persarmenian general Narses (not to be confused with his namesake, the eunuch Narses, later commander in Italy). Theodosius had exchanged letters with SEVERUS OF ANTIOCH; in 536 they exchanged letters of communion with the sympathetic Anthimus of Constantinople. But Justinian now took a strict Chalcedonian line (judgment based on the statement of the Catholic faith made by the Council of CHALCEDON of 451). Anthimus was deposed, and in 537 Theodosius was summoned to the capital and offered the choice of Chalcedon or exile from his see. He chose the latter, and for the rest of his life was interned in or near Constantinople, and for some time before Theodora's death at her monastery in the palace of Hormisdas.

As a confessor for Coptic orthodoxy, Theodosius gradually won the support that he had previously lacked. After the death of Severus in 538, he was the leading theologian and ranking hierarch of the anti-Chalcedonian party. Later Copts were willing to accept the name Theodosians, perhaps originally given by their opponents. Theodosius guided his church by correspondence, but was restrained from specifically episcopal functions. However, in 543 he was able, with the support of the Arab prince Ḥārith (Arethas), to consecrate a bishop for the Arabs, and more significantly, to consecrate JACOB BARADAEUS with a roving commission to ordain and consecrate, including some bishops for Egypt. About the same time, Theodosius commissioned the priest Julian for the Nubian mission. The theology of Theodosius followed that of Severus. He recognized the full humanity of Christ while also asserting the single will of Christ. His writings included a theological *Tome* to Theodora, and later he condemned the eccentric heresy of the tritheists, who argued that one person and one nature in Christ implied three natures and three persons in the Trinity. After Justinian's death in 565 Theodosius was honorably received by the new emperor, Justinian II, but died himself shortly afterward. Almost his last action was to authorize the consecration of LONGINUS, a priest of his entourage, as bishop for Nubia.

BIBLIOGRAPHY

Amann, E. "Théodose d'Alexandrie." In *Dictionnaire de Théologie catholique,* Vol. 15, pp. 325–28. Paris, 1946.

Bardenhewer, O. *Geschichte der altkirchlichen Literatur,* Vol. 5, pp. 1–9. Freiburg, 1932.

Frend, W. H. C. *The Rise of the Monophysite Movement,* chap. 7. Cambridge, 1972.

Hardy, E. R. *Christian Egypt,* pp. 130–43. New York, 1952.

______. "The Egyptian Policy of Justinian." *Dumbarton Oaks Papers* 22 (1968):22–41.

Maspero, J. *Histoire des Patriarches d'Alexandrie,* chaps. 4–6. Paris, 1923.

Wigram, W. A. *The Separation of the Monophysites,* chaps. 9, 10. London, 1923.

EDWARD R. HARDY

THEODOSIUS II, seventy-ninth patriarch of the See of Saint Mark (1294–1300). His original name was ʿAbd al-Masīḥ. He was a native of the town of Minyat Khaṣīm when he became a monk of Dayr Abū Fānā at an unspecified date. There he was elevated to the priesthood before his selection for the patriarchate, during the first reign of Sultan al-Naṣir Muḥammad ibn Qalāwūn in 1294. He was also a contemporary of al-ʿĀdil Kiṭbughā (1294–1296) and Ḥusām al Dīn Lājīn (1296–1299). It was a time of great confusion, in which one Mamluk killed the other. The sultanate of Lājīn was memorable for an expedition carried out against Lesser Armenia. On the local scene, a new reorganization of the landed property was enforced and caused a great uproar among the population. A Copt was accused of engineering the reorganization, which must have intensified the hostility against the Copts in general. After Lājīn was murdered, al-Nāṣir succeeded him in his second reign (1299–1309), although the real power behind the throne rested with the Mamluk amir and viceroy Salār.

This state of confusion encouraged the Mongols to revive their old scheme of the conquest of Syria, which they crowned with the possession of the capital city of Damascus. However, the fort of Damascus itself remained in Mamluk hands until the return of the Mamluk batallions. The financial pressures caused by these expensive campaigns forced the ruling class to tax up to one-third of the general income of all subjects, Muslim and Christian alike. This situation incited local unrest. The patriarch is said to have been prone to corruption in order to meet the royal pressures for funds, and the bishops and the clergy suffered from the interminable imposts. The situation of the country as a whole was worsened by the outbreak of a plague that is said to have killed 17,500 people in a single month toward the end of 1300. Theodosius died in that year and was buried in the Nestorian monastery (DAYR AL-NASṬŪR), previously recovered by the Copts from that heretical sect. The throne of Saint Mark remained vacant after his death for only a few days. His biography occupies only a few lines in the HISTORY OF THE PATRIARCHS.

BIBLIOGRAPHY

Lane-Poole, S. *History of Egypt in the Middle Ages.* London, 1901.

———. *The Mohammadan Dynasties.* Paris, 1901.

SUBHI Y. LABIB

THEODOSIUS OF JERUSALEM, fifth-century bishop of Jerusalem who was exiled. He was the opponent of Juvenal of Jerusalem after the Council of CHALCEDON; head of the side opposed to the decisions of the council, he was bishop of Jerusalem between 451 and 453, when Juvenal was forcibly restored by Marcian (Frend, 1972, pp. 149, 151). He is spoken of especially in the *Vita Petri Iberi* (ed. Raabe, 1895, p. 54) but also in Chapter 27 of the *Vita Euthymii* of Cyril of Scythopolis. He consecrated many anti-Chalcedonian bishops, among them Peter the Iberian, to the see of Maiuma. When Juvenal was restored to his throne, Theodosius accepted the sentence of exile without putting up a fight.

The Coptic tradition remembers him among the opponents of Chalcedonian doctrine. However, the two works attributed to him in Coptic are late forgeries of the period of the CYCLES.

The first is a homily *In Honor of Victor,* existing in a complete codex (or complete in the relevant section) from the White Monastery (DAYR ANBĀ SHINŪDAH) (ed. Bouriant, 1893, pp. 243–63). Victor is praised in the prologue. He is compared in virtue and courage to various biblical characters, and moral exhortations are made. This is followed by a brief description of miracles performed by him in Jerusalem. There is no epilogue. The text is poorly written.

The second work attributed to Theodosius is *The Miracles of Saint George* (Bodleian Library, Oxford, Marshall 23, fols. 83–95; John Rylands Library, Manchester, Copt 61, fols. 59–148; ed. Budge, 1888). This is a collection of miracles, similar to many circulating at that time, barely dressed up as a homily by means of a short prologue. Here, too, there is no epilogue, which may mean that the same person was responsible for the redaction of both texts. The miracles take place around the work of building the shrine of the saint at Ioppe (Jaffa) and are of various types (healings, restitution of stolen goods, etc.).

BIBLIOGRAPHY

Bouriant, U. "L'Eloge de l'apa Victor fils de Romanos." *Mémoires publiés par les membres de la mission archéologique française au Caire* 8 (1893):145–268.

Budge, E. A. W. *The Martyrdom and Miracles of Saint George of Cappadocia.* London, 1888.

Frend, W. H. C. *The Rise of the Monophysite Movement.* Cambridge, 1972.

Raabe, R. *Petrus der Iberer.* Leipzig, 1895.

TITO ORLANDI

THEODOTUS OF ANCYRA, bishop of Ancyra (Galatia) (d. c. 445). After being a supporter of Nestorius, he became an opponent, taking the side of CYRIL at the Council of EPHESUS. This was probably why his memory continued to live on in the Coptic literary tradition and why he was attributed with the authorship of a homily in honor of the martyr George. Historically, he wrote six books *Against Nestorius* (none of which has survived), an *Explanation of the Council of Nicaea,* and various homilies.

The homily preserved in the Coptic tradition, *In Georgium martyrem,* has survived in a full codex in Bohairic (Vatican Library, Rome, Coptica 63, 5, ed. Budge, 1888; Balestri and Hyvernat, 1908, Vol. 2, pp. 183–269). The saint is praised in the prologue, with the usual rhetorical convention of the fear of writing about him. This is followed by an account of his martyrdom, in accord with the well-known version of the *Passio Georgii,* followed by the translation of his relics to Diospolis Parva by the servant Pasicrates, the legend of the blindness of DIOCLETIAN, and the advent of CONSTANTINE. The conclusion refers to the consecration of the church of George.

The style and content of the homily clearly show that the text was produced in the late period of the CYCLES, that is, the seventh to the eighth century.

BIBLIOGRAPHY

Balestri, I., and H. Hyvernat. *Acta Martyrum,* 2 vols. CSCO 43, 44. Paris, 1908.

Budge, E. A. W. *The Martyrdom and Miracles of Saint George of Cappadocia.* London, 1888.

TITO ORLANDI

THEOGNOSTA, SAINT, fifth-century virgin who introduced Christianity to Georgia (feast day: 17 Tūt). The legend of the conversion of Georgia to Christianity has in Coptic one of its most complex and impressive witnesses. But as often happens in Coptic sources, the legend, unrecognizable in the scattered Sahidic fragments, is not told in its entirety in a coherent manner, except in the succinct résumé of the Copto-Arabic SYNAXARION of Mīkhā'īl Malīj. In the remarkable case of Theognosta, to read only this Arabic résumé, which mentions India, would not suggest that it concerned the Caucasus. Here, then, is a general survey of the legend for 17 Tūt in the Synaxarion.

Theognosta lived during the reigns of the great emperors Honorius and Arcadius (395–408). Representatives of the king of India come to Constantinople and on the way back seize the virgin Theognosta, who is engrossed in reading a book. In her country of exile, she is placed at the head of the royal family's gynaeceum as a prisoner. The king's son, when ill, is cured by the sign of the cross. The captive's reputation causes her to leave the rank of mere servant. In the course of a campaign the king is caught in fog, but, when he has made the sign of the cross according to the saint's rite, a wind scatters the fog, restores the light, and allows the king to win a victory over his enemies. Immediately on his return he asks the virgin for the grace of baptism. She refuses to baptize him herself. A delegation is sent to Honorius asking him to send a priest. A hermit is chosen, ordained, and sent. He baptizes them all and builds a monastery where Theognosta and many virgins live. The emperor rejoices at the conversion of the kingdom and gives them the hermit as bishop. They build a huge church by borrowing the pillars from a neighboring pagan temple. Through the virgin's prayer, the pillars are transported to the church. Thus the people of the country come to the knowledge of God (theognosia). The virgin lives and dies in peace surrounded by other religious women.

The Coptic fragments of the legend are preserved in very scattered conditions. There are at least three manuscripts.

1. I. Guidi first published in 1893 two leaves from the Coptic codex Borgia 162, which have the original pagination 151–52 and 161–62. In 1899, O. von Lemm first noticed that the country Tiberia mentioned there has nothing to do with the town Tiberias, but represents Iberia, preceded by the Coptic feminine article. In 1934 W. Till found two other leaves from the same codex in the Rainer collection in Vienna (K 9622 and 9452, with the pagination 147–50). Finally H. Munier published folios 135–36 of the same codex, according to the Cairo fragments 9236/7 in his catalogue (published in 1916, pp. 39–42). This codex alone restores twelve consecutive columns, then after ten missing pages, four more columns.

2. In 1906, Von Lemm took up the subject again and published a leaf from Paris (132.1, fol. 13), badly mutilated, but including the title of the piece and the upper part of the first four columns.

3. In the same article, Von Lemm published a codex, still more mutilated (Tischendorf's no. 3 at the Hermitage; Leningrad, dated A.D. 952), of which only some passages are really legible, although twelve columns can be identified.

In spite of the very poor condition of the fragments, it is clear that this third manuscript does not reproduce exactly the legend that is summarized by the Synaxarion, whereas the first two correspond perfectly.

From these fragments, one learns that the story takes place under Honorius and Arcadius. The letter from the Georgian princes is addressed to Honorius alone, and part of it is preserved. The hermit's name is Theophanes. Honorius summons him personally and speaks to him at length, then has him ordained in the town. Then they all set off for Iberia, to the archon of the country, without Honorius. Taken to the Blessed Theognosta, they hear from her of the miracles worked by the Cross of Christ, and notably the luminous cross that appeared in the darkness and led the king toward the town. Theophanes then gives a discourse on the creation, fall, and redemption. Following the gap in the manuscript Theophanes is seen ordained as archbishop in the town of Honorius, which is not named. The new prelate returns to Iberia and finds the church built, and he is told how it was constructed, thanks to Theognosta's prayer and the power of Christ and His cross. Theophanes immediately sends a letter to the emperor, telling the story of the two pillars from the temple of Apollo that nobody could move. The fragment ends at this point.

By contrast, the third text appears to presuppose a martyrdom, though whose is unclear. Theognosta is engaged in burying dead bodies. The bishop who sends Theognosta is called Eustathius. The placename Iberia does not appear.

The parallel constituted by the account written by Rufinus in his supplement to the Latin translation of the *Ecclesiastical History* of Eusebius (10.2), written about 402 and reproduced by the historian Socrates (1.20), is striking. The same story is inserted in the Greek Synaxarion for 27 October. But there the captive's name is not given, nor that of the hermit. In this tradition all place the event under Constantine, and therefore also under the bishop Eustathius of Antioch, according to the third Coptic manuscript.

There is, therefore, reason to question the most widespread Coptic account. There is no doubt about its age. The historian JOHN OF NIKIOU, in the seventh century, inserted it into his *Ecclesiastical History* (pub. Zotenberg, 1883, p. 201), where Iberia, doubtless through the medium of Ethiopic, is already transformed into the Yemen or India. The principal account contains an anomaly. It is virtually later than 408, the death of Arcadius, for Honorius is the only protagonist in the exchanges of letters and the sending of the priest, then of the bishop. At this time Honorius was in Ravenna, the plaything of Alaric, and was to die in 423 without ever having anything whatever to do in the Eastern empire. One can only remind oneself that Rufinus had his account from General Bacurius, a Georgian prince, who fought in 393 in the West beside Theodosius and Honorius, and thanks to a providential north wind, won a decisive victory over the pagan usurper Eugenius in September 394. From 395, on the death of Theodosius, Honorius necessarily became the interlocutor of Bacurius.

The Coptic legend that mentions Honorius and Arcadius seems to be a rereading and updating of an older account that mentioned Constantine, from which the Tischendorf fragment and Rufinus have preserved only a little.

It is difficult to sum up here the Georgian sources, properly so called, because their considerable complexity makes interpretation of the collection still more delicate. In Georgia, the virgin is always called Nino, and the captive of Rufinus becomes a king's daughter. But the problems raised by Georgian historiography are beyond the scope of this article.

BIBLIOGRAPHY

Guidi, I. "Di alcune pergamene saidiche della collezione Borgiana." *Rendiconti della real accademia dei Lincei*, ser. 5, 2 (1893):525–28.

Kekelidze, K. "Die Bekehrung Georgiens zum Christentum." *Morgenland* 18 (1928):1–51.

Lemm, O. von. "Kleine koptische Studien." *Bulletin de l'Académie des Sciences de Saint-Pétersbourg* 5, 10 (1899):416–34.

______. "Iberica." *Mémoires de l'Académie impériale des Sciences de Saint-Pétersbourg* 8, 7 (1906):19–32.

Munier, H. *Manuscrits coptes*. Catalogue générale des antiquités égyptiennes du Musée du Caire 9201–9304 [Vol. 74]. Cairo, 1916.

Till, W. *Koptische Pergamente theologischen Inhalts*, pp. 45–50. Vienna, 1934.

Zotenberg, H. "Mémoire sur la chronique byzantine de Jean, évêque de Nikiou." *Journal asiatique* ser. 7, 10 (1877):451–517; 12 (1878):245–347; 13 (1879):291–386.

MICHEL VAN ESBROECK

THEONAS, sixteenth patriarch of the See of Saint Mark (282–300). Theonas was a contemporary of Roman emperors Carus (282–283), Numerianus (283–284), and DIOCLETIAN (284–305). After the death of Patriarch Maximus, it took the faithful some months to find a worthy successor. Finally they elected Theonas, who was the head of the

CATECHETICAL SCHOOL OF ALEXANDRIA, succeeding DIONYSIUS THE GREAT (*Historia ecclesiastica* 7.32). At the time, Egypt seems to have been experiencing a breathing space from outright persecution under Emperor Probus, who treated the Christians leniently and allowed them to practice their religion undisturbed. Probus was rather more interested in the maintenance of the deteriorating public works in the country than fighting the spread of Christianity. Unhappily, he was assassinated by some of his own legionaries in 282, the year of Theonas' succession to the See of Saint Mark. But his policies of appeasement survived him under the rule of his son Numerianus, whose reign unfortunately did not last long, for he was murdered at Chalcedon after an abortive Persian expedition.

From the atmosphere of intrigue and conspiratorial strife prevailing in the Roman empire emerged a new successor in the person of Diocletian in 284. The opening years of his reign were marked by tolerance, while in his later years he became the severest of all persecutors of Christians. Had Diocletian died before the year 303, he would have passed into history as a pagan sponsor of Christians. Had Diocletian died before the year 303, he would have passed into history as a pagan sponsor of Christians. It was those early years of tolerance that coincided with Theonas' episcopate. The Egyptians were encouraged by his early leniency to aspire not only to more religious tolerance but also to political freedom from Rome, a movement that in the long run brought forth immeasurable calamities on the Egyptian people.

The political freedom movement found a leader in a Christian by the name of Achilleus, from the Thebaid in the interior of Upper Egypt. Later, Achilleus was made a presbyter in Alexandria, and it is said that he was nominated to head the Catechetical School (*Historia ecclesiastica* 7.32.30), which tied the church more closely to the nascent drive toward liberty.

On the religious front, the growing enfranchisement of the Christians enabled Theonas to contemplate openly the establishment of a new cathedral in Alexandria, which was built within sight of the pagan populace. He dedicated this new church to Mary, Mother of God (*Theotokos*), thereby inadvertently inviting trouble from hostile citizens, who feared for their idols.

The situation called for action from Rome. In fact, Diocletian organized two separate expeditions against Alexandria. The first, swift and relatively mild, aimed at stifling the tendency toward liberty and independence. This was accomplished without difficulty, and the leader Achilleus fled from Diocletian, who then retired from Alexandria to devote his attention to reorganizing the empire and to dealing with barbarian incursions on his distant frontiers. This provided the Christians with a period of respite, during which the patriarch aimed at courting favor with the state by the issuance of a conciliatory epistle to a Christian notable named Lucianus in the imperial administration.

Lucianus held the position of high chamberlain (*praepositus cubiculariorum*) at the imperial court, and Theonas wanted through him to designate the patriarchal guidelines for all Christians in the service of the state, with an eye on loyalty to the emperor in order to ensure freedom of worship for his flock and eventually terminate Christian persecutions. First published in the seventeenth century by a certain D'Archy, this interesting document has since been reproduced in translation by others (see Neale, 1897, pp. 85–88; Butcher, 1897, Vol. 1, pp. 112–14). A survey of its contents throws light on the diplomatic skill of Theonas and the situation of the Christians during his episcopate. Its preamble reads: "The peace which the churches now enjoy is granted to this end, that the good works of Christians may shine out before pagans, and that thence our Father which is in heaven may be glorified." He maintained that a Christian in office should carry out his duties in all humility as a model in the sight of the prince and all other authorities. He must avoid bribery, avarice, unworthy gain, and duplicity. He should never use evil or immodest language, but deal with others kindly, courteously, and with justice. He must fulfill his tasks with fear toward God and love toward the emperor. He must put on patience as a robe.

After a chain of exhortations, Theonas enters into the details of the expected performance of a Christian subject in a specific post. The keeper of the privy purse should meticulously retain a full record of his accounts, "never trusting to memory." The keeper of the robes and ornaments must have a complete register of his trust with the ability to find the whereabouts of every article without difficulty. The patriarch then devotes some space to the post of palace librarian, which seems to have been vacant at the time, in the hope that it might be filled by a Christian. The candidate should be knowledgeable on books and all details pertaining to librarianship. He should be acquainted with the principal orators, poets, and historians of antiquity, in readiness to furnish the emperor with his requirements.

The librarian should aim at the acquisition of such tomes as the Septuagint and the manuscript codices of works related to Christ, in the hope that he might be summoned to read them for the emperor and other authorities, thereby introducing the true faith to the inner circles of the imperial court. All the Christian servants in the administration must always be clean, neat, "bright faced," and respectful.

In fact, it would seem from this epistle that a considerable number of Christian civil servants filled the departments of the imperial government in the early years of Diocletian's reign. The same seems to apply to the army, where many legionaires were converted to Christianity. The tide of conversions seems to have been on the increase since Emperor Gallienus issued his edict of 259 placing Christianity among the *religiones licitae* (permitted religions), thus giving Christians for the first time legal status in the eyes of Roman authorities. Notables in the imperial house such as Dorotheus and Gorgonius were highly respected members of the imperial administration and both were pious converts (*Historia ecclesiastica* 7.1). Even within the domestic life of the imperial house, Diocletian's wife, Prisca, and his daughter, Valeria, aroused questions among people when they refrained from appearing at the state functions of sacrifice to the idols. News of their possible conversion to Christianity began to circulate freely among pagan onlookers at these official ceremonies. Indeed, the last years of Theonas' episcopate could have passed as a golden interlude of tolerance toward Christians under Roman paganism. Thus we begin to see Christians emerging from their habitual concealment to hold open meetings and build churches.

From another perspective, however, this period appears as the calm before the gathering storm. First, the pagan populace, which was still in a majority, began to show signs of discontent and unrest toward the temerity of their Christian neighbors, who constituted a real danger to the official gods. Second, the release of some of the pressure on the Christian congregations seems to have broken the unity that had brought them together as a forceful front in the face of their common oppressors. In Christian ranks, heretofore unknown problems started to emerge, such as envy, lack of concern for past troubles, and heretical argumentation, which weakened the church. Third, authorities who remained faithful to the old pagan gods succeeded in prevailing upon the emperor to turn the tide of tolerance toward the Christians into a policy of brutal repression in defense of the official religion of the empire. Fourth, the freedom movement led by Achilleus in Alexandria, which was largely identified with the Christian church, left no room for Diocletian to avoid striking a deadly blow against the Egyptian metropolis, which was gradually becoming a fortress for the faith. His two expeditions against Alexandria ended in the total defeat of the rebels, who were subsequently subjected to the most rigorous punishment for their insubordination and for their religion. Thus Diocletian issued his memorable edict of 23 February 303, signaling the inauguration of the worst of all the persecutions, which bathed the latter years of his reign in Christian blood until his abdication. But this bloody chapter belongs to the next patriarchate, of PETER I, who lost his head in the persecution and became identified as the "Seal of the Martyrs."

Apart from the building of numerous churches to cope with the expanding congregations, the internal activity of Theonas is demonstrated by his support of the Catechetical School, which he had headed at one time. His appointee to its presidency, Pierius, who succeeded the famous Theognostus, proved to be a tremendous force in upholding the faith and in homiletic and theological activities. JEROME called Pierius "Origen Junior" (*De viris illustribus* 76), who shook the metropolis with his resounding homilies. His written works include *On the Beginning of Osee*, *On the Gospel of Luke*, *On the Mother of God*, and *The Life of Saint Pamphilus*. The last work was a great eulogy of one of his old pupils who was martyred in the presecution of Diocletian. Some reports indicate that Pierius passed his later years in Rome, while others claim that he won the crown of martyrdom in Alexandria in the reign of Diocletian.

After approximately nineteen years at the head of the church, Theonas died in bed. He is commemorated in the Coptic SYNAXARION on 2 Kiyahk, which was probably the date of his death.

BIBLIOGRAPHY

Altaner, B. *Patrology*, trans. Hilda Graef. London, 1958.

Bardenhewer, O. *Geschichte der altkirchlichen Literatur*, 3 vols. Freiburg, 1902–1912.

Butcher, E. L. *The Story of the Church of Egypt*, 2 vols. London, 1897.

Duchesne, L. *Early History of the Christian Church*, Vol. 1, pp. 341ff. London, 1909.

Jerome. *De viris illustribus*, trans. E. C. Richardson. In *A Select Library of the Nicene and Post-Nicene*

Fathers of the Christian Church, series 2, ed. Philip Schaff and Henry Wace. Grand Rapids, Mich., 1892.
Neale, J. M. *The Patriarchate of Alexandria.* London, 1897.
Quasten, J. *Patrology,* 3 vols, Utrecht and Antwerp, 1975.
Smith, W., and H. Wace. *Dictionary of Christian Biography,* 4 vols. New York, 1974.

AZIZ S. ATIYA

THEOPHANES, sixtieth patriarch of the See of Saint Mark (952–956). Theophanes was already an old man from the city of Alexandria when invested with this high office. His biography, with its tragic ending, is succinctly cited in the HISTORY OF THE PATRIARCHS. It is said that the patriarchs at that time were expected to pay their electors the sum of 1,000 dinars every year. When at one time Theophanes was unable to meet their demand, a dispute arose between him and his electorate, ending with his repudiation of the patriarchal garb. He ultimately threw it in their faces. Apparently the infuriated Theophanes became mad, or, according to the *History of the Patriarchs,* was filled with an evil spirit. Thus, his electors chained him in iron fetters and took him in a boat destined for Miṣr (al-Fusṭāṭ). On the way they placed him in the hold of the ship, where one of the disciples of the bishops placed a wet pillow on his face and sat on it until he died. Thus ended a patriarchate lasting four years and six months.

SUBHI Y. LABIB

THEOPHILOS I, Coptic archbishop of Jerusalem (1935–1945). He was born in 1893 in the village of al-Maṭahrah, Egypt. He joined the Monastery of Saint Antony (DAYR ANBĀ ANṬŪNIYŪS) in the Eastern Desert, becoming a monk in 1910 and adopting the name Buṭrus. In 1915 he was ordained and then appointed HEGUMENOS. After serving as pastor of the Coptic community at Kom Ombo, where he caused a large church to be built, he was appointed abbot in 1931 of Cairo's Monastery of Saint Antony and the Resurrection. During the same year he became abbot of the Monastery of Saint Antony in the Eastern Desert. In 1935 he succeeded Basilios III as archbishop of Jerusalem, taking the name Theophilos. Shortly after his consecration, he was restored to the abbacy of the Monastery of Saint Antony. He constructed a new church at this monastery and opened two schools, one for boys and one for girls, in Būsh near the administrative headquarters of the monastery. He also built houses for the endowment of the monastery in Cairo and bought about twenty *feddans* (a little more than twenty acres) of land near Banī Suef, annexing them to the endowment of Saint Antony's. He was responsible for the construction of churches in the governorates of Sharqiyyah and the Canal as well as in his home town near Minyā. He also built the Church of Saint George at al-ʿArīsh and bought land near the river Jordan to build a monastery.

He was fatally wounded by a gunshot on 1 October 1945, while visiting farms near the monastery in Būsh in the governorate of Banī Suef.

ARCHBISHOP BASILIOS

THEOPHILUS, twenty-third patriarch of the See of Saint Mark (385–412). A complex and controversial patriarch, Theophilus was much admired for his many writings, his destruction of pagan temples and subsequent church-building program, as well as his important role as a mediator of schisms at Antioch, Bostra, and Jerusalem during the early part of his tenure. Nonetheless, he acquired a lasting and perhaps deserved infamy for his persecution of the monks of NITRIA and SCETIS and his banishment of JOHN CHRYSOSTOM, archbishop of Constantinople. Theophilus is the villain in PALLADIUS' biography of Chrysostom and bears the epithet *amphallax,* "two-faced" (Palladius, *Dialogue* 21; Coleman-Norton, 1928, 34.13).

Theophilus fares no better among several ancient historians, such as SOCRATES Scholasticus, SOZOMEN, and ISIDORUS OF PELUSIUM, who had valid reasons for their criticisms. The patriarch's quarrels probably arose more from spite than from substantial issues. For his integral part in the deposition of Chrysostom at the so-called Council of the Oak, Theophilus was excommunicated by Pope Innocent I. The notoriety of Theophilus in this affair was apparently so great that later generations had to restore his image. In a Coptic homily (Amélineau, 1888, pp. 188–91) attributed to his nephew, CYRIL I, Theophilus apologizes to John's ghost. The stand of Theophilus against Origenism, however, won for him the admiration of other persons such as LEO I; JEROME; SYNESIUS of Cyrene; THEODORET; the compiler of the Alexandrian SYNAXARION, JOHN, the eighth-century bishop of Nikiou in Upper Egypt; and SĀWĪRUS IBN AL-MUQAFFAʿ, tenth-century bishop of al-Ashmūnayn.

He appears as a saint in both the Coptic and Syrian churches, and his festival day is fixed on 18 Bābah (Forget, 1921, p. 72).

Childhood and Early Career

According to an Ethiopic text of John of Nikiou's *Chronicle* 79 (Zotenberg, 1879, pp. 315–17; Charles, 1916, 75–76), Theophilus and his sister were born in Memphis and orphaned early. As a portent of Theophilus' later destruction of the pagan temples, the idols in a Memphite temple fell to the ground and broke into pieces when Theophilus and his sister entered. In Alexandria the two orphans came under the protection of Patriarch ATHANASIUS. The sister later bore CYRIL I. Theophilus studied under Athanasius and distinguished himself both in piety and scholarship.

In his career as patriarch, Theophilus razed several pagan places of worship at Alexandria and elsewhere, the most famous of which were the Serapion and the Mithraion. His destruction of the Serapion merited him an illustration in the *Alexandrian World Chronicle,* now in the Pushkin State Museum of Fine Arts, Moscow (Bauer and Strzygowski, 1906, pp. 56–58, 121–22). Socrates states (*Historia ecclesiastica* 5.16) that the emperor, Theodosius I, granted Theophilus' request for the destruction of the temples.

Theophilus was responsible for building more than seven churches (Orlandi, 1970, pp. 100–106). Theodosius allowed him to convert the temple of Dionysius to a church (Sozomen, *Historia ecclesiastica* 7.15). The Alexandrian Synaxarion has reference to seven churches, but names only those sacred to the Virgin, Raphael, and John the Baptist and Elisha (Forget, 1921, pp. 72–73; 1926, pp. 111–12, 292). Eutychius of Alexandria mentions the Church of Saint Mary in his *Annals* (PG 111.1026). The Raphael church is known from *History of the Patriarchs* (Vol. 2, p. 430), and the Sahidic text of Theophilus' dedication thereof. The Synaxarion (Forget, 1921, p. 77), a Syriac text of Theophilus' alleged vision of the Holy Family (Geerard, 1974, p. 125, no. 2628), and a Bohairic homily attributed to Theophilus with an Ethiopic version thereof (Geerard, 1974, p. 124, no. 2626) each mention Theophilus' supposed consecration of a seventh church to the Three Children of Babylon. Theophilus began the great church of ABŪ MĪNĀ, in Maryūt, which was finished by TIMOTHY II AELURUS (Sāwīrus 3. 122).

In the Syriac text about the Holy Family, the patriarch claims to have built a church dedicated to John the Baptist, which figures prominently at the end of another Syriac text on the life of John the Baptist (Mingana, 1927, pp. 256–57). Theophilus also converted the Serapion into a glorious church (John of Nikiou, *Chronicle,* 78; Zotenberg, 1879, pp. 314–315; Charles, 1916, pp. 74–75; Rufinus, *Historia ecclesiastica,* 2.17, PL 21.536). He later brought the body and head of the saint for reinterment in a tomb within that church. The church or martyrium may have been the subject of one of Theophilus' homilies (van Lantschoot, 1931; Orlandi, 1969a, p. 23; Orlandi, 1970, pp. 100–102).

To the emperors Theodosius I and his son Arcadius, Theophilus built two churches. Theophilus also built or renovated several other churches and monasteries beyond Alexandria (Eutychius, *Annals* 528, PG 111.1026; Sozomen 7.15; Zacharias Rhetor, *Historia ecclesiastica,* 5.6; Brooks, 1924, pp. 154–155; Favale, 1956, pp. 532–35; Orlandi, 1970, pp. 104–106).

According to several sources, the emperor Theodosius I gave Theophilus the keys to all the pagan temples in Egypt, from Alexandria to Aswan, with permission to build churches with whatever riches found therein. In several accounts, Theophilus finds an inscription with three *thetas,* signifying God (*theos*), the emperor Theodosius I, and Theophilus. Although the accounts are highly fanciful, they suggest that Theodosius I, as Constantius II and Julian before him, had indeed entrusted the keys of certain pagan temples to a bishop (Dölger, 1932, p. 191).

Not everyone approved of Theophilus' building activity. Palladius called the patriarch a "lithomaniac" (*Dialogue,* 22; Coleman-Norton, 1928, 35.19) and compared him to a pharaoh in his zeal for constructing grand buildings. Isidorus of Pelusium labels him a "money worshiper, crazy about stone" (*Epistles,* 1.152, PG 78.284–85). The author of the Syriac text about Theophilus' vision of the Holy Family may have had these or similar charges in mind and, in an attempt to defend Theophilus' reputation, claimed that he spent the money he found in the pagan temples on the poor and needy, not on churches.

The Schisms at Antioch (c. 392 and 394)

According to Ambrose of Milan (Epistle 56, PL 16.1220–22), Theophilus was named mediator at a synod in Capua because of his impartiality in the dispute between Flavian and EVAGRIUS, both of Antioch. Flavian had the support of the emperor but not the pope. Evagrius was the champion of the influential Melitian faction at Antioch. Ambrose apparently thought little of both. Flavian refused the request of Theophilus to attend a council of arbitration. Answering Theophilus' inquiry, Ambrose encouraged him to summon Flavian again, and if he still refused, the archbishop should consult Pope Siricus. Evagrius died not long afterward, but Flavian was not accepted until 398, when in a highly unusual incident of cooperation, Theophilus worked with John Chrysostom to end the schism and to reconcile Flavian with Pope Siricus.

In 394 a schism arose between Rufinus of Aquileia and John of Jerusalem on the one side and Jerome and Epiphanius of Constantia in Cyprus on the other. Epiphanius was charged with improperly ordaining Jerome's brother, Paulinus, as bishop. Both sides accused the other of Origenism. Theophilus corresponded with both factions and appears to have been sympathetic to them equally. Although the result of the controversy is not clear, the concern of Theophilus for the welfare of the church and maintenance of the orthodox faith is richly documented in Jerome's letters (Nautin, 1974).

The Bostra Affair (394)

Meanwhile, to determine the rightful claimant to the See of Bostra in Arabia, Theophilus negotiated with Flavian of Antioch, Nectarius of Constantinople, GREGORY OF NYSSA, and THEODORUS OF MOPSUESTIA, among others, in the capital. One Bagadius had been deposed by two bishops, who died by the time the meeting convened. Agapius was the replacement. With the concurrence of Nectarius and Flavian, Theophilus judged that although he could not comment on the actions of the dead, in the future at least three bishops, and preferably all their colleagues, should pronounce depositions. He therefore presumably accepted the appointment of Agapius. The meeting and apparent concord between Theophilus and Flavian while they were at odds is perhaps explained by their attending the consecration of the church of Peter and Paul near Chalcedon, where Theophilus was to have his infamous Council of the Oak in 403. By this interpretation, the judgment concerning Bostra was a development from the consecration; it was not the major event (Pelagius, *In defensione trium capitulorum;* see Geerard, 1974, p. 132, no. 2677[3]; Duchesne, 1885; Batiffol, 1924, pp. 283–86; Bright, 1887, p. 1001).

Theophilus' Relationship with the Monks and the Anthropomorphite Controversy (399–403)

Throughout his career, Theophilus was on good terms with various groups of ascetics in Nitria and Scetis. Even after his rancorous disputes with ISIDORUS and the Tall Brothers, the archbishop commanded the loyalty of the more simple-minded inhabitants of the monastic settlements. Jerome observes (*Epistle* 82) that the monks rushed to greet Theophilus on the occasion of his visits. In both the Coptic and Greek versions of the APOPHTHEGMATA PATRUM (Chaîne, 1960, nos. 19, 114; PG 65.95–96, 197–202, 221–22), the patriarch and the monks consult each other. According to one apothegm, the patriarch enlisted the help of the monks for the destruction of the Serapion at Alexandria (PG 65.199–200, no. 3). In the HISTORY OF THE PATRIARCHS (2.425–26) Theophilus sent monks from the Pachomian communities in Upper Egypt to drive out pagans from Jerusalem, perhaps an allusion to his persecution of the "Origenist" monks, who fled from Egypt to Palestine and then to Constantinople. He also sent his nephew and successor, Cyril, to study with the monks, especially the learned Serapion, in Nitria. ARSENIUS, too, was held in such high esteem that Theophilus in his dying words praised him (PG 65.201–202, no. 82).

The argument of Theophilus with Isidorus over a gift of money complicated these amicable relations. Fearing the wrath of Theophilus, Isidorus fled to the valley of Nitria where he had many friends, particularly Dioscorus, Ammonius, Euthymius, and Eusebius, collectively known as the "Tall Brothers" because of their stature. The jealousy of Theophilus over the hospitality accorded Isidorus, and not his concern for the monks' alleged belief in Origenism, was the source of the controversy. The ensuing conflict is well known from ancient and modern sources (Socrates, *Historia ecclesiastica* 6.7, 9, 11–14; Sozomen 8.11–14; Palladius, *Dialogue* 23–4, Coleman-Norton, 1928, 38.9–40.7; Baur, 1960, pp. 192–206).

Before the problems with Isidorus, Theophilus had been quite friendly with the Tall Brothers and had awarded them important posts. For example, Theophilus appointed Dioscorus to the bishopric of Hermopolis Parva in Lower Egypt, a position he accepted reluctantly. Later, the four monks became disaffected with the materialism of Theophilus (Socrates, 6.7), and perhaps with his zeal for building churches. They returned to the Nitrian communities. Stung by their ostensible disloyalty and, according to Sozomen (8.12), their generosity to Isidorus, the patriarch turned on these friends.

Heretofore, Theophilus had not paid attention to the monks' supposed Origenist beliefs or to their opinions about God's form. Theophilus' good friend and frequent correspondent, Jerome, readily admitted (*Epistle* 82) to the patriarch that he read ORIGEN's works and admired his exegetical abilities, although he by no means agreed with all of his opinions. Theophilus never censured him. Sozomen (8.11–12, 14) and especially Socrates (6.7–9, 13–14) state that Theophilus, as well as the Tall Brothers, accepted Origen's opinion about God's incorporeality. Further, Theophilus had read and continued to read Origen's works long after the controversy was over (Socrates 6.17). He cleverly refrained from publicizing his concurrence with Origen over the nature of God's existence and played instead upon the volatile emotions of the less learned monks in Nitria and Scetis by charging the Tall Brothers with Origenism. This accusation was a battle cry for the simple-minded monks, who adhered to "anthropomorphiticism" or the belief in God's human form and quickly rallied round the patriarch. Theophilus' Paschal letter of 399 was directed against the Anthropomorphites.

Using Origenism as a convenient, if hypocritical, means by which to ruin the Tall Brothers, Theophilus made a great show of his tenacity to the orthodox faith. In his Paschal letter of 402 (Jerome, *Epistle* 98, PL 22.799), he referred to Origen as the "hydra of heresies." According to Palladius (*Dialogue* 23–24; Coleman-Norton, 1928, 38.9–40.7; see also Sozomen 8.12), Theophilus' forcible expulsion of the monks involved bloodshed.

The Tall Brothers fled first to Palestine and then, with fifty of their colleagues, to Constantinople, where they sought refuge with John, later known as Chrysostom (Socrates 6.11; Sozomen 8.12). The important and balanced eyewitness account of Sulpicius Severus of the situation prevalent at Alexandria shortly after the Tall Brothers had left (*Dialogues* 1.6–7; PL 20.187–89) corroborates Palladius', Socrates', and Sozomen's statements.

Opposition to John Chrysostom

Prior to the dispute with the Tall Brothers, Theophilus had nominated his presbyter Isidorus for the archiepiscopate of Constantinople upon the death of Nectarius late in 397. On several occasions Isidorus had proven his discretion and his loyalty to the elected patriarch. Nonetheless, John, then bishop at Antioch, was elected early in 398. Although Theophilus initially sought to discredit him, he acquiesced to John's election when faced with the possibility of answering unspecified charges made against him. He even supported John in his efforts to end the schism at Antioch. Once the four Tall Brothers and their colleagues fled to Constantinople and found shelter with him, however, the ill will of Theophilus was renewed (Socrates 6.2; Sozomen 8.2; Bright, 1887, p. 1000).

Like the debacle with the monks, the struggle with John is well documented, especially by Palladius and in a letter written by Chrysostom himself and preserved by Palladius, who reports (*Dialogue* 24–25, Coleman-Norton, 1928, 40.13–41.22) that John was well disposed toward the monks but did not receive them at communion for fear of offending Theophilus. John sent a letter to Alexandria and asked his colleague to honor him by forgiving the monks. Although Sozomen denies (8.13) that Theophilus returned an answer, Palladius claims (*Dialogue* 25, Coleman-Norton, 1928, 41.22–42.9) that Theophilus replied by sending the same clergy back with false documents proving that the monks were reprehensible. At this, the Tall Brothers wrote to the patriarch at Alexandria, stating that they anathematized all incorrect doctrine, and to John, with a list of the grievous injuries they had suffered from Theophilus. Their accusations must have been shocking, because Palladius, never one to spare Theophilus an unkind word, emphatically refrains from detailing the contents of their petition lest his audience doubt his credibility (*Dialogue* 25; Coleman-Norton, 1928, 42.9–11).

The monks went to the empress EUDOXIA, who complied with their request for a trial, at Constantinople, of Theophilus and the clergy who had borne the false documents. A counter council at Constantinople was also envisaged to try John. Theophilus urged Epiphanius of Cyprus and his eastern colleagues to attend, thus violating the sixteenth canon of the Nicene council that he had previously accused John of transgressing. This canon prohibited clergy from interfering in the affairs of other churches. Epiphanius ordained a deacon in John's church without his permission (Socrates 6.12), heedless of the second canon laid down at Constantinople in 381, which forbade bishops from performing ordinations outside their dioceses. Meanwhile, Theophilus set off for the capital (see Coleman-Norton, 1928, p. 165, note on Palladius, 26).

Heretofore, John had ignored the actions of Theophilus and Epiphanius. When Epiphanius announced that he would not meet with him until he denounced Origen and expelled the Tall Brothers, John finally retorted that he would deal further with Epiphanius only after the council originally summoned by Eudoxia against Theophilus had been convened. Shortly thereafter, the Tall Brothers met with Epiphanius and asked whether he had actually read any of their works. Epiphanius had not and was finally convinced of their innocence. After harsh words with John, he set sail for Cyprus, only to die at sea (Socrates 6.14; Sozomen 8.15).

Having stopped at Chalcedon en route to Constantinople, Theophilus gathered various bishops hostile to John and urged them to hasten to the capital. John, meanwhile, fell out of Eudoxia's favor because of a sermon on the vanity of women.

Disguising his intentions, Theophilus then arrived in the capital "like a dung-beetle laden with Egypt's and India's best, emitting a sweet smell instead of the stink of jealousy" (Palladius, *Dialogue* 26, Coleman-Norton, 1928, 44.3–5). He set about organizing the infamous "Council of the Oak," just outside Chalcedon. John refused to appear at the "council" or "synod" until his enemies were removed from the bench and replaced by more impartial judges. This request was never granted.

Many of the twenty-nine charges recorded against John by Photius (PG 103.105–10; Baur, 1960, pp. 246–48) are rather petty. In fact, John's failure to appear was the only reason for his downfall (Socrates 6.15; Sozomen 8.17). John went into exile three days later, only to be recalled almost immediately. Meanwhile Theophilus refused the emperor's summons to the capital for the trial of his own conduct that had been planned much earlier. Not long after, opinion once more turned against John at a second synod convened by Arcadius, which confirmed his condemnation.

Theophilus himself was in trouble. John denounced him in a letter to Pope Innocent I (Palladius, *Dialogue* 8–12), and Theophilus also notified the pope of his actions. Possibly at this time Theophilus composed his famous condemnation of John, which survives in three Latin translations (Baur, 1960, pp. 328–29). Angered by the arrogance of Theophilus, Innocent called for a synod wherein the patriarch was to substantiate his claims against John on pain of excommunication (Palladius, *Dialogue* 8, 12, 78). Innocent prevailed upon the emperor, Honorius, to call for a synod. The emperor wrote to his brother and colleague, Arcadius, giving his assent and labeling Theophilus as the culprit in the whole affair (Palladius, *Dialogue* 14–15). Whether such a council was held is unknown (see Baur, 1960, pp. 396–406).

Writings

Despite Theophilus' fame as a writer, no critical edition of his works exists, other than the very incomplete collection in Patrologia Graeca (65.33–68). His writings were admired by Pope Gelasius I (PL 59.171–72). Pope Leo I recommends the sermons of Theophilus to the anti-Eutychians (*Epistles* 117, PL 54.1038, 1076). Theodoret has kind words for him (Epistle 83, PG 83.1271–72). The fame of Theophilus as an exegete is apparent from the number of quotations from his works (Richard, 1938; Reuss, 1957, pp. 151–52). He was often imitated (Gennadius, *De Viris Illustribus* 33, PL 58.1077). The list of his spurious writings is truly impressive (Richard, 1939, p. 15; Geerard, 1974, pp. 124–31; Delobel and Richard, 1946, col. 526). His work has four divisions: Paschal letters, other correspondence, homilies, and other miscellaneous items (Opitz, 1934, cols. 2159–65; Richard, 1939; Delobel and Richard, 1946, cols. 524–27; Geerard, 1974, pp. 112–34; Crum, 1915, pp. xvi–xvii; Favale, 1956, pp. 218–38; Orlandi, 1970, pp. 97–98).

Around 390, Theophilus sent Theodosius I a Paschal canon establishing the Easter cycle for one hundred years to make the Alexandrian schedule universal (PG 65.48–52). Despite his friendship with the emperor (PG 111.1025–26), the ambitions of Theophilus were disappointed. Nonetheless, the canon was widely used and admired long after his death by persons such as Pope Leo I and Proterius of Alexandria (PL 54.929, 1085, 1100). As late as the eighth century, Bede recalls (*Historia ecclesiastica* 5.21) this Paschal canon.

Of the annual Paschal letters written by Theophilus throughout his tenure, many fragments survive. Latin translations exist in Jerome's letters, and various Oriental recensions are known, excluding Coptic. References or allusions to the Easter epistles of Theophilus are scattered throughout late antique literature (Richard, 1939, pp. 35–38; Geerard, 1974, pp. 112–17; Delobel and Richard, 1946, col. 524).

Numerous other letters survive, in whole or in part. These attest to a wide range of important civil and religious authorities. His correspondence with

Jerome, preserved in the latter's *Epistles* 87, 92, 96, 98, 100 (PL 22), in particular is a rich and important source for reconstructing not only the aftermath of the quarrel of Theophilus with the "Origenist" monks of Nitria and Scetis, but also his efforts to end the schism between Rufinus and John of Jerusalem on the one side and Epiphanius and Jerome on the other (Nautin, 1974). At least five of the letters of Theophilus were addressed to monks, and these support the picture of close contacts with the monks presented in the *Apophthegmata Patrum.*

Including twenty-seven Armenian translations, more than fifty homilies remain, most of which are of uncertain authenticity (Geerard, 1974, pp. 122–31). Two tracts mentioned by Gennadius (*De viris illustribus* 33; PL 58.1077–78), *Against Origen* and *Against the Anthropomorphites,* may be among the homilies tallied under different names, as is perhaps true also of work against Origen, cited by Theodoret in the second dialogue of his *Eranistes* (PG 83.197–98). John CASSIAN reports (*Collationes* 10.2) that the Paschal letter of 399 was directed against the Anthropomorphites.

Several of the homilies, some spurious, are preserved in Coptic (Richard, 1939, pp. 43–44; Geerard, 1974, pp. 123–25). These are: *The Crucifixion and the Good Thief, On Penitence and Abstinence, On the Assumption of the Virgin Mary, On the Three Children of Babylon,* a sermon on the church dedicated to the archangel RAPHAEL and another on JOHN THE BAPTIST (Orlandi, 1972; van Lantschoot, 1931, pp. 235–54).

Of Theophilus' many other writings, perhaps the most important is the diatribe against John Chrysostom, preserved in part by Jerome (Geerard, pp. 131–34).

Reputation

Embroiled as he was in several disputes, Theophilus is either hero or villain in many histories of the early church (Favale, 1956, pp. 239–46), depending on the gullibility or sympathies of the writer, particularly with regard to the works of Origen. Theophilus is consistently praised, however, in Oriental literature.

Jerome was the most loyal supporter of Theophilus; he always addresses him as "father" and "master." Rufinus boasts of having been a student of Theophilus (Jerome, *Apologia contra Rufinum* 3.18), and Synesius of Cyrene lauds him for the scholarship of his annual Paschal letters (*Epistle* 9, PG 66.1345–47). Theodoret (*Historia ecclesiastica* 5.22) regards him as a "man of sound wisdom and lofty courage" and quotes him approvingly in the second dialogue of his *Eranistes* (PG 83.198) for his anti-Origenist stance and his belief in the immortality of the soul. Pope Leo I commends Theophilus as well as Athanasius and Cyril for their orthodoxy (*Epistle* 130, PL 54.1076, 1079). TIMOTHY AELURUS, Monophysite patriarch of Alexandria (d. 477), excerpts the twenty-second Paschal letter of Theophilus for the same purpose (Ebied and Wickham, 1970, pp. 355–56). Sāwīrus' remarkably hagiographical entry for Theophilus is full of praise for his energy in driving out the pagans and in building churches (2.425–30).

The energy with which Theophilus pursued his various ambitions also earned him disrepute among many other writers such as Sozomen and Palladius. Socrates describes him as a "hothead" (*Historia ecclesiastica* 6.7; see also Palladius, *Dialogue* 23, Coleman-Norton, 1928, 37.22–38.5). This temper may have been the reason for the conspicuous reluctance of several monks to serve as bishops under Theophilus. Among these monks were Aphou (Florovsky, 1965, p. 280), Evagrius (Socrates 4.23), Nilammon (Sozomen 8.19), and Dioscorus. Their hesitation corroborates the remark of Palladius (*Dialogue* 19, Coleman-Norton, 1928, 31.10–13) that Theophilus sought to control his bishops as "mindless" persons.

Conspicuous too was his hypocrisy. He accused the Tall Brothers of Origenism yet he himself read Origen's works. He broke conciliar law despite his denunciations of John for doing the same. Isidorus of Pelusium faulted Cyril I for behaving like his uncle Theophilus (*Epistle* 1.310, PG 78.361–62). No doubt inspired by these accounts, Gibbon wrote of Theophilus that he was "the perpetual enemy of peace and virtue, a bold bad man, whose hands were alternately polluted with gold and with blood" (Gibbon, 1900, p. 200).

BIBLIOGRAPHY

Altaner, B., and A. Stuiber. *Patrologie: Leben, Schriften und Lehre der Kirchenväter.* Freiburg, 1966.

Amélineau, E. *Monuments pour servir à l'histoire de l'Égypte chrétienne au IVe, Ve, VIe, et VIIe siecles.* Paris, 1888.

Batiffol, P. *La Siège apostolique.* Paris, 1924.

Bauer, A., and J. Strzygowski. *Eine Alexandrinische Weltchronik, Text und Miniaturen eines griechischen Papyrus der Sammlung W. Goleniscev.* Vienna, 1906.

Baur, C. *John Chrysostom and His Time. Vol. 2, Constantinople,* trans. M. Gonzaga. Westminster, Md., 1960.
Bright, W. "Theophilus." In DCB 4, pp. 999–1008.
Brooks, E. W., ed. *Zacharias Rhetor. Historia Ecclesiastica.* CSCO 87. Scriptores Syriaci, ser. 3, 5. Louvain, 1924.
Chaîne, M. *Le manuscrit de la version copte en dialecte Sahidique des "Apophthegmata Patrum."* Institut français d'Archéologie orientale, Bibliothèque d'Etudes Coptes 6. Cairo, 1960.
Charles, R. H. *The Chronicle of John, Bishop of Nikiu.* London, 1916.
Coleman-Norton, P. R., ed. *Palladii Dialogus de Vita S. Joannis Chrysostomi.* Cambridge, 1928.
Crum, W. E., and A. Erhard. *Der Papyruscodex saec. VI–VII der Phillippsbibliothek in Cheltenham. Koptische theologische Schriften.* Schriften der Wissenschaftlichen Gesellschaft in Strassburg, Heft 18. Strasbourg, 1915.
Delobel, R., and M. Richard. "Théophile d'Alexandrie." In *Dictionnaire de Théologie Catholique,* Vol. 15, Pt. 1, cols. 523–30. Paris, 1946.
Dölger, F. J. *Antike und Christentum. Vol. 3.* Münster, 1932.
Duchesne, L. "Le Pape Sirice et le siège de Bostra (un appel au Pape au VIe siècle)." *Annales de philosophie chrétienne* 13/111 (1885):280–84.
Ebied, R. Y., and L. R. Wickham. "A Collection of Unpublished Syriac Letters of Timothy Aelurus." *Journal of Theological Studies* 21(1970):321–69.
Favale, A. "Teofilo d'Alessandria (345c.–412)." *Salesianum* 18 (1956):215–46, 498–535; 19 (1957):34–82, 215–72, 452–86.
Florovsky, G. "Theophilus of Alexandria and Apa Aphou of Pemdje: The Anthropomorphites in the Egyptian Desert, II." In *Harry Austryn Wolfson Jubilee Volume: On the Occasion of His Seventy-fifth Birthday,* Vol. 1, pp. 275–310. Jerusalem, 1965.
Forget, J., ed. *Synaxarium Alexandrinum, I–II.* CSCO 78, 90. Scriptores Arabici, ser. 3, 18–19. Louvain, 1921, 1926.
Geerard, M. *Clavis Patrum Graecorum, Vol. 2: Ab Athanasio ad Chrysostomus.* Turnhout, Belgium, 1974.
Gibbon, E. *The Decline and Fall of the Roman Empire,* ed. J. B. Bury. New York, 1900.
Hamilton, F. J., and E. W. Brooks. *The Syriac Chronicle Known as That of Zacharias of Mytilene.* London, 1899.
van Lantschoot, A. "Fragments coptes d'un panégyrique de S. Jean-Baptiste." *Le Muséon* 44 (1931):235–54.
Lazzati, G. *Teofilo d'Alessandria.* Publicazioni della Università cattolica del Sacro Cuore, ser. IVa, Scienze filologiche, 19. Milan, 1935.
Mingana, A. *Woodbrooke Studies,* Vol. 1. Cambridge, 1927.
Nautin, P. "La Lettre de Théophile d'Alexandrie à l'église de Jérusalem et la réponse de Jean de Jérusalem (Juin-Juillet 396)." *Revue d'histoire ecclésiastique* 69 (1974):365–95.
Opitz, H. G. "Theophilus von Alexandrien." *Paulys Real-Encyclopädie der classischen Altertumswissenschaft.* Vol. 5, Pt. 2, cols. 2149–65. Stuttgart, 1934.
Orlandi, T. "Un Frammento copto di Teofilo di Alessandria." *Rivista degli studi orientali* 44 (1969a):23–26.
______. "Uno scritto di Teofilo alessandrino sulla distruzione del Serapeum?" *La Parola del passato* 121 (1969b):295–304.
______. *Storia della chiesa di Alessandria. Vol. 2. Da Teofilo a Timoteo II.* Milan, 1970.
______. "Un encomio copto di Raffaele Arcangelo ('Relatio Theophili')." *Rivista degli studi orientali* 47 (1972):211–33.
Quasten, J., *Patrology, Vol. 3: The Golden Age of Patristic Literature from the Council of Nicaea to the Council of Chalcedon.* Westminster, Maryland, 1965.
Reuss, J. *Matthäus-Kommentare aus der griechischen Kirche.* Texte und Untersuchungen 61. Berlin, 1957.
Richard, M. "Une Homélie de Théophile d'Alexandrie sur l'Institution de l'Euchariste." *Revue d'histoire ecclésiastique* 33 (1937):46–56.
Richard, M. "Les Fragments exégétiques de Théophile d'Alexandrie et de Théophile d'Antioche." *Revue Biblique* 47 (1938):387–97.
______. "Les Écrits de Théophile d'Alexandrie." *Le Muséon* 52 (1939):33–50.
Zotenberg, H., ed. *Mémoire sur la chronique byzantine de Jean, évêque de Nikiou.* Paris, 1879.

DONALD B. SPANEL

THEOPHILUS, SAINT, monk and the only son of King Tamulawus, ruler of a Greek island. He received a Christian education. At the age of twelve, having read in the Gospel, "He who would be perfect, let him leave all his goods and follow me," Theophilus disguised himself and left his father, journeying to Egypt and the monastery of the ENATON. The abbot, Victor, received him and gave him the monastic habit. Ten years later, soldiers sent by Theophilus' father arrived at the monastery and seized the abbot, demanding that he deliver the king's son to them. Theophilus surrendered to the soldiers, who took him home. His father did not recognize him, however, because of the effects of his austerities on his body. Theodorus succeeded in persuading his father, who entrusted his kingdom to his brother, and, accompanied by his wife, came with his son to the monastery of the Enaton. The abbot received the mother and entrusted her to a women's convent, and gave the king the monk's habit.

The arrival of the king was reported to the governor, who feared that he and his son might be Greek spies. He put them in irons, and sent a report to Caliph ʿAbd al-Malik (685–705) in Damascus. However, they were released by an angel and returned to the monastery. The governor, believing they had escaped through the laxity of the guards, had the guards tortured. Tamulawus and Theodorus left the monastery and explained that their liberation was not due to any fault of the soldiers. The governor sent them back to the monastery with gifts, asking the monks for their blessing.

Some days later the abbot visited the father and son in their cell, and Tamulawus announced that he would die the following night. This occurred as a great light illuminated the cell. Three days later, Theodorus died.

The story of Theophilus is related by the SYNAXARION of the Copts in two manuscripts of Lower Egyptian recension.

Theophilus' feast day is 14 Ṭūbah.

RENÉ-GEORGES COQUIN

THEOPISTUS OF ALEXANDRIA. Theopistus accompanied DIOSCORUS I of Alexandria (444–458) to the Council of CHALCEDON. After Dioscorus was sentenced to exile in Gangra, Theopistus went to the Pentapolis where he wrote an account of the events of the council, challenging its decisions.

He is named in the *Panegyric of Macarius of Tkow*, which is attributed to the same Dioscorus. In this text (ed. Johnson, 1983, chap. 1, pp. 10–13), the bishop-monk Macarius is portrayed as an uneducated holy man who did not know Greek, just as Dioscorus did not know Coptic. When he saw that an interpreter was needed in order to talk with Dioscorus, Theopistus asked Dioscorus why he had brought Macarius to the council; Dioscorus replied that Macarius was the superior of either of them.

It seems clear that a Coptic-monastic tradition sought to exalt a specific monk (as in the case of Victor at the Council of EPHESUS), thus introducing some alteration in the "official" Greek tradition of the patriarchate, which was also anti-Chalcedonian. However, Theopistus is a well-attested historical character.

As a literary writer, Theopistus is known as the author of the so-called *Life of Dioscorus*. Internal references lead one to suppose that he produced it in Greek in the Pentapolis (perhaps at Cyrene about 455). The Greek original has been lost; a complete Syriac version has survived (ed. Nau, 1903) and also various fragments from a papyrus codex now in London (British Library, Or. 7561, 85, 87, 90–102; ed. Crum, 1903; Wenstedt, 1906). As far as comparison can indicate, the Coptic and Syriac texts both appear to have their source in the same Greek version.

The content of the text reflects the tastes of the time, and especially that of the anti-Chalcedonian circles in which Timothy moved. They produced such works as the *Plerophoriae* of JOHN OF MAYUMA and the *Life of Peter the Iberian*, in which historical facts that were actually the basis of the accounts tended to be replaced by the miraculous element and "pious fraud" of a polemico-theological type. The text is not a true life of Dioscorus but an account (fictitious and polemical) of the Council of Chalcedon, including the opening stages of the council, its actual celebration, the condemnation of Dioscorus, and his exile to Gangra and death.

BIBLIOGRAPHY

Crum, W. E. "Coptic Texts Relating to Dioscorus of Alexandria." *Proceedings of the Society of Biblical Archaeology* 25 (1903):267–76.

Haase, F. *Patriarch Dioscur I von Alexandrie*. Kirchengeschichtliche Abhandlungen 6 (1908). Also published separately, Breslau, 1909.

Johnson, D. W. *A Panegyric on Macarius Bishop of Tkow Attributed to Dioscorus of Alexandria*. CSCO, 415, 416. Louvain, 1983.

Nau, F. "Histoire de Dioscore." *Journal Asiatique*, ser. 10, 1 (1903):5–108, 241–310.

Winstedt, E. O. "Some Munich Coptic Fragments." *Proceedings of the Society of Biblical Archaeology* 28 (1906):137–42, 229–37.

TITO ORLANDI

THEOTOKION, hymn in praise of the Blessed Virgin, Mother of God (Greek, *theotókos*), that celebrates in plain and simple language the mystery of Christ's incarnation and His miraculous nativity. They are used both in the Canonical Hours and in the service of PSALMODIA, of which they are an essential part.

In the canonical hours, two *Theotokia* are regularly sung during the third, sixth, and ninth hours, and may or may not be sung during Vespers and Compline. As to vespers and compline, the *Theotokia* texts are sometimes given in both Coptic and Arabic. The text in some recent Arabic editions of the *Ajbiyah* (Book of Canonical Hours) differs from the Coptic and is probably of modern compilation. In the prayer of the veil, the text, if given in the Coptic *Ajbiyah,* is the same as the second *Theotokion* of compline.

In psalmodia, the *Theotokia* consist of seven sets of metrical hymns, one set for each day of the week, with each set followed by a LŌBSH (crown, consummation), which serves as a conclusion. Each *Theotokion* is preceded by its PSALI (short hymn), which varies for each day of the week.

During the month of Kiyahk, the monasteries and a few city churches sing the prescribed sets of *Theotokia* daily. But in most churches, since it is not easy to assemble a congregation every night, it has become the custom to sing the seven sets of *Theotokia* (plus the *Lōbsh, Psali,* and Arabic *Ṭarḥ* [explanation] assigned to each *Theotokion*) together with the Four Odes (*hōsāt,* sing. HŌS) on Saturday night. This practice has given rise to the Arabic ecclesiastical idiom SAB'AH WA-ARBA'AH (seven and four) referring to the seven *Theotokia* and four odes.

[*See also:* Music: Description of the Corpus and Musical Practice.]

BIBLIOGRAPHY

Burmester, O. H. E. "The Canonical Hours of the Coptic Church." *Orientalia Christiana Periodica* 2, nos. 1–2 (1936):78–100.

______. *The Egyptian or Coptic Church,* pp. 96–111. Cairo, 1967.

______. *The Horologion of the Egyptian Church, Coptic and Arabic Text from a Mediaeval Manuscript.* Cairo, 1973.

O'Leary, De L. *The Coptic Theotokia.* London, 1923.

______. "The Coptic Theotokia." In *Coptic Studies in Honor of Walter Ewing Crum,* pp. 417, 420. Boston, 1950.

EMILE MAHER ISHAQ

THEOTOKOS, Greek term meaning "God-bearer." This title of the Virgin Mary was used by Greek and especially Alexandrian church fathers and writers from ORIGEN on and perhaps even by Hippolytus of Rome. In any case, CLEMENT OF ALEXANDRIA (c. 110–c. 220) used the expression *Marias tes metros tou kyriou* (Mary the Mother of the Lord [of God]) (*Stromateis* 1.21). From theological speculation, this title entered slowly but surely into popular devotion. Despite the effort to find evidence of it elsewhere, there is reason to believe that it originated in Alexandria, where it seems to have been in harmony with the general tradition. The earliest incontestable occurrence of the term "Theotokos" was in the encyclical letter of ALEXANDER I of Alexandria, which he issued against ARIANISM in 324 and which became the official position of the Alexandrian patriarchate. Relating to the liturgy and popular devotion, in an earlier Greek version (written in Coptic characters) from the third century, we have the troparion "Sub tuum praesidium confugimus, sancta Dei Genitrix . . ." (Papyrus 476, John Rylands Library, Manchester), the fourth line of which contains the term *Theotoke* (vocative case) for the first time. It is also known that Pope Theonas (282–300) built the first church in Alexandria and dedicated it to the Holy Virgin Mary as *theometor.*

The term was quietly accepted in the church until 429, when it was refused by NESTORIUS, patriarch of Constantinople, and his supporters as incompatible with the full humanity of Christ. According to his Christological doctrines, Nestorius proposed to substitute for *Theotokos* the new term *Christotokos.* The term *Theotokos,* however, found a formidable champion in CYRIL I OF ALEXANDRIA, who secured its formal and dogmatic status in the liturgy at the Council of EPHESUS in 431; this was reconfirmed at the Council of CHALCEDON in 451. This was a major Christological victory for the See of Saint Mark through the centuries. It has remained the accepted Alexandrian doctrine of the COMMUNICATIO IDIOMATUM as applied to Mariology-Christology. Writing to the Egyptian monks in defense of the *Theotokos,* Saint Cyril of Alexandria counseled them to follow in the steps of the holy fathers who preserved the faith as it was handed down by the apostles. Henceforward the orthodoxy of the Alexandrian apostolic see in the East and the West was undisputed in the church, and the Alexandrian term *Theotokos* has remained the accepted dogmatic Christological truth.

BIBLIOGRAPHY

Dölger, F.-J. "Zum Theotokos-Namen." *Antike und Christentum* 1 (1929):118–23.

Giamberardini, G. *Il culto mariano in Egitto,* Vol. 1. Jerusalem, 1975.

Rahner, H. "Hippolyt von Rom als Zeuge für den Ausdruck Θεοτόκος." *Zeitschrift für katholische Theologie* 59 (1935):73–81; 60 (1936):577–90.

MARTINIANO PELLEGRINO RONCAGLIA

THEOTOKOS, FEASTS OF THE. The high reverence for the Virgin Mary by the Copts is best expressed in the Coptic SYNAXARION where she is described as "the sovereign of the universe, the queen of all womanhood, through whom we have grace." Thus the Copts celebrate seven feasts for her. Dates are here given according to the Coptic Calendar, with their equivalents in the Gregorian calendar.

1. The Annunciation by the archangel Gabriel to her father Joachim and her mother Hannah (who was barren) that she would conceive and give birth to a daughter, 7 Misrā/13 August.

2. The Nativity of the Virgin Mary at Nazareth, 1 Bashans/9 May.

3. The Presentation of the Virgin Mary at the temple, 3 Kiyahk/12 December. Hannah had vowed to offer her daughter to the service of God. When Mary was three she was presented at the temple. Her father Joachim died when she was six, and her mother when she was eight. Mary spent twelve years at the temple, with other virgins.

4. The Dormition of the Virgin Mary, 21 Ṭūbah/29 January. The Virgin slept in the Lord at the age of fifty-eight years, eight months, and sixteen days, attended by the disciples and her female companions. In an effulgence of divine light, Christ appeared, with angels and archangels, received her soul, and entrusted it to the archangel Michael.

5. The Assumption of the Virgin's body. The bodily taking up into heaven of the Theotokos occurred three days after her burial, on 24 Ṭūbah/1 February.

The Coptic church, however, celebrates this feast on 16 Misrā/22 August, at the end of the fifteen-day fast devoted to the Theotokos. The only apostle who had witnessed the assumption of the Virgin's body was Thomas. According to a Coptic tradition, on his way back from India to Jerusalem, Thomas saw the Theotokos' body carried on the wings of angels, above the mountain of Akhmīm in Upper Egypt. The other apostles, desirous of seeing it as well, kept a fast with prayers and were promised by Christ to have their wish granted. This came to pass on a day that was adopted by the Coptic church to be the Feast of the Assumption of the Theotokos, 16 Misrā.

6. Feast of the Theotokos the iron-dissolver (21 Ba'ūnah/28 July). On this day the apostle Matthias, who had been chosen to replace Judas Iscariot (Acts 1:26), was released from prison through the Theotokos' prayers that were fervid enough to dissolve the iron used in the making of chains and fetters. Likewise on this day the Coptic church celebrates the consecration of the first church to be dedicated to the Theotokos, at the city of Philippi.

7. Feast of the Apparition of the Virgin at Zaytūn, Cairo, 24 Baramhāt/2 April. This event took place in 1968 (see VIRGIN MARY, APPARITION OF).

In addition to the above, in medieval times Abū al-Barakāt IBN KABAR, the author of an encyclopedic work on theology in the early part of the fourteenth century, mentions another feast of the Virgin, which does not figure in the Synaxarion. This is the Annunciation.

BIBLIOGRAPHY

Fenoyl, M. de. *Sanctoral le Copte*. Beirut, 1960.

Kabes, J. "La Dévotion de la Sainte Vierge dans l'église copte." *Les Cahiers coptes* 2 (1952).

Wassef, C. W. *Pratiques rituelles et alimentaires*. Cairo, 1971.

BISHOP GREGORIOS

THERENOUTIS. *See* Tarnūṭ.

THETIS. *See* Mythological Subjects in Coptic Art.

THIQAH IBN AL-DUHAYRI, AL-. *See* Ibn al-Dahīri.

THMUIS. See Tmuis.

THOMAS, SAINT. We know little about this anchorite who was held in great esteem by Apa SHENUTE, in whose life he is mentioned twice (Amélineau, 1888, pp. 462–66). He was a contemporary of Apa Shenute and died before him, having lived a holy life. His cult is still alive in his church in the neighborhood of AKHMĪM at Shinsīf.

Our chief source of information is the typika of the White Monastery (DAYR ANBĀ SHINŪDAH), which mention this saint (London, British Library, Or. 3580A, 3, frag. A, ed. Crum, no. 146; Vienna, Nationalbibliothek, K9734). His feast day, 25 Bashans, is often confused with that of Thomas the apostle, which falls on the following day.

A fragment of Thomas's Life survives in Arabic (Troupeau, 1972, p. 230). His complete Life has been published by al-Manqabādī.

BIBLIOGRAPHY

Amélineau, E. *Monuments pour servir à l'histoire de l'Egypte chrétienne.* Mémoires de la Mission Archéologique Française du Caire 4. Paris, 1888.

Crum, W. E. *Catalogue of the Coptic Manuscripts in the British Museum.* London, 1905.

Troupeau, G. *Catalogue des manuscrits arabes,* Vol. 1. Paris, 1972.

RENÉ-GEORGES COQUIN

THOMAS, SUNDAY OF. *See* Feasts, Minor.

THOMPSON, HENRY FRANCIS HERBERT (1859–1944), English Coptologist and demotic scholar. He took up Egyptology at the age of forty under the influence of Flinders Petrie, and studied at University College, Cambridge. After training in Egyptology, he specialized in Coptic and demotic. He published many independent works and assisted W. E. Crum in the completion of his Coptic dictionary. He was a generous supporter of archaeology as well and presented his library to the Egypt Exploration Fund in 1919. His Coptic and demotic works include *The Demotic Magical Papyrus of London and Leiden* (with F. L. Griffith, 3 vols., London, 1904–1909). He also contributed chapters to Petrie's *Gizeh and Rifeh* and J. E. Quibell's *Monastery of Apa Jeremias*; by his will he founded a chair of Egyptology at Cambridge.

BIBLIOGRAPHY

Dawson, W. R., and E. P. Uphill. *Who Was Who in Egyptology,* pp. 286–87. London, 1972.

Kammerer, W., comp. *A Coptic Bibliography.* Ann Arbor, Mich., 1950; repr. New York, 1969.

AZIZ S. ATIYA

THOUGHT OF NOREA. The second tractate from Codex IX of the NAG HAMMADI LIBRARY, the *Thought of Norea* (27.11–29.5), is untitled in the manuscript and has been given its present title on the basis of the phrase "the thought of Norea" found near the end of the document at 29.3. The protagonist in this short text is Norea herself, a character depicted in several Gnostic sources as the daughter of Adam and Eve, and the wife of Seth, Noah, or Shem. In the *Hypostasis of the Archons* (NHC II, 4) for instance, Norea the virgin daughter of Eve, is refused passage aboard Noah's ark and consequently destroys it with her fiery breath. The object of the lust of the archons, Norea calls out for help and is saved by the great angel Eleleth, who reveals true *gnosis* to her. Birger Pearson has demonstrated that the name and role of Norea are derived from Jewish legends about the daughter of Lamech and sister of Tubal-cain, Na'amah (lovely; Gn. 4:22) and that the original form of Norea's name must have been Horaia (cf. also *On the Origin of the World* [NHC II, 5] 102.24–25; Epiphanius *Panarion* 39.5.2; Hegemonius *Acta Archelai* 9).

The *Thought of Norea* opens with an invocation of the "Father of the All" and his glorious comrades (cf. the familiar "trinity" of the Father, the Mother, and the Son). Norea, it is said, cries out to them for aid. Like Sophia (wisdom) in other Gnostic sources, Norea must be restored to her heavenly place. Through the intercession of "the four holy helpers" (unnamed here, but probably Harmozel, Oroiael, Daveithe, and Eleleth), she is brought from deficiency to fullness (the pleroma), and thus she is saved together with the Gnostics, that is, "all the Adams who possess the thought of Norea" (29.1–3).

BIBLIOGRAPHY

Facsimile Edition of the Nag Hammadi Codices: Codices IX and X. Leiden, 1977.

Pearson, B. A. "The Figure of Norea in Gnostic Literature." In *Proceedings of the International Colloquium on Gnosticism,* ed. G. Widengren. Stockholm, 1977.

______, ed. "IX, 2: The Thought of Norea." In *Nag Hammadi Codices IX and X,* ed. B. A. Pearson. Nag Hammadi Studies 15. Leiden, 1980.

Pearson, B. A., and S. Giversen. "The Thought of Norea (IX, 2)." In *The Nag Hammadi Library in English,* ed. J. M. Robinson. Leiden and San Francisco, 1977.

Roberge, M. *Noréa (NH IX, 2).* Bibliothèque copte de Nag Hammadi, Section "Textes" 5, pp. 149–71. Quebec, 1980. Bound with Bernard Barc, *L'Hypostase des Archontes, NH II, 4,* pp. 1–147.

MARVIN W. MEYER

THREE GRACES. *See* Mythological Subjects in Coptic Art.

THREE HEBREWS IN THE FURNACE. According to the book of Daniel three young men in Babylon at the time of Nebuchadnezzar were cast into a fiery furnace, guided by a guardian angel

(Dn. 3:8–30). Six Coptic documents are devoted to the fate of the relics of the three young men:

1. The narrative of the journey to the sepulcher of the saints by JOHN COLOBOS is among the Sahidic extracts of the saint's life included in two Vienna Nationalbibliothek folios edited by W. C. Till (1938, pp. 230–39).
2. A Sahidic fragment in the Cairo Museum was published by H. Munier in 1916.
3. A fragmentary homily preserved in the Vatican Library (Coptica 69, fols. 103r–129v) and parallel to the Tischendorf fragments in Leipzig and others in Cairo, was published by H. Devis in 1929.
4. A panegyric for the three saints attributed to THEOPHILUS OF ALEXANDRIA (385–412), for the day of their commemoration on 10 Bashans, was also published by H. Devis.
5. Another panegyric for 10 Bashans, by Saint CYRIL I OF ALEXANDRIA (412–444), consists of two homilies on the miracles and prodigies at the time of the construction of the oratory in Alexandria (Vatican Library, Coptica 62, fols. 143r–88r, published by H. Devis).
6. Seven unpublished leaves of a homily in which reference is made to a monk Bacheus (Zoega no. 264) is in the Naples National Library.

From the summary account in the SYNAXARION for 10 Bashans it clearly emerges that the attempt by John Colobos to bring back the relics of the three young men at the request of Theophilus, who had built the church without having the relics, ended in failure. The three saints declared to John Colobos, who had got as far as the place of their burial under the image of Nebuchadnezzar, that they were not permitted to leave that place, but that they would appear through the lamps lit in their church.

The Munier fragment shows that the complete narrative underlying this account was fairly complex. Here Jechonias gives the following report: The three young men have been carried into heaven on a chariot, and Nebuchadnezzar remains inconsolable. He honors them all his life, and at the point of death the three inform him that his place is among them. The account of Bacheus specifies that 10 Bashans is the day on which the three young men came out of the furnace. A homily, the beginning of which is lost (ed. Devis, pp. 64–120), is rather an exegetical commentary, not without some reflection in the manner of midrashim. SEVERUS OF ANTIOCH is there cited as "the greatest among the patriarchs," and anti-Gaianite polemic is clearly present. One must admire the adroitness of the author, who makes the three young men sons of Joachim, brothers of Jechonias, and uncles of Daniel.

The panegyric attributed to Theophilus (ed. Devis, pp. 124–57) is totally different. This is the story of the appearance of ATHANASIUS to Theophilus, after the latter has completed the martyria of JOHN THE BAPTIST, Elisha, and the three young men. The latter come the following Sunday to give instructions to Theophilus for obtaining their relics. They ask him to send John Colobos to Babylonia. Theophilus at once dictates to his secretary, the future Cyril, a letter addressed to John Colobos. John comes first to Alexandria, where seven months later Theophilus builds the house of the three saints, before John returns from his journey.

The sites visited by John in Jerusalem are typically those of the anti-Chalcedonian resistance, Saint Mary of Josaphat and the cenacle of the apostles on the Mount of Olives. John's journey requires his prayers to tame large numbers of dangerous animals; in fact, for miracles John's story passes all bounds of extravagance. John sees the gold image built by Nebuchadnezzar as preserved by God for the confounding of his memory. Finally, on the banks of the river of Babylon, he meets the three saints, who lead him to the place of the furnace, now transformed into crystal. Last of all, they show him the cavern of their burial, a place filled with splendor. But the saints explain that they cannot give him any material relic. They will appear in the lamps, which are not to be lit. Later, the saints do come themselves, heralded by a demoniac, and perform a series of cures.

The last panegyric, attributed to Cyril (ed. Devis, pp. 60–202), is of a very different nature. It relates eight miracles wrought during the construction of the martyrium. The most curious is the story of an aged man who has no children, and who promises fifty pieces of gold if he has a son, twenty-five if he has a daughter. The saints give to him and his wife twins, a son and a daughter, but the man pays only for the son. In time he becomes especially attached to the daughter for whom he did not pay. She falls ill, and to cure her the man hands over the additional twenty-five pieces to the saints.

The complete Coptic dossier about the "three children," its links with the life of John Colobos, and the adoption of some episodes in the history of SĀWĪRUS IBN AL-MUQAFFA' all contribute to give countenance to the cult of the three young men under Theophilus. But there is a series of parallel documents on the Chalcedonian side, which make the authenticity of the Coptic pieces suspect. In Armenian and Georgian there is a history of the discovery of the three young men in Persia, published by G. Garitte in 1959 and 1961. The emperor LEO I (457–474) had caused the relics deposited on the tomb of Daniel the Stylite by the patriarch Euphemius (490–496) to be brought from Babylon. What is more, Apollinarius, the Chalcedonian patriarch of Alexandria (551–570), had the hand of one of the three young men deposited at Alexandria. In the Life of Saint Macarius the Roman (*Bibliotheca Hagiographica Graeca,* 1004–1005h) the pilgrims gather at the tomb of the three young men at Ctesiphon. The story of the discovery takes place under Bahram V (420–438/439), probably in 422 since there is reference to a notable Christian rehabilitated after seven months in prison, according to the actual facts of history. The Armeno-Georgian discovery is not encumbered by anything miraculous. It relates how a *hegumenos,* a deacon, and a Jewish Christian succeeded in deceiving the Jewish guardians of the house in which miracles took place in Babylon. They stole the relics of the three saints. Indeed, in addition to the relics demanded by Leo I, other relics of the three young men were deposited in two chapels in Jerusalem, one on 25 August in the building of the patriarch Juvenal (422–458), the other in the building of Flavia, a monastery founded on the Mount of Olives in 454/455. All these foundations are strictly Chalcedonian. Therefore it was necessary to refurbish and even accentuate the tradition concerning John Colobos and Theophilus. If it is very probable that Theophilus built a chapel under Theodosius the Great, it seems also evident that mention of the relics on the opposing side must have entailed the creation of various pieces to justify the priority of the cult at Alexandria, thus laying exclusive claim to any relics of the three.

[*See also:* Biblical Subjects in Coptic Art.]

BIBLIOGRAPHY

Devis, H. *Homélies coptes de la Vaticane,* Vol. 2. Copenhagen, 1929.

Garitte, G. "L'Invention géorgienne des trois enfants de Babylone." *Le Muséon* 72 (1959):69–100.

______. "Le Texte arménien de l'invention des trois enfants de Babylone." *Le Muséon* 74 (1961):91–108.

Munier, H. "Recueil de manuscrits coptes de l'Ancien et du Nouveau Testament." *Bulletin de l'Institut français d'archéologie orientale* 12 (1916):243–257.

Till, W. C. "Ein Sahidischer Bericht der Reise des Apa Johannes nach Babylon." *Zeitschrift für die neutestamentliche Wissenschaft* 37 (1938):130–39.

MICHEL VAN ESBROECK

THREE STELAE OF SETH. The *Three Stelae* (Codex VII, tractate 5, of the NAG HAMMADI LIBRARY) belongs to a group of tractates associated with Sethianism. Seth is the third son of Adam and Eve (Gn. 4: 25–26), appointed as another seed in place of Abel.

The *Three Stelae of Seth* is a series of hymnic prayers and blessings, each of which is addressed to a person of the Gnostic divine triad (Father-Mother-Son) in conjunction with a communal liturgical practice. A short prologue (118.10–24) introduces Dositheos, the revealer of the three stelae. Whether or not this Dositheos is the disciple of John the Baptist, a Samaritan sect founder, and the godfather in the formation of Gnostic schools, is unclear (Pseudo-Clement, *Recognitiones* 1.54–63 and 2.8; *Homiliae* 2.15–25; Origen, *In Evangelium Joannis Commentariorum* 13.27).

The short tractate is subdivided into three sections consciously structured to parallel each other (e.g., benedictions close each section). The subdivisions also correspond to the Sethian threefold nature of God and the stages of visionary ascent and descent. The tractate concludes with a description of the practice: "from the third they bless the second; after these the first. The way of ascent is the way of descent" (127.18–22). The background of this descent–ascent may reflect aspects of the baptismal rite, spiritualized (Turner, 1986). The transmission of these three didactic hymns to the community serves to provide a vision of the heavenly world to the Gnostic community and to support the individual believer in elevating himself to the pleroma through prayer. The tractate ends with a scribal note, a colophon, in all likelihood intended to apply to the whole codex (127.29–33).

The importance of Seth to gnosticism as well as Seth's relationship to religious and philosophical currents of the day make the *Three Stelae of Seth* most appealing. In particular, the tractate has no traces of Christian content; in its place is Neoplatonic metaphysics. The structure of the divine world and contemplative/mystical ascent has parallels with the Platonists of the third century. Two other tractates, *Zostrianos* and *Allogenes,* noted by Porphyry in his *Life of Plotinus,* are very similar in terminology and vocabulary to the *Three Stelae of*

Seth. All exhibit a tendency toward ontological monism. This literary cluster acts as a unit and helps in deducing the evolution of the Sethian treatises and in placing the *Three Stelae* chronologically. One theory is that the *Three Stelae of Seth* was redacted twice (Claude, 1983).

The Gnostic theme of bisexuality, an expression of perfection, is also present in this tractate. Barbelo, the female aspect of the Father, is called "the first male virginal aeon" (121.21–22).

BIBLIOGRAPHY

Böhlig, A. "Zum 'Pluralismus' in den Schriften von Nag Hammadi: Die Behandlung des Adamas in den Drei Stelen des Seth und im Ägypterevangelium." In *Essays on the Nag Hammadi Texts: In Honor of Pahor Labib*, ed. M. Krause. Nag Hammadi Studies 6. Leiden, 1975.

Claude, P. *Les Trois stèles de Seth: Hymne gnostique à la Triade (NHS 7, 5)*. Bibliothèque Copte de Nag Hammadi 8. Quebec, 1983.

Krause, M., and V. Girgis. "Die drei Stelen des Seth." In *Christentum am Roten Meer*, Vol. 2, ed. F. Altheim and R. Stiehl. Berlin, 1973.

Robinson, J. M. "*The Three Steles of Seth* and the Gnostics of Plotinus." In *Proceedings of the International Colloquium on Gnosticism*, ed. G. Widengren. Filologisk-filosofiska serien 17. Stockholm, 1977.

Stroumsa, G. *Another Seed: Studies in Sethian Gnosticism*. Nag Hammadi Studies 24. Leiden, 1984.

Tardieu, M. "Les Trois stèles de Seth: Un écrit gnostique retrouvé a Nag Hammadi." *Revue des sciences philosophiques et théologiques* 57 (1973): 545–75.

Turner, J. "Sethian Gnosticism: A Literary History." In *Nag Hammadi, Gnosticism and Early Christianity*, ed. C. Hedrick and R. Hodgson, Jr. Peabody, Mass., 1986.

Wisse, F. "The Three Steles of Seth." In *The Nag Hammadi Library*, ed. J. M. Robinson. San Francisco, 1977.

HENRY A. GREEN

THUNDER, PERFECT MIND, the second treatise in Codex VI of the NAG HAMMADI LIBRARY. The text consists of a revelatory discourse uttered by an unnamed female deity who speaks chiefly about herself. Using the phrase "I am . . ." to point out her essential qualities, she ascribes to herself such diverging characteristics as: "I am senseless and I am wise" (15.29–30), and "I am the bride and the bridegroom" (13.27–28). It is this contradictory style of self-disclosure that makes this document unique.

Even though this short piece is preserved only among the Christian Gnostic texts from Nag Hammadi, it exhibits no distinctively Christian traits. While it does manifest ties to a Gnostic world of thought—parallels to selected passages in the Nag Hammadi Library have been adduced (MacRae, 1988; Arthur, 1984)—not any of the expected elements of a Gnostic myth are present. As a result, the treatise is to be considered a document with a pre-Christian origin, possessing features that would commend it to Gnostics and also find readers among Christians.

Concerning possible ties to Jewish thought, links to the divine Wisdom—in association with the Egyptian goddess Isis—have been proposed (Quispel, 1975; Arthur, 1984). To be sure, the literary style that employs the "I am" phraseology stands closest to the aretologies of Isis, the Egyptian goddess whose functions are richly diverse. But similarities to the Isis inscriptions remain without certainty because of the uniquely contradictory tone of what is said about the deity features in *Thunder*. At best, the threads that would assist in locating the origin of this piece in place and time are thin and weak. In a word, *Thunder* is a unique work, which has so far resisted categorization.

BIBLIOGRAPHY

Arthur, R. H. *The Wisdom Goddess: Feminine Motifs in Eight Nag Hammadi Documents*. New York, 1984.

MacRae, G. "The Thunder: Perfect Mind." In *Protocol of the Fifth Colloquy of the Center for Hermeneutical Studies*, ed. W. Wuellner. Berkeley, Calif., 1973.

MacRae, G., and D. M. Parrott. "The Thunder: Perfect Mind (VI,*2*), Introduction and Translation." In *The Nag Hammadi Library*, 3rd ed., ed. J. M. Robinson. San Francisco, 1988.

Quispel, G. "Jewish Gnosis and Mandaean Gnosticism: Some Reflections on the Writing Brontė." In *Les Textes de Nag Hammadi*, ed. J.-E. Ménard. Leiden, 1975.

S. KENT BROWN

ṬIḤNĀ AL-JABAL. About 6.5 miles (10 km) northeast of Minyā are the ruins of an ancient Egyptian town, Tehni, with its necropolis. At the same place there was, it is believed, a town of the Hellenistic period called Achoris, also with its necropolis. There was also a Muslim cemetery. There were Christian anchorites at Achoris very early, as is attested by the HISTORIA MONACHORUM IN AEGYPTO. This work, however, does not say precisely where they had their abode—merely "in the district of Achoris."

Greek and Coptic inscriptions have been found that prove monastic occupation of the necropolis. On this point, reference may be made to the excavators, who give the plan of the tombs: Aḥmad Kamāl (pp. 232–341), Lefèbvre and Barri (pp. 141–58), and Lesquier (pp. 132–33). The hypogea have yielded Greek and Coptic inscriptions that have been published by G. Lefèbvre (1903, pp. 369–72; 1907, nos. 117–65). Several are indubitably of monastic origin (1907, nos. 121, 149, 162, 164). Lefèbvre has published three inscriptions, the better part of which are of monastic origin ("Inscriptions chrétiennes," pp. 92–94).

Two rock temples to the north and to the south were fitted out by the hermits with a prayer niche to the east, a niche serving as a cupboard, holes for the hanging of lamps, and other amenities.

BIBLIOGRAPHY

Festugière, A. J., ed. *Historia monachorum in Aegypto.* Subsidia Hagiographica 53. Brussels, 1971.

Kamāl, Aḥmāḍ, "Fouilles à Tehneh." *Annales du Service des antiquités de l'Egypte* 4 (1903):232–41.

Lefèbvre, G. "Inscriptions chrétiennes du Musée du Caire." *Bulletin de l'Institut français d'archéologie orientale* 3 (1903):69–95.

______. "Inscriptions grècques de Tehneh." *Bulletin de correspondance hellénique* 27 (1903):369–82.

______. *Recueil des incriptions grecques chrétiènnes d'Egypte.* Cairo, 1907.

Lefèbvre, G., and L. Barri. "Rapport sur les fouilles executées à Tehneh." *Annales du Service des antiquités de l'Egypte* 6 (1905):141–58.

Lesquier, J. "Fouilles à Tehneh." *Bulletin de l'Institut français d'archéologie orientale* 8 (1908):113–33.

RENÉ-GEORGES COQUIN
MAURICE MARTIN, S.J.

TIL,

TIL, or Apa Til or Apatil, third-century martyr dealt with in a legend (Bibliotheca Hagiographica Orientalis 75/76) in the style of the type of martyr's life predominant in Egypt. According to the legend, Til was a soldier in the camp at Babylon. In the persecution of DIOCLETIAN, he was sent by ARIANUS after unsuccessful torture to the *praeses* Pompius (Pompeius) in Pelusium. We find in the legend the well-known scenes of repeated rescues and miraculous healings performed by the martyr. After the sentence of beheading is pronounced, the saint prays for the ascent of his soul to be free from peril. His father and his brother transfer the corpse to his home town of Sabaru in the Delta. In that area there must have been a martyr's *topos* (place) consecrated to him. The legend gives as the date of his death 7 Amshīr, and as the day of his burial in Sabaru it gives 16 Abīb. The legend could have been composed to be read at his grave on the martyr's feast day.

BIBLIOGRAPHY

Balestri, I., and H. Hyvernat. *Acta martyrum,* Vol. 1. CSCO 43, Scriptores Coptici 3, pp. 89–109. Louvain, 1955.

Baumeister, T. *Martyr invictus,* pp. 103f. Münster, 1972.

Crum, W. E. "Egyptian Martyrs." *The Journal of Theological Studies* (1909):459–65, esp. 461f.

Delehaye, H. "Les Martyrs d'Egypte." *Analecta Bollandiana* 40 (1922):5–154; 299–364, esp. p. 108f.

Gordini, C. D. "Apatil." *Bibliotheca Sanctorum II* (1962):226f.

THEOFRIED BAUMEISTER

TILL, WALTER CURT FRANZ THEODOR KARL ALOIS

TILL, WALTER CURT FRANZ THEODOR KARL ALOIS (1894–1963), Austrian Coptologist. He became a lecturer in Egyptology at the University of Vienna in 1928. He was professor at Vienna (1939–1945) and in charge of papyri in the Austrian National Library (1931–1951). He was senior lecturer in Coptic at the University of Manchester (1951–1959). Till wrote an excellent Sahidic grammar and a number of studies relating to the biblical prophets and stories of the saints. A list of his works may be found in *A Coptic Bibliography* (Kammerer, 1950, 1969).

BIBLIOGRAPHY

Dawson, W. R., and E. P. Uphill. *Who Was Who in Egyptology,* pp. 287–88. London, 1972.

Kammerer, W., comp. *A Coptic Bibliography.* Ann Arbor, Mich., 1950; repr. New York, 1969.

AZIZ S. ATIYA

TIMOTHEOS I, Coptic archbishop of Jerusalem (1899–1925). He was born in Zaqāzīq in 1865 with the name Michael. He studied Arabic and French at the school of the Frères de la Salle. He was ordained a monk in the Monastery of Saint Antony (DAYR ANBĀ ANṬŪNIYŪS) in 1885. When Basilios II, archbishop of Jerusalem, asked for monks to serve in the Coptic churches in Jerusalem, Michael was appointed to serve in the Holy Sepulcher. In 1892, he became both an archpriest and secretary to the archbishop. When Basilios II became too ill to perform his duties, he asked Pope CYRIL V to consecrate Michael as a suffragan bishop. When this was done in 1896, he took the name Timotheos. He succeeded Basilios as archbishop in 1899. During his term in office, he traveled to Turkey to defend (successfully) the Copts' possession of Dayr al-Sulṭān. He renovated the Church of Saint Antony in the patriarchate of Jerusalem, furnishing it with lamps, bells, and icons. He also renovated the Monastery of Saint George in Jerusalem and built the Monastery, and Church, of Saint John the Baptist near Jericho. In his diocese in Egypt, he built a number of churches and schools, while at the same time restoring and enlarging the convent of the martyr Sitt Dimyānah in the north of the Nile Delta.

When World War I broke out, Timotheos remained in Jerusalem to watch over the church until he was evacuated to Damascus with other ecclesiastical leaders. He returned to Jerusalem at the end of 1918 and continued to serve until his death on June 9, 1925.

ARCHBISHOP BASILIOS

TIMOTHEUS, SAINT, anchorite (23 Kiyahk). The Life of this saint is inserted into the Lower Egyptian recension of the Arabic SYNAXARION of the Copts at 23 Kiyahk and from there passed into the Ethiopian Synaxarion. Its source, however, is the story of a search for hermits living in the desert, attributed to one PAPHNUTIUS and presented within the Life of ONOPHRIUS, although the text concerning the latter occupies only half the work by Paphnutius. The passage concerning Timotheus was included in some versions of the APOPHTHEGMATA PATRUM.

After a journey of four days and four nights in the inner desert (the desert most distant from the Nile; from several indications, this could be in the neighborhood of the oasis of Oxyrhynchus, today al-Baḥariyyah), Paphnutius arrives at a cave where he finds the skeleton of a monk. After burying him, he continues on his way and comes to another cave. Although it is empty Paphnutius sees traces of footprints and waits for evening, thinking that the occupant will return. At sunset he sees a herd of bubals (a type of antelope) approaching, and among them is a naked brother with long hair. Fearing that he is seeing a spirit, the latter recites the Lord's Prayer, but Paphnutius reassures him and puts three questions to him: How long has he been in the desert? What does he eat and drink? Why is he naked?

The hermit then tells his story. He had been a monk in a *cenobium* in the Thebaid, following the trade of linen weaver, work also carried on in the Pachomian monasteries (Halkin, 1932, pp. 107–108). When the idea came to him to live alone, he had built a hermitage not far from the monastery; there he continued his trade, and gave alms to strangers and to the poor. The devil became jealous and set out to tempt him, entering the body of a nun who entrusted him with modest tasks. From their habitual contacts, familiarity grew between the monk and the nun, and they lived together for six months.

However, Timotheus—he reveals his name to Paphnutius at the end of the story—was stricken with remorse and reflected on the torments of hell that awaited him if he remained in sin: "the outer darkness, the gnashing of teeth, the inextinguishable fire, the worm that does not sleep [instead of "does not die"; cf. Mark 9:48, the expression found in some Egyptian texts] and devours the soul of the impious." Hence he decided to separate from the woman and went off into the desert. There he found a cave with a spring and a date palm, elements also occurring in the Life of Saint PAUL OF THEBES. This date palm has given him a cluster of dates every month; he never eats bread, and his hair has grown long to replace his worn-out garments. He does not suffer from cold, for the climate is of an even temperature. He was, however, afflicted by a malady of the liver—for four years, the Synaxarion says. A man of glory—the Synaxarion says an angel—appeared to him, massaged his side, opened it, and took out the liver, from which he removed the ulcers, then put the organ back in place and closed the opening, saying to him, "Henceforward, sin no more."

This episode, which sets the liver in relation to the passions, presupposes the Greek conception of the three parts of the soul, in which the liver is the seat of concupiscence. In proof of his statements, Timotheus shows Paphnutius the ulcers removed by the man of glory. Paphnutius wishes to remain with Timotheus, but the latter dissuades him: "Your strength is not enough to sustain the attacks of the demons." After receiving the blessing of Timotheus, Paphnutius leaves him and pursues his search for the desert hermits.

This passage in the work of Paphnutius is interesting, for it presents a wandering monk: his presence among the bubals is revealing; we know of Apa Pshosh (the Bubal), later bishop of Oxyrhynchus, and the *Apophthegmata patrum* mentions anchorites living among the bubals. Paphnutius Kephalas, a monk at Scetis, was also named "the Bubal," or vagrant animal because of his great love for the most secret and inaccessible solitude, where he remained hidden for days on end (John Cassian *Collationes* 3.1, 3, and 18.15).

Timotheus lives naked, in contrast with Onophrius, who wears a girdle of foliage. This nudity, which does not seem due to Gnostic influence, expresses complete contempt for the world, such as appears in several Egyptian monastic texts, but it is also the sign of a paradisiacal life, which is suggested as well by the hermit's food. He never eats bread, an earthly food, but only the fruit of a date palm that miraculously furnishes him with a cluster every month; nor does he suffer from the climate, for it is always temperate. Despite this somewhat novelistic aspect, the story retains some realistic features: the underlying misogyny—woman is the devil's instrument to make the hermit fall—and the desert, the favorite abode of the demons, chosen for that reason by Timotheus.

[*See also:* Onophrius, Saint; Paphnutius of Scetis, Saint.]

BIBLIOGRAPHY

Halkin, F. *Sancti Pachomii vitae graecae.* Hagiographi Bollandiani 19. Brussels, 1932.

Nau, F. "Le chapître 'peri tôn anachôrètôn agiôn' et les sources de la vie de Paul de Thèbes." *Revue de l'Orient Chrétien* 10 (1905):387–417.

______. "Histoire des Solitaires égyptiens." *Revue de l'Orient Chrétien* 12 (1907): 43–69; 171–81; 393–404 [text only]; 49–69 [trans. on right pages]; 181–89, 404–13 [trans. only].

Williams, C. A. *Oriental Affinities of the Legend of the Hairy Anchorite.* University of Illinois Studies 10, 2 and 11, 4. Urbana, 1925–1926.

RENÉ-GEORGES COQUIN

TIMOTHY I, SAINT, twenty-second patriarch of the See of Saint Mark (380–385). Timothy was unanimously elected to succeed PETER II. An elderly man at the time of his election, Timothy was associated with ATHANASIUS in his earlier years and must have been profoundly influenced by his theology. He is known to have disposed of all his worldly possessions in favor of the church and the poorer folks of his Christian community.

His reign was relatively peaceful, and the major event of his time was the famous Council of CONSTANTINOPLE. The council was summoned in May 381 by Emperor Theodosius I, who was eager to ensure the unity of the church within the empire after the defeat of the Arians, the triumph of Athanasian orthodoxy, and the confirmation of the Nicene Creed. Participants in the council numbered 150 Orthodox bishops and 36 Macedonians, who were regarded as heretics. The Egyptian patriarch and his suffragan bishops arrived a little late to find GREGORY OF NAZIANZUS, bishop of Constantinople, and Melitius, bishop of Antioch, presiding over the council, which seems to have irked the Egyptian delegation. However, Melitius died during the meeting and Gregory resigned from his see. The appointment of Nectarius to succeed Gregory as bishop of the Byzantine capital was ratified by the council. It would seem that Timothy assumed the presidency of the council in that period. Although Rome was not represented at the council, its decisions were binding to East and West. The Nicene doctrine concerning the divinity and humanity of the person of Jesus was ratified and the heresy of APOLLINARIANISM was condemned. The question of the indivisibility of the Holy Spirit from the Father and the Son was also settled at this council. On the ecclesiastical front, Flavian rather than Paulinus was nominated to succeed Melitius as bishop of Antioch. The problem of episcopal ranks was discussed, and the primacy of Rome was confirmed. Henceforth, the bishop of Constantinople came second, the bishop of Alexandria third, the bishop of Antioch fourth, and the bishop of Jerusalem fifth.

Timothy was a great supporter of monastic orders, and he is known to have recorded the lives of eminent monks, now lost and known only through the work of SOZOMEN, who used them as sources. Timothy is also known to have made a number of responses to clerical questions, and his answers became part of the church legal system.

AZIZ S. ATIYA

TIMOTHY II AELURUS, twenty-sixth patriarch of the See of Saint Mark (457–477). Along with Philoxenus of Mabbug and SEVERUS OF ANTIOCH,

Timothy was the preeminent champion of MONOPHYSITISM. He adhered to CYRIL'S well-known formula "one incarnate nature of the divine Logos" and took up DIOSCORUS' cause when the latter was deposed at CHALCEDON.

Consecrated patriarch on 16 March 457 in opposition to Proterius, a supporter of the Council of Chalcedon, Timothy was regarded by many of his contemporaries and by later writers as an intruder into the Alexandrian See. Less than a fortnight after Timothy's consecration, Proterius was murdered by a Monophysite mob. For his alleged complicity, the questionable legitimacy of his episcopal appointment, and his opposition to the Council of Chalcedon, Timothy spent most of his patriarchate in exile. Even after his recall by the emperor Basiliscus in 475, he fell out with Acacius, patriarch of Constantinople, and would certainly have been banished once more, had he not died just in time, on 31 July 477.

Several modern writers (e.g., Bright, 1887; Opitz, 1937) have described Timothy as a ruthless opportunist. Their accounts derive primarily from the writings of his critics, among them the various eastern metropolitan bishops whose letters comprise the *Codex Encyclicus*, THEOPHANES, JUSTINIAN, and Pope LEO I. In his own letters and other works Timothy appears as a remarkably moderate person ever ready to make peace with his opponents. These letters lend support to Zacharias Rhetor's account of Timothy's willingness to accept into communion Proterius' followers (*Historia ecclesiastica* 5.4). His several writings, composed during exile, clarify his opposition to the Council of Chalcedon and are excellent statements of Monophysite beliefs, which played an important part in the development of the Armenian church (Sarkissian, 1965; Akinian, 1909). His unusual sobriquet, Aelurus, is ambiguous in Greek and is often translated "cat" but should be rendered "weasel" (Ebied and Wickham, 1985, p. 115, n. 1). Zacharias Rhetor (4.1) claims that his slender build gave rise to the epithet. Others such as Theodore Lector (*Historia ecclesiastica* 1.8, PG 86, pp. 169–72) and Theophanes (*Chronographia*, Anno Mundi 5949) attribute the nickname "weasel" to his ostensible practice of slinking about Alexandria at night to solicit support for his episcopal appointment from the monks.

Life

Zacharias Rhetor (3.1–5.7), EVAGRIUS (*Historia ecclesiastica* 2.5–3.7), Michael the Syrian (Chabot, 1963, pp. 91, 126–40, 145–47), Liberatus (*Breviarium ad Causas Nestorii et Eutychianorum* 13–16, Schwartz, 1936, pp. 98–141), Theophanes (*Chronographia*, Anno Mundi 5949–5952, no. 5967), John Rufus (*Vita Petri Iberi;* Raabe, 1895, pp. 59–72), Theodore Lector (*Historia ecclesiastica* 1.8–9, 30–34, PG 86, pp. 169–72, 179–80), and JOHN OF NIKIOU (*Chronicles* 88) describe Timothy's career. The *History of the Patriarchs of the Coptic Church* has a brief but almost entirely accurate account of Timothy's career (Vol. 2, p. 445) remarkably free of the anecdotes so frequent in the other entries. The author does not recognize the archepiscopates of either Proterius or TIMOTHY SALOFACIOLUS and his statements about the length of time Timothy served in exile are at variance with all other records.

Having been a monk, Timothy was ordained a presbyter by Cyril I and served in this capacity under Dioscorus. He accompanied the latter to the Second Council of Ephesus (the so-called "Robber Council" or *Latrocinium*) in 449, at which Eutyches of Constantinople was restored. Neither Dioscorus nor Timothy accepted, however, Eutyches' refusal to believe in Christ's consubstantiality with humans (Zacharias, *Historia ecclesiastica*, 4.1, 5.4; Raabe, 1895, p. 65; Sellers, 1953, pp. 258, n. 1, 262).

Thereafter, Timothy's life was marred by conflict. He was made patriarch by two bishops previously outlawed, Eusebius of Pelusium and Peter of Iberia. John of Nikiou incorrectly states (*Chronicles* 88.14–16) that the emperor, Leo, appointed Timothy patriarch. Soon after, he was banished by Dionysius the Roman governor, but returned to Alexandria almost immediately and later capitalized on popular dislike for Proterius. Zacharias (4.1) relates an interesting story about the number of persons the two Alexandrian patriarchs baptized at Easter. The multitudes of converts received by Timothy wearied the clerks recording their names. Proterius received only five candidates. He was murdered in his own church very shortly after Timothy's consecration, and if his assassination occurred on Maundy Thursday, as Liberatus claims (Schwartz, 1936, p. 134), Zacharias' account of the Easter baptisms cannot be true, though it may well be valid evidence of Timothy's popular support.

According to Emperor Leo in a letter to Anatolius, the archbishop of Constantinople, Timothy set about ridding Egypt of the Proterian and Eutychian clergy (Schwartz, 1936, pp. 17–21). Evagrius (*Historia ecclesiastica*, 2.8) claims that Timothy's followers were responsible for the assassination of Proterius but notes that Zacharias believed that the

Roman military carried out the deed. Timothy himself was blamed in a *libellus* quoted by Evagrius (2.8) and Zacharias (4.4), sent to the emperor by several Egyptian clerics, who also protested Timothy's ordination. This letter forged a lengthy concatenation of indictments against Timothy. Upon receipt of the letter, the emperor wrote to Anatolius. Despite the influence of Timothy's party at the capital, the emperor's inclination toward Timothy, and the considerable favor of Leo's military commander, Aspar, under pressure from Anatolius, the emperor did not call a general synod to resolve the matter of Timothy's consecration. Instead, he requested the opinions of Pope Leo as well as Anatolius together with sixty eastern metropolitan bishops and three renowned monks, about the Council of Chalcedon and the legitimacy of Timothy's consecration (Zacharias, 4.5; Evagrius, 2.9, Theophanes, *Chronographia,* Anno Mundi 5951; Schwartz, 1936, pp. 9–11, 22–24).

The numerous replies from the clerics were later collected in a single volume, known as the *Codex Encyclicus* (Schwartz, 1936, pp. 24–79, 84–98; nos. 12–39, 41–48). It is an invaluable indication of eastern acceptance of the conciliar decrees. Only Amphilochius of Side in Anatolia, who had supported Dioscorus at Chalcedon, refused to give approval to the conciliar decisions but even he joined in the unanimous condemnation of Timothy (Zacharias, 3.1, 4.7; Chabot, 1963, pp. 145–46; Evagrius, 2.10). Zacharias claims (4.7) that Anatolius instigated their disapproval and sent his own bitter opinion to the emperor. John of Nikiou has the interesting remark (*Chronicles* 88.17–21) that Amphilochius and Eustathius of Berytus alone dared tell the emperor the truth of what had occurred at Chalcedon, all the other clerics having feared imperial wrath. Pope Leo, in calling Timothy "the unholy parricide" (Epistle 169; PL 54, p. 1212; cf. Epistle 150; PL 54, p. 1121), set the tone for the other letters by charging Timothy with responsibility for his mob's actions. Many of the Oriental bishops spoke of Timothy's "tyranny" and "cruelty." John of Damascus, echoing his colleagues' sentiments, called Timothy "not the pastor of Christ's sheep but an intolerable wolf, not a father but a parricide, not the betrothed [of the church] but the rapist of the bride." Such vilification earned for Timothy the reputation of an Antichrist both in his own time and even later (Leo, Epistle 171; Theophanes, *Chronographia,* Anno Mundi 5950).

Probably as a result of the overwhelming support for Chalcedon from the East, Pope Leo felt compelled to demonstrate Western assent in two letters Epistles 156 and 165 (PL 54, pp. 1127–32, 1155–90), the second of which is the so-called Second Tome. Despite the universal condemnation of Timothy, Emperor Leo was slow to act. He sent a copy of the Second Tome to Timothy, who not only rejected it but reviled the First Tome and the council as well. His long reply is recorded by Zacharias (4.6). He emphatically disagreed with those who divided Christ into natures and hypostases. He was excommunicated as "murderer and heretic" (Theophanes, *Chronographia,* Anno Mundi 5952) and finally banished to Gangra in Paphlagonia, where Dioscorus had also spent his exile. Timothy Salofaciolus, a partisan of the Proterian faction, was ordained archbishop in his place. He was promptly excommunicated by Pope Leo (Zacharias, 4.7–9; Raabe, 1895, pp. 69–70; Evagrius, 2, 8, 10; John of Nikiu 88.23; Schwartz, 1936, pp. 46–50).

Timothy spent four years in Gangra (460–464/465). Because of his generosity and piety in Gangra, he won the jealousy of both the local bishop and Gennadius, patriarch of Constantinople, and he was sent to Cherson in the Crimea, where he spent the next eleven years.

Throughout his exile, Timothy continued to write against the conciliar decisions of Chalcedon, the Tome of Leo, the Eutychians, and the Nestorians. Zacharias (4.12) preserves a very long letter directed against two Egyptian clerics, Isaiah, bishop of Hermopolis, and Theophilus, presbyter of Alexandria, whom he excommunicated for their Eutychian beliefs. This letter is also found in another Syriac manuscript.

When Basiliscus usurped Zeno and became emperor early in 475, he pardoned Timothy, who thereupon went to the capital. He was so well received (Zacharias, 5.1) that Pope Simplicius wondered how people could honor a person of Cain's status (Epistle 4; PL 58, p. 38). Timothy persuaded the emperor to send an encyclical to all bishops anathematizing the Council of Chalcedon and Leo's Tome.

On his return to Alexandria, Timothy stopped in Ephesus and restored the patriarchate that had been taken away at Chalcedon. This action offended Acacius, archbishop of Constantinople, because it encroached on the prerogatives awarded to the capital at Chalcedon. Meanwhile, with Timothy's restoration to the See of Alexandria, Timothy Salofaciolus retired to a monastery in Canopus. Timothy Aelurus was quick to forgive the Proterian faction (Zacharias, 5.4). Acacius initiated sedition against

Basiliscus, who then recanted his encyclical and his support for Timothy. Liberatus claims that Timothy drank poison to escape further banishment (Schwartz, 1936; see also John of Nikiou, *Chronicles* 88). He was succeeded by PETER III MONGUS.

At some point in his career, Timothy finished the great church of ABŪ MĪNĀ in the Maryūt that had been begun by THEOPHILUS (*History of the Patriarchs*, vol. 3, p. 122).

Writings

Timothy's literary activity was considerable, to judge from a Coptic source: "Timothy being in exile, produced 512 commentaries written in two books, [wherein] he spoke of many passages of the Scriptures, expounding them excellently" (Crum, 1902, p. 81). Zacharias notes (4.11) that his literary productivity while in exile was immense. He is frequently quoted by later critics such as Justinian, Leontius of Byzantium, and Anastasius of the Sinai (PG 86, pp. 903–4, 1127–30).

Of the numerous works attributed to him, the majority survive in Syriac and Armenian translations. Only two minor works are in Coptic, and their authenticity is uncertain. One (Crum, 1902, pp. 68–84) is a historical narrative describing briefly the events from the *Latrocinium* to about 475. Some ancient authors make reference to Timothy's works of historical character, and a Syriac treatise is important evidence of Timothy's historical interests (PO 8, pp. 83–85; Lebon, 1909, pp. 103–11). The second Coptic text is a sermon, very likely spurious, on the dedication of a Pachomian monastery (van Lantschoot, 1934, pp. 13–56).

By far the most important manuscript containing Timothy's works is British Library Add. MS 12,156, a Syriac text written before 562. It includes two great treatises, which comprise Timothy's *summa theologica*. One of the two tracts is sometimes called *Refutation of the Synod of Chalcedon* or *Against Those Who Speak of Two Natures*, but is more accurately stated *On the Unity of Christ* (Ebied and Wickham, 1985, p. 118). It survives in a complete Armenian version (ed. Ter-Mekerttschian and Ter-Minassiantz, 1908) and in a Syriac epitome (PO 13, pp. 202–218; see also Ebied and Wickham, 1970, p. 323; Geerard, 1979, p. 62, no. 5475).

Timothy's other great work is *Against the Definition of the Council of Chalcedon* (PO 13, pp. 218–36; Ebied and Wickham, 1985; Geerard, 1979, p. 64, no. 5482). A carefully composed, richly documented florilegium, it contains much more than the title suggests. Following a line-by-line rebuttal of the conciliar articles of faith, it has an extensive criticism of Pope Leo's Tome, a summary of the decisions reached at the First Council of Ephesus in 449, and a final section with many quotations from the fathers.

From exile, Timothy wrote at least six letters, also found in the London manuscript. He defended his beliefs and condemned both the decisions of the Council of Chalcedon and especially Eutychianism (Ebied and Wickham, 1970; Geerard, 1979, pp. 63–64). They are remarkable for their charitable spirit. The first of these, written to the residents of Constantinople, is an important condemnation of the Eutychian heresy. The second letter is directed against one Isaiah, bishop of Hermopolis, and Theophilus, presbyter of Alexandria, whose heresy occasioned the first epistle. Timothy's humanity, almost completely unrecognized until the publication of these letters, emerges clearly from his willingness to forgive his two clerics if only they would renounce their heterodoxy.

Although Timothy's claim may seem to be a self-serving rhetorical device, its sincerity is corroborated by his instructions to his clergy to receive with charity all converts from diphysitism after one year's penance (Zacharias, 4.12). These terms of penance lend support to Zacharias' claim (5.4) that when Timothy was restored to the patriarchate in 475, he readmitted penitent Proterians under the terms stipulated from his exile. In the fourth letter, his goodwill extends to lapsed clergy and foreigners. His generous spirit is everywhere apparent in the fifth letter to his deacon Faustinus, whom Timothy instructs to be sparing in his treatment of the simple and innocent converts from diphysitism. The sixth letter is a condemnation of Eutychianism.

Christology

Throughout his writings, Timothy insists that Christ has but one nature and is consubstantial with both God and man. By assuming our flesh at the Incarnation, He did not lose His divinity. This belief was in accord with Dioscorus' sentiments (see, e.g., Zacharias, 3.1). Few, if any, of his extant works were written for purely exegetical or contemplative purposes, but rather as exposés of heresy. Consequently, Timothy was more pamphleteer than theologian. His sole mission was to condemn the perversion wrought on the Council of Ephesus by Leo's Tome and by the decisions reached at Chalcedon. He instructs his faithful to be on guard against Eutychianism and Nestorianism. In his *Against the Definition of the Council of Chalcedon*, Timothy quotes EUTYCHES as saying, "I confess that our Lord was of two natures before the union, but after the union, I confess one nature" (Ebied and Wickham, 1985, p. 157). Timothy believed, on the contrary, that the Eternal Logos was consubstantial with the Father and was immutable in its divinity that became man in the person of Christ. Christ's flesh was the same as ours. His opinion is stated concisely in the treatise *On the Unity of Christ* (fol. 19r): "We anathematize those who speak of two natures or of two *ousiai* (beings) in respect of Christ" (Lebon, 1908, p. 687). He rejected the Nestorians, too, because they spoke of two natures (*Against the Definition of the Council of Chalcedon,* fol. 41v; PO 13, p. 231). The title of the letter to the city of Constantinople is also a succinct explanation of his faith. It was "written against the heretics [the Eutychians] who do not confess that God the Word who is consubstantial in his Godhead with the Father, is consubstantial in the flesh with us . . ." (Ebied and Wickham, 1970, p. 351). For Timothy divinity and flesh had but one immutable nature in the person of Christ:

> The divine Logos, not [yet] incarnate, was conceived in the womb of the holy Virgin, and was then incarnate of the flesh of the holy Virgin, in a manner that he alone knew, while remaining without change and without conversion as God; and he is one with his flesh. In fact, the flesh had neither *hypostasis* nor *ousia* before the conception of God the Logos, that it equally could be called a nature, separate and [existing] by itself.
> (Ebied and Wickham, 1970, pp. 228–29)

Also in *Against the Definition of the Council of Chalcedon,* Timothy faulted Pope Leo for his inconsistency with regard to Christ's nature. He praises the pope (fol. 43r) for the words:

> For when God is believed to be Almighty and Father, the Son is shown to be co-eternal with him, differing in nothing from his Father because as God from God, almighty from almighty and from eternity has he been begotten as co-eternal, not temporally younger, not less in power, not different in glory or separate in substance but the eternal only-begotten of the eternal Father has been born of the Holy Ghost and Mary the Virgin; and this temporal birth neither detracted from nor added to his divine, eternal nature.
> (Ebied and Wickham, 1985, pp. 143–44)

Later, Timothy quotes Leo as writing that at the Incarnation, two natures, divinity and humanity, became one. Here Timothy finds traces of Nestorianism. The rest of the document is full of similar charges.

BIBLIOGRAPHY

Akinian, P. N. *Timothy Ailuros in der armenischen Literatur.* Vienna, 1909.

Bright, W. "Timotheus." In DCB 4, pp. 1031–33.

Chabot, J.-B., ed. *Documenta ad Origines Monophysitarum Illustrandas.* CSCO 103, *Scriptores Syriaci,* 52. Louvain, 1954.

______. *Michel le Syrien: Chronique,* Vol. 2. Paris, 1963.

Conybeare, T. C. "The Patristic Testimonia of Timotheus Aelurus." *Journal of Theological Studies* 15 (1913–1914):432–42.

Crum, W. E. "Eusebius and Coptic Church Histories." *Proceedings of the Society of Biblical Archaeology* 24 (1902):68–84.

Ebied, R. Y., and L. R. Wickham. "A Collection of Unpublished Syriac Letters of Timothy Aelurus." *Journal of Theological Studies* 21 (1970):321–69.

______. "Timothy Aelurus: Against the Definition of the Council of Chalcedon." In *After Chalcedon: Studies in Theology and Church History Offered to Professor Albert Van Roey for His Seventieth Birthday,* ed. C. Laga, J. A. Munitiz, and L. Van Rompay, pp. 115–66. Orientalia Lovaniensia Analecta 18. Louvain, 1985.

Frend, W. H. C. *The Rise of the Monophysite Movement: Chapters in the History of the Church in the Fifth and Sixth Centuries.* Cambridge, 1972.

Geerard, M. *Clavis Patrum Graecorum, Vol. 3: A Cyrillo Alexandrino ad Johannem Damascenum.* Turnhout, Belgium, 1979.

Hamilton, F. J., and E. W. Brooks. *The Syriac Chronicle Known as That of Zacharias of Mytilene.* London, 1899.

Lantschoot, A. van. "Allocution de Timothée d'Alexandrie prononcée à l'occasion de la dédicace de l'église de Pachome à Pboou." *Le Muséon* 47 (1934):13–56.

Lebon, J. "La christologie de Timothée Aelure." *Revue d'histoire ecclésiastique* 9 (1908):677–702.

______. "Le monophysisme sévérien: Etude historique, littéraire et théologique sur la résistance monophysite au concile de Chalcédoine jusqu'à la constitution de l'église jacobite." Universitas Catholica Lovaniensis Dissertationes, Ser. 2, 4. Louvain, 1909.

______. "Version arménienne et version syriaque de Timothée Elure." *Handes Amsorya: Monatsschrift für Armenische Philologie* 41 (1927):713–22.

______. "La christologie du monophysisme syrien." In *Das Konzil von Chalkedon: Geschichte und Gegenwart, Vol. I: Der Glaube von Chalkedon,* ed. A. Grillmeier and H. Bacht, pp. 425–580. Würzburg, 1951–1954.

Moberg, A. *On Some Syriac Fragments of the Book of Timotheus Ailuros Against the Synod of Chalcedon.* Lund, 1928.

Nau, F. "Sur la christologie de Timothée Aelure."

Revue de l'orient chrétien, 2nd ser., 4 (14) (1909):99–103.

Opitz, H. G. "Timotheus." *Paulys Real-Encyclopädie der classischen Altertumswissenschaft,* Ser. 2, Vol. 6, pt. 2, cols. 1355–57. Stuttgart, 1937.

Raabe, R., ed. *Petrus Iberer. Eine Characterbild zur Kirchen- und Sittengeschichte des fünften Jahrhunderts.* Leipzig, 1895.

Sarkissian, K. *The Council of Chalcedon and the Armenian Church.* London, 1965.

Schwartz, E. *Codex Vaticanus gr. 1431: Eine antichalkedonische Sammlung aus der Zeit Kaiser Zenos.* Abhandlungen der Bayerischen Akademie der Wissenschaften, phil.-hist. Kl., Vol. 32, Fasc. 6. Munich, 1927.

______. *Publizistische Sammlungen zum Acacianischen Schisma.* Abhandlungen der Bayerischen Akademie der Wissenschaften, Neue Folge, Vol. 10. Munich, 1934.

______. Acta Conciliorum Oecumenicorum. Vol. II, Fasc. 5. Berlin and Leipzig, 1936.

Sellers, R.V. *The Council of Chalcedon: A Historical and Doctrinal Survey.* London, 1953.

Ter-Mekerttschian, K., and E. Ter-Minassiantz. *Timotheus Älurus, des Patriarchen von Alexandrien: Widerlegung der auf der Synode zu Chalcedon festgesetzter Lehre.* Leipzig, 1908.

Theophanes. *Chronographia,* ed. C. de Boor. Leipzig, 1883.

Zotenberg, H., ed. *La Chronique de Jean, Evêque de Nikiou.* Paris, 1879. Trans. by R. H. Charles as *The Chronicle of John, Bishop of Nikiu.* London, 1916.

DONALD B. SPANEL

TIMOTHY III, thirty-second patriarch of the See of Saint Mark (517–535) and the last ruler of an undivided Egyptian church. On the Emperor Justin's accession in 518, the Chalcedonian faith was proclaimed in the Eastern empire generally, but Timothy was left in peace in a church and province loyal to its own orthodoxy. He doubtless profited from the support of THEODORA, empress from 527, who is said to have claimed him as her spiritual father. He was used by the government as a means of communication with the Ethiopian kingdom of Axum, and is reported to have assembled a council to assure the Axumite king, Caleb (or Elesbaas), of imperial support, at least for launching his expedition in defense of the Christians of Yemen. Timothy was able to welcome refugees from the Chalcedonian persecution elsewhere, conspicuous among them SEVERUS OF ANTIOCH and JULIAN OF HALICARNASSUS, whose theological difference on the corruptibility or incorruptibility by nature of the humanity of Christ thus entered the Egyptian church.

Timothy's theology is known from polemical quotations. Like Severus he asserted the full humanity of Christ, and is quoted in this sense by the Nestorian (or Nestorianizing) COSMAS INDICOPLEUSTES. In one example, a Christmas sermon on 30 Kiyahk of the tenth indication (517 or 532), he writes, "the Virgin brought forth a perfect man, without sin," and again, "the Lord became man in nature and truth and not in appearance." Timothy's excellent government was praised by Maximian, bishop of Ravenna. But he does not seem to have realized the intensity of the difference between the supporters of Severus and those of the more extreme Monophysite Julian, who predominated in monastic circles for a while so that Severan monks needed the protection of a powerful lay patron.

BIBLIOGRAPHY

Hardy, E. R. *Christian Egypt,* pp. 127–32. New York, 1952.

Maspero, J. *Histoire des patriarches d'Alexandrie,* chap. 3. Paris, 1923.

Vasiliev, A. *Justin the First,* pp. 224–27, 284–99. Cambridge, Mass. 1950.

Wigram, W. A. *The Separation of the Monophysites,* pp. 95, 151–54, 203. London, 1923.

EDWARD R. HARDY

TIMOTHY SALOFACIOLUS, Chalcedonian patriarch of Alexandria (460–482). A one-time steward of the church of Alexandria, he was consecrated patriarch after the expulsion of TIMOTHY II AELURUS ("the Cat") in 459. His nickname may be derived from Coptic with a "dog Latin" ending meaning "wearer of a white turban" or "wobbling turban." He was the recipient of some of Pope Leo's last recorded letters, one (*Letter* 171 of 18 August 460) exhorting him to exert himself against the remnants of Eutychian and Nestorian heresy. For sixteen years he was able to hold his position through innate reasonableness and gentleness of character, which made him popular with pro- and anti-Chalcedonians alike. The Carthaginian deacon Liberatus records in the next century (*Breviarium* 16) that the Alexandrians told him, "Even if we do not communicate with you, we love you." He restored the name of Patriarch Dioscorus to the diptychs, an act that increased the affection in which he was held even by opponents.

In 476, however, Emperor ZENO was in exile from Constantinople and the anti-Chalcedonian usurper Basilisceus ruled in his stead. Timothy "the Cat" returned to Alexandria; Timothy Salofaciolus retired to the Pachomian monastery of Canopus in the suburbs of Alexandria. On the death of Timothy "the Cat," the anti-Chalcedonians elected PETER III MONGUS patriarch (480–488), but on the intervention of the prefect Anthemius he was removed and Timothy Salofaciolus restored.

Timothy entered into relations with Zeno, who had been restored to the throne (August 476), and with Pope Simplicius (468–483), whom he assured of his orthodoxy and his cancellation of his commemoration of Dioscorus.

In 481 Timothy made provision for the continuance of the Chalcedonian succession by sending an embassy to Emperor Zeno under his steward, John Talaia. John, however, behaved imprudently and was suspected of contacting the powerful Iranian general Illus, whom Zeno feared, not unreasonably, as a possible rival. As a result, Zeno, while agreeing to the appointment of a successor to Timothy, stipulated that John should remove all claim to that position. John complied, but on the death of Timothy, probably in February 482, went back on his word and allowed himself to be consecrated patriarch. Zeno thereupon accepted Peter Mongus as patriarch, on condition that he admit pro-Chalcedonians to communion and subscribe to the letter that Zeno sent to the church of Alexandria on 28 July 482, known as the HENOTICON of Zeno.

The career of Timothy shows how deep were the divisions among Cyril's clergy, and how they were exacerbated by the autocratic rule of Dioscorus. No amount of conciliation, however, could bring the Western and Eastern, the pro- and anti-Chalcedonian factions, in Alexandria together. That Timothy remained in office for so long and that, unlike his predecessor Proterius, he died peacefully says much for his fair-minded and conciliatory nature. That he failed was no fault of his.

BIBLIOGRAPHY

Besant, W. "Timotheus." DCB 4, pp. 1033–34.

Stein, E. *Histoire du Bas Empire,* Vol. 2. Paris, Brussels, and Amsterdam, 1949.

W. H. C. FREND

TINNIS, city located on an island in the southeastern part of Lake Manzalah in the province of Daqahliyyah, the site of which is now known as Kom Tinnis.

Tinnis was a bishopric at least as early as the first third of the fifth century as evidenced by the mention of Bishop Heracleides (Heraclius in the Coptic version) of Tinnis in the lists of bishops who attended the First Council of EPHESUS in 431 (Munier, 1943, p. 17).

[*See also:* Mikhā'īl.]

BIBLIOGRAPHY

Kosack, W. *Historisches Kartenwerk Ägyptens.* Bonn, 1971.

Munier, H. *Recueil des listes épiscopales de l'église copte.* Cairo, 1943.

RANDALL STEWART

TIRSĀ, a town in Egypt located in the vicinity of al-Minyā. On 9 Kiyahk the SYNAXARION commemorates Saint PAMIN, who is said to have hailed from "Minyat al-Khaṣīb, from the area of al-Ashmūnayn, near Tirsā." Inasmuch as Tirsā is given as a reference point for Minyat al-Khaṣīb, it is reasonable to assume that in Pamin's day, or at least at the time the Synaxarion was composed, Tirsā was the more significant of the two towns. Minyat al-Khaṣīb is the modern al-Minyā, but there is no dwelling named Tirsā in the surrounding area and there are no other attestations of the town in ancient, medieval, or modern literature.

BIBLIOGRAPHY

Timm, S. *Das christlich-koptische Ägypten in arabischer Zeit,* pt. 5. Wiesbaden, 1988.

RANDALL STEWART

TISCHENDORF, KONSTANTIN VON (1815–1874), German Lutheran theologian. In 1851 he became professor of New Testament studies at Leipzig. On his travels he discovered, and later collated and edited, many biblical manuscripts and palimpsests. Well known is his discovery of the *Codex Sinaiticus* at Saint Catherine's Monastery on Mount Sinai, published in Leipzig, 1859. His edition of the New Testament rests above all on this codex and on the *Codex Vaticanus.* His critical edition (Leipzig, 1869–1972), with its extensive apparatus, is a standard tool of New Testament textual criticism.

BIBLIOGRAPHY

Junack, K. "Constantin Tischendorf in seiner Bedeutung für die neutestamentliche Textkritik." *Das Altertum* 2 (1956):48–56.

Kenyon, F. G. *Der Text der griechischen Bibel.* Berlin, 1952; 2nd ed., 1962.

Schneller, L. *Tischendorf-Erinnerungen.* Leipzig, 1927; repr. 1954.

Sevčenko, I. "New Documents on Constantin Tischendorf and the Codex Sinaiticus." *Scriptorium* 18 (1964):55–58.

MARTIN KRAUSE

TISSERANT, EUGENE (1884–1972), French clergyman and Orientalist. He was a cardinal and member of the Institut de France. He was scriptor orientalis and then proprefect of the Vatican Library (1908–1936). He helped prepare his own bibliography: "Bibliographie de son Eminence le Cardinal Eugène Tisserant (1907–1964)" (with P. Hennequin, *Mélanges Eug. Tisserant,* Vol. 1, Vatican City, 1964, pp. 7–18).

BIBLIOGRAPHY

Bourguet, P. du. "Le Cardinal Eugène Tisserant (1884–1972)." *Bulletin de la Société d'archéologie copte* 21 (1971–1973):223–33 (with a bibliography).

Raes, A. "In memoriam: Eugène, Cardinal Tisserant (1884–1972)." *Rendiconti atti della Pontificia accademia romana di archeologia* 45 (1974):1–9.

Vida, G. Levi della. "L'Activité scientifique du Cardinal Tisserant." In *Recueil Cardinal Tisserant "Ab Oriente et Occidente,"* Vol. 1, pp. 1–11. Louvain, 1955.

RENÉ-GEORGES COQUIN

TITKOOH. *See* Bāwīṭ.

TMOUSHONS. *See* Bakhānis-Tmoushons.

TMUIS, city in the Eastern Delta, now known as Tall ʿAbd al-Salām. It lies southwest of the village of Timay in the province of Daqahliyyah approximately 12 miles (19 km) southeast of al-MANṢŪRAH.

Tmuis was one of the first Christian cities of Egypt. Ammonius was bishop of Tmuis before the middle of the third century. He was succeeded by Philippus. Around 306 the bishop of Tmuis was a man named Phileas. When Phileas suffered martyrdom, his successor was Donatus. In 325, at the time of the Council of NICAEA, Tmuis had a Melitian bishop named Ephraim as well as an orthodox bishop. The name of this orthodox bishop is not known with certainty because the lists of the bishops at the council are discrepant.

One of the most famous bishops of Tmuis was Serapion, a pupil of ANTONY, the author of the Life of MACARIUS THE EGYPTIAN, and a staunch supporter of orthodoxy. He wrote against Manichaeism and in 356, he led a delegation in support of ATHANASIUS to Constantinople. In 359, however, Serapion was removed from office and replaced by Ptolemaeus, an anti-Athanasian.

From the time of the Council of EPHESUS (431) when Aristobulus was bishop of Tmuis until the ARAB CONQUEST OF EGYPT in the seventh century, there are few attestations of Christianity in the city. Although the sources for the Arabic period are more plentiful, MENAS is still the only bishop of Tmuis from this era whose chronological position can be ascertained. He was a contemporary of the patriarch ISAAC (686–689), but he was still in office in 744 at which time he attended the synod in Cairo that chose KHĀ'ĪL I (744–767) to be the forty-sixth patriarch. The SYNAXARION lists the commemoration of Menas on 7 Hatūr, stating that he hailed from Samannūd, had been a monk in the Monastery of Macarius (see DAYR ANBĀ MAQĀR) in Wādī al-Naṭrūn, and was the spiritual father of the patriarchs ALEXANDER II (705–730), COSMAS I (730–731), THEODORE (731–743), and Kha'īl I. Under the date 30 Kiyahk the Synaxarion adds that Menas had also been a student of John of Scetis (see FORTY-NINE MARTYRS OF SCETIS).

By the end of the tenth century Tmuis seems to have joined with DAQAHLAH to form an ecclesiastical administrative unit. During the tenure of the patriarch ZACHARIAS (1104–1032), when Tmuis had apparently lost its standing as a bishopric, Bishop Mercurius of Tilbānah became ill and made a pilgrimage to Tmuis where there was a renowned church of the Virgin Mary. At that time Tmuis belonged to the diocese of Bishop Mercurius.

BIBLIOGRAPHY

Amélineau, E. *La Géographie de l'Egypte à l'époque copte,* pp. 500–502. Paris, 1893.

Casey, R. P. *Serapion of Thmuis Against the Manichees.* Cambridge, Mass., 1931.

Harnack, A. von. *Mission und Ausbreitung des Christentums in den ersten drei Jahrhunderten,* Vol. 2. Leipzig, 1924.

Le Quien, M. *Oriens Christianus,* 3 vols. Graz, 1958. Reprint of Paris, 1740.

Munier, H. *Recueil des listes épiscopales de l'église copte.* Cairo, 1943.

Timm, S. *Das christlich-koptische Ägypten in arabischer Zeit,* pt. 5. Wiesbaden, 1988.

RANDALL STEWART

TOILET ARTICLES. *See* Wood, Uses of.

TOLEMAUS, SAINT, a martyr in the persecution under DIOCLETIAN (feast day: 11 Kiyahk). The text of his Passion has come down to us in two codices in Sahidic (Rossi, 1893, p. 5, in the Pierpont Morgan Library, New York, M 581, phot. 32). The account found in the Morgan codex, which is also given in the Arabic SYNAXARION (trans. Forget, Vol. 1, pp. 207–210) is derived from a late expansion on the older text that has come down in Coptic.

According to the Synaxarion, Tolemaus is a soldier from Dandarah, who is converted by the famous monk Paphnutius and sent by the latter to Antinoopolis to confess his faith. This part seems to be foreign to the Coptic text, which tells us only of the events at Antinoopolis, where Tolemaus, after refusing to offer sacrifice, has the usual exchange of words with the prefect ARIANUS, is tortured, recovers various times, and is finally put to death.

The original story was probably part of the older nucleus of epic passions built around the figure of the prefect Arianus; the later expansion places the martyr within the cycle of monk-martyrs, one of whom was Paphnutius of Dandarah.

BIBLIOGRAPHY

Rossi, F., ed. "Un nuovo codice copto del Museo Egizio di Torino." *Atti Accademia dei Lincei,* ser. 5, 1 (1893).

TITO ORLANDI

TOPONYMY, COPTIC. The study of ancient place-names is one of the most interesting domains of historical research, since the names of hamlets, villages, and towns of the past often give brief but valuable indications, usually absent from historical records, about the creation of those urban centers and the reasons for their founding, whether economic, political, religious, or otherwise. This is especially true in regard to Coptic Egypt, inasmuch as historical texts pertaining to these centers are scanty and form only a small percentage of the available data, most of it biblical or liturgical. Coptic toponymy is an important link in the long chain of recorded toponymy of Egypt from the pharaonic period down to the present. Together the links of this chain—ancient Egyptian, Demotic, Greek, Coptic, and Arabic documents—provide a rich mass of place-names that have survived four thousand years. Gauthier's *Dictionnaire des noms géographiques contenus dans les textes hiéroglyphiques* (1925–1931), in seven volumes, illustrates the extraordinary richness of the toponymy of ancient Egypt, and Amélineau's *La Géographie de l'Egypte à l'époque copte* (1893; 1973), which is always informative despite being incomplete and in need of revision, gives an idea of the relative abundance of Coptic place-names. Naturally, one cannot take into consideration the names of the various more or less big estates, which, like the *'izbas* in modern Egypt, were named in ancient and Coptic Egypt after their successive proprietors. One should also exclude the names of small districts of a rather too local use and concentrate on names of localities that had a reasonable economic and urban infrastructure. This information has also to be examined in the light of two Mamluk surveys of agricultural land, *al-Rūk al-Ḥusāmī,* ordered by Ḥusām al-Dīn Rājūn (1297–1299), and *al-Rūk al-Naṣirī,* ordered by al-Nāṣir Muḥammad ibn Qalawūn (1309–1340). They give valuable indications about the toponymy of Egypt in the late Middle Ages. It is hoped that the recent work on these surveys would enhance research on Egyptian toponymy in general and especially on Coptic place-names.

The privileged position of Coptic toponymy in this long chain has always attracted etymologists. In spite of the normal alteration due to the long history of these place-names, to the diversity of the phonetic characteristics of the languages in question (Egyptian, Coptic, Greek, Egyptian Arabic), and to the diversity of their scripts, one could trace the evolution of place-names. This helped to identify and localize many ancient Egyptian names and to link them to the actual toponymy of Egypt, thus throwing light on the survival, the shifting, or the disappearance of urban centers, not only in the Coptic period but through the centuries. Coptic etymological dictionaries by Spiegelberg (1921), Černy (1976), Westendorf (1977), and Vycichl (1983), as well as the tremendous work of Crum (1939), illustrate the fruits of these researches, an identification that is certain in many cases but only probable, possible, or doubtful in others.

There is no doubt that in the Coptic period, when Christianity had already triumphed over the deities of pharaonic Egypt and temples had ceased to celebrate their cults, very few Egyptians realized that a great number of their towns bore names that glorified pagan deities. This is also true for the Muslim period and for modern Egypt. No concerted, native movement to change those pagan names has been recorded, and it is certain that none has been successful. Such names have continued to be used and borrowed for centuries.

Following are the different categories of names that illustrate the rich heritage of the past and examples of each. Their literal translation derives from ancient Egyptian through the Coptic names.

Towns Named After a Divinity

1. ⲉⲣⲙⲟⲛⲧ (Ermont), *Inū* of (the god) Montu, now Armant or Erment in Upper Egypt.
2. ϯⲙⲓⲛϩⲱⲣ (Timinhōr), town of (the god) Horus, now Damanhūr in the Delta.

Towns Named After a Temple

ⲡⲟⲩⲥⲓⲣⲉ (Pousire), House (or temple) of (the god) Osiris, an abbreviation of full names as they appear in Arabic Būṣīr or Abūṣīr. Such full names are ABŪṢĪR BANĀ or ABŪṢĪR AL-MALAK.

Towns Named After Mansions of Deities

1. ϩⲱ (Hō), from *Ḥwt,* an abbreviation of full names like *Ḥwt-Shm,* mansion, now HIW in Upper Egypt.
2. ⲁⲑⲣⲏⲃⲓ (Athrēbi), mansion of the Land of the Middle, now ATRĪB (Atripe) in the Delta, also called Kom al-Atrīb or Tall Atrīb (*tall* and *kom* are synonyms; the first is Arabic, the second is given by the inhabitants to mounds of old villages or towns and is derived from the term *kōmé,* which the Greeks used to designate small villages inhabited by Egyptians).

Towns Named After Chapels

ⲧⲁⲃⲉⲛⲛⲏⲥⲓ (Tabennēsi), Chapel of (the goddess) Isis, probably Dafānī, which is an island in the Nile near the aforementioned Hiw.

Towns Named After Their "Land"

ⲡⲧⲉⲛⲉⲧⲱ (Ptenetō), "The Land of (the goddess) Edjō, now Kom al-Dinṭaw in the Delta.

Towns Named After Their Islands

ⲡⲟⲩⲛⲉⲙⲟⲩ (Pounemou), the Island of Amūn, now Tall al-Balāmūn in the Delta.

Towns Named for the Creation of Divinities

ⲡⲉⲣⲉⲙⲟⲩⲛ (Peremoun), that which Amūn has made, al-Faramā or Tall al-Faramā in the Delta.

Towns Named After Gifts from the Gods

ⲡⲉⲧⲉⲙⲟⲩⲧ (Petemout), (the town of him) whom (the goddess) Mūt has given, Madamūd or Tall al-Madamūd in Upper Egypt.

It is important to remark here that the number of such place-names greatly exceeds that of those named after ancient Egyptian kings, such as ⲥⲃⲱⲛ (sbōn), mansion of (King) Snefru, now Aṣfūn al-Mataʿnah in Upper Egypt. From this fact, one can deduce that religion was a more important factor than politics in Egyptian civilization.

The geographical, topographical, and economic factors that usually condition the choice of place-names were also found in Coptic toponymy. But here again, in spite of the fact that the same factors were at play during the Coptic period, such place-names were used in ancient Egypt, and most of them still survive, as is shown by the following examples:

1. ⲧⲃⲉⲣϭⲱⲧ (Tbercōt), a loanword from the Semitic, commonly used in the toponymy of the New Kingdom to mean "pond," now Farshūṭ in Upper Egypt.
2. ⲗⲉϩⲱⲛⲉ (Lehōne), mouth of the lake (of the Fayyūm), now al-Lāhūn in the Fayyūm.
3. ⲫⲓⲟⲙ (Phiom), the sea (i.e., the lake of Fayyūm), now al-Fayyūm.
4. ⲥⲟⲃⲧ (Sobt), wall or fortress, an abbreviation of full names with additions to identify the "walls" of different localities, now Ṣaft, as in Ṣaft Maydūm and Ṣaft al-Ḥinnah.
5. ⲥⲟⲩⲁⲛ (Souan), the name of the city of Aswan, at the southern border of Egypt, which served in ancient Egypt as a market.
6. ⲧⲕⲱⲟⲩ (Tkōou), high mountain, Qāw al-Kiblī in Middle Egypt, where the eastern mountain is a prominent element.
7. ⲧⲟⲩϩⲟ (Touho), the settlement, now Ṭahā, in Upper Egypt.
8. ⲧⲉϩⲛⲉ (Tehne), the peak, now Ṭihnā in Middle Egypt.

Toponymic survival is evident in almost all the cases of important towns in the Coptic period. And apart from the towns that were created by the foreign masters of Egypt, those urban centers continued to have more or less the same political, economic, or administrative importance as before. Each was the seat of a bishop. A large number of these towns is also noticed in modern Egypt, where they are the center of administrative divisions. Here are but a few examples:

1. ⲕⲉϥⲧ (Keft), now Qifṭ in Upper Egypt
2. ⲉⲙⲃⲱ (Embō), now Kom Ombo in Upper Egypt

3. ⲉⲥⲛⲏ (Esnē), now Isnā in Upper Egypt
4. ⲥⲓⲱⲟⲩⲧ (Siōout), now Asyūṭ in Upper Egypt

Apart from the aforementioned categories of place-names that belong in fact to one and the same Egyptian substratum, Coptic toponymy provides the historian with other groups of equally interesting names. One of these groups presents only very few examples, which, while being Coptic, are built differently from all those above. Other groups are formed with special loanwords added to Coptic designations.

Place-Names with the Prefix ⲙⲁⲛ- (Man-)

The prefix *man-*, "place of," is added to a second element, which, while not always easy to translate, seems to have been a designation of the characteristic product of the locality in question. Three examples are attested:

1. ⲙⲁⲛⲃⲁⲗⲟⲧ (Manbalot), translated as Mawḍiʿ al-Farā ('), place of fleeces, now Manfalūṭ in Upper Egypt. Manfalūṭ is the center of an area that produces the well-known *kilīms* (rugs made of wool).
2. ⲙⲁⲛⲕⲁⲡⲱⲧ (Mankapōt), translated as "place of pots," now MANQABĀD (but locally pronounced Mangabād also) in Upper Egypt.
3. ⲙⲁⲛⲗⲁⲩ (Manlau), place of the textile (ⲗⲁⲩ), probably Mallawī, in Upper Egypt. This town is known for its textile industry.

Further research may more precisely date these "economic" place-names and determine whether they replaced older Egyptian names of the towns. They may also initially have been given to new workshops or markets for these products at or near these towns before being extended to the whole locality. If these three names deal with wool or woolen rugs, pottery, and textiles—which were, in fact, the main industrial products of Egypt—the limited percentage of these place-names (only three are attested) could perhaps be an indication that the appearance of new centers of those industries, or perhaps the shifting of existing ones to new places, was a limited phenomenon at that time. This conclusion seems to be in harmony with the gradual deterioration of the economic situation in the Arabic period.

Place-Names Formed with the Loanword ϫⲉⲫⲣⲟ- (Jephro-)

This loanword, from the Semitic word meaning "village" (originally, "farmstead") and related to the Egyptian Arabic *kafr*, forms the first element in several place-names. The second element could either be a geographical designation, as in ϫⲉⲫⲣⲟⲛⲣⲏⲥ (Jephronrēs), or otherwise, as in ϫⲉⲃⲣⲟⲙⲉⲛⲉⲥⲓⲛⲁ (Jebromenesina). Papyrological and Coptic sources seem to shed little light on the origin and date of these villages or their original inhabitants. But it seems that the Semitic origin of the word means that these names were given to settlements inhabited at least at the beginning by Semitic elements, either partly or totally. These elements, either peacefully or with invading Persian or Greek armies, were later sent with the garrisons that settled in the country. It is more plausible than attributing the origin of these settlements to bedouin tribes that the Umayyads transplanted from North Arabia to different places in Egypt to serve as paramilitary forces after the first series of Coptic revolts. Such places were named after the nome of the tribe in question, either with a *nisbah* (affiliation) form or with the prefix *banī* (tribe) attached to it.

It seems that these settlements did not disappear in the Arab period. The numerous examples given by the Arab geographer Yaqūt show the relatively high number of so-called villages in his time. The majority of the names he mentioned have Coptic designations starting with *shubra*, village, as in Shubra Bakhūm and Shubra Damanhūr. Others with Arabic designations seem to have been drawn from the flora, as is often the case in toponymy in general: Shubra Nakhlah (Village of the Palm Tree), Shubra Zaytūn (Village of the Olive Trees), Shubra Nabaq (Village of the Jujube Tree). This is a promising subject for future research, which might determine why these Shubras are concentrated in the northern part of Egypt (the Delta and Giza). Is it an indication of Semitic elements? Some of these places have lost their importance, but others do survive, in the form found in the Coptic period, as with Shubramant (Shubra Raḥmah from ϭⲁⲡⲣⲟϩⲃⲱ, Caprohbō); with Egyptian Arabic designations, as with Shubra al-Khaymah (Village of the Tent) and Shubra al-Naḥlah (Village of the Bee); or only the abbreviated form Shubra, an important suburb of Cairo.

Place-Names Formed with the Loanword ⲧⲙⲟⲟⲛⲉ- (Tmoone-) or ⲑⲙⲟⲛⲏ- (Thmonē-) from the Greek mone

The long Greco-Roman presence in Egypt left its mark in Coptic toponymy in the form of place-names beginning with the above prefixes and their variants, which mean "a stopping place of a journey, a hostel" or a "monastery." These places normally developed small settlements around them with a more or less limited infrastructure that would grow in time, under favorable circumstances. This explains the number of such localities. But once more the actual data do not allow the historian to define the social or economic reasons that favored the formation of these ⲧⲙⲟⲟⲛⲉ- (Tmoone-) localities and the real differences or resemblances between them and the ϭⲱⲡⲣⲟ- (Cōpro-) localities. Was the first category initially begun by Greek elements (perhaps among the merchants who dominated the commerce of the country), or was it merely inhabited by a higher percentage of Greeks? What was the role of administrative considerations? Or is it only a question of loanwords that had nothing to do with the composition of the population of these localities or with their administrative status? This leads to the delicate question of the raison d'etre of loanwords, which is particularly complicated in the case of place-names, and to the problem of the social, economic, or political factors that concurred in maintaining them.

Perhaps one should consider in this regard the difficult economic circumstances and particularly the crushing burden of taxes that pushed many people to become FUGITIVES, that is, to give up their fields and houses, leave the villages in which they were registered, and roam around the country trying to find a place in which to settle. This problem, which had its beginnings in the Roman period, flared up again in the Umayyad period, and it may have been one of the factors behind the formation of the *tmoone*-villages, which numbered more than 250 in the Middle Ages. Some of them still flourish, such as Al-Minyā in Middle Egypt and other towns elsewhere, whose names have changed little since the Coptic period.

Coptic Toponymy and Foreign Place-Names

For over one thousand years—from the Ptolemaic period until the end of the Byzantine period—the Greek administration in Egypt had the habit of transcribing the majority of Egyptian place names in Greek with certain modifications more or less pronounced in accordance with the phonetic differences between the two languages. This habit produced varying results as is shown by the following examples: PR-WSİR > Dem. P-WS'R ⲃⲟⲩⲥⲓⲣⲉ, Bousire (S), ⲡⲟⲩⲥⲓⲣⲉ, Pousire (B) was transcribed in Greek as Βούσιρις, Boúsiris, which is not really different; ḪNT-MN ϣⲙⲓⲛ, Shmin (SB), ⲭⲙⲓⲛ, Khmin (S), was transcribed as Χέμμις, Khémmis, by Herodotus; and GBTYW ⲕⲏⲃⲧ, Kēbt (S), ⲕⲉϥⲧ, Keft (B) gave the Greek Kóptos; ṮB-NṮR (var. Ṯbn-nṯr) ϫⲉⲙⲛⲟϯ, Jemnoti (B) became Sebénnytos and Ḏ'NT > Dem. Ḏ'NY > ϫⲁⲛⲛⲉ, Janne (S), ϫⲁⲛⲏ, Janē (B) was altered in the Greek form to Tánis.

This is not the place to discuss conclusions about these alterations and their phonetic significance for the toponymy of Egypt in the Coptic period, nor to define their guidelines. But it is perhaps interesting to note that they bear comparison to the modifications effected by twentieth century Greek residents of Egypt in their pronunciation of present day Egyptian toponymy and proper names.

The administrative system's practice of rendering more or less faithfully Coptic toponymy for almost a thousand years apparently did not affect Coptic place-names, which continued to be close to their initially transmitted forms.

In certain cases, Greeks diverted from this general rule and gave to some place-names purely Greek equivalents, as with Thebai or Dios Polis for Egyptian *níwt* > ⲛⲏ (nē) and (Thebes) Laton Polis or Latopolis for Egyptian *Sn* > ⲉⲥⲛⲏ (Esnē, Isnā). But here again Copts only used the original toponymy, which resisted this modification.

In the case of totally new place-names, Copts transcribed them into Coptic: ⲁⲗⲉⲝⲁⲛⲇⲣⲓⲁ (Aleksandria) for Alexandria, ⲧⲁⲡⲟⲑⲏⲕⲏ (Tapothēkē) for Apotheke (Abutīg), and ⲫⲩⲥⲧⲁⲧⲱⲛ (Phystatōn) (al-Fustāt), the first Arab capital of Egypt.

BIBLIOGRAPHY

Amélineau, E. *La Géographie de l'Egypte à l'époque copte.* Paris, 1893; 2nd ed., Osnabrück, 1973.

Gauthier, H. *Dictionnaire des noms geógraphiques contenus dans les textes hieroglyphiques.* 7 vols. Cairo, 1925–1931.

Černy, J. *Coptic Etymological Dictionary.* Cambridge, 1976.

Crum, W. E. *A Coptic Dictionary.* Oxford, 1939.

Roquet, G., *Toponymes et lieux-dits égyptiens, enregistrés dans le Dictionnaire Copte de W. E. Crum.* Cairo, 1973.

Spiegelberg, W. *Koptisches Handwörterbuch.* Heidelberg, 1921.

Vycichl, W. *Dictionnaire étymologique de la langue copte.* Louvain, 1983.

Westendorf, W. *Koptisches Handwörterbuch.* Heidelberg, 1977.

MOUNIR MEGALLY

TOPOS AL-MALAK MIKHĀ'ĪL (IDFŪ). *See* Dayr al-Malāk Mikhā'īl (Idfū).

TOPOS AL-QIDDIS YUHANNIS. *See* Dayr al-Sāqiyah.

TOYS AND GAMES. *See* Metalwork, Coptic; Ceramics, Coptic; Wood, Uses of.

TRANSEPT. *See* Basilica.

TRANSFIGURATION, FEAST OF THE. *See* Feasts, Minor.

TREATISE ON THE RESURRECTION (*Codices Gnosticorum* I, 4, 43.25–50.18), the fourth tractate of Codex I from the NAG HAMMADI LIBRARY. This tractate is a brief, personal communiqué from an unknown Gnostic teacher to his pupil "Rheginos" (43.25). Written in response to the pupil's questions regarding the nature, means, and goals of personal resurrection from the dead, the document propounds a view of realized eschatology ("already you have the resurrection," 49.15–16; cf. 49.22–26) which bears remarkable resemblance to the heresy combated in 2 Timothy 2:18.

With respect to physical characteristics, the 262 lines of text (43.25–50. 18; fols. 22–25) are cast in a preclassical form of the Subakhmimic dialect, the same dialect used for all tractates in Codices I, X, and the first half of XI. This is a Coptic translation, the original having been composed in Greek—as certain puns, high incidence of Greek loanwords, and syntactical patterns make clear. Further, the orthography of script reveals that this tractate was copied by the same scribe responsible for the first two tractates in Codex XI. With minor exceptions, the eight papyrus sheets are well-preserved and the text is little damaged.

The tractate is cast in the form of a personal letter, even though a *praescriptio* naming sender and receiver is missing. However, the indisputable presence of the Cynic-Stoic diatribe style and the use of a commonplace philosophical vocabulary in places have led some scholars (notably Martin, 1971; Layton, 1979; and Dehandschutter, 1973) to conclude that it is not a true letter but rather a philosophical tract, a lecture, or a homily. Whatever the resolution, a prior relationship between teacher and pupil (as indicated by the form of address, "son" and "sons," 43.24; 46.6; 50.2–3; and by a personal rebuke, 49.28–30) suggest that its personal tone is not wholly fabricated.

The author-teacher—whose ideas reflect influences from Valentinian gnosticism (Eastern), Pauline eschatology, and Middle Platonic thought—offers three major teachings: (1) that individual resurrection, though philosophically indemonstrable and seeming fantasy, is, because of Christ's resurrection, a certain reality for one having "faith" (46.3–47. 10; 48.3–38); (2) that resurrection involves, immediately at death, the shedding of physical flesh and the ascent to the pleroma of an inward, spiritual body ("members") which retains the personal identity of the deceased (47.4–8; 47.38–48.11—note the use of the Transfiguration as a proof); and (3) that since one knows the inevitability of physical death and participates now in the resurrection-ascension of Christ, he should live as having "already been raised" (49.16–36). Presupposed by both author and reader is a cosmogonic myth (probably Valentinian) according to which this world has come into being through a split in the heavenly pleroma (which had included the preexistent Elect, 46.38–47.1; cf. 47.26–27) and a consequent devolution of the Divine (48.34–49.5). This makes the "spiritual resurrection" of individuals actually part of a cosmic process of "restoration" of the disrupted Pleroma (44.30–33; 45.36–40).

Though the first editors of the text (Puech and Quispel; see Malinine et al., 1963), held that it was probably written by the arch-Gnostic Valentinus himself around 140–165, most scholars today affirm an anonymous Gnostic teacher to have been the author. Still, the presence of an allusion to Valentinian speculation about the aeon (45.11–13), a fragment of a cosmogonic hymn (46.35–47.1), and Valentinian symbolism (48.34–49.5) make manifest Valentinian associations of the *Treatise*. Most scholars date it to the late second century.

BIBLIOGRAPHY

Bazán, F. G. "Sobre la Resurrección (Epístola a Reginos): Traducción, Introducción y Commentario." *Revisita Biblica* 38 (1976):147–78.

Gaffron, H. G. "Eine gnostische Apologie des Auferstehungsglaubens: Bemerkungen zur 'Epistula ad Rheginum.'" In *Die Zeit Jesu: Festschrift für Heinrich Schlier,* ed. G. Bornkamm. Freiburg, 1970.

Haardt, R. "'Die Abhandlung über die Auferstehung' des Codex Jung aus der Bibliothek gnostischer koptischer Schriften von Nag Hammadi: Bemerkungen zu ausgewählten Motiven, I und II," *Kairos. Zeitschrift für Religionwissenschaft und Theologie* 11 (1969):1–5; 12 (1970):241–69.

Layton, B. *The Gnostic Treatise on the Resurrection from Nag Hammadi.* Missoula, Mont., 1979.

———. "Vision and Revision: A Gnostic View of the Resurrection." *Colloque international sur les textes de Nag Hammadi (Quebec, 22–25 août 1978)*, ed. B. Barc, pp. 190–217. Bibliothèque copte de Nag Hammadi, Section "Etudes" No. 1. Quebec and Louvain, 1981.

Malinine, M.; H. Ch. Puech; and G. Quispel, eds. *De Resurrectione*. Zurich, 1963. The *editio princeps*.

Martin, L. H. "The Anti-philosophical Polemic and Gnostic Soteriology in 'The Treatise on the Resurrection' (CG I,3)." *Numen* 20, (1973):20–37.

Menard, J.-E. "'L'Epître à Rhèginos et la résurrection.'" In *Proceedings of the XIIth International Congress of the International Association for the History of Religions . . . Stockholm, Sweden, August 16–22, 1970*, ed. J. Bleeker et al. pp. 189–99. Leiden, 1975.

Peel, Malcolm L. "Gnostic Eschatology and the New Testament." *Novum Testamentum* 12 (1970):141–65.

———. *The Epistle to Rheginos: A Valentinian Letter on the Resurrection—Introduction, Translation, Analysis*. Philadelphia and London, 1969. Revised German ed.; *Gnosis und Auferstehung*. Neukirchen-Vluyn, 1974.

———. "NHC I, 4: The Treatise on the Resurrection: Introduction, Text and Translation." *Nag Hammadi Codex I (The Jung Codex): Introductions, Texts, Translations, Indices*, ed. H. W. Attridge. Nag Hammadi Studies 22, ed. M. Krause et al., pp. 123–57; "Notes to the Treatise on the Resurrection." Nag Hammadi Studies 23, pp. 137–215. Leiden, 1985.

Peretto, E. "L'Epistola a Rheginos: il posta del corpo nella risurrezione." *Augustinianum* 18 (1978):63–74.

Unnik, W. C. van. "The Newly Discovered Gnostic 'Epistle to Rheginos' on the Resurrection: I and II." *Journal of Ecclesiastical History* 15, ser. 1 (1964):141–67.

MALCOLM L. PEEL

TRIANGLE. *See* Music, Coptic: Musical Instruments.

TRIBUNE. *See* Synthronon.

TRICONCH. *See* Architectural Elements of Churches.

TRIMORPHIC PROTENNOIA (Nag Hammadi Codex XIII. 1). This short Coptic text (sixteen pages of papyrus) forms a small booklet, clearly detached from a larger whole and slipped inside the leather cover of Codex II of the NAG HAMMADI LIBRARY. On its last page, the beginning of another Nag Hammadi treatise can be recognized, the anonymous treatise from Codex II of which Codex XIII no doubt contained a second version. The text of the *Protennoia* is probably complete, but the manuscript is badly damaged, containing considerable lacunae that hinder the interpretation of a work already very obscure.

The work is a kind of hymn of revelation, of the "I am" type, strongly marked by mythological gnosticism. The work appears to belong to the same Gnostic sect as the APOCRYPHON OF JOHN, with which it has several points in common, and also could well be almost contemporary. The revelation consists of three clearly separated parts, each having a subtitle in the manuscript. The speaker is always Protennoia, that is, the First Thought of the Invisible. The three parts begin, respectively: (1) "I am the Protennoia, the Thought . . ."; (2) "I am the Voice which was manifested . . ."; and (3) "I am the Word [Logos]. . . ." This tripartite division broadly corresponds to the three modes of the manifestation of Protennoia, although the latter are not so sharply distinguished (in fact, the first section already introduces the threefold aspect of Protennoia). Like the Revealer in the Apocryphon of John, Protennoia is at once the Father, the Mother, and the Son. She descends on three occasions from the world of light, each time in a form corresponding to the sphere that she comes to save: "Among the angels I manifested myself in their likeness, and among the powers as one among them, and among the sons of men as a son of man" (49.15–20). She is life, has produced the All, and lives in all. Her second coming had as its aim to put an end to fate (43.4–27). Accordingly, she put breath into those who were her own but ascended back to heaven without her "branch" (45.29–34). In the final segment, the Logos comes to enlighten those who are in darkness (46.30–33) and to teach the decrees of the Father to the sons of light. Protennoia puts Jesus on the cross, then takes him down from the cross and establishes him in the dwelling places of his Father. Finally, she declares, she will establish her "seed" in the holy light, in an inaccessible silence.

The work is much more complex than this summary might lead one to believe, apparently having undergone several reworkings. Related not only to the Apocryphon of John but also to other Coptic Gnostic texts now rediscovered, it presents additionally literary contacts with the New Testament. Assuming that the work was purely Gnostic in origin, and only subsequently Christianized, it has been thought to represent—particularly in its third section, which concerns the Logos—a Gnostic source for the prologue of John's Gospel. This possibility has formed one of the principal foci of interest in this treatise. But on this subject exegetes remain far from unanimous.

BIBLIOGRAPHY

Evans, C. A. "On the Prologue of John and the *Trimorphic Protennoia.*" New Testament Studies 27 (1980–1981):395–401.

Janssens, Y. *La Prôtennoia Trimorphe, Bibliothèque Copte de Nag Hammadi.* Université Laval, Section: "Textes," fasc. 4. Quebec, 1978.

———. "The Trimorphic Protennoia and the Fourth Gospel." In *The New Testament and Gnosis,* ed. A. H. B. Logan and A. J. M. Wedderburn. Edinburgh, 1983.

Robinson, J. M. "Sethians and Johannine Thought: The Trimorphic Protennoia and the Gospel of John." In *The Rediscovery of Gnosticism,* Vol. 2, ed. B. Layton. Numen Supplement 41. Leiden, 1981.

YVONNE JANSSENS

TRIPARTITE TRACTATE. One of longest (138 pp.) and best-preserved documents of the NAG HAMMADI LIBRARY, the *Tripartite Tractate* (codex I, tractate 5) offers an original Gnostic theological treatise on creation and redemption. Beginning from praise of the primal Father, it relates how all being derives from him as its source. From him derives, above all, the "first-born and only Son" (57.19) who "existed from the beginning" (57.33). The love between Father and Son, in turn, brings into being the primordial church, forming a primal trinity.

After describing the dynamic emanation of divine being, the author of the Tripartite Tractate relates how the Logos initiates a process that results in the creation of the world. Although he describes the action of the Logos as a kind of primordial transgression (he "attempted an act beyond his power," 76.7) the author is concerned to show that the action of the Logos did not violate the Father's will. Since the Logos "intended what is good," and acted, if precipitously, "from an abundant love" (76.20), his action is beyond criticism (77.6–7); it brought into being "a system that was destined to come about" (77.10–11)—cosmic creation.

The second part of the Tripartite Tractate interprets Genesis 1–3 to account for the human condition. That the spiritual Logos participated with the demiurge and his angels in creating Adam explains for this author the composite character of the human soul. Adam's soul received its spiritual element from the Logos, its psychic element from the demiurge, and its hylic (material) element from the lower powers. Yet each human soul bears all three potentialities. One's spiritual development depends on which potential one realizes in response to Christ's coming.

The third part of the tractate describes the *oikonomia* (arrangement) of salvation. In passages that emphasize the reality of the Incarnation, the author explains that the eternal Logos "came into being in the flesh" (113.38), was born "as an infant in body and soul" (115.10–11), and suffered passion and death to redeem humankind.

Comparison with other evidence suggests that the author of the Tripartite Tractate, although probably a theologian of the Western Valentinian tradition, attempts, in this treatise, a bold revision of earlier Valentinian theology. This author intends to accommodate his theology to that of the "great church" to demonstrate that it offers no essential contradiction.

His revision includes six major theses. First, this author stresses the uniqueness of the Father, describing him as the single One who "created the universe" (52.4–6). Second, in place of the primal dyad that Irenaeus attributes to Valentinus' teaching, here the Father generates the "only begotten Son." Third, instead of attributing creation to Sophia's fall, he traces it instead to the Logos's activity, interpreted in terms of theodicy. Fourth, like the Valentinian teacher Heracleon, this author describes the demiurge in relatively positive terms, as the Logos's (and, hence, ultimately, the Father's) agent in creation. Fifth, this author describes the "three natures" of humanity as potentials within every human being, which each realizes differently in response to the revelation in Christ. Finally, this author describes both pneumatic and psychic Christians—both the elect and the called—as members of the same church, who share a common hope for their eschatological reunion with Christ. If, as the text suggests, its author is responding to such orthodox critics as Irenaeus, bishop of Lyons (c. 160–180), the Tripartite Tractate probably dates from the third or early fourth century.

BIBLIOGRAPHY

Attridge, H. W., and E. H. Pagels. *The Tripartite Tractate (CG I, 5).* Nag Hammadi Series 1. Leiden, 1982.

Devoti, D. "Una summa di teologia gnostica; il Tractatus Tripartitus." *Rivista di storia e letterature religiosa* 13 (1977):326–53.

Emmel, S. "Unique Photographic Evidence for Nag Hammadi Texts, CG I, 1–5." *Bulletin de l'Académie des Sciences de St. Petersbourg* 15 (1978):251–61.

Kasser, R., et al. *Tractatus Tripartitus, Pars I: De supernis*. Bern, 1973.

______. *Tractatus Tripartitus, Pars II: De creatione hominis: Pars III: De generibus tribus*. Bern, 1975.

Luz, U. "Der dreiteilige Traktat von Nag Hammadi," *Theologie en Zielzorg* 33 (1977):384–93.

Orbe, A. "En torno a un tratado gnostico." *Gregorianum* 56 (1975):558–66.

Puech, H.-C. and G. Quispel. "Les Ecrits gnostiques du Codex Jung." *Verbum Caro* 8 (1954):1–51.

______. "Le Quatrième écrit du Codex Jung." *Verbum caro* 9 (1955):65–102.

Schenke, H. -M. "Zum sogenannten Tractatus Tripartitus des Codex Jung." *Zeitschrift für ägyptische Sprache und Altertumskunde* 105 (1978):133–41.

Thomassen, E. "The Structure of the Transcendent World in the Tripartite Tractate." *Verbum Caro* 34 (1980):358–75.

Zandee, J. *The Terminology of Plotinus and of Some Gnostic Writings, Mainly the Fourth Treatise of the Jung Codex*. Istanbul, 1961.

______. "Die Person der Sophia in der vierten Schrift des Codex Jung." In *Le Origini dello Gnosticismo, Colloquio de Messino, 13–18 Aprile 1966*. Studies in the History of Religions; Supplement to *Numen* 12, pp. 203–14. Leiden, 1967.

HAROLD W. ATTRIDGE
ELAINE H. PAGELS

TRISAGION, Greek for "thrice-holy," a hymn used in Coptic worship. The Byzantine form of the Trisagion is as follows: "Holy God, Holy Mighty One, Holy Immortal One, have mercy upon us," to be reiterated three times, followed by the lesser doxology. But the Coptic form of the Trisagion is as follows (verses 1–5 are in Greek; verses 6–10 are in Coptic):

> (1) Holy God, Holy Mighty One, Holy Immortal One, Who wast borne of a virgin, have mercy upon us. (2) Holy God, etc., Who wast crucified for us, have mercy upon us. (3) Holy God, etc., Who rose from the dead and ascended into the heavens, have mercy upon us. (4) Glory be to the Father and to the Son and to the Holy Spirit, both now and always and unto the ages of the ages. Amen. (5) Holy Trinity, have mercy upon us. (6) All-Holy Trinity, have mercy upon us; Holy Trinity, have mercy upon us. (7) Lord, forgive us our sins; Lord, forgive us our iniquities; Lord, forgive us our transgressions. (8) Visit, Lord, the sick of Thy people, heal them for Thy Holy Name's sake. Our fathers and our brethren who have fallen asleep, Lord give rest to their souls. (9) Sinless Lord, have mercy upon us: Sinless Lord, aid us, receive our prayer. (10) For to thee belongeth glory and power and the Trisagion: Lord, have mercy. Lord, have mercy. Lord, bless us. Amen.

The whole hymn is understood as being addressed to Christ. The choice of verses varies according to the service and the holiday. For example, verses 1–10 are recited during the canonical hours, whereas verses 1–5 are sung in the Divine Liturgy before the prayer of the Gospel; from Christmas Eve to the Feast of the Circumcision, the first verse is repeated thrice, followed by the fourth and fifth verses (without the singing of the second and third verses), and so on. It is sung before the prayer of the Gospel in many church services.

According to the Byzantine tradition, it was in the time of Saint Proclus, bishop of Constantinople (434–446), that the Trisagion came into use (Salmon, 1974).

Saint Peter the Fuller (d. 488), patriarch of Antioch, is chiefly remembered for his addition to the Trisagion of the clause *Ho staurotheis di humas* ("Who wast crucified for us").

In the thirteenth century, however, Ibn Sibāʿ in his *Kitāb al-Jawharah* noted a tradition that Saints Joseph of Arimathea and Nicodemus, while giving burial to the body of Christ, heard the angels saying, "Holy God, Holy Mighty One, Holy Immortal One," and at the words "Holy Immortal One," Christ opened His eyes in their face. Then Joseph and Nicodemus said, "Who wast crucified for us, have mercy upon us."

Ibn Sibāʿ also said that the Trisagion is repeated thrice to accord with the number of the Holy Trinity and that the word "Holy" in the Trisagion (verses 1–3) is repeated nine times in reference to the nine angelic orders, whose worship in heaven is the prototype of the worship of the church. Hence, the dignitary present (whether he be a senior priest, a bishop, or the patriarch), as a head of the earthly angels or heavenly men, alone says the first verse of the Trisagion, "Holy God . . . , Who wast borne of a virgin, have mercy upon us," and the people sing the rest.

[*See also:* Music: Description of the Corpus and Musical Practice.]

BIBLIOGRAPHY

Burmester, O. H. E. "The Canonical Hours of the Coptic Church." *Orientalia Christiana Periodica* 1-2 (1936):78-100.

———. *The Horologion of the Egyptian Church: Coptic and Arabic Text.* Cairo, 1973.

Daniell, F. H. B. "Proclus." In DCB, 4, pp. 483-84. Millwood, N.Y., 1974.

Yassa ʿAbd al-Masīḥ. "Doxologies in the Coptic Church." *Bulletin de la Société d'archéologie copte* 4 (1938):97-113.

EMILE MAHER ISHAQ

TRIUMPHAL ARCH. *See* Architectural Elements of Churches.

TSE. *See* Akhmīm.

ṬUBḤ, an Egyptian Arabic term (plural *ṭobḥāt*) meaning "prayer," from Coptic ⲧⲱⲃϩ (Tōbh, pray, prayer). It is an ecclesiastical term used in the plural for the litany of intercessions in the midnight psalmody consisting of a listing of saints (Arabic, *majmaʿ al-qiddīsīn*) and a series of prayers, each beginning with ⲧⲱⲃϩ ⲙ̀ⲡϭ̅ⲥ̅ (*ṭobḥ amebshays*), meaning "Pray to the Lord." The *Ṭobḥāt* in the midnight psalmody for the whole year consist of seventy-four verses or prayers, but for the month of Kiyahk they consist of eighty-three verses or prayers. The *Ṭobḥāt,* like the Doxologies, are sung to a melody type called WĀṬUS, which varies according to the season.

On all feasts of Our Lord, the *Ṭobḥāt* are sung only as far as the verse "Pray to the Lord for us, Lord Claudius and Theodore and Apa Iskhīron and Apa Isaac, that He may forgive us our sins" or the verse of Saint George according to the ritual manuscript *Tartīb al-Biʿah,* (The Order of the Church), after which are added the last three verses of the *Ṭobḥāt.*

The intercessions recited after reading the Gospel and ṬARḤ in the canonical hours of Holy Week are also known as *Ṭobḥāt.* The *Tartīb al-Biʿah* says that the *Ṭobḥāt* are to be recited in each canonical hour of Holy Week (especially in monasteries), except the first and third hours of the night, because the people are not then fasting and cannot perform prostrations.

Some of the deacon's responses, exclamations, and interpositions in the Divine Liturgy and other rites are called *Ṭobḥāt,* as in the *Ṭobḥ* in the Prayer of Thanksgiving and in the Prayer of the Waters, Seeds, and Airs of Heaven.

BIBLIOGRAPHY

Ibn Sibāʿ Yūḥannā ibn Abī Zakarīyā. *Kitāb al-Jawharah al-Nafīsah fī ʿUlūm al-Kanīsah,* ed. Viktūr Manṣūr. Cairo, 1902. Latin version *Pretiosa Margarita de Scientiis Ecclesiasticis,* trans. Vincent Mistrīḥ, pp. 325, esp. note, and 327. Cairo, 1966.

EMILE MAHER ISHAQ

ṬŪD, an old cultic center of the Theban local god Month, going back to the time of Userkaf (Fifth Dynasty). It is located on the east bank of the Nile, about 12 miles (19 km) south of Luxor. The temple ruins that have survived are, however, essentially no earlier than the Ptolemaic and Roman periods. The destruction of this temple began in the fifth century A.D. with the increasing spread of Christianity, and it was overlaid by three successive layers of settlement belonging to the fifth, eighth, and thirteenth centuries. Over the Month temple of Sesostris I (Twelfth Dynasty), which was razed and its limestone material burned for lime, a basilica of simple mud bricks was erected in the eighth century (Bisson de la Roque, 1937, pp. 41-45). Of the atrium, or western entrance court, only small parts of the outer side walls have survived. The three-aisled naos, on the other hand, can be readily surveyed. The remarkable inner buttresses on the west wall may have stood in some relation to the foundations of the western return aisle. The sanctuary has a richly developed spatial plan with two rooms on each of the two sides of the apse. On the right was, perhaps, the baptistery. The curve of the apse is adorned with a continuous row of applied columns. In front of the apse is a forechoir, seldom seen in the Christian architecture of the Nile Valley. How long this church remained in existence is not known. In the thirteenth century a new building was erected on the same spot, its quarry stone foundations still following roughly the course of the outer walls of the older church. Otherwise no further details have survived. On the strength of the fifth-century sculptured materials (capitals and decorated vaulting-stones) found in the filling under the church, the excavators have assumed a second church of the fifth century so far not located.

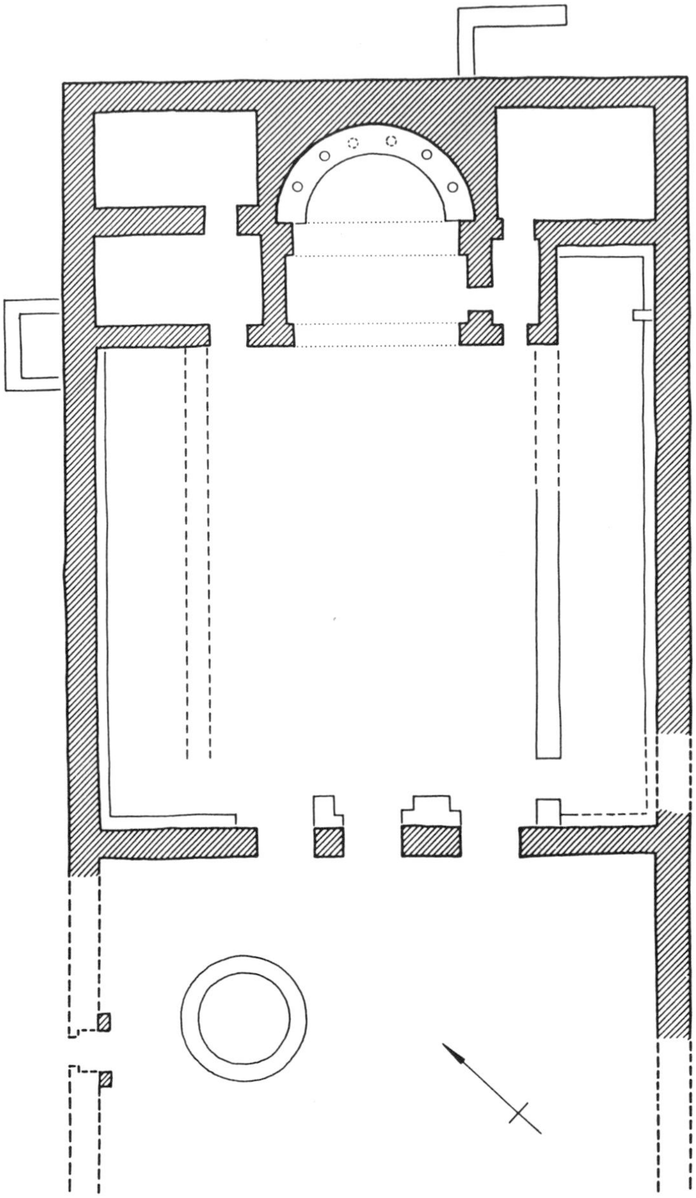

Plan of the eighth-century church at Ṭūd.

A third church was discovered in the winter of 1948/1949, but because of a mosque in the neighborhood and the objection of Muslims, it had to be filled in again only a few days after the beginning of the excavation. It contained very fine limestone fragments, friezes, capitals, and various kinds of woodwork. Of the architectural layout of the building, however, nothing is known.

BIBLIOGRAPHY

Bisson de la Roque, F. *Tod (1934 à 1936).* Fouilles de l'Institut français du Caire 17. Cairo, 1937.

Vercoutter, J. "Tod (1946–1949)." *Bulletin de l'institut français d'Archéologie orientale* 50 (1959): 83–84.

PETER GROSSMANN

TUKH AL-NASARA. *See* Pilgrimages.

TUKH TANBISHA. *See* Pilgrimages.

TULUNIDS AND IKHSHIDS, COPTS UNDER THE. Under the Abbasid caliphate in Baghdad, the Turkish viceroy Aḥmad ibn Ṭūlūn (870–884) was appointed to rule Egypt. He aimed at governing the country independently and at establishing his own dynasty, though nominally under the titular rule of the Abbasids. On assuming the reins of power in Egypt, Ibn Ṭūlūn followed a completely different policy from that of his Abbasid predecessor, ibn al-Mudabbir, whose greed had milked the country dry with excessive taxation. Ibn Ṭūlūn, on the contrary, lifted the burden of his predecessor's imposts from Muslims and Copts alike, who began to enjoy a breathing space from administrative pressures and could devote their energy to positive productivity. In fact, for the first time since the Ptolemies, all Egyptians, the Copts included, had a feeling of independence and local prosperity, as is evident from the rate of taxation. Under Aḥmad ibn al-Mudabbir, tax revenues had reached 4.3 million dinars annually, whereas it fell to 800,000 dinars in the first year of Ibn Ṭūlūn's reign.

Ibn Ṭūlūn favored the Turks over other Muslims and the Melchites over the Jacobite Copts. Thus, he pursued a totally different policy with the Coptic patriarch, whom he arrested and incarcerated until he received a heavy ransom, which he sorely needed to subsidize a Syrian campaign. Ibn Ṭūlūn's policy was double-pronged—leniency with the Coptic community in general, but harshness with the patriarch and the church. His position toward the church was dictated partly by the treacherous report supplied to him by one of the bishops hostile to Anbā KHĀ'ĪL III (880–907) who told Ibn Ṭūlūn that the patriarch concealed an immense treasure. Thus, Ibn Ṭūlūn seized the patriarch and demanded the deposition of his wealth in the public treasury. After a year, two Coptic archons, Yuḥannā and Ibrahim Mūsā, both secretaries in the Tulunid administration, succeeded in freeing the patriarch by signing a document that promised the payment of

20,000 dinars in two installments, of which the first was raised with difficulty from the Coptic community. Only the death of Ibn Ṭulūn and the succession of his son, the more lenient Khumarawayh, relieved the patriarch of payment of the second installment.

In spite of these policies, Ibn Ṭūlūn continued to favor some segments of the Coptic community, and he used to retire to the Monastery of al-Quṣayr, in the neighborhood of Ḥilwān, for contemplation and for consultation on his state problems with one of its monks, Andūnah.

Khumarawayh was, as noted, even more lenient toward the Copts than his father, but his extravagant policies were opposed by the caliphate in Baghdad, who finally struck Egypt with an iron hand. To replace the Tulunids, the caliph appointed a new governor in the person of the Ikhshid Muḥammad ibn Ṭughk, like Ibn Ṭūlūn, a Turk, but more docile in his relations with the Abbasid caliphate. Ikhshid rule was relatively short and marked by harsher financial treatment of Egypt, and the Copts in particular, though socially the governor shared with the Copts the celebration of their feasts. The Muslim historian al-Mas'ūdī (1861, Vol. 1, pp. 212–13) recorded that in the Epiphany evening of the year 941–942, Ibn Ṭughk participated with the Copts in their annual celebrations by ordering that a thousand torches be lit in addition to the Coptic torches on the Nile banks at the island of Rodah and the city of al-Fusṭāṭ (Old Cairo). In the end, however, Kafūr, an Abyssinian eunuch and the mentor of Ibn Ṭughk's young successors, seized power, and his reign tolled the knell of the Ikhshids, from whose hands the Shi'ite North African Fatimids were able to wrest the kingdom of Egypt.

One must remember that most of the important positions in the Islamic administration of both the Tulunids and the Ikhshids were occupied by Coptic scribes, who were mainly responsible for the finances of the country.

BIBLIOGRAPHY

Hitti, P. *History of the Arabs*. London, 1946.
Huart, C. *Histoire des arabes*. 2 vols. Paris, 1912.
Lane-Poole, S. *History of Egypt in the Middle Ages*. London, 1925.

AZIZ S. ATIYA

TŪMĀ IBN AL-NAJĪB LUṬFALLĀH, fourteenth-century monk known from two manuscripts that he copied.

Tūmā's name is given in two colophons of Vatican Arabic 158 with the addition "known as (*al-ma'rūf bi-*) al-Maḥallī," which suggests he came from al-Maḥallah in the Delta. The same colophons also record that he was a monk at the monastery of Saint Mercurius, known as Dayr Shahrān, which is situated near Ṭurah at about 7 miles (11 km) south of Old Cairo. It was there that he copied his manuscript.

The manuscript was copied between November 1356 and November 1357, for his own use (cf. fol. 23a). This explains the rather careless handwriting. He copied it in five stages from five different and rare manuscripts that were not found in his monastery but in nearby places such as Ṭurah, Miṣr, or Cairo. These parts are each dated in the Coptic and Muslim calendars, giving the day of the week without the slightest error, which is extremely rare.

His manuscript is composed of independent fascicules of ten sheets, assembled as he went along. In this way he constituted five separate small manuscripts, each numbered beginning with 1. The whole was not bound, which explains why the first two sheets containing the table of contents and the last are now lost. Originally, the collection contained at least 210 sheets. What remains is now found in two manuscripts (Vatican Library, Arabic 158, 177 sheets; and Vatican Library, Arabic 159, fols. 1–28, the rest belonging to a Munich manuscript).

The manuscripts contain ten extremely interesting texts.

1. Two treatises justifying Coptic usages by MĪKHĀ'ĪL, bishop of Damietta at the end of the twelfth century, against Abū al-Fakhr Murqus ibn Qanbar, a blind Coptic reformer priest who became a Melchite and died in 1208. These two texts are found only in this manuscript, where they are now in disorder; the order should be: B (Vatican Arabic 159, fols. 3–9); A (Vatican Arabic 158, fols. 2–3), B, fols. 9–18, and A, fols. 4–13. The second text is in A, fols. 14–22.

2. Folios 24a–25a contain two pages on the profession of faith of the Good Thief, not mentioned in G. Graf's *Geschichte der christlichen arabischen Literatur*.

3. Folios 25b–98a contain a treatise by Elias, Nestorian bishop of Nisibis (975–1004). Tūmā twice calls the Nestorian bishop *al-Qiddīs Mār Iliyyā* (the Saint Mār Elia), since the text copied is of a high spiritual tenor.

4. Folios 99b–111b report the vision of Saint Athanasius. Only one other manuscript is known of this text; it is also Coptic, but much more recent (National Library, Paris, Arabic 153, copied in the seventeenth century).

5. Folios 112b–27a describe the vision of Samū'īl of Qalamūn. Here too, only one older manuscript of this text is known (National Library, Paris, Arabic 205, dated 1344).

6. Folios 128b–47b are notes concerning the twenty-four prophets and twelve apostles. These are missing in Graf's *Geschichte der christlichen arabischen Literatur,* which suggests that they are found only in this manuscript.

7. Folios 148a–57b include a commentary on the Creed of Abū al-Majd ibn Yu'annis, priest of Minyat Banī Khaṣīb. This is the oldest known manuscript of this text.

8. Folios 158a–67a include a collection of monastic texts, beginning with a series of brief questions and answers addressed to Saint Basil. No equivalent of this text can be found in Graf's *Geschichte der christlichen arabischen Literatur.*

9. Folios 168a–77b and Vatican Arabic 159, folios 20a–27b and 19a–19b contain the Life of Saint Just (Yusṭus) and his son Apollo (Abūlī). This text was the model for the Ethiopian version mentioned in *Bibliotheca Hagiographica Orientalis* (no. 554) and edited by M. Esteves Pereira in 1907. Only one witness to this text is known; it is also Coptic, but far more recent (National Library, Paris, Arabic 4775, nineteenth century).

As is evident, Tūmā in his personal manuscript collected rare or even unique texts. In order to do so, he undertook a regular manuscript hunt, traces of which have been left by him in the colophons.

Thus, the two texts of Michael of Damietta were copied from a manuscript belonging to the Shaykh Amīn al-Mulk ibn al-Akram al-Ṭawīl, a still unidentified Coptic dignitary, who lived in Cairo in 1356. He completed his copy on Friday, 25 November 1356 (fol. 22b).

The text of Elias of Nisibis was completed on Friday, 9 December 1356, copied from a manuscript copied at Qaṣr al-Jama' in Old Cairo on Wednesday, 11 November 1327, but given as a bequest to the monastery of Mārī Jirjis.

On folio 13b we find a page by a contemporary reader, dated Monday, 4 Ba'ūnah A.M. 1073/29 May 1357, stating that the deacon Jirjis read this "book" (*kitāb*). At this date, only the first three texts mentioned had been copied.

The two visions of Athanasius and of Samū'īl were completed on Tuesday, 31 October 1357, on the basis of a manuscript belonging to Ya'qūb 'Alām, (or Ghulām) al-Tāj, son of the Qummuṣ Fakhr al-Dawlah ibn Dāniyāl, who was at that time living at the Church of the Angel Gabriel (fol. 127a), probably that of Miṣr. Tūmā further tells us that he returned the manuscript to him, and this indicates that he copied it where he was living, at Dayr Shahrān. These other notables of Cairo are also still unidentified.

The notes concerning the twenty-four prophets, the commentary on the creed, and the collection of monastic texts, were all copied in one week from a manuscript belonging to 'Ubayd (?) ibn al-Ḥājj Manṣūr the monk, who was at that time living at Bāb al-Baḥr in Cairo (cf. fol. 167a). They were completed respectively on 31 October, 2 November, and 6 November 1357.

It is unclear from which manuscript the biography of Saints Just and Apollo was copied, as the end of the manuscript is missing.

KHALIL SAMIR, S.J.

TUNICS. *See* Costume, Civil.

TURAEV, BORIS ALEXANDROVITCH (1868–1920), Russian Egyptologist. He studied first in St. Petersburg and later under Adolf Erman in Berlin. On returning to Russia, he was appointed professor of ancient history at the University of St. Petersburg. He was also made keeper of Egyptian antiquities in the Moscow Museum when it acquired the Golenischeff collection. In 1918 he was elected a member of the Russian Academy of Sciences. He had assembled a large collection of antiquities, which he had intented to bequeath to the Moscow Museum, but instead, it was acquired by the Hermitage in 1920. He published *Der Ostergottesdienst der koptischen Kirche* (St. Petersburg, 1897); *Description de la section égyptienne du Musée d'antiquitiés de Kazan* (St. Petersburg, 1903); *Koptische Aufsätze* (Petrograd, 1907); and *Opisanie Egiepetskago sobraniya,* Vol. 1, *Statui i statuetki golenischevskago sobraniya* (1917).

BIBLIOGRAPHY

Dawson, W. R., and E. P. Uphill. *Who Was Who in Egyptology.* London, 1972.

Kammerer, W., comp. *A Coptic Bibliography.* Ann Arbor, Mich., 1950; repr. New York, 1969.

M. L. BIERBRIER

ṬURAH. *See* Dayr al-Quṣayr (Ṭūrāh).

TUṬŪN, village situated in the district of Iṭsā, south of the Fayyūm in the middle of cultivated lands. The ancient town (Coptic, Touton) of the same name was near the desert. It was very probably the site today called Umm al-Barayjāt, of which the Greek name was Tebtunis, about 2.5 miles (4 km) south of the present Tuṭūn.

The name of this village occurs quite often in the subscript to Coptic manuscripts, in which the scribes added a prayer at the end of the copy for the donor and the church or monastery to which the manuscript was offered, as well as their own name. The oldest mention of a copyist from Tuṭūn is from 861/862 (Van Lantschoot, 1929, pp. 22–24), and the most recent is from 1014, although in the latter case it is a reader's note (Hebbelynck and Van Lantschoot, 1937, pp. 510–11). Some donors, natives of the same village, also are mentioned. All these manuscripts—thirteen cataloged by Van Lantschoot (1929)—derive either from the library of the monastery of Dayr al-Malāk Mīkhā'īl (Fayyūm) or from that of Dayr al-Abyaḍ (Suhāj). They are dated between 861/862 and 940, the most recent being those of Dayr al-Abyaḍ.

It has sometimes been said that these manuscripts were copied in the scriptorium of a monastery at Tuṭūn. However, there is no justification for this statement. A single copyist, the priest Zacharias, presents himself as calligrapher of the monastery of Qalamūn (Van Lantschoot, nos. 3 and 4, pp. 6–10). In contrast, none of the copyists native to Tuṭūn presents himself as a monk in a monastery. The name of the village Toutōn is given only as their place of origin. On the other hand, though these scribes are often clerics, deacons, subdeacons, singers, or even priests, they work in large measure at home. Basil and the deacon Peter are brothers, as are the deacons Stephen and Qalamūn. Moses, a deacon, wrote with Menas, a subdeacon, his brother; the deacon Basil, with his son Samuel, also a deacon. There are, however, some isolated copyists: John, brother of the deacon Menas; the deacon Matthew; the deacon Peter (perhaps the brother of Basil); and the priest Theodorus, son of the deacon Luke.

The donors said to be natives of Tuṭūn are not described by the title of monk, as is done in the colophons numbered 51, 52, and 53 (Van Lantschoot, pp. 78–86), all three donors of which bore the name Shenute and offered the manuscripts to the monastery of Shenute (Dayr al-Abyaḍ) at Suhāj, a very long way from Tuṭūn. It seems thus much more probable that the scriptoria of Tuṭūn were small family workshops or those of individual copyists.

Outside of Tuṭūn, there were copyists native to and no doubt also residing in the following towns and villages of the Fayyūm: Miktol, Perpnoute, and Ptepouhar.

BIBLIOGRAPHY

Hebbelynck, A., and A. Van Lantschoot. *Codices coptici Vaticani.* Codices Coptici. Vatican City, 1937.

Lantschoot, A. van. *Recueil des colophons des manuscrits chrétiens d'Egypte.* Vol. 1, *Les colophons coptes des manuscrits sahidiques.* Bibliothèque du Muséon 1. Louvain, 1929.

Petersen, T. "The Paragraph Mark in Coptic Illuminated Ornament." In *Studies in Art and Literature for Belle da Costa Green.* Princeton, N.J., 1954.

RENÉ-GEORGES COQUIN

TWENTY-FOUR ELDERS. *See* Christian Subjects in Coptic Art.

TYPES. In I Corinthians 10:6–13, Paul teaches that while the people of Israel wandered in the wilderness (Ex. 13:21–22; 14:22–29; 16:4, 35), certain events occurred as "types," or examples, for the Christians of the apostolic period. He further claimed that such happenings were intended "typically" to forewarn Christians about the coming of Christ and the consequences of His ministry. In Romans 5:14 he suggests that Adam was a "type" of the Christ who was to come. Such explanations illuminate the New Testament idea that certain incidents during the old dispensation predicted the major events of the career of Jesus Christ and of the early church, which relived them in a Christian sense. Most obvious analogies concern the flood and the ark, the liberation of the people of Israel from Egypt (the Exodus), the wandering in the wilderness, the crossing of the River Jordan, the later return from exile, and the rebuilding of Jerusalem. Actual historical episodes were thought to foreshadow later events not in a literal but in a spiritual sense; thus, the liberation from Egypt was paralleled in Christ's freeing us from our sins.

These types were perpetuated and enormously increased in the writings of the ancient Christian fathers. Indeed, the Bible was ransacked to extract types regarded as fulfilled in the Christian dispensation, some of them absurd and farfetched. Early

Christian art displays innumerable examples of types, though in a more restricted range than in literature. Early Christian sarcophagi, for instance, display again and again Abraham's sacrifice of Isaac, Daniel in the lion's den, and Noah in the ark. It is possible that the list of types used in art derived from a range of examples of God's deliverance used in Jewish prayers. The use of types in this manner may be said to have entered deeply into Christian prayer, worship, hymnology, and piety generally.

Christian theologians today are cautious about using types, partly because of critical doubts raised concerning the historical authenticity of some of the events serving as types, and partly because of the subjectivity of all typology. Nevertheless, types still contribute largely to the piety and worship of many individual Christians and of the church as a community.

BIBLIOGRAPHY

Daniélou, J. *From Shadows to Reality: Studies in the Biblical Typology of the Fathers*. London, 1950.

Hanson, R., and P. Crosland. *Allegory and Event*, chaps. 1–4. London, 1959.

Lampe, G. W. H., and K. J. Woolcombe. *Essays in Typology*. London, 1957.

Simon, M. *Verus Israel*. Paris, 1948.

R. P. C. Hanson

U

ULPHILAS (c. 311–381), the Apostle of the Goths, who was responsible for the conversion of the Goths to Arian Christianity (see ARIANISM). According to the ecclesiastical historian Philostorgius (*Historia ecclesiastica* 2.5), the Goths descended on the eastern provinces of the empire and crossed the Bosporus to Asia Minor and Cappadocia in the third century, during the reigns of Valerian and Gallienus. After ravaging these provinces, they returned to Dacia with many prisoners, including Ulphilas, who happened to be Arians. These Cappadocians eventually became missionaries of Arian Christianity amid their barbarian masters. Ulphilas is known to have been born in Dacia to Cappadocian parents around 311, and he labored all his life among the Goths, whose language he mastered in addition to his native Greek.

Little is known about the life of Ulphilas beyond the gleanings collected from Philostorgius and a newly discovered manuscript of an *Epistle* written by his former pupil Auxentius, Arian bishop of Dorostorum (Silistria) in the Louvre, Paris. Apart from his preaching of the gospel in Dacia he was selected by the Gothic monarchs to go to Constantinople as their ambassador around 340, apparently because of his knowledge of Greek. It was during his visit to the Byzantine capital that Ulphilas was elevated to the rank of bishop by Eusebius of Nicomedia, who was also a follower of ARIUS. Afterward he returned to Dacia, where he resumed his missionary activity.

In 360, Ulphilas is said to have been in Constantinople to attend a synod where the Acacian party (*see* ACACIAN SCHISM) scored a triumph in devising a middle-of-the-road formula intended to bring orthodox Christians and Arians closer together and end their quarrels over the nature of Christ. A new term, *homoios,* was devised as a substitute for the terms *homoousios* and *homoiousios,* where the root of the trouble lay. The "Homoeans" maintained that the Son was "like" the Father, and this similarity was confirmed by Ulphilas, who described Jesus as the image of the invisible God. This led to the creation of a new party of orthodox "semi-Arians" who seem to have suffered, perhaps temporarily, a wave of local persecution at the hands of the Arian Athanaric the Goth during the period 372–375. This persecution affected Ulphilas until Arianism was completely restored among the Goths before their final descent into the Roman empire.

On the authority of Auxentius, Ulphilas found time to write a number of literary and theological treatises that are all lost save a Latin Homoean Mass creed and a baptismal creed reproduced in the *Epistola* of Bishop Auxentius. His masterpiece was the monumental translation of the Bible into the Gothic tongue, which has survived and is available in print. Noteworthy in the text of the Gothic Bible is Ulphilas' omission of the Books of Kings, which he deliberately left out in order not to encourage the warlike nature of the Goths through the example of scripture.

The latter years of the life of Ulphilas are shrouded in obscurity. He is said to have returned to Constantinople in 380 on an unknown mission and died early in 381.

BIBLIOGRAPHY

Altaner, B. *Patrology.* Trans. H. Graef. London, 1958.

Bardenhewer, O. *Geschichte der altkirchlichen Literatur,* Vol. 3. Freiburg, 1912.

Friedrichsen, G. W. S. *The Gothic Version of the Gospels.* Oxford, 1939.

AZIZ S. ATIYA

UMAR TUSSUN. *See* Omar Toussoun.

UMAYYAD FLEET, COPTIC CONTRIBUTION TO. Arabic, Greek, and Coptic documents from the Umayyad period (661–750) indicate the contribution of Christian Egyptians, including Copts, in the building and the manning of the Muslim fleet. The extent of this participation is unclear, since these documents contain sparse and fragmentary information, and are insufficient for a thorough study of this topic. It is evident that the Arabs, in their effort to counter Byzantine maritime supremacy in the Mediterranean, made use of available skilled labor in building or refitting naval vessels after their conquest of Egypt in 641.

A number of Arabic medieval accounts—including those of al-Bakrī, al-Raqīq al-Qayrawānī, and al-Tījānī—report that the Umayyad caliph ʿAbd al-Malik ibn Marwān (685–705) ordered his brother ʿAbd al-ʿAzīz (governor of Egypt, 685–705) to dispatch to Ḥassān ibn al-Nuʿmān (commander of the Arab forces in North Africa) one thousand Copts with their families to help with the construction of the shipyard and the building of the fleet in Tunis. This is the only historical text in which Copts are specifically mentioned. Other texts either refer to Christians or to non-Muslim Egyptians in general, or include information that implies that Copts are meant.

The chronicle of the Byzantine historian Theophanes (d. 818) comprises an account of the Arab naval assault on Constantinople in 717–718, during the rule of Emperor Leo III (717–741). It states that the main fleet sailed from Egypt and was later reinforced from Africa (Tunisia). The Arab assault ended in disaster not only because the Byzantines used Greek fire but also, according to Theophanes (p. 89), because the "Egyptians . . . took the merchant ships' light boats, and . . . fled to the city," thus providing the Byzantines with information about the Muslim fleet. "Egyptians" is a reference to non-Arab sailors, and the mention of "merchant ships" in this passage indicates that Christian sailors were manning supply ships. The question of their actual participation in the fighting is left unanswered.

A number of relevant Greek and Coptic papyri from Aphrodito, the majority dating back to the governorship of Qurrah ibn Sharīk (709–714) in Egypt, have been reproduced by H. I. Bell and W. E. Crum in the fourth volume of *Greek Papyri in the British Museum.* These documents leave no doubt that Christian manpower was used in the maintenance of the fleet. In Papyrus 1350 (dated 710, pp. 24–25), Qurrah requests Basilius, pagarch of Aphrodito, to supply information regarding the whereabouts of sailors who were part of a fleet that sailed to North Africa under the orders of ʿAṭā ibn Rāfiʿ. The latter was the commander of a raid against Sicily in 703–704. In Papyrus 1353 (dated 710, pp. 27–28), the same governor orders Basilius to dispatch sailors and shipbuilders, probably to Alexandria. Papyri 1355, 1371, 1376, 1386, 1393, 1451, 1452, and 1456, all Greek, contain requisitions for sailors, workmen, money, or provisions, or for all of these together, to meet the needs of the fleet. This is confirmed by the contents of some of the Coptic papyri in the same collection that are reproduced by Crum (pp. 435–450).

Christian contributions to Arab naval works continued after the fall of the Umayyads in 750. SĀWĪRUS IBN AL-MUQAFFAʿ (tenth century), bishop of al-Ashmūnayn and first compiler of the *History of the Patriarchs,* complains of the conscription of Christian sailors by the governor of Egypt during the rule of the Abbasid caliph al-Mutawakkil (847–861), following a Byzantine attack on Damietta in 853. He states that Christian workmen took part in building and refitting ships, and that Christian sailors were forced to join the fleet, receiving no pay and being provided food rations only. This implies that Christian conscripts who were in the service of the fleet were usually paid only in kind for their labor, an interpretation that is supported by the content of Coptic Papyrus 1501, edited by Crum.

BIBLIOGRAPHY

Greek Papyri in the British Museum. Catalogue, with Texts, Vol. 4, ed. H. I. Bell, with *Appendix of Coptic Papyri,* ed. W. E. Crum. London, 1910.

Lewis, A. R. *Naval Power and Trade in the Mediterranean.* pp. 60–75. Princeton, 1951.

Sebag, P. "Les travaux maritimes de Ḥasan [*sic*] Ibn Nuʿman." *Revue de l'Institut des belles-lettres arabes* (Tunis) 33 (1970):41–56.

ADEL ALLOUCHE

UMAYYADS, COPTS UNDER THE. The Umayyads (661–750), named after the Banū Umayyah, a merchant family of Mecca, following a civil war established the first dynasty to rule the Islamic world. Under Umayyad rule the Islamic empire attained its greatest extent, reaching as far as France in the west and India in the east. The Umayyads moved the capital of the Islamic world, and therefore the center of gravity, from Mecca to Damascus, whence Egypt was ruled as a province of Syria by ethnic Arab governors appointed by the caliph.

Umayyad rule has been most fully examined as it affected Syria, Iraq, and the Persian-speaking East. There, Umayyad favoritism toward ethnic Arabs resulted in discrimination against non-Arab converts to Islam, hence the literature often refers to the Umayyad empire as the "Arab Empire." Discontent among converts led to the overthrow of the Umayyads and their replacement by the Abbasid dynasty (A.H. 132–656/A.D. 750–1258), which brought in its wake increasing ethnic Persian influence. Under the Abbasids not only were the Umayyads physically hunted down and eliminated but also the history of the Umayyads was written as propaganda justifying their overthrow. With the beginnings of European historiographical interest in Egypt in the nineteenth century, Abbasid depiction of a cruel and tyrannical Umayyad reign in Egypt was accepted and compounded by an imperial mind-set that saw Islam as the cause of the decline of Egypt's fortunes following the decline of the Roman world.

As a corrective to this double distortion of Umayyad rule in Egypt, the *Qurrah Papyri* (written in Arabic and Greek) contradict the later Abbasid narrative sources, which misrepresent the character of Umayyad administration in Egypt. These provincial Egyptian documents indicate, for example, that the governor Qurrah ibn Sharīk (ruled 709–714) was a careful and effective administrator and not the godless tyrant portrayed by Abbasid historians.

Agrarian Administration and Land Tenure

From Greek, Coptic, and Arabic papyri we know that following the Arab conquest Egypt was administered largely through the Coptic church and provincial Coptic notables. This was of necessity as no Arabs, other than a few high-level personnel, settled in Egypt until a half century later. Egypt's agrarian wealth was legendary. Umayyad interest in Egypt was fiscal, the wealth yielded by agricultural taxation as well as the poll tax levied on non-Muslims. Fiscal interest in agricultural taxation led the Umayyads to interfere in Coptic–Arab (Arab and Muslim are synonymous in Umayyad Egypt) administrative and ultimately social relations.

From about 715 to 740 the Umayyad administration took a radical step to increase tax remittance to the fisc. It changed the tax status of the land of Egypt from treaty to nontreaty (Noth, 1984). This change reputedly doubled the tax rate. The precise juridical term used to indicate land conquered without treaty, *kharāj,* is unknown in the Umayyad papyri. This change in tax status probably accounts for the endemic tax revolts by, first, Copts, then both Arabs and Copts, which began in 725 and continued periodically into the Abbasid period.

At about the same time as the change in the tax status of the land, intrusion of the central government at the local level was felt in two other, interrelated ways. The government began to assess peasant farmers individually, and it launched an effort to replace Coptic administrative personnel with Muslims beginning around 717. This was a very slow process, according to the testimony of documents, which indicate that Coptic officials continued in place well into the eighth century, and long after that according to narrative sources.

Previously, Arab officials of the central government determined a gross assessment figure for each of the various agrarian administrative districts. Then, at the local level, a native Egyptian notable, often a churchman, apportioned the district's assessment by assessing the individual villagers in his district. This same native Egyptian notable collected the individually assessed taxes from the local population and remitted them to the Arab officials of the Umayyad administration.

The documents show that reliance on native Egyptian administrators had its shortcomings. At the village level the fisc was sometimes confronted with group noncompliance, or only partial remittance of the tax assessment by the native Egyptian notables. Lack of control over agricultural assessment and collection perhaps accounts for the comparatively high levels of poll tax in the first century and a half of Islamic rule in Egypt and the later inclusion of poll tax as an incidental element of agrarian assessment and collection.

The change in administrative personnel who assessed taxes at the local level, from third-party native Egyptian notables to Muslim bureaucrats appointed by the Umayyad government, was intended to address noncompliance and partial remittance. Previously, the individual who had worked the land had been liable to the local, native Egyptian notable, and the notable had in turn been liable to the central government. Now the individual who worked the land was directly liable to the central government's official and, therefore, to the Umayyad government itself.

This establishment of individual liability was tantamount to a change in land tenure from group to individual tenure. As far as the state was concerned, whoever was directly liable for taxes held tenure to that land. In addition, Arabs liable for taxes on land begin to appear in the documents dating from this period. This entirely new group of landholders resulted from subsidized Arab immigration into Egypt from Syria, which began in 728.

The transfer of tenure based on the change from indirect to direct liability vis-à-vis the Umayyad government implied a social revolution. The local Egyptian notable, frequently a churchman, had formerly exercised influence over the community by apportioning the district's tax assessment among the peasants, who were then liable to him for individual assessments. With individual assessment by the state, and individual liability directly to the state, the Egyptian notable and the Coptic church began to lose their influence with the peasant population. The notables and churchmen no longer occupied the same position of economic and political influence over the villagers. This transfer of tenure from church to tenant farmer, on paper as it were, also was to lead to the church physically losing some of its land.

The change from native notables to Arab personnel in local administration did not solve the problem of partial remittance. The root cause lay in the fact that, under both personnel systems, the administrator who collected taxes directly from the peasants was the very same official who had assessed the taxes on those individuals. Transferring this dual power to assess and collect from native administrators to Arab officials had a devastating effect on the individual peasant, and ultimately the fisc.

Previously, the local notable, through his role as an agrarian administrator, had not only been able to exercise considerable influence upon the peasantry but had also acted as an intermediary between the peasant and the Umayyad state. Local Egyptian notables had stood as a buffer between the peasant and taxation. With the change in personnel, the individual landholder, whether Coptic peasant or Arab immigrant, now had to deal directly with the state's local tax official. Whereas the local Egyptian notable had been a member of the community with long-term interests within that community, the Arab official was often an outsider who was only on temporary assignment from his home in Syria. The individual landholder now stood defenseless against the potential for abuse, which was inherent in the tax official's dual powers of assessment and collection.

It is well attested in narrative sources, and alluded to in the documents, that in dealing directly with the peasant farmer, first Copt and later Arab as well, tax officials abused their authority. By the middle of the eighth century we hear that the state's local tax officials pocketed taxes that they collected from peasant farmers, while alleging that the peasants were in arrears or that crops had failed. Tax assessors also "shortened the measuring rod" (overmeasured) or were bribed to "measure gently." Arbitrary taxes were levied. Much of this fraudulently assessed tax was collected but not reported, again ending in the tax official's pocket rather than in Umayyad coffers.

When tax officials succeeded in extracting excessive taxes, peasants stood to be abused to the point of abandoning the land. Officials reputedly deliberately overassessed landholders in some instances in order to dispossess them and then take over their lands. In the case of tenant farmers on church lands, it led to the church's loss of that land.

Conversion

Coptic church sources viewed their loss of tenure and the loss of their position as intermediaries between the state and the peasant as religious persecution. While many historians have focused on the emphasis on religious persecution in Coptic sources as the likely reason for conversion, it has been suggested that the church's weakening economic and social status was a more demonstrable and likely factor. In this interpretation, conversion can be seen as a means of joining the new ruling class in an attempt to protect one's property. Whatever the motives for conversion, its progress is remarkable for its glacial pace.

Parties to published Arabic legal documents dating from as late as the eleventh century continue to be Copts overwhelmingly, by the evidence of their names and genealogies. These documents also provide an indication that the means of conversion among the provincial population, too humble to have come to the attention of Muslim biographers resident in capital cities, was intermarriage. According to Islamic jurisprudence, witnesses were required to be Muslim. Some of the witnesses who signed the contracts referred to may have been recent converts, or from families recently converted. Some have Muslim patronymics and non-Muslim first names, suggesting intermarriage between Muslim men and Christian women. Similarly, the parties to contracts indicate intermarriage; for example, a woman with a Coptic patronymic marries a man with a Muslim first name and patronymic. A state functionary bears a Muslim name and patronymic, while his mother's name and patronymic are both Coptic.

Arabization and Law

Documents indicate a lack of arabization in provincial Egypt as much as three centuries after the Arab conquest, well beyond the Umayyad period. First, private documents continued to be written in Coptic in the eighth century. In legal documents, parties to contracts had a choice of language in which to have their documents recorded, and they opted for Coptic. Tenth-century documents from the Fayyūm expressly state that the contract in question had been "read to the seller in Arabic and explained to him in the 'foreign language.'" The fact that even oral Arabic had to be "explained" to the parties to these contracts suggests the slow pace of arabization in Egypt.

According to a body of documentary litigation dating from the eighth century, Muslims adjudicated between Christians on the basis of contracts written in Coptic and in Greek. Significantly, as mentioned above, Umayyad officials continued to give the option of having a contract written in Coptic as late as fifteen years after their assumption of judicial authority around 718, thus demonstrating not only their familiarity with the Coptic formulary but also its acceptance as valid before Muslim jurists.

Such acceptance, along with the chronological overlap in the practice of the two systems, Arabic and Coptic, suggests commonality between the two. While there are many parallels between the Coptic and Arabic formularies, as well as between the Greek and Arabic, they are not identical. Arabic contracts from Umayyad Egypt contain unique clauses as well as modification of phrases making earlier Egyptian formularies conform to Islamic norms.

BIBLIOGRAPHY

Abbott, N. *The Ḳurrah Papyri from Aphrodito in the Oriental Institute.* Chicago, 1938.

Cahen, C. "Darība." In *Encyclopaedia of Islam,* new ed., Vol. 2, pp. 142–45. Leiden, 1965.

______. "Djizya." In *Encyclopaedia of Islam,* new ed., Vol. 2, pp. 559–62. Leiden, 1965.

______. "Kharādj." In *Encyclopaedia of Islam,* new ed., Vol. 4, pp. 1030–34. Leiden, 1978.

Frantz-Murphy, G. "Agricultural Tax Assessment and Liability in Early Islamic Egypt." In *Atti del XVII Congresso Internazionale di Papirologia,* Vol. 3, pp. 1405–1414. Naples, 1984.

______. "Land Tenure and Social Transformation in Early Islamic Egypt." In *Land Tenure and Social Transformation in the Near East,* ed. T. Khalidi, pp. 131–39. Beirut, 1984.

______. "A Comparison of Arabic and Earlier Egyptian Contract Formularies: Part II, Terminology in the Arabic Warranty and the Idiom of Clearing/Cleaning." *Journal of Near Eastern Studies* 44 (1985):99–114.

______. *The Agrarian Administration of Egypt from the Arabs to the Ottomans.* Cairo, 1986.

Noth, A. "Some Remarks on the 'Nationalization' of Conquered Lands at the Time of the Umayyads." In *Land Tenure and Social Transformation in the Near East,* ed. T. Khalidi, pp. 223–28. Beirut, 1984.

______. "Zum Verhältnis von kalifer Zentralgewalt und Provinzen in umayyadischer Zeit; die ṣulḥ'-anwa'-Traditionen für Ägypten und den Iraq." *Die Welt des Islams,* n.s. 14 (1973):150–62.

GLADYS FRANTZ-MURPHY

UMM AL-BARAKĀT (Tebtynis), site where numerous Ptolemaic to Byzantine papyri were found.

Ancient Tebtynis, situated on the southeastern edge of the Fayyūm, belongs to the settlements that sprang up in the vicinity of a temple—in this case of the crocodile deity Suchos. The origins of the settlement probably reach back to the period of the Twelfth Dynasty. The settlement reached its peak development in the Ptolemaic-Roman period, the period to which the temple also belonged. The quarters laid out in the Ptolemaic period to the north of the temple, on both sides of the great processional way, have a system of street planning similar to that found in other Hellenistic towns in the eastern half of the Mediterranean. The Roman and late Roman quarters to the northeast are considerably more irregular. In late antiquity a military unit was established within the temple, a contributing factor in the settlement's continuation into the Christian period. A number of uniformly shaped rooms that belonged to the buildings where the soldiers were billeted are visible, chiefly along the western enclosure wall of the temple.

In the section of the town belonging to the late antique period three early Christian churches, all built on the lines of a basilica, were found. In each instance the buildings were extremely provincial, and their architectural embellishment was made up entirely of reused and even ill-matched working

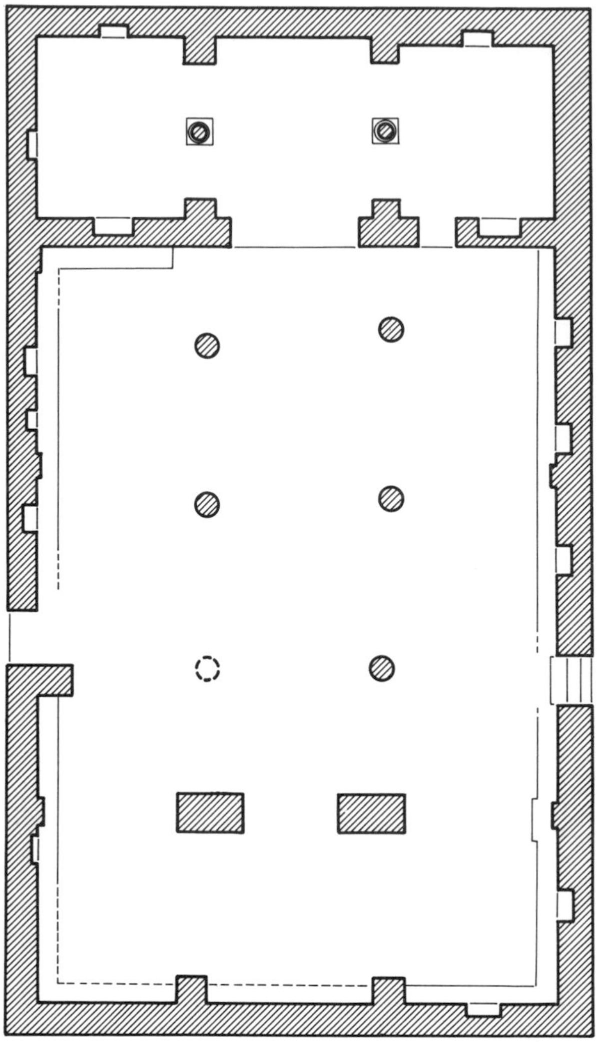

Plan of Church A, Umm al-Barakāt. *Courtesy Peter Grossmann.*

materials. None of the churches possessed an apse; they made do with more or less regular rectangular exedras. They can all be placed approximately in the seventh century.

Church A is three pillar-axes long. The very narrow central nave is bordered on the west end by two transverse brick pillars, beyond which lies the western return aisle. The three rooms of the sanctuary are separated from each other by double-arched passageways each with intermediate columns. In addition, both the side rooms are connected with the side aisle by arched windows, a feature that is unparalleled in the early Christian architecture of Egypt. Besides that, only the south side room still features a connecting door to the south aisle.

Of church B only a few sections of the wall were visible, and these of no great height. Both rows of columns end in the west in angular columns built with fired bricks. The contiguous transverse arch nearby on the south side is from a later date. Finally, most unusual is the division of rooms in the sanctuary with a large central room reaching on both sides beyond the width of the middle aisle.

Church C is the best preserved of the three churches and is especially renowned for its fine interior paintings, parts of which are today in the Coptic Museum, Cairo (Jarry, 1968, pp. 139–42). The church appears to have had a later narthex added on externally. The sanctuary is constructed asymmetrically with a south side room probably

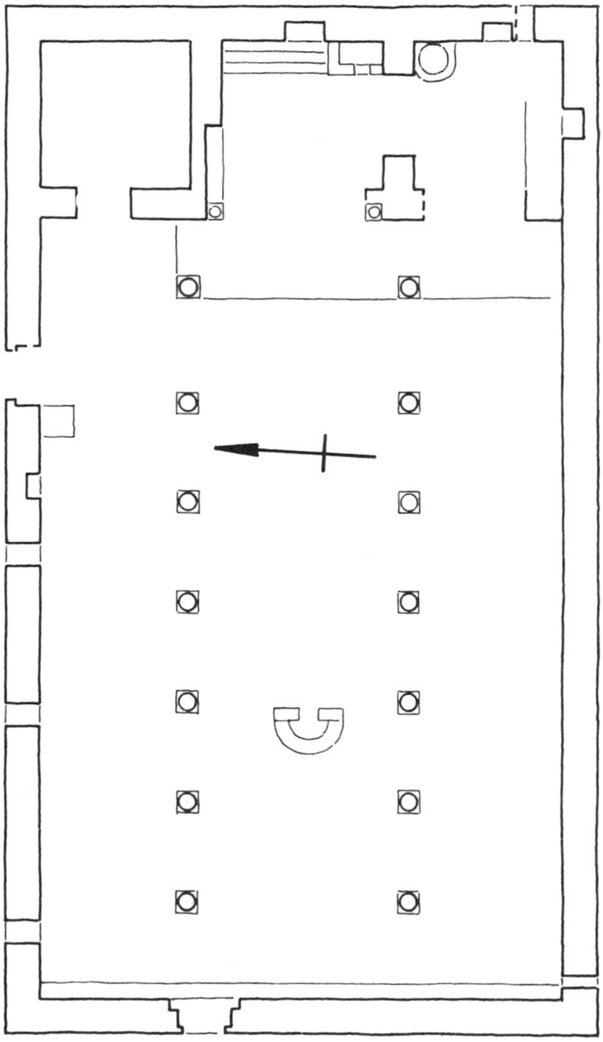

Plan of Church C, Umm al-Barakāt. *Courtesy Peter Grossmann.*

used as a baptistery and connected to the central main room by a broad arch.

BIBLIOGRAPHY

Jarry, J. "Reflexions sur la portée théologique d'une fresque d'Umm el-Baragat (Tebtunis)." *Bulletin de l'Institut français d'Archéologie orientale* 66 (1968):139–42.

Kees, H. "Tebtynis." In *Realencyclopädie der classischen Altertumswissenschaft,* ser. 2, Vol. 5. Stuttgart, 1934.

PETER GROSSMANN

UMM DABADĪB, remarkably well-preserved village, also called the oasis of ʿAbbās, about 28 miles (45 km) northwest of Khargah. In addition to the village, the site includes an imposing fortress consisting of a central keep flanked by two trapezoidal towers 65 × 65 feet (20 × 20 m) and a square outer rampart 328 feet (100 m) along the sides. The present height varies between 32 and 41 feet (10 and 13 m). Between the keep and the rampart to the east, in the interior of the fortress, is a small, three-aisled church with stuccoed and painted columns, oriented from west to east (apparent length of the nave is 33 feet [10 m]). The decorated half-dome of the apse is preserved, and includes numerous Greek and Coptic grafitti, for example, "Lord Jesus Christ, help the hapless Paphnoute"; "John son of Sergius, Amen, 30th Thot, the 6th indiction"; and so forth.

BIBLIOGRAPHY

Blundell, H. W. "Notes sur une excursion à Khargueh, Dakhleh, Farafrah et Behariyeh." *Bulletin de la Société khédiviale de géographie* 4 (1894):272ff.

Gascou, J., and G. Wagner. "Deux voyages archéologiques dans l'Oasis de Khargeh." In *Bulletin de l'Institut français d'Archéologie orientale* 79 (1979):15–16.

GUY WAGNER

UNCTION OF THE SICK, HOLY SACRAMENT OF THE, a sacrament instituted by Jesus Christ and carried out by the apostles, who, as attested by Mark 6:13, "anointed with oil many that were sick and healed them." It was also commended by the Epistle of James: "Is any among you sick? Let him call for the elders of the church, and let them pray over him, anointing him with oil in the name of the Lord; and the prayer of faith will save the sick man, and the Lord will raise him up; and if he has committed sins, he will be forgiven" (Jas. 5:14–15). The apostles received this sacrament from Jesus Christ, who had actually healed many sick people Himself, and they continued to exercise this power of healing in the course of their ministry.

Testimonies of the Fathers

Expounding the various means by which our sins can be forgiven, ORIGEN (c. 185–c. 254) speaks of baptism, the suffering of martyrdom, almsgiving, forgiving others their sins, converting other sinners from the error of their ways, and philanthropy. Finally he cites a "seventh, albeit hard and laborious: the remission of sins through penance, when the sinner washes his pillow in tears, when tears are day and night his nourishment, and when he does not shrink from declaring his sin to a priest of the Lord and from seeking medicine, after the manner of him who says, 'I said, "To the Lord I will accuse myself of my iniquity," and You forgave the disloyalty of my heart' [Ps. 32:5]. In this way there is fulfilled that too, which the Apostle James says, 'If, then, there is anyone sick, let him call the presbyters of the Church, and let them impose hands upon him, anointing him with oil in the name of the Lord; and the prayer of faith will save the sick man, and if he be in sins, they shall be forgiven him'" *(Homilies on Leviticus,* 1970, p. 207).

Two points deserve particular attention in Origen's homily: (1) With reference to the verse from James, he substitutes "impose hands upon" for "pray over" a sick person, thereby referring to the procedure followed in administering this sacrament, and still in current usage. (2) He links the two sacraments of penance and the unction of the sick, thus indicating that the former is a requisite for the latter, and that before the reception of the sacrament of unction and the performance of its service, the sick person is required to make a confession of his sins.

Dwelling upon the spiritual and physical efficacy of the sacrament of unction of the sick, Saint JOHN CHRYSOSTOM draws a comparison between spiritual fathers and parents:

> God has bestowed a power on priests greater than that of our natural parents. The two indeed differ as much as the present and the future life. For our natural parents generate us unto this life only, but the others unto that which is to come.

And the former would not be able to avert death from their offspring, or to repel the assaults of disease; but these others have often saved a sick soul, or one which was on the point of perishing, procuring for some a milder chastisement, and preventing others from falling altogether, not only by instruction and admonition, but also by the assistance wrought through prayers. For not only at the time of regeneration, but afterwards also, they have authority to forgive sins. "Is any sick among you? Let him call in the priests of the church, and let them pray over him, anointing him with oil in the name of the Lord. . . ."

(*On the Priesthood* 3.6, 1956, p. 46)

Finally, Saint Cyril of Alexandria (d. 444) says:

But you, if some part of your body is suffering, and you really believe that saying the words "Lord Sabaoth!" or some such appellation which divine Scripture attributes to God in respect to His nature has the power to drive that evil from you, go ahead and pronounce those words, making them a prayer for yourself. You will be doing better than you would by just uttering those names, and you will be giving the glory to God and not to impure spirits. I recall also the saying in the divinely inspired Scripture: "Is anyone among you ill? Let him call in the presbyters of the Church and let them pray over him, anointing him with oil in the name of the Lord. . . ."

(1979, p. 217)

Elements of the Sacrament

Like all other sacraments, unction of the sick has three basic constituents: (1) the consecrated priest (or, a fortiori, the bishop); originally this sacrament, including seven prayers, was administered by seven priests, but there is no restriction to a minimum number who can take part; (2) the sick recipient of the sacrament, who makes a confession of his or her sins to the priest, and has full faith in the efficacy of the sacrament; and (3) oil, as the visible material element, preferably olive oil; from the scriptures we gather that certain therapeutic values were attached to oil, and that it was a common remedial agent among the Jews, besides its sacerdotal applications, and prophets, kings, and priests were anointed with oil (Ex. 29:7; I Sm. 9:16, 10:1, 16:1, 12, 13; I Kgs. 19:16; Mk. 6:13; Lk. 10:30–34).

With the exception of the paschal week, during which no incense may be used in services, the sacrament of the unction of the sick can be administered any day throughout the year. In addition, this service is also performed publicly in all churches on the Friday preceding the Saturday of Lazarus, the eve of Palm Sunday. On this occasion, the service is held immediately before the start of the Divine Liturgy.

Whereas repentance was instituted as a sacrament by which we obtain remission of sins, unction of the sick is a means of physical, as well as spiritual, healing. As such, it was practiced in all churches of Christendom until the twelfth century, when a change came about in the Western church, whereby the use of oil was restricted to the anointing of people on the brink of death, not as a means of their recovery but for the purpose of the remission of their sins. In addition, it was denied to those who had not reached the age of discretion.

BIBLIOGRAPHY

Ḥabīb Jirjis. *Asrār al-Kanīsah al-Sab'ah,* 2nd ed., pp. 155–63. Cairo, 1950.

Iqladiyūs Yūhannā Labīb. *Kitāb al-Mashah al-Muqaddasah, ay al-Qandīl.* Cairo, 1909.

Jerasimus Masarrah al-Lādhiqī. *Al-Anwār fī Al-Asrār,* pp. 256–71. Beirut, 1888.

Mīkhā'il Mīnā. *'Ilm al-Lāhūt,* Vol. 2, pp. 483–91. Cairo, 1936.

Origen. *Homilies on Leviticus* 2.4. In *The Faith of the Early Fathers,* Vol. 1, p. 207, ed. W. A. Jurgens. Collegeville, Minn., 1970.

ARCHBISHOP BASILIOS

UNDERWEAR. *See* Costume, Civil.

UNION PARTY. *See* Political Parties.

UQSURAYN, AL-. *See* Luxor.

URSUS OF SOLOTHURN, SAINT, fourth-century Egyptian who was a member of the THEBAN LEGION martyred in Switzerland under the emperors Maximian and DIOCLETIAN (feast day: 30 September). Foremost among sources specifically naming Ursus are the records left by Saint Eucherius, the fifth-century bishop of Lyons, *Passio Agaunensium martyrum* and an anonymous *Passio sancti Mauritii et sociorum ejus . . .* (Codex 256, in the Monastery of Einsiedeln). The early chronicle of Fredegar (c. 600) furnishes further confirmation of the events of the martyrdom at Solothurn. Relatively later descriptions are in Codex 569 in the Library of the Convent of Saint Gall and in the *Codex Signacensis,* originally from the Monastery of Signy, in Rheims. Though both codices are dated in the ninth century, it is quite clear that they are copies of much earlier sources. The martyrdom of Saint Ursus is also mentioned in the ninth-century *Martyrology of Ado,* by the archbishop of Vienne (c. 800–875), and in the *Vitae sanctorum* by the sixteenth-century Carthusian L. Surius.

Like the other members of the Theban Legion, Ursus and Saint VICTOR OF SOLOTHURN refused to obey the imperial command to sacrifice to the heathen gods and to take part in shedding the blood of innocent Christians. Therefore, Hirtacus, the Roman governor of Solothurn, had them brutally tortured. During this savage event, several miracles occurred, which filled the spectators with wonder. Enraged by this demonstration, Hirtacus ordered the beheading of the Thebans. Without the slightest resistance, they offered their necks to the executioners. According to the *Codex Signacensis,* the saints, who had been thrown into the river Aar after their decapitation, stepped out of the river, walked a short distance, and then knelt to pray. Their bodies were buried, and the Chapel of Saint Peter was later built on that spot.

Archaeological excavations have revealed that the present chapel was constructed over another dating from the fifth century. During the first half of the eighth century, Queen Bertrada, wife of Pepin the Short and mother of Charlemagne, founded a monastery there. The present Cathedral of Saint Ursus in Solothurn was built in the tenth century by Queen Bertha, daughter of Burchard of Swabia and wife of Rudolph of Burgundy, and it housed the relics of seventeen Theban martyrs whose bodies were found at the spot of the martyrdom. In 1473, during the restoration of the Chapel of Saint Peter, the remains of thirty-four more martyrs were discovered, and in the presence of two papal commissioners, their bones were deposited with those of their other Theban brethren in the Cathedral of Saint Ursus. In 1479, additional bodies were discovered, raising the number of the martyrs at that spot to over sixty. According to Sirius, the figure of sixty-six martyrs is mentioned at Solothurn, which seems to be confirmed by the discoveries of relics in modern times.

Though a number of scholars have cast some doubt on the Theban origin of Ursus, contrary to established traditions and the earliest sources, which had specifically linked him to his Theban brethren (Eucherius and the anonymous account), the ethnological construction of the name seems to indicate an Egyptian origin. The names Orsos or Orseus and Orsis are frequent in the Copto-Greek papyri; the first two are derivatives of the dynastic deity Horus, while the last means Horus, the son of Isis.

Ursus has always been highly venerated, especially in the canton and town of Solothurn. His image in armor, as well as his resurrected body standing upright with head in hand, were reproduced in the earliest coats of arms of the medieval Convent of Saint Ursus (St. Ursenstift, 1 December 1208), and of the town of Solothurn (28 July 1230). Among the churches consecrated in his name, in addition to Cathedral of Solothurn, the church of Subingen and the church of Kestenholz (originally Saint Peter's) are still in existence.

BIBLIOGRAPHY

Girgis, S. F. *The Coptic Contribution to the Early Evangelization of Switzerland.* Zurich, 1984.

______. *Die thebäische Legion im Lichte der koptischen Quellen sowie der koptisch-griechischen und altägyptischen Etymologie.* Zurich, 1984.

SAMIR F. GIRGIS

V

VALENTINIAN EXPOSITION. *A Valentinian Exposition* (Codex XV, tractate 2, of the NAG HAMMADI LIBRARY) presents itself as a document of revelation intended for a restricted elite: "I will speak my mystery to those who are mine and to those who will be mine." This revelation concerns first of all the Father, then the Son, the tetrad, the pleroma, Sophia, the demiurge, and the heavenly syzygies. By its presentation this treatise takes its place alongside other revelation documents from the *Nag Hammadi Library,* the hermetic writings of ALLOGENES and ZOSTRIANUS, with which, moreover, it has certain traits in common.

The first lines of the *Exposition* are devoted to the Father, who is described according to the canons of the negative theology current among the Gnostics as in the philosophical schools of Middle Platonism in the first centuries A.D. (Festugière, 1942–1953). The Father is called "the Ineffable One who dwells in the Monad. He dwells alone in silence, and silence is tranquillity since, after all, he was a Monad and no one was before him; he dwells in the Dyad and in the Pair and his Pair is Silence. And he possesses the all dwelling within him" (22.20–28).

This section on the Father should be compared with those, much more complete, in *Allogenes* (NHC XI, 3) and the THREE STELES OF SETH (NHC VII, 5). The Father is there described as the Ineffable (*All.* 47.18; 61.15), the first to exist (*Stel. Seth* 119.18), associated with silence and with rest (*All.* 61.21; 62.25). But the text most nearly akin to the *Valentinian Exposition* is that which Irenaeus devotes to the Valentinians (*Adversus omnes haereses* 1.1–8.4). The Father is described as being pre-existent, living in rest and solitude. His partner is called Grace and Silence.

After the figure of the Father, *A Valentinian Exposition* turns to that of the Son. He is called "the Mind of the All, coming from the Root of All, a spring which exists in Silence and speaks only with himself" (22.31–23.23). Above all, "he is the projector of the All and the very hypostasis of the Father" (24.22–23).

In what follows, *A Valentinian Exposition* enumerates a number of hypostases, among whom Horos plays a role of the first order, being "the Mind of the Son" and having the function of separating Bythos from the aeons (27.35–37).

Christ is described as "not manifest but invisible while he remains within limit," and he "possesses four powers, a separator, a confirmer, a form-provider and a substance-provider" (26.29–34). Then follows the description of a tetrad formed by Word, Life, Man, and Church. Let us recall here the composition of the second tetrad in the account of Irenaeus of the Valentinians: Word, Life, Man, and Church (1.8.6 and 1.1.1). This created tetrad resembles and reproduces, the author of the *Exposition* tells us, the superior uncreated tetrad. All these elements make up the pleroma (31.25–29), which is formed by 360 hypostases, equivalent to the 360 days of the year of the Lord (30.30–39, cf. *Eugnostos* III 3.83.15–20, where the powers of the heavens are 360 in number). We are here faced with speculations based on the lunar year (for the 360 hypostases, cf. Agapius, *Kitab al-Unvan, histoire du Maudit Ibn-Daican (Bardesanes),* fol. 29 in Patrologia Orientalis 7, ed. A. Scher, 1909, p. 520; and *Chronique de Michel le Syrien,* Patrologia Orientalis 1, 1899, ed. B. Chabot, para. 110, p. 184).

Beginning with page 33 of the *Exposition,* in a text full of lacunae, we meet with the story of Sophia, marked once more by Valentinian features. Through brief allusions the author of the *Exposition* evokes the sufferings of Sophia (33.36–38), her repentance, her invocation of the Father, her pangs of conscience (cf. Irenaeus 1.2.3): "Granted that I have left my consort. Therefore I am beyond confirmation as well. I deserve the passions I suffer." Sophia recalls the existence she led in heaven: "I used to dwell in the pleroma putting forth the Aeons and bearing fruit with my consort." She knows what she was and what she has become (34.31–32; cf. *Excerpta ex Theodoto* 78). The children of Sophia are abortions, "incomplete and formless" (35.12–14; cf. Irenaeus 1.2.3). The author specifies that these things take place without the will of the Father, for "this is the will of the Father: not to allow anything to happen in the pleroma apart from a syzygy. Again the will of the Father is: always produce and bear fruit. That she should suffer, then, was not the will of the Father, for she dwells in herself alone without her consort" (36.29–38). The story of Sophia ends in classic fashion (cf. *Exegesis on the Soul* 133.12–16), and the author underlines the joy of her reunion with her bridegroom, as well as the unity and reconciliation of the pleroma (39.30–35).

Finally, pages 40–44 of the *Exposition* are devoted to the sacraments of unction, baptism, and the Eucharist. They constitute teaching for the Gnostic community to which the author addresses himself and are put in the mouth of Christ and presented as "the full content of the summary of knowledge which was revealed to us by our Lord Jesus Christ."

Two themes of Jewish origin deserve to be briefly singled out from the *Exposition*. At page 38.27–28 we read: "and there took place the struggle with the apostasy of the angels and mankind, those of the right with those of the left, and those in heaven with those on the earth, the spirits with the carnal and the devil against God. Therefore the angels lusted after the daughters of men and came down to flesh so that god would cause a flood." The series of oppositions in which the first member is positive, the second negative, finds a parallel in the TRIPARTITE TRACTATE 38.14–22 and in the GOSPEL OF PHILIP, paragraph 40. The fundamental text for these speculations on the contraries is the teaching on the two spirits in the scroll of the *Qumrān Rule* (I *QS* III, 19–26). More precisely the contrast of "right" and "left" (i.e., the way of good and the way of evil), for which the classic text, of clearly Jewish inspiration, remains the *Shepherd* of Hermas 9.9, is also found in the Gnostic texts (*Excerpta ex Theodoto* 34.1; 43.1; 47.2 where earthly equals left and heavenly equals right; Irenaeus, *Adversus omnes haereses* 1.5.1.2: *Gospel of Truth* 31.35–32.20; Tripartite Tractate 104.10; 105.7; 106.21, 108.14, 21–23 . . .; *Pistis Sophia* 128, 354, 361, 362, etc.). The author of the *Valentinian Exposition* recalls briefly the fall of the angels and their sin consummated with the daughters of men. This myth, which had a considerable vogue in Jewish and later Christian literature (Martin, 1906), was the object of attentive exegesis among the Gnostics (cf. *Apocryphon of John* II 29.17–30.11; *On the Origin of the World* 123.9–15; Tripartite Tractate 135.1–15; Gospel of the Egyptians 61.20–22; *Testimony of Truth* 41.1–5; Scopello, 1980).

The other passage of the *Exposition* that calls for comment concerns the "Day of Atonement." The high priest's entry into the holy of holies is placed on the level of the pleroma, and recalls the mystical exegesis of Philo of the day on Yom Kippur (Goodenough, 1935; cf. *De gigantibus* 52–55; *De vita Mosis* II, 99; *Specialibus legibus* 71–72; *Quaestiones in Exodum* 93ff.; cf. also the tractate *Yoma*, according to Mishna and Talmud; for Nag Hammadi, see the GOSPEL OF PHILIP, paras. 76, 125; see also *Excerpta ex Theodoto* 27.1; 38.2).

BIBLIOGRAPHY

Festugière, A. J. *La Révelation d'Hermès Trismégiste*, Vols. 1–4, especially Vol. 2. Paris, 1942–1953.

Ginzberg, L. *The Legends of the Jews*, Vol. 7, p. 35. Philadelphia, 1946. On the fallen angels.

Goodenough, E. R. *By Light, Light; The Mystic Gospel of Hellenistic Judaism*, pp. 95–120. New Haven, 1935.

Martin, F. *Le Livre d'Hénoch*, pp. 122–39. Paris, 1906.

Scopello, M. "Le Mythe de la chute des anges dans l'Apocryphon de Jean de Nag Hammadi." *Revue des sciences religieuses* 54 (1980):220–30.

MADELEINE SCOPELLO

VALENTINUS, founder of a Gnostic sect that bears his name. He was born at Phrebonis in the Nile Delta (c. A.D. 100) and educated in Alexandria. He was well trained in rhetoric and philosophy, perhaps including familiarity with some of the allegorical writings of Philo Judaeus (c. 20 B.C.–c. A.D. 50). After teaching for some years in Alexandria, he migrated to Rome about 140 and, because of his intellectual prowess, had some hope of being elected bishop there (Tertullian *Adversus Valentinianos* 4). Disappointed in his attempt to gain the episcopate, Valentinus is said to have broken with the true faith, although Epiphanius states that his apostasy occurred years later, when he had moved to Cyprus (Epiphanius *Panarion* 31). Either assertion presents difficulties for describing how the so-called Gnostic heresy associated with Valentinus came to be centered in Egypt if he never returned to Africa after founding his heretical sect. One must admit, therefore, that uncertainty prevails concerning both his ecclesiastical career and the time and place of the founding of Valentinian gnosticism. The date of Valentinus' death is unknown but is placed between 165 and 185.

As uncertain as are the historical dates and events in Valentinus' life, so also are the writings and doctrines that are associated with him. The popularity of the Valentinian sect was not disputed in antiquity (Tertullian, *Adversus Valentinianos* 1, describes them as *frequentissimum collegium inter haereticos*, "a very large group among the heretics"), and most of what is known about the Valentinians has been transmitted through disciples rather than the founder himself, somewhat as with Pythagoras and the Pythagoreans. The acknowledged secrecy of the doctrines of the sect, the disavowal of the name Valentinian by its adherents, and the charge by Tertullian that succeeding generations became more spiritually and doctrinally promiscuous combine to make difficult, if not impossible, the task of ascribing particular doctrines or writings to Valentinus. Recent discoveries of manuscripts, especially *The Gospel of Truth* in the NAG HAMMADI LIBRARY, and the efforts of many scholars have clarified the matter somewhat, but much remains unknown.

The essential characteristics of Valentinian gnosticism include an involved cosmological speculation consisting of a heavenly realm, the Pleroma, comprised of thirty or more worlds or aeons. Irenaeus claims that Pythagoras was the originator of the number systems that describe the emanations within the aeons (*Adversus omnes haereses* 2.14), and the emanations are described as tripartite, being divided into an Ogdoad, a Decad, and a Duadecad (*Adversus omnes haereses* 1.1–2). One emanation within the Pleroma, Sophia, brought about the Fall and, eventually, the creation of the world. Redemption became possible through one aeon, Christ, who became united with the mortal Jesus to bring knowledge (*gnosis*) to mankind. Only the "pneumatic" Valentinians can receive the *gnosis* and be fully saved, while the "psychic" other Christians receive partial salvation, and the "hylic" remainder of the human family will be eternally damned. One of the requirements for full salvation as a "pneumatic" was marriage (Tertullian *Adversus Valentinianos* 30; Irenaeus *Adversus omnes haereses* 1.46.4), which Clement (*Stromateis* 3.29) notes is after the pattern of sacred marriages among the gods.

Although many followers of Valentinus can be named in the second and third centuries, two main branches of Valentinianism appear to have emerged: the Eastern segment, identified at first with Theodotus and Mark, and the Western segment, founded by Ptolemy and Heracleon. These sects cannot be traced with certainty, but Valentinians can be found in all parts of the Roman empire, including Gaul, Asia (Turkey), Syria, Mesopotamia, Carthage, and, of course, Egypt. Commentaries on scripture and speculative works were produced by adherents of this Gnostic movement, a characteristic feature of such writings being the use of allegorical interpretation.

BIBLIOGRAPHY

Bardy, G. "Valentin." In *Dictionnaire de théologie catholique*, Vol. 15, pt. 2. Paris, 1950.

Förster, W. *Gnosis*, Vol. 1. Oxford, 1972.

Layton, B. *The Gnostic Scriptures*. New York, 1987.

______, ed. *The Rediscovery of Gnosticism: Proceedings of the International Conference on Gnosticism at Yale, New Haven, Connecticut, March 28–31, 1978*, Vol. 1, *The School of Valentinus*. Studies in the History of Religions no. 41, vol. 1. Leiden, 1980.

Robinson, J. M., ed. *The Nag Hammadi Library*. New York, 1977. See esp. *Gospel of Truth* and *Gospel of Philip*.

C. WILFRED GRIGGS

VALERIAN (Publius Licinius Valerianus), Roman emperor (253–260). He was named emperor by the legions on the death of Trebonianus Gallus and was associated with his son Gallienus as co-emperor. During his reign there were almost continuous conflicts to defend the frontier of the empire, first against the attacks of the Franks and the Alemanni on the Rhine frontier, and then, with increasing severity, against the attacks by Shapur I on the Roman Euphrates frontier with Persia. At the same time Germanic tribes, such as the Goths and the Borani, dwelling in what is now southern Russia, invaded parts of Asia Minor by sea, bringing anarchy and misery in their wake. Valerian was lured into a personal conference with the Persian king outside Edessa, which he recaptured in 256–258. He ended his days as a captive.

Valerian's relations with the Christians, especially as they affected Egypt, are described by Bishop DIONYSIUS of Alexandria in a letter to Hermammon, a bishop whose see is not known (Eusebius *Historia ecclesiastica* 7.10). Apparently Valerian, in contrast to his predecessors, DECIUS and Gallus, began his reign well-disposed toward the Christians (7.10.3). By 257, however, he had changed. Dionysius attributes this to the machinations of Macrianus, the former imperial financial officer (*rationalis*) in Egypt, who was now "master and ruler of the synagogue of the Egyptian magicians," and perceived the Christians as rivals possessing a more powerful magic than he could command (Eusebius, 7.10.4), and no doubt casting an envious eye on the wealth of the church.

Probably in August 257 a joint edict was issued in the name of Valerian and Gallienus. Letters were sent to provincial governors ordering that "those who do not venerate the Roman religion should acknowledge the Roman ceremonies." The emphasis was on "Roman" religion and a demonstration of respect toward it. On 30 August 257 Cyprian of Carthage was summoned to the *secretarium* of the proconsul of Carthage, informed of the terms of the edict, and, on his refusal to observe them and his further refusal to name his presbyters, put under house arrest at Curubis on the Gulf of Hammamat. The interview of Dionysius with Aemilianus, the vice-prefect, recorded in the letter of Dionysius to Bishop Germanus (Eusebius, 7.ii) was more courteous but came to the same conclusion. Christians were forbidden to hold assemblies and to enter (Christian) cemeteries. Dionysius was exiled to Cephro (the oasis of Kufrah), and sent on his way the same day.

At Cephro, Dionysius was able to make some conversions among the inhabitants. He was moved, perhaps in January 258 (see *Papyrus Oxyrhynchus* 3112), to the village of Collution in Mareotis, nearer Alexandria, which was less friendly to Christians.

In August 258, Valerian and Gallienus promulgated a further edict that provided the death penalty for clergy and loss of dignities for influential laymen (Cyprian, *Letters* 80 and 81). Cyprian was executed at Carthage on 13 September 258 (*Acta proconsularia* 4), and both Catholics and Marcionites were executed in Palestine. In Egypt, Dionysius may have been in the process of being led to a trial for his life when he was rescued by individuals he does not say were Christians, and spent the remainder of the persecution "in a lonely parched spot in Libya" (Eusebius, 11.23). Valerian's persecution continued to claim victims through 259. Dionysius comments that Aemilianus continued to have Christians put to death even during the plague that struck the country (Eusebius, 11.24). A papyrus (*Papyrus Oxyrhynchus* 3119) dated to 259 indicates the possibility of an official scrutiny (*exstasis*) of Christians in the Saitic nome, in the seventh year of Valerian, that is, the systematic continuation of the persecution throughout Egypt. In the West, the persecution was probably the longest and the worst ever suffered, exceeding, at least in the deaths of senior clergy, the Great Persecution.

Valerian's reign, then, involved a major test of strength between the empire and its protecting gods, and the Christians. The church's resilience and ability to weather the storm, not least in Egypt, boded ill for any future major attack on it by the imperial authorities.

BIBLIOGRAPHY

Andresen, C. "Siegreiche Kirche. 387–458." In *Aufstieg des Christentums. Untersuchungen zu Eusebius von Caesarea und Dionysios von Alexandrien. Aufstieg und Niedergang der römischen Welt,* ed. Temporini und W. Haase. Berlin and New York, 1979.

Healey, J. *The Valerian Persecution: A Study of the Relations Between Church and State in the Third Century.* London, 1905.

Sordi, M. *Il cristianesimo e Roma.* Bologna, 1965.

———. "Dionisio di Alessandria e le vicende della persecuzione di Valeriano in Egitto." In *Paradoxos politeia, Studi patristici in onore di Giuseppe Lazzati.* Milan, 1979.

W. H. C. FREND

VAN LANTSCHOOT, ARNOLD (1889–1969),

Belgian Orientalist, principally in Syriac, Coptic, and Ethiopian. He was scriptor orientalis and then vice prefect of the Vatican Library (1936–1965).

BIBLIOGRAPHY

"In memoriam Rmi A. A. van Lantschoot." *Analecta Praemonstratensia* 45 (1969):109–116; also in *Le Muséon* 82 (1969):249–58.

Garitte, G. "Bibliographie d'A. van Lantschoot." *Le Muséon* 82 (1969):259–64.

Malak, P. H. "Arnold van Lantschoot, 1889–1969." *Bulletin de la Société d'archéologie copte* 20 (1969–1970):305–308.

RENÉ-GEORGES COQUIN

VANSLEB (WANSLEBEN), JOHANN MICHAEL (d. 1679), German Orientalist. After intensive studies in Oriental languages, especially Ethiopic and Arabic, he went to Egypt for the first time in 1664–1665 with the intention of going on to Ethiopia, but the patriarch MATTHEW IV dissuaded him. He then went to Rome, converted to Catholicism, and joined the Dominican order.

Later in Paris, Colbert commissioned him to go to the Orient to buy manuscripts for the Royal Library. In Egypt for the second time, he resided there from June 1672 to October 1673. He then moved to Istanbul, where he wrote his *Histoire de l'église d'Alexandrie* (Paris, 1677). He returned to France in 1676 and died in disgrace three years later. He was accused by Colbert of lingering too long in Istanbul and not attempting to reach Ethiopia.

His great skill at discovering manuscripts of great value puts him in the forefront of those who introduced Christian Egypt to the West, while these manuscripts became useful for his own work. *Miṣbah al-Zulmah,* by Abū al-Barakāt; *History of the Patriarchs of the Egyptian Church;* and *The Churches and Monasteries of Egypt and Some Neighbouring Countries* were among 355 codices acquired in Egypt that consisted of *scalae* (comprehensive lexicons of all available Coptic terms and their Arabic equivalents), canonical records, and liturgical books. These manuscripts helped Eusèbe Renaudot to write his *Historia Patriarcharum Alexandrinorum Jacobitarum* (Paris, 1713) and *Liturgiarum Orientalium Collectio* (Paris, 1716), which remain classic references on the subject to this day.

Two of Vansleb's publications are of special interest to Coptologists. The *Histoire de l'église d'Alexandrie* is a brief description of the hierarchical structure of the Alexandrian Coptic church, its customs, liturgy, theology, and canon law. To it, two lists were attached, one about the patriarchs of the church and the other about the "illustrious men of the Coptic nation," meaning its writers in the Arabic language and their works. This presentation taken from manuscripts listed by Vansleb shows objectivity, scientific approach, and a lack of polemical commentary. The same qualities are found in his *Nouvelle Relation en forme de journal d'un voyage fait en Egypte en 1672 et 1673* (Paris, 1677).

Vansleb's interest in the affairs of the church resulted in works that provide firsthand information on the condition of the Monastery of Saint Antony, on the pilgrimage of Sitt Dimyānah, of the precarious situation of the patriarch and the bishop of Fayyūm, the number of churches in the province of Manfalūṭ, and so on. Particularly moving is the account of the pastoral visit of the bishop of Asyūṭ to the White Monastery (DAYR ANBĀ SHINŪDAH) on the west bank of the Nile. Vansleb accompanied him and thus came to travel farther south in Egypt than any European up to that time.

BIBLIOGRAPHY

Carré, J.-M. *Voyageurs et écrivains français en Egypte,* Vol. 1, pp. 29–36. Cairo, 1956.

Kammerer, W., comp. *A Coptic Bibliography.* Ann Arbor, Mich., 1950; repr. New York, 1969.

Martin, M. "Note sur la communauté copte entre 1650 et 1850." *Annales islamologiques* 18 (1982):193–215.

Omont, H. *Missions archéologiques françaises en Orient aux XVIIe et XVIIIe siècles,* pp. 54–174, 883–951. Paris, 1902.

Pougeois, A. *Vie et voyages de Vansleb, savant orientaliste et voyageur.* Paris, 1869.

Ouetif, J., and J. Ichard. *Scriptores Ordinis Praedicatorum,* pp. 70 et seq. Paris, 1721

MAURICE MARTIN, S.J.

VATICAN MUSEUM, COPTIC TEXTILE COLLECTION. *See* Museums, Coptic Collections in.

VAULT. *See* Architectural Elements of Churches.

VEILS. *See* Eucharistic Veils.

VERENA, SAINT, fourth-century Egyptian holy woman associated with the THEBAN LEGION martyred in Switzerland (feast days: 1 September and Easter Tuesday). Verena's unwavering faith, long life of Christian charity, and many miracles contributed greatly to the spread of Christianity among the Alemanni in what is now Canton Argau, Switzerland. Her status in the German part of Switzerland and in southwest Germany can be compared with that of Saint Ursula in the Rhineland, Saint Odilia in Alsace, and Saint Bridget in Sweden.

In addition to numerous accounts of her life in various martyrologies dating before 1000, there are two early records of Saint Verena, the *Vita prior* and the *Vita posterior.* The oldest known manuscript of the *Vita prior* is dated 888, and was written by Abbot Hatto of Reichenau, later archbishop of Mainz and counselor of the German king Arnulf. It served as the basis for the later and larger *Vita posterior,* which was prepared by a writer who was well acquainted with the region of Zurzach about a century after the *Vita prior.*

The only daughter of a distinguished Theban family in Upper Egypt, Verena was entrusted in her early years to a bishop named Chaeremon, who was to provide her with the necessary religious instruction for baptism. After Chaeremon perished during the persecution under the emperor DECIUS, Verena journeyed with some Christians toward Lower Egypt, where a large number of believers had been assembled for military service under the emperors DIOCLETIAN and Maximian. Among them were members of the Theban Legion commanded by Saint MAURITIUS, some of whom were her close relatives.

In keeping with an old Coptic custom whereby women followed their legionnaire menfolk to give them spiritual support and relief, Verena went with the Theban Legion into Italy as far as Milan. (It is noteworthy in this connection to mention that remains of female persons were discovered amid the graves of martyred Theban legionnaires.) In Milan she stayed at the home of a holy man named Maximus for some years, frequenting prisons and martyrdom sites to comfort the beleaguered saints. Upon hearing of the martyrdom of Saint VICTOR OF SOLOTHURN and his Theban brethren, Verena crossed the Alps to Agaunum (present-day Saint Maurice en Valais) and went on to a place beyond the Aar River not far from Castrum Salodurum (Solothurn). She stayed at the home of a Theban fugitive, spending all her time fasting and praying, ever striving for eternal salvation. To this end, she retired to a narrow cave, where she led the ascetic and austere life of a nun, torturing her body to save her soul. She lived by means of her handwork, which an old Christian woman in the neighborhood sold for her to the heathen Alemanni.

A highly venerated virgin, Verena came to be regarded as "the mother of maidens," to whom she devoted much of her time, trying to guide them into the paths of Christian virtue and piety, as well as to teach them proper hygienic practices. She also performed many miracles of healing and restoration of vision, thereby converting many to Christianity. At one time she was arrested by the Roman authorities for a few days, during which she had a vision of Saint Mauritius, who came to comfort her. She was, however, released by the Roman governor, whom she had miraculously healed. When her fame spread on account of her miracles, she decided to flee from that region and sought seclusion on a small island at the confluence of the Aar and the Rhine. She freed the island from its countless serpents and nursed the sick and healed the blind and the lame.

Later Verena went to Tenedo (present-day Zurzach), where she found a church dedicated to Our Lady and decided to spend the rest of her life. She lived at the local priest's house, but his complete trust in her aroused the jealousy of the other villagers. Even though she spent her time caring for the poor and nursing the lepers, the villagers repeatedly tried to discredit her with the priest. As a result, she begged him to build her a segregated cell where she could spend the rest of her days in seclusion. Verena retired there for a solitary life of severe austerity, which lasted eleven years. During that time she continued to heal the sick and assisted all who sought her help. On the day of her death, she was spiritually strengthened by a vision of the Virgin. Afterward her remains were enshrined in the crypt built on the spot of her death, which became one of the most frequented pilgrimage centers in that region. Round her tomb, the first cloister of Canton Aargau was founded.

The high place that Saint Verena occupied in Switzerland is attested by the number of religious foundations and churches consecrated in her name. Though it is hard to make a precise inventory of these foundations, it is known that there were at least eighty-two scattered in the various cantons. In Germany, fourteen chapels were consecrated in her name. Her relics were honored as far away as Helmgersberg in East Prussia and in Vienna.

In modern times, the imperial house of the Hapsburgs adopted Verena as one of the main patrons of the dynasty. Her image appears in Swiss religious statuary, where she is represented with a double comb in her left hand and a water jug in the right, signifying her care for girls and her use of healing water for the sick and the lepers. The same representation appears on the arms of the city of Stäfa in Canton Zurich. Among the very popular pilgrimage centers of the saint are Saint Verena's cavern (Verenaschlucht) between Oberdorf and Fallern near Solothurn and her chapel in Coblenz.

Contemporary Coptic sources contribute considerably to verifying the historicity of Verena's story and confirm specific details related to Egypt. At the beginning of the fourth century, Eusebius of Caesarea confirmed, in his work on the history of the Coptic church, the existence of Bishop Chaeremon of Nilos at the place and time given in European sources. He even quoted the account of his death

Coat of arms of the city of Stäfa, Canton Zurich, showing Saint Verena. *Courtesy The Chancellery of the State of Canton Zurich.*

during the Decian persecutions given by the contemporary patriarch of Alexandria, Saint DIONYSIUS THE GREAT, in his letter to Bishop Fabius of Antioch. Moreover, the name Chaeremon is of ancient Egyptian origin and means "Son of Amon." The name Verena could be identified as the popular Coptic short form of the Ptolemaic Berenice. The Copts omitted the Greek suffixes *ioc* and *ic* and replaced them with *e* or *a* (according to Heuser); and the letter *b* in Coptic reads *v* when followed by a vowel. The name Verena could also be of ancient Egyptian origin, a compound of the Coptic and ancient Egyptian words *vre* ("seed") and *ne* ("town or *the* town," Thebes), that is, Seed of Thebes.

BIBLIOGRAPHY

Heusser, G. *Die Personennamen der Kopten.* Studien zur Epigraphik und Papyrus Kunde, Vol. 1. Leipzig, 1929.

Reinle, A. *Die heilige Verena von Zurzach.* Basel, 1948.

SAMIR F. GIRGIS

VESPERS, the prayers of the eleventh Canonical Hour, corresponding to five o'clock in the afternoon and, accordingly, called in Arabic *ṣalāt al-ghurūb,* the sunset prayer. It was instituted to commemorate the removal of the body of Christ from the cross, its enshrouding in linen and its anointment with spices (Mt. 27:57; Mk. 15:42–45; Lk. 23:50–52; Jn. 19:38). It is also a reminder of the evanescence of human life and of the importance of being ready at all times for the hour of death.

ARCHBISHOP BASILIOS

VESTRY. *See* Architectural Elements of Churches: Sacristy.

VICTOR, abbot of the Enaton, listed in the SYNAXARION as the author of two "histories of monks" at 7 Ṭūbah (recension from Upper Egypt) and 14 Ṭūbah (recension from Lower Egypt). He is probably the author of the narratives of monastic history celebrated in the Middle Ages, from which the author(s) of the two recensions of the Synaxarion drew. This was necessary when he (they) did not have suitable documents to compose a notice for a particular day, as had been done in other synaxaria, or to compose extracts from various narratives and sermons.

It is known only that Victor was "abbot" of the LAURA, the group of several monasteries having a church and several buildings in common, something rare in Egypt. His was the ENATON, which was situated, as its name indicates, nine miles west of Alexandria.

Victor's dates can be stated precisely, for in a story that he reports as an eyewitness, he speaks of Marwān II, the last Umayyad caliph. But the Synaxarion speaks of Marwān ibn ʿAbd al-ʿAzīz, which in all probability is a metathesis by the author for ʿAbd al-ʿAzīz ibn Marwān, who became governor of Egypt (684–685) and was a son of the Marwān who ruled as caliph in Damascus, for the text speaks later of the patriarch John, probably JOHN III (677–686).

It was perhaps the same person who wrote the story preserved in the recension from Upper Egypt at 30 Hātūr, although he speaks only of SCETIS and not of the Enaton, though the story is under the name of "Victor."

Finally, a Victor "the secretary" (he may be the same person) transmitted a collection of four stories of saints of the same genre (National Library, Paris, archives 305, fols. 344v–354v) in a sole manuscript dated to 1609.

BIBLIOGRAPHY

Troupeau, G. *Catalogue des manuscrits arabes.* Vol. 1, *Manuscrits chrétiens.* Paris, 1972.

RENÉ-GEORGES COQUIN

VICTOR OF PBOW. *See* Victor of Tabennēsē.

VICTOR OF SHŪ, early-fourth-century saint. Victor was born in Asyūṭ. He served as a soldier in the fortress of Shū (Qaṣr Shū) south of Asyūṭ, at the age of twelve. In accordance with the rescript of Diocletian, he was asked to offer sacrifice to the idols, but refused. His superior tried to persuade him kindly, but since he remained adamant, Victor was cast into the jail of the fortress, where his parents visited him and encouraged him to remain dauntless. His superior, unable to persuade him to follow instructions, sent him to the governor in Asyūṭ. The governor attempted to gain the cooperation of Victor by making lavish promises, which Victor refused, bringing upon himself severe tortures.

Finally, after he prayed and an angel comforted him, he was thrown into the furnace of the baths at Mūshah, south of Asyūṭ. Christians came to take away his body, which they found intact. At Mūshah they built over the body a church, which was still in existence in the thirteenth century as the Synaxarion states. Many miracles were worked there.

A more detailed account of the martyrdom of Saint Victor of Shū, for 5 Kiyahk, is found in a manuscript copied in Cairo around 1370 by Jirjis Abū al-Barakāt ibn Rizqallāh, great-grandson of the Coptic encyclopedist Abū al-Barakāt IBN KABAR (d. 1324). Since this text is unique and as yet unpublished, the incipit, after the conventional preface, may be translated as: "It came to pass that, under the reign of the impious king Diocletian and Maximian, . . . orders were sent to all the places subject to their rule, to close the churches."

The same copyist transmitted another manuscript copied in 1360–1363, with an anonymous homily on the invention of the body of Saint Victor of Shū, on the building and dedication of his church in Mūshah, and on the miracles that occurred there on 5 Ba'ūnah. This dedication is not mentioned in the Synaxarion. The incipit may be translated as: "It came to pass that, after the martyrdom of the holy and glorious martyr Mār Buqṭur and the building of his church at Mūshah to the South of Asyūṭ, people came in great numbers and from all parts on account of the powers and miracles. . . ."

BIBLIOGRAPHY

Amélineau, E. *La Géographie de L'Egypte*. Paris, 1893.

Graf, G. *Catalogue de manuscripts arabes chrétiens conservés au Caire,* Vatican City, 1934.

Simaykah, M., and Y. ʿAbd al-Masīḥ. *Catalogue of the Coptic and Arabic Manuscripts in the Coptic Museum,* Vol. 1. Cairo, 1939.

KHALIL SAMIR, S.J.

VICTOR OF SOLOTHURN AND GENEVA, SAINT, member of the THEBAN LEGION, a large number of whom were martyred in Switzerland. Victor was killed at Solothurn during the reign of Emperor DIOCLETIAN (284–305), on the spot where the Chapel of Saint Peter later arose. His name appears in the *Passio Agaumensium martyrum* of Saint Eucherius, bishop of Lyons (434–450) as well as in the anonymous account entitled *Passio sancti Mauritii et sociorum ejus,* of the monastery of Einsiedeln. According to Fredegar's *Chronicle* (602), Saint Victor's relics were transferred from the Chapel of Saint Peter to a basilica built in his honor outside Geneva, whereupon he became the patron saint of that city. Citation of his martyrdom was frequent in medieval times. In the ninth century, both Codex 569 of the Library of the Convent of Saint Gall (fols. 224–31) and the *Codex Signacensis,* originally from the monastery of Signy at Rheims (published by the Bollandists in *Acta sanctorum,* 30 September), refer to Saint Victor's story. Moreover, the *Martyrologium Romanum* of Ado, archbishop of Vienne (800–875), published at Paris in 1645, and the *Vitae sanctorum* of the Carthusian L. Surius (1522–1578) cite the Victor story under September 30.

The legend of the martyrdom of Victor and Ursus states that, on their refusal to obey the imperial command of Emperor Maximian (286–305) to sacrifice to the heathen gods and slaughter innocent Christian natives, the Roman governor of Solothurn, Hirtacus, subjected them to barbarous tortures, during which miracles occurred. The saints' shackles broke, and as they were made to walk on blazing embers, the fire was instantaneously extinguished. In the end Hirtacus ordered them beheaded. Both approached their executioner without resistance, and their headless bodies emitted dazzling light before they were thrown into the river Aar. Afterward, according to Surius and to the *Codex Signacensis,* the saints stepped out of the water with their heads in their hands, walked a distance from the bank, then knelt and prayed at the spot of their burial, where the Chapel of Saint Peter arose over their tomb. A monastery was founded there by order of Queen Bertrada, wife of Pepin the Short and mother of Charlemagne, in the first half of the eighth century.

In 602 the identification of Saint Victor's remains at his new resting place near Geneva was made by Bishop Hiconius in the presence of King Theodoric II (587–613). At the beginning of the eleventh century, the saint's relics were placed under the altar. However, in the Calvinistic upheavals of the sixteenth century, the church was demolished (1534). In 1721, a leaden coffin containing bones was discovered; it was inscribed with the Roman numerals 8–30, which were interpreted as 30 September, commemoration day of Saint Victor.

There is hardly any doubt about the ethnic origin of Saint Victor of Solothurn. He not only is mentioned among the Thebans in the earliest sources (Saint Eucherius and the anonymous account of Einsiedeln), but his name has always been familiar among the Copts and still is today. It is written Buktor but reads Victor because the letter *b* is pronounced *v* when followed by a vowel.

BIBLIOGRAPHY

Abel, D. *Die Kronik Fredegars und der Frankenkönige und deren Fortsetzung bis zum Jahre 736.* Berlin, 1849. Fredegar's *Chronicle* also ed. B. Krusch, in *Monumenta Germaniae Historica, Scriptores rerum Merovingicarum,* Vol. 2. Hannover, 1888. Latin text in PL 71. Paris, 1879.

Baulaere, L. *Oeuvres historiques et littéraires de L. Baulaere 1728–1756,* ed. Edouard Mallet. Paris, 1857.

Blavignac, J. D. *Histoire de l'architecture sacrée du quatrième au sixième siecle dans les anciens évêchés de Genève, Lausanne et Sion.* Paris, 1853.

Blondel, L. *Origine et développement des lieux habités de Genève et environs.* Paris, 1853.

Crum, W. E. *Varia coptica.* Aberdeen, 1939.

Preisigke, F. *Sammelbuch griechischer Urkunden aus Aegypten,* 2 vols. Strasbourg, 1913.

______. *Namenbuch.* Heidelberg, 1922.

SAMIR F. GIRGIS

VICTOR STRATELATES, SAINT, or Victor the General.

[*This son of the Roman governor Romanus miraculously survived death three times before being martyred during the persecution under Diocletian (feast day: 27 Baramūdah). This entry consists of two articles:* Coptic Tradition, *and* Copto-Arabic Tradition.]

Coptic Tradition

About Victor Stratelates we have four complete accounts and several that are incomplete.

1. The martyrdom itself was published by E. Wallis Budge in 1914 from the manuscript in the British Museum (Or. 7022) dated A.D. 951.

2. The panegyric attributed to CELESTINUS OF ROME is attached to the *Acts* in the same manuscript and in the same edition.

3. Another panegyric attributed to THEODOSIUS OF JERUSALEM was published by U. Bouriant in 1893, from a Paris codex dated 941 (Bibliotheca Hagiographica Orientalis 1243, pp. 247–82) in the original Coptic pagination.

4. The Pierpont Morgan codex (in Volume 41 of the photographic edition) offers a panegyric on Victor by Theopemptus of Antioch, which has been neither edited nor published. In addition, four leaves from Vienna were edited by W. Till in 1934; these are connected rather with the panegyric of Celestinus, but might also belong to another type of martyrdom. Bouriant's codex contains, moreover, a very long panegyric, which must be attributed to JOHN CHRYSOSTOM (Bibliotheca Hagiographica Orientalis 1242) according to a passage in the text, for the title is lost. In view of the lacunae in the original codex (1–34, 37–96, 125–128, and 245–246), it is not possible to verify even one item in the Paris codex. O. von Lemm published leaves 125–26, which were at Saint Petersburg. F. Rossi also published some columns in 1893, according to the Turin fragments. From reading the Ethiopic derivatives, one infers that other Coptic items have undoubtedly disappeared.

The hagiographic record of Victor, son of Romanus, is typically Coptic. What has ended up in the Greco-Latin tradition on 11 November is minimal, considering the importance of the Coptic records. The following is an outline of the martyrdom, in which the fundamental concepts of Christianity are personified and represented as in a geometrical drawing. DIOCLETIAN, with his tetrarchy consisting of BASILIDES, Romanus, and Euaios, institutes the cult of seventy divinities, among whom Apollo and Artemis are prominent. Victor, twenty years old, is the son of Romanus, and has been promised by his parents to the daughter of Basilides. Romanus himself has proceeded from Antioch to Alexandria. Victor, although tempted by Satan disguised as a soldier, privately renounces all the advantages of his rank to his father. His father, therefore, finally hands him over to Armenius, duke of Rakote. The four soldiers who take him away submit him to harsh questioning on 1 Baramūdah. The interview with Victor's mother (whose name, Martha, is not quoted) is longer and more moving.

Victor reaches Armenius, whose appointment in rank close to his father he had formerly approved. But this wicked man returns evil for good. He submits Victor to torture on the wheel, which he endures with the help of the archangel MICHAEL, Victor's soul having already been carried off up to heaven during the torture. Subsequently, Victor is burned with lamps and thrown in vain into the furnace. Finally, Armenius sends him back to Eutychianus, duke of the Thebaid. On 20 Baramūdah, he reaches ANTINOOPOLIS, but the duke awaits him still farther south. Eutychianus improvises a tribunal and submits him to the tortures (which resemble those to which Saint George is subjected in the Coptic and Nubian cycles of this martyrdom) of the cutting of his tongue and ears, of needles in the skin, and iron helmet over burning coal, and boiling bitumen in the throat. Then he exiles him to a desert camp at Hierakon, still farther south, where Christ, in the form of an old man, comes in person to aid Victor, who is fasting every day in solitude.

Finally, Sebastianus, along with the praetor Asterius and the duke Soterichos, submits him to a last trial. Victor remains inflexible while he is eviscerated, treated with boiling oil with ashes and vinegar in his mouth, with red-hot knives in his skin, while his eyes and his tongue are pulled out, and he is finally dispatched by the sword. At this moment a fifteen-year-old girl, the daughter of a soldier, Stephanou, proclaims her faith and is also martyred. Horion, the executioner, beheads the girl, but she does receive Victor's blessing. Only this last episode has passed into the Greek in the *Martyrdom of Victor and Stephanis* (Bibliotheca Hagiographica Graeca 1864), the entirety being placed under the emperor Antoninus, under Sebastianus, governor of Italy at Damascus (*sic*). This text exists also in Latin (*Analecta Bollandiana* 2, 1883, pp. 291–99), as E. Galtier already noted in 1905, quoting the martyrdom of Victor and Corona. The same author draws up a family tree of the family of Basilides and his cycle.

The two published panegyrics have a similar structure: a classic eulogy, provided with *synkriseis* (comparisons) according to the rules of sophistry, surrounds the account of some miracles. Thus for Theodosius of Jerusalem there are cures at Victor's chapel—a man made blind by illness, a rich epicure who had fallen from his terrace and been attacked by gangrene, a mason rescued in mid-air during a fall from the wall of the saint's chapel, a woman ill with dropsy. In these accounts, Victor appears as the healer, wearing his general's uniform. The miracles in Celestine's panegyric are more original. A child dedicated to Saint Victor by his parents is redeemed by them for forty gold pieces, since they find him too handsome to surrender the boy. Victor strikes the boy with illness, and the child is saved only by prayer. After that the boy commits himself to the religious life as before promised by his parents. Kalliotropia, the niece of Honorius, is healed of an incurable illness. The architect of the saint's chapel in Rome is also cured, as well as a patrician. One of Constantine's generals, the founder of the cult of Victor in Rome, sets off to drink the saint's water in the chapel at Antioch, but is sent back to drink it in Rome where it has the same curative virtues. A rich man, nearly 100 years old, is cured of elephantiasis as is a blind man, and both undertake the service of the chapel. An invasion by the Sabans is stopped just after Constantine has left the front in Armenia. Finally, a rich and generous man whose grape harvests are blessed by Saint Victor exhorts his son to generosity. Since the son does not follow his father's example, the wine is spoiled and the son is obliged to do penance in the saint's chapel, after which prosperity is restored to him. The panegyric attributed to John Chrysostom is of a different kind. It has to do with scriptural, theological, and moral developments in the text of the Passion.

Celestinus, the fifth-century anti-Nestorian champion, quotes his predecessors, Eusebius (but here it is a question of the fictitious substitute for Eusebius of Nicomedia, the baptizer of Constantine), Julius, and Innocent. The three panegyrics touch Rome, Antioch, and Jerusalem, despite the fact that the existence of the cult of Saint Victor in these cities is highly improbable. Theodosius of Jerusalem is the antipatriarch opposed to Juvenal after the Council of CHALCEDON in 451 (cf. Rufus, PO 8, 1912, p. 62). The support of these patrons gives to the cult of Saint Victor a strongly anti-Chalcedonian tone. Constantinople is excluded, as well as Pope LEO, in the name of an orthodoxy that is projected back into the era of the martyrs under Diocletian. We shall not go far wrong in allowing the dawn of this speculation at the end of the fifth century, at the time when no shadow separated Antioch from Alexandria.

BIBLIOGRAPHY

Bouriant, U. "L'Eloge de L'Apa Victor, fils de Romanos." *Mémoires de la Mission archéologique française au Caire* 8 (1893):145–266.

Budge, E. A. W., ed. and trans *Coptic Martyrdoms*

etc., in the Dialect of Upper Egypt, pp. 1–101. London, 1914.

Galtier, E. "Contributions à l'étude de la littérature arabe-copte. III. Les Actes de Victor fils de Romanos." *Bulletin de l'Institut français d'Archéologie orientale* 4 (1905):127–40.

Rossi, F. "Di alcuni manoscritti copti che si conservano nella Biblioteca Nazionale di Torino." *Memorie della Reale Accademia di Torino,* ser. 2, 43 (1893):326–29.

Till. W. *Koptische Heiligen- und Märtyrerlegenden.* Orientalia Christiana Analecta 102. Rome, 1935.

MICHEL VAN ESBROECK

Copto-Arabic Tradition

The Copto-Arabic tradition concerning Saint Victor Stratelates, son of Romanus, is particularly rich. Unfortunately, none of it has as yet been edited, and it is hence practically unknown. Graf (1944, p. 540) collected a considerable portion of the material; however, his classification of the manuscripts has resulted in more confusion than clarification. What is more, he mixed this material up with that concerning Saint VICTOR OF SHŪ without realizing it. As for Sauget (1969) he practically ignores the Arabic tradition (cf. Bibliotheca hagiographica orientalis, 1910, pp. 269–270, nos. 1242–44).

To clarify matters a little we must distinguish the various pieces. In order to do this, until the texts are published, the incipit (insofar as it is given by the manuscript catalogs) is the only more or less reliable criterion. This is because the other elements, such as authors or titles, are anonymous or subject to modification. Hence, for each piece we shall transliterate a few words from the beginning of the real Arabic incipit (leaving aside the prologues or initial formulas), followed by its translation in full.

Here we have collected two types of texts. On the one hand, we have five different accounts of the martyrdom of Saint Victor; these are panegyrics (encomia) for his feast on 27 Baramūdah. On the other hand, we have two different accounts of miracles for the anniversary of the dedication of his church on 27 Hātūr.

Panegyric by Cyriacus of al-Bahnasā

The panegyric by Cyriacus is the one most frequently encountered in the manuscripts. In the two oldest manuscripts it is attributed to Cyriacus, Coptic bishop of al-Bahnasā; in the four nineteenth-century manuscripts it is attributed to Demetrius, patriarch of Antioch. This text is particularly developed, taking up over 200 pages in certain manuscripts. Graf (1944, p. 476) mentions the first two manuscripts, questioning the authenticity of the attribution.

The incipit, according to the manuscript in Paris (Arabe 212), reads in Arabic: *"Hasanan dhahara lanā al-yawm"* which may be translated, "Beautifully appeared for us to-day the source of perfumed flowers, in this month of Baramūdah, o my dear friends."

The manuscripts containing this text are the following (but see also below), in chronological order:

Paris Arabe 212 (Egypt, A.D. 1601), fols. 149r–212v

Cairo, Coptic Patriarchate Hist. 27 (Egypt, A.D. 1723), fols. 1r–44v (Graf no. 470; Simaika no. 614)

Paris Arabe 4782 (Egypt, nineteenth century), fols. 65v–166r

Paris Arabe 4793 (Egypt, nineteenth century), fols. 163r–164v, 159r–162v, and 165r–234v

Paris Arabe 4877 (Egypt, nineteenth century), 142 fols.

Paris Arabe 4879 (Egypt, nineteenth century), fols. 84r–111v.

Panegyric by Demetrius of Antioch

A second panegyric, attributed to a certain (unknown) Demetrius, patriarch of Antioch (cf. Graf, 1944, p. 354, no. 8; but the "Nützliches über den Neujahrstag" is rightly attributed to Demetrius, the twelfth Coptic patriarch, who reigned from 189 to 231), is found in two complete manuscripts. This text is also highly developed, indeed even longer than the foregoing.

The incipit, according to the manuscript in Paris (Arabe 131), which opens in Arabic: *"Tabārak ism al-rabb,"* may be translated as "Blessed be the name of our Lord who has made us worthy today to gather in this holy place to commemorate Him whom God has glorified in heaven and on earth."

The two manuscripts are:

Paris Arabe 131 (Egypt, A.D. 1440), fols. 2v–71v

Cairo, Coptic Patriarchate Hist. 27 (Egypt, A.D. 1723), fols. 90v–126v (Graf 470; Simaika 614).

Panegyric by Celestinus of Rome

A third panegyric, attested by one complete manuscript and one incomplete one, is attributed to

"Saint Celestinus, Archbishop of Rome." This text is shorter than the foregoing ones. It may be the translation of the Sahidic Coptic text published by E. A. Wallis Budge under the title *The Encomium of Celestinus, Archbishop of Rome, on Victor the General.*

The incipit, according to the manuscript in Paris (Arabe 4782), which opens in Arabic, *"ʿIndamā arādā Allāh al-Khāliq,"* may be translated as "When God the Creator, who made everything, wished . . . to remember us, the work of his hands. . . ."

The two manuscripts referred to above pose certain problems. The text of Graf 470 is incomplete, and the Paris manuscript Arabe 4782 contains an account of miracles contained also in the Paris Arabic manuscript 150 (cf. the section on the *Building of the Church,* below). However, these may not belong to our panegyric but to the text preceding it (fols. 166v–249v), which contains the account of the miracles of Saint Victor, which, however, lacks the very same miracles 3 to 10.

Panegyric by Theopemptos of Antioch

The fourth panegyric is found in one manuscript, kept at the Coptic Patriarchate of Cairo, and described by Graf (1934, p. 179) as follows: "Mīmar concerning Saint Victor, composed by Tābunṭus Archbishop of Antioch." However, ten years later, Graf doubted his own reading and wrote (1944, p. 540, lines 22–23): "from (?), Archbishop of Antioch."

Actually, the name was not so deformed in Arabic. We find in the Pierpont Morgan Library (Coptic 591, Vol. 28 of the photographic edition) a panegyric of Saint Victor composed by Theopemptos of Antioch. This is probably the same text as Caro's.

Unfortunately, Graf omitted to give an incipit for this text in his catalog, which would have enabled us to identify it. The only known manuscript is the *Cairo Coptic Patriarchate* (Hist. 27 [Egypt, A.D. 1723], fols. 45r–80r; Graf 470; Simaika 614). On the basis of the calligraphy of this manuscript, the present text corresponds to 80 percent of the length of the panegyric attributed to Cyriacus of Bahnasā (above).

Biographical Note by Michael of Atrīb and Malīj

A brief note, only three pages long, for the feast of Saint Victor on 27 Baramūdah, composed by Mīkhāʾīl (Michael), bishop of Atrīb and Malīj, in the mid-thirteenth century, appears in the second half of the Coptic-Arabic Synaxarion. This text has been edited twice (by R. Basset and J. Forget) and translated into French and Latin.

The incipit (according to Basset, pp. [980]–[983]), which opens in Arabic: *"Hadhā al-Qiddīs kān yuqāl abūh Rūmānus,"* may be translated as "The father of this saint was called Romanus, minister of the Emperor Diocletian and his counsellor. He shared [Basset translates against the sense here: "he was against"] the Emperor's [Basset: "the prince's"] opinion concerning the cult of idols" (Forget omits to translate the second sentence; cf. Forget, II, p. 92).

The Building of the Church of Saint Victor and His Miracles by Demetrius of Antioch

The title of this text is customarily given as "Homily of Saint Demetrius, Patriarch of Antioch, on the building of the Church of Saint Victor, son of the Vizier Romanus, and on his miracles." The text is in fact two pieces joined together: a homily on the building of the church and the account of the miracles (generally fourteen) that accompanied this event. As we read in the only text edited to date, that is, the account of the Synaxarion for 27 Hātūr (see the section on the Synaxarion, below), miracles occurred when the two churches dedicated to the saint were consecrated in Antioch and in Upper Egypt.

The text usually begins with a long preamble (four pages in the Paris manuscript Arabe 150), the incipit of which begins in Arabic: *"al-Majd lillāh al-wāhid bi-al-dhāt,"* which may be translated as "Glory to God, One in His Essence." The preamble does not belong to the original text. It was composed directly in Arabic, as is evident from the style, whereas the rest is translated. It is not found in all the manuscripts (it is lacking, for example, in the Paris manuscript Arabe 4782). It is also found as a prologue to other pieces (we have discovered in the only catalog of Christian Arabic manuscripts in Paris twenty or so different pieces beginning in this way).

The true incipit (according to the only two manuscripts the incipits of which are given by the catalogs—the Coptic Museum manuscript and the Paris Arabe 150) reads in Arabic: *"Hasanan huwa qudūm shahr barmūdah . . .,"* which may be translated as "Beautiful is the advent of the month of Baramūdah toward us, o my dear friends, for it is full of joy and delight."

This incipit poses two problems. On the one

hand, it is reminiscent of that of the panegyric of Cyriacus of al-Bahnasā (see the section on the *Panegyric by Cyriacus,* above). On the other hand, it speaks of the month of Baramūdah, as in this panegyric, whereas all the manuscripts attribute this homily to 27 Hātūr, the date of the commemoration of the dedication. This may be an adaptation of the panegyric of Cyriacus in abridged form, to which was added the account of the fourteen miracles.

We have four manuscripts of this homily: Coptic Museum, Cairo, History 471 (Egypt, fourteenth century; 31 pages, not numbered; Graf, no. 714/5th; Simaika no. 100/4th); Paris, Arabe 150 (Egypt, A.D. 1606; fols. 49r–92v); Paris, Arabe 4782 (Egypt, fourteenth century; fols. 166v–233r, without the preamble; the sheets are out of order and should be rearranged as follows: [1] homily; fols. 167–70, 172–210, and 216–20; [2] miracles 1–2: fols. 221–23; [3] miracles 11–14: fols. 170–72, 210–16, 223–33; as for miracles 3–10, they are inserted somewhere in fols. 251–85: cf. the discussion of the *Panegyric by Celestinus,* above); and Paris, Arabe 4887 (Egypt, nineteenth century; fols. 143v–262r).

In certain manuscripts there is a fifteenth miracle (not numbered) added after the others, entitled: "Miracle worked at the occasion of the dedication of his church." It is found in two manuscripts: Paris Arabe 150 (fols. 93r–100v) and Paris Arabe 4782 (fols. 233v–249v). The incipit (according to the Paris Arabe 150), reads in Arabic: *"Kān rajul shammās,"* which may be translated as "There was a man who was a deacon, in the region *[kūrah]* of Miṣr, of the people of the city of Akhmīm; his name was Samuel."

Account of the Construction of the Two Churches, in the Synaxarion

The author of the first half of the Coptic-Arabic Synaxarion (who was not Michael, bishop of Atrīb and Malīj), recounts on 27 Hātūr the building of two churches in honor of Saint Victor, as reported by his mother, Martha. The first was in Antioch, under the patriarch Theodore; the second was in Upper Egypt, in the palace of al-Barīqūn [sic], where the saint had spent a whole year before his martyrdom.

At each of these two consecrations the miracles of Saint Victor are evoked. At Antioch, oil was exuded from his body on the day of his feast, "and all who were ill and were anointed with this oil recovered immediately" (Basset; p. [270]/11). In Upper Egypt, immediately following the divine liturgy of consecration of the new church, "all those who had various illnesses went up to Saint Victor's reliquary and were cured of their illnesses. . . . This took place on 27th Hātūr, and countless miracles and wonders were manifested in this Church" (Basset, p. [272]/9–12).

Unidentified Texts

There are also manuscripts dealing with Victor the General the identification of which is impossible or uncertain because of the excessively vague information given by the catalogs. They are Birmingham, Mingana Christian Arabic Add. 265 (Egypt, A.D. 1749); catalog: Mingana no. 258; fragment [nine sheets] of a life of Saint Victor, numbered 14–18, 70–71, and 138–39); Coptic Museum, Cairo, History 482 (Egypt, seventeenth century; catalog: Graf, 726, Simaika, 113; fragment of fifteen sheets, numbered 23–27, of a life of Saint Victor); Coptic Patriarchate, Cairo, History 79 (Egypt, eighteenth century?; Simaika, 680; 210 folios, containing *The Life of Saint Victor Son of Romanus* and *His Miracles and Wonderworkings* [incomplete at the end]); Louvain, *Fonds Lefort Arabe A 7* (burned in 1940; miracles of Saint Victor).

Churches and Monasteries Dedicated to Saint Victor

The following data have been gleaned from medieval Coptic-Arabic texts concerning churches and monasteries named for Saint Victor. Most come from the *History of the Churches and Monasteries of Egypt* attributed to ABŪ ṢĀLIḤ THE ARMENIAN around 1210. In geographical order, from north to south, they are:

- Church at Arḍ al-Ḥabash, near Cairo (Abū Ṣāliḥ, fol. 41b; Amelineau, pp. 579/6 and 581/7) Church opposite the afore-mentioned (Abū Ṣāliḥ, fol. 42a)
- Church at al-Jīzah (Abū Ṣāliḥ, fol. 59a)
- Church at Jalfah, in the district of Banī Mazār (Abū Ṣāliḥ, fol. 74a)
- Church at al-Qalandamūn, near Antinoopolis, in the province of al-Ashmūnayn (fol. 92a)
- Church at Sāqiyat Mūsā, south of al-Ashmūnayn, in the district of Itlīdim (Abū Ṣāliḥ, fol. 92a)
- Church at al-Khuṣūs, east of Asyūṭ, in the mountains, where his body is conserved (Abū Ṣāliḥ), fol. 90a; this may be the same monastery of Saint Victor to which the ninety-seventh Coptic patriarch GABRIEL VIII [1587–1603] withdrew

when he composed, in January 1597, his profession of faith of union with the church of Rome [Graf, 1951, p. 122]; this monastery was situated in the vicinity of Abnūb)

Church at Qifṭ (Abū Ṣāliḥ, fol. 103a)

Church and monastery at Qamūlah, in the district of Qūṣ (Abū Ṣāliḥ, fol. 104a; it was here that Athanasius, bishop of Qūṣ, the author of the famous Coptic grammar who lived at the end of the thirteenth and the beginning of the fourteenth century, became a monk [cf. Graf, 1947, p. 445]).

BIBLIOGRAPHY

Budge, E. A. W., ed. and trans. *Coptic Martyrdoms, etc., in the Dialect of Upper Egypt.* London, 1914.
Sauget, J.-M. "Victore il generale." In *Bibliotheca Sanctorum,* Vol. 12, cols. 1258–1260. Rome, 1969.

KHALIL SAMIR, S.J.

VICTOR OF TABENNĒSĒ, SAINT (feast day: 18 Bābah). Saint Victor is known as abbot general of the Tabennesiotes (see MONASTICISM, PACHOMIAN) and local abbot of PBOW. According to the Coptic sources, he was present at the Council of Ephesus (431) with Saint CYRIL and Saint SHENUTE. According to the same sources, he was the natural son of Emperor Theodosius II (408–450), which explains the favor he enjoyed with the emperor. With the support of the emperor, he began to build a church named for Saint PACHOMIUS at Pbow, but died both before Theodosius and before the dedication of this church, which was organized by his successor Martyrius.

Victor was celebrated at the White Monastery (DAYR ANBĀ SHINŪDĀH), as is shown by the typika preserved at Leiden (Insinger 39, ed. Pleyte and Boeser, p. 215), Cologne (Westermann, no. 10206), and Vienna (K9735).

An Arabic manuscript recounts the consecration of the church, which was begun by Apa Victor and was completed by his successor Martyrius (van Lantschoot).

BIBLIOGRAPHY

Lantschoot, A. van. "Allocution de Timothée d'Alexandrie." *Le Muséon* 47 (1934):13–56.
Pleyte, W., and P. A. A. Boeser. *Manuscrits coptes du Musée des antiquités des Pays-Bas à Leide.* Leiden, 1897.
Westermann, W. L. *Upon Slavery in Ptolemaic Egypt.* New York, 1929.

RENÉ-GEORGES COQUIN

VIGIL, nocturnal prayers or services on the eve of the Sabbath in preparation for the Sunday eucharistic celebration, including Easter. In the monasteries, it became a daily practice for the midnight offices. Vigils were observed on special occasions, such as at times of affliction or persecution and on momentous occasions in the church, such as the election of a new patriarch.

Vigils are more or less the order of the day in Coptic monasteries, though habitually they are left to the individual monks in their cells. Anbā Bishoi is known to have had his hair tied to a ring in the ceiling of his solitary chapel (still to be seen in his monastery in Wādī al-Naṭrūn) so that when he dozed in the midst of his nocturnal vigil, he would be awakened by the pull at the top of his head. Associated with the vigil is abstinence, which is a penitential practice implying refraining from one or all categories of food for a given period.

BIBLIOGRAPHY

Baumstark, A., and O. Heiming. *Nocturna Laus: Typen frühchristlicher Vigilienfeier und ihr Fortleben vor allem im römischen und monastischen Ritus.* Münster, 1957.
Callewaert, C. "De Vigiliarum Origine." *Collationes Brugenses* 23 (1923):425–66.
Gastoué, A. "Les Vigiles nocturnes." *Science et Religion* 295 (1908).
Leclercq, H. "Vigiles." In *Dictionnaire d'archéologie et de liturgie,* Vol. 15, pt. 2, cols. 3108–13. Paris, 1953.

AZIZ S. ATIYA

VILLECOURT, LOUIS (1869–1928), French Arabist, Coptologist, and specialist in Syriac. He was a Benedictine monk of Farnborough, Hampshire, England.

RENÉ-GEORGES COQUIN

VIRGIN ENTHRONED. *See* Christian Subjects in Coptic Art.

VIRGIN MARY, APPARITION OF THE.
The Coptic Orthodox church in the Cairo suburb of

Icon of the Virgin. Tapestry. Sixth century. 110 × 178 cm. *Courtesy Cleveland Museum of Art, Leonard C. Hanna, Jr. Fund, 67.144.*

Zaytūn was named after the Holy Mother. On the evening of 2 April 1968, it became the scene of the first apparition of the Virgin Mary above its domes. It was witnessed by municipal garage employees across the road, and they immediately reported the event to the priest. These apparitions, in which the Virgin was often seen accompanied by doves, recurred numerous times until the beginning of September. Those of 4 May to 5 May and 7 July were particularly noteworthy. People of all creeds and denominations came to witness the miraculous scene, often waiting through the night for the occurrence. Many songs were composed to celebrate the event. A liturgical feast of the Transfiguration of the Virgin Mary at Zaytūn was sanctioned in 1969 by the late Patriarch Cyril VI (1959–1971). It is celebrated on 24 Baramhāt, which, according to the Coptic calendar, marks the anniversary of the first appearance.

BIBLIOGRAPHY

"Apparition miraculeuse de la Sainte Vierge à Zeitoun." *Le Monde copte* 1 (1977):23–32.

Ishak, Fayek M. "The Appearance of the Most Holy Mother of God at Zeytoun, Egypt." *The Orthodox Word* 5 (July-Aug. 1969):128–33.

______. *Philosophic and Spiritual Tidings Behind the Zeytounian Holy Appearance,* no. 16. Toronto, 1970.

Viaud, G. *Les Pèlerinages coptes en Egypte, d'après les notes du Qommos Jacob Muyser,* p. 35. Cairo, 1979.

Zaki, P. *Our Lord's Mother Visits Egypt in 1968.* Cairo, 1977.

FAYEK ISHAK

VIRGIN MARY, FAST OF THE. *See* Fasts.

VIRTUES, THE TWELVE. The hymn of the Twelve Virtues is usually chanted by the deacons on occasions when the pope or a bishop is present during the celebration of the Divine Liturgy.

After reading the Pauline epistle, which is the first of the liturgical lections, the hymn starts with the following petition: "May the Twelve Virtues of the Holy Spirit, as recorded in the Holy Scripture, come upon our blessed father the Patriarch, Pope [name] and his co-partner in the Apostolic Ministry, Metropolitan (or Bishop) [name]. May the Lord God establish him upon his See for many peaceful years, and bring his adversaries under his feet." Two groups of deacons then take turns in singing the hymn, each reciting three virtues at a time.

These virtues are the sum total of the attributes of Christian perfection, distilled from the teachings of Christ and the apostles and, together, make the perfect head of the church. The virtues and some of their biblical sources are as follows:

1. Love, the greatest of all virtues: Matthew 22:37–40; Mark 12:30–31; Luke 10:27; John 15:12; 1 Corinthians 13:13; 1 Timothy 1:5.
2. Hope: 1 Thessalonians 5:8; 1 Timothy 4:10; Titus 2:13; Hebrews 6:18.
3. Faith: Matthew 23:23; Ephesians 6:16; 1 Thessalonians 5:8.
4. Purity: 2 Corinthians 6:6; 1 Thessalonians 2:10; 1 Timothy 4:12.
5. Chastity: Matthew 19:12; 1 Corinthians 7:8, 32–33.
6. Love of peace: Matthew 5:9; Romans 10:15; 2 Corinthians 13:11; Hebrews 12:14; 1 Peter 3:11.
7. Wisdom: Matthew 10:16, 24:45; Luke 12:42, 21:15; Acts 6:3; Ephesians 5:5; Colossians 4:5; James 3:13.
8. Righteousness: Matthew 3:15; Luke 1:74–75; Acts 10:35; Romans 4:3, 5, 9, 22; Galatians 3:6; James 2:23.
9. Meekness: Matthew 11:29, 21:5; 2 Corinthians 10:1; Galatians 5:22–23.
10. Patience: Luke 8:15, 21:19; 2 Corinthians 6:4; 1 Timothy 6:11; 2 Timothy 3:10; James 5:11; Revelations 1:9, 2:2–3.
11. Forbearance: Romans 2:4, 9:22; Corinthians 6:6; Galatians 5:22; Ephesians 4:1–2.
12. Asceticism: Titus 1:7–8; 1 Corinthians 9:25.

BISHOP GREGORIOS

VOCALISE. *See* Music, Coptic: Description.

W

WĀDĪ HABIB. *See* Scetis.

WĀḌIH IBN RAJĀ', AL- (c. 1000), a Coptic monk and priest from SCETIS. He took the name Paul after his conversion from Islam to Christianity. He was the author of four apologetic, polemical works, three of which have not yet been investigated. The only source for biographical information on him is the insertion of a biography into a *Lives of the Patriarchs* made by Mīkhā'īl, bishop of Tinnis, from the verbal account of a deacon, Theodosius, a secretary to the patriarch Philotheus (979–1003). It says he and SĀWĪRUS IBN AL-MUQAFFA' were friends and shared an interest in apologetic literature. The two holy men spent most of their time in discussion and study of the Bible until they knew how to interpret the holy books. Then, al-Wāḍiḥ composed two books in Arabic refuting errors from the Qur'ān.

His preserved works are *Kitāb al-Wāḍiḥ* (Book of Evidence), *Nawādir al-Mufassirīn Wataḥrīf al-Mukhālifīn* (Rare Points of the Interpreter), *Kitāb al-Ibānah fī Tanāquḍ al-Hadīth* (Disclosing the Contradictions in the Hadīth), and *Hatk al-Maḥjūb* (Unveiling the Veiled).

VINCENT FREDERICK

WĀDĪ AL-NAṬRŪN. *See* Scetis.

WĀDĪ AL-RAYYĀN (Fayyūm), valley (*wādī*) connected to the great depression of the Fayyūm, of which it forms an extension to the southwest with Wādī al-Muwayliḥ, where DAYR ANBĀ SAMŪ'ĪL of QALAMŪN is situated. There are three wells and a small grove of palms; it is frequented by the camel caravans that link the Fayyūm with the oasis of al-Bahriyyah.

The *wādī* seems to have been inhabited and cultivated in the Roman period, as is attested by remains of brick walls with plaster. Caves, either natural or dug in the eastern face of the part of the Libyan plateau called Munqār al-Rayyān, were used by hermits, as is shown by crosses and Coptic graffiti traced on the walls of one of them (Meinardus, 1966, fig. 7–9); unfortunately they are not dated.

The Coptic Life of Samuel reports that the founder of the monastery of Qalamūn often withdrew to the oasis of Piliheu, west of the monastery, returning to the monastery once every three months. *The Churches and Monasteries of Egypt* specifies that the place was called al-Rayyān. It is therefore probable that Samuel lived in one of these caves.

Numerous European travelers have visited the site, and geological studies have been published, notably on the possible utilization of the depression as a reservoir for water (Meinardus, pp. 299–301).

From 1960 to 1969 these caves were reoccupied by a dozen hermits led by P. Mattā al-Miskīn; they were later asked to restore the DAYR ANBĀ MAQĀR in Wādī al-Naṭrūn.

BIBLIOGRAPHY

Fakhry, A. "Wadi al-Rayān." *Annales du Service des antiquités de l'Egypte* 46 (1947):1–19.

Meinardus, O. "The Hermits of Wādī Rayān." *Studia Orientalia Christiana Collectanea* 11 (1966): 293–317.

______. "The Caves of the Wadi Rayan." *Christian Egypt, Ancient and Modern*, 2nd ed., pp. 468–82. Cairo, 1977. (Same text as preceding article, without map or plates.)

RENÉ-GEORGES COQUIN
MAURICE MARTIN, S.J.

WĀDĪ SARJAH, a fairly narrow valley about 220 yards (200 m) wide that opens up about a mile (1.5 km) from the cultivable lands and 5 miles (8 km) south of Dayr al-Balay'zah. It is about a mile (1.5 km) long, but the inhabitants developed only its mouth. There are some quarries equipped as a church with frescoes, and cells were constructed on the slopes.

This site was excavated by an English team from the Byzantine Research Fund during the winter of 1913/1914. Unfortunately World War I dispersed the excavators, who were unable to publish the full results of their work. We have the introduction to *The Excavations at Wadi Sarga* by R. Campbell Thomson, director of the excavations, and the texts. The general plan of the site was published with an introduction to the excavations (Crum and Bell, 1922, pp. 1–5). The essential question was posed by Crum (p. 10): whether it is a site of a cenobium or of a colony of anchorites. There are indications that it was a cenobium, for in the texts there is a superior who has the title of archimandrite and acts in the name of the council of the monastery. A wall of large stones was erected around the buildings. The monks used and decorated ancient quarries, out of which they made their church. The paintings in this church have not been published.

The Greek and Coptic texts have been published (Crum and Bell, 1922). A fresco representing the three young men in the furnace has been restored and placed in the British Museum. It derives from a neighboring site, and has often been reproduced.

The state of the ruins today is presented by Meinardus (1965, pp. 288–89; 1977, pp. 398–99).

BIBLIOGRAPHY

Crum, W. E., and H. I. Bell. *The Excavations at Wādī Sarga*. Coptica 3. Copenhagen, 1922.

Dalton, O. M. "A Coptic Wall-painting from Wādī Sarga." *Journal of Egyptian Archeology* 3 (1916):35–37.

Meinardus, O. *Christian Egypt, Ancient and Modern*. Cairo, 1965; 2nd ed., 1977.

RENÉ-GEORGES COQUIN
MAURICE MARTIN, S.J.

WĀDĪ SHAYKH ʿALĪ, a rather narrow and inaccessible ravine running roughly north–south into the Dishnā plain in the area of Nag Hammadi in Upper Egypt; it apparently was named after the nearby village of Shaykh ʿAlī. Opening off the northwestern perimeter of the desert and flanked by the Jabal al-Ṭārif to the west and the Jabal Abū Mīnā to the east, this wash leads back some distance into the Eastern Desert. Its rugged character and the northerly direction of access suggest that, unlike major wadis such as Wādī Ḥāmmamāt and Wādī Qinā, Wādī Shaykh ʿAlī most likely was not used as an overland commercial route to the Red Sea. This wadi yields little evidence of previous use or occupation other than the anticipated fossils from prehistoric times, an unfinished obelisk and cut stone observable part of the way up the wadi, and the most important archaeological feature of the wadi: a site, located approximately 2 miles (3 km) from the mouth, painted and incised with inscriptions. The numerous inscriptions are located in a compact area on the western overhang of the canyon wall, on both the exposed exterior and the underside of the overhang. While some modern Arabic inscriptions show that local villagers occasionally left their marks on the wadi walls, the site is dominated by dozens of Coptic graffiti.

The Wādī Shaykh ʿAlī provides evidence of at least two periods of occupation or usage: Coptic and Old Kingdom. Painted on the face of the overhang in red paint, and occasionally scratched into the soft stone with a sharp instrument, are many Coptic graffiti of a monastic sort. Such pious graffiti are well known from other locations (cf. W. E. Crum and H. G. Evelyn-White, *The Monastery of Epiphanius at Thebes*, Vol. 2, pp. 141–47, 326–30 [New York, 1973]).

A multitude of graffiti in Sahidic Coptic contain the names of Phoibammon, Pekin, Fakire, Solomon, David, Philotheus son of David, Chael, and Stauros. Their inscriptions are similar in content. "Pray for me in love" is customary. "Jesus Christ, help me" also occurs.

A stone chip 8 × 2 × 1 inches (20 × 5 × 2.5 cm) found just below the western overhang of Wādī Shaykh ʿAlī is inscribed in red paint; the paint traces on the sides and bottom of the chip show it to have been inscribed after it had broken off. It may have functioned in a manner analogous to papyri and ostraca left in temples and holy centers. The bottom line, in Sahidic Coptic, reads: "I am Archeleos. Remember in love."

Additional indications of a Coptic presence at this location include an incised representation of a monk named John. Shown as orant, with beard and robe, the monk is identified by means of a Coptic inscription that seems to read "I am faithful John or "I, John, am faithful." Furthermore, a number of Byzantine bricks and many Byzantine shards have been found, including some resembling the fourth/fifth century painted red slipware found throughout the region.

Other graffiti from the wadi indicate a much earlier Egyptian presence at this overhang. Drawings scratched into the rock depict hunters and animals such as the ibex, lion, and ram, along with boats (with poles or oars) and hunting enclosures. In one instance a lion, with mane, is portrayed attacking a hunter, with spear; the lion appears to be overcoming the hunter. These hunting graffiti have a simple, direct character, and one might speculate that they could be prehistoric in origin, since they resemble prehistoric and predynastic drawings found at such Upper Egyptian sites as Hierakopolis and decorations on such pottery as late Naqādah ware. Although such a conclusion is not impossible, further evidence from the Wādī Shaykh 'Alī suggests a date during the early historical period, for among the hieroglyphs that are identifiable on the western wall of the wadi is a cartouche of Menkaure, the famous pharaoh of the Fourth Dynasty and the builder of the third great pyramid at Giza.

A tentative interpretation of these data from the wadi suggests the following scenario. Early stonecutters and quarriers used the wadi (confirmed by the obelisk and worked stone therein). Hunters naturally accompanied them, and scratched typical hunting graffiti onto the western face of the wadi cliff, where the overhang provided shade from the afternoon sun and perhaps shelter for the evening. Many centuries later, Coptic monks must have happened upon the scenes and rededicated the site, in their usual fashion, by means of Christian graffiti while possibly using it for pilgrimage or retreat. Whether or not a substantial installation, or even a burial of a holy personage, existed at the Coptic site is impossible to say without further exploration.

BIBLIOGRAPHY

Meyer, M. W. "Wadi Sheikh Ali Survey, December 1980." *American Research Center in Egypt Newsletter* 117 (1982):22–24.

______. "Archaeological Survey of the Wadi Sheikh Ali: December 1980." *Göttinger Miszellen* 64 (1983):77–82.

MARVIN W. MEYER

WAFD, NEW. *See* Political Parties.

WAFDIST BLOC. *See* Political Parties.

WAFD PARTY. *See* Political Parties.

WĀHAM (plural *wāhamāt* or *wōhamāti*), from Coptic ⲃⲱϩⲉⲙ (bōhem), song, air, tune, hymn, LAḤN. This is an ecclesiastical term found only in ritual manuscripts. *Wāham* is properly pronounced *wōham* and means "air," "tune," "hymn" (see MUSIC, COPTIC).

EMILE MAHER ISHAQ

WANSLEBEN, JOHAN M. *See* Vansleb (Wansleben), Johann Michael.

WAQ'AT AL-KANĀ'IS (the Incident of the Churches), the first demonstration of the presence of widely organized Muslim religious brotherhoods in Egypt and of their deep impact on the populace, which they manipulated in the Mamluk period. On one day in 1321, the populace, incited and led by members of these brotherhoods, destroyed, pillaged, and burned over sixty of the main churches and monasteries in all the important cities and towns throughout the country—hence, the historical importance of this crisis not only for the history of Egyptian Christianity, to which it was a severe blow, but also for the long and interesting history of brotherhoods, particularly their influence on different layers of the population and their continuous political interference in Egypt. In addition, this crisis indicates the scale of the political power of the populace, which one can trace from the Fatimid period, and its effect on other components of the social structure, particularly on Copts, a power that endured until the nineteenth century and that would take other forms later.

Undoubtedly, this crisis was not the only one of its kind and could be compared to others, particularly to an earlier crisis that resulted in the systematic destruction of a still greater number of edifices in the time of the Fatimid caliph al-Ḥākim at the beginning of the eleventh century. But in spite of the fact that the Mamluk crisis resulted in the destruction of a smaller number of churches, it has proved to have been historically much more important and its effects more serious.

In fact, the decision of al-Ḥākim was more or less

the action of a bizarre, unpopular, and isolated caliph whose many instances of irrational behavior, the proclamation of his own divinity being but one example, were condemned by Egyptians and criticized by Arab historians. If, for demagogic reasons, he invited the population to attack churches, it was a relatively long campaign, and being an official movement, its effects have to be considered in the same way as other governmental decisions at that period, that is, against a background of skeptical acceptance by the population of the decisions of foreign rulers who followed one another as masters of the country and, in particular, of the oddities of al-Ḥākim, who acted erratically. And though the populace and certain members of his entourage profited from his policy, it was destined to be short-lived, as were his other schemes.

The Mamluk case, on the contrary, was the fruit of a deliberate plan and well-organized preparation of an active part of the population and profited from the laxity and the avidity of the governors and from the circumstances of the populace. The success of the action reflected a certain political development that rallied the rigorists; most of the jurists; and in particular the amirs and high officials who were looking after their rival interests. There was also the sultan Muḥammad ibn Qalāwūn (1310–1341), who accepted the eruption of the populace apparently as a way out of the serious difficulties Egypt confronted at that moment. It is just one more example of the old habit of governors of Egypt, especially weak and unpopular ones, of finding an easy scapegoat in the rich domain of intolerance against the Copts. This consensus no doubt gave the population the false idea that the events were ordered by the sultan. Al-MAQRĪZĪ wrote that amirs told the sultan, who was alarmed by the spreading eruption, that it was not the work of man but the intervention of God's will, since even the sultan could never have achieved the same result, had he ordered it. Al-Maqrīzī, like other historians of his period, who all shared the rigorists' point of view, went into ecstasies about the strangeness of the events, as if they had been miraculous.

All this explains how this crisis, which was in fact only one of a series of grave events that took place between the end of the thirteenth century and the late fourteenth century, came to have such serious and lasting effects. The sultan, who intended to punish the populace because it acted without his order, finished by agreeing to receive its cheering and to give it free rein. As far as churches are concerned, the Mamluks apparently did not agree to reopen any church in return for the money paid by Copts or the rich gifts Christian sovereigns sent them, as in 1303. (Al-Maqrīzī referred to a sum of 500,000 golden coins that was to be levied on Copts at the end of the crisis.) Later the Ottomans were more tolerant than the Mamluks, but it was not until the advent of the MUḤAMMAD ʻALĪ dynasty in the nineteenth century that the Copts became the beneficiaries of a more liberal attitude.

This crisis, like all crises of the Mamluk period in which Copts were involved, adds interesting material to the important dossier on religion and politics in Egypt. But one difference is to be noted in this case: whereas in other crises in which Copts were personally the target, where their rights, their properties, and their posts were attacked, no manifestly violent action is recorded, here the churches, the symbol of their identity, became the object of widespread violence. One thinks of the results of the persecution by the Byzantines when they confiscated Coptic churches and gave them to the Melchites. The arrival of the new masters, who were trying to extend their new faith, must have underlined the importance of this symbol and rendered the question more delicate. This seems to explain why the alleged treaty that the Arabs concluded with the Egyptians contained a clause concerning the security of churches and crosses. But by the time of the rigorists and the mounting intolerance, the situation of churches must have become a problem. Their security, as well as the situation of Christians in general, began to be interpreted in a restrictive way, evolving into what was called the COVENANT OF ʻUMAR, which prohibited the building of new churches. During periods of tension, this interpretation was asserted by rigorists to deny the right of restoring decaying churches.

The rigorists took churches as a subject for their polemic works and *fatwās* (legal opinions) well before the end of the Ayyubid dynasty and, in particular, during the agitated Mamluk period. As early as 1243, in his *Tārīkh al-Fayyūm* (History of the Fayyūm), al-Nabulsī gave a list of the churches and monasteries there, stating that his aim in recording them was to prevent Copts from building new edifices. Again during the crisis of the very first years of the fourteenth century, Qāḍī Aḥmad ibn Muḥammad ibn al-Rafʻah issued a *fatwā* authorizing the destruction of certain churches and would have executed it had he not been stopped by Qāḍī al-Quḍāh Taqiy al-Dīn Muḥammad ibn Daqīq al-ʻĪd. This same rigorist *qāḍī*, who was at one time a *muḥtassib* (a jurist whose function was to see if the Muslim laws, or *sharīʿah,* were respected) of Cairo, was mentioned by al-Ṣuyūṭī among the important theologians and authorities on interpretation and is famous for a book he wrote in 1308 called *Al-Nafāʾis fī Hadm al-Kanāʾis* (Chronicles Concerning the Destruction of Churches). To the same polemic category belong the anti-Christian *fatwās* of the theologian and jurist Ibn Taymiyyah (1263–1328).

But nearer to the populace than the official clergy or the eminent rigorist jurists were the brotherhoods, whose members had a more direct influence on it. These brotherhoods, which have flourished in Egypt since the thirteenth century, had more or less the same political and religious attitudes as other brotherhoods that appeared in certain Muslim countries in the same period and used the same means to recruit members and to attract the population. Apparently, it was owing to them that the hashish (Indian hemp) they used regularly became so widespread among the lower strata of the population that the Mamluk sultan Baybars had to prohibit its use. Al-Maqrīzī spoke about a certain Kurānī who used to send his followers from the same low social castes (pages, blacks, etc.) to the streets of Cairo at night to attack shops and even soldiers and incite them to revolt against the government.

The populace itself had already become a dangerous power in the social structure of towns. It was incited by the permanent economic difficulties and the continuous political disorder. Life had become difficult for the lower classes because of the effect of long wars, famines, epidemics, high taxes, and corruption. Many people were forced to leave villages for towns where work was not always available. At one time, the government had to assign poor people to be fed by rich persons or amirs. The political climate of the Mamluk period, with amirs plotting against each other and sending their armed bands of Mamluks to attack their rivals and sometimes the population and to sack and pillage shops, must have added to the difficulties and pushed the populace to join in or to riot, motivated either by revenge or hopes of benefiting from the pillage. No wonder that the masses began to be feared and coveted by political powers in the Mamluk period. They were all trying to manipulate them and to use their eruptions. This also explains the evident consensus of all these political powers and religious circles with the populace not only during this crisis but also in later ones. It also explains why the power of the populace governed the streets of Cairo for a long time. The anti-Christian *fatwas* and polemics of the rigorists produced among these masses an atmosphere of continuous excitation, which could easily turn into outbursts against Copts.

In 1308 the Copts obtained from the sultan Muḥammad ibn Qalāwūn permission to restore a decaying church in ḤĀRIT AL-RŪM in Cairo, the Church of Saint Barbara. The restoration, which seems to have embellished the church, angered the rigorists, who complained to the sultan that a new part had been added to the edifice. The sultan decided to send his officials to remove the new part, but the population, which had been informed, crowded around the church, while elements of the populace began to pull down the whole building without waiting for the officials, who had purposely delayed their arrival, and then built a *miḥrāb* (a niche indicating the direction to Mecca) in its place and called for prayer. This did not last long, for the sultan, who felt his authority threatened, ordered the removal of the *miḥrāb,* a solution that did not ease the tension.

The populace seized the occasion of certain transformations in Cairo in 1320 to dig around a neighboring church (the Church of al-Zuhrī), but did not succeed in causing it to fall by itself or in convincing the amirs to destroy it. This excitation culminated a week later when this church and sixty others all over Egypt were attacked at the same time. In all these places, the pattern was the same: just after the Friday prayer in important mosques a *faqīr* appealed for an attack and then entered a trance. Outside, people could see the dust and smoke of churches being destroyed and burned and elements of the populace carrying away what they robbed. Details were given by al-Maqrīzī about the eruption and the consequences of the noninterference of the authorities: the spoliation, the assaults, the enslavement of nuns, and so on.

Al-Maqrīzī described how the officials lingered in applying the orders of the sultan before convincing him not to punish the populace. This was why the appeals of his personal treasurer, Qāḍī Karīm al-Dīn, a converted Copt, to punish the instigators were futile and did nothing but increase the anger of the rigorists, other high officials, and the population against him. The repeated direct attack of rigorists, historians, and, in particular, al-Maqrīzī on that converted Copt underlines a certain development in beliefs concerning the conditions of conversion to Islam (see EGYPT, ISLAMIZATION OF). Apparently, pronouncing the two essential formulas concerning the divinity of Allah and the Prophet was no longer considered a sufficient act of faith in these moments of tension, as if the rigorists could not forget or forgive the past of the converts. So it was not only a matter of jealousy between other high officials and the converted treasurer or of the usual hatred by the population for the persons responsible for the fiscal system. Polemic and sarcastic poems circulated in Cairo at that time about the genuineness and the validity of conversions, an atmosphere that explains why the sultan's treasurer was publicly attacked in the streets of Cairo. No wonder that this development prepared for the new measures applied by rigorists during the next crisis, in the year 1354, when they obliged new converts to undergo confinement in mosques and a total physical and juridicial isolation from their background.

This consensus and the fact that the historians were far from being impartial make one of the recorded consequences of this crisis difficult to judge. Al-Maqrīzī relates in detail how fire broke out in several places in Cairo a month after the events, burning and destroying many storehouses and buildings such as mosques, *madrasas* (schools), and even houses and offices of high officials. This last reference was given by al-Maqrīzī to justify the people's suspicion that the Christians were responsible for it, as well as the assertion that monks were arrested while about to start, or after having started, fires. They are even said to have confessed that other monks were behind the plan. But the fact that fire broke out in the house and office of the treasurer in question, the only high official who opposed the rigorists and advocated punishment of the arsonists, seems to create doubt about the veracity of the accusation and of the confessions.

These circumstances make it difficult to draw historical conclusions about the crisis. Was it after all an act of some exasperated monks who were trying to avenge the destruction of the churches or could one see in these fires another plan of the rigorists to stir up the population against the Copts, to justify the harsh measures that they were pushing for and that were strictly applied after the fires? Al-Maqrīzī and other historians wrote about these measures and especially about the point of interest here, namely, the fact that many churches in Upper Egypt were transformed into mosques.

This question, which cannot be easily or definitely answered, is important because of the historical significance of the conclusions one could draw about an eventual change in the outlines of the response of Copts to crises. Coptic history plainly shows that in other more or less similar crises Copts maintained the same peaceful demeanor they had always adopted. When one reads through Coptic history, one can easily characterize the attitude and reaction of the church in moments of tension and crisis: the patriarchs and the clergy always preferred to endure difficulties and asked people for more prayers and to turn the other cheek. This attitude often succeeded. It moderated, if not disarmed, the zeal of rigorists and isolated them as much as possible from the peaceful mass of Egyptians and from moderate governors, who would finally agree to ease the tough measure by one means or another.

An interesting detail is to be found in the relation of the events by al-Maqrīzī. When the patriarch was told about the confessions of the monks, he wept and said, "Insolent Christians who wanted to act like insolent Muslims who destroyed churches." He accepted the harsh and expensive measure imposed upon him. The excitation slowly calmed down.

Thus, if it is true that monks were responsible for the fires, one should wonder about the factors that changed the general attitude and rendered these monks "insolent," adopting an attitude similar to that of the members of the brotherhoods. It is true that both were less bound by the multiple rules binding the established clergy on both sides. It is also true that monks in the past had played an active role in the protection of Christianity and the beliefs of the church, as in the time of Apa SHENUTE II and of certain patriarchs of Alexandria. Was the sudden destruction of churches a sufficient reason for the monks to take action in the Mamluk period, or was there another change not recorded in history?

MOUNIR MEGALLY

WAQʿAT AL-NAṢĀRĀ (Christian encounter), a name given by Arab writers to a grave crisis or, more precisely, a series of crises caused by a buildup of tension against the Copts in the thirteenth and fourteenth centuries during the first Baḥrī Mamluk dynasty (Baḥrides). These events, which coincided with a general consensus against Christians in the Muslim world, of which Egypt was the leading power at that time, are important for Coptic history. They illustrate the change that had already begun with the ARAB CONQUEST OF EGYPT and by which Coptic history ceased to be dependent solely on local events and became exposed to decisive external factors pertaining to the evolution of Muslim society in different countries and to its animated relations with the non-Muslim communities, such as Jews and Christians, living in the same countries.

The tension against the Copts was inflamed not only by the local situation in the agitated Mamluk period—that is, by extremists like Qāḍī Aḥmad ibn Muḥammad ibn al-Raf'ah (see WAQ'AT AL-KANĀ'IS) or, in the fourteenth-century, Ibn al-Naqqāsh, with their polemical *fatwās* (legal opinions) and publications—but also by a group of rigorists from outside Egypt, such as the theologian Ibn Taymiyyah of Damascus, and by other foreign appeals to Mamluks against Copts.

This explains why the duration of these crises was out of proportion to their causes and why their consequences were grave. They were the coup de grâce of a particular phase in the history of Christianity in Egypt, with massive conversions to Islam and the destruction of the majority of churches and monasteries. They reduced Copts to the poor state in which they remained until the nineteenth century, that of an isolated minority with very limited participation in the active life of the country, with marginal social activity, and consequently with low economic possibilities. Travelers described this state from the sixteenth century on.

Al-Nuwayrī and al-MAQRĪZĪ could be considered the principal recorders of these crises, although many other writers from the Mamluk period, both Egyptian and Arab, mentioned them. The importance of the evidence of these two Egyptian historians is due not only to the fact that al-Nuwayrī was contemporary with the events and wrote a history of Egypt up to 1331, the year before his death, and that al-Maqrīzī lived in the aftermath of these crises and reported on their consequences for the Copts, but also because of the high positions they held.

Al-Nuwayrī, who descended from a family of civil servants, became one of the important statesmen of the Mamluk period, a *nāẓir al-jaysh* (secretary of war) and *nāẓir al-diwān* (secretary of state) before becoming one of the favorites of the sultan Muḥammad ibn Qalāwūn, in whose reign the important events occurred. His attitude is identical with that of the amirs and heads of the administration, who did not really want to stop the eruption of the populace against the Copts. Al-Maqrīzī, on the other hand, was born of a family of *qāḍis* (magistrates) and jurists. Before he decided to give up his career to devote himself to writing, he was nominated to the chancellery (Diwān al-Inshā') and then as a *muḥtasib* of Cairo (an official who supervised the application of *shari'ah,* or Islamic law), a position that gave him power to control the non-Muslims. Later he was a preacher in the Mosque of 'Amr and the Madrasah of al-Ḥassan and finally an *imam* and professor of *ḥadīth* (science of the Muslim traditions). He thus belonged to the religious circles that were no less influential in the sociopolitical structure than was the administration and that also played an active role in the events. Thus, it is evident that these two historians belonged to groups that always have been, and still are, very powerful in Egypt—the administration and the clergy.

The political conditions of the Mamluk period and the circumstances of the Muslim world at that time greatly reinforced the role of these two groups and introduced changes in their structure and in their relationship with the population. The administration, which had always been a monolithic body in Egypt under the control of one powerful hand, began to mirror the features of Mamluk military society and the precarious equilibrium of power between the sultan and other high members of the government, such as amirs. There persisted an air of suspicion, rivalry, and dissension between these Mamluks and their armed bands, which were eventually paid only by pillage. The sultan Ibn Qalāwūn himself, to give one example, was forced to leave his throne twice under the pressure of rival amirs. These heads of government were as avid as their bands, which joined the populace attacking people and shops in Cairo. At one time, when the amirs decided to close down some churches under pressure from the rigorists, they agreed to reopen the one or another in return for money paid by Copts or rich gifts sent by Christian sovereigns, as in 1303. They also seized the occasion in the crisis of 1354 to confiscate the properties of the churches. No wonder that corruption and high taxes were among the results of the inability of the Mamluks to direct the country in any orderly way, apart from the military activities. The population suffered from their management, the precarious economy, epidemics, famines, and extra taxes to finance the war. The population naturally paid the price, and the Copts, being the weaker party, had to pay the bigger part. To please the population, the Mamluk government adopted the practice (used by other governors as well) of punishing or imprisoning one of the high officials in the fiscal administration. He usually happened to be a Copt. Such scapegoating gave the population the impression that Coptic officials were responsible for the corruption and thereby intensified anti-Coptic feelings.

There was also an important change in the structure of religious circles. The clergy with its hard elements of rigorist theologians and jurists was no longer the only religious power in the country. In the thirteenth century, Muslim brotherhoods began to flourish in Egypt. They had in common political aims and the habit of exploiting religious or related problems, such as the antagonism between the Shiʻites and the Sunnites. Historians speak about the members of one of these brotherhoods who descended on the streets of Cairo at night profaning the Shiʻites, attacking shops and even soldiers, and inciting the population to revolt against the government. Naturally these brotherhoods were closer to the population than most of the official clergy, which formed, in fact, a part of the administration and was loyal to the government of the Mamluks, who were blamed for the difficulties.

These developments in Egypt coincided with a still greater tension against the Christians in the Muslim world at large, which was being attacked from outside at that time by the Mongols and the Crusaders. Christian elements in the Mongol army were hard on Muslims in Syria, in retaliation for their attacks on churches. The greater danger came at one time from the Crusaders, who debarked twice in the Delta. No wonder a certain hardening of the attitude of Muslims against Christians began to set in as a normal reaction against the pressure of Christian Europe. In Egypt this attitude became a unifying factor. The government proclaimed the country an "Islamic kingdom," in response to the *fatwās* that had already appeared in Egypt against the Christians and the polemic tone of books of jurisprudence by certain rigorists. There appeared in other countries *fatwās* against the Christians. The same attitude characterizes the histories, poems, and other works from that period. But naturally the response was greatest in the lower layers of the population; and in spite of the fact that this movement was a political reaction to consolidate the response of the Muslims to the aggression of Christian Europe and was not publicly or officially declared against the Christians living in Egypt, they were to suffer its consequences. Not everyone would disassociate the Copts, who were always loyal to their masters and who shared a general dislike of the European Christians.

It is interesting to draw the outlines of these crises from the evidence of historians of the Mamluk period. The first important crisis, which al-Maqrīzī calls *waqʻat al-naṣārā*, was that of 1283, in the reign of al-Malik al-Ashraf Khalīl, followed by others in 1300, 1318, 1320, and 1354. No direct explanation in the strict sense of the term is given except for the crisis of 1318, which began when rigorists destroyed a church that had been restored by Copts. But in all these crises, the real reason seems to have been, at least at the beginning, essentially social and economic. The rigorists did not like to see Copts occupying important positions or having authority over Muslims, with even historians complaining melodramatically about Coptic scribes being well dressed or boldly asking people to pay their debts. The sultan, to whom the rigorists complained, asked his subordinates to investigate. He ordered the dismissal of all the Copts engaged in the state administration, and in certain cases those who had not converted to Islam were to be killed or exiled.

The populace applied its own law. Without any interference by officials, who usually lingered around to maintain order at that time, the people attacked the Copts, mistreated them, and pillaged their houses, sometimes killing them and enslaving their women and children. When the situation became alarming because it threatened the whole city, orders were given to stop the eruption. It is difficult to know exactly the dimensions of such attacks or the number of victims; al-Maqrīzī, who did not hide his anti-Coptic attitude, is not free from exaggeration. At any rate, many Copts converted to Islam in each crisis. Those who chose to keep their faith were forced to accept the decision of the consensus of *qādis*, officials, and rigorists to reinforce the harsh prescriptions of the famous COVENANT OF ʻUMAR, which greatly limited their rights, liberties, professional activities, and economic possibilities, and thus pushed them to a marginal state in the society.

But what pleased the rigorists could not be maintained for long. When the excitement subsided, the authorities were usually forced to reintegrate Coptic officials and scribes, because they were badly needed to do the administrative work, which others could not do, especially in fiscal matters. Naturally, they were given the necessary responsibilities to do the job. Once more this angered the rigorists, tensions mounted, and a new crises began to take form. This explains the chain of crises that lasted for a century.

It follows that successive crises gave the rigorists more possibilities to improve their measures. The crisis of 1354, the last one during the reign of the first Mamluk dynasty, was the hardest against Copts. The government decided to confiscate all the properties of the churches in Egypt, over 25,000 *feddans* (acres), to exact more money from them, to consider the state as the only heir to heirless Copts, and not to hire them, even if they converted. But the populace carried out what the government did not proclaim. Al-Maqrīzī spoke about the fires that were kindled to force conversion; churches were destroyed, and the authorities interfered only when a church for non-Coptic Christians was threatened. There was a series of massive conversions all over the country: Traditional popular feasts with Coptic connotations were prohibited. The results of this crisis finally reduced Copts in Egypt to a "lonely minority."

MOUNIR MEGALLY

WAQF, COPTIC, an Arabic term (plural *awqāf*) that has a meaning similar to "estate in mortmain," the inalienable possession of property, or tenure of land, by an ecclesiastical or charitable organization. The *waqf* is a legal system derived from Islamic jurisprudence, which was applied in Egypt after the ARAB CONQUEST (A.D. 641).

Awqāf are of two categories: charitable endowments for religious institutions, churches, monasteries, etcetera; and family endowments made in favor of children and grandchildren of the deceased. According to Egyptian Law No. 48, issued in 1946, a non-Muslim may thus dispose of his property, providing the purpose thereof is compatible with Islamic religious law.

Many Coptic benefactors have disposed of property, agricultural lands, or other possessions, specifying a certain proportion of the usufruct for the poor, a charitable society, a church, monastery, or the patriarchate. Accordingly, the property thus endowed cannot be used for any other purpose, nor can it be liable to confiscation or seizure.

Following the Egyptian revolution of 1952, two laws were promulgated. Law No. 178 limited agricultural land ownership to 200 *feddans* (acres), and compensated the owners or beneficiaries for the excess appropriated by the state. Law No. 180 abrogated family endowmnents, keeping only charitable ones.

The administration of Coptic charitable *awqāf* was for many years the subject of dispute between the COMMUNITY COUNCIL and the abbots of monasteries, who acted as trustees in accordance with the provisions of the relevant *waqf* documents. This dispute was resolved in 1960 during the patriarchate of Pope Cyril VI (1959–1971) by the promulgation of laws No. 264 and 1433, which provided for the establishment of a board to administer these *awqāf*. The board is under the presidency of the pope, with six metropolitans and six competent Coptic laymen as members. It has the legal capacity to receive appropriate compensation from the state in lieu of excess ownership of land, administer all Coptic *awqāf*, supervise their trustees, and apportion their usufruct as it sees fit.

BIBLIOGRAPHY

"Waqfs." In *Encyclopedia of Islam,* Vol. 8, p. 1096. Leiden and New York, 1987.

ADEL AZER BESTAWROS

WARRIORS IN COPTIC ART. The warrior cannot be considered a general theme in Coptic art. The subject is rare and particularized. We must distinguish from it the occasional figure of Alexander on horseback (see BYZANTINE INFLUENCES ON COPTIC ART) and the frequent theme of the mounted saints. The latter, while attesting to a Byzantine iconographic influence, pertains to hagiography rather than to the military arts.

Two pieces are practically all that we can cite; both date from the fourth century. The first, in the Louvre Museum, is the statuette (painted limestone, 18 inches [45 cm] high; 7 inches [18 cm] wide; 5 inches [12.5 cm] thick) of a soldier in the Roman army, without helmet or sword. He is clad in a short tunic, girded by a belt, in which is set a dagger; the torso is protected below a polished gorget by a cuirass of scales, ornamented with a Gorgon's head, as is his shield. His right hand, raised to middle height, is gripped round a space that must have been filled by a throwing weapon in a different material, now lost. His breeches appear to be of coarse sacking. The almond eyes, among other features, show that he is an Egyptian. The hairstyle is contemporary with DIOCLETIAN (284–305).

The other piece, in the Staatliche Museen, Berlin, is, in contrast, a group of soldiers (on horseback and on foot) liberating a fortress (wood, 18 inches [45 cm] high; 9 inches [22 cm] wide; 8 inches [20 cm] thick). Its treatment in very high relief justifies placing it in the area of statuary. It originated from al-Ashmūnayn in Upper Egypt. It could be a late rendering of a biblical battle scene among those sustained during the Exodus. The clothes and weapons are imperial. One of the soldiers carries the labarum with the chi-rho monogram.

Both the treatment and the details and style are characteristic of a period when the recruitment of auxiliaries, but also of legionnaires, was carried on among the citizens of Egypt, from the beginning of the second century. The state of subjection and even oppression to which the Copts were more and more exposed readily explains why the subject was not taken up again later.

BIBLIOGRAPHY

Bourguet, P. du. "A Propos d'un militaire égyptien de la période romaine." *Bulletin de la Société française d'égyptologie* 68 (October 1973):10–16.

Christentum am Nil. Koptische Kunst, Supplement no. 588, fig. 13. Zurich, 1963.

PIERRE DU BOURGUET, S.J.

WATER JUGS AND STANDS. Throughout the Egyptian countryside one often sees water jugs in front of houses, supported either by stands of solid stonework or by wooden tripods. These jugs are filled with water, then carefully plugged so that the contents are protected from insects and dust. The water, which seeps through the porous bottom of the vase, runs into a small receptacle placed on the ground below. This simple and ingenious system serves to assure a supply of fresh water throughout the day. Frequently there is a ladle or a tin mug attached to the edge of the jug for dipping up the water directly. In Arabic this combination of water jug and stand is called *zīr,* a term that originally designated a large pitcher with or without two handles, and that was very narrow at the top.

Water jugs and stand, known in Arabic as *zīr. Courtesy Louvre Museum, Paris.*

The *zīr* represents a very ancient tradition dating from pharaonic times, when each house had a space especially constructed for it. During the Coptic era, it became the custom to erect stands in stone, which were supported by quadrangular legs, for removable jugs. There were also some examples in terra-cotta. The top of the stand was hollowed out with circular cavities arranged so as to hold the vases. These were connected by perforations through which the water ran into a human mask or lion's head sculpted upon the anterior side and serving as an outlet for it. The libation tables from the Greek and Roman eras, themselves derived from the ancient pharaonic sacrificial tables, no doubt foreshadowed the form of the Coptic stands. Like their prototypes, the latter were often decorated by bas-relief sculptures of animals, curling vines, interlacing ribbons, crosses, or inscriptions. The sculpted lion heads, no matter how stylized, trace their origins to the gargoyles of the temples from the late dynastic period. As a symbol of both fertility and resurrection, the lion was related to the Nile flood; as protector of the gods, the lion, in the form of rainstorms and tempests, could destroy the enemy.

BIBLIOGRAPHY

Badawy, A. M. "The Prototype of the Coptic Water-Jug Stand." *Archaeology* 20 (1967):56–61.

Rutschowscaya, M.-H. *La Sculpture copte.* Petits guides des grands musées 84. Paris, 1981.

MARIE-HÉLÈNE RUTSCHOWSCAYA

WATUN, AL-. *See* Press, Coptic.

WĀṬUS, Coptic chanting term, one of the two leading melody types in the music of the Coptic church. This melody type (*laḥn wāṭus*) receives its name from the opening words of the Thursday THEOTOKIA, which begins, "*Pibatos . . .*" ("The bush that Moses saw in the desert").

If the day is one of the last four days of the week, that is, Wednesday to Saturday, the *theotokia* of the day, its PSALI (and similarly the feast *psali*), the LOBSH, the DIFNĀR, and the ṬARḤ are sung to a *laḥn wāṭus.*

The Third HŌS (Ode), the two *psali* following it, the ṬUBḤĀT, and the DOXOLOGIES are, however, sung every day of the week to a *laḥn wāṭus*. Similarly the *aspasmos wāṭus* is to be sung in the anaphora each day.

[*See also:* Music: Description of the Corpus and Musical Practice.]

EMILE MAHER ISHAQ

WEAVERS' COMBS. *See* Woodwork, Coptic.

WEAVERS' SHUTTLES. *See* Woodwork, Coptic.

WEAVING. *See* Textiles: Manufacturing Techniques.

WEDNESDAY AND FRIDAY FASTS. *See* Fasts.

WEIGHTS AND BALANCES. *See* Metalwork, Coptic.

WESSELY, CARL FRANZ JOSEF (1860–1931), Austrian papyrologist. He studied at the University of Vienna. Between 1883 and 1888 he visited Paris, Leipzig, Dresden, and Berlin to study Greek papyri. From 1883 he was an assistant in the Archduke Rainer's collection, which in 1899 was incorporated in the Court Library, Vienna. He became privatdocent in paleography and papyrology at the University of Vienna in 1919. He made many contributions to papyrological literature, his two memoirs on the magical papyri (1888, 1893) being perhaps the best known. His contributions to the field of Coptic studies can be found in W. Kammerer, *A Coptic Bibliography* (1950, 1969).

BIBLIOGRAPHY

Dawson, W. R., and E. P. Uphill. *Who Was Who in Egyptology,* p. 302. London, 1972.

Kammerer, W., comp. *A Coptic Bibliography.* Ann Arbor, Mich., 1950; repr. New York, 1969.

M. L. BIERBRIER

WHITE MONASTERY. *See* Dayr Anbā Shinūdah (Suhāj).

WHITSUNDAY. *See* Feasts, Major: Pentecost.

WHITTEMORE, THOMAS (1871–1950), American archaeologist and Byzantine scholar. He was director of the Byzantine Institute of America, which published the *Coptic Studies in Honor of Walter Ewing Crum* (Boston, 1950). From 1911 to 1926 he was the American representative of the Egypt Exploration Society and excavated in Egypt. From 1930 to 1931 he led an archaeological expedition to the monasteries of Saint Antony and Saint Paul in the Eastern Desert. All its material (notes, copies of the frescoes and inscriptions, photos) is unpublished.

BIBLIOGRAPHY

Dawson, W. R., and E. P. Uphill. *Who Was Who in Egyptology,* p. 303. London, 1972.

Kammerer, W., comp. *A Coptic Bibliography.* Ann Arbor, Mich., 1950; repr. New York, 1969.

Piankoff, A. "Thomas Whittemore." *Les Cahiers coptes* 7–8 (1954):19–20.

MARTIN KRAUSE

WIESMANN, HERMANN (1871–1948), German exegete. He entered the Society of Jesus on 30 September 1890 and was ordained priest on 2 February 1913. Wiesmann was professor of exegesis and of Oriental languages at the Institute of Philosophy and Theology in Frankfurt-am-Main. Besides works on various languages of the Near East, he published some twenty studies on Coptic grammar and vocabulary.

PIERRE DU BOURGUET, S.J.

WIET, GASTON (1887–1971), French Arabist and specialist in Islamic studies. He was professor of Arabic and Turkish at the University of Lyons (1911–1931); director of the Islamic Museum of Art in Cairo (1926–1951); professor of geography and history of the Near East at the Ecole des Langues orientales of Paris (1931–1951); professor of the history of Islamic art at the Ecole du Louvre (1936–1951); and professor of Arabic language and literature at the Collège de France (1951–1960).

BIBLIOGRAPHY

Elisséeff, N. "Gaston Wiet (1887–1971)." *Journal asiatique* 259 (1971):1–9.

Raymond, A. "Bibliographie de l'oeuvre scientifique de M. Gaston Wiet." *Bulletin de l'Institut français d'Archéologie orientale* 59 (1960):9–24.

RENÉ-GEORGES COQUIN

WILCKEN, ULRICH (1862–1944), founder of papyrology in Germany. He studied Egyptology (with Georg Ebers), Oriental languages, and ancient history at Leipzig. In Berlin he became a pupil of Theodor Mommsen, Eduard Meyer, and Adolf Erman. After being lecturer at several German universities, he was professor at Munich (1889–1915) and Berlin (1917–1931). He was a member of many academies in Europe, founded the journal *Archiv für Papyrus-forschung,* and published many papyri, among them *Griechische Ostraka aus Ägypten und Nubien* (2 vols., Leipzig and Berlin, 1899). His *Grundzüge und Chrestomathie der Papyruskunde* (with L. Mitteis, 2 vols., Leipzig and Berlin, 1912) became the handbook of papyrologists.

BIBLIOGRAPHY

Preaux, C. "Ulrich Wilcken." *Chronique d'Egypte* 45/46 (1948):250–56.

MARTIN KRAUSE

WILKE (WILKIUS, WILKINS), DAVID (1685–1745), English clergyman and scholar. He was born of Prussian parentage and was educated at the universities of Berlin, Rome, Vienna, Paris, Amsterdam, Oxford, and Cambridge. In October 1717 he was awarded a doctorate in divinity at Cambridge and ordained in the Church of England. In 1724 he was appointed professor of Arabic at Cambridge. He published many books. Most important and still useful is his *Concilia Magnae Britanniae et Hibernae a Synodo Verulamiensi* A.D. *446 ad Londinensem* A.D. *1717* . . . (4 vols., London, 1737). He was the first scholar who published books of the Coptic Old Testament, among them *Quinque Libri Moysis Prophetae in Lingua Aegyptia ex MSS. Vaticano, Parisiensi et Bodleiano Descripsit ac Latine Vertit* (Five Books of Moses the Prophet in the Egyptian Language from Manuscripts of the Vatican, Paris, and the Bodleian Library Published with Latin Translation; London, 1731), and the Coptic New Testament, *Novum Testamentum Aegyptium Vulgo Copticum ex MSS. Bodleianis Descripsit, cum Vaticanis et Parisiensibus Contulit, et in Latinum Sermonem Convertit* (The Egyptian or Coptic New Testament from Manuscripts in the Bodleian Library, Collated with Manuscripts in the Vatican and in Paris, and Published with Latin Translation; Oxford, 1716). A part of his correspondence with M. V. La Croze has been published (La Croze, *Thesauri Epistolia Lacroziani.* 3 vols. in 2, ed. J. L. Uhlius, Leipzig, 1742–1746).

BIBLIOGRAPHY

Douglas, D. C. *English Scholars.* pp. 276–84. London, 1939.
Quatremère, E. M. *Recherches critiques et historiques sur la langue et la littérature de l'Egypte,* pp. 80–83. Paris, 1808.

MARTIN KRAUSE

WISSA WASSEF (1873–1931), Egyptian politician. He was born in Ṭahṭā in Upper Egypt. In 1880 his family moved to Cairo, where Wissa finished his secondary education in foreign language schools, which then were numerous in Cairo. His achievement won him a scholarship to France in 1889. In Paris he was admitted to the Ecole normale primaire de Versailles. Three years later he joined the Ecole normale supérieure de St. Cloud, where in 1894 he obtained the teaching qualifications from these schools.

Back in Egypt, he became a teacher of science at Ra's al-Tīn School in Alexandria. An ardent patriot, he watched the heavy hand applied by the British colonial administration as all schools came under the supervision of British inspectors. Harassed by one of the inspectors, the young Wissa decided to study law as a means of combating British policies toward education. In the summer of 1902 he departed for France to take his exams. Consequently, he resigned his post as teacher and was the first Egyptian to be admitted as a lawyer before the Mixed Tribunal in Cairo.

In 1904 he started publishing articles in English in *The Egyptian Gazette,* established a private law practice, and joined the faculty of the French School of Law in Cairo. In 1925 he resigned from the Mixed Tribunal and devoted himself entirely to politics.

Wissa Wassef joined the Egyptian Nationalist Party in 1906, inspired by the leader Muṣṭafā Kāmil, whose ideas and ideals he shared. He was the first Egyptian Christian to join the party and was followed by a colleague, Murqus Ḥannā, later to become one of its executive members. He was stigmatized by the Coptic community for joining a party that advocated allegiance to the Ottoman empire, an unacceptable choice to the Copts, whose rights had been completely ignored by the Sublime Porte (government offices in Istanbul during the reign of the sultan).

On 16 June 1908, in a series of articles in the organ of the Nationalist Party, Shaykh ʿAbd al-ʿAzīz Jāwīsh attacked the Copts, accusing them of considering "Islam a foreign religion in its own country." Wissa Wassef and Murqus Ḥannā resigned from the party as religious tensions rose. The assassination of Boutros Ghālī Pasha by a fanatic Muslim led to the convening of the COPTIC CONGRESS OF ASYŪṬ in March 1911.

When the Wafd Party, headed by SAʿD ZAGHLŪL, came into existence soon after the armistice in 1918, the Copts sought to be represented in it, and the choice fell on Wissa Wassef, who declined in favor of Wāṣif Bouṭros Ghālī. Differences with the British colonialists soon led to the exile of Saʿd Zaghlūl and members of his party to Malta. Wissa Wassef was recruited as counselor to the group because of his oratorical skills, his perfect French, and his thorough knowledge of the "Egyptian question." Following that meeting, he was unanimously proclaimed full member of the Wafd and thereafter actively participated in the struggle against British rule. When Saʿd Zaghlūl was deported to the Seychelles for a second term of exile (1921–1923), Wissa Wassef along with Wāṣif Ghālī took control of the Wafd and advocated Egypt's boycott of all British goods.

In response British authorities incarcerated Wissa Wassef. After being released a few days later, he again incited the population to fight the British occupiers, whereupon he was arrested once more, brought before a military court, and sentenced to death. The sentence was later commuted to seven years in prison and a fine of five thousand pounds. He in fact served ten months and paid a fine of fifteen hundred pounds. His liberation, together with the return of Saʿd Zaghlūl and other detainees from the Seychelles, relaxed the tension between British authorities and Egyptian nationalists. Martial law was abrogated and the constitution promulgated on 19 April 1923 was accepted by the Wafd. Elections gave the Wafd a landslide victory and Wissa Wassef became deputy of Maṭariyyat al-Manzalah in the Delta, where he owned land. The proposal of his nomination as minister of education was rejected by King FOUAD on the ground that a Christian could not head an Islamic institution such as Al-Azhar University.

After the assassination of the sirdar, Parliament was closed and new elections ordered. The Wafd was once again victorious and, although Saʿd Zaghlūl was rejected as prime minister by the British, he won the presidency of the Chamber of Deputies. Serving with him as vice-presidents were Wissa Wassef and MUSṬAFĀ AL-NAḤḤĀS. Wissa Wassef championed many social, educational, and cultural projects.

When Saʿd Zaghlūl died on 24 August 1927, Wissa Wassef was nominated as his successor as speaker of the House.

Wissa Wassef decided to pursue the cause of an independent Egypt internationally. In August 1928 he went to Berlin via Paris, despite obstacles set up by the government of Egypt to stop him and the group he headed from attending the twenty-fifth Inter-parliamentary Conference. This was an occasion for him to attack the intolerable meddlings of the British colonialists in Egypt's parliamentary affairs. Subsequent to his speech of 24 August, it was unanimously decided to call that day the Day of the Oppressed Nations. The following day, 25 August 1928, an act condemning suspension of parliamentary governments was signed by representatives of thirty-eight nations, including Britain. That day was called the Egyptian Day. At the conference that followed in London in July 1930, the secretary-general of the Parliamentary Union emphasized international concern over parliamentary freedoms, citing Egypt's stand at the 1928 Berlin conference as an example of success.

Some sort of stabilization seemed to follow with the coming to power of the Labour Party in London in May 1929, which authorized new elections in Egypt. The Wafd won by a landslide—230 of the 235 seats—and the opening parliamentary session on 11 June 1930 gave a vote of confidence to Wissa Wassef, reinstating him with a comfortable majority as president of the Chamber of Deputies. In thanking his colleagues, he made a plea to all patriots to join hands in working toward national unity.

These events, however, met with opposition from King Fouad causing Naḥḥās Pasha to resign. Sidqī Pasha was nominated in his stead and issued new decrees restricting parliamentary activities. When protests followed, Sidqī Pasha ordered the doors of Parliament to be locked with chains. Wissa Wassef was put under house arrest. Outmaneuvering the guards around his house, however, he reached the Parliament buildings, where members of the House were already gathered. He ordered the guards to break the chains, which had been installed in violation of the constitution, denouncing this step as illegal interference by Sidqī Pasha. He then read the decrees issued by Sidqī Pasha to the assembled members of Parliament, who renewed their allegiance to the constitution. Wassef then called a meeting of Parliament for 21 July. This won him the epithet the "Chain-breaker."

The situation in Egypt was reaching an explosive state, as was made apparent by Wissa Wassef in the Interparliamentary Conference held in London on 14 July 1930, as well as at a meeting of the League for Human Rights on July 30 of that year in Paris. Meanwhile, a new constitution issued in October 1930 without a referendum was denounced by the Wafd and the Liberal Movement, who decided to boycott the elections of May 1931. Violent demonstrations followed these events.

On 27 May 1931, Wissa Wassef died of food poisoning, said by some to have been intentional. His funeral was attended by over a million people, proof of the popularity he had gained.

[*See also:* Political Parties.]

BIBLIOGRAPHY

Abd' al-Raḥman al-Rāfiʿī. *Thawrat Sanat 1919.* Cairo, 1946.

Ahmad, J. M. *The Intellectual Origins of Egyptian Nationalism.* London and New York, 1960; repr., 1968.

Darwin, J. *Britain, Egypt and the Middle East: Imperial Policy in the Aftermath of War, 1918–1922.* London, 1961.

Ghali, M. B. *The Policy of Tomorrow.* Washington, 1953.

Muḥammad Ahmad Amin. *Dirāsāt fī Wathā'iq Thawrat 1919.* Cairo, 1963.

Quraishi, Z. M. *Liberal Nationalism in Egypt: Rise and Fall of the Wafd.* Allahabad, 1967.

Rifaat, M. *The Awakening of Modern Egypt.* Lahore, 1976.

Tignor, R. *Modernization and British Rule in Egypt, 1882–1914.* Princeton, N.J., 1966.

CÉRÈS WISSA WASSEF

WOIDE, CHARLES GODFREY (1725–1790),

Polish Oriental scholar. He studied at the universities of Frankfurt an der Oder and Leiden, and was ordained in the Socinian church in Lissa, Poland. At Leiden in 1750 he copied the Coptic dictionary of LA CROZE. Christian Scholtz taught him Bohairic. In the libraries of Paris he studied Oriental manuscripts for four months in 1773 and 1774. He learned the Sahidic dialect by himself, and in 1775 he edited La Croze's *Lexicon Aegyptiaco-Latinum,* which Scholtz had revised, adding notes and indexes. After reducing Scholtz's *Grammatica Aegyptiaca (Utriusque Dialecti quam Breviavit, Illustravit, Edidit)* from four volumes into one and adding the Sahidic portion, he was appointed assistant librarian of the British Museum. He also contributed to the facsimile edition of the *Novum Testamentum Graecum codice Ms. Alexandrino* (London, 1786), and in the appendix of this publication (1799) he published fragments of the New Testament in the Sahidic dialect, mostly from manuscripts at Oxford.

BIBLIOGRAPHY

Courtney, W. P. "Woide, Charles Godfrey." *In Dictionary of National Bibliography,* pp. 289–90. London, 1950.

Quatremère, E. *Recherches critiques et historiques sur la langue et la littérature de l'Egypte,* pp. 94–102. Paris, 1808.

MARTIN KRAUSE

WOMEN'S RELIGIOUS COMMUNITIES.

From the earliest years in the history of Christianity, there have existed communities of virgins, who dedicated their lives to the service of the Lord, free from all family ties. However, in Egypt some young women preferred to remain with their families while performing such sacred duties toward others. One of the most prominent examples is the fourth-century virgin who offered her abode to shelter Saint ATHANASIUS the Apostolic during one of his exiles. She herself carried his missives to his church following in Alexandria.

Other examples of women who selected the monastic way of life, in what may be described as nunneries, existed even earlier during the ages of Christian persecutions. One of the most cherished examples among the Copts is the story of the rise and fall of Sitt (Lady) Dimyānah (see DIMYĀNAH AND HER FORTY VIRGINS). She was the daughter of Marcus, Roman governor of the province of Burullus in the Delta, a Christian who recanted under pressure during the reign of Emperor DIOCLETIAN (284–305) but later declared his adherence to the faith and was martyred.

His daughter Dimyānah had refused all proposals of marriage and decided to lead a life of Christian asceticism in the wasteland near the city of Damietta. Forty devout virgins followed her. Her father built for her what later became a nunnery. Eventually, like her father, she, along with all her companions, suffered martyrdom under Diocletian. Diocletian had in vain offered her safety if only she would offer incense and a libation to his image. The site of her retirement and martyrdom is still a favorite center of pilgrimage among the Copts. Her memory is celebrated by them on 12–20 May; curiously, the Copts are joined by Muslims in these national festivities. Another prominent example is that of Saint Catherine of Alexandria, a highly lettered young woman whose martyrdom occurred in 307 during the persecution of Maximinus. The monastery bearing her name on Mount Sinai is said to have been erected by Justinian (327–365) on the spot to which her body had presumably been carried by the angels of the Lord (see MOUNT SINAI MONASTERY OF SAINT CATHERINE). This monastery has survived as a center of enlightenment and sanctity.

When Saint ANTONY THE GREAT, founder of monastic rule, decided to retire to the Eastern Desert in the late third century, he entrusted his young sister to a community of pious virgins in Middle Egypt. Saint PACHOMIUS (c. 290–348), father of Coptic cenobitism, is said to have established a convent for his sister Miryam, who was joined by four hundred sisters. That convent was situated about twelve miles from his own monastery at TABENNĒSĒ, near the city of Qinā. Pachomius also founded another convent at al-Fakhūrah, one mile from a monastery near Idfū. He appointed a monk of mature age and sanctity for the guidance of each of those foundations. As a rule, the sites for convents were selected in the neighborhood of cities and villages within the Nile Valley, and not in the remote desert wilderness where monastic establishments were favored.

The biography of Anbā Maqrophios (Dayr al-Suryān manuscript 268) enumerates a series of nunneries in the sixth century. Other convents appeared later in Lower Egypt, though a precise survey of them is hard to make because of a lack of sources.

Records from the later Middle Ages reveal the existence of nunneries. In the fifteenth century the Muslim historian of the Copts al-MAQRĪZĪ mentioned four convents at ḤĀRIT AL-RŪM and ḤĀRIT ZUWAYLAH in Cairo as well as Saint Barbara and the Church of the Virgin known as al-MU'ALLAQAH in Old Cairo. In the nineteenth century, the Coptic historian ʿAbd-al-Masīḥ al-Masʿūdī mentions five of these institutions: two at Ḥārit Zuwaylah, and one at Ḥārit al-Rūm, together with DAYR MĀR JIRJIS and DAYR ABŪ SAYFAYN (Saint Mercurius) in Old Cairo. Those attached to Saint Barbara's church and al-Muʿallaqah have disappeared. The following six convents have survived to our day:

1. Dayr Sitt Dimyānah in Bilqās, Gharbiyyah Province
2. Dayr Mār Jirjis in Old Cairo
3. Dayr al-Amīr Tadrus al-Shūṭbī (Convent of Saint Theodore) in Ḥārit al-Rūm, near the Church of Our Lady
4. The Convent of the Holy Virgin Mary at Ḥārit Zuwaylah
5. DAYR AL-BANĀT (Convent of Virgins) in the vicinity of the Church of Saint Mercurius in DAYR ABŪ SAYFAYN
6. a convent founded in the name of Saint George at Ḥārit Zuwaylah in the old Coptic quarter of the city of Cairo.

Bishop Andarāwus of Damietta (d. 1978) started a female religious group at the sanctuary of Sitt Dimyānah. Independent groups of nuns, dedicated but without affiliation and often living at home, lead contemplative lives and participate in services. Others volunteer for mundane activities such as baking bread, cleaning house, or serving in orphanages and benevolent institutions.

Since 1965, in the city of BANĪ SUEF, there has arisen the Daughters of Saint Mary, a growing community whose members are consecrated in two stages. The first stage, that of novice, is not binding for life, and during it, a member can leave at will. The second stage is that of nunhood, and its occupant, once consecrated, is committed to service for her whole life. These nuns render service in senior citizen homes in both Banī Suef and Cairo. They also offer help in clinics and nurseries. The order has established ecumenical relations with similar Roman Catholic and Protestant institutions in other parts of the world.

BIBLIOGRAPHY

Atiya, A. S. *A History of Eastern Christianity.* London, 1968.

Burmester, O. H. E. *A Guide to the Ancient Coptic Churches.* Cairo, 1956.

Meinardus, O. *Christian Egypt, Ancient and Modern.* Cairo, 1977.

ATHANASIUS, BISHOP OF BANĪ SUEF AND AL-BAHNASĀ

WOOD SPECIES. *See* Woodwork, Coptic.

WOODWORK, COPTIC, functional objects and sculpture made of wood in Egypt from the fourth century into the Middle Ages. By virtue of its geological past, Egypt originally had plentiful and varied supplies of wood, but it was rapidly used. Shortages were already evident in the pharaonic period. Ptolemaic rulers put into operation a policy of afforestation, and they regulated the felling of trees. These measures were continued by Byzantine emperors and Arab governors. According to the forestry zones drawn up in the second half of the twelfth century by Ibn Mammatī, general controller of the Egyptian ministries, the wooded resources of the country were in the regions of al-Bahnasā, al-Ashmūnayn, Asyūṭ, Akhmīm, and Zūs. These regions probably corresponded to the wooded regions of earlier periods.

Nevertheless, the shortage of wood was accentuated from the fourth to the seventh century, probably owing to the general impoverishment of the country under Byzantine rule. Afforestation declined along the coast, which meant that timber had to be sought farther and farther inland. The luxury trade, using imported wood, was essentially centered in Alexandria. Inland areas had to depend on local supplies.

The collection of Coptic woodwork in the Louvre Museum, Paris, is the only one that has been systematically studied, by the Centre Forestier Tropical. The relatively large number of objects (380 approximately) and their variety provide much information.

Kinds of Wood

Native Species. Tamarisk (*Tamarix* sp.) was found in most areas. It was used for decorative friezes or objects (for personal use such as kohl pots and seals). The Egyptian sycamore (*Ficus sycomorus*), next in importance, could be carved or painted. Acacia (*Acacia* sp.) yielded big beams from which lintels with carving and inscriptions were made. The kariti, or butter tree (*Vitellaria paradoxa*), and a variety called *nilotica*, supplied wood for such objects as friezes and combs. The jujube tree (*Ziziphus* sp.), very common in Egypt, was used especially in the Copto-Arab period. Willow (*Salix* sp.) and carob (*Ceratonia siliqua*) were seldom used except in some friezes and a lintel. Fragments of reeds, in place of rushes in the Greco-Roman period, were used to make calami (reed pens), hundreds of which have been brought to light.

Imported Species. A number of woods were imported from the Middle East. Pine (*Pinus* sp.) was used to carve some friezes; beech (*Fagus sylvatica*), cedar (*Cedrus* sp.), spruce (*Picea orientalis carr.*), lemon wood (*Citrus* sp.), and oak (*Quercus* sp.) were used for other pieces. Box (*Buxus sempervirens*), which grows in Europe, western Asia, and North Africa, was already being used in pharaonic times (perhaps in the *longifolia* variety) to make small precious objects such as statuettes and boxes. Olive wood (*Olea europaea*) was used for such objects as three seals and a box lid. Ebony (*Diospyros*), whose name is derived from the Egyptian word *hebeny*, probably had to be imported from tropical Africa through Ethiopia and Nubia. It is attested in a comb from Idfū. Only one species from a more distant region, jacaranda from India (*Dalbergia latifolia*), was used, in a small panel from the tenth to twelfth century.

Craftsmen

The activity of craftsmen in general and in the domain of work in wood in particular is difficult to discern because of the lack of adequate epigraphic and archaeological documentation. In addition, the subject is complex, including carpenters, joiners, cabinetmakers, and sculptors. Each category of craftsman, in fact, demanded specific technical and economic structures in the choice of materials as well as in space for workshops and types of clientele. Only some carpenters' names have come down to us on stelae, one of which, preserved in the Coptic Museum in Cairo, presents an adze placed under an aedicula (shrine) with a pediment. Another stela in the same museum mentions a carpenter priest. Papyri tell us that Dayr Epiphanius at Thebes had established contracts with carpenters for the repair of a cart and the construction of a door.

The inscription situated on the left upright of the entrance to the south church at Dayr Apa Apollo, Bāwīṭ, exhorts the pilgrim to pray for the soul of Joseph the sculptor. Among the rich sculptures in stone are mingled pieces of carved woodwork, for which Joseph was perhaps also responsible.

Techniques

Carpentry. Traces of tools—saws, chisels, knives, and drills—are numerous on the surface of wooden objects, when, of course, they have not been carefully polished down. Egypt has yielded a good number of tools in bronze or iron, dating for the most part from the Roman period, whose forms have endured to the present day. They include hammers, graving tools, augers driven by a bow, gimlets, planes, saws, and axes. Coptic stelae sometimes mention the dead man's profession as a carpenter; one of them, preserved in Cairo, offers the image of an adze between two ankhs.

The carpenter's work consists not only of squaring and preparing pieces of wood but also fitting them together. Mortises and tenons were the most common means of assembling panels for furniture and architecture. But nails were used to fasten veneers, as, for example, on a lintel in the Louvre, in which two panels in tamarisk wood were nailed to the main beam of acacia. Smaller objects in general were held together by pegs or nails.

In place of assembly by mortises and tenons, carpenters frequently used grooves and tongues, a system that allowed a strengthening of the whole object. A coffer in the Coptic Museum in Cairo is formed of carved panels joined by this method and reinforced by tenons and pegs. Doors such as a ninth-century one from Dayr Apa Apollo in the Louvre and doors of churches in Cairo were also constructed in this fashion. The casing is formed of laths connected by mortises and tenons, enclosing panels that may or may not be decorated.

Screens and balustrades, such as those in the Coptic Museum, Cairo, and the State Museum of Berlin, appear as veritable trellises, formed of laths mitered together and often covered with incised geometric motifs. This type of structure, which appeared long before in windows and furniture, was common in the Arab period under the name *mashrabiyyah*. Pulpits, doors, and furniture were made of polygonal panels joined by grooves and tongues or mortises and tenons mounted in a framework or resting on a frame. The Louvre possesses two square twelfth-century panels composed of mortised hexagonal elements, covered with arabesques forming a Greek cross. The underlying frame serves to integrate the hexagonal elements.

Small rounded utilitarian objects, such as ointment boxes, kohl tubes, or castanets, in the pharaonic period were shaped by rotation by means of a drill and bow. The introduction of the lathe in the Hellenistic period meant that they could be turned more efficiently. Turning was also used for balusters. Balusters strengthened at each end by tenons inserted into the uprights of the frame were used to make balustrades, such as are in the Coptic Museum, Cairo, or important pieces of furniture. Balusters sawn lengthwise in two or four pieces were incorporated into *mashrabiyyah* screens, to be seen from the front, or attached with nails or pegs to furniture, such as the fifth-century coffin of Aurelius Colluthus from Antinoopolis, in the Royal Museum of Art and History, Brussels.

Owing to its scarcity, wood must have been very frequently reused, although that is difficult to detect. Two weaver's combs preserved in the Louvre bear the marks of reuse and of ancient repairs, evidence of the carpenter's daily work. The surfaces of the breaks were pierced with mortises to take the pegs. One of them was even reinforced at the level of the handle by two plaques of bronze fastened by rivets.

Sculpture. Although carving in the round played practically no role in Coptic sculpture in stone or wood, it was employed for making small, everyday objects such as toy dolls or horsemen or figurines of a magical or apotropaic character, numerous examples of which are preserved in the Louvre.

Relief sculpture, however, was important. Examples of very high relief are a fifth-century console with Daniel among the lions and a fifth-century piece showing the capture of a city, both in the State Museum of Berlin. A vigorously modeled low relief adorns the fourth-century lintel of the Church of al-Mu'allaqah in thc Coptic Museum, Cairo. Friezes of scroll pattern from Dayr Apa Apollo and Saqqara, from the sixth to eighth century, are low reliefs on a flat plane. Sunken carving (intaglio) forms the figures and inscriptions on seals.

Reliefs were achieved by cutting away the background to reveal the motif, which might be further carved in relief, as on a sixth-century lintel in the Louvre, or left on a flat plane, as on a sixth-century comb showing Daniel in the State Museum of Berlin. The flat-plane technique was very often combined with engraving, which allowed the marking of details. Engraving was equally used by itself for decorating such small objects as combs, spindles, and boxes.

Combs were frequently decorated with latticelike cutwork. The central zone presents silhouettes of people or animals with schematized angular profiles. Interlacing work or geometrical tracery treated in network was employed in veneers, as on a sixth-century lintel from Dayr Apa Apollo in the Louvre.

Decoration on Wood. The majority of the architectural sculptures were intended to be enhanced by painting. Traces of color on many reliefs in stone may still be seen, for example on the south church of Dayr Apa Apollo. Numerous panels and friezes in wood present either the remains of a whitish wash or important colored areas showing black, blue, green, ocher, red, and rose, as in a fifth-century Virgin of the Annunciation, in the Louvre, and a fifth-to-sixth-century frieze in the State Museum of Berlin.

Certain precious objects were covered with a veneer of ivory, mother-of-pearl, wood, metal, leather, or glass. Some games of the Roman or Coptic period were covered with ivory rods adorned with "pointed circles," a motif much used by the Copts that goes back to the Middle Empire. A sixth-century box for weights in the Louvre is veneered with cut leaves of copper fixed by rivets, showing putti (cupids) holding a medallion occupied by an eagle and adorned with geometric motifs or engraved inscriptions. Another box for weights in the Louvre, from the seventh to eighth century, presents marquetry decoration in which triangular motifs alternate in precious wood and in ivory. There are also combs encrusted with lozenges of glass, ebony, or ivory.

Veneers were also used on elements fitted into pieces of furniture or architecture. Examples include wooden plaques whose ivory veneer is ornamented with arabesques in Copto-Arabic style and a lintel in the Louvre bearing in the center an ivory cross placed between an alpha and an omega set in a band of lead.

A curious object from Antinoopolis preserved in the Louvre, whose purpose is still unknown, bears a geometric motif made of inlays of wood and ivory, surmounted by an aedicula with an ivory pediment sheltering a cross in mother-of-pearl. A reliquary cross in the Coptic Museum, Cairo, has a wooden core covered with a band of cut leather, which allows studs of colored glass to show through; one of the studs is adorned with a painted, haloed head.

The majority of these veneers, whatever the material, as well as the body of the objects (the combs in particular) are often marked with series of "pointed circles," either engraved or hollowed out. The *Daremberg-Saglio Dictionary of Greek and Roman Archaeology* affirms, with reference to a Roman disk in bronze preserved in the National Archaeological Museum of Umbria, Perugia, that this motif was probably achieved with the aid of a trephine (instrument for cutting out circular sections). The motif was probably executed with the same tool in all materials. Numerous tubes and pots for kohl, and also castanets, in turned wood, frequently carry a simple decoration of incised concentric circles.

Functional Objects

Functional wooden objects range from practical implements, such as spindles and weight boxes, to religious items such as crosses, to games and implements for grooming.

Altar. The only surviving ancient Coptic altar in wood (pine) dating from the fourth to the sixth century, comes from the Church of Abū Sarjah (Saint Sergius) in Old Cairo and is now in the Coptic Museum, Cairo. Rectangular in plan, its sides are composed of arcading (three arches on the long sides, one on the short) resting on small twisted columns with Corinthian capitals. The intercolumniations are surmounted by spandrels in the form of shells enclosing the cross; the covings are filled with foliage. The angle ties are carved in relief with vegetable motifs and animals and with crosses inscribed in crowns. The external uprights of the altar are covered with scroll patterns, a large part of which is damaged.

Altar from the Church of St. Sergius (Abū Sarjah). Pine wood ornamented with crosses, birds and shells. Fourth century. *Courtesy Coptic Museum, Cairo.*

Boxes and Caskets. Food, cosmetics, jewelry, relics, and implements were commonly stored in boxes or caskets. Their form and decoration were naturally determined by their contents. It is not always casy, however, to ascertain the function of some of these containers. A large casket from Kom Ishqāw in Middle Egypt, preserved in the Coptic Museum, is supported by four uprights adorned with wavy lines punctuated by pearls and with a row of hearts. Each face consists of six panels fitted into one another, as well as into the uprights, by grooves and tongues, fastened by pegs. Only one side is adorned with carving in low relief. The lower horizontal mounting is bordered with a row of hearts and a frieze of wavy lines alternating with pearls, interrupted by a row of leaves alternating with pearls. The central panel portrays a lion leaping in foliage, surmounted by a hare. The narrower side panels are edged by friezes of wavy lines with pearls and by leaves alternating with pearls, while those at the ends are occupied by lozenges and triangles filled with leaves and half-leaves. Unfortunately, the top and the lid of the casket have disappeared.

Several of these large caskets in the Coptic Museum, particularly sumptuous and covered with ivory plaques with engraved decoration of profane or mythological scenes, were intended to be offered as wedding presents.

Other smaller caskets, also in the Coptic Museum, probably served to keep toilet articles in order. They take the form of rectangular boxes, with or without feet, with hinged or sliding lids. Their decoration consists of rods and veneers of ivory simply adorned with incised "pointed circles." Some of these examples, in the State Museum of Berlin and the Louvre, are cut from a single piece of wood and are provided with a sliding lid engraved with a cross.

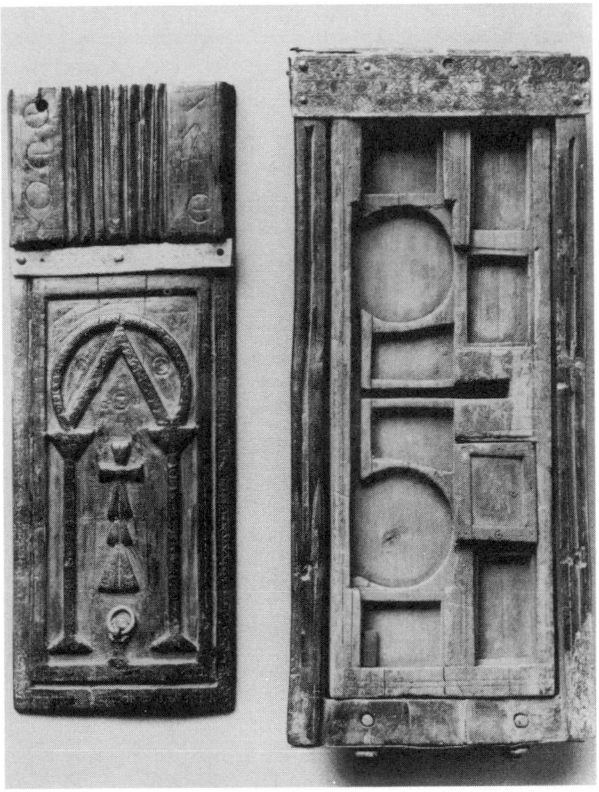

Small casket with sliding lid engraved with a cross. *Courtesy Louvre Museum, Paris.*

Two small boxes, one ornamented with "pointed circles" in the Coptic Museum, Cairo, the other decorated with a stylized scroll pattern in the State Museum of Berlin, were provided with sockets containing coloring materials. In their present state, it is difficult to say whether this was paint or cosmetics. As a general rule, however, rouge and kohl were preserved in small round boxes or cases (see below).

A series of boxes, of very specific forms, served to protect implements for weighing. A very fine example described by Flinders Petrie (1927) consists of two parts: the body of the box, cut from a solid block, and a removable board intended to offer a second level for arranging. These two parts are hollowed out to form square sockets containing weights, coins, and tweezers, as well as into circular and rectilinear hollows exactly fitting the form of a balance: the beam, the vertical rod with ring for suspension, and two scale pans in copper.

Five of these boxes for weights, still holding part of their contents, are preserved in University College, London. The sliding lids are adorned with "pointed circles" either grouped or in rows. These, like the five preserved in the Louvre and the one in the Cairo Museum, show that variation could occur: square, rectangular, or round hollows, sometimes provided with a diminutive lid; a system for fastening, with or without a copper lock; inscriptions invoking God or the saints. On the finest examples, the lid is adorned with a cross in relief, sometimes housed within an aedicula and dotted with "pointed circles." One of the examples in the Louvre has inlays of wood and ivory. The ends of several boxes in the Louvre are covered with veneers of copper with engraved or carved decoration: interlacing work, wavy lines, and two winged putti supporting a crown containing an eagle. A box of the sixth to seventh century in the Metropolitan Museum of Art, New York, is quite original not only for its oval form but also for its system of fastening, on the long sides by means of hinges and a metal clasp.

Liturgical objects and relics were generally deposited in coffers. An example found in the tower of Dayr al-Suryān, Wādī al-Naṭrūn, but certainly from the choir of the Church of al-ʿAdhrā' in this monastery, is rectangular and rests upon four small, shaped feet. The ebony body (early tenth century) presents on its long sides Christ and the Virgin surrounded by holy personages standing under arcades. Originally inlays of ivory, the greater part of which has disappeared, filled out the silhouettes, as did the inscriptions identifying them. The pine lid (twelfth or thirteenth century), equipped with

Vessel likely used to hold the flask containing the wine used for the liturgy. Wood. *Courtesy Coptic Museum, Cairo.*

bronze clasps and hinges, is adorned with two square panels in a frame of scroll patterns. One contains a Coptic cross, the other a bird; they alternate with two friezes of fretwork and crosses.

A large sixth-century casket preserved in the State Museum of Berlin belongs to the same category. Square in form and resting on four square feet, it is surmounted by a flat lid adorned in encaustic painting with a bust of the young Christ the Savior placed in a medallion. The sides present, two by two, the four archangels and the saints Luke, Thomas, Faustus, and Cosmas. It is possible that other painted panels, now isolated, in the Coptic Museum, Cairo, and the Dumbarton Oaks Collection, Washington, D.C., belonged to this type of casket.

Coffins. The mode of burial varied in accordance with the wealth of the deceased. This fact is substantiated by A. Gayet (1902) in his description of the necropolises of Antinoopolis. Most of the bodies were laid out on a plank or even placed directly on the sand, without any protection. A few senior officials, however, who had a vault constructed or excavated, were sometimes able to have a wooden coffin made for themselves. The traces of plain, undecorated coffins have not attracted the attention of excavators. A few rare, decorated pieces—very fragmentary, unfortunately—have been preserved.

The most important coffin remains are those of Colluthus previously cited. All that is left is one side consisting of three superimposed panels probably held together by mortise-and-tenon joints. Each of the two lower panels is decorated by a row of demi-balusters attached to uprights framing undecorated, square areas. The topmost panel, shaped like a pediment, has its center hollowed out in the shape of a large demirosette flanked by two rows of vertical tongues of wood.

The Louvre has four other fragments of coffins from Antinoopolis, one of which, according to Gayet, was that of Thaïs, famous mistress of Alexander the Great. The one surviving side, in a poor state of preservation, consists of three frame panels enclosing incised vegetable motifs. The other three fragments, in even worse condition, are also likely to be remains of coffins. One is decorated with an ankh engraved with crosshatched motifs, with a Greek cross in its loop. The second, which has a labarum (imperial Roman standard), was probably recut at a later date according to the form of the labarum; it still retains fragments of material stuck to the edge and its underside. The third preserves a two-line inscription preceded by a cross with branched ends, which reads "May God establish . . ."

Gayet also described a coffin lid with the monogram ⲭ ⲙ ⲅ drawn in ink on it.

The scantiness of these remains clearly demonstrates that the most common custom, even for the well-to-do, was to consign bodies to the desert sand. Indeed, at the time of his excavations in 1899–1900, Gayet wrote, "Exceptionally the bodies of Colluthus and Tisoia had been put in coffins, the only such interment I have encountered among about ten thousand others" (p. 133).

The painted wooden sarcophagus discovered at Qarārah, Middle Egypt, during the excavations of 1913–1914 by the University of Heidelberg poses a tricky problem of dating—either the fourth to fifth century or the eighth century. It is exceptional not just because of its painted decoration but also because of its excellent state of preservation and its form, the face of the deceased being positioned under one end of the lid, with a little saddleback roof over it. There is a decorative foliated scroll around the base, while the shorter sides of the roof and lid are studded with medallions enclosing Umayyad-style arabesques. The two longer sides of the roof display a peacock standing upright with a pearl necklace in its beak, a detail betraying unmistakable Sassanid influence. Since Muslims do not use coffins, the complete absence of any kind of Christian symbolism makes it more difficult to pass any judgment on the identity of the owner of such a magnificent sarcophagus.

Crosses. The existence of wooden crosses, marking the position of tombs, does not seem to have been noticed by the excavators a the time of the clearing of the necropolises, for example, at Antinoopolis or Bāwīṭ. These fragile objects were probably for the most part destroyed or carried off. Some of them, however, still preserved in museums, quite certainly marked tombs. The foot, without decoration but sometimes provided with perforations, must have been driven directly into the ground or nailed to a transverse beam to hold it more firmly.

The only decoration consists of stylized florets in low relief at the end of the branches and in the center of the crosses when they adopt the Latin form, as do those in the State Museum of Berlin, or of engraved geometrical motifs when they take the form of the ankh, as do those in the Coptic Museum, Cairo.

A cross in the State Museum of Berlin, still in a good state of preservation, carries a long epitaph, engraved on each of the branches and the foot, consecrated to the blessed Theodorus, who died in 799. One branch mentions a name (perhaps) accompanied by the sign "amen"; the other branch mentions the name of Jeremiah, which is preceded by "amen" and the name of Jesus Christ.

A stela in the form of a cross, preserved in the Louvre and recalling the ankh, is covered by an inscription engraved on the principal face and the two side faces: it belonged to a certain Pantoleus, who died in 1025. Three crosses of the same type, unfortunately fragmentary, were given to the museum of Périgueux by J. Clédat in 1904. Their provenance is Bāwīṭ, although one of them was purchased at Akhmīm. Only the uprights are still in part preserved. They carry inscriptions, the most complete of which invokes Apa Ramoun, Saint Apollo, Saint Phib, and Saint Anub.

A reliquary cross of Latin form in the Coptic Museum in Cairo, deriving from Akhmīm, is formed of a core of wood covered in leather. On the branches of the cross and on the foot, square spaces marked off by gilded stamping are occupied by alveoli (hollows) set with glass cabochons, alternately circular and quadrangular. At the foot of the cross, the leather widens to reveal a medallion adorned with a painted head, with a halo, wearing a beard and dark blue hair. The Coptic Museum possesses numerous other crosses of various forms and sizes. They are engraved with representations of angels or saints. Sometimes Christ appears in the form of a portrait located within a medallion or as crucified, a late iconography.

Bolt in the shape of a cross. Wood. Tenth century. *Courtesy Coptic Museum, Cairo.*

A pendant in the Louvre in the form of the ankh must have been used in a collar or bracelet. It was probably hung by means of a cord through the perforation wrought in the ring.

Doors. Because of the scarcity and cost of wood, few ordinary people could afford the luxury of a door; most had to be content with a piece of rush matting or a curtain, as is still true today in rural areas. A considerable number of doors of late date (tenth to thirteenth century) are still in situ in the churches of Old Cairo or Wādī al-Naṭrūn. They provide access to the choir and the sanctuary and are often set in a large screen also of carved wood, marking off the sanctuary and concealing it from the faithful.

Smaller doors must have belonged either to window apertures cut in such screens as in the Church of Cairo, to reliquaries like the one in the Brooklyn Museum decorated with a praying figure, or to cupboards, such as the remains of a doorframe in Dayr Epiphanius, Thebes.

The smallest doors often had only a single leaf, while the massive entrance doors of churches were double. Their jambs were fitted with a hinge at the top, and the bottom carved from the solid block; the leaves consisted of panels of varying sizes connected to each other by tongue-and-groove joints.

Doors were secured by means of either a simple latch, or a lock with a wooden or iron key, of a design that seems to be of Greek origin and is still in use today. There is a fixed wooden element with teeth that engage in the perforations of a movable element set across the opening. The long-handled key has similar teeth to allow it to push back the teeth of the fixed element and thus engage it in a cavity shaped for this purpose. Such keys come from Dayr Epiphanius and monasteries of the Wādī al-Naṭrūn. H. E. Winlock and W. E. Crum (1926) are of the opinion that such a lock system made its appearance in the Greek world as early as the sixth century B.C. under the appellation "Laconian lock" and spread throughout the Mediterranean basin from then on.

Door from the Church of Sitt Barbārah. Upper part of oblong panel on the back, showing lattice of vine fronds sprouting from bases. *Courtesy Coptic Museum, Cairo.*

Detail of the foregoing: central part of the same oblong panel. *Courtesy Coptic Museum, Cairo.*

A number of uprights decorated with cross motifs, inscriptions, or simply with multisectioned panels set within frames, in the Coptic Museum, Cairo, and in the Louvre, should probably be regarded as fragments of doors.

Undoubtedly the most important example from the fourth to the seventh century is the sixth-century door of the Church of Sitt Barbārah in Cairo now in the Coptic Museum. The lower section has been damaged by moisture, but in the center of each of the upper panels there is still an evangelist carved in relief topped by a bust of Christ wearing a crown, supported by two angels and flanked by two apostles. The lower frieze depicts Christ on a throne surrounded by the twelve apostles. The oblong panels on the back are covered by a lattice of vine fronds sprouting from vases, like those of Maximian's sixth-century throne in the National Museum of Ravenna.

A door leaf probably dating from the eighth or ninth century, now in the Louvre, was discovered by Clédat in the north church of Dayr Apa Apollo. Unfortunately, it is in very damaged condition; it originally consisted of ten rectangular panels framed by friezes of incised foliated scrollwork.

The churches of Sitt Barbārah and Abū Sayfayn in Old Cairo and Mār Jirjis's chapel near Abū Sayfayn once had screens equipped with doors (now in the Coptic Museum, Cairo) that are made up entirely of small panels decorated with Fatimid-style ara-

Door with a single leaf. *Courtesy Louvre Museum, Paris.*

besques that frequently depict people or animals. The same architectural and decorative features occur on the doors of the monasteries of Wādī al-Naṭrūn, which at times attain a level of great richness. The ivory-encrusted tenth-century doors of the Church of al-ʿAdhrā' at Dayr al-Suryān, combining the representation of figures of Christ and the Virgin accompanied by saints with complex geometric ornamentation, are enhanced by a Syriac inscription naming the person who commissioned them and their date of execution. Even though Islamic influence was already predominant, it was not until the thirteenth century that Coptic art finally cut itself off from its roots, giving way both to the Islamic style and to the Byzantine tradition represented by the cedar door panels of the Church of al-Muʿallaqah in Old Cairo, now in the British Museum, London. Four of the panels are decorated with Ayyubid-style arabesques. Six others illustrate episodes from the life of Christ: the Annunciation and the Baptism, the Nativity and the Adoration of the Magi, the Entry into Jerusalem, the Descent to Hell, the Ascension, and Pentecost.

Musical Instruments. Coptic textiles and sculptures abound in representations of musicians playing for dancers. Fortunately, some of the actual instruments have survived, although their fragility has often reduced them to fragments.

A seventh-to-eighth-century *lute* found at Qarārah and preserved in the University of Heidelberg Egyptian Institute has a wooden sound box with hollowed edges. Its long neck terminates in a tenon for the attachment of the strings (now disappeared). At half its length there is a groove occupied by a bridge. The board of the drum, which was either of wood or of skin, has not been preserved. The form of this lute appears to be entirely new and seems to have no historical antecedents in pharaonic Egypt.

The simple or double *flutes* of reed, in the Egyptian Institute and the Coptic Museum, Cairo, which are very common, are the direct descendants of pharaonic flutes. Formed from a single stalk of reed, they are simply perforated by a series of holes on one face.

A *clapper* in the Coptic Museum, Cairo, in wood or ivory, has a handle adorned with stripes and ending in a small fixed board, made of one piece. Two other movable small boards, attached by a string or rivets, clash against the central board. Fragments of another are in the Louvre. Clappers were never portrayed. It seems that they were used as an alarm or to indicate the different activities of the day in Coptic monasteries.

Pairs of *castanets* are made of a piece of wood in the shape of an arm, a bottle, or a pineapple, turned on a lathe, split into two and hollowed out inside. One extremity is pierced or provided with hinges in bronze to bind the two halves together. Castanets, preserved in the Louvre and the Coptic Museum, appeared toward the second century, but we do not know whether they are of Greek or pharaonic origin; their use continued down to the Arab period.

Crotala are pincers in bronze, more rarely in wood, between whose branches are inserted two small bronze cymbals. Examples are in the Louvre; the Coptic Museum, Cairo; and the Municipal Collections, Freiburg, West Germany. These instruments, introduced into Egypt by the Romans, appear commonly in the hands of dancers on the

Musical instruments. Left to right: castanet and clapper. *Courtesy Coptic Museum, Cairo.*

textiles, bronzes, and stone sculptures of the Coptic period (see MUSIC: Musical Instruments).

Screens. A wooden screen or wall was fitted up in front of the sanctuary to separate the faithful from the most sacred part of the church. Many have disappeared, particularly the oldest, but there are screens from the Arab period, still in place, that have the same form. Such screens rise to about one-third of the height of the vault or the ceiling, so that the upper part of the apse remains visible from the nave. The center is pierced by a door and the side spaces by doors or windowlike openings. The top piece is most often formed of one or two rows of painted icons of recent date.

The most ancient traces of screens do not seem to be earlier than the ninth century. These are fragments of woodwork in the Louvre carved with scroll patterns that, according to H. Torp (1970), would be the evidence for the screen of the sanctuary of the north church of Dayr Apa Apollo.

The screens of the churches of Sitt Barbārah and Abū Sayfayn in Old Cairo date from the Fatimid period. That of Sitt Barbārah, preserved in the Coptic Museum in Cairo, is adorned by forty-five panels and a central arcade. It is carved with scroll patterns representing scenes of hunting and of war, horsemen, musicians, and a multitude of animals—lions, jackals, camels, griffins, deer, and birds of all kinds. The antique character of the patterns and the realism of the figures allow us to date it to the end of the tenth century, a period of religious tolerance under the first Fatimids that encouraged the creation of works of high quality. The screen of Abū Sayfayn, in a more abstract style with a tendency to the elimination of figures and the withering of the decoration, must be dated between the end of the eleventh and the course of the twelfth century. Sixty-six panels as well as the central arcade and the lintel are adorned with geometrical scroll patterns populated by birds, animals, and crosses. Sixteen other small panels are carved with figures of standing monks, holding a book in their hands; of mounted saints; or of angels holding the cross.

A screen is preserved in the chapel of Saint John the Baptist, Cairo. Thirty-eight panels are covered with interlacing work or with floral scroll patterns reduced to geometrical form. Forty panels treat in sketchy fashion figures of monks or saints carrying a book. The even more accentuated geometrical form of the elements of the decoration and the workmanship of the figures lead us to date it to the end of the Fatimid period, which is marked by the progressive abandonment of images and the deforming of the Byzantine models.

The churches of Old Cairo possess other screens, from the twelfth to the eighteenth century, consisting essentially of panels of geometric forms varied with arabesque decorations in wood or ivory. These are the churches of al-Muʿallaqah, Abū Sarjah, Sitt Barbārah, the Virgin in Dayr al-Daraj in Babylon, Saint Theodorus, Dayr Abū Sayfayn, Dayr Anbā Shinūdah, and those of the Virgin at al-Damshīriyyah, Ḥārit al-Rūm, and Ḥārit Zuwaylah. In the screen of the Church of Abū Sarjah from the twelfth to thirteenth century, five panels with figured scenes have been inserted that date from the tenth century: the Nativity, the Last Supper, a mounted saint, and two saints.

Churches and chapels in the monasteries of Wādī al-Naṭrūn possess numerous screens, all of the Arab period.

Seals. Seals, in metal or in wood, were intended either for marking an object or for marking a soft clay or wax closing. These uses, which date from pagan antiquity, allow us to distinguish several types of seals among the examples in wood from the Coptic period.

Stamp seals in the form of a medallion served to

mark the stoppers of jars for wine. They also marked loaves of bread, a custom that is still very much alive in the Coptic church. At Antinoopolis the marks of seals have been found on potter's clay fixed to braids that held a mummy's shroud in place. Some stamp seals with a medallion were provided with a handle. They carry, engraved or hollowed out, a monogram, the Christogram, other inscriptions, or figures of birds, felines, and other quadrupeds. Some cylindrical seals present medallions at both ends, often each bearing different motifs.

Small, rectangular stamp seals (between 2 and 8 inches [5 and 20 cm]) are marked only on a single face, the other being occupied by a handle that is full or perforated. The smallest may have been used to stamp the closing of vases, but they could also have been applied to tiles, bricks, or stucco.

Also rectangular are large stamp seals measuring between 16 and 24 inches (40 and 60 cm); they have heavy perforated handles. It appears that they were used to mark the closing of the doors of granaries or to imprint heaps of flour in order to prevent theft. The majority of these rectangular seals bear the names of the proprietors or perhaps of holy personages. Some bear invocations to God. One series presents typically Egyptian figures: a hand, a crouching monkey, ostrich plumes, a solar disk.

Spindles and Spindle Whorls. Although it is possible to spin without an implement, the spindle seems to have appeared at a very early period, at the same time as the first weaving techniques (see TEXTILES, COPTIC). It might have been just a plain wooden stick, but most of the time it was fitted with a whorl of wood, bone, ivory, stone, or baked clay. As is often the case with such humble tools, the spindle has undergone very little development. From Middle Empire models and the New Empire examples discovered at Dayr al-Madīnah, Luxor, one concludes that the sticks were provided with a whorl in the form of a flattened disk. During the Roman and Coptic periods, whorls were very often double, the lower flattened whorl of wood supporting an upper, round one in a different material such as stone or bone, often decorated with incised or carved lines. The latter is often fitted with an iron hook for attaching the end of the thread. Several examples, two of which are in the Louvre, consist of a stick with a disk at one end carved out of the body of the stick at right angles to it: stick and disk are decorated with incised or hollowed-out concentric circles.

Screen of a sanctuary from the Church of Saint Barbara. Tenth century. Central arcade and ornamented panels. *Courtesy Coptic Museum, Cairo.*

Stelae. The position of each tomb was, as a general rule, marked by a stela in stone. Nevertheless, there are also stelae of wood, examples of which are much more rare. At Dayr Apa Apollo, these stelae consisted of a long piece of wood roughly squared, held at the base by a small plaque nailed transversely. The upper part, which rose above the ground, carried in engraving a short invocation or a wish addressed to the deceased.

Three examples, of very different types, belong to

Cylindrical seals. *Courtesy Louvre Museum, Paris.*

Rectangular seals. *Courtesy Louvre Museum, Paris.*

the Louvre. The stela of Cyrus, who died at the age of eight on 7 Ṭūbah, offers simply a Greek inscription on a panel with a roughly rounded top. The stela may have come from Akhmīm. A panel from Dayr Apa Apollo in a much more elaborate style, with a curved top and equipped with tenons at the extremities and mortises at the base, presents a decoration common in stone stelae. An eagle with outspread wings, placed below a band of interlacing work, is encircled by an inscription mentioning a certain Banus. Stelae in the form of a cross, in

Seals for marking (sealing) the sacred bread. Seventh century. Left: monogram of Christ; right: cross. *Courtesy Coptic Museum, Cairo.*

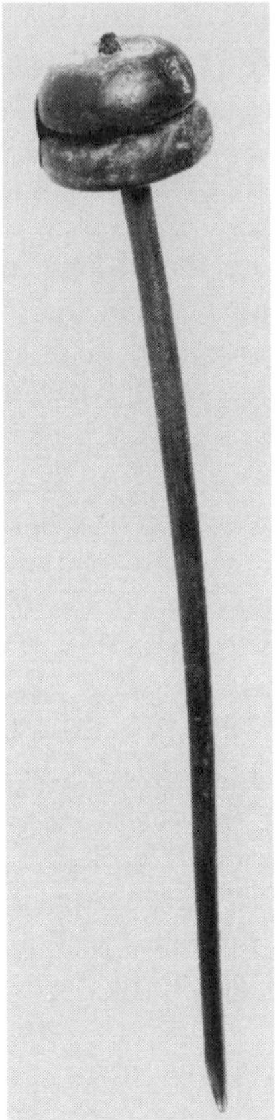

Spindle and spindle whorl. *Courtesy Louvre Museum, Paris.*

the Louvre and the Museum of Périgueux, carry inscriptions engraved over their entire height.

Toilet Articles. Utensils for personal grooming have been found in large numbers. They are the very personal objects that accompany the deceased in their last resting place.

Combs in ivory or wood are the most common. At Antinoopolis some were even placed on the dead person's chest. While combs in the pharaonic period had only a single row of teeth, from the Greek period onward there were combs with a double row of teeth, which continued in use down to the Arab period. The large widely spaced teeth at one end served to disentangle the hair; the fine, close-set teeth at the other enabled it to be cleaned and smoothed. Some examples, however, have only widely spaced teeth. The rectangular central zone was given ornamentation, often on both faces—low-relief carving, openwork, and engraved or painted decorations. Motifs include people, animals, vegetation, geometrical decorations, and crosses. Some combs show encrustations with glass roundels.

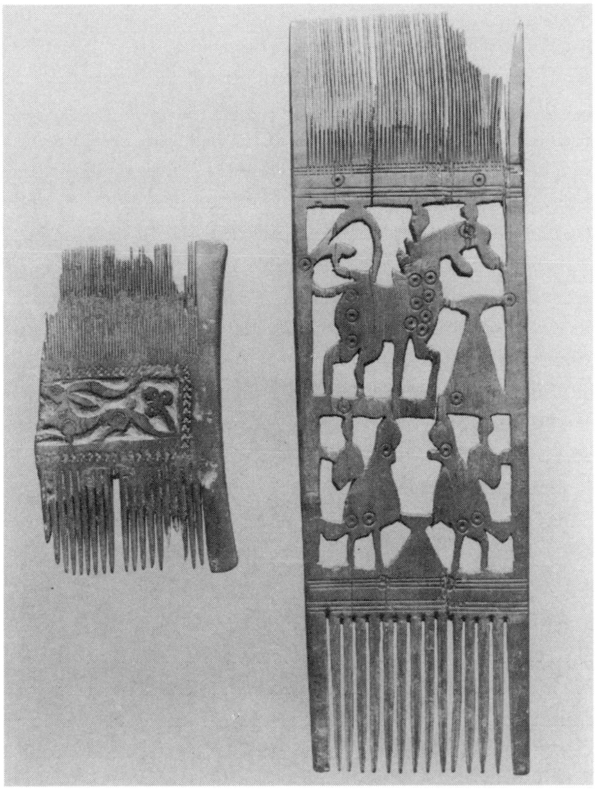

Ornamented comb. *Courtesy Louvre Museum, Paris.*

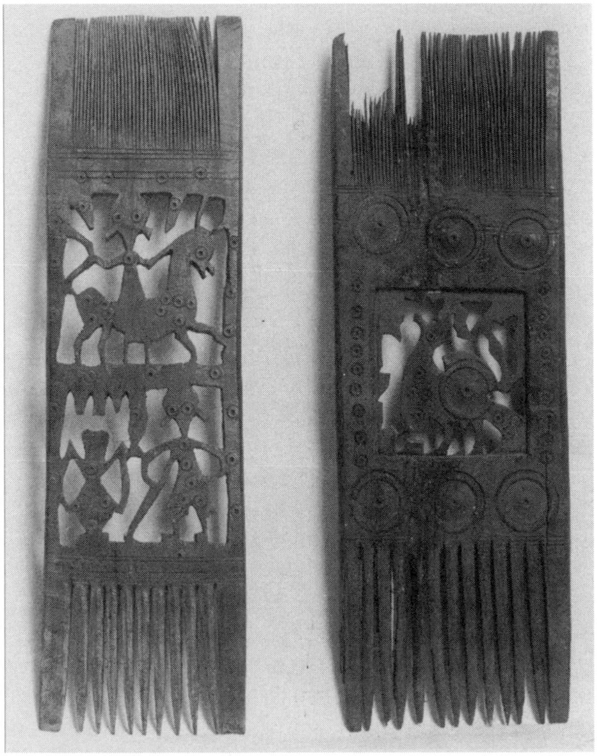

Ornamented combs. Left: man on horseback above acrobatic figures; right: fabulous bird. *Courtesy Coptic Museum, Cairo.*

Study of the so-called liturgical combs led F. Swoboda to distinguish two geographical zones of manufacture according to the form of the combs. Combs from Italy, represented by a few examples in the Louvre, are wider than they are high. Combs from North Africa, including Egypt, are higher than they are wide.

Up to now it has not been possible to identify a "liturgical" comb from a secular one, for the presence of a Christian symbol does not necessarily entail a liturgical use but simply a protective purpose for the one who possessed it. Nevertheless, it is tempting to think that the sixth-century comb in the State Museum of Berlin depicting Saint Thecla and Daniel among the lions could have served a priest preparing to present himself at the altar. On several stelae in the Louvre and the Coptic Museum, Cairo, combs are represented sheltered under an aedicula symbolizing a chapel. The funerary context invites us to see here a reminiscence of the rite of liturgical cleanliness, required of the priest, then of the deceased, prior to appearing before God. On a bas-relief in the Coptic Museum the scene of the bath of the Child is surmounted by an enormous comb engraved with three crosses, in keeping with the toilet of the newborn.

Among existing secular combs, some may originally have been offered as wedding gifts. Others without doubt have never been used.

Painting around the eyes with kohl is a very common and ancient practice in Egypt, by reason of its protective function against dust and insects. Statues of the pharaonic period still preserve around the eyes green traces that suggest the use of malachite. From the Roman period on, malachite was replaced by powdered galena, a gray or blackish substance, which was mixed with a medium. Laboratory tests have discovered traces of galena in the kohl boxes belonging to the Louvre. Small sticks of bone, wood, or bronze were used to mix and apply the kohl. The forms of the *kohl boxes* are inherited from those of the pharaonic period. The materials are stone, faience, bronze, wood, and in particular stalks of reed, which naturally lent themselves to the purpose of boxes. From the Greek period on, wood, shaped or turned on a lathe, was the sole material used for kohl boxes. Some boxes are in the form of tubes, resting on an annular foot and provided with a stopper, which has often disappeared. They are simply adorned with concentric

engraved lines or with bands painted in red, green, and yellow. Other tubes are covered with a network motif engraved on a background of dark paint. The strangest boxes, in the form of more or less potbellied amphorae, rest on small pedestals with four feet, cut from a solid piece of wood. They are adorned with a network of engraved lines, small tongues, stylized vegetable motifs, or crosses. Some are backed by small plaques, the verso of which presents figured decorations: goddesses, dancers, birds. The stoppers are generally conical or carved in the form of heads, as are examples in the University of Mainz, Institute of Art History. The handles of the amphorae or the perforations made in the plaques were intended for the passage of leather thongs, which allowed the boxes to be carried or hung up. Examples are in the Louvre; the University of Heidelberg; the University of Mainz; and the Walters Art Gallery, Baltimore. Two examples with a double tube, in the Coptic Museum, Cairo, and the University of Heidelberg, are hollowed into the back of cases originally closed with a sliding lid, in which the kohl sticks must have been arranged.

In addition to making up their eyes, the Egyptians painted their faces with red ocher, traces of which have been found in small, round boxes. Fibers of wool mixed with this matter perhaps indicate the use of pads for application. These *ocher boxes* are turned and have a wide rim pierced with holes, which correspond to perforations in the cover. Leather thongs threaded through the holes held the covers in place. These covers, surmounted by a central knob for gripping, are engraved simply with concentric circles.

Mirrors, aids to beauty, were in ancient times formed of disks of metal cast and then polished and provided with a handle in wood or ivory. From the Roman period other types appear, made of plaster or wood, set with a round piece of silver-plated glass. The Coptic Museum in Cairo possesses an example still in a fairly good state of preservation. The rectangular wooden support, provided with a handle, is hollowed into a circular socket occupied by a round piece of silver-plated glass fixed by a filling of stucco. The Louvre has only four of these supports, in which the glass has disappeared, but one can still distinguish on the edge of the frame traces of painted decoration: undulating black lines dotted by red and white points, and large black and white points.

Box for holding eye cosmetics. *Courtesy Louvre Museum, Paris.*

Box for holding eye cosmetics, with the tube in the form of an amphora. *Courtesy Louvre Museum, Paris.*

Toys and Games. The only games that have survived appear in the form of rectangular tablets of wood with three steps, which increase in size from the upper level to the lower. The surface is covered with a veneer of ivory, which has very often partly disappeared. Each step is provided with series of perforations. The examples known at present—one in the Coptic Museum in Cairo, one in the Royal Museums of Art and History in Brussels, two in the Louvre—all show the same series of perforations, except in the central spaces of the upper steps: two rows of four, two rows of five, and four rows of ten perforations. The top step is often provided in its center with an ivory knob. The presence of two series of perforations may imply a game for two players, who had to finish at the common goal formed by the central perforations. As E. Drioton thought, it is not impossible that the form of these games and their rules were inherited from the ancient pharaonic game of *senet,* which resembles the games of checkers and chess. The same author, however, also compares them with games, dating from the beginning of the Middle Empire, that continued in use in the form of "bucklers," then of "frogs." These games belong to the same type as two other specimens of board game, one from the twelfth century B.C. found at Susa and one from the fourth century B.C. found in Ur.

The game must have been played with pegs and counters, marked with points in bone or ivory, which have been found in large numbers. On the back of the gameboard was fitted a drawer closed by a sliding cover, intended no doubt for storing counters and pegs. One of the examples in the Louvre, deriving from Antinoopolis, presents on this face an engraved cross with forked branches, flanked by two alphas and two omegas. The name "God" inscribed vertically is not necessarily contemporary with it.

The tombs of children at Antinoopolis have yielded two kinds of toys: horsemen and dolls. Other types of toys do not seem to have been identified on other sites. The horsemen appear in two forms. In one, a figurine without feet is held in place by tenons between two small plaques, very probably suggesting the two sides of the same horse. On the lower part of these plaques are mounted four wheels fixed by thin rods and tenons. Only the outer faces of these plaques have been carefully smoothed and covered with red, white, and black

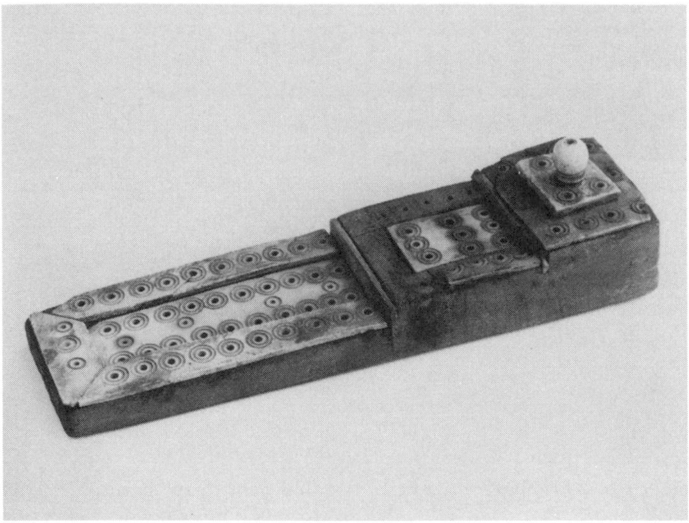

Game. *Courtesy Louvre Museum, Paris.*

painting that details the saddle, the harness, the hair, and the eyes, as in examples in the Louvre. The other type can be reconstructed on the basis of fragments recovered. The horseman, similar to the preceding one, is provided with two legs, which allows him to be mounted on a single plaque, both faces of which are smoothed. The horses are stylized in the extreme: very simplified silhouettes, without hooves or tails. The horsemen are roughly outlined by means of a series of excisions effected with a chisel or a knife. The two arms, crossed on the chest, appear to hold the reins. The face is cut

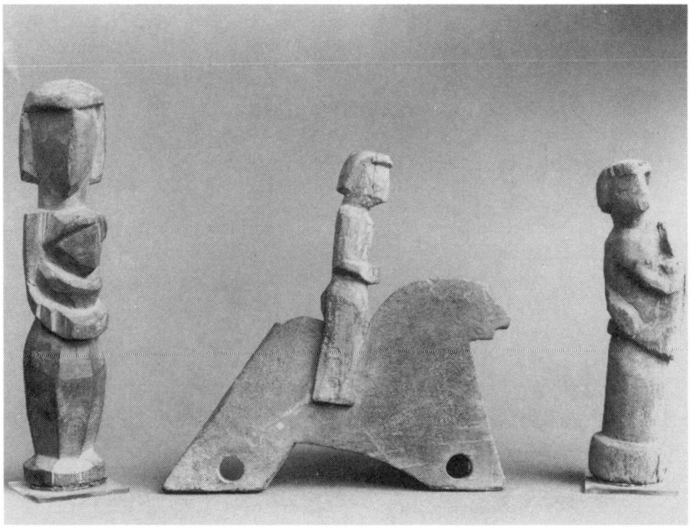

Toy horseman and dolls. *Courtesy Louvre Museum, Paris.*

Toy horseman. *Courtesy Louvre Museum, Paris.*

in two planes that meet at the nasal axis. A small skullcap forms the headdress.

The same characteristics were applied in the manufacture of dolls. They are presented standing on a small pedestal, the feet and legs veiled by a heavy garment with blunted angles. Some cross their hands at the level of the waist; others carry a child in front of the chest, either in a strictly frontal position or slightly twisted.

Weaver's Combs. Weavers used special combs to compress the threads of the weft and to maintain the regular spacing of the warp threads. These combs were mostly carved from a hardwood, such as box, which allowed the thrust involved to be transmitted with less risk of damage. They consist of a rectangular block with a handle, projecting from the middle of one of the long sides, that is carved from the same piece of wood. The opposite side has a row of teeth with the gaps between beveled on the working surface to prevent damage to the weft threads during use. They often show signs of wear, and many of them have teeth missing. Some broken ones appear to have been repaired in antiquity by means of bronze ligatures. One comb

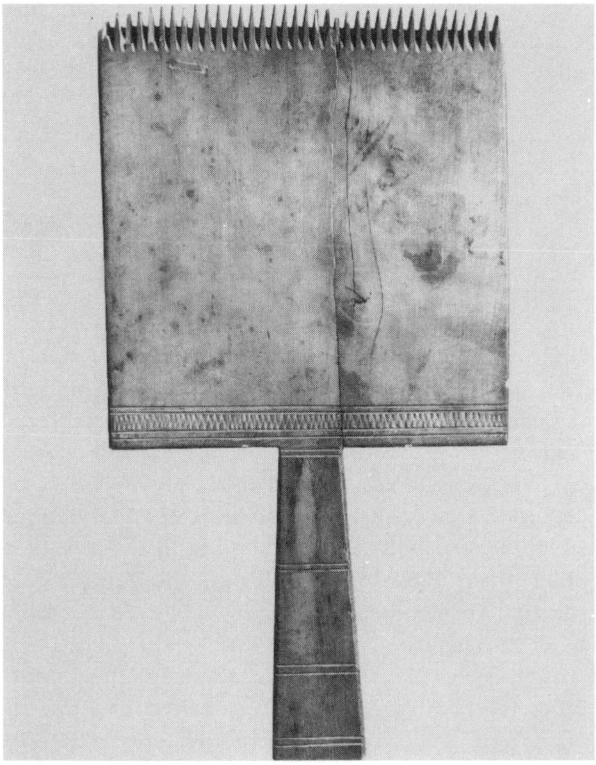

Weaver's comb. *Courtesy Louvre Museum, Paris.*

Weaver's comb ornamented with animals. *Courtesy Coptic Museum, Cairo.*

in the Louvre was probably made from broken fragments fitted together by tenons and pegs.

Weaver's combs come in an enormous variety of sizes depending on the sizes of the warp. They accommodate a larger or smaller number of teeth with varying spacing, according to the examples in the State Museum of Berlin and the Louvre.

The very sketchy decoration is found chiefly on one side of the block and the handle: groups of incised lines in parallels or cruciform, series of chevrons, or pricked-out circles. Two combs, however, one in a private collection, the other in the Coptic Museum in Cairo, carved with animals in relief, demonstrate that such utilitarian implements could sometimes be elaborately decorated.

Weaver's Shuttle. Everyday, unadorned implements are rarely preserved. One example of a weaver's shuttle is in the Louvre; two are at University College, London. One of the London pieces consists of a baton slit at the two ends. The thread, still preserved, is twined crosswise at three points on the shuttle.

The two other pieces, ovoid in shape, are hollowed out in their central part to prepare for the positioning of the bobbin. The London example is ballasted with pegs of lead, allowing for a more effective throwing of the shuttle.

Sculptured Architectural Decoration

As in the times of pharaonic Egypt, so also in the Coptic period, only public buildings in carefully squared stone received sumptuous painted or sculpted decoration. Private houses were constructed of unbaked clay, washed with white lime, and sometimes enhanced by a few paintings. The attention of the decorators was directed chiefly to the churches. Sculpted works in stone or in wood, often painted, adorn the interior as well as the exterior of the south church at Dayr Apa Apollo. They include friezes, lintels, brackets, pilasters, and panels.

Friezes. The most common decorative elements are the long friezes running right round the building, often on several levels. They reproduce in large part the same ornaments of acanthus scroll patterns

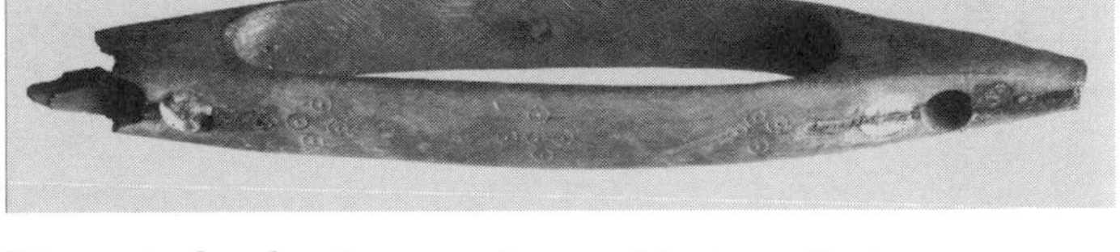

Weaver's shuttle. *Courtesy Louvre Museum, Paris.*

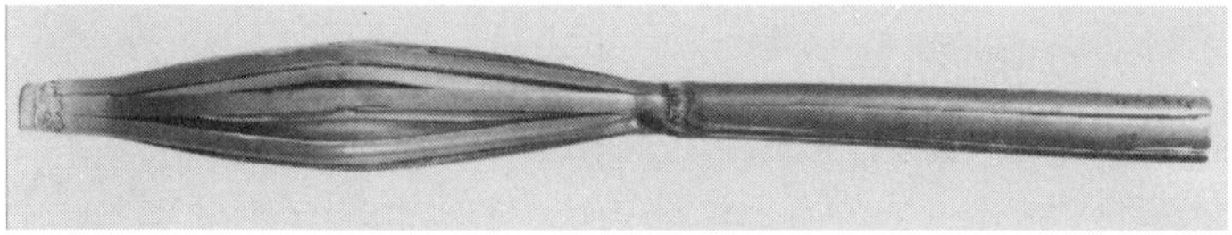

Weaver's shuttle. *Courtesy Louvre Museum, Paris.*

or vine leaves as on stone friezes in the Louvre, the Coptic Museum in Cairo, and the State Museum of Berlin. Nevertheless, the foliage scroll pattern forming wheels occupied by flowers, fruit, or animals that appears so often in the stone friezes is practically absent in friezes of wood. The choice of this motif, which entails the hollowing out of the background to obtain a genuine lacework effect, was probably ignored by the sculptors in wood, whose material lent itself less readily to this form of carving.

These other motifs, common to all the lands of the Mediterranean basin from the Greco-Roman period on, take on a variety of invention in their treatment that is typical of the decorative character of Coptic sculpture.

Carved in relief, leaves, flowers, and fruits are either naturalized or stylized in the extreme, to the point of being no more than almost geometrical forms. The branches run through the woodwork in undulating lines or form hoops or ovals. When they are symmetrical, they often emerge from the pedestal of a vase that marks their center, a motif coming originally from the Orient. Elements alien to the nature of the vegetation represented often occupy the spaces left free. Fruits, flowers, beads, and trefoils are used, as are human or angel busts, full-length figures, fawns, or birds. The birds are constantly represented in the act of pecking the flowers or the fruits. This theme, of Oriental origin, spread throughout the Mediterranean basin from the Greco-Roman period, and was to know an extraordinary expansion both in space and time.

Choir enclosures. *Courtesy Louvre Museum, Paris.*

Naturalistic or stylized, the palmette reigns everywhere. It is used in friezes but also in borders or in framing. Although less frequent than the scroll pattern, meanders (frets) appear in the form of ribbons adorned with beads or bands occupied by florets. The spaces between the angles are occupied by vegetable or human elements. This geometrical decoration on wood includes rows of beads, waves, or denticles (small tooth projections). The same decoration on stone or in painting seems intended to imitate the technique of carving in wood, e.g., a pillar from Dayr Apa Apollo in the Louvre and paintings in geometrical tracery from the necropolis of al-Bagawāt.

Figurative subjects are not wanting; they sometimes interrupt the regular connection of a vegetable or geometric frieze; for example, angels holding up the cross or busts enclosed in garlands as in the Louvre. The animal decoration seems much more frequent and varied: a lion bounding in foliage; felines following one another, biting the tail of the one in front; peacocks; or quails, as in the Louvre. More rarely, a browsing hare appears on a frieze in company with birds pecking at grapes, for example in the State Museum of Berlin.

Mythological and Nilotic scenes, in the Louvre and the Coptic Museum in Cairo, form an abundant and varied iconography, offering in turn realistic or fantastic animal representations gamboling in the midst of putti, nymphs, or goddesses.

Lintels. Some thirty lintels in wood are known at present. The majority consist of a single large beam. The decoration is situated on one of the principal faces but may equally cover the lower face where this area remains visible. Tenons and mortises, often still in place, served to fix the lintels on uprights or wedge them into the masonry. The use of veneering held by nails or the superimposition of several friezes makes it possible to give them a richer appearance. They must have belonged to the doors of churches, monks' cells, or funerary chapels. At Dayr Apa Apollo, a lintel now in the Louvre was found in situ at the entrance of a chamber situated between the north and south churches.

Lintel from the Church of al-Mu'allaqqah (Old Cairo). Wood. Fourth–sixth century. Entry of Christ into Jerusalem and the Ascension. *Courtesy Coptic Museum, Cairo.*

The sculptured decoration of wooden lintels is analogous to that of lintels in stone. The center most often takes the form of a Latin or Greek cross, carved in relief, embossed, or inset with a strip of lead, as in examples in the Louvre, the State Museum of Berlin, and the Coptic Museum in Cairo. This cross may be placed against a shell and sheltered under an aedicula with a pediment, upheld by two columns. On a lintel in the State Museum of Berlin it is upheld by two angels. Two lintels, probably deriving from the Fayyūm, are preserved at the French Institute of Oriental Archaeology in Cairo. In one, a cross with branches in the form of leaves is inscribed in a medallion with knotted ribbons. In the other, a cross fleury is inscribed in a simple circle.

The lateral areas of the lintels are occupied either by alpha and omega, engraved or inset in lead, or by garlands enclosing a rosette. Some pieces, however, offer more varied decorations. A lintel in the Louvre presents Greek crosses inserted among hexagonal and octagonal motifs, adorned with flowers as well as two rosettes, one in the form of a floret, the other in full flower with four petals, enclosed within garlands. The lower face is adorned with a Greek fret. An example in the same museum carries panels veneered at the extremities and adorned with fawns bounding among bushes.

Figural scenes, although less frequent, are sometimes simply limited to busts of angels, of holy personages, or of Christ, enclosed within garlands. Two angels frequently uphold the cross or the bust of Christ, as on a lintel in the State Museum of Berlin.

One example in the Louvre, with its reliefs severely rubbed away, still allows us to perceive in the central zone a seated figure faced by two other figures. At the extremities, pieces at right angles are adorned—one with Moses, perhaps, receiving the tables of the law, the other with Saint Menas as an

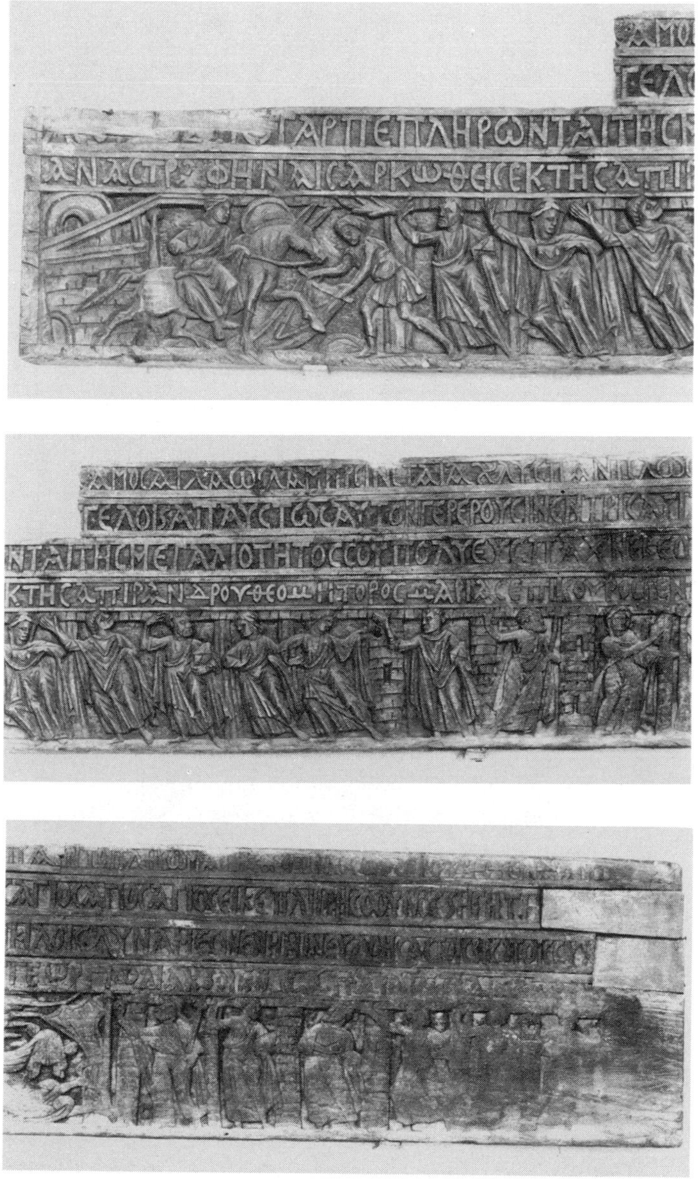

Detail from the above lintel. *Top and middle:* Entry into Jerusalem (left half). *Bottom:* Ascension (far right). *Courtesy Coptic Museum, Cairo.*

orant (praying figure) between camels, a single one of which survives.

Only two lintels offer great narrative scenes, treated on a single register over their whole length. A lintel deriving from the Fayyūm now in the State Museum of Recklinghausen, West Germany, bears the entry of Christ into Jerusalem, treated in a style simplified to the extreme. By contrast, the fourth-to-sixth century lintel of the Church of al-Muʿallaqah, now in the Coptic Museum, Cairo, presents classical forms that link it to the Alexandrian style, although the harshness of the drapery and of the faces sets them apart from that tradition. The frieze, disposed on a single register, is surmounted by a four-line inscription in finely worked Greek uncial letters, in which the abbot Theodore and the deacon George address a hymn to Christ. The left part is occupied by the entry into Jerusalem, the right by the Ascension. The graphic style of the drapery and the disposition of the personages in front of gates flanked by towers cannot but recall the Greco-Roman sarcophagi called "At the Town Gates" in the Louvre or some sarcophagi with columns from Asia Minor also in the Louvre.

Corbels. Corbels are supportive architectural elements characterized by their rectangular form with beveled edging and by their flattened upper face without decoration, which were intended to receive a section of wall. Half or one-third of the corbel, roughly squared, was introduced into the wall in order to fix the element in place. Only the lower face was therefore visible and carried ornamentation.

Some examples from Dayr Apa Apollo are covered with geometrical tracery consisting of octagons and overlapping crosses, as seen in the Coptic Museum in Cairo, or of meanders, on the examples in the Louvre. Others imitate the capitals of columns and pilasters with the use of laurel leaves or vine and acanthus leaves, the extremities of which are curled back. Acanthus adorns a double corbel in the Coptic Museum in Cairo, the two sculpted extremities of which are separated by the supportive area, which has no decoration.

Several examples were adorned with figured motifs or scenes. Two fifth-to-sixth-century corbels from Dayr Apa Apollo, now in the Coptic Museum, each present a holy personage, one of whom holds the book of the Gospels, sheltered by an arcade. The arcade is surmounted by a garland enclosing a cross. From the same site a corbel in the State Museum of Berlin offers under the same type of arcade a representation of Daniel among the lions, clothed in Persian costume (Phrygian bonnet, leggings, and tunic with triangular flaps); the head stands out against a conch shell.

Corbel. *Courtesy Louvre Museum, Paris.*

A unique fourth-to-fifth-century corbel from al-Ashmūnayn, now in the State Museum of Berlin, is sculpted in very high relief with a scene of the capture of a town. The composition is in several registers depicting a dead prisoner, trampled by foot soldiers and horsemen, and prisoners pilloried in front of the ramparts of the town, which are furnished with towers. On these ramparts appears a row of soldiers. Behind them rises the citadel, the bastions of which are surmounted by busts. Two personages appear under the arcade of the entrance. The presence of a standard-bearer carrying the labarum leads one to interpret this assault as a symbol of the triumph of Christianity over paganism. The very stylized rounded faces and heavy drapery bring this small monument close to the sculptures of late antiquity, for example, the fourth-century porphyry sarcophagus called that of Saint

Helena in the Vatican Museums, or the fourth-century group of the Tetrarchs in Venice.

Small Columns and Pilasters. Small pillars and pilasters, essentially movable objects, served either to support arcades as in the fourth-to-sixth century wooden altar of the Church of Abū Sarjah in Cairo, or as the uprights in furniture or balustrades.

The Louvre has several of these objects, which unfortunately are separated from their context. One small column, whose capital has two rows of stylized leaves, has a shaft of two different shapes. One half is cylindrical, the other half is hexagonal. Similarly one-third of the height of another fine small column is square in section, another third is hexagonal, and the last third is circular; three groups of indentations form its ornamentation. The lower half of the shaft of another small column is square in section, while the upper half presents three oblique faces; the front face is adorned with a row of waves between two engraved lines. A small column, square in section, has a capital adorned by a flower with four petals inscribed in a lozenge and framed by flutes, leaves alternating with pearls, and indentations. Two-thirds of the shaft is occupied by a floral frieze between two series of indentations.

Slender boards served for the execution of pilasters. The shafts were usually covered by a scroll pattern, emerging from the base, that included leaves, pomegranates, and rosettes.

Panels. In the majority of cases it has proved impossible to replace panels in their original context. Only some panels from Dayr Apa Apollo have been restored to their place in the south church, which has been partially reconstructed in the Coptic rooms of the Louvre. In particular, on either side of the door of the church two sculptured "pictures" in wood were fitted in, carrying borders with leaves and palmettes or other vegetable motifs. This inlay technique, which goes back to the Ptolemaic and Roman periods, allows the introduction of contrasts in materials and in colors. Some of the panels in the Louvre and the State Museum of Berlin present at their center a perforation, which may or may not pass through the thickness of the panel, the purpose of which has not yet been determined.

Small column. *Courtesy Louvre Museum, Paris.*

Panel with animal motif. *Courtesy Louvre Museum, Paris.*

Panel delimited by borders. *Courtesy Louvre Museum, Paris.*

The center may be adorned with geometrical and vegetable motifs, such as Greek frets, conches, garlands, scroll patterns, leaves, and pearls, which for the most part delimit the spaces occupied by figured representations. But often the field is decorated with animal motifs such as birds in the Louvre and leaping lions and an eagle in the State Museum of Berlin, or human figures such as holy personages and angels, and mounted saints placed face-to-face, in the Louvre.

A series of rectangular panels, delimited by borders in the form of bands or adorned with scroll patterns, could have belonged either to movable objects or to architectural elements such as doors or screens in front of the sanctuary.

Panel depicting a saint between two angels. Sycamore wood. Fifth century. *Courtesy Coptic Museum, Cairo.*

A fifth-to-sixth-century panel in the Coptic Museum in Cairo presents a cultic scene difficult to identify, perhaps the dance of Salome. A musician, seated and playing her flute, accompanies a dancer holding cymbals performing before a seated personage; behind, a bust, possibly the head of Saint John the Baptist, is placed on a stool of repentance.

Dating from the same period, a fragmentary panel also in the Coptic Museum still allows us to recognize the upper part of the scene of the Baptism of Christ. Saint John the Baptist pours water on the head of Christ, toward whom a dove descends.

The small fifth-century Virgin of the Annunciation in the Louvre still preserves part of its many colors —black, violet, and rose. She is seated on a high stool and spins purple thread for the veil of the Temple. With her large, fixed black eyes she looks at the observer, while the archangel Gabriel, of whom no more than a foot remains, makes his announcement to her.

Panel depicting the Annunciation. *Courtesy Louvre Museum, Paris.*

Other panels date from the Arab period. An eleventh-to-twelfth-century sacrifice of Isaac in the Kevorkian Collection, New York, presents in a quite Islamic style the traditional scene of Abraham on the point of sacrificing the little Isaac, lying on the altar. Behind him the ram entangles its horns in the branches of a tree, which occupies the whole background of the panel, although the face of the angel sent by God to stop Abraham's action does appear.

In the eleventh-century iconostasis of the Church of Abū Sarjah in Old Cairo, panels are inserted representing the Nativity, the Last Supper, and three saints on horseback. There, too, Christian iconography is wedded to pure Islamic decoration, made of stylized palmettes and arabesques. Other examples in the Louvre consist of panels with or without holy personages.

BIBLIOGRAPHY

Badawy, A. *Koptische Kunst—Christentum am Nil,* Catalog 152, pp. 116–21. Essen, 1963.

Bahgat, A. "Les forêts en Egypte et leur administration au moyen age." *Bulletin de l'Institut d'Egypte,* 4th ser. 1 (1900):141–58.

Beckwith, J. *Coptic Sculpture,* figs. 97, 135–137, 141–147. London, 1963.

Coquin, C. *Les Edifices chrétiens du Vieux-Caire.* Cairo, 1974.

Drioton, E. "Un ancien jeu Copte." *Bulletin de la Société d'Archéologie copte* 6 (1940):177–206.

Evelyn-White, H. G. *The Monasteries of the Wādī'n Natrūn,* Part 3. *The Architecture and Archeology,* ed. W. Hauser, New York, 1933.

______. *The Monasteries of the Wādī'n Natrūn,* pp. 195–96, pl. 63. New York, 1938.

Fikhman, I. F. *L'Egypte entre deux époques, artisans et travail artisanal du IVe au milieu de VIIe siècle.* Moscow, 1965. Reviewed by E. Wipszycka in *Journal of Juristic Papyrology* 16–17 (1971):217–36.

Forbes, R. J. *Studies in Ancient Technology,* Vol. 4. Leiden, 1956.

Galavaris, G. *Bread and the Liturgy.* London, 1970.

Gayet, A. "L'Exploration des nécropoles gréco-byzantines d'Antinoé." *Annales du Musée Guimet* 30, parts 2 and 3. Paris, 1902.

Habib, R. *The Ancient Coptic Churches of Cairo: A Short Account.* Cairo, 1967.

______. *Feminine Coquetry and Headdresses,* p. 2. Cairo, n.d.

______. *The Coptic Museum: A General Guide.* Cairo, 1967.

Hickmann, H. "La Cliquette, un Instrument de percussion Egyptien de l'époque Copte." *Bulletin de la Société d'archéologie copte* 13 (1948–1949):1–12.

______. *Instruments de musique.* Catalogue général des antiquités égyptiennes du Musée dù Caire. Cairo, 1949.

______. "La Castagnette égyptienne." *Bulletin de la Société d'archéologie copte* 14 (1950–1957): 37–49.

Kötzsche, L. "Reliquienbehälter oder Toilettegeräte." *Gesta* 18 (1979):157–62.

Lombard, M. *Epaces et réseaux du haut moyen age,* pp. 107–76. Mouton edition. Paris, 1972.

Lucas, A., and J. R. Harris. *Ancient Egyptian Materials and Industries.* London, 1962.

Pauty, E. *Bois sculptés de églises coptes (époque fatimide).* Cairo, 1930.

Petrie, F. *Arts and Crafts of Ancient Egypt.* London, 1909.

______. *Tools and Weapons,* London, 1917.

______. *Objects of Daily Use.* London, 1927.

Rutschowscaya, M.-H. "Objets de toilette d'époque copte." *Revue du Louvre* 1 (1976):1–5.

______. "Introduction à l'ètude des bois coptes du Musée du Louvre." *Enchoria* 8 (1978):123–125.

______. "Boîtes à poids d'époque copte." *Revue du Louvre* 1 (1979):1–5.

______. *Musée du Louvre—Bois de l'Egypte copte,* nos. 399, 446, 447. p. 101. Reunion des Musées nationaux. Paris, 1986.

Strzygowski, J. *Koptische Kunst.* Catalogue général des antiquités égyptiennes du Musée du Caire 12, pp. 133, 139–140, 147–49, 230, 235. Vienna, 1904.

Swoboda, F. *Die liturgischen Kämme.* Dissertation, Tübingen, 1963.

Torp, H. "The Carved Decorations of the North and South Churches at Bawit." *Kolloquium über spätantike und frühmittelalterliche Skulptur* (1970):35–41.

Winlock, H. E., and W. E. Crum. *The Monastery of Epiphanius,* Part 1, pp. 57–60. New York, 1926.

Wulff, O. *Altchristliche und mittelalterliche, byzantinische und italienische Bildwerke. Vol. 1, Altchristliche Bildwerke.* Berlin, 1909.

______. *Altchristlich und mittelalterliche Bildwerke,* nos. 331–332; 1604. Köngliche Museen zu Berlin 1. Berlin, 1909.

Ziegler, C. *Instruments de musique égyptiens au Musée du Louvre.* Paris, 1979.

MARIE-HÉLÈNE RUTSCHOWSCAYA

WOODWORK, PRESERVATION OF. *See* Art Preservation.

WOOL. *See* Textiles, Coptic: Yarns.

WORRELL, WILLIAM HOYT (1879–1952), American Coptologist. He was educated at the universities of Michigan, Berlin, and Leipzig. He taught at Hartford Seminary (1910–1924) and was an associate professor and later professor of Semitics at the University of Michigan (1925–1949).

BIBLIOGRAPHY

Dawson, W. R., and E. P. Uphill. *Who Was Who in Egyptology,* p. 311. London, 1972.

Kammerer, W., comp. *A Coptic Bibliography.* Ann Arbor, Mich., 1950; repr. New York, 1969.

M. L. BIERBRIER

WÜSTENFELD, FERDINAND (1808–1899), German Orientalist. He received his doctorate in 1831 at Göttingen and was habilitated there in 1832. Above all, he was active as a librarian. He edited and translated Arabic historians and geographers. Worthy of mention for Christian Egypt are his *Makrizi's Geschichte der Copten aus den Handschriften zu Gotha und Wien mit Übersetzung und Anmerkungen* (Göttingen, 1845); *Das Synaxarium, das ist Heiligen-Kalender der coptischen Christen aus dem Arabischen übersetzt* (Gotha, 1879); and his manuscript catalog "Coptisch-arabische Handschriften der königlichen Universitätsbibliothek" (*Nachrichten der Göttinger Gesellschaft,* 1878, pp. 285–325).

BIBLIOGRAPHY

Wellhausen, J. "Ferdinand Wüstenfeld." In *Allgemeine deutsche Biographie,* Vol. 55, pp. 139–40. Berlin, 1910.

MARTIN KRAUSE

Y

YACOBOS II, archbishop of Jerusalem (1946–1956). He was born in the village of al-Muṭī'ah in 1908. In 1939 he resigned from the civil service and entered the CLERICAL COLLEGE in Cairo, from which he graduated in 1942. He joined the Monastery of Saint Antony (DAYR ANBĀ ANṬŪNIYŪS), where he took the name Ṣalīb al-Anṭūnī. In 1944 he was ordained a priest and was promoted to HEGUMENOS in 1945. During the following year, he became deputy of the archbishop of al-Balyanā and remained in this post until he was consecrated archbishop of the See of Jerusalem and the Near East in September 1946. The see consisted of Jerusalem, the Sinai, Palestine, and all other countries of the Near East.

In 1946, Yacobos built a road along the Jordan River with shelters for Coptic pilgrims. He also established a farm on the bank of the river and a monastery on a piece of land nearby given to the patriarchate in the time of THEOPHILUS I. He inaugurated the Coptic Antonian Church in Jerusalem in 1947, where Christian children study. In the same year, he opened another church at Rafaḥ in Sinai.

The next year, the Palestinian war of 1948 broke out. As a result of this war, many Coptic families deserted their homes in Haifa, Jaffa, and other towns, taking refuge in the Coptic Patriarchate in Jerusalem and in various monasteries. With so many refugees to look after, the see was strained financially. The situation was worsened both by the interruption of the flow of Coptic pilgrims and by the loss of the large orchards of the Coptic monastery in Jaffa, whose fruit provided revenue for the expenses of monasteries, churches, and other activities.

In 1949 he laid the foundation stone of the Coptic church in Nazareth. Four years later, the archbishop inaugurated the Coptic College of the Martyr Sitt Dimyanah in Jerusalem and initiated the building of the Coptic Orthodox cathedral in East Qantarah. Yacobos died in a train accident on 22 March 1956.

ARCHBISHOP BASILIOS

YA'QUB. *See* Ethiopian Prelates.

YA'QŪB, GENERAL (1745–1801). Financial commissioner, then military leader, a *mu'allim* become a general, Ya'qūb died young, and we have little information about his remarkable career. His role is thus debated: collaborator in the French occupation of Egypt, or pioneer of national independence? His contemporary al-Jabartī—who was a member of the *diwan* that collaborated with the French—presents him as a revanchist defender of the Coptic minority, a view repeated more than a century and a half later in the polemical writings of Muslim extremists. This is in contrast with the modernist ideology ascribed to him by Louis 'Awaḍ.

In 1924 Georges Douin brought to light the 1801 project for the independence of Egypt, attributed to Ya'qūb, from documents in the British Foreign Office. Copts recognized here early manifestations of the same nationalism they had shown, along with their Muslim compatriots, in the revolution of 1919. However, with the proclamation of a constitutional government at Cairo under King Fouad, the reality of this project was played down by a man with a grudge, the French-speaking Greek journalist Alexander Hadjivassiliou, who used the pseudonym Auriant. 'Abd al-Raḥmān al-Rāfi'ī does not mention Ya'qūb in his *History of the National Movement,* no doubt to avoid alluding to a confessional conflict; but in a thick booklet the historian Shafīq Ghurbāl demonstrates the mature political sense of Yaʿqūb, who could visualize the objective foundations of a viable independence when more popular leaders (ʿUmar Makram, al-Maḥrūqī, al-Sādāt, certain dervishes) did not go beyond a sterile and ephemeral demagogy. The only biography of Yaʿqūb, written in 1921 by Gaston Homsy, one of his descendants in Marseilles, is chiefly concerned with establishing the glories of a provincial family.

For the study of the genesis and destiny of the Coptic Legion, the principal sources are the French archives: those of the Ministry of External Relations in Paris and particularly those of the Service historique de l'Armée de Terre at Vincennes, as well as the departmental and municipal archives in Marseilles.

Yaʿqūb (Yacoub, Jacob) was born at Mallawī in 1745. All we know of his civic status are the names of his parents: Maryam Tawfīq Ghazāl and *Muʿallim* Ḥannā, an abbreviation of Yuḥannā (John). We do not know whether his father was a bookkeeper, in the tradition of the Coptic scribes who kept the records of the land survey, or a merchant. Mallawī had a famous market that supplied a region of Middle Egypt with corn, spices, molasses, oil, linen, and cotton fabrics. It was also the center of a lucrative small principality that belonged to the chief of Mecca's pilgrim caravan, Amīr al-Ḥajj, the highest dignitary in the Mamluk hierarchy after Shaykh al-Balad, the commandant of Cairo. His representative, a *sirdar,* at once a civil and a military governor, was aided by a Coptic bureaucracy in the main task of raising the annual tribute in grain, which was transported via Cairo, Suez, and the Red Sea to Arabia. Though there is no precise information about Yaʿqūb's upbringing, his subsequent activities testify to experience as a merchant and as a scribe. His originality was in the integration of these two domains of economic life, contrary to the customary separation of those professions, which reserved trade for foreigners—Europeans or people under the jurisdiction of the Ottoman Empire—and reserved the administration of fiscal policy to the Copts.

Yaʿqūb crossed these boundaries, beginning with his post as commissioner general of Sulaymān Bey, *kāshif* (governor) of the province of Asyūṭ. Sulaymān was one of eighteen new Mamluks promoted by ʿAlī Bey al-Kabīr, who had just seized Egypt from Turkish domination (1767) and wished to establish his authority through a staff of his own. Yaʿqūb, assisted by a hierarchy of scribes, managed the bey's establishment and the territory held in rent. Al-Jabartī calls attention to the astute exploitation of this *muqāta'ah* (land rented out): waterwheels irrigated the orchards, and extensive pastures allowed the raising of large flocks of sheep. Their wool was shorn and spun by peasants liable to statutory labor and was woven for the benefit of the bey, who sold the weavers' work to tailors and clothes merchants. The initiative of the *mubāshir* (commissioner general) was responsible for this economic rationalization, aimed at an exchange economy. The wide range of the Asyūṭ market favored the development of his business.

An ancient desert port on the Nile, Asyūṭ added to the bey's rural resources those of the customhouse, which dealt with the boats in transit on the river, and rights over the merchandise brought by the important caravans of Darfur: four or five thousand camels, led twice every year by two or three hundred people. Yaʿqūb presided over the tax collectors, evaluated the transactions, and, no doubt, invested capital in this intercontinental traffic. In exchange for African products the caravans carried fabrics from Asyūṭ, silks and soap from Syria, cloths and iron goods from Europe, and rice from the Delta.

After the death of his first wife, in 1782 Yaʿqūb married Maryam Niʿmat-Allāh Babutshī, daughter of a Syrian Christian from Aleppo. This intrusion of a Syrian into a Coptic family reflects the spread of Syrian merchants over Egypt between 1776 and 1798. ʿAlī Bey al-Kabīr had approved this expansion as early as 1769 by wrestling the rent of the customs dues from the Jews to give it to the Catholic Syrians Mīkhā'īl Fakhr and Yusuf Bītār al-Ḥalabī. No doubt this was with the intention of winning the financial resources of their community at a time when he was launching his costly annexation policy. In the pashaliks of Syria, which ʿAlī Bey coveted, the Greek Catholic community had dissented from the local Melchite orthodoxy and had ostensibly attached itself to Rome in order to avert Ottoman exactions; at the same time they retained the Arabic language in worship in order to safeguard autonomy. Welcomed to economic activity by a Muslim power, the Greek Catholic community thus defended the prosperity it had gained in trade. This occurred notably at Aleppo, a station on the route between the Mediterranean and the Indian Ocean, which received and redistributed articles manufactured in Europe, raw materials from Asia, and the products of its own vast hinterland.

While a Uniate diaspora, often from Aleppo, installed itself in Livorno (Leghorn) or Venice or Trieste in the interests of an expanding east–west trade, in Egypt the common lot of Christian minorities in the Ottoman provinces was recurring persecution and brought together the great Syrian customs officers as well as the Coptic financial commissioners. Yaʿqūb dealt with Anton Cassis Pharaon, the chief customs officer, and the Venetian Carlo Rossetti, a future consul of Austria. The commercial houses of Cairo and Aleppo jointly monopolized the movement of merchandise between Europe and the commercial ports of the East. Marriages sanctified commercial alliances, and before the last decade of the eighteenth century, the network of credit established between Syrian and European traders was extended, discreetly, to the upper stratum of the Copts. The Syrians lived in Cairo between the Coptic quarter and the Frank, in which they frequented two Catholic churches, thus ensuring in residential terms the links they had in business.

The Coptic patriarch refused to bless Yaʿqūb's marriage, which he felt to be a desertion to Aleppo and synonymous with the Catholic advance in Egypt in the eighteenth century. But the movement toward modern times brought the lines of confessional separation to a new reality. The cathedral of the Coptic patriarchate in Cairo was built in 1800 on ground offered by Yaʿqūb, a year before his death, and his widow contributed generously to the building of the Greek Catholic church in Marseilles.

On the surface, the political system was dominated by the distant Ottoman sultan and by the local rivalries of the Mamluks. In practice, the scribes of the Coptic minority exercised a degree of effective power. Yaʿqūb carried this situation of the Copts to its limits. He had great assurance because his roots were in Upper Egypt, where the real fulcrum of political power was. The Mamluk chiefs sought refuge there with powerful allies in order to renew their forces, the better to conquer Cairo. After the settlement of the Hawwārah bedouin to the south, the beys of Jirjā enjoyed an autonomy that brought Upper Egypt the prosperity built up under its last amir, Hammām, whose rule ʿAlī Bey had destroyed in 1769. Yaʿqūb was present at ʿAlī Bey's lightning ascent and at many events in the struggle between the Mamluks after his death.

Except for his status as a member of a minority, Yaʿqūb possessed all the attributes of command, as he was brilliantly to show during the three years of the French expedition. In August 1798 a fellow Copt, JIRJIS AL-JAWHARĪ, the commissioner general under Napoleon, appointed him to accompany General Desaix's division against the fleeing beys in the south. Charged with the revictualing of these troops and the organization of the camps, he also distinguished himself by feats of prowess on the battlefield—especially at ʿAyn al-Qūṣiyyah, where his quick reaction saved the advance guard from a fatal ambush. For this exploit Desaix awarded him a sword of honor. His superiority to his former masters was recognized. The Mamluks, seeking his mediation with the French, wrote through Sulaymān Bey that if the general of the division wished to lay down his arms, Murād Bey would yield to him a province in Upper Egypt or furnish him with vessels to travel to France. Yaʿqūb advised them to ask for peace themselves, and history was to prove him right. It was Murād Bey who, concluding with General Kléber the treaty of 5 April 1800, had to accept the condition of governing the province of Jirjā "with the charge of paying to the French Republic the *mīrī* [land tax] due to the sovereign of Egypt."

During the eighteen months of this campaign, Yaʿqūb assessed the reversal that was taking place and that he had thought basically settled, since he had received the French in Upper Egypt as his guests. From January 1799 it fell to him, starting from Desaix's headquarters at Jirjā, to organize the postal service necessary to link the garrisons scattered over the region.

A month after Napoleon's departure for France, General Kléber faced a catastrophic financial situation. He had to discharge the arrears in the troops' pay. Upon returning to Cairo in September 1799, Yaʿqūb was charged with accelerating the raising of contributions.

The Turks had just broken the treaty of al-ʿArīsh, and while Kléber was doing battle with them at Heliopolis, some of their cavalry slipped into Cairo and roused the population. The Coptic quarter was the target for attacks by an enraged mob led by Ḥasan Bey al-Jiddāwī. Instead of fleeing to Old Cairo and begging the protection of the Turks, as some rich Copts did, Yaʿqūb barricaded himself and defended his quarter during twenty days of siege. On 17 April 1800, Kléber decreed that all Copts should remain in their quarter, those who had fled to Old Cairo being forced to return to their homes. If its house had been burned or otherwise destroyed, a family was to be received into the nearest house. Yaʿqūb was charged with the execution of the order and was given the title agha of the Coptic nation. He was to have a guard of thirty French troops for his personal security and to ensure French respect for his authority.

The Coptic Legion was an outcome of this resistance, and is thus distinguished from other "auxiliary" units grouped within the French army by Napoleon, who had been cut off from his base (1 August 1798) by the destruction of his fleet at Aboukir (Abū Qīr) and compelled to recruit on the spot. The Coptic Legion was born of the need for self-defense and gave expression to a national vocation. Yaʿqūb had a fortress built, with towers and ramparts like those encircling the city. In Cairo and in Upper Egypt he recruited young Copts, whom French instructors trained. The legion was to consist of six companies, to be augmented as a sufficient number of men presented themselves. The figure of 800 given by the chronicler Nicolas Turc is approximate. On 23 September 1800 there were 896 men, including officers, which seems to be the largest number attained.

Yaʿqūb died suddenly of dysentery on 17 August 1801. He was buried in Marseilles.

BIBLIOGRAPHY

Documents in archives

Public Record Office, London. F. O. 78, Turkey, vol. 33.

Archives du ministère des Relations Extérieures, Paris. Correspondance politique, Turquie, vols. 203, 204, 205, 206, 208, 218.

Archives Nationales, Paris. Série AF^{iv}.

Service historique de l'armée de terre, Vincennes. Orientalis (1798–1815); Army of the Orient: correspondance, situations, registers.

Archives départementales des Bouches-du-Rhône, Marseilles. 200 876, 892. L 338.

Archives communales, Marseilles. *Etat civil;* land survey; Egyptian refugees.

Books and articles

Atiya, A. S. *A History of Eastern Christianity*. London, 1968.

Auriant. "Maallem Yakoub, dit le 'Général Jacob,' commandant la Légion Copte (1798–1801)." *L'Acropole*, 6 (1931):137–146.

______. *La vie du chevalier Théodore Lascaris ou l'Imposteur malgré lui.* Paris, 1940.

ʿAwad, L. *Al-Mu'aththirāt al-Ajnabiyyah fī al-Adab al-ʿArabī al-Ḥadīth 2, al-Fikr al-Siyāsī wa al-Ijtimāʿī.* Cairo, 1966.

Bachatly, C. "Un membre oriental du premier Institut d'Egypte: Don Raphaël (1759–1831)." *Bulletin de l'Institut d'Égypte*, 17, 2 (1934–1935):237–260.

Belliard, A.-D. *Mémoires du comte Belliard publiés par Vinet.* Paris, 1842.

Chevalier, M. *La politique financière de l'Expédition d'Egypte (1798–1801) (Cahiers d'histoire égyptienne.* 7–8). June 1955–July 1956.

Dehérain, H. *L'Egypte turque. Pachas et Mamelouks du XVIe au XVIIIe siècle. L'Expedition du général Bonaparte (Histoire de la Nation Egyptienne* 5). Paris, 1934.

Douin, G. *L'Egypte indépendante. Projet de 1801.* Cairo, 1924.

Gibb, H. A. R., and Harold Bowen. *Islamic Society and the West.* 2 vols. Oxford, 1950–1957.

Gozlan, L. "Les Réfugiés Egyptiens à Marseille." *La Revue Contemporaine* (January 1866):31–47.

Guemard, G. "Les auxiliaires de l'armée de Bonaparte en Egypte." *Bulletin de l'Institut d'Egypte* 19 (1926):1–17.

Haddad, G. A. "A Project for the Independence of Egypt, 1801." *Journal of the American Oriental Society*, 90, no. 2 (1970):169–183.

Haddad, R. M. *Syrian Christians in Muslim Society.* Princeton, N.J., 1970.

Hourani, A. H. "The Changing Face of the Fertile Crescent in the XVIIIth century." *Studia Islamica* 8 (1957):89–122.

______. "The Syrians in Egypt in the Eighteenth and Nineteenth Centuries." In *Colloque international sur l'histoire du Caire*, pp. 221–233. 1969.

Al-Jabartī, ʿAbd al-Rahmān. *ʿAjā'ib al-Āthār fī al-Tarājim wa al-Akhbār*, Būlāq 1297/1879. 4 vols. Translation by A. Cardin.

Kayata, P. *Monographie de l'église grecque catholique de Marseille.* Marseilles, 1901.

Kishk, M. J. *Wa Dakhalat al-Khayl al-Azhar.* Beirut, 1971.

Louca, A. *Voyageurs et écrivains égyptiens en France au XIXe siècle.* Paris, 1970.

______. "Militaires coptes en Egypte au XIXe siècle." In *Minorités, techniques et métiers.* Aix-en-Provence, 1980.

______. "Les cinquante jours à Marseille de Rifāʿah al-Tahṭāwī". In *L'Orient des Provençaux dans l'histoire.* Marseilles, 1982.

______. "Les sources marseillaises de l'Orient romantique." In *Le miroir égyptien.* Marseilles 1984, pp. 243–257.

ʿAbd al-Rahmān al-Rāfiʿī. *Tārīkh al-Ḥarakah al-Qawmiyyah*, 2 vols. Cairo, 1938.

Raymond, A. *Artisans et commerçants au Caire au XVIIIe siècle*, 2 vols. Damascus, 1973.

Reynaud, G. "Les données de l'état civil et du cadastre (1801–1833)." In *L'Orient des Provençaux dans l'histoire.* Marseilles, 1982.

Saman, E. "L'église Saint-Nicolas de Myre de Marseille et les collaborateurs orientaux de Bonaparte." *Marseilles revue municipale* 124 (1981): 50–59.
Savant, J. *Les Mamelouks de Napoléon*. Paris, 1949.
Turc, N. *Chronique d'Egypte (1798–1804)*, trans. G. Wiet. Cairo, 1950.
Volney, C. F. Chasseboeuf comte de. *Voyage en Syrie et en Égypte [1782–1785]*. Published by Jean Gaulmier. Paris–La Haye, 1959.

ANWAR LOUCA

YAʻQŪB NAKHLAH RUFAYLAH (1847–1908), Egyptian historian. He was born in Cairo and received his early education in a primitive Coptic school, where he learned Italian and English while perfecting his knowledge of Coptic. He was appointed teacher at the Coptic School of Hārit al-Saqqāyīn, from which many celebrated personalities graduated prior to the foundation of the COPTIC COLLEGE. Later he left the field of education and became a proofreader for the Būlāq Government Press. This experience proved to be invaluable for him in the establishment of the Coptic printing presses of the daily newspaper *Al-Waṭan* and the Tawfīq Society.

He occupied several government posts. Later, he moved to the Fayyūm Province, where he was appointed secretary of the Fayyūm Railways Company and founded welfare societies and two schools, one for boys and one for girls.

Throughout his educational and administrative career, he retained his literary interests and wrote numerous books on the teaching of Arabic to English-speakers and on the teaching of English to his native countrymen. But his masterpiece was a Coptic history in Arabic entitled *Tārīkh al-Ummah al-Qibṭiyyah* (History of the Coptic Nation, Cairo, 1899).

Notwithstanding his official duties and his literary productivity, Rufaylah found time to participate in community affairs and in the reform movements of his age. He was the founder of numerous religious societies and clubs for the edification of the Coptic youth. Moreover, he was an active member of the Coptic COMMUNITY COUNCIL. He was undoubtedly one of the most effective members of the Coptic community in the nineteenth century.

BIBLIOGRAPHY

Ramzī Tadrus. *Al-Aqbāṭ fī al-Qarn al-ʻIshrīn*, 5 vols. Cairo, 1911–1919.
Tawfīq Iskarūs. *Nawābigh al-Aqbāṭ wa'Mashāhiruhum fī al-Qarn al-Tāsī ʻAshar*, 2 vols. Cairo, 1910–1913.

AZIZ S. ATIYA

YARNS. *See* Textiles, Coptic: Manufacturing Techniques.

YASSA ʻABD AL-MASĪḤ (1898–1959), Egyptian scholar, with special knowledge of ecclesiastical Arabic. Although his higher education was limited to diplomas in theological studies from the Coptic Clerical College (1922) and in archaeology from the Egyptian University, now Cairo University, he distinguished himself through his own independent efforts in the study of the Coptic language. He became an internationally recognized scholar in this field.

He started his career as a teacher at Thamarat al-Tawfīq Coptic School (1918–1922). He then became librarian of the Coptic Museum in Old Cairo (1922–1957). In 1951 he was selected to assist in the American expedition for microfilming the manuscripts of the MOUNT SINAI MONASTERY OF SAINT CATHERINE. He taught Coptic at the CLERICAL COLLEGE and the HIGHER INSTITUTE OF COPTIC STUDIES.

His publications include *Catalogue of the Coptic and Arabic Manuscripts in the Coptic Museum, the Patriarchate, the Principal Churches in Cairo and Alexandria, and the Monasteries of Egypt* (with Murqus Simaykah Pasha, 3 vols., Cairo, 1939–1942); an unedited Bohairic letter of Abgar (*Bulletin de l'Institut français d'Archéologie orientale* 45, 1946, pp. 65–80); a Sahidic fragment of the Martyrdom of Saint Philotheus (*Orientalia Christiana Periodica* 4, 1938, pp. 584–90); "Saint Cyrille dans la liturgie de l'église copte" (*Kyrelliana*, 1947); "Doxologies in the Coptic Church" (*Bulletin de la Société d'archéologie copte* 4, 1938, pp. 97–113; 5, 1939, pp. 175–91; 6, 1940, pp. 19–76; 8, 1942, pp. 31–61); letter from a bishop of al-Fayyūm (*Bulletin de la Société d'archéologie copte* 7, 1941, pp. 15–18); *History of the Patriarchs of the Egyptian Church* (trans., with O. H. E. Burmester, of the *History of the Holy Church*, by Sāwīrus ibn al-Muqaffaʻ, Vol. 2, pt. 1, Cairo, 1943; and with Aziz Suryal Atiya and O. H. E. Burmester, Vol. 2, pts. 2–3, Cairo, 1948–1949); and *The Gospel According to Thomas* (ed. and trans. with A. Guillaumont, H. C. Puech, and W. C. Till, New York, 1959).

BIBLIOGRAPHY

Burmester, O. H. E. Obituary. *Bulletin de la Société d'archéologie copte* 15 (1958–1960):191–92.

Kammerer, W. *A Coptic Bibliography.* Ann Arbor, Mich., 1950.

Khater, A. "Bibliographie de Yassa ʿAbd al-Masīḥ." *Bulletin de la Société d'archéologie copte* 15 (1958–1960):167.

MIRRIT BOUTROS GHALI
MUNIR BASTA

YESHAQ I. *See* Ethiopian Prelates.

YESHAQ II. *See* Ethiopian Prelates.

YOHANNES I. *See* Ethiopian Prelates.

YOHANNES II. *See* Ethiopian Prelates.

YOHANNES III. *See* Ethiopian Prelates.

YOSAB I. *See* Ethiopian Prelates.

YOSAB II. *See* Ethiopian Prelates.

YOUTH OF EGYPT (al-Shabībah al-Miṣriyyah), a clandestine society formed in Alexandria toward the end of Khedive Ismāʿīl's rule (1863–1879), under the influence of the reformer Jamal al-Afghānī. The society's original members were said to have been representative of the cream of the youth of Alexandria's Christian and Jewish families.

Conflicting accounts are given of the person who sponsored the society. While some claim it was Sharif Pasha, others say it was Prince ʿAbbās Ḥalīm.

The society came into the open early in September 1879 when a reform scheme calling for a secular state was submitted to Khedive Tawfīq, whom some members considered an advocate of reform and expected much of. The society's scheme advocated the distribution of power through the maintenance of equality before the law, all Egyptians qualifying for government employment without any discrimination as to religion or origin.

Furthermore, the scheme contained constitutional and other demands regarding education, political rights, individual freedoms, freedom of the press, and freedom of the people to elect their deputies. The scheme spelled out the executive, the judicial, and the legislative power.

A bilingual newspaper called *La Jeune Egypte* was put out by the society for the prime purpose of advocating internal political reforms. The newspaper was mostly in French; the Arabic was translated from the French text. Subjected to the oppressive policies of Riyāḍ Pasha, the newspaper was eventually confiscated and disappeared. This led to the disappearance of the society itself.

BIBLIOGRAPHY

Salīm Naqqāsh. *Miṣr lil-Miṣriyyīn*, 9 vols. Alexandria, 1886.

Schölch, A. *Egypt for the Egyptians: The Socio-Political Crisis in Egypt, 1878–1882.* London, 1981.

Ṭāhir al-Ṭanāḥī, ed. *Mudhakkirāt al-Shaykh Muḥammad ʿAbdū.* Cairo, 1963.

YŪNĀN LABIB RIZQ

YOUTH MOVEMENTS. Coptic youth movements started to appear at the end of the nineteenth century under Pope CYRIL V (1874–1927). The 112th patriarch of the Coptic church stressed the importance of religious education and moral teachings, among the young especially. Archdeacon ḤABĪB JIRJIS played a significant role in encouraging such trends. In 1900, with the help of some of his friends, the archdeacon formed a youth organization with branches all over Egypt. Its aim was to provide Christian education to Christian students attending public schools. Ḥabīb Jirjis was especially interested in the students of the CLERICAL COLLEGE, in whom he saw the future leaders of these movements.

In 1909 in Fajjālah, a district of Cairo, a special center was dedicated to youth services. It later became the Society of the Friends of the Bible, whose founder, Basīlī Buṭrus, was a graduate of the Clerical College. Concentrating on youth activities, its branches spread all over Egypt. By 1928 the students of the Clerical College had formed the Society for the Spread of the Word of Salvation, with nine centers in Cairo aimed at young people. Some of these centers were later turned into churches.

In 1937 another group of the Clerical College

founded a similar association, Soldiers of the Coptic Church, with eighty branches extending from Giza, south of Cairo, to many of the northern dioceses. The main purpose of these centers was to promote Christian knowledge and church attendance among isolated Christian communities that had become Christian in name only. Special attention was given to those who lived in rural areas away from established churches. Weekly gatherings were organized for religious instruction and the distribution of free Bibles. General education was also provided for the eradication of illiteracy by establishing modest centers with libraries. The appearance of Sunday schools in 1927 played an important role in offering fundamental Christian education in areas where it was most needed.

In 1946, the Society of Coptic Students and the Sunday School Organization jointly issued a list of aims, rules, and regulations for their associations. Different groups were assigned to various activities, to serve the religious, spiritual, social, intellectual, artistic, and athletic needs of Coptic youth. This created an unprecedented religious awareness among young men and young women, resulting in the mobilization of a youth force dedicated to religious and social services. Young people, many of them university graduates, participated in these activities. Some joined monasteries and became monks. Some were raised to the rank of bishop and archbishop. Pope SHENOUDA III was chosen from these groups in 1971. He later established a special bishopric for the supervision of the various youth activities all over the country.

For these activities, wise leadership is essential. Books are provided for different needs in different disciplines, while tutoring is offered to those in secondary schools and universities by professional volunteers. Several camps are available for Christian communal living, and cultural activities are encouraged throughout the year. Youth organizations have become a vital arm of the Coptic church, stressing ecumenism and tolerance among its members.

BIBLIOGRAPHY

Ḥabīb Jirjis. *Al-Iklirīkiyyah bayn al-Māḍī wa-al-Ḥaḍir.* Cairo, 1928.

Al-Manhaj al-ʿĀm li-Madāris al-Aḥad al-Qibṭiyyah. Cairo, 1948.

ANBĀ MUSĀ

YU'ANNIS. *See also under* John.

YU'ANNIS, thirteenth-century (?) bishop of Asyūṭ, known for having edited the panegyric of the martyrs of Isnā who died under Maximian (286–310): Saint Dīlājī and her four children, Eusebius and his brothers, as well as their companions.

The panegyric occupies 182 pages, with twelve lines per page. It is found in at least three Arabic manuscripts from Egypt: (1) Cairo, collection of Qummuṣ 'Abd al-Masīḥ Ṣalīb al-Baramūsī al-Mas'ūdī; (2) National Library, Paris, Arabe 780, a copy finished in the month of Bashans, A.M. 1236/April–May A.D. 1520, for the Coptic patriarch John XIII; fols. 23a–115a; and (3) National Library, Paris, Arabe 4887, Egypt, nineteenth century, fols. 63a–143a; the text is identical to that of the preceding manuscript.

BIBLIOGRAPHY

Cheikho, L. *Catalogue des manuscrits des auteurs arabes chrétiens depuis l'Islam.* Beirut, 1924.

Graf, G. *Catalogue de manuscrits arabes chrétiens conservés au Caire.* Vatican City, 1934.

Sbath, P. *Al-Fihris* (*Catalogue de manuscrits arabes*), Vol. 1. Cairo, 1938.

______. "Manuscrits arabes d'auteurs coptes." *Bulletin de la Société d'archéologie copte* 5 (1939): 159–73.

Slane, W. McG. baron de. *Catalogue des manuscrits arabes de la Bibliothèque Nationale.* Paris, 1883–1895.

Troupeau, G. *Catalogue des manuscrits arabes* [de Paris], Vol. 2. Paris, 1974.

KHALIL SAMIR, S.J.

YŪḤANNĀ. *See also under* John.

YŪḤANNĀ, bishop of Samannūd (c. 1240), one of the first four bishops consecrated on 29 July 1235 by the patriarch Cyril (1235–1243) in the CHURCH OF ABŪ SAYFAYN in Old Cairo. As bishop, he signed a new judicial code (3 September 1238) and was first signatory of a protocol on the ranking of bishops (28 June 1240) and on the closing of a meeting in the Cairo citadel (8 September 1240). He worked along with the monk Yūsāb for the reconciliation of the resisting monks of DAYR ANBĀ MAQĀR with the patriarch, and after the death of Cyril, he and Yūsāb, by then bishop of Fuwwah, took a decisive part in the disputed choice of the new patriarch, Athanasius ibn Kalīl. He was still alive in 1257, and in the introduction to his dictionary Abū al-

MU'TAMAN Ibn al-'Assal mentioned him with high praise. Yūḥannā was mostly occupied with the composition of aids to the understanding of the Coptic language. The list of the extant transmitted material is long.

Yūḥannā's works include a grammar, *Muqaddimat al-Sullam* (Introduction to the Ladder), which presents an inventory of the elementary components of the Coptic language, chiefly the Bohairic dialect. The articles, suffixes for nouns and verbs, prepositional and adverbial particles, and elements of conjugation are explained. An elaboration with similar treatment of the Sahidic dialect is more likely the supplementary work of a later writer. The introduction was translated into Latin and Italian in the early seventeenth century by Thomas Obicini (A. van Lantschoot, 1948; Latin trans. Kircher, 1643).

Al-Sullam al-Kanā'isī (The Ecclesiastical Ladder), the vocabulary for which the *Muqaddimat* is the grammatical introduction, takes the most important words from the books in use in the church and translates them into a sort of glossary, following the order of the texts themselves: New Testament, with John, Matthew, Mark, Luke, Epistles, and Revelation; Old Testament, with Psalms and extracts from Sirach and the other Wisdom books.

A separate history (*Akhbār*) of the martyrs who were killed in the city of Samannūd appears under the name of the same Yūḥannā.

A translation of a theological compendium from an undetermined Greek original is attributed to Yūḥannā. It is in the popular form of questions from a student and answers from a teacher.

BIBLIOGRAPHY

Lantschoot, A. van. *Un précurseur d'Athanase Kircher, Thomas Obicini et la Scala.* Vatican Copte 71. Bibliothèque du Muséon 22. Louvain, 1948.

Simaykah, M., and Y. 'Abd al-Masīḥ. *Catalogue of the Coptic and Arabic Manuscripts in the Coptic Museum, the Patriarchate, the Principal Churches of Cairo and the Monasteries of Egypt,* Vol. 2. Cairo, 1942.

VINCENT FREDERICK

YUḤANNĀ, scribe of Shenute I. Originally the spiritual son and disciple of MĪNĀ I (767–774), the forty-seventh patriarch, Yuḥannā later became the scribe of SHENUTE I (858–880), fifty-fifth patriarch. Apparently he lived to be a centenarian and wrote the biographies of contemporary patriarchs, nine in number, including, besides the aforementioned two, JOHN IV (775–799), MARK II (799–819), JACOB (819–830), SIMON II (830), YŪSĀB I (830–849), KHĀ'ĪL II (849–851), and COSMAS II (851–858). His record of the forty-seventh to the fifty-fifth patriarchs was discovered in Dayr Nahyā by SĀWĪRUS IBN AL-MUQAFFA', bishop of al-Ashmūnayn, who included its contents in his HISTORY OF THE PATRIARCHS, but the original appears to have been lost since then. He must have lived through the Abbasid period from Caliph al-Manṣūr (754–775) to al-Muhtadī (869–870), and he must also have witnessed the rise of Aḥmad ibn Ṭūlūn (870–881), under whom Egypt attained local independence. He was a close companion of all these patriarchs, and he states that he was incarcerated with Shenute I. The name of the author emerges occasionally in the course of the text, and he often refers to himself as an eyewitness of the events that he describes in detail.

AZIZ S. ATIYA

YŪḤANNĀ THE DEACON, also known as Yūḥannā ibn Moesis, the spiritual son and disciple of Anbā Moesis, the saintly bishop of Awsīm. He lived around the middle of the eighth century, during the rule of the Umayyad caliphate. He compiled a series of patriarchal biographies up to his own time, and his work was utilized by SĀWĪRUS IBN AL-MUQAFFA' in his HISTORY OF THE PATRIARCHS. The original work, which is lost, appears to have been derived at least in part from another source by a certain Archdeacon Abū Jirjah, who lived in the seventh century and was a personal friend of SIMON I, forty-second patriarch (689–701). This Abū Jirjah compiled the patriarchal biographies from CYRIL I (412–444) to ALEXANDER II (705–730), covering the period of the later ecumenical movement as well as the rise of Islam and the Arab conquest of Egypt. Also lost but incorporated in Yūḥannā's work, it continued the biographies down to the patriarchate of Theodore (731–743), which appears only in outline.

The real contribution of Yūḥannā appears in the elaborate biography of Theodore's successor, KHĀ'ĪL I (744–767). Being his contemporary, Yūḥannā was able to assemble the major events of his patriarchate, which spanned the reigns of al-Walīd ibn Yazīd (743–744) to the last Umayyad caliph, Marwān II (744–750), and the early Abbasid caliphs al-Saffāḥ (750–754) and al-Manṣūr (754–775). This is probably one of the richest and fullest biographies in the *History of the Patriarchs*. It abounds in details that throw a flood of light not only on the internal history of the church and eighth-century Egypt in general but also on the foreign relations of other patriarchates and of the whole caliphate. The name of his spiritual mentor, Anbā Moesis, appears continuously in his story, and they both figure as the primary movers of the selection of Khā'īl to the throne of Saint Mark from among the monks of the monastery of Saint Macarius in Wādī al-Naṭrūn. His work abounds in interesting details and deserves a special analytical study.

BIBLIOGRAPHY

Kāmil Ṣāliḥ Nakhlah. *Kitāb Tārīkh wa-Jadāwil Baṭārikat al-Iskandariyyah al-Qibṭ.* Cairo, 1943.

AZIZ S. ATIYA

YŪḤANNĀ AL-ḤĀDHIQ AL-QIBṬĪ (MU'ALLIM), seventeenth-century author of a history of the world from the creation to the age of the apostles, called *Kitāb Akhbār al-Zamān*. He intended the work as an apology, as indicated in the introduction, rather than a historical treatise. Yūḥannā once had a discussion with a Jew concerning the Christian faith and the life of Jesus. Because the Jew denied the advent of the Messiah, Yūḥannā resolved to prove Christ's existence by appealing to the Old Testament. He also employed as proof the work of another Jew, Yūsuf ibn Kuryūn (Joseph ben Gorion), written in the ninth century. This work was translated into Arabic in the tenth century by the Yemeni Jew Zakariyyā ibn Sa'īd, and was known widely in the Coptic church during the Middle Ages. Yūḥannā also referred to Christian works such as those by Epiphanius of Salamis, Sa'īd ibn al-Biṭrīq, the Melchite patriarch, and "the eighty-one books of the Jacobite Christians."

After reviewing the history of the kings of Israel, the Persians, Alexander, the Seleucids, and the Roman emperors, Yūḥannā sought to establish Jesus' divinity by appealing to His miracles in the Gospels and to the missions of the apostles. He ended his work on this enigmatic note: "I then turned around and saw this Jew no longer. To this day I do not know where he went." Contrary to what he said in the preface—that the history would continue to 1020—he stopped with the missions of the apostles.

G. Graf at first considered Yūḥannā to be Melchite Orthodox, then classified him among Coptic authors. Naṣrallāh rejected the possibility that he might be Melchite. The employment of Coptic dates in his book and the contents of the book itself confirm that he belonged to the Coptic community. This is further substantiated by the fact that the only two existing manuscripts known of this history are of Coptic origin.

As for the date of this work, one could consider that it was written shortly after 1612, if the Arabic date 1020, noted in its preface, is correct.

There are two known manuscripts, one in Cairo, in the private collection of Jirjis 'Abd al-Masīḥ, and the other in the National Library, Paris (Arabe 6702). This latter manuscript was copied by the priest Yūḥannā of Ḥārit al-Rūm in Cairo; it was finished on 15 Tūt A.M. 1503/October 1785. He may have been the same priest who, in October 1806, copied the manuscript now in the Coptic Museum (Liturgy 295) and bequeathed it to the Church of the Virgin of Ḥārit al-Rūm.

BIBLIOGRAPHY

Blochet, E. *Catalogue des manuscrits arabes des nouvelles acquisitions (1884–1924).* Paris, 1925.

Cheikho, L. *Catalogue des manuscrits des auteurs arabes chrétiens depuis l'Islam.* Beirut, 1924.

Nasrallāh, J. *Histoire du mouvement littéraire dans l'église melchite du Ve an XXe siècle,* Vol. 4: *Période ottomane (1516–1900),* pt. 1: 1516–1724. Louvain and Paris, 1979.

Sbath, P. *Al-Fihris (Catalogue de manuscrits arabes),* Supplement. Cairo, 1940.

Troupeau, G. *Catalogue des manuscrits arabes,* Vol. 2, pt. 1, *Manuscrits chrétiens.* Paris, 1974.

KHALIL SAMIR, S.J.

YŪḤANNĀ IBN SĀWĪRUS, the author of a single work, *Kitāb al-'Ilm wa-al-'Amal* (Book of Theory and Practice). The oldest manuscript dates from 1323, and he is mentioned in the author index of Abū al-Barakāt IBN KABAR, so that he probably lived before the first quarter of the fourteenth century. The additions to his name in the heading to his work indicate that he came from Cairo or spent most of his life there in some official post known as *al-kātib al-Miṣrī* (Egyptian secretarial official).

Yūḥannā's work, instigated by the Muslim teacher Abū 'Alī ibn al-Ḥasan (or al-Husayn) ibn Mawhūb, is a counterpart of numerous Islamic writings on theoretical and practical ethics. From the longing for immortality that mankind has, recognizing that this can be realized only in the next world, and assuming the desirability of a virtuous life in this world, the writer arrives at an apologia for Christianity. He gives fifteen arguments based on Christian moral doctrine. Reasons for accepting the rules of Christian law are the existence of miracles and the moral benefit derived from the rules, which provide a greater benefit than philosophy does. Theoretical knowledge is requisite to practical activity, and so Yūḥannā gave ways and means of achieving both. The whole work is a fundamental exposition of Christian moral doctrine made up from rational considerations and evangelical testimony.

VINCENT FREDERICK

YŪḤANNĀ IBN ZAKARIYYĀ IBN ABI SIBA'. *See* Ibn Sibā' Yūḥannā Ibn Abī Zakariyyā.

YŪḤANNĀ AL-MAQSĪ, fourteenth-century hieromonk at DAYR AL-BARAMŪS in the Wādī al-Naṭrūn. Yūḥannā lived for a certain period at DAYR AL-QUṢAYR, which was situated at Ṭurah about 15 miles (24 km) south of Old Cairo at a monastery he calls "the mount of Saint Arsenios, known as the 'cells.'" It was there in 1329 that he copied the NOMOCANON of al-Ṣafī IBN AL-'ASSĀL, completing his work in June 1329.

The manuscript is now at the Monastery of Saint Macarius in the Wādī al-Naṭrūn. On folio 245v we find the colophon in Arabic, accompanied by a cryptogram in Coptic characters, which explains the ethnic surname of this monk. At the beginning of the twentieth century, the abbot 'Abd al-Masīḥ Ṣalīb al-Masū'dī al-Baramūsī read it as *al-Muqassī* (with a *shaddah,* cf. note to fol. 1). The name indicates that the monk came from the port town of al-Maqs, outside the city of Cairo, the fortress of which forms the west corner of the north wall built by Saladin (Ṣalāḥ al-Dīn) between 1176 and 1193 in order to encircle the city of Cairo.

BIBLIOGRAPHY

Zanetti, U. "Un Cryptogramme copte de Pierre V d'Alexandrie." *Analecta Bollandiana* 100 (1982): 692–700.

KHALIL SAMIR, S.J.

YUḤANNIS IBN BUQṬUR AL-DIMYĀṬĪ, a Melchite from Damietta who became a monk at the monastery of Sinai in the year A.H. 374/A.D. 984/985. He subsequently became a priest.

In 995, he copied a gospel book for the feasts of the year, in two columns, Greek and Arabic. His Arabic handwriting, halfway between *kūfī* and *naskhī* script, is very clear. His orthography and grammar leave something to be desired. His Greek hand is entirely in capitals, rather angular, but cultivated. A reproduction of folios 1v–2r may be found in figure 17 of Atiya and Youssef (1970, p. 228).

BIBLIOGRAPHY

Atiya, A. S., and J. N. Youssef. *Catalogue Raisonné of the Mount Sinai Manuscripts.* Alexandria, 1970.

KHALIL SAMIR, S.J.

YŪNĀ (JONAS) OF ARMANT (feast day: 2 Ṭūbah). Of this monk, who came from and lived near the town of Armant in Upper Egypt, we know only what is said by the recension of the SYNAXARION of the Copts from Upper Egypt.

Yūnā's birth was miraculous, brought about by the prayers and ascetic practices of his maternal uncle, a monk of the Dayr Anbā Ḥiziqyāl (Ezekiel) in the inner desert (the most remote from the Nile Valley). This was like the birth of the prophet Samuel, with the explicit promise that he would be dedicated from the age of three. As soon as he had been weaned, at the age of three, his mother also dedicated him and entrusted him to her brother, Anbā Victor. His uncle brought him up in the knowledge of the scriptures, and instilled in him all the practices of asceticism. From this narrative we learn the existence of two monasteries no doubt not very far apart: DAYR ANBĀ DARYŪS and DAYR AL-MALĀK GHUBRĪYĀL, where Yūnā sometimes went. The first appears to have been his usual residence, and it was there that his uncle was buried.

Several miracles are related, and we learn from these accounts that the civil power was Muslim, which shows that Yūnā lived after the Muslim conquest. There is reference to the monastery of Saint Mattāwus (Matthew) of Isnā, no doubt the one today called DAYR AL-FAKHŪRI, and the founder is mentioned in the Life of the patriarch ALEXANDER II (705–730) in the HISTORY OF THE PATRIARCHS. It can be deduced that this Saint Yūnā or Jonas lived in the seventh or eighth century.

As his death approached, Yūnā had the vision of numerous saints, and expired peacefully at the age, it is precisely stated, of seventy-two years and four months. He was buried beside the church, no doubt that of the monastery of Anbā Daryūs, where his uncle had been buried.

BIBLIOGRAPHY

Amélineau, E. *La Géographie de l'Egypte à l'époque copte.* Paris, 1893.

RENÉ-GEORGES COQUIN

YŪSĀB, thirteenth-century bishop of Akhmīm. No biographical note exists concerning this bishop. Information about him is scattered through various sources. His name appears for the first time in 1250 on the occasion of the consecration of ATHANASIUS III, the seventy-sixth patriarch. He was described on that occasion as the senior bishop of Upper Egypt, and he seems to have been the consecrating bishop.

In 1257 he was present at the consecration of the chrism performed by Athanasius III (cf. Munier, 1943, p. 35).

In 1260, or a little earlier, Yūsāb asked Buṭrus al-Sadamantī to compose a treatise of moral theology to complement that on faith. Buṭrus fulfilled his request, completing the treatise on 12 May 1260. In his preamble, Buṭrus calls Bishop Yūsāb "the sincere friend, brother and companion in divine service, partner in common life and spiritual formation." This suggests that they lived in the same monastery. Thus Yūsāb must at first have been a monk in the Dayr Mār Jirjis of Sadamant (or Sidmant) in the Fayyūm region (van den Akker, 1972, pp. 18 and 24–25).

In 1262, Yūsāb consecrated JOHN VII, the seventy-seventh patriarch. He no longer appears at the consecration of GABRIEL III, the seventy-eighth patriarch, in 1268; this may have been on account of internal conflicts in the community prompted by this election.

In 1294, Yūsāb was present at the consecration of THEODOSIOS II, the seventy-ninth patriarch. However, on this occasion the ordaining prelate was Anbā Buṭrus Ḥasaballāh, bishop of Shanshā in Lower Egypt.

In 1299, no bishop of Akhmīm took part in the consecration of the chrism on 12 April, which was described at length by Abū al-Barakāt IBN KABAR in chapter 9 of his encyclopedia. Yūsāb was probably too aged to take part in so tiring a ceremony. The list of the twelve bishops present is given in Munier (1943, p. 36).

In 1300 he was again present at the consecration of JOHN VIII, the eightieth patriarch, with fourteen other bishops. On this occasion he signed himself "bishop of Akhmīm and Abū Tīj," thus combining two sees (van Lantschoot, 1932, p. 229, no. 2). This combination of the sees was only provisional, as in 1257 Anbā Yu'annis held the title of Abū Tīj (Munier, 1943, p. 35); and in 1305 and 1320 Anbā Marqus held the title of Abū Tīj (Munier, 1943, pp. 38 and 39). Thus by 1305 Yūsāb was already dead.

Yūsāb may have been born around 1210, maybe in the Fayyūm region. As an adult he became a monk at DAYR MĀR JIRJIS in the mountains of Sadamant. Between 1240 and 1250, after the protracted vacancy of the patriarchal see that lasted from 1216 to 1235, during which period most of the bishops died, he was appointed as bishop of Akhmīm in Upper Egypt. He died at an advanced age, soon after February 1300.

BIBLIOGRAPHY

Akker, P. van den. *Buṭrus as-Sadamantī, Introduction sur l'herméneutique.* Beirut, 1972.

Graf, G. "Die Rangordnung der Bischöfe Ägyptens nach einem protokollarischen Bericht des Patriarchen Kyrillos ibn Laḳlaḳ." *Oriens Christianus* 24 (1927):306–337.

Lantschoot, A. van. "Le ms. Vatican copte 44 et le livre du chrême (ms. Paris arabe 100)." *Le Muséon* 45 (1932):181–234.

Miṣbāḥ al-Ẓulmah fī Īḍāḥ al-Khidmah. li-Shams al-Riyāsah Abī al-Barakāt al ma'ruf bi-Ibn Kabar, ed. Khalil Samir, S.J., Cairo, 1971.

Munier, H. *Recueil des listes épiscopales de l'église copte.* Cairo, 1943.

Muyser, Jacob. "Contribution à l'étude des listes épiscopales de l'église copte." *Bulletin de la Société d'archéologie copte* 10 (1944):115–76.

KHALIL SAMIR, S.J.

YŪSĀB, fifteenth-century bishop of Akhmīm. It is not certain if a Yūsāb, bishop of Akhmīm, ever existed in the fifteenth century, as no lists of Coptic bishops from this century exist.

However, in 1938 P. Sbath mentioned four works attributed to a certain Yūsāb, bishop of Akhmīm, in various manuscripts, stating he was a "Coptic author of the fifteenth century" although he gave no basis for this assertion.

In 1944, J. Muyser (p. 156) attributed these treatises to YŪSĀB, the thirteenth-century bishop, although he, too, gave no basis for his statement. In 1947, independently of Muyser, Graf made the same attribution; however, four years later he corrected what he had written and attributed these works to the eighteenth-century YŪSĀB, bishop of Jirjā and Akhmīm; again, he gave no basis for his choice.

One of these works is contained in a manuscript belonging to the *qummuṣ* Armāniyūs Ḥabashī of Cairo, who is said to have copied it in 1507. This would rule out the eighteenth-century bishop, who is, furthermore, always described in the manuscripts as "bishop of Dirjā [sic] and Akhmīm." As for the attribution to the thirteenth-century bishop, it is possible but entirely unfounded.

The following hypothesis may be advanced: the first work, the only one attested in the manuscript copied in 1507, may be attributed to Yūsāb of the fifteenth century (or the thirteenth-century Yūsāb), whereas the three others could well have been written by the eighteenth-century Yūsāb.

The titles of the four works are: (1) *Apology for the Christian Religion* (manuscripts of the *qummuṣ* ʿAbd al-Masīḥ Ṣalīb al-Baramūsī al-Masūʿdī, and of the *qummuṣ* Armāniyūs Ḥabashī); (2) *Treatise on the Trinity* (manuscript belonging to Abd al-Masīḥ Ṣalīb); (3) *Treatise on the Incarnation of the Word of God;* and (4) *Controversy with a Muslim* (three undated manuscripts belonging to Copts of Cairo, namely the two *qummuṣ* mentioned above and Jirjis ʿAbd al-Masīḥ).

BIBLIOGRAPHY

Muyser, J. "Contribution à l'étude des listes épiscopales de l'église copte." *Bulletin de la Société d'archéologie copte* 10 (1944):115–76.

Sbath, P. *Al-Fihris* (*Catalogue de manuscrits arabes*), Vols. 1, 3. Cairo, 1938, 1940.

KHALIL SAMIR, S.J.

YŪSĀB (1735–1826), bishop of Jirjā and Akhmīm. Yūsāb was born in al-Nukhaylah (province of Asyūṭ); his name was originally Yūsuf. In 1760 he became a monk at the Monastery of Saint Antony on the Red Sea. In 1791, the 107th patriarch, JOHN XVIII (1769–1796), who belonged once to the Monastery of Saint Antony, consecrated him bishop for the double diocese of Jirjā and Akhmīm, with residence at Jirjā. He was full of zeal for the moral and spiritual renewal of the faithful and for the struggle against the Catholic missionary propaganda campaign which was active at that period in his diocese. He died in 1826 at the age of ninety-one, and the SYNAXARION commemorates him on account of the sanctity of his life.

Yūsāb was the author of over thirty brief treatises on exegesis, moral theology, pastoral theology, and liturgy. They were collected, and usually appear in the manuscripts with the title *Silāḥ al-Mu'minīn* (The Weapon of the Faithful). In the two Paris manuscripts they appear under the title *Kitāb al-Maqālāt* (Book of Treatises). No particular system is evident in the order of these collections, and it may be purely chronological. This would mean Yūsāb added his treatises to a manuscript gradually, as he wrote them. These collections are usually preceded by a long preface, written after all the treatises were completed and absent in the oldest manuscript of all (National Library, Paris, Arabe 4711).

The most complete of these series contains thirty-one treatises. It is given in three manuscripts of the Coptic Patriarchate, Cairo (Theology 137, Theology 226, and Theology 316). The Paris manuscript contains twenty-seven treatises, the first nineteen of which correspond to the first nineteen of other collections. It also includes one treatise (the twenty-second) not found elsewhere. Another manuscript in the Coptic Patriarchate (Theology 138) contains the first eighteen and also a new item (the thirty-third in our list). A second manuscript in Paris (Arabe 4790) contains only treatises 1, 13, and 17 in our list. Certain treatises attributed to YŪSĀB, bishop of Akhmīm (fifteenth century), could simply be treatises 1, 2, and 13 by the present author.

The style of these treatises is very casual, both on account of the language, which is full of grammatical errors and vulgarisms, and on account of the redaction, which contains numerous repetitions and sentences that are often incomprehensible.

An inventory of the treatises follows. The order comes from the most complete manuscript (Coptic Patriarchate, Cairo, Theology 137). The number of the treatise in the Paris Arabe 4711, when the order differs from the Cairo manuscript, is indicated in parentheses. Three treatises or letters contained in other manuscripts are listed at the end.

1. The existence of the Creator, and the Trinity, and His attributes.
2. The incarnation of Christ.
3. On Matthew 18:7: "Woe to the world on account of scandals!"
4. On Matthew 18:9: "If your eye scandalizes you, tear it out."
5. On Romans 9:6: "This does not of course mean that the word of God has failed. For all the descendants of Israel are not Israel."
6. On 1 Corinthians 15:23ff: "Each according to his rank; at the head, Christ."
7. On Ecclesiasticus 24:1–4: "I am the mother of pure love, of fear, of knowledge, and of worthy hope."

8. Discourse addressed to those Copts who have abandoned their church in order to follow that of the Franks, dealing in particular with the two natures in Christ, the sacraments, and liturgical innovations.
9. On the last judgment.
10. Against the heretics who deny the resurrection of the just and their individual judgment.
11. Against those who habitually commit, without being aware, the sins of pride, slander, and attachment to wealth.
12. Against the Abyssinians who claim that the Holy Spirit anointed Christ (falsely interpreting the expression in the Creed "conceived by the Holy Spirit"), and go on to say that this is why Christ is called the "son of grace."
13. Account of a controversy between a Muslim sage and a bishop (namely, Yūsāb), on the occasion of a visit to a prominent Copt, on the Trinity and the Incarnation.
14. Against the custom of celebrating martyrs by large banquets, for which musicians, singers, and poets are hired, out of vainglory, and to which the poor are not invited, thus leading to jealousy and base rivalries.
15. Against abuses current in churches: games, chitchat, disputes, and tumults.
16. Reproaches to the priests concerning the Wednesday and Friday fast and disputes that arise among them on account of confession.
17. Panegyric of John XVIII (1769–1796) for the day of his death, which occurred on 7 June 1796; and panegyric of Ibrāhīm al-Jawharī.
18. On the sins that derive from pride and on the benefits of humility.
19. On confession, and the dispositions of the confessor and the penitent, an interesting and very rich treatise.
20. On medals ("icons") struck in the image of the saints and the martyrs, and the respect they should be accorded for fear of scandal (this is a reply to a question posed by Yuwāṣāf ibn Ilyās al-Birmāwī; Paris, Arabe 27).
21. Concerning the scapegoat mentioned in Leviticus 16:5–10 (not in Paris manuscript).
22. On Matthew 15:13: "Every plant not planted by my Father will be uprooted," and on John 17:12b: "I have watched over them, and none of them has been lost, save the son of perdition," and on John 14:6: "I am the way, the truth and the life" (Paris, Arabe 20).
23. Against the faithful who fast on their own authority, without the counsel of their ecclesiastical pastors (Paris, Arabe 21).
24. On the prince of darkness (not in Paris).
25. On the prayer of Christ in his agony: "Father, if it be possible, may this cup be taken away from me" (Mt. 26:39 and parallels; Paris, Arabe 24).
26. How was it possible that the soul of the prophet Samuel appeared at the command of the prophetess before Saul? (not in Paris).
27. On penance and the absolution of sins (probably Paris, Arabe 25: On the mercy of God toward sinners. Text taken from the *Master of the Vineyard*).
28. On haughtiness, the love of dominion, and pride (not in Paris).
29. On patience and perseverance in time of trials and tribulations (Paris, Arabe 26).
30. On the resurrection, and against those Copts who have followed the Chalcedonians, who claim that the saints and the martyrs will be crowned already before the resurrection (Paris, Arabe 23).
31. On the fall of Satan and the disobedience of Adam and Eve (not in Paris).
32. On the unjust judge and the second coming of Christ, according to Luke 18:18 (not in the Cairo manuscript, but in Paris, Arabe 22).
33. Letter of Father Bartholemew [Storz, O.F.M.] to the 107th patriarch, JOHN XVIII (1769–1796), suggesting he write to the pope of Rome, and the reply of Yūsāb to Bartholemew, in the name of the patriarch (this exchange is found in the Coptic Patriarchate, Theology 138, end of the eighteenth century; also in the Theology 125 of the Monastery of Saint Antony, copied in the year 1800.
34. Letter to the 107th patriarch, John XVIII, concerning questions of discipline, and the patriarch's reply. This exchange is found in two manuscripts of the Coptic Patriarchate: Theology 134 and Theology 113, and probably in Theology 54 of the Monastery of Saint Macarius).

BIBLIOGRAPHY

Amīr Naṣr. *Al-Qiddīs Anbā Yūsāb al-Abaḥḥ Usquf Jirjā wa-Akhmīm.* Cairo, 1985.

Graf, G. *Catalogue de manuscrits arabes chrétiens conservés au Caire.* Vatican City, 1934.

Griveau, R. "Notices des manuscrits arabes chrétiens entrés à la Bibliothèque Nationale depuis la publication du catalogue." *Revue de l'Orient chrétien* 14 (1909):174–88, 276–81, 337–56.

Īrīs Ḥabib el-Maṣrī. *Qissat al-Kanīsah al-Qibṭiyyah,* Vol. 4: 1517–1870. Cairo, 1975.

Kāmil Ṣāliḥ Naklah. *Silsilat Tārīkh al-Bābawāt Baṭārikat al-Kursī al-Iskandarī,* Vol. 5. Cairo, 1954.

Simaykah, M., and Y. ʿAbd al-Masīḥ. *Catalogue of the Coptic and Arabic Manuscripts in the Coptic Museum, the Patriarchate, and the Principal Churches of Cairo and Alexandria and the Monasteries of Egypt.* Cairo, 1939–1942.

KHALIL SAMIR, S.J.

YŪSĀB I, saint and fifty-second patriarch of the See of Saint Mark (830–849). Yūsāb was an orphaned child born in the city of Upper Minūf (MINŪF AL-ʿULYĀ). He was adopted by a Coptic archon from Nikiou, where he lived to the age of maturity and began to aspire to monastic life and the flight to the wilderness of Wādī Habīb. Tadrus, his sponsor, took him to Alexandria, where he introduced him to Pope MARK II, who took charge of his education. Mark entrusted him to one of his deacons to teach him Greek and acquaint him with the Byzantine world before sending him to the monastery of Saint Macarius (DAYR ANBĀ MAQĀR). There, again, Mark entrusted him to an enlightened HEGUMENOS by the name of Paul, who continued his instruction, not only in Coptic but also in Coptic church rites and traditions. In due course, he was made a deacon and ultimately became a priest, confirmed by Pope Mark himself. He spent most of his time in prayer and studying the lives of the great fathers of the church. His sanctity and Christian humility, as well as his theological knowledge, became known to his colleagues and to the archons and clergy in the valley. Nevertheless, after the death of his mentor, the *hegumenos* Paul, he led the life of a recluse until the time came when the bishops decided to recruit him for the patriarchate.

Following the death of Simon II, the clergy and the bishops as well as the archons in Alexandria were divided on the question of nomination to the throne of Saint Mark, and a strong party was lured by the immense wealth of a certain Coptic layman residing in al-Fusṭāṭ (Cairo) named Isḥāq ibn Andūnah, who coveted the throne of Saint Mark, which he was offered. He himself approached the Muslim governor of Alexandria, ʿAbdallah ibn Yazīd, and promised him a thousand dinars if he could help him attain that dignity by dissuading other bishops from the search for another candidate. But Isḥāq was a married man with children, not just a layman, and this would constitute a serious departure from established church tradition. Hence, the older bishops, including Mīkhāʾīl, bishop of Bilbeis; Mikhāʾīl, bishop of Ṣā; John, bishop of Banā; and others, decided to call a general synod to consider the situation. The bishops supporting Isḥāq ibn Andūnah included Zacharias, bishop of Awsīm, and Tadrus, bishop of Miṣr, who were silenced and put to shame for the breach of church tradition. When a decision was reached, the loyal bishops informed the local governor of Alexandria that they would go to al-Fusṭāṭ to put their case before the governor of the whole of Egypt. Thus, the intimidated local governor had no choice but to sanction their request.

After the solution of this rather bizarre problem, the loyal bishops proceeded to the monastery of Saint Macarius and approached the monk Yūsāb in his solitary cell, offering him the throne of Saint Mark. He protested their request in all humility and said in tears that he was below that dignity. The delegation insisted, put Yūsāb in chains, and conducted him by force to Alexandria, where he was consecrated against his will on 21 Hātūr.

After his inauguration, Yūsāb first devoted his attention to the material welfare of the church, which was dwindling. He sponsored the cultivation of vineyards and the establishment of mills and oil presses, rather than using the funds of the church in church building, which seemed to infuriate some of the faithful who thought that the Muslim administration might be tempted to exploit these lucrative foundations. The persons commissioned with the levy of the *kharāj* tax at the time were Aḥmad ibn al-Asbaṭ and Ibrāhīm ibn Tamīm, who laid a heavy hand on the patriarch and the community while a sudden wave of famine and pestilence befell the country. People were perishing like flies and were stricken by such hunger as to offer their children for sale just to survive. The inhabitants rebelled against these humiliating pressures and extraordinary financial imposts.

The contemporary caliphs were al-Maʾmūn (813–833); al-Muʿtaṣim (833–842), known in the HISTORY OF THE PATRIARCHS as Ibrāhīm; al-Wāthiq (842–847); and al-Mutawakkil (847–861), all members of the Abbasid dynasty. During the reign of al-Maʾmūn the Coptic rebellion flared up in Egypt, its most dangerous center being the marshland of the Bashmurites, who were able to kill the Muslim soldiers and flee behind their unapproachable marshes in the north Delta of the Nile. Al-Maʾmūn dispatched his strong battalions under the leadership of one of his ablest generals, al-Afshīn, who slew the conspirators and rebels from the Eastern part of Egypt until he reached Alexandria. Yūsāb, in profound grief, could only watch the murder of his flock. The situation was worsened by the outbreak of pestilence and famine. So serious was the situation that al-Ma'mūn himself had to come to Egypt. He brought with him Dionysius, patriarch of Antioch, and summoned Yūsāb for an audience to command him to prevail upon his Bashmurite flock to desist from the killing of Muslim soldiers and to live in peace. Apparently the patriarch undertook the mission ordained by the caliph, but without ostensible results, for the Bashmurites continued their conflict with the Muslim soldiers. Eventually, al-Ma'mūn mustered greater armies and with the help of local villagers, notably those of Tandah and Shubra-Sanbūṭ, sought to discover the hiding places of the Bashmurites. In this way, the Bashmurites were defeated and massacred and their homes and villages put to flames.

All this happened within sight of the grieving patriarch, whose reign turned out to be a sorry age for the community of the faithful. The *History of the Patriarchs* records an episode that sheds light on the character of Yūsāb: in an attempt to conciliate his old rival Isḥāq ibn Andūnah, Yūsāb made him a deacon of the church. Nevertheless, the two disloyal bishops who had supported the nomination of Isḥāq continued to stir up trouble against Yūsāb and were consequently deposed and excommunicated. One of the two visited al-Afshīn, the military commander, to persuade him to kill Yūsāb, but his maneuver failed, and the patriarch remained safe and secure until his death. Caliph al-Ma'mūn issued a special decree requesting patriarchal mediation for the pacification of the remaining Bashmurites, which he did in his later years. He also mediated with Nubia and Abyssinia on behalf of the Muslim state. Within the church, he filled the void caused by the deposition of the bishops of Miṣr and Awsīm. He entrusted the episcopal seat of Miṣr to his old rival Isḥāq ibn Andūnah, while also consecrating him as bishop of Awsīm. Apparently Ibn Andūnah retained the two bishoprics until his death.

BIBLIOGRAPHY

Hitti, P. K. *History of the Arabs.* London, 1946.

Holt, P. M.; A. K. S. Lambton; and B. Lewis, eds. *The Cambridge History of Islam,* 2 vols. Cambridge, 1970.

Lane-Poole, S. *History of Egypt in the Middle Ages.* London, 1901.

SUBHI Y. LABIB

YŪSĀB I (archbishop of Jerusalem). *See* Jerusalem, Coptic See of.

YŪSĀB II, 115th patriarch of the See of Saint Mark (1946–1956).

He was born in 1880 at Dayr al-Tafatīsh, a village near al-Balyanā in the province of Jirjā. He entered DAYR ANBĀ ANṬŪNIYŪS, in the Eastern Desert, at the age of seventeen, and was made priest and HEGUMENOS in 1901. From 1902 to 1905 he was sent on an educational mission to Greece, where he studied at the Theological College in Athens. On his return he was appointed abbot of Dayr Anbā Anṭūniyūs and subsequently became metropolitan of Jirjā. He twice served as patriarchal deputy, once when JOHN XIX traveled to Europe, and a second time after John's death in 1942.

He also twice visited Ethiopia, first in the company of John XIX in 1930, and later when he represented the pope in the following year at the coronation of HAILE SELASSIE.

At the death of MACARIUS III in 1945, he was nominated as patriarchal deputy, and was later elected patriarch. His election was contested by a group of young Coptic zealots under the leadership of Hegumenos SARJĪYŪS of the church in the district of al-Qulalī, who was known as an eloquent public speaker. He used his own periodical *Al-Manārah al-Murqusiyyah* to spread the word against the patriarch. In the face of these unremitting attacks on the patriarch, the Holy Synod finally met and excommunicated Sarjīyūs who, in defiance, established his own independent Coptic Orthodox Church.

Toward the end of his pontificate, more sections of the community became disenchanted with his conduct and that of his personal assistant, Melek. Early in the morning of 24 July 1954, a party of young men forced their way into the patriarch's bedroom and compelled him to sign a document of abdication. Afterward they took him to a monastery in Wādī al-Naṭrūn, where he stayed until his death on 13 November 1956. During this period a committee of metropolitans was formed to conduct the affairs of the church. The abductors were later tried, each receiving a three-year sentence for the charges of obtaining an unlicensed weapon and carrying an individual by force.

During Yūsāb's patriarchate, it was decided for the first time to send a delegation of two clerics and a layman to represent the Coptic church in the World Council of Churches (WCC) held at Evanston, Illinois, in 1954. The Copts became a force in the central committee of the WCC through its elected representative, Makārī al-Suryānī, later Bishop SAMUEL, who was assassinated with President Anwar al-Sadat in 1981.

BIBLIOGRAPHY

Atiya, A. S. *History of Eastern Christianity*. London, 1968.

MOUNIR SHOUCRI

YŪSUF ABŪ DAQN, sixteenth–seventeenth-century linguist and historian. A native of Cairo, Yūsuf was sent to Rome in 1595 by Patriarch GABRIEL VIII (1586–1601), an event to be viewed within the context of the intensive ecumenical relations between the Coptic church of Egypt and the Catholic church of Rome at the time of this patriarch. It may be assumed that Abū Daqn was then about thirty years of age, and hence was born around 1565.

For reasons unknown, Abū Daqn became a Catholic soon after his arrival in Rome (de Vocht, 1946, p. 671, n. 4). He latinized his name to Abudacnus, or translated it directly to Barbatus, adding by way of a surname "Memphiticus."

In Rome Abū Daqn devoted himself to intensive study, concentrating particularly on ancient and modern languages, for which he showed a remarkable talent. He already knew Arabic (his mother tongue), Turkish (the current official language of the Egyptian administration), and Coptic, his liturgical language. In addition, he learned Greek, Latin, Hebrew, Chaldean, and Syriac. As to the modern Western languages, he studied Italian, Spanish, and French. It appears that he also learned Modern Greek at that time. This knowledge of languages determined the course of his life. He became the first in a line of Orientalists who taught Near Eastern languages in the West.

In about 1600, he was in Paris as a translator at the court of King Henry IV. At this time, Thomas van Erpe, the Dutch Arabist, better known as Erpenius (1584–1624), studied conversational Arabic with Abū Daqn, making such progress that he was able to write in Arabic to William Bedwell (1562–1622) after only nine months of study.

In 1603 Abū Daqn embarked for England, and on 12 July 1603, thanks to the recommendation of John Whitgift, archbishop of Canterbury, he was engaged to teach Arabic at Oxford University. A few months later he wrote in Latin his history of the Coptic church, *Historia Jacobitarum seu Coptorum in Aegypto, Lybia* [sic] *Aithiopia tota, et Cypri insulae parte habitantium opera Iosephi Abudacni, seu Barbati, nati Memphis Aegypti Metropoli.* Abū Daqn never saw this work in print, for it was only in 1675, long after his death, that Thomas Marshall, then rector of Lincoln College, published the text at Oxford as a small book of seventy-three pages. In 1693 Sir Edward Sadleir published a translation of it in London, *The History of the Copts under the Dominion of the Turk and Abyssinian Emperors.* In 1733, Johan Henri de Seelen reedited the Latin text in Lübeck as a small volume of sixty-five pages, preceded by thirty pages of introduction; and in 1740, Siegebert Haverkamp produced a new edition in Leiden, augmented with erudite notes compiled by Johann Nicolai of Tübingen, which brought the work to a total of some 215 pages.

Such great posthumous success was due in large part to the author's clear and simple method of exposition. Abū Daqn showed a marvelous talent for simplification, for in twenty-three chapters, he explained the salient points of the Coptic church: its origin, history, hierarchical structure, liturgy, and customs.

It is interesting to note that E. L. Butcher, who knew nothing of Abū Daqn, wrote in 1897 about this history: "His book is remarkable for its dispassionate tone, though it is evidently written to point out the differences of ritual and discipline between the Church of Egypt and the Church of Rome" (Butcher, 1897, p. 280). Butcher used the work largely to describe the situation of the seventeenth-century Copts, and, believing that it had been written in Arabic, wondered how it could have come into the library at Oxford. All Butcher's assertions were repeated later by the two Coptic historians who discussed the history: Ya'qūb Nakhlah Rūfaylah (1898) and Kāmil Ṣāliḥ Nakhlah (1954).

It is said that during Abū Daqn's sojourn at Oxford, he translated the New Testament into Bohairic Coptic (de Vocht, 1946, p. 672). However, this may have been a transcription rather than a translation. Abū Daqn also copied the Coptic text of the ancient Coptic liturgies for use in his teaching, which would indicate that he taught Coptic. The manuscripts are likely still at Oxford. About 1611, Abū Daqn also transcribed the Arabic text of the New Testament from a manuscript at Oxford, and sent it to Leiden, perhaps to his former pupil, Erpenius. This text was published by Johannes Antonides in 1612 at Leiden, where the latter taught Arabic, under the title of *D. Pauli Apostoli Epistola ad Titum.*

Abū Daqn remained at Oxford for ten years. He then taught Oriental languages to the monks and priests of Antwerp, as well as to future missionaries and a few merchants. Abū Daqn also taught Hebrew at Louvain.

During his sojourn in Belgium, Abū Daqn prepared many volumes in Arabic, of which the first was an Arabic-Latin lexicon. Soon thereafter, he translated from Latin into Arabic the work of Dia Sanche d'Avila—a Discalced Carmelite better known as Thomas de Jésus. That work had just appeared in Antwerp in 1613 under the title *Thesaurus Sapientiae Divinae, in Gentium omnium Salute procuranda . . . Impiissimarum Sectarum, maxime Orientalium, Ritus ad Historiae Fidem XII Libris enarrans, Errores ad Veritatis Lucem confutans.*

In addition to this work, considered by modern authors as the foundation of all future missionary study, Abū Daqn prepared the edition of a Psalter in four languages: Hebrew, Arabic, Greek, and Latin. Lastly, he translated a work of mathematics from Latin into Arabic for an unknown reason.

From 1618 to 1620 he lived in Munich, where he worked at the ducal library. A manuscript dated 1620 and containing an abridgment of his Arabic grammar is conserved at the library of Vienna, which could indicate that he went from Munich to Vienna at this time. He died about 1630.

BIBLIOGRAPHY

Butcher, E. L. *The Story of the Church of Egypt,* vol. 2. London, 1897.

Essen, L. van der. "Joseph Abudacnus ou Barbatus, Arabe né au Caire, professeur de langues orientales à l'Université de Louvain (1615–1617)." *Le Muséon* 37 (1924):121–37.

Fueck, J. *Die arabischen Studien in Europa bis an den Anfang des 20. Jahrhunderts.* Leipzig, 1955.

Kāmil Ṣāliḥ Nakhlah. *Silsilat Tārīkh al-Bābawāt Baṭārikat al-Kursī al-Iskandarī,* Vol. 4. Cairo, 1954.

Sommervogel, C. *Bibliothèque de la Compagnie de Jésus,* Vols. 1, 5, 6. Paris, 1890, 1894, 1895.

Vocht, H. de. "Oriental Languages in Louvain in the XVIIth Century. Abudacnus and le Wyt de Luysant." *Le Muséon* 59 (1946):671–83.

Ya'qūb Nakhlah Rūfaylah. *Tārīkh al-Ummah al-Qibṭiyyah.* Cairo, 1898.

KHALIL SAMIR, S.J.

YŪSUF AL-QIBṬĪ, seventeenth-century Copt who lived in Rome. About 1624, Yūsuf al-Qibṭī submitted a petition to Pope Urban VIII (1623–1644) to be employed as a *scriptor* at the Vatican Library and to correct proofs of books printed in Greek and in Arabic (Barberini Greek 280, fol. 29). This shows that Yūsuf, who had probably become a Catholic priest in the meantime, had a good knowledge of Greek; it is this fact that led Levi Della Vida to believe he was a Melchite.

In 1624–1625, Yūsuf copied several Arabic manuscripts that are now in the Vatican Library. In his catalog of the Arabic manuscripts of the Vatican, Joseph Simon Assemani calls Yūsuf al-Qibṭī Ioseph Aegyptius.

BIBLIOGRAPHY

Levi Della Vida, G. *Richerche sulla formazione del più antico fondo dei manoscritti orientali della Biblioteca Vaticana.* Studi e Testi, Vol. 92. Vatican City, 1939.

KHALIL SAMIR, S.J.

Z

ZACHARIAS, sixty-fourth patriarch of the See of Saint Mark (1004–1032). Zacharias was a contemporary of the rulers of Egypt al-HĀKIM BI-AMR ALLĀH (996–1021) and al-Ẓāhir Abū al-Ḥasan ʿAlī (1021–1035).

He was a poor priest in Alexandria, and no one knew much about him. His selection occurred in rather unusual circumstances. When the bishops and the clergy met in Alexandria to elect a new patriarch, they were undecided about a candidate. A rich merchant by the name of Ibrāhīm ibn Bishr coveted the patriarchal dignity for himself, even donating some of his wealth to the Islamic administration to help him in securing the office by a decree from the caliph. When the bishops, who were convened in a synod, learned of his manipulation, they were alarmed and hastened to look for a clerical candidate before the layman arrived with a formal decree from the caliph.

It so happened that a poor priest by the name of Zacharias was acting as the servant of the convened synod. While running around to meet the requirements of the bishops, he stumbled and fell on the stairs. The urn he was carrying remained intact. The perplexed bishops saw in this a miracle and a sign for them to adopt the poor and impecunious priest as the new patriarch. They hastened to consecrate him before Ibrāhīm ibn Bishr arrived with a caliphal decree. Ibrāhīm was conciliated later by being invested with the episcopate of Upper Minūf. At the time, the moral position of the church was at a low ebb due to the sale of the priesthood and episcopal seats to unworthy candidates, who were ready to pay for them in cash. Nevertheless, the community of the faithful clung to their church. The advent of a new patriarch who was both poor and impervious to corruption helped to save the church from perdition at a time when a mortal enemy of Christianity held the throne of Egypt. During the reign of al-Ḥākim the Copts and their patriarch suffered many tortures. The peace and prosperity that Egypt experienced during the reigns of the immediate predecessors of al-Ḥākim were reversed during his caliphate, whose history is related in the HISTORY OF THE PATRIARCHS. He issued decrees that could only have come from an insane man.

During al-Ḥākim's rule church bells were silenced and all crosses were ordered destroyed. Christians had to wear girdles (*zunnārs*) and black turbans to distinguish them from Muslims. They were required to hang a wooden cross around their necks, first measuring the span of a hand, later increased to a full cubit (about 23 inches [58 cm]). These humiliating orders were followed by a decree for the destruction of churches throughout the country and the arrest of the patriarch, Zacharias, who was threatened with being thrown to wild beasts if he did not apostatize to Islam. For three months he remained under this threat.

The defiance of the Copts was illustrated by the case of a former secretary in the caliphal administration, Buqayrah, known as the bearer of the cross, who gave up his position and carried a cross to the threshold of the royal palace crying "Jesus is the Son of God." On hearing him, al-Ḥākim had him arrested and tortured. Curiously, al-Ḥākim finally freed Buqayrah, probably on account of his personal admiration for his tenacity. The patriarch was also freed, after having been incarcerated for three months, after which the congregation advised him to flee from his persecutor to the peace of the desert in Wādī Habīb.

This phase of al-Hākim's rule came to an end just as abruptly as it had begun. In A.D. 1021 a new decree was issued permitting the ringing of church bells. Christians were relieved of wearing distinct dark clothing and carrying a weighty wooden cross around their necks, and they resumed the building and restoration of churches. It was also in the course of that year that al-Ḥākim was wont to roam in the hills outside al-Fusṭāṭ (Cairo). One night, riding a donkey in the company of a single guard, he reached the desert at ḤILWĀN. There, he abandoned his beast and ordered the guard to break its legs and return to the palace, leaving the caliph alone. The following morning al-Ḥākim could not be found. His son, known as al-Ẓāhir Abū al-Ḥasan ʿAlī (1020–1035), succeeded him. Peace and security were again established throughout Egypt during the remaining years of the papacy of Zacharias, who died in the city of Damrū after ruling during one of the most precarious periods for the Copts since DIOCLETIAN.

BIBLIOGRAPHY

Lane-Pool, S. *History of Egypt in the Middle Ages.* London, 1901.

———. *The Mohammadan Dynasties.* Paris, 1925.

SUBHI Y. LABIB

ZACHARIAS, SAINT, eighth-century bishop of Sakhā (feast day: 21 Amshīr). The son of a presbyter, Zacharias received adequate training in profane and ecclesiastical letters to open for himself a career as secretary of the *diwan.* Arabic was prescribed for official documents in 706, which would indicate that Zacharias was proficient in Arabic and Greek as well as in his native Coptic, still the spoken language of Egypt in the first century of Arab rule.

Disenchanted with service at the *diwan,* he and his friend and companion Aplatas, governor of Sakhā, decided to take vows in the monastery of JOHN COLOBOS in the wilderness of SCETIS. Their ascetic training was performed under ABRAHAM AND GEORGE of that monastery.

In his search for men of spiritual excellence and profound learning for the episcopate, SIMON I, late seventh-century patriarch of Alexandria, selected Zacharias and ordained him bishop of Salchā, where he is reported to have served thirty years. Since his homily on Jonah and Nineveh is dated in the year 715, he must still have been active under Patriarch ALEXANDER II in the early eighth century. Testimony of his gifts as a writer and preacher are the homilies, which survive until the present.

One of his major works concerned John Colobos, the saint of his monastery. Zacharias not only produced an edifying homily for the memorial day of that saint, 20 Bābah, but he developed it into a comprehensive historical treatise as well. This work may be classified as a biography in the form of a panegyric. Zacharias recorded written sources for his work, including the APOPHTHEGMATA PATRUM of older times, obviously an epitome of the great Greek book, as well as a separate tradition from POEMEN. He also quoted oral information transmitted from patristic sources and inserted a piece of anti-Chalcedonian polemic in his work composed in full harmony with the prevailing rules of classical Coptic rhetoric. A Bohairic version of this work is known, as well as a partial Sahidic one; there is also an extant Arabic recension.

Further treatises on the spiritual life and history of his monastery can be found in the *Panegyrics of Zacharias,* notably those related to his mentors, Apa Abraham and Apa George, which were transmitted in Arabic.

The consolation homily on Jonah is an example of the attempt of Zacharias to explain the Bible. Because of two epidemic diseases that devastated great parts of Lower Egypt, Zacharias was prompted to deal with Jonah and his tribulations. Zacharias wrote another famous homily in a Coptic (Bohairic) original in which he discusses Jesus' presentation in the Temple and the blessing of Simeon (Lk. 2:22–35). The comments of Zacharias on the Incarnation are extant as well as comments on the exchange between Simeon and Mary, the Eucharist (with a special prayer), and the deportment of Christians after receiving the Eucharist. He describes in eloquent terms the connection between Simeon holding the Infant Jesus and the Christians receiving the eucharistic elements.

Several Arabic recensions of an extensive homily on the Holy Family in Egypt are still extant. In surveying the journey of the Holy Family, Zacharias chronicles every site known to him.

Zacharias is an important figure in Coptic literature (especially Bohairic) and he was a fine preacher, a master in the use of faultless rhetoric, filling his homilies with historical and ascetic pronouncements. Arabic translations of his works indicate the esteem with which he was regarded even during his lifetime. In fact, many details of Zacharias' illustrious career still remain to be brought to light.

BIBLIOGRAPHY

Amélineau, E. *Histoire des monastères de la Basse-Egypte, vie des Saints Paul, Antoine, Macaire, Maxime et Domèce,* ed. Jean Le Nain. Annales du Musée Guimet 25, pp. 316–410; 411–25. Paris, 1894.

Evelyn-White, H. G., and W. Hauser. *The Monasteries of the Wadi 'n Natrun,* Part 2, p. 285. New York, 1932.

Hebbelynck, A., and A. van Lantschoot. *Codices Coptici Vaticani, Barberiniani, Borgiani, Rossiani,* Vol. 1, pp. 386–87, 393–94, 503–506. Vatican City, 1937.

Hopfner, T. *Über die koptisch-sa'idischen Apophthegmata Patrum Aegyptiorum.* Kaiserliche Akademie der Wissenschaften in Wien, Philosophisch-historische Klasse, Denkschriften 61, Part 2: Abhandlung, pp. 33–37. Vienna, 1918. But Zacharias wrote no book of the holy elders of the desert; see H. J. Polotsky, in *Orientalistische Literaturzeitung,* Vol. 33, 1930, cols. 871–81, especially col. 872, now also in *Collected Papers,* pp. 342–347, Jerusalem, 1971. This work is a recension of Vis, below.

Müller, C. D. G. *Die alte koptische Predigt (Versuch eines Überblicks).* Ph. D. diss. Heidelberg, 1953, pp. 23–24, 61–74, 300–49; published in Darmstadt, 1954.

______. "Einige Bemerkungen zur ars praedicandi der alten koptischen Kirche." *Le Muséon* 67 (1954):231–70.

Vis, H. de. *Homélies coptes de la Vaticane.* Coptica 2, pp. 1–30, 31–57. Copenhagen, 1929.

Wüstenfeld, F. *Synaxarium das ist Heiligen-Kalender der Coptischen Christen,* pp. 309–10. Gotha, 1979.

C. DETLEF G. MÜLLER

ZACHARIAS I. *See* Jerusalem, Coptic See of.

ZACHARIAS OF SCETIS (fourteenth century), the son of Carion, who must not be confused with his namesake, the disciple of SILVANUS OF SCETIS, who followed his master into Sinai and the region of Gaza. Carion had left his wife and two children, a boy and a girl, to come to Scetis and be a monk. When a famine occurred, his wife brought the two children to their father. Carion kept the boy and brought him up. When the youngster became a handsome adolescent, there were rumors about him; to quell suspicion, he dived into a pool of niter and emerged disfigured. Zacharias quickly came to surpass Carion in virtue, and was favored by visions, the divine origin of which was recognized by POEMEN. Carion said modestly, "I have carried through many more labors than Zacharias, my son, yet I have not attained to his perfect humility and silence." One day MOSES THE BLACK, coming to the well to draw water, noticed Zacharias praying, with the Holy Spirit hovering like a dove above him. He fell at his feet and asked him how to become a monk.

Zacharias died fairly young, for Moses was present during his last moments and at that time received from him a final lesson in silence and humility. To his question "What do you see?" the dying man's answer was "Is it not best, Father, to say nothing?" Zacharias was at once proclaimed blessed by the abbā Isidorus, and he is mentioned in the SYNAXARION on 13 Bābah.

BIBLIOGRAPHY

Arras, V., ed. *Collectio monastica* 14, 34f. CSCO 328, pp. 117ff. Louvain, 1963.

Cotelier, J. B., ed. *Apophthegmata patrum.* PG 65, pp. 177–80, 249–52. Paris, 1864.

LUCIEN REGNAULT

ZAYTUN. *See* Virgin Mary, Apparition of the.

ZENO, Roman emperor (474–491). An Isaurian chieftain by birth, he came to Constantinople and in 466 or 467 married the daughter of Emperor LEO I (457–474). He changed his almost unpronounceable name, Tarasicodissa, to Zeno; and when Leo I died in February 474, he maneuvered his way into becoming a joint ruler with his young son, Leo II. The latter died in November 474, and Zeno became sole emperor. Within three months he was displaced by a court intrigue headed by his mother-in-law, Empress Verina, and was forced to find refuge in his native Isauria (9 January 475). Verina set her brother, Basiliscus, on the throne, and for eighteen months Zeno's chances of regaining power seemed dim.

Basiliscus and his wife, Zenonis, however, were both strongly anti-Chalcedonian. They were influenced by TIMOTHY AELURUS II "the Cat," the anti-Chalcedonian patriarch of Alexandria who had come to Constantinople to plead his cause against his Chalcedonian rival. Basiliscus threw his weight against his own patriarch, Acacius (471–489), to the extent of allowing the bishoprics of Asia, including Ephesus, to withdraw from control of the patriarchate of Constantinople. Citizens and clergy were outraged, and though Basiliscus recalled the most anti-Chalcedonian of his decrees (spring 476), the populace, spurred on by Daniel the Stylite, became increasingly restless. In August 476 Zeno returned to his capital in triumph; Basiliscus was arrested and eventually put to death. On 17 December 476 an edict restored the ecclesiastical status quo and prerogatives of the see of Constantinople, now described as "the mother of our Piety and of all Christians of the orthodox religion" (*Codex Justinianus* 1.2.16). The bond between emperor and patriarch was sealed as never before, and Zeno was determined not to travel again.

The ecclesiastical problems remained, especially those connected with Egypt. In the next two years the main opponents of Chalcedon in the provinces were exiled, and on 31 July 477 Timothy "the Cat" died in Alexandria before he suffered a similar fate. However, the anti-Chalcedonian line was continued in the person of PETER III MONGUS (477–488). The first reaction of Acacius to his election was to refuse Mongus recognition and to denounce him to Pope Simplicius (468–483) as a "friend of darkness" and one who had "subverted the canons of the fathers" (Acacius, ed. Schwartz, 1934, pp. 4–5). Second thoughts, however, prevailed. Peter Mongus was supported by a considerable proportion of the monks in Egypt, and it was clear that some reconciliation between Alexandria and Constantinople must take place if a threat to the unity of the eastern provinces of the empire was to be avoided.

In 480 Zeno patched up relations with the Vandal kingdom in North Africa (Vitensis, 7.2.2–6). A Catholic bishop was allowed to function in Carthage once more, though only for three years. In 481 Zeno turned to the situation in Egypt. At the end of 481, the aging Chalcedonian patriarch of Alexandria, TIMOTHY SALOFACIOLUS, sent his fellow Pachomian monk John Talaia to the capital to discuss the succession to the see. The request that John brought was that the successor should be sought from among the Egyptian clergy who were loyal to CHALCEDON, among whom John himself, as *oeconomus* to the patriarch, would have been a strong candidate (Evagrius *Historia ecclesiastica* 3.12). To this the emperor agreed. Unfortunately, John Talaia also approached Zeno's potential rival for the throne, the powerful Isaurian general Illus. This was discovered, and before he left Constantinople, John was forced to swear an oath that he would not accept the patriarchate for himself. Timothy died in February 482, but John went back on his word and, helped by liberal use of money, had himself elected patriarch in the Chalcedonian succession (Evagrius 3.12; Liberatus *Breviarium* 15.2.111). The result was that the emperor and his patriarch decided that John was impossible, and that agreement must be sought with Peter Mongus. In June, John Talaia fled Alexandria for Rome and the emperor accepted Peter Mongus as patriarch of Alexandria, on condition that he admit the pro-Chalcedonians to communion and subscribe to a document known as the HENOTICON. This instrument of union took the form of an edict addressed, on 28 July 482, to "the bishops and clergy and monks and laity" of Alexandria, Egypt, and Cyrenaica. Peace and the restoration of communion between Alexandria and Constantinople were to be established on the basis of a common acceptance of the councils of NICAEA, CONSTANTINOPLE, and EPHESUS, together with the Twelve Anathemas of Cyril. NESTORIUS and EUTYCHES were condemned, and Chalcedon was relegated to the status of a disciplinary council concerned with their condemnation. The emperor went as far as he could to accept the one-nature theology of Alexandria without condemning Chalcedon explicitly.

Broadly speaking, the *Henoticon* preserved the unity of the east Roman provinces for thirty-five years. Secure in their loyalty, Zeno was able to attend to external threats to his authority. The Ostrogoths under their young king, Theodoric, were first bribed into accepting settlement in parts of Dacia (modern Romania) and Moesia (modern Bulgaria) and in 489 were diverted into Italy to wrest the kingdom from the Herulian king Odovacar (Odoacer). A year earlier, in 488, Zeno had at last disposed of a formidable coalition consisting of Illus, the dowager empress Verina, and the patrician Leontius. Though Zeno left no direct heir, and his personal character was regarded as despicable, he showed a statesmanlike instinct in consolidating the empire around its eastern provinces both politically and ecclesiastically. The latter was based on harmony between Constantinople and Alexandria, and the dominance of the theology of Cyril. On his death, on 9 April 491, his successor, Anastasius, continued his policies.

BIBLIOGRAPHY

Bury, J. B. *History of the Later Roman Empire,* Vol. 1. New York, 1958.

______. *The Later Roman Empire.* New York, 1958.

Stein, E. *Histoire du Bas-empire,* Vol. 2. Paris, Brussels, and Amsterdam, 1949.

W. H. C. FREND

ZENOBIOS, archimandrite and a man of great culture. He wrote in the period of Nestorius in Greek. The secretary of Apa SHENUTE and a physician, he became archimandrite on the death of BESA (Kuhn, p. 38). He founded a convent of nuns in the land of Akhmīm. He was buried in the monastery where he died, perhaps the White Monastery (DAYR ANBĀ SHINŪDAH).

Zenobios was celebrated at the White Monastery, as witnessed by the typika preserved in Leiden (Insinger, 38c–d and 40, ed. Pleyte and Boeser, pp. 197–224), Venice (ed. Mingarelli, vol. 2, pp. 50–55), and Vienna (Nationalbibliothek K9731, ed. Wessely, no. 264).

His Life existed in Coptic at the White Monastery. Crum has cited several leaves of it, and TILL has published the Vienna fragments (pp. 125–33) and drawn attention in a general way to the Michigan fragments (p. 179). The SYNAXARION of Upper Egypt commemorates him at 6 Amshīr (Basset, p. 795; Forget, text, p. 453, trans., p. 476). It does not seem that his Life has been preserved in Arabic.

BIBLIOGRAPHY

Kuhn, K. "A Fifth-century Egyptian Abbot." *Journal of Theological Studies* n.s. 5 (1954):36–48, 174–87, and n.s. 6 (1955):35–48.
Mingarelli, L. G. *Aegyptiorum codicum reliquiae Venetiis in Bibliotheca Naniana asservatae,* Vol. 2. Bologna, 1785.
Pleyte, W., and P. A. A. Boeser, *Manuscrits coptes du Musée d'antiquités des Pays-Bas à Leyde.* Leiden, 1897.
Till, W. *Koptische Heiligen- und Martyrerlegenden,* Vol. 1. Rome, 1935.
Wessely, K. *Studien zur Palaeographie und Papyruskunde,* Vol. 18. Leipzig, 1917.

RENÉ-GEORGES COQUIN

ZINIYYAH. *See* Coptic Language, Spoken.

ZOEGA, GEORG (JORGEN) (1755–1809), Danish antiquarian and scholar. He was educated at the University of Göttingen (1773). In 1782, while classifying the coins in the national collection at Copenhagen, he was sent on a mission in connection with numismatics, but the journey became a prolonged Roman residence which lasted for the rest of his life. He never went back to Denmark. In 1783 he came to the notice of Cardinal Stefano Borgia in Rome, secured his patronage, and later published a catalog of the Borgia Egyptian coins. He became interested in the decipherment of hieroglyphs and learned Coptic to assist his studies. He died in Rome in 1809. His *Catalogus Codicum Copticorum Manuscriptorum* (*in Museo Borgiano*) was published posthumously (Rome, 1810).

BIBLIOGRAPHY

Dawson, W. R., and E. P. Uphill. *Who Was Who in Egyptology,* p. 314. London, 1972.
Kammerer, W., comp. *A Coptic Bibliography.* Ann Arbor, Mich., 1950; repr. New York, 1969.

AZIZ S. ATIYA

ZOSIMUS OF PANOPOLIS probably lived in the fourth century in Alexandria, where he worked as a gnostic Christian and alchemist. A twenty-eight-volume alchemistic work, Χημευτικά (*Khēmeutiká*), is traced back to him, but apart from Volume 24 only fragments have survived.

BIBLIOGRAPHY

Bertolet, M., and E. Ruelle. *Collection des anciens alchimistes grecs,* 3 vols. Paris, 1887–1888.
Lippmann, E. O. von. *Entstehung und Ausbreitung der Alchemie,* 3 vols. Hildesheim, 1919–1954.

MARTIN KRAUSE

ZOSTRIANUS. *Zostrianus* is the major tractate (1) in Codex VIII of the NAG HAMMADI LIBRARY. The name is linked with the magical tradition of the famous Persian Zoroaster by means of a second colophon to the tractate (cf. Arnobius, 1871, I, 52). The work is likely to be the apocalypse of Zostrianus referred to by Porphyry (1946, p. 16). The text of *Zostrianus* is poorly preserved. Since only the opening and closing sections are relatively intact, a lucid translation is difficult.

The book recounts a heavenly journey by Zostrianus. He is called from this world, ascends into the heavens, and learns from various revealers a secret *gnosis.* The content of that knowledge consists largely of the names of the mythological beings in the heavens and of their interrelationships. Attention centers on an intermediate realm called the Barbelo aeon. This aeon in turn contains three constituent aeons (Kalyptos or Hidden, Protophanes or

First-Visible, and Autogenes or Self-Begotten), each of which possesses four illuminators or lights. Knowledge of these heavenly beings provides the key for escape from the physical world. When the journey is over and the revelations are complete, Zostrianus is pictured as descending to this world, where he writes down his *gnosis* and exhorts his readers to escape from their bondage to matter.

The worldview presented by *Zostrianus* is thoroughly Gnostic. A basic dualism between matter and spirit is assumed. Human life represents the imprisonment of the soul within matter; salvation means to be rescued from this world. The mythological aeons are intended to explain how this evil world came into existence from the one, good Spirit.

The relationship of the gnosticism of *Zostrianus* to that of other Gnostic works is difficult to ascertain. *Zostrianus* addresses itself to a select group called "the living elect" and "the sons of Seth." Its cultic materials suggest the existence of a group or community. Yet its teachings do not easily fit those of the Sethians described by Irenaeus and Hippolytus. From the *Nag Hammadi Library* close parallels can be found with the THREE STELES OF SETH (VII, 5) and ALLOGENES (XI, 3), and to a lesser degree with MARSANES (X, 1). These four non-Christian works in turn share some mythological ties, especially in the Autogenes aeon, with the GOSPEL OF THE EGYPTIANS (III, 2 and IV, 2), APOCRYPHON OF JOHN (II, 1; III, 1; IV, 1), and the Untitled Text of the Bruce Codex. Thus it would appear that Gnostic groups of varying persuasions felt at liberty to utilize and alter common traditions to suit their needs.

Zostrianus is also related to the philosophical discussions of the late Middle Platonic period. The Barbelo aeons are expressly identified with the philosophical triad of Existence, Life, and Mind. Other philosophical terms and categories are also frequently employed. Furthermore, parallels with the arguments of the essay of Plotinus *Against the Gnostics* (Enneads II, 9.6–10) indicate that *Zostrianus* was one of the Gnostic works that Plotinus disputed.

Jewish and Christian influences on *Zostrianus* are secondary. *Zostrianus* approves of creation by a word, but it provides no exegesis of or reference to the Genesis texts. Though it uses a heavenly journey format similar to that in the Enochian literature of the Pseudepigrapha (especially 2 Enoch), the contents of the revelation are totally dissimilar. There is an allusion to the Pauline triad of faith, hope, and love, but without specific reference to the Pauline passage. Unless one Greek abbreviation stands for Christ, that name receives no mention at all; likewise, the name of one angelic being may preserve the name Jesus without special interest in it. One brief reference to a man who cannot suffer but does could also reflect later Christian teachings.

In conclusion, *Zostrianus* is best described as an apocalypse of the heavenly journey type. It intends to show that its mythological *gnosis* provides the interpretive keys for those interested in a correct understanding of Platonic philosophy. Thus, the tractate most likely originated in one of the centers of Middle Platonism late in the second century A.D. or early in the third.

BIBLIOGRAPHY

Arnobius of Sicca. *Adversus nationes*, trans. A. H. Bryce and H. Campbell. Edinburgh, 1871. Reprinted, trans. G. E. McCracken, Wilmington, 1979, and trans. H. Le Bonniec, Paris, 1982.

Doresse, J. "Les Apocalypses de Zoroastre, de Zostrien de Nicothée. . . ." In *Coptic Studies in Honor of Walter Ewing Crum*, Boston, 1950.

Plotinus, *The Enneads*, trans. S. MacKenna. London, 1969.

Porphyry. *Vita di Plotini ed ordine dei suoi libri*, ed. G. Macchiaroli. Naples, 1946.

Robinson, J. M. "The Three Steles of Seth and the Gnostics of Plotinus." In *Proceedings of the International Colloquium on Gnosticism*, ed. G. Widengren. Leiden, 1977.

Scopello, M. "The Apocalypse of Zostrianos (Nag Hammadi VIII.1) and the Book of the Secrets of Enoch." *Vigiliae Christianae* 34 (1980):376–85.

Sieber, J. H. "An Introduction to the Tractate Zostrianos from Nag Hammadi." *Novum Testamentum* 15 (1973):233–40.

______. "The Barbelo Aeon as Sophia in Zostrianos and Related Tractates." In *The Rediscovery of Gnosticism*, Vol. 2, ed. B. Layton. Leiden, 1981.

JOHN H. SIEBER